QBasic

EXAMPLE

QUE

Greg Perry

QBasic by Example

For information, address Que, 11711 N. College Ave., Carmel, IN 46032.

Library of Congress Catalog Card Number: 91-66200

ISBN: 0-88022-811-3

96 95 94 93 92 8 7 6 5 4 3 2

Interpretation of the printing code: the rightmost double-digit number is the year of the book's printing; the rightmost single-digit number, the number of the book's printing. For example, a printing code of 92-1 shows that the first printing of the book occurred in 1992.

The examples in this book should work with QBasic 1.0 (included with DOS 5.0).

Publisher
Richard K. Swadley

Publishing Manager
Joseph Wikert

Managing Editor
Neweleen A. Trebnik

Development Editor
Paula Northam Grady

Technical Editor
David Leithauser

Production Editors
Cheri Clark
Katherine Stuart Ewing

Copy Editors
Lori Cates
Becky Freeman

Editorial Assistant
Rosemarie Graham

Formatter
San Dee Phillips

Cover Design
Jean Bisesi

Book Designer
Michele Laseau

Indexer
Tina Trettin

Production
Jeff Baker
Claudia Bell
Brad Chinn
Michelle Cleary
Keith Davenport
Mark Enochs
Brook Farling
Denny Hager
Betty Kish
Phil Kitchel
Juli Pavey
Cindy Phipps
Joe Ramon
Caroline Roop
Dennis Sheehan
Louise Shinault
Kevin Spear
Bruce Steed
Phil Worthington
Christine Young

Production Coordinator
Mary Beth Wakefield

Composed in Palatino and MCP Digital by Prentice Hall Computer Publishing.
Screen reproductions in this book were created by means of the program Collage Plus from Inner Media, Inc., Hollis, NH.

Dedication

I've saved this, my best book, for Mr. Richard Chambers. He taught me how to love books and all they teach. Thanks, Mr. C.

G.M.P.

About the Author

Greg Perry has been a programmer and trainer for the past 14 years. He received his first degree in computer science and then a Masters in corporate finance. He currently is a professor of computer science at Tulsa Junior College as well as a computer consultant and lecturer. Greg Perry is the author of ten other computer books. In addition, he has published articles in several publications, including *PC World, Data Training,* and *Inside First Publisher.* He has traveled in several countries attending computer conferences and trade shows, and he is fluent in nine computer languages.

Acknowledgments

This book began in 1978 when I first turned on a computer and opened a BASIC manual to page 1, having never touched a computer before. Since then, I have continued to learn and teach BASIC. From that first Microsoft BASIC language, I taught many others, but Microsoft's variants of BASIC continue to be my favorites and "old standbys." I am glad that Mr. Gates and his crew at Microsoft continue to support this language, and it looks as though they are dedicated, more than ever, to keeping the BASIC flame alive with QBasic.

Joe Wikert and Paula Grady at Prentice Hall had enough faith in me to ask for my authorship, for which I am grateful. The rest of my editors, David Leithauser, Cheri Clark, and Lori Cates, kept me on track so the readers can have an accurate and readable text.

The Tulsa Junior College administration has been nothing but supportive of my writing. They realize that writing helps my teaching, and teaching helps my writing. Diane Moore is more than just a department head; she is first and foremost a friend, and a more important figure in my life than she realizes.

I have the following three people to thank for my professional career: Dr. Richard C. Burgess, Dr. Roger Wainwright, and my dearest friend, Michael Stapp.

Lloyd Berry, Mike Fenner, and Leo Berry kept me on my feet during some hectic times and had patience when others might not. Thanks, guys.

My beautiful bride, Jayne, seems to have much more patience than I do when I'm furiously trying to finish a book. Somehow her love for me seems to grow each day, a miracle I will never understand but will gladly accept. Jayne, every book is as much your work as it is mine; thanks for sharing my love and life.

Most important, I've mentioned my parents, Glen and Bettye Perry, in every one of my books for the simple reason that they have supported every endeavor in my life. If I succeed at anything, it is solely because of them.

Greg M. Perry, January 1992

Trademark Acknowledgments

Que Corporation has made every attempt to supply trademark information about company names, products, and services mentioned in the book. Trademarks indicated below were derived from various sources. Que Corporation cannot attest to the accuracy of this information.

GW-BASIC, Microsoft, Microsoft Windows, and MS-DOS are registered trademarks of Microsoft Corporation. QBasic and Windows are trademarks of Microsoft Corporation.

IBM is a registered trademark of International Business Corporation.

WordStar is a registered trademark of Micropro International Corporation.

Overview

Part I Introduction to QBasic 1

1 Welcome to QBasic 11
2 The QBasic Environment 31
3 What Is a Program? 55
4 Working with Your Program File 79

Part II Primary QBasic Language Elements 91

5 Understanding Numeric Variables and Constants 93
6 REMarks and Additional PRINT Options 115
7 QBasic's Math Operators 141
8 String Variables 159

Part III Input/Output 179

9 Inputting Values 181
10 Producing Better Output 207
11 Comparing Data 235
12 READ and DATA Statements 261

Part IV Control Statements 281

13 FOR-NEXT Loops 283
14 The WHILE-WEND Loop, the DO Loop, and the EXIT DO Statement 307
15 The Block IF-THEN-ELSE 325
16 The SELECT CASE Statement 343

Part V Data Structures: Arrays 365

17 Introduction to Arrays 367
18 Multidimensional Arrays 393

Part VI Subroutines and Functions 411

19 Numeric Functions 413
20 String Functions 441

21 User-Defined Functions 469
22 Subroutines and Function Procedures 489
23 Variable Scope 517

Part VII Disk File Processing 541

24 Reading and Writing to Disk 543
25 Sequential Disk Processing 555
26 Random-Access Disk Processing 579

Part VIII Graphics and Sound 609

27 Drawing with QBasic 611
28 Adding Colors to Graphics 635
29 Making Music and Special Sounds 655

Part IX Appendixes 669

A ASCII Code Character Set 671
B Answers to the Review Questions 677
C Keyword Reference 699
D Comparing QBasic and GW-BASIC 701
E The Complete Application 707
Glossary 729
Index 745

Contents

Introduction 1

Who Should Use This Book 1
The Book's Philosophy 2
Overview 3
Part I: Introduction to QBasic 3
Part II: Primary QBasic Language Elements 3
Part III: Input/Output 3
Part IV: Control Statements 4
Part V: Data Structures: Arrays 4
Part VI: Subroutines and Functions 4
Part VII: Disk File Processing 4
Part VIII: Graphics and Sound 5
Part IX: Appendixes 5
Conventions Used 5
Index to the Icons 6
The Book's Diagrams 6

Part I Introduction to QBasic

1 Welcome to QBasic 11

What QBasic Can Do for You 11
The Background of BASIC 12
BASIC and Microcomputers 13
The Evolution of BASIC 14
An Overview of Your Computer 15
The Computer's Hardware 15
The Computer's Software 26
Summary 29
Review Questions 30

2 The QBasic Environment 31

Starting QBasic 32
Starting QBasic from Windows 34
Starting QBasic with Command-Line Options 34
Examples 36
The QBasic Screen 37
Selecting from QBasic's Menus 39
Choosing an Option 40
Menu Shortcut Keys 41
Using Dialog Boxes 42
Getting Help 46
The Help Survival Guide 46
Help About Help 47
The Help Menu 48
Quitting QBasic 51
Summary 52
Review Questions 52

3 What Is a Program? 55

Computer Programs 56
Running the DOS QBasic Programs 57
Example 58
Stopping a QBasic Program 59
Program Design 61
Using the Program Editor 62
Typing a Program 62
Example 64
If There Are Errors 65
Working with a Longer Program 67
Advanced Editing 68
Summary 76
Review Questions 77

4 Working with Your Program File 79

Loading Program Files from the Disk 80
Saving Programs to Disk 81
Erasing the Program Editing Window 82
Printing a Program 83

Writing a QBasic Program 84
Spacing in Programs 84
Example 85
Searching for Text in Your Programs 86
Replacing Text in Your Programs 88
Summary 90
Review Questions 90

Part II Primary QBasic Language Elements

5 Understanding Numeric Variables and Constants 93
QBasic Data 94
Variables 94
Examples 99
Using QBasic Constants 102
Scientific Notation 102
Examples 104
Viewing Output 105
The PRINT Statement 105
Examples 106
Clearing the Screen 109
The CLS Command 109
Example 110
Using the END Command 110
Examples 111
Summary 112
Review Questions 112
Review Exercises 113

6 REMarks and Additional PRINT Options 115
Program REMarks 116
Examples 116
The REM Shortcut 118
Examples 118
Use Helpful REMarks 119
More with PRINT 120
PRINTing String Constants 120
Examples 121

Printing More Than One Value on a Line 124
Examples 126
Printing with TAB 131
Examples 132
Printing to Paper 135
The LPRINT Command 135
Example 136
Summary 136
Review Questions 137
Review Exercises 138

7 QBasic's Math Operators 141

The Math Operators 142
The Four Primary Operators 142
Integer Division, Modulus, and Exponentiation 143
The Assignment of Formulas to Variables 145
Examples 146
The Order of Operators 147
Examples 148
Parentheses 150
Examples 150
Printing Calculations 152
Examples 152
Summary 156
Review Questions 156
Review Exercises 157

8 String Variables 159

Creating String Variables 160
Naming String Variables 160
Examples 161
Storing Data in String Variables 162
Examples 163
Printing String Variables 164
Separating Spaces 164
Examples 165
String Concatenation 168
Examples 169
Do Not Mix Types 171

Other String Features 173
Summary 175
Review Questions 175
Review Exercises 176

Part III Input/Output

9 Inputting Values 181

The INPUT Statement 182
INPUT Fills Variables with Values 182
Examples 182
Improving the Use of INPUT 186
Examples 187
Prompting with INPUT 191
Examples 192
Inputting Strings 193
Examples 193
Match the INPUT Variables 195
Eliminating the Question Mark 196
The LINE INPUT Statement 196
Differences Between LINE INPUT and INPUT 197
Examples 197
INPUT and LINE INPUT Cursor Control 199
Examples 200
Summary 204
Review Questions 204
Review Exercises 206

10 Producing Better Output 207

The PRINT USING Statement 208
Printing Strings with PRINT USING 208
Examples 209
Printing Numbers with PRINT USING 211
Examples 213
Printing with SPC 216
Examples 217
Using BEEP 219
Example 219
Printing Special Characters 219

Examples 222
Printing with Color 223
Example 225
The GOTO Statement 226
Examples 228
The LOCATE Statement 230
Example 231
Summary 231
Review Questions 232
Review Exercises 234

11 Comparing Data 235
Comparison Operators 236
Examples 237
The IF Statement 238
Examples 240
String Comparisons 242
Examples 244
Compound Logical Operators 246
Examples 247
The Complete Order of Operators 250
Counters and Totals 251
Counting with QBasic 251
Examples 252
Producing Totals 255
Summary 257
Review Questions 257
Review Exercises 259

12 READ and DATA Statements 261
READ and DATA Overview 262
Examples 262
Using READ and DATA 263
Multiple READ-DATA Values 264
Match READ and DATA Types 266
Example 267
The Trailer DATA Statement 269
Examples 269
The RESTORE Statement 276

Examples 276
Summary 278
Review Questions 279
Review Exercises 280

Part IV Control Statements

13 FOR-NEXT Loops 283
The FOR and NEXT Statements 284
The Concept of FOR Loops 285
Examples 286
Other FOR-NEXT Options 292
Examples 293
Nested FOR-NEXT Loops 295
Examples 297
The EXIT FOR Statement 300
Examples 301
Summary 304
Review Questions 304
Review Exercises 305

14 The WHILE-WEND Loop, the DO Loop, and the EXIT DO Statement 307
The WHILE-WEND Loop 308
Examples 309
The DO Loop 311
The DO WHILE-LOOP 311
Example 311
The DO-LOOP WHILE 312
Examples 312
The DO UNTIL-LOOP 314
Examples 314
The DO-LOOP UNTIL 318
Examples 318
The EXIT DO Statement 320
Example 321
Summary 322
Review Questions 323
Review Exercises 324

15 The Block IF-THEN-ELSE 325

Multiple Statements on a Line 326
    Examples 326
The ELSE Statement 329
    Examples 330
The Block IF-THEN-ELSE 332
    Examples 333
The ELSEIF Statement 336
    Examples 336
Summary 339
Review Questions 339
Review Exercises 340

16 The SELECT CASE Statement 343

Introducing SELECT CASE 343
    Examples 345
Relational SELECT CASE Choices 352
    Examples 352
The Range of SELECT CASE Choices 355
    Examples 356
The STOP Statement 358
    Examples 358
Summary 360
Review Questions 361
Review Exercises 362

Part V Data Structures: Arrays

17 Introduction to Arrays 367

What Is an Array 368
Good Array Candidates 368
Using DIM to Set Up Arrays 371
    Examples 374
The OPTION BASE Statement 380
    Examples 380
Searching and Sorting Arrays 381
    Searching for Values 382
    Examples 383
    Sorting Arrays 384

Examples 385
Advanced DIM Options 387
The ERASE Statement 388
Example 389
Summary 390
Review Questions 391
Review Exercises 391

18 Multidimensional Arrays 393

What Multidimensional Arrays Are 394
Dimensioning Multidimensional Arrays 395
Tables and FOR-NEXT Loops 397
Example 398
Summary 407
Review Questions 408
Review Exercises 409

Part VI Subroutines and Functions

19 Numeric Functions 413

Overview of Functions 414
Integer Functions 415
Example 418
Common Mathematical Functions 420
Examples 422
Noninteger Precision Functions 423
Trigonometric Functions 425
Logarithm and e Functions 427
The LEN Function 428
The TIMER Function 429
Example 430
Random-Number Processing 430
Using RND 431
The RANDOMIZE Statement 434
Using the Random-Number Generator for Applications 434
Examples 436
Summary 439
Review Questions 439

Review Exercises 440

20 String Functions 441

ASCII String Functions 442
Examples 445
String Conversion Functions 447
String Character Functions 450
Examples 455
Justifying String Statements 457
The MID$() Statement 458
Working with Date and Time Values 459
Example 461
The INKEY$ Input Function 464
Examples 465
Summary 466
Review Questions 467
Review Exercises 468

21 User-Defined Functions 469

Overview of User-Defined Functions 470
Single-Line DEF FN() Statements 470
Examples 472
Adding Parameters to Single-Line Functions 474
Examples 476
Multiple-Line DEF FN() Statements 479
Examples 483
Summary 486
Review Questions 487
Review Exercises 487

22 Subroutines and Function Procedures 489

An Overview of Subroutines 490
The SUB Subroutine Procedure 494
A Subroutine Procedure Example 496
Wrapping Up Subroutine Procedures 503
FUNCTION Procedures 508
A Function Procedure Example 509
Building Your Own Library 514
Summary 514

Review Questions 515
Review Exercises 515

23 Variable Scope 517

The CONST Statement 518
Examples 519
Advanced Array Subscripting 520
Global and Local Variables 521
Local and Global Variable Example 523
The Need for Passing Variables 524
Passing by Address 527
Passing by Address Example 529
The LBOUND() and UBOUND() Functions 530
Passing by Value 532
Passing by Value Example 533
Automatic and STATIC Variables 534
Summary 537
Review Questions 537
Review Exercises 538

Part VII Disk File Processing

24 Reading and Writing to Disk 543

Why Use a Disk? 544
Data Files and File Names 546
Computer File Example 546
Records and Fields 548
File Names 551
Types of Disk File Access 552
Summary 553
Review Questions 553

25 Sequential Disk Processing 555

The OPEN Statement 556
Examples 557
The FREEFILE Function 558
An Alternative OPEN Statement 559
The CLOSE Statement 560
Creating Sequential Files 561
Examples 564

Reading Sequential Files 569
Examples 570
Appending to Sequential Files 573
Examples 573
Summary 575
Review Questions 575
Review Exercises 576

26 Random-Access Disk Processing 579

Random File Records 580
The Random-Access OPEN Statement 581
The TYPE Statement 582
Declaring Record Variables from Your TYPE 584
Accessing Fields in a Record 585
Examples 587
The FIELD Statement 589
Examples 592
Reading and Writing to Random-Access Files 593
Creating Random-Access File Data 594
Examples 594
Reading Random-Access Files 597
Examples 598
Changing a Random-Access File 604
Examples 604
Summary 607
Review Questions 607
Review Exercises 608

Part VIII Graphics and Sound

27 Drawing with QBasic 611

Your Screen 612
Examples 615
Drawing Pixels on the Screen 616
Examples 617
Drawing Lines and Boxes 621
Drawing Straight Lines with LINE 622
Examples 623
Drawing Boxes with LINE 625

Examples 625
Drawing Circles and Ellipses 626
Examples 627
Randomly Drawing with DRAW 628
Examples 630
Summary 632
Review Questions 633
Review Exercises 633

28 Adding Colors to Graphics 635

QBasic and Color 636
Adding Colors to Graphics Statements 638
Examples 639
Example Color Setup Program 641
Changing the Foreground and Background Colors 643
CGA COLOR Mode Examples 643
EGA and VGA COLOR Mode Examples 645
Examples 646
The PALETTE Statement 647
The PAINT Statement 649
Examples 649
Summary 652
Review Questions 652
Review Exercises 653

29 Making Music and Special Sounds 655

The SOUND Statement 655
Examples 656
The PLAY Statement 659
Examples 662
Summary 665
Review Questions 666
Review Exercises 666

Part IX Appendixes

A ASCII Code Character Set 671

B Answers to the Review Questions 677

C Keyword Reference 699

D Comparing QBasic and GW-BASIC 701

The QBasic Environment 701
Converting GW-BASIC Programs to QBasic Programs 705
Conclusion 705

E The Complete Application 707

Glossary 729

Index 745

Introduction

QBasic by Example is one of several books in Que's new line of "By Example" titles. The philosophy of these books is a simple one: Computer programming concepts are best taught with multiple examples. Command descriptions, format syntax, and language references are not enough for a newcomer to truly learn a programming language. Only by looking at numerous examples, in which new commands are immediately used, and by running sample programs, can programming students get more than just a feel for the language.

Who Should Use This Book

This book teaches at the following three levels: beginning, intermediate, and advanced. Text and numerous examples are aimed at each level. If you are new to QBasic, and even if you are new to computers, this book attempts to put you at ease and gradually builds QBasic programming skills. If you are an expert at another BASIC language and need to see how QBasic differs, this book is for you also.

The Book's Philosophy

This book focuses entirely on programming *correctly* in QBasic by teaching structured programming techniques and proper program design. Emphasis is always placed on a program's readability rather than "tricks of the trade" code examples. In this changing world, programs should be clear, properly structured, and well-documented. This book does not waver from the importance of this philosophy.

This book will teach you QBasic with a holistic approach; not only will you learn the mechanics of the language, but you will learn tips and warnings, how to use QBasic for different types of applications, and a little of the history and interesting asides of the computing industry.

Whereas many other books build single applications, adding to them a little at a time with each chapter, the chapters of this book are stand-alone chapters that show you complete programs that fully illustrate commands shown in the chapter. There are programs for every level of reader, from beginning to advanced.

This book contains more than 200 sample program listings. These programs show ways that QBasic can be used for personal finance, school and business record keeping, math and science, and general-purpose applications that almost everybody with a computer can use. This wide variety of programs shows you that QBasic is a very powerful language that is easy to learn and use. Experienced programmers can learn what they need by skipping to those programs that demonstrate specific commands.

At the end of the book (Appendix E), you will find a complete application that is much longer than any of the other programs in the book. This application tries to bring your entire working knowledge of QBasic together. The application is a computerized book-collector's inventory system. You will learn how each part of the program works throughout the chapters that come before it. You might want to modify the program to better suit your own needs. You could change it to keep track of other information, such as a compact disc and record collection, as well.

Overview

This book is divided into nine parts. Part I introduces you to the environment of QBasic. Starting with Part II, the book presents the QBasic programming language, divided into seven logical parts. The final section, Part IX, comprises the appendixes. After mastering the language, you can then use the book as a handy reference. When you need help with a specific QBasic programming problem, turn to the appropriate area which describes that part of the language to see numerous examples of code.

To give you an idea of the book's layout, here is a description of each part of the book:

Part I: Introduction to QBasic

This part explains what QBasic is by describing a brief history of the BASIC programming language and then presenting an overview of QBasic's advantages over its predecessors. This part describes your computer's hardware, how you start and end QBasic, and the fundamentals of using the QBasic editor to enter and run programs.

Part II: Primary QBasic Language Elements

This part teaches the rudimentary QBasic language elements, including variables, remarks, math and string operators, and introductory output commands. You will write your first QBasic programs starting in the earliest chapter while learning the foundation of the QBasic language.

Part III: Input/Output

Without the ability to receive input from the user and display results, QBasic would be limiting. Fortunately, QBasic supplies a rich assortment of commands that enable you to enter and display information in whatever format best serves your application. You learn how to store and compare data, as well as format your output to the screen and printer.

Part IV: Control Statements

QBasic data processing is most powerful due to the looping, comparison, and selection constructs it offers. This part of the book shows you how to write programs that correctly flow and control computations to produce accurate and readable code.

Part V: Data Structures: Arrays

QBasic offers single- and multidimensional arrays that hold multiple occurrences of repeating data but that do not require a great deal of effort on your part to process. By learning the fundamentals of sorting and searching parallel arrays, you begin to build powerful routines you can use later in your own programs.

Part VI: Subroutines and Functions

The reusability of a language determines whether programmers continue to use it or discard it for another. The authors of QBasic produced a block-structured, fully separate subroutine and function procedural language that enables you to define the scope and visibility of variables and how you want to pass them between procedures. Along with the built-in numeric and string functions, this part of the book describes the many options available when you start to create your own library of procedures.

Part VII: Disk File Processing

Your computer would be too limiting if you could not store data to the disk and retrieve that data into your programs. Disk files are required by most real-world applications. This part of the book describes how QBasic processes sequential and random-access files and teaches the fundamental principles needed to effectively save data to the disk.

Part VIII: Graphics and Sound

The artist in you will come out when you learn how to create colorful drawings in this part of the book. You will also learn how to add a musical melody or sound effects to your QBasic pictures to ensure that you will grab your user's attention.

Part IX: Appendixes

The appendixes supply support information for the rest of the book. You will find a comprehensive ASCII table, answers to all the Review Questions from the ends of the chapters, a keyword reference, and a detailed comparison of QBasic and GW-BASIC to help you convert any existing GW-BASIC applications you have. Appendix E includes the complete program listing for the book collector's inventory system.

Conventions Used

The following typographic conventions are used in this book:

- Command and function names are in `UPPERCASE MONOSPACE`. In addition to code lines, variable names and any text you would see on the screen are also in `monospace`.
- Placeholders within code are in *`italic monospace`*.
- User input following a prompt is in **`bold monospace`**.
- File names are in regular text.
- New terms, which can be found in the Glossary, are in *italic*.

Index to the Icons

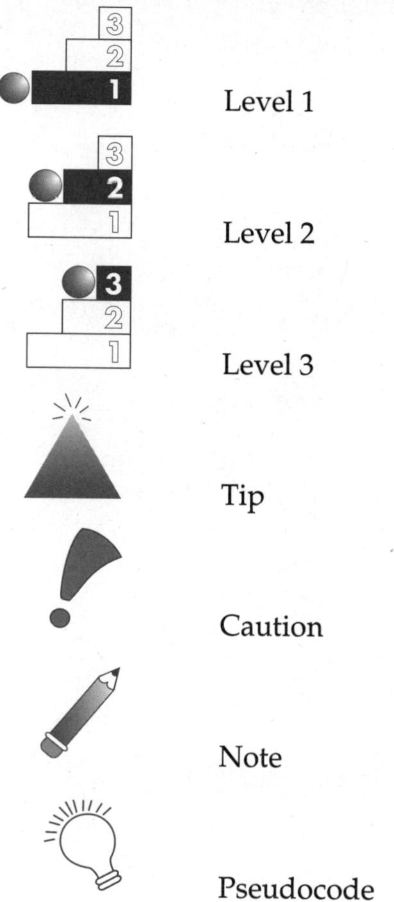

The Book's Diagrams

To further help your understanding of QBasic, this book includes numerous *margin graphics*. These margin graphics are similar to *flowcharts* you might have seen before. Both employ standard symbols to represent program logic. You might have heard the adage "A picture is worth a thousand words." Instead of wading through a lot of code, you sometimes can more easily look at our margin graphics to get a feel for the overall logic before dissecting programs line-by-line.

Throughout this book, these margin graphics are used in two places. Some graphics appear when a new command is introduced, to show you how the command works. Others are placed where new commands are shown in example programs for the first time.

No attempt is made to give you complete, detailed graphics of every statement in each program. The margin graphics are kept simple to give you an overview of the statements you are reading about at the time.

The symbols used are shown on the following page. Their meanings are listed next to each.

You will find the graphics presented here easy to interpret. Their goal is to be self-explanatory, even if you have not fully learned the commands they represent. The margin graphics, the program listings, the program comments, and the program descriptions presented in this book should give you many vehicles for learning the QBasic programming language.

Terminal symbol (BEGIN, END, END SUB, END FUNCTION...)

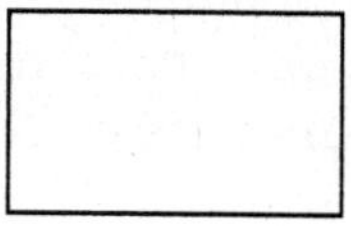

Assignment statement (total = total + newvalue; ctr = ctr + 1;...)

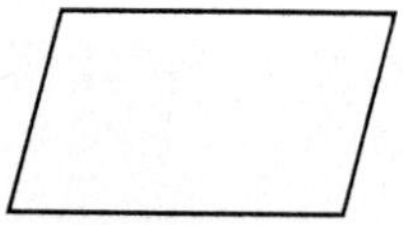

Input/output (READ, PRINT, LPRINT, WRITE...)

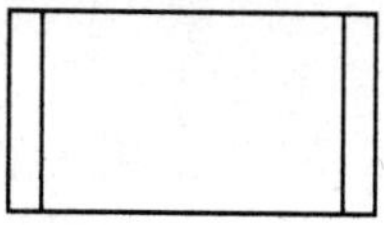

Calling a procedure/function (CALL subname...)

Small circle; loop begin

Large dot; beginning and end of IF-THEN, IF-THEN-ELSE, and CASE

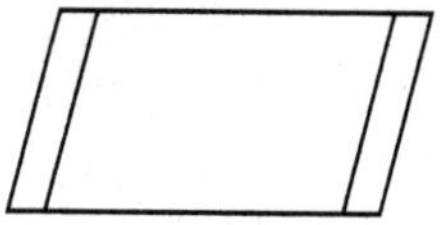

Input/output of arrays; assumes implied FOR loop(s) needed to deal with array I/0

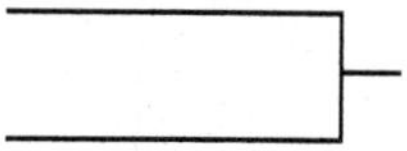

Comment bracket; used for added info, such as name of a subroutine/function

Part I

Introduction to QBasic

Welcome to QBasic

QBasic is the new version of the BASIC programming language supplied with every version of MS-DOS 5.0. QBasic makes programming easier than it was with GW-BASIC, QBasic's predecessor. Whether you are a novice, an intermediate, or an expert programmer, QBasic has the programming tools you need to make your computer do what you want. This chapter introduces you to QBasic, briefly describes the history of the BASIC programming language, shows the advantages of using QBasic, and ends with an introduction to hardware and software concepts.

What QBasic Can Do for You

Have you ever wished that your computer could do exactly what you want? Maybe you have looked for a program that keeps track of your household budget exactly as you prefer to do it, or you want to track the records of a small business (or a large one) with your computer, but nothing is available that prints reports the way you like them. Maybe you have thought of a new use for a computer and would like to implement that idea. QBasic gives you the power to develop new uses for your computer.

QBasic is actually a new implementation of an old concept, namely the BASIC programming language. Unlike GW-BASIC and BASICA (the two versions of BASIC supplied with versions 1.0 through 4.01 of MS-DOS and PC DOS), QBasic supplies superior programming tools to help you concentrate on the important job: the program you are writing. QBasic takes the tedium out of programming by supplying a full-screen editor, on-line help, mouse support, and extensions to the previous versions of BASIC, extensions that add structure, power, and flexibility to the language.

TIP: If you have programmed before in either GW-BASIC or BASICA, you might want to turn now to Appendix E to see how QBasic's commands compare with the commands in these other versions.

If you have never programmed a computer before, you will see that programming in QBasic is rewarding. Becoming an expert programmer in QBasic or any other computer language takes some time and dedication on your part. Nevertheless, you can start writing simple programs with very little effort. When you learn the fundamentals of QBasic programming, you can build on what you've learned and hone your programming skills. As you write more powerful programs, you will start to see new uses for your computer and will use your programming skills to develop programs that others can use as well.

The Background of BASIC

Before jumping into QBasic, you should know a little about the origins and evolution of the BASIC programming language. The first thing you should know about BASIC is what its name means: BASIC stands for *Beginner's All-Purpose Symbolic Instruction Code.* That's a mouthful. BASIC (as its abbreviated name implies), however, was designed for beginning programmers.

The first BASIC programming language was written by professors at Dartmouth College in the 1950s. Programming computers in the 1950s was complex at best. Several programming languages were available, such as COBOL, FORTRAN, and Assembler, but each of these languages was confusing to beginning programmers and hard to learn. The authors of BASIC saw the need for an easy-to-use computer language. The professors were well-versed in FORTRAN, so they used it as the basis for this newer, but simpler, language named BASIC.

One of the benefits the BASIC language provided was its quick response time for programmers. For example, programmers writing in COBOL sometimes waited several hours to get the results of their programs. Because BASIC ran *interactively,* however, as soon as programmers wrote programs in BASIC, they could instruct the computer to execute that program. When programmers had errors in BASIC programs, they could detect and correct those errors quickly. Probably the biggest advantage of BASIC was that people who never programmed computers before could begin writing simple programs with little introduction to BASIC.

BASIC and Microcomputers

For 20 years, BASIC continued to be used by students and beginning computer programmers. One of the trade-offs in using BASIC over one of the other languages of the time was its lack of real computing power and efficiency. Businesses needed to use computer programs written in more powerful languages, such as COBOL. BASIC had its place (it was good for beginners), but it played a relatively small role in the world of programming. BASIC's role in computers would not be better defined until the invention of the microcomputer.

In the 1970s, NASA created the *microchip,* a small wafer of silicon that occupies less space than a postage stamp. Because computer components could be placed on small microchips, the computers did not need to take up much space. NASA produced these small computers in response to the need to send rocket ships to the moon with computers aboard. The computers on Earth could not give split-second accuracy to the rockets because radio waves take a few seconds to travel between the Earth and the moon. Through development, these microchips became small enough that a computer could travel with a rocket and accurately compute the rocket's trajectory.

The space program was not the only beneficiary of the miniaturization of computers. The microchip was used also as the heart of the *microcomputer.* For the first time, computers could fit on desktops. These microcomputers were much less expensive than their larger counterparts. Many people started buying them, which helped create the home and small-business computer market.

Today, a microcomputer typically is called a PC, which stands for *personal computer.* The early PCs did not have the memory capacity of the large computers used by big businesses and government. The owners of these computers needed a way to program them, however. BASIC was the first programming language chosen, because it was a smaller language than many of the others and would fit inside the memory constraints of the smallest PCs. Because many computer purchasers were novices, they also benefitted from learning BASIC.

PC usage continued to grow into the multimillion-dollar industry it is today. No one expected the tremendous growth and power increases that followed these early computers. One thing remains constant as PCs continue to be placed in more people's hands: BASIC is still supplied with almost every new computer. BASIC is considered a PC standard and now is available on more computers than any other language in the world.

The Evolution of BASIC

The number of BASIC installations is enough to justify learning BASIC. A more important reason exists to learn and use BASIC, however: It has evolved continually from those early days into an extremely powerful, command-rich language that rivals other languages. BASIC is not solely a beginner's language. Many businesses use computers programmed almost exclusively in BASIC.

As BASIC improved, PCs also got more powerful. Today, the large amount of memory and computing power that comes with computers is complemented by newer versions of BASIC written to take advantage of that added computing power.

QBasic is the result of the evolution of BASIC. PC users now have the most powerful version of BASIC that has ever been supplied with MS-DOS. QBasic contains a complete programming environment and includes many helpful features that aid programmers. Nevertheless, the authors of QBasic, the Microsoft Corporation, have not forgotten the origins of BASIC. Beginners still can create simple programs with little introduction. QBasic programs produce results quickly. It is easy to find and remove errors in QBasic programs. QBasic is actually fun to use because its authors never deviated from BASIC's original goal of being easy to learn and use.

Before diving into QBasic, take a few moments to familiarize yourself with some of the hardware and software components of your PC. The next section, "An Overview of Your Computer," introduces you to parts of the computer that QBasic interacts with, such as the operating system, memory, disks, and input/output devices connected to your PC. If you are already familiar with your computer's hardware and software, you might want to skip to Chapter 2, "The QBasic Environment," and begin using QBasic.

An Overview of Your Computer

Your computer system consists of two parts: the *hardware* and the *software.* The hardware is all the physical parts of the machine. Hardware has been defined as "anything you can kick." Although this definition is coarse, it helps illustrate that your computer's hardware consists of the things you can see. Software is the data and programs that interact with your hardware. The QBasic language is an example of software. You will use QBasic to create even more software programs and data.

The Computer's Hardware

Figure 1.1 shows a typical PC system. Before using QBasic, you should have a general understanding of what hardware is and how your hardware components work together.

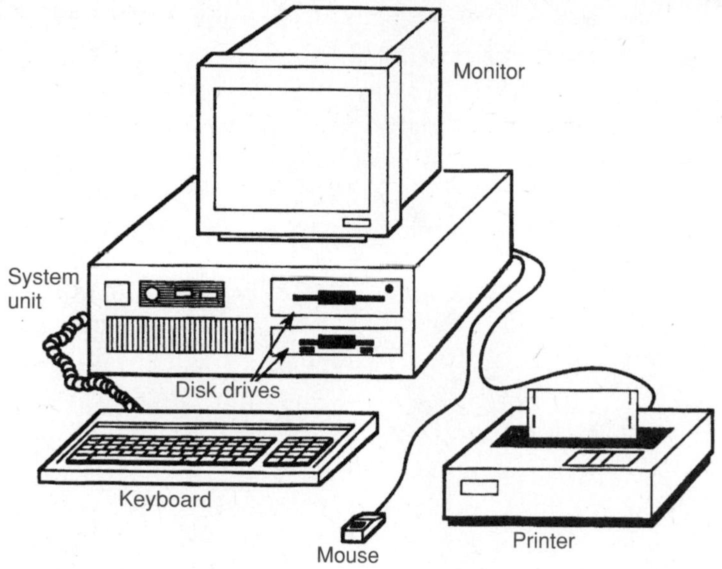

Figure 1.1. A typical PC system.

The System Unit and Memory

The *system unit* is the large box component of the computer. The system unit houses the PC's microchip. You might hear the system unit called the *CPU,* because its more formal name is the *central processing unit.* The CPU acts in a manner similar to a traffic cop: It controls every operation of the computer system. The CPU is analogous to the human brain. When you use the computer, you actually are interacting with the CPU. The rest of the hardware enables the CPU to send results to you (through the monitor and printer). You also give instructions to the CPU through the hardware (the keyboard).

The system unit houses the computer's internal *memory* as well. The memory has several names. You commonly hear it referred to as *RAM* (for random-access memory). The CPU looks for software and data in the RAM. When you run a QBasic program, you are instructing your computer's CPU to look in RAM for the program and carry out the program's instructions. QBasic takes some of your RAM when you start it.

RAM is one of the most important components of your computer's hardware. Without RAM, your computer would have no place for its instructions and data. The more RAM your computer has, generally, the more work the computer can do. The amount of RAM in your computer also can affect the speed of the computer. In general, the more RAM your computer has, the faster it processes data.

BYTE: The amount of memory taken up by one character.

The amount of RAM is measured by the number of characters RAM can hold. PCs usually hold a maximum of about 1 million characters in RAM. A character in computer terminology is called a *byte,* which can be a letter, a number, or a special character such as an exclamation point or a question mark. QBasic can only work in "conventional" RAM, which is 640,000 bytes. If your computer has 640,000 bytes of RAM, it holds a total of 640,000 characters.

All of those zeros following RAM measurements get cumbersome. You often see the shortcut notation, *K* (which comes from the metric system's *kilo,* meaning 1,000), in place of the last three zeros. Therefore, 640K means 640,000 bytes of RAM.

Tape is to music as RAM is to characters.

The limit of RAM is similar to a music cassette tape's storage limit. If a cassette tape is manufactured to hold 60 minutes of music, it does not hold 75 minutes of music. The total characters that make up your program, the QBasic data, and the computer's system programs cannot exceed your RAM's limit (unless you save some of it to disk).

QBasic programs cannot exceed 160K in size, but you need more RAM than that to hold QBasic, its data, and the system programs. Generally, 640K is ample room for anything you would want to do in QBasic. Computer RAM is relatively inexpensive today. If your computer has fewer than 640K of memory, you should consider purchasing additional memory to bring its total RAM to 640K. You can put more than 640K in most PCs. This additional RAM is called *extended* or *expanded* memory. You cannot access this extra RAM without special programs. Most QBasic programmers do not need to worry about RAM past 640K.

The computer stores QBasic programs to RAM as you write them. If you have used a word processor before, you have used RAM. As you typed words in your word-processed documents, the words appeared on the video screen. The words also went to RAM for storage.

The Power of 2

Although K means approximately 1,000 bytes of memory, in reality, K equates to 1,024 bytes of memory. Computers are based on **off** and **on** states of electricity. These are called *binary* states of electricity. At its lowest level, a computer does nothing more than turn electricity on and off with millions of switches, called *transistors*. Because these switches have two possibilities, the total number of states of electricity in the computer is a power of 2.

The closest power of 2 to 1,000 is 1,024 (which is 2 to the 10th power). The inventors of computers designed memory so that it always is added in kilobytes or multiples of 1,024 bytes at a time. Therefore, if you add 128K of RAM to a computer, you actually are adding a total of 131,072 bytes of RAM (128 multiplied by 1,024 equals 131,072).

Because K actually means more than 1,000, you always get a little more memory than you bargain for. Although your computer might be rated at 640K, it really holds more than 640,000 bytes—655,360 to be exact.

Despite RAM's importance, it is only one type of memory in your computer. RAM is *volatile.* In other words, when you turn the computer off, all the RAM is erased. Therefore, you must store the contents of RAM to a nonvolatile, more permanent memory device (such as a disk) before turning off your computer, or you lose your work.

Disk Storage

A *disk* is another type of computer memory, sometimes called *external memory.* Disk storage is nonvolatile. When you turn off your computer, the disk's contents do not go away. This is important: After typing a long QBasic program into RAM, you do not want to retype that program every time you turn your computer on. Therefore, after creating a QBasic program, you save the program to the disk. It remains there until you are ready to retrieve it.

Disk storage differs from RAM in ways other than volatility. Disk storage cannot be processed by the CPU. If you have a program or some data on disk that you want to use, you must transfer it from the disk into RAM. That is the only way the CPU can work with the program or data. Luckily, most disks hold many times more data than the RAM's 640K. Therefore, if you fill up RAM, you can store it on a disk and continue working. As RAM continues to fill up, you or your QBasic program can keep storing the data to disk.

If all of this sounds complicated, you only have to understand the general idea that data must be brought into RAM before your computer can process it. Most of the time, a QBasic program runs in RAM and brings in data from the disk as it needs it. Later in the book, you will see that working with disk files is not difficult.

There are two types of disks: *hard disks* and *floppy disks.* Hard disks (sometimes called *fixed disks*) hold much more data and are many times faster than floppy disks. Most of your QBasic programs and data are stored on your hard disk. Floppy disks are good for making backup copies of information on hard disks and for transferring data and programs from one computer to another. The removable floppy disks often are called *diskettes.* Figure 1.2 shows two common diskette sizes, the 5 1/4-inch diskette and the 3 1/2-inch diskette. Before using a new box of diskettes, you must format them for use on your computer. This writes a pattern of paths called *tracks* where your data and programs will go. Before you use new diskettes, check the *MS-DOS Reference Manual* that came with your computer.

> **TIP:** Some disks are already formatted when you buy them to save you the time and trouble of formatting them yourself.

Disk drives contain the disks in your computer. Usually, the disk drives are stored in your system unit. The hard disk stays sealed inside the hard disk drive and you never remove it. You must insert and remove floppy diskettes to and from exterior disk drives.

Disk drives have names. The computer's first floppy disk drive is called `A:`. The second floppy disk drive, if you have one, is called `B:`. The first hard disk (many computers have only one) is called `C:`. If you have more than one hard disk, the rest are named `D:`, `E:`, and so on.

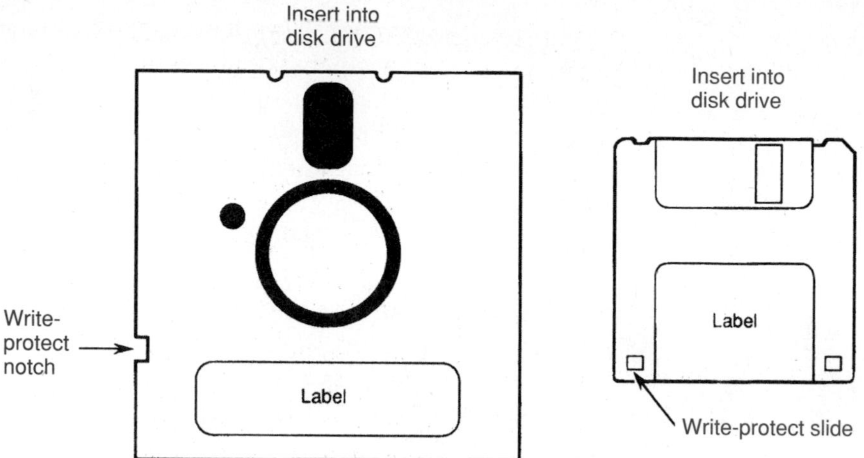

Figure 1.2. A 5¼-inch diskette and a 3½-inch diskette.

The size of the disk is measured in bytes, just as RAM is. Because disk drives hold more data than RAM does, disks can hold millions of bytes of data. A 40-million-byte hard disk is common. In computer terminology, a million bytes is a *megabyte.* Therefore, if your hard disk is a 20-megabyte hard disk, it holds about 20 million characters of data before it runs out of space.

The Monitor

The television-like screen is called the *monitor.* It is sometimes called the *CRT* (which stands for the primary component of the monitor, the *cathode ray tube*). The monitor is one place to which the output of the computer can be sent. If you want to look at a list of names and addresses, you could write a QBasic program to list the information on the monitor.

The advantage of reading output on screen over printing on paper is that screen output is faster and does not waste paper. Screen output, however, is not permanent. When text is *scrolled* off the screen (displaced by additional text being sent), it is gone and you might not be able to see it again.

All monitors have a *cursor,* which is usually a blinking underline. The cursor moves when you type letters, which appear on the screen, and marks the location of the next character you will type.

Monitors that can display pictures are called *graphics monitors.* Most PC monitors are capable of displaying graphics and text. Some can display only text. QBasic gives you the ability to draw your own pictures on a graphics monitor. If your monitor cannot display colors, it is called a *monochrome* monitor.

Your monitor plugs into a *display adapter* located in the system unit. The display adapter determines the amount of *resolution* and the possible number of colors on the screen. The resolution refers to the number of row and column intersections there are. The higher the resolution, the sharper the graphics and text appear. Some common display adapters are the Hercules, MDA, CGA, EGA, and VGA display adapters.

The Printer

The *printer* provides a more permanent way of recording your computer's results. It is the "typewriter" of the computer. The printer prints QBasic program output to paper. You usually can print anything that appears on your screen. You even can use your printer to print checks and envelopes.

The two most common PC printers are the *dot-matrix* printer and the *laser* printer. A dot-matrix printer is inexpensive and fast; it uses a series of small dots to represent printed text and graphics. Most laser printers are even faster than dot-matrix printers. Laser printer output is much sharper than that of a dot-matrix printer, because a laser beam actually burns toner ink into the paper. Laser printers are more expensive than dot-matrix printers, so their speed and quality come with a price. For many people, a dot-matrix printer provides all the quality and speed needed for most applications. QBasic can send output to either type of printer.

The Keyboard

Figure 1.3 shows three typical PC keyboards. Most of the keys are the same as on a standard typewriter. The letters and numbers in the large center of the keyboard produce the characters that you type on the screen. When you want to type an uppercase letter, press one of the Shift keys before typing the letter. Pressing the Caps Lock key makes every letter you type an uppercase letter. When you want to type one of the special characters above a number, press the Shift key. For instance, to type the percent sign (%), press Shift+5.

You can use the Alt and Ctrl keys in conjunction with other keys, just as you did with the Shift key. Some QBasic commands and programs require you to hold down the Alt or Ctrl key while pressing another key. For instance, when QBasic prompts you to press Alt+F, you should press the Alt key, then press the F key while still holding Alt. Then let up on both keys. Do not hold them both down for long, or the computer repeats the keystroke as though you had typed it more than once.

The key marked Esc is called the *Escape* key. In QBasic, you press this key to escape from something you have started. For instance, if you prompt QBasic for help and then you no longer need the help message, pressing Esc removes the help message from the screen.

The group of numbers and arrows on the far right side of the keyboard is called the *numeric keypad.* People familiar with a 10-key machine might prefer to enter numbers from the keypad rather than from the top of the alphabetic key section. The numbers on the keypad work only when you press the Num Lock key. Pressing the Num Lock key a second time makes the arrow keys but not the numbers work. Many keyboards have separate arrow keys that allow for directional movement of the cursor while the keypad is being used solely for numbers.

The arrows help you move around the screen. You use the arrows to move the cursor from one area of the screen to another. To move the cursor toward the top of the screen, you need to press the up arrow. To move the cursor to the right, press the right arrow key, and so on. Do not confuse the Backspace key with the left arrow key. Backspace moves the cursor back a character and erases as it moves. The left arrow key simply moves the cursor backward without erasing.

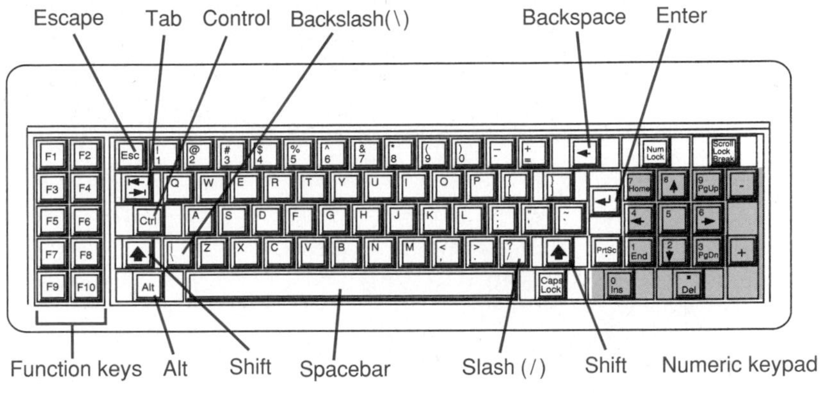

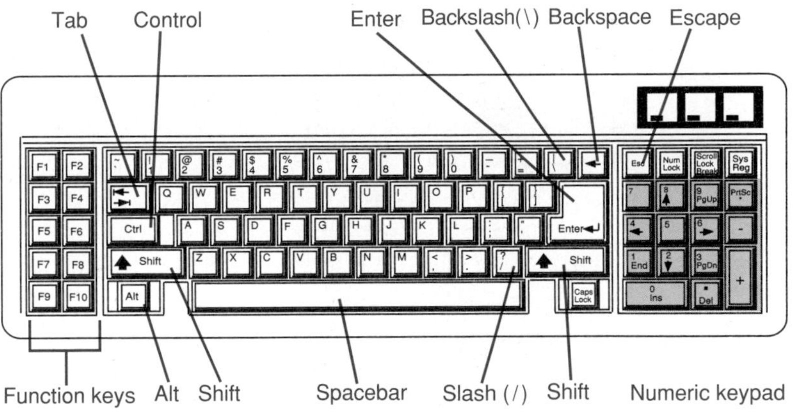

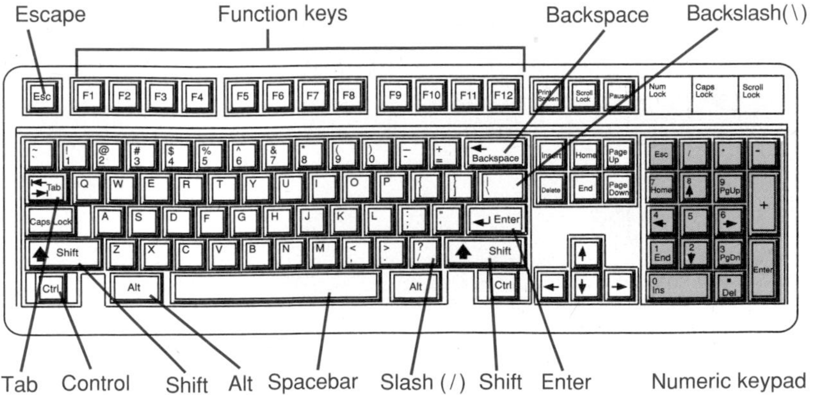

Figure 1.3. Three PC keyboards.

The keys marked Insert and Delete are the editing keys on the keyboard. Later, you will see how to change program text within QBasic using these keys. If you have used a word processor before, Insert and Delete work on QBasic programs in the same manner that they work in the word processor's text. If you do not have separate keys labeled Insert and Delete, you may have to press the Num Lock key and use the keypad keys 0 (or Ins) and period (or Del) to perform text insertion and deletion.

PgUp and PgDn are the keys you press when you want to scroll the screen (move text on the screen) up and down. (On some keyboards, additional keys read Page Up and Page Down.) Your screen acts like a camera that scans your QBasic programs up and down. You can move the screen down the text (like panning a camera) by pressing the PgDn key, and up the text with the PgUp key. Like Insert and Delete, you might have to use the keypad if these actions are not on keys by themselves.

The keys labeled F1 through F12 (some keyboards only go to F10) are called *function keys.* The function keys are located either across the top of your alphabetic section or to the left of it. These keys perform advanced functions. When you press one of them, you usually want to issue a complex command to QBasic, such as searching for a specific word in a program. The QBasic function keys do not produce the same results as they might in another program such as your word processor. They are *application specific.*

Later, you will see examples that use the keyboard for different commands and functions in QBasic.

CAUTION: Because computer keyboards have a key for number *1*, do not substitute the lowercase *l* to represent a *1* as you do on many typewriters. To QBasic, a *1* is different from the letter *l*. You also should be careful to use *0* when you mean zero, and *O* when you want the uppercase letter *O*.

The Mouse

The mouse is a relatively new input device. The mouse moves the mouse cursor to any location on the screen. If you have never used a mouse before, you should take time to become skillful in moving the cursor with it. Chapter 2, "The QBasic Environment," explains the mouse's use in QBasic. You also can issue QBasic commands and select items on the screen by pointing to them with the mouse and pressing a button on the mouse.

Some mouse devices have two buttons, whereas others have three. Most of the time, pressing the third key produces the same result as simultaneously pressing both keys on a two-button mouse.

The Modem

The PC's *modem* lets your PC communicate with other computers over telephone lines. Some modems sit in a box outside your computer. Such modems are called *external modems. Internal modems* reside inside the system unit. It does not matter which one you have, because they operate identically.

A modem is frequently used to speed things up by overcoming the distance between two computers.

Many people have modems so that they can share data between their computer and a friend's or coworker's computer. You can write programs in QBasic that communicate with your modem.

A Modem by Any Other Name...

You probably have heard the term *digital computers.* This term comes from the fact that your computer operates on binary (**on** and **off**) digital impulses of electricity. These digital states of electricity are perfect for your computer's equipment, but they cannot be sent over normal telephone lines. Telephone signals are called *analog signals,* which are much different from the binary digital signals used by your PC.

Telephone lines are fine for analog signals, but they do poorly when they send digital signals. Therefore, before your computer can transmit data over a telephone line, the information to be sent must be *modulated* (converted) into analog signals. The receiving computer then must have a way to *demodulate* (convert back) those signals to digital.

The modem is the means by which your computer signals are *mo*dulated and *dem*odulated from digital to analog. Thus, the name of the device that modulates and demodulates these signals is *modem.*

The Computer's Software

No matter how fast, large, and powerful your computer's hardware is, the software determines what work actually gets done and how the computer does it. Software is to a computer what music is to a stereo system. You store software on the computer's disks and load it into your computer's memory when you are ready to process it, much like you store music on cassettes and compact disks so that you can play it later.

Programs and Data

No doubt you have heard of *data processing*. This is what computers really do: They take data and manipulate it into meaningful output. The meaningful output is called *information.* Figure 1.4 shows the *input-process-output* model. This input-process-output model is the foundation of everything that happens in your computer.

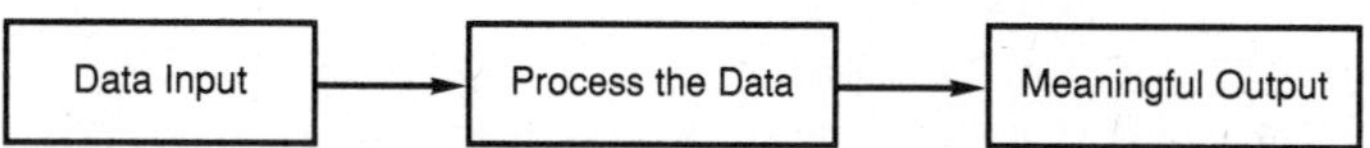

Figure 1.4. Data processing at its most elementary level.

In Chapter 2, "The QBasic Environment," you learn the mechanics of programs. For now, you should know that programs you write in QBasic process the data you input into those programs. Both data and programs make up the software. The hardware is there just to act as a vehicle to gather the input and produce the output. Without software, computers would be worthless, just as an expensive stereo would be useless without some way of getting music into it so that you could hear it.

The input comes from input devices, such as keyboards, modems, and disk drives. The CPU processes the input and sends the results to the output devices, such as the printer and monitor. A QBasic payroll program might get its input (the hours an employee worked) from the keyboard. It then would instruct the CPU to calculate the payroll amounts for each employee in the disk files. After processing the payroll, the program would print checks on the printer.

MS-DOS—The Operating System

MS-DOS must be loaded into your computer's RAM before you can do anything with the computer. MS-DOS stands for *Microsoft Disk Operating System.* MS-DOS, commonly called *DOS* for short, is a system program that lets your QBasic programs interact with hardware. DOS always is loaded into RAM when you power-up your computer. DOS really controls more than just the disks; DOS is there so that your programs can communicate with all the hardware on the computer, including the monitor, keyboard, and printer.

Figure 1.5 illustrates the concept of DOS. It is the "go-between" for your computer's hardware and software. Because DOS understands how to control every device hooked to your computer, it stays in RAM and waits for a hardware request. For instance, printing the words "QBasic is fun!" on your printer takes many computer instructions. You do not have to worry about all of those instructions, however. When your QBasic program wants to print something, it actually tells DOS what to print. Because DOS always knows how to send information to your printer, it takes your QBasic program requests and does the dirty work of routing that data to the printer.

Many people have programmed computers for years without taking the time to learn why DOS is really there. You do not have to be an expert in DOS, or even know more than a few simple DOS commands, to be proficient with your PC. Nevertheless, DOS does some things better than QBasic can, such as formatting diskettes and copying files to your disks. As you learn more about the computer, you might see the need to better understand DOS. For a good introduction to using DOS, check *Using MS-DOS 5,* Second Edition, published by Que Corporation.

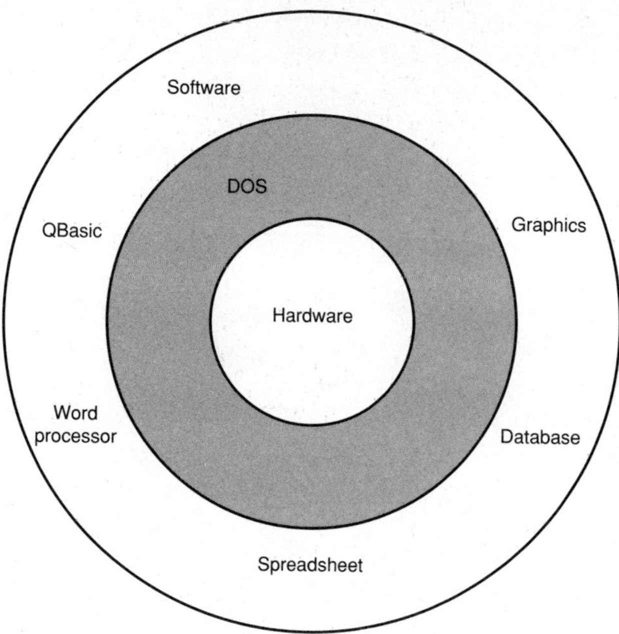

Figure 1.5. MS-DOS is the intermediary between the software and the hardware.

NOTE: As mentioned earlier, DOS always resides in RAM and is loaded when you start the computer. This is done automatically, so you can use your computer and program in QBasic without worrying about how to get DOS into RAM. It is important to remember that DOS always takes some of your total RAM.

Figure 1.6 shows you the placement of DOS and its relationship to QBasic and your QBasic program area in RAM. The 640K of RAM usually is pictured as in Figure 1.6: a bunch of boxes stacked on top of each other. Each memory location (each byte) has a unique *address,* just as everybody's house has a unique address. The first address in memory is 0, the second RAM location's address is 1, and so on until the last RAM location (which comes thousands of bytes later).

DOS takes part of the first few thousand bytes of memory. The amount of RAM that DOS takes varies with each computer's configuration. When working in QBasic, the QBasic system sits on top of DOS, leaving you with the remainder of RAM for your program and data. This explains why you can have a total of 512K of RAM and still not have enough memory to run some programs; DOS is taking some of the memory for itself.

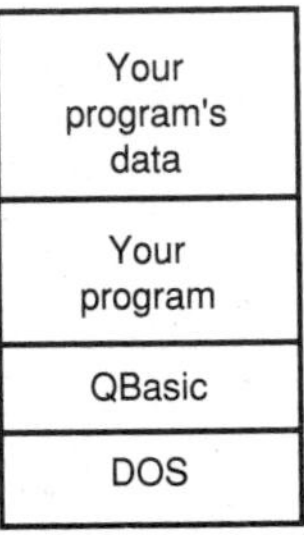

Figure 1.6. After MS-DOS, QBasic, and a QBasic program take memory, the remaining space is all you have for data.

Summary

Whether you are new to QBasic or are an experienced programmer, QBasic is a new language to suit almost all of your programming needs. QBasic is the only programming language supplied with MS-DOS 5.0, but it is all you need to produce computer programs that make the computer work the way you want it to.

This chapter presented the background of QBasic by walking you through the history of the BASIC programming language. QBasic did not forget its roots, so it is an easy language for beginning programmers to learn. QBasic, however, offers some of the most advanced programming language commands that exist today. The rest of this book is devoted to teaching QBasic. Chapter 2, "The QBasic Environment," explains the QBasic screen and environment so that you can start writing QBasic programs.

Review Questions

Answers to the Review Questions are in Appendix B.

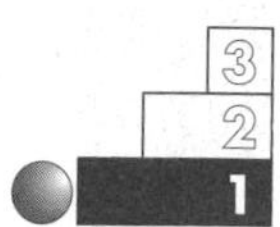

1. What is the name of the programming language that comes with MS-DOS 5?
2. In what decade was BASIC developed?
3. TRUE or FALSE: QBasic is not as powerful as the BASIC programming language.
4. Which usually holds more data: RAM or the hard disk?
5. What is the name of the device your PC uses to communicate over telephone lines?

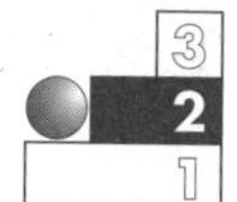

6. What type of device is the mouse?

   A. Storage device
   B. Input device
   C. Output device
   D. Processing device

7. What key would you press to turn off the numbers on the numeric keypad?
8. What does the acronym *BASIC* stand for?
9. What language was the model for BASIC?
10. TRUE or FALSE: BASIC runs interactively.
11. Why do we say that RAM is volatile?

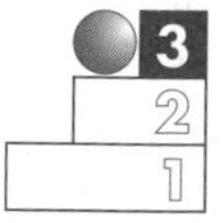

12. TRUE or FALSE: The greater the resolution, the better graphics look on the screen.
13. How many bytes is 512K?
14. What does *modem* stand for?

2

The QBasic Environment

The QBasic environment is different from that of its predecessors, GW-BASIC and BASICA. QBasic offers an array of helpful tools, such as a full-screen editor, pull-down menus, helpful advice, and mouse support.

This chapter introduces the following topics:

- Starting QBasic
- Understanding QBasic's screen
- Using QBasic's menus
- Getting help in QBasic
- Leaving QBasic

This chapter equips you with the tools you require to begin entering QBasic programs.

Starting QBasic

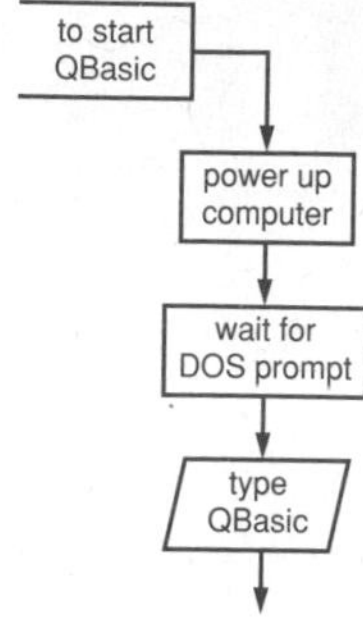

To begin using QBasic, power-up your computer. On most systems, a DOS prompt appears, similar to

```
C:\
```

If your PC displays a menu on power-up, you can't start QBasic until you choose the menu option that exits the menu and takes you to DOS. If you use QBasic often, you might want to add the QBasic start-up command to your menu. If you do not know how to do this, you should contact the person who installed the menu program on your computer.

QBasic is in the DOS directory on your hard disk. Usually, the DOS directory is named \DOS. To load QBasic on most computers, you only have to type QBASIC in either uppercase or lowercase letters. After you type QBASIC, the QBasic opening screen appears (see Figure 2.1).

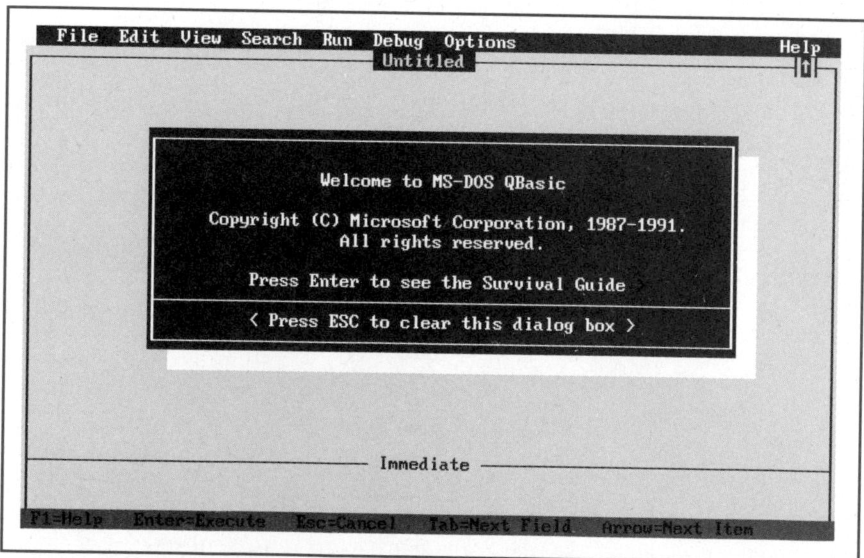

Figure 2.1. The QBasic opening screen.

If you get an error message, the path to the \DOS directory might not be set properly. You might have to change to the \DOS directory by typing CD\DOS. Now you can type QBASIC to load QBasic in memory. If this procedure does not work, either you do not have MS-DOS 5.0 installed on your computer, or the directory that contains DOS is named something other than \DOS. In such a case, you might have to contact the person who set up your computer to find where QBasic is installed. QBasic is supplied with MS-DOS 5.0, so be certain you have MS-DOS 5.0 installed on your system. If you type VER at the DOS prompt, you can see your operating system's version number.

You should add the \DOS path to your PATH command in AUTOEXEC.BAT. After adding this path, you can start QBasic or execute the many other DOS commands from any directory on your disk. See Que's *Using MS-DOS 5* for more information on your PATH.

Power-Up Properly

There is a proper sequence to follow when turning on your computer. The sequence is easy to remember with the following rule:

The boss always comes to work last and is the first to go home.

Have you had bosses like that? Your computer's power-on sequence should follow that rule: The system unit (the "boss" that holds the CPU) should come to work last. In other words, turn on everything else first, including the printer, monitor, and modem. Only then can you turn on the system unit. This keeps system unit power surges to a minimum and protects the circuits inside the unit.

When you are ready to turn off the computer, turn off the system unit first (the boss goes home first). Then, turn off the rest of the equipment in whatever order is most convenient.

TIP: If your computer equipment is plugged into a switched surge protector, it is fine to use the single switch for all your equipment, including your system unit. The surge protector ensures that power gets to the system unit as evenly as possible.

Starting QBasic from Windows

If you use Microsoft Windows, one of the easiest ways to start QBasic is to select the File Manager, open the \DOS subdirectory, and click twice on QBASIC.EXE. Figure 2.2 shows QBasic being started from the File Manager screen.

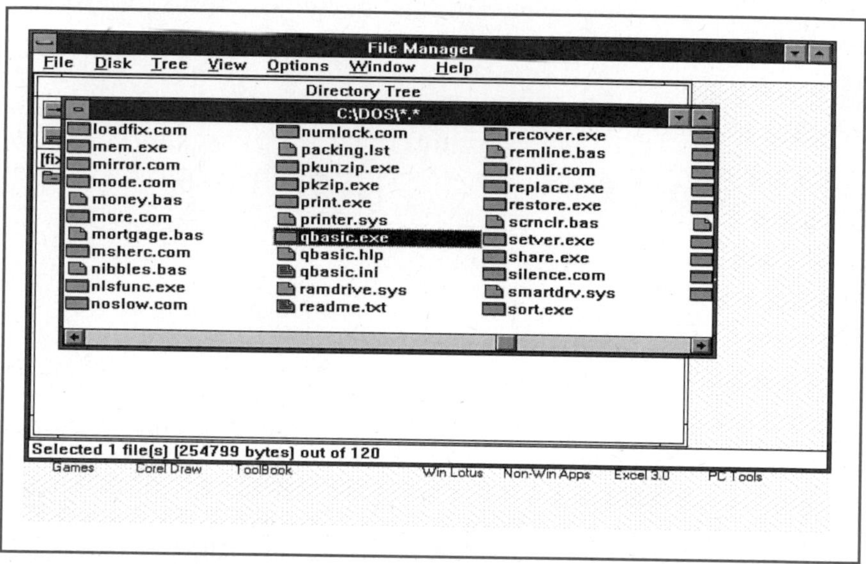

Figure 2.2. Starting QBasic from the Windows File Manager.

QBasic works in all three Windows modes: real, standard, and enhanced. A QBasic .PIF file is not supplied with QBasic, however, and no Window icon for QBasic exists. You can, however, switch from QBasic to another Windows application by pressing Ctrl+Esc, just as you do with any Windows-based application.

Starting QBasic with Command-Line Options

You can add several options to the QBasic start-up command. These options, which are listed in Table 2.1, change the QBasic environment to change the way it starts. Some of them make more sense as you learn more about QBasic.

Table 2.1. QBasic start-up command-line options.

Option	*Meaning*
`/B`	Use this option if you have a monochrome monitor and a color graphics adapter. Laptop users might prefer this option if they have an LCD screen.
`/EDITOR`	This option uses the MS-DOS text editor, which is called *Editor*. Otherwise, the QBasic text editor is used. The editors are similar; many commands and keystrokes are common to both.
`/ED`	This is the abbreviated form of the previous `/EDITOR` command-line option.
`/G`	If you have a CGA (Color Graphics Adapter) screen that flickers or is snowy when text scrolls, set this command-line option to update the screen more slowly, which eliminates the flickering.
`/H`	This option sets the number of lines for the QBasic screen to the maximum your video adapter allows. For instance, VGA screens can display up to 50 lines of text at the same time. The `/H` option automatically sets a VGA screen to 50 lines. The default is 25.
`/MBF`	This option is used for numeric conversions. Without it, QBasic stores numbers with more precision, as defined by the Institute of Electrical and Electronics Engineers (IEEE), and is better suited for math coprocessors. This option maintains compatibility with some previous versions of BASIC that stored numbers in the Microsoft binary format.
`/NOHI`	Use this option if your monitor does not support high-intensity (bold) characters.

continues

Table 2.1. continued

Option	*Meaning*
`filename`	This loads the ASCII QBasic program called `filename` into the editor when QBasic starts. This is faster than starting QBasic and then selecting menu options to load the program. The `filename` must be a valid QBasic program with a .BAS extension.
`/RUN filename`	This option loads the ASCII QBasic program called `filename` into QBasic when QBasic starts, and then automatically runs that program. The filename must be a valid QBasic program.

TIP: If you forget these command-line options, type `QBASIC/?` at the DOS prompt, and QBasic displays all the possible options and their meanings.

Examples

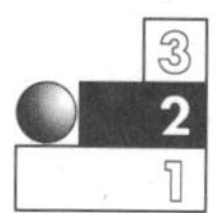

1. To start QBasic and load a program called MYFILE.BAS into the QBasic editor at your monitor's highest resolution, type the following at the DOS prompt:

   ```
   C:\QBASIC /H MYFILE.BAS
   ```

   You can type the options in any order, as well as use uppercase or lowercase characters.

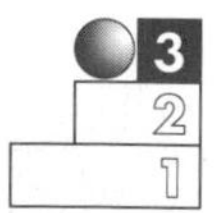

2. To start QBasic on an LCD laptop that does not have color, you might make QBasic more readable by starting it with

   ```
   C:\QBASIC /NOHI /B
   ```

   The preceding line starts QBasic on computers that do not have high-intensity capabilities and that have a CGA card with a monochrome monitor.

The QBasic Screen

Figure 2.3 shows the parts of the QBasic screen. From this screen you create, modify, and execute QBasic programs. After you start the QBasic program, press Esc to clear the copyright message. You see the QBasic screen. If you have a mouse, move it around on your desk so that you can see the mouse cursor.

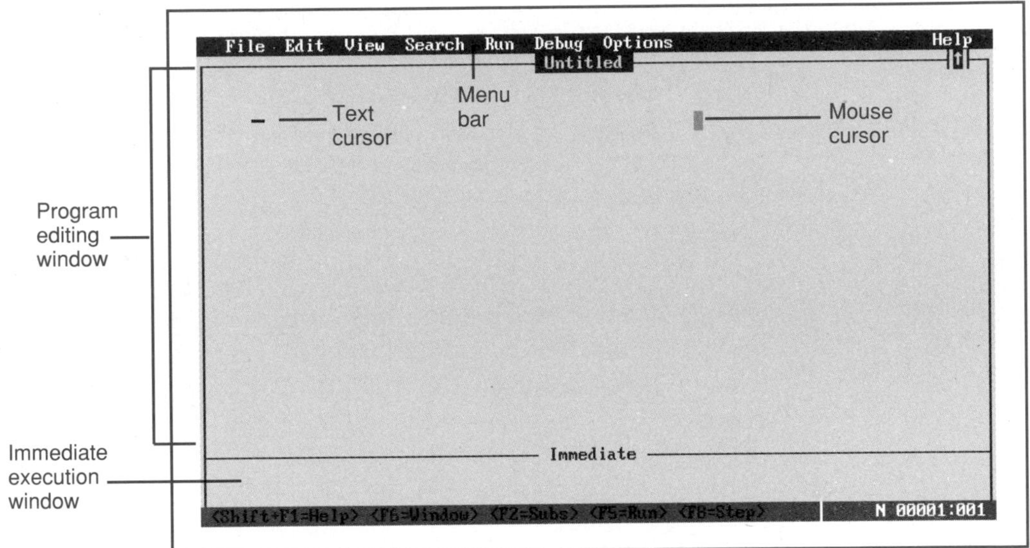

Figure 2.3. The parts of the QBasic screen.

You will see several more screen elements as you use QBasic. These elements are discussed in later sections of this book.

The most important part of the screen is the *program editing window*, in which you work with QBasic programs. The window acts like a word processor's document-editing area. You can move the cursor with the arrow keys or mouse and make any necessary changes to the text.

The *menu bar* at the top of the screen makes using QBasic easy. With older versions of BASIC, you had to memorize many commands, such as `LOAD`, `SAVE`, `LIST`, and `RUN`. QBasic programmers only have to select what they want from the menu bar.

Using the Mouse

You use the mouse to move around the screen quickly. Before mouse devices became common, users had to press the arrow keys continuously to move the cursor from one location to another. Now they can move the cursor by moving the mouse across the desktop and clicking the cursor at the desired position.

Throughout this book, I ask you to perform certain actions with the mouse. These require moving the mouse and using a mouse button. Press only the left button, even if you have a two- or three-button mouse. QBasic does not require you to press more than the left button.

When I ask you to *click* the mouse button, press and immediately release the left mouse button. Clicking the mouse might select an item from a menu or move the text cursor around the screen. Sometimes you click the mouse button after moving the mouse cursor over a **Yes** or **No** answer in response to a question.

Double-clicking the mouse button means pressing the left mouse button twice in rapid succession. You might need to double-click the mouse to execute a menu command.

When you are asked to *drag* the mouse, press and hold the left mouse button without letting up and move the mouse cursor across the screen. Usually the area you drag the mouse across is highlighted on the screen so that you can see the path the mouse leaves. When you are finished marking the path, release the mouse button. This is one way to select several lines from a QBasic program so that you can move or erase them.

Throughout this book you learn many uses for the QBasic screen. For now, familiarize yourself with the names of the different parts of the screen. The rest of the book refers to these names.

Selecting from QBasic's Menus

How do you know what to order when you go to a new restaurant? You choose from a menu. Restaurant owners know that people who eat in their restaurants have not memorized everything the restaurant serves. In the same way, the authors of QBasic understood that users would not want to memorize the commands that control QBasic. They would rather look at a list of possible commands and select the command desired.

The QBasic menu bar displays the words **F**ile, **E**dit, **V**iew, **S**earch, **R**un, **D**ebug, and **O**ptions. You can select these items from the QBasic screen. These items are not commands but are headings for additional *pull-down menus.* These items are called pull-down menus because of their resemblance to a window shade being pulled down. For example, Figure 2.4 shows what happens if you select the **F**ile pull-down menu.

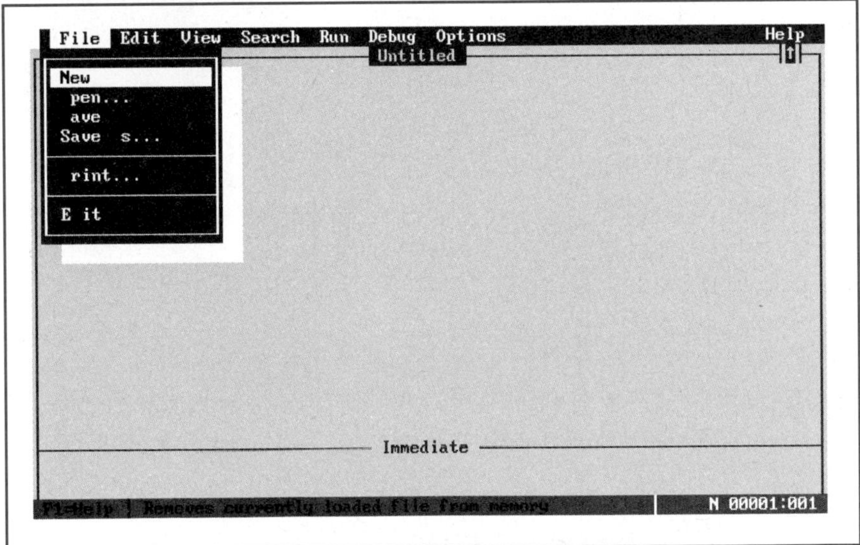

Figure 2.4. Viewing the complete **F**ile pull-down menu.

When you want to look at any of the menus, you can use either the mouse or the keyboard. To display a pull-down menu with the mouse, move the mouse cursor over a menu bar item and click (see the sidebar "Using the Mouse"). If you click each of the rest of the words on the menu bar, you see the remaining pull-down menus in succession.

Displaying a pull-down menu from the keyboard is just as easy as displaying it with the mouse. Press the Alt key followed by the first letter of the menu you want to see. For example, to display the **E**dit pull-down menu, press Alt+E.

If you change your mind, you can press Esc to remove a displayed menu. You are, in effect, escaping from the command you started.

TIP: To display a menu, mouse users sometimes prefer the keyboard's Alt+*key* combination to clicking the mouse. Because your hands are already on the keyboard, pressing Alt+S for **S**earch might be faster than pointing with the mouse and clicking.

Choosing an Option

When you display a pull-down menu, you must tell QBasic which command on the menu's list to perform. For example, the **F**ile pull-down menu lists several commands. You can request the command you want in one of three ways:

- Click with the mouse.
- Point with the keyboard arrow keys.
- Press the command's highlighted letter.

For example, to request the **N**ew command, mouse users move the mouse cursor until it sits anywhere on the word **N**ew. One click of the mouse chooses the **N**ew command. Keyboard users press the down arrow until the **N**ew command is highlighted. Pressing the Enter key carries out the command. Keyboard users also have a shortcut: simply typing the highlighted letter of the command they want. By pressing **N**, the keyboard user can execute the **N**ew command. You can use either uppercase or lowercase letters to select any command.

If you begin to select from a menu, but then change your mind, press Esc to close the menu and return to the program editing window. Mouse users only have to click the mouse outside the pull-down menu area to close the menu.

TIP: The best way to learn how to choose from QBasic's pull-down menus is to experiment. As long as you do not save anything to disk, you do not harm existing QBasic program files or data.

Sometimes commands appear in gray and are not as readable as others. For example, Figure 2.5 shows the **E**dit pull-down menu. Notice that most of the options on the menu are in gray and have no highlighted letter. You cannot choose any of these commands. QBasic displays these commands so that you remember where the commands are when you need them. These commands return to their normal colors when they make more sense in the context of your QBasic session.

Menu Shortcut Keys

After using QBasic for a while, you become familiar with the commands on the pull-down menus. Despite the ease of using QBasic menus, there is a faster way to select some of the commands. QBasic's *shortcut keys* are easier to use than the menus, whether you use a mouse or a keyboard.

Many of the function keys execute menu commands when you press them. Table 2.2 lists these shortcuts. For example, to choose **V**iew **O**utput Screen, you could display the **V**iew pull-down menu and then select **O**utput Screen. The **V**iew **O**utput Screen menu option, however, has F4 listed to the right of it. The listing to the right of the option is the shortcut key for this menu option. Instead of going through the menu steps, you can press F4 and immediately run the **O**utput Screen command. You will understand the function of each of these shortcut keys as you learn more about QBasic.

Table 2.2. QBasic menu shortcut keys.

Key	*Menu Command*
F1	**H**elp
F2	**S**UBs...
F3	**R**epeat Last Find
F4	View **O**utput Screen
F5	**R**un **C**ontinue
F8	Debug **S**tep
F9	Debug **T**oggle Breakpoint
F10	Debug **P**rocedure Step
Del	Edit Cl**e**ar (erase selected text)
Shift+F1	**H**elp Using **H**elp
Shift+F5	**R**un **S**tart
Shift+Del	Edit Cu**t**
Ctrl+Ins	Edit **C**opy to clipboard
Shift+Ins	Edit **P**aste from clipboard

Using Dialog Boxes

Not all menu commands execute when you select them. Some are followed by an ellipsis (...), such as the **F**ile **O**pen... command. If you choose one of these commands, a *dialog box* opens in the middle of the screen. You must type more information before QBasic can carry out the command.

This extra information might be a number, a word, a file name, or the selection of one option from several. Sometimes, a dialog box requires a combination of several things from you.

Figure 2.6 shows the **O**ptions **D**isplay... dialog box. This is a good time to practice using a dialog box and changing QBasic's screen colors at the same time (assuming you have a color monitor). Select **D**isplay... from the **O**ptions menu. Notice that each of the three options on the left (Normal Text, Current Statement, and Breakpoint Lines) has a circle next to it and that one of the three circles has a dot in it. To the right are two lists of colors, labeled Foreground and Background. With this dialog box, you can control the colors of the three kinds of text in QBasic.

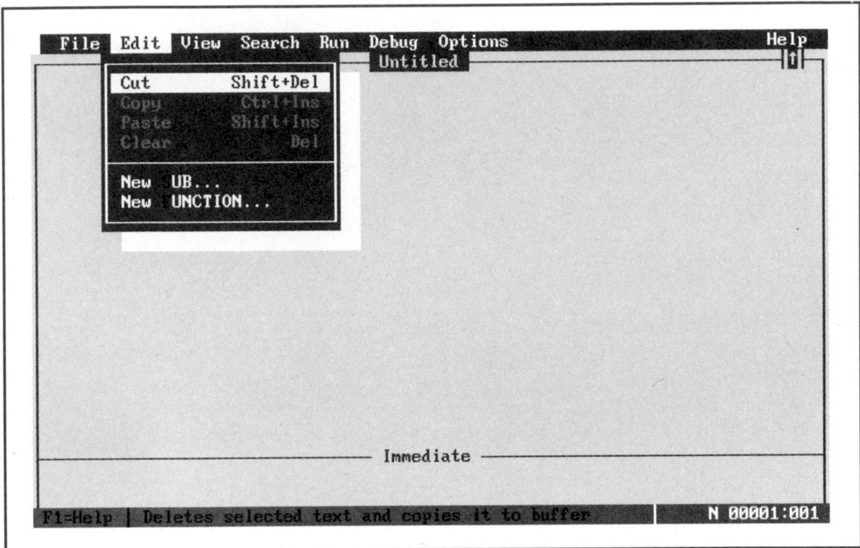

Figure 2.5. The **E**dit pull-down menu.

The Foreground option enables you to change the color of the characters on the screen, whereas the Background option enables you to change the color of the screen behind the characters.

To change the normal text colors on the screen, be certain the circle next to Normal Text is marked with a dot. To mark the circle (and all similar dialog box selections), press the up arrow or the down arrow to move the dot among the selections until it marks Normal Text. This process is even easier with a mouse. You only have to point to the appropriate circle and click to mark your selection.

Now, move to the foreground color chart by pressing Tab or by clicking on the color chart with the mouse. (This is how you move between sections of a dialog box.) Press the up arrow or the down arrow to highlight the foreground color you prefer. As you continue to press the arrows, the color list scrolls to show you the colors at the bottom of the list.

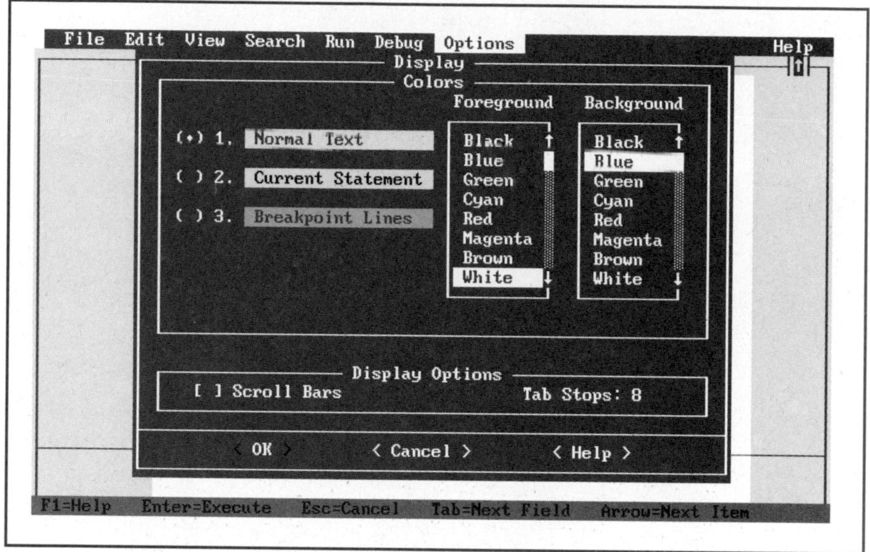

Figure 2.6. The **O**ptions **D**isplay... dialog box.

Press Enter to choose the highlighted color for the foreground. As with most lists, you can select a color also with a mouse click. When you finish with the Foreground box, Tab to Background and select a background color. The text and screen of your QBasic programs now are the colors you selected. You can change the colors at any time.

Notice the shaded bar to the right of the Background box and the one to the right of the Foreground box. These are called the *scroll bars*. They show the relative position of the selected item in a list. The scroll bars are helpful if you have a mouse. When you point to the down arrow on a scroll bar and click the mouse, the list of colors scrolls upward. Conversely, clicking the up arrow of a scroll bar scrolls the list of colors downward. This is faster than using the arrow keys to scroll a list of items in a dialog box.

For now, don't change the colors of the Current Statement and the Breakpoint Lines. When you start working with QBasic and learn how to use the debugging tools, you might want to come back to the **O**ptions **D**isplay... dialog box and change these colors. Debugging tools help you find and correct errors in programs.

To see another type of dialog box, move (with Tab or the mouse) to the box marked Display Options. You can set two options here: Scroll Bars and Tab Stops. Whenever you see brackets to the left of a dialog box choice, you only can turn that choice on or off. An *X* in the brackets turns the option on, and a blank turns it off. For example, to turn off the scroll bars in the program editing window, Tab to the brackets and press the space bar to remove the *X* you see. Mouse users can click with the left mouse button. When you leave the dialog box, the scroll bar to the right of the program editing window disappears. (Because scroll bars are helpful only for mouse users, keyboard users might want to turn off the scroll bar.) Conversely, pressing the space bar at the empty brackets of a dialog box choice marks that choice with the *X*. In this case, if you marked the brackets with an *X*, the scroll bar will remain in the program editing window when you leave the dialog box.

The Tab Stops option illustrates the last type of dialog box. You can set the number of spaces each Tab keystroke moves the cursor when you are writing QBasic programs. The default, or the setting used unless you specify otherwise, is eight spaces. You can replace the default by moving to the *8* and typing another number. If you leave the dialog box and start typing a QBasic program, the Tab key moves the cursor the number of spaces you requested every time you press the key.

> **TIP:** Setting the Tab Stops to three spaces usually is sufficient. Too many Tab spaces can make programs pour over the right side of the screen. This book's QBasic program listings use *3* as the Tab Stop setting.

When you have completed a dialog box, press Enter or click OK to put the dialog box selections in effect. If you change your mind, even after changing the options in the dialog box, you can press Esc or click Cancel to make the dialog box disappear and keep the original options in effect. Clicking Help displays a help screen that explains everything you can do in this dialog box. More of QBasic's on-line Help feature is explained in the next section.

Getting Help

When using QBasic, you can get help at any time by using the on-line Help feature. Help explains virtually every aspect of QBasic. The QBasic Help system gives several kinds of help. Depending on your request, QBasic helps you with whatever you need and even offers example programs that you can merge into your own programs.

The Help Survival Guide

QBasic's *Help Survival Guide* appears every time you start QBasic from the DOS prompt. After you become familiar with QBasic, you can bypass the Help Survival Guide by pressing Esc when the guide appears. New users of QBasic, however, find the Help Survival Guide helpful. The opening copyright screen is the beginning of the Help Survival Guide. After starting QBasic from the DOS prompt, you see the copyright screen with the message

```
<Press Enter to see the Survival Guide>
```

Pressing Enter displays the Survival Guide's control screen, which is shown in Figure 2.7.

The top part of the Survival Guide screen explains how to choose from the menu bar. You already learned how to do that in an earlier section of this book. The rest of the screen explains the Help system in detail. You can access the three options, **I**ndex, **C**ontents, and Using **H**elp, from the **H**elp pull-down menu and from elsewhere in the program. The next few sections explain these three options in more detail. Feel free to browse through the Survival Guide. When you are finished, press Esc to leave the Survival Guide and return to QBasic.

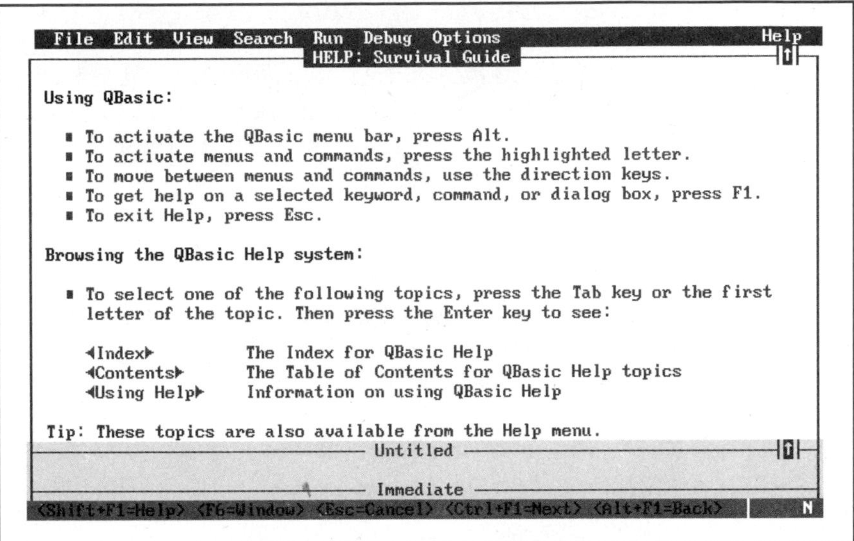

File Edit View Search Run Debug Options Help
HELP: Survival Guide
Using QBasic:
▪ To activate the QBasic menu bar, press Alt.
▪ To activate menus and commands, press the highlighted letter.
▪ To move between menus and commands, use the direction keys.
▪ To get help on a selected keyword, command, or dialog box, press F1.
▪ To exit Help, press Esc.
Browsing the QBasic Help system:
▪ To select one of the following topics, press the Tab key or the first letter of the topic. Then press the Enter key to see:
◄Index► The Index for QBasic Help
◄Contents► The Table of Contents for QBasic Help topics
◄Using Help► Information on using QBasic Help
Tip: These topics are also available from the Help menu.
Untitled
Immediate
<Shift+F1=Help> <F6=Window> <Esc=Cancel> <Ctrl+F1=Next> <Alt+F1=Back>
N

Figure 2.7. The Help Survival Guide control screen.

Help About Help

The QBasic on-line help system is so complete that it even gives you help about using Help. The Survival Guide's Using **H**elp option explains the many ways to get help from QBasic. Selecting Using **H**elp with a mouse click or tabbing to this option and pressing Enter produces the screen shown in Figure 2.8. You can press the up arrow, the down arrow, PgUp, and PgDn to scroll through the text on the screen. Mouse users can click the scroll bar to scroll the text.

Clicking or tabbing on **C**ontents takes you to Help's table of contents. Clicking or tabbing on **I**ndex takes you to the index of QBasic keywords, and selecting Back takes you back to QBasic's first Help screen.

The *Help* Menu

Figure 2.9 shows the **H**elp pull-down menu. Notice that this menu contains three of the same commands as the Survival Guide: **I**ndex, **C**ontents, and Using **H**elp. In addition, you can access the help **T**opic command from the Help menu (although pressing F1 is easier).

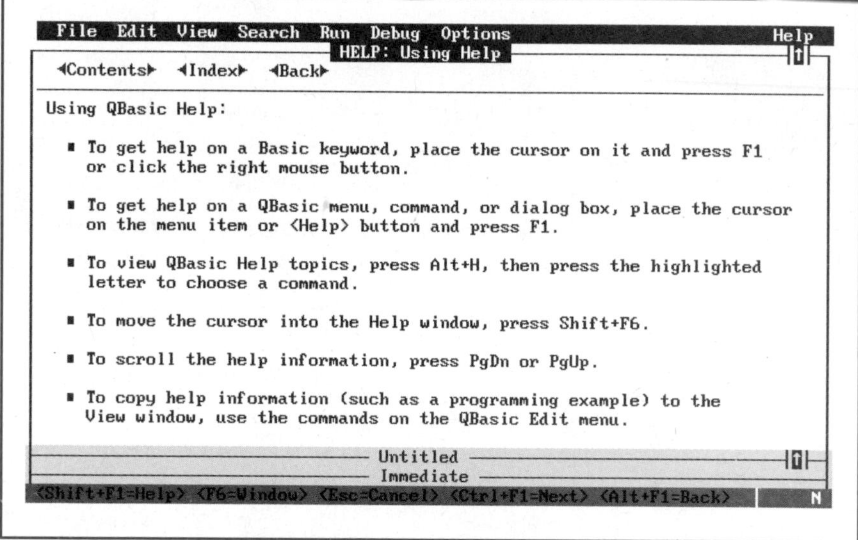

Figure 2.8. Getting help with the Help system.

The *Help* Index

Choosing **I**ndex from the **H**elp menu displays a list of the more than 100 commands used in QBasic. At this point, most of the commands probably make little sense to you. As you learn more about the QBasic programming language, however, you will understand these commands better. As shown in Figure 2.10, only a few of the commands fit on the screen at one time.

The index is more than just a list of command names. You can click any command on the list or tab to any command. A detailed explanation for that command appears, with actual QBasic program sections that use the command. As with all the help screens, pressing Esc returns you to the program editing window.

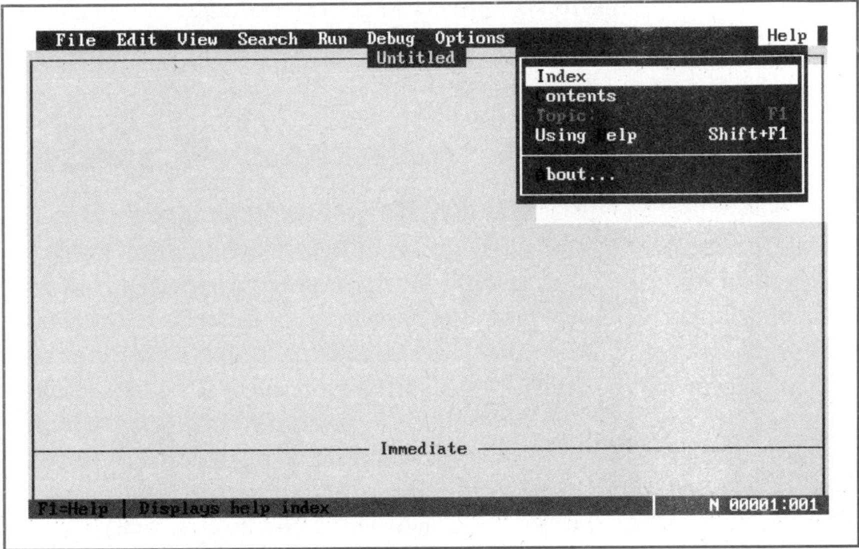

Figure 2.9. The **H**elp pull-down menu.

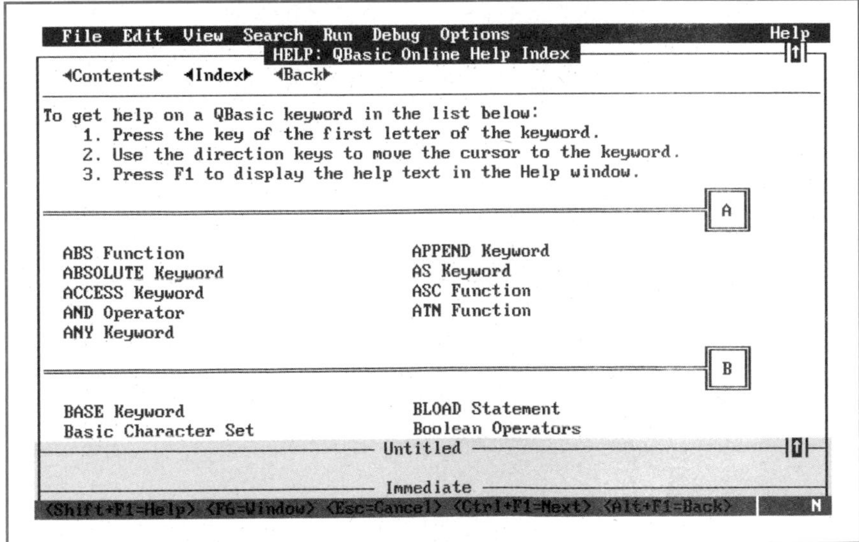

Figure 2.10. The **H**elp Index.

The *H*elp Table of Contents

Selecting **H**elp **C**ontents displays the screen shown in Figure 2.11. The Contents screen displays help on various parts of QBasic by subject: Orientation, Keys, Using QBasic, and Quick Reference. Throughout this book, sections refer you to the Help Contents screen when it might be useful as you program in QBasic.

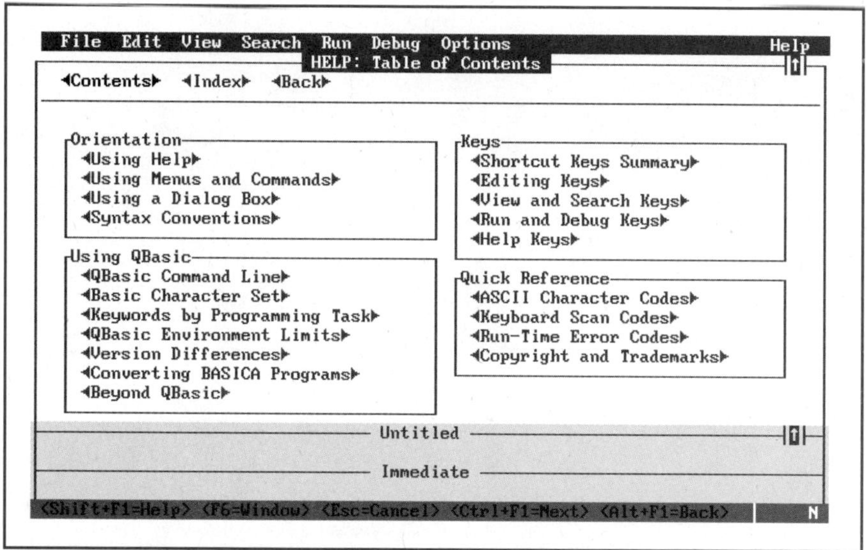

Figure 2.11. The **H**elp Table of Contents.

*T*opic and the Context-Sensitive Help

When you become familiar with QBasic, the *context-sensitive help* feature relieves some of your programming frustration. Whenever you request context-sensitive help by pressing F1 or choosing **H**elp **T**opic, QBasic "looks" at what you are doing and gives you help with your problem. For example, if you are working on the QBasic PRINT statement and the cursor is resting over the word PRINT when you press F1, QBasic displays help on the PRINT command. If you want help on the **S**earch menu, display the **S**earch menu and press F1.

Help About...

Selecting **H**elp **A**bout... displays a dialog box in the center of the screen that shows the version number of QBasic you are using. This is helpful if you call Microsoft for support and need to supply the version number of QBasic you are using. Pressing Enter or clicking OK removes the dialog box from the screen and returns you to the program editing window.

Quitting QBasic

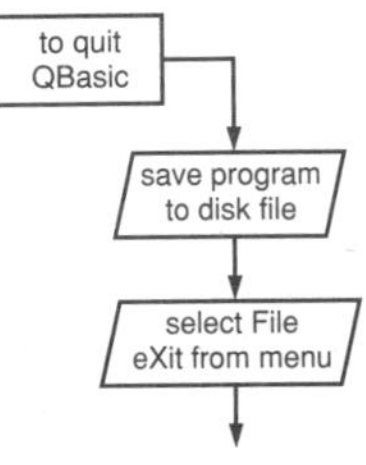

When you finish your QBasic session, you can exit QBasic and return to DOS by choosing **F**ile E**x**it. It is important to exit to DOS before powering-off your computer because you could lose some of your work if you do not. If you made changes to a QBasic program and you try to exit to DOS without saving those changes to disk, QBasic displays the warning message dialog box shown in Figure 2.12.

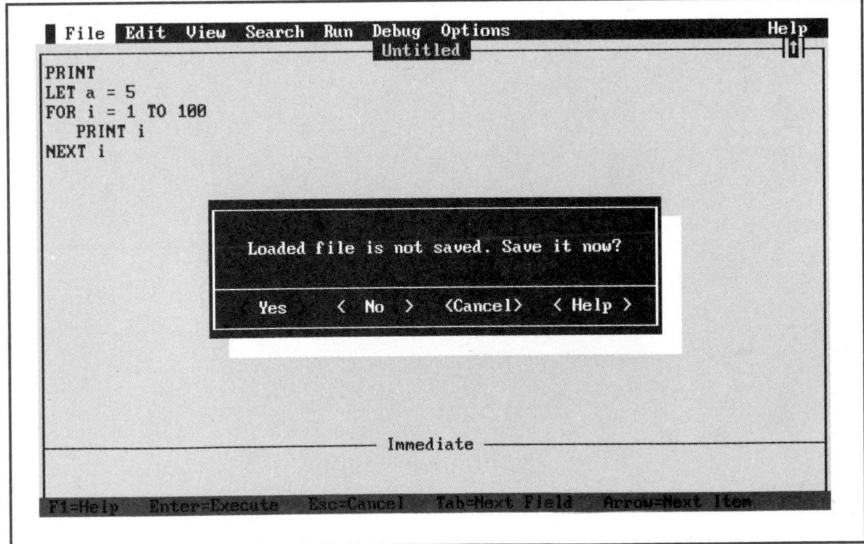

Figure 2.12. The QBasic warning message to save a file.

If you choose **Yes**, QBasic prompts you for a file name under which to save the file. Choosing **No** instructs QBasic that you want to exit to DOS without saving the file, although the latest changes are not recorded. **Cancel** instructs QBasic to return to the program editing window, and **Help** displays a description of the warning message.

Summary

This chapter familiarized you with the QBasic environment. The major advantages of QBasic over its predecessors are the screen's menus and on-line help system. You learned how to start QBasic, use the menus, request on-line help, and exit the program. With its intuitive interface, QBasic makes working easy, whether you have a mouse or a keyboard.

This chapter prepares you for Chapter 3, "What Is a Program?" in which you learn the mechanics of programming, how to use the QBasic editor, and what you need to know to run your first QBasic program.

Review Questions

Answers to the Review Questions are in Appendix B.

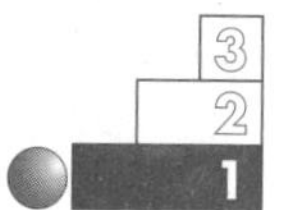

1. TRUE or FALSE: You can find QBasic in your \DOS subdirectory.
2. Which part of the QBasic screen retains the program as you type it?
3. What are the differences among clicking, double-clicking, and dragging your mouse?
4. Do you need to remember command names so that QBasic can execute them? Why or why not?
5. How do you display the Help Survival Guide?
6. What does *context-sensitive help* mean?

7. Why should you exit QBasic and return to DOS before turning off your computer?

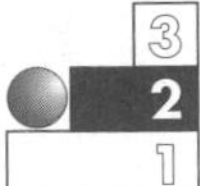

8. What are two ways to get help in QBasic?
9. What key do you use to delete the character to the left of the cursor?

   A. F1
   B. Esc
   C. Backspace
   D. Right arrow

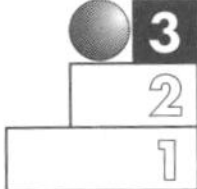

10. What are command-line options used for?
11. What are the keyboard shortcut keys used for?

3

What Is a Program?

Programming computers has been described by different people at different times as rewarding, challenging, easy, difficult, fast, and slow. Programming is a combination of each of these. Programming your computer takes time, but you have fun along the way, especially with help from QBasic. Writing more advanced programs takes time and can be frustrating, but when you make a complex program work, the feeling is gratifying.

This chapter describes the concept of programming, from a program's inception to its execution on the PC. The most difficult part of programming is breaking the problem into logical steps that the computer can carry out. In this chapter, you type and execute your first QBasic program.

This chapter covers the following topics:

- ♦ The concept of programming
- ♦ Running the programs included with QBasic
- ♦ Program design
- ♦ Using the QBasic editor
- ♦ Typing and running your first QBasic program

After completing this chapter, you will be ready for the next section of the book, which explains how to manage your QBasic program files.

Computer Programs

PROGRAM: A collection of instructions that makes the computer do things.

Before you can make QBasic work for you, you need to write a QBasic program. So far, you have seen the word *program* used several times in this book. Now is a good time to define a program as a group of instructions that makes the computer do things.

Keep in mind that computers are machines. They are not smart—quite the opposite. Computers cannot do anything until you give them detailed instructions. When you use your computer for word processing, the word processor is a program that someone wrote (in a language such as QBasic) telling the computer exactly how to behave when you type words.

If you ever have followed a recipe, you are familiar with the concept of programming. A recipe is just a program (a set of instructions) telling the cook how to make a certain dish. A good recipe gives these instructions in the proper order, completely describes how to cook the dish, and makes no assumptions that the cook knows anything about the dish in advance.

If you want your computer to help with your budget, keep track of names and addresses, or compute gas mileage for your travels, you must provide a program that tells the computer how to do those things. There are two ways to supply that program for your computer. You can

- Buy a program that somebody else wrote that does the job you want.

or

- Write the program yourself.

Writing the program yourself has a big advantage for many applications: The program does exactly what you want it to do. If you buy one that is written already, you must adapt your needs to the needs of the program's designers. That's where QBasic comes into the picture. With QBasic (and a little study), you can make your computer perform any task.

Because computers are machines that do not think, the instructions you write in QBasic are detailed. You cannot assume the computer understands what to do if the instruction is not in your program.

After you write a QBasic program, you then must *run,* or *execute,* it. Otherwise, your computer doesn't know that you want it to follow the instructions in the program. Just as a cook must follow a recipe's instructions before a dish is made, your computer must execute the program's instructions before it can accomplish what you want.

Microsoft supplies several QBasic programs with each copy of DOS 5.0. To better understand the process of running a program's instructions, take some time (and have some fun doing it) to run these QBasic programs. The next section explains the process.

Running the DOS QBasic Programs

DOS 5.0 includes several programs that you can load into QBasic and run immediately. As explained in Chapter 1, "Welcome to QBasic," your computer must transfer programs from the disk to RAM before your CPU can execute the program's instructions. Before learning more about how to write your own programs, you can get a good idea of what QBasic does by looking at the instructions supplied with DOS.

Table 3.1 describes the DOS 5.0 QBasic programs and their disk file names. The file names are important because without them QBasic doesn't know which program you want to run. (You can run only one program at a time.)

Notice that all QBasic file names end in the .BAS extension. When you save a QBasic program to disk and QBasic prompts you for a file name, the file name assumes the .BAS extension without requiring you to type it.

Table 3.1. DOS 5.0 QBasic programs.

File Name	*Description*
GORILLA.BAS	A game of two Empire State Building gorillas battling each other by throwing bananas. GORILLA.BAS is a good game for two people.
MONEY.BAS	A simple budgeting program to track expenses and income.
NIBBLES.BAS	A game that pits two snakes against each other, with each snake eating up points.
REMLINE.BAS	A utility program to help you convert GW-BASIC and BASICA programs to QBasic's format.

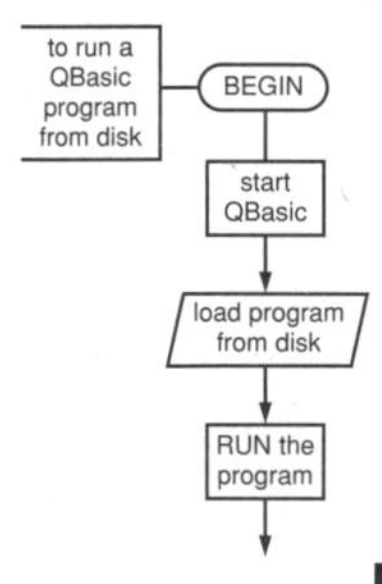

To run a QBasic program that is stored on disk, you must

- Start QBasic.
- Load the program into QBasic's program editing window.
- Run the program.

Example

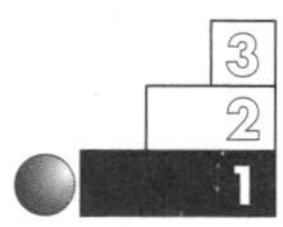

You can run the program by selecting from the menus. For example, run the GORILLA.BAS program using the following steps:

1. Start QBasic by typing `QBASIC` at the DOS prompt.
2. Press Esc to clear the Survival Guide.
3. Select **O**pen... from the **F**ile pull-down menu. You see the **F**ile **O**pen... dialog box as shown in Figure 3.1. QBasic displays a list of the files on the hard disk that have the .BAS extension. Select GORILLA.BAS in one of the following ways: Click on GORILLA.BAS with the mouse, type the file name, or tab to the Files box and press the keyboard's arrow keys until GORILLA.BAS is highlighted. Then press Enter.

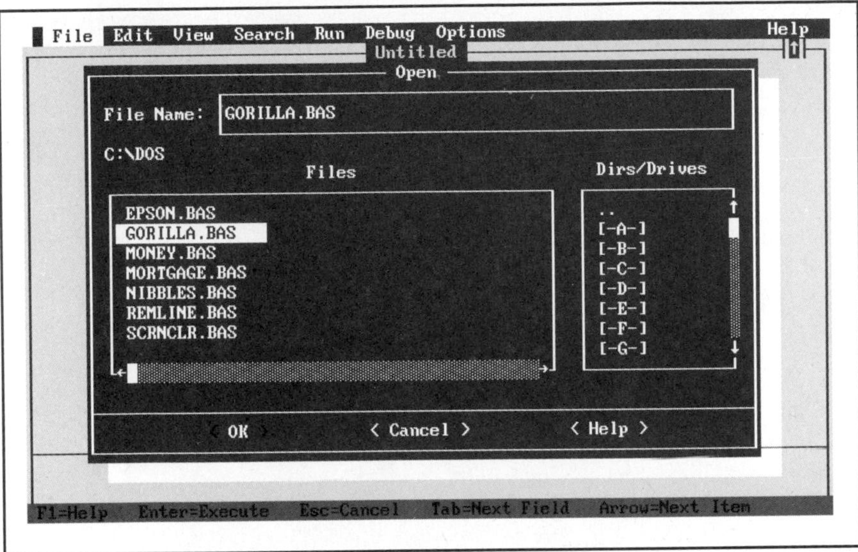

Figure 3.1. Selecting from the **F**ile **O**pen... dialog box.

4. After a brief pause, the program editing window is filled with the GORILLA.BAS program from the disk. The program's file name appears in the center of the bar above the program editing area. If this is the first time you have seen a QBasic program, you might want to look through the program to get an idea of a large QBasic program. This book helps you understand every command in this program.

5. Select **S**tart from the **R**un pull-down menu, or press F5. The game begins with a melody, and then the start-up screen appears. Read through the game's instructions and play the game for a while. Figure 3.2 shows a game of GORILLA.BAS in progress. Who said working with computers doesn't include a little monkey business?

Stopping a QBasic Program

Most QBasic programs give you a chance to quit when you come to a logical stopping place. For example, the GORILLA.BAS program lets you quit the game after you play through and destroy a gorilla. Sometimes, however, you might want to stop a QBasic program in the middle of its execution.

Figure 3.2. The GORILLA.BAS game during play.

Stopping a QBasic program during its progress is simple. When you press Ctrl+Break, the program stops and the program editing window reappears. You then can load another program, select **R**un **S**tart (Shift+F5), or exit to DOS.

The Program and Its Output

While programming, remember the difference between the program and its output. Your program contains the instructions you write using QBasic. Only after you run the program does QBasic follow your instructions.

OUTPUT DEVICE: Where the results of a computer program go.

Throughout this book, you see a program listing (the QBasic instructions in the program) followed by the results that occur when you run the program. The results are the output of the program. They go to an *output device* such as the screen, the printer, or a disk file.

> **TIP:** If you stop a program with Ctrl+Break and decide you want to restart the program at the same place, select **R**un **C**ontinue. The program resumes its previous execution.

Program Design

Design your programs before typing them.

You must plan your programs before you type them. When carpenters build houses, they don't get hammers and nails and start building. Carpenters first find out what the owner of the house wants, draw up the plans, order the materials, gather the workers, and *then* start hammering the nails.

The hardest part of writing a program is breaking it into logical steps that the computer can follow. Learning the language is a requirement; however, the language is not the only thing to consider. Learning the formal program-writing procedure makes your programming job easier. To write a program you should

1. **Define the problem to be solved with the computer.**
2. **Design the output of the program (what the user sees).**
3. **Break the problem into logical steps to achieve the problem's solution.**
4. **Write the program (this is where QBasic comes into play).**
5. **Test the program to make sure it performs as expected.**

As you can see, the actual typing of the program occurs toward the end of programming. You *must plan* how to tell a computer to perform certain tasks.

Your computer can perform instructions only step-by-step. You must assume that your computer has no previous knowledge of the problem and that you must supply the computer with that knowledge. That is what good recipes do: A recipe for baking a cake that simply said, "Bake the cake" wouldn't be a very good one because it assumes entirely too much on the part of the cook. Even if the recipe is written step-by-step, you must take proper care to ensure that the steps are in sequence (by planning in advance). Putting the ingredients in the oven *before* stirring them wouldn't be prudent.

This book follows the same step-by-step process that a computer program and a good recipe should follow. Before you see a program, the book shows you the thought process behind it. The book tells you the goals of the program, breaks them into logical steps, and then shows the written program.

Designing the program in advance makes the entire program structure more accurate and keeps you from having to change it much. A builder knows that a room is much harder to add after the house is built than before. When you do not plan properly and think out every step of your program, creating the final working program takes longer. It is harder to make major changes to a program if you have written the program already than it would be if you made the change in the design stage.

Developing programs using these five steps becomes more important to you as you write longer and more complicated programs. Throughout this book, you see tips for program design. Now, you can jump into QBasic and see what it's like to type and run your own program.

Using the Program Editor

QBasic's program editor is one of its biggest improvements over its predecessors. The program editor is like a word processor. You can type a program, change it, move parts of it around, and erase pieces of it. You do most of these functions from the menu bar, so you do not need to remember command names.

Typing a Program

QBasic programs appear in the large program editor window as you type them. After typing the program's instructions, you should run the program to see the results and fix any problems that might arise. Before worrying about QBasic's instructions, type a program in the program editing window. The most important thing to understand is how to move the cursor. Keep in mind the following helpful hints:

- The cursor shows you where the *next* character you type appears.
- Press Enter after each line in the program.
- Backspace moves the cursor to the left and erases as it moves.
- Use the arrow keys, PgUp, and PgDn to move the cursor left, right, up, and down the screen one character or one screen at a time.
- If you leave out a letter, word, or phrase, move the cursor to the place you want to insert the missing text. Type the missing text. The rest of the line moves over to the right so that there is room for the inserted characters. The cursor turns into a block cursor if you press Ins. Pressing Ins toggles you between *insert* mode and *overtype* mode. Overtype mode replaces letters on the screen as you type.
- If you type an extra letter, word, or phrase, move the cursor over the extra text and press Del. The rest of the line moves to the left to fill the gap left by the deleted character.
- If the program takes more than one screen, the program editing window scrolls upward to make room for the new text. If you want to see the text that has scrolled off the screen, press the up arrow, press PgUp, or click on the top of the scroll bar with the mouse. Pressing the down arrow, pressing PgDn, or clicking on the bottom of the scroll bar moves the bottom portion of the text back into view.

Later in this chapter, Table 3.2 gives a more detailed list of editing commands.

TIP: Many of QBasic's shortcut keys, such as the cursor movement keystrokes, are the same as the ones used in the WordStar word processing program.

Example

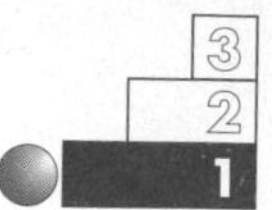

1. Type the following program in your program editing window. This program takes less than one screen, so the program doesn't scroll. Do not worry about understanding the program. The rest of this book focuses on the QBasic language. For now, just practice using the editor.

```
REM My first QBasic program
REM
REM This program displays a message on the screen
REM
CLS
PRINT "Hello!  I am your computer."
PRINT
PRINT "Press a key to clear the screen..."
REM Wait for a keystroke
WHILE (A$ = "")
   A$ = INKEY$
WEND
CLS
END
```

After you type the program, your screen looks like the one in Figure 3.3. Make sure you type the program exactly as it appears here. When you type the commands (the words that are in uppercase) in lowercase letters, the QBasic program editor converts them to uppercase so that you can see them better.

If you used the `/EDITOR` command-line option to start QBasic (which would put the MS-DOS editor, `Editor`, in effect), the characters are not converted to uppercase because only the QBasic program editor does conversion.

You can see the results of this program by running it, just as you ran the GORILLA.BAS program earlier. Select **S**tart from the **R**un pull-down menu. Your screen clears and you see the output of the program.

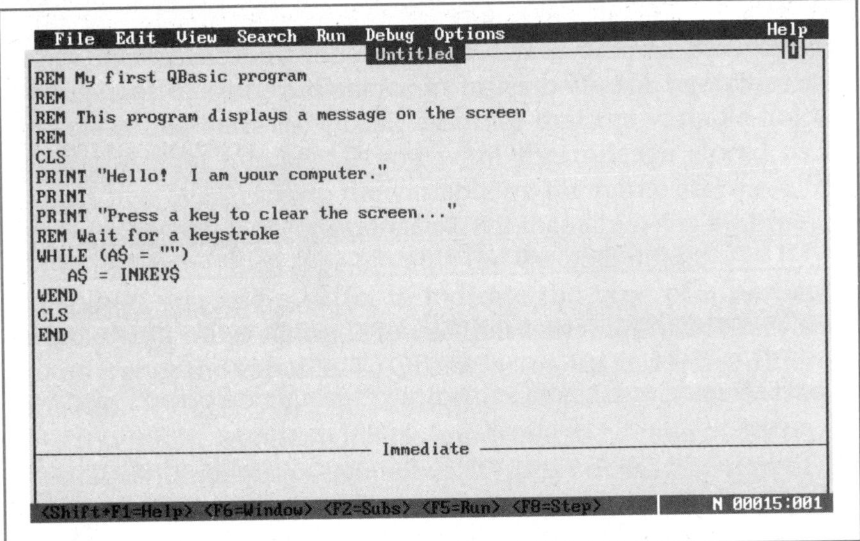
File Edit View Search Run Debug Options Help
Untitled
REM My first QBasic program
REM
REM This program displays a message on the screen
REM
CLS
PRINT "Hello! I am your computer."
PRINT
PRINT "Press a key to clear the screen..."
REM Wait for a keystroke
WHILE (A$ = "")
A$ = INKEY$
WEND
CLS
END
Immediate
<Shift+F1=Help> <F6=Window> <F2=Subs> <F5=Run> <F8=Step>
N 00015:001

Figure 3.3. The program editing window after you type your first QBasic program.

NOTE: QBasic always displays the message

```
Press any key to continue
```

at the bottom of the screen before returning to the QBasic editor. This gives you the chance to see the last of a program's output before QBasic clears it and the QBasic editor returns to the screen.

If There Are Errors

Because you are typing instructions for a machine, you must be accurate. If you misspell a word, leave out a quotation mark, or make another mistake, QBasic informs you with a dialog box that pops up in the middle of the screen (see Figure 3.4). The word or line of the program in which QBasic first spotted the error is highlighted. The most common error is a *syntax error,* which usually means you've misspelled a word.

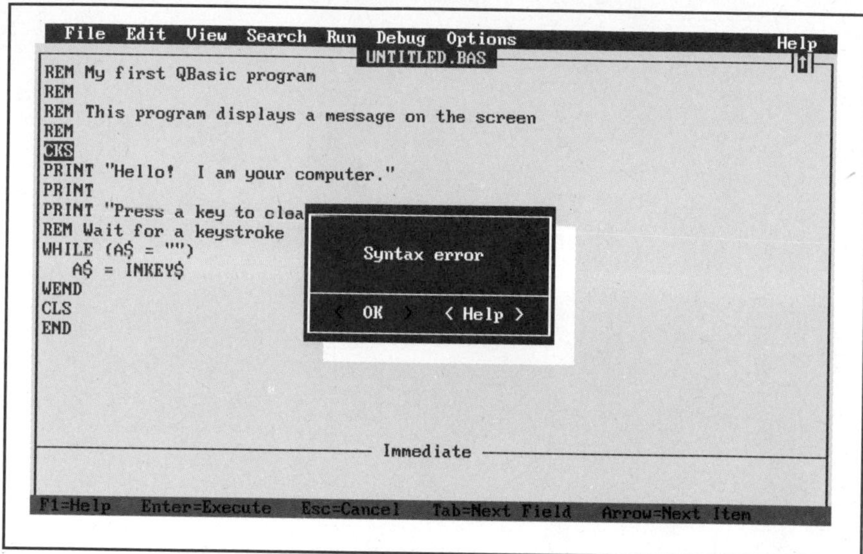
File Edit View Search Run Debug Options Help
UNTITLED.BAS
REM My first QBasic program
REM
REM This program displays a message on the screen
REM
CKS
PRINT "Hello! I am your computer."
PRINT
PRINT "Press a key to clea
REM Wait for a keystroke
WHILE (A$ = "")
A$ = INKEY$
WEND
CLS
END
Syntax error
< OK > < Help >
Immediate
F1=Help Enter=Execute Esc=Cancel Tab=Next Field Arrow=Next Item

Figure 3.4. The error message dialog box.

If you get an error message, you can select OK to return to the program editor and fix the problem. If you don't understand the error, select **H**elp to get an idea what the error message means.

This example program illustrates the difference between the program and its output. You must type the program (or load it from disk) and then run the program to see its output.

Clear this program from memory by selecting **F**ile **N**ew. Select **N**o when QBasic asks whether you want to save the file to disk.

You do not always have to run the program to find syntax errors. The QBasic program editor can check for syntax errors in your program *as you type.* For example, if you leave off a closing parenthesis, QBasic lets you know about the omission when you press Enter after typing the line. You can turn on and turn off this feature by selecting **S**yntax Checking from the **O**ptions pull-down menu.

Getting the Bugs Out

One of the first computers, which was owned by the military, would not print some important data one day. After programmers spent many hours trying to find the solution within the program, a lady named *Grace Hopper* decided to check the printer.

She found a small moth lodged between two wires. When she removed the moth, the printer began working perfectly (although the moth didn't have as much luck).

The late Grace Hopper retired from the Navy as a rear admiral. Although she was responsible for developing many important computer concepts (she was the author of the original COBOL language), she might be remembered best for discovering the first computer *bug*.

Because a bug was discovered to be the culprit, errors in computer programs are known as computer bugs. When you test a program, you might have to *debug* it—remove the bugs, or errors—by fixing your typing errors and changing the logic so that the program does exactly what you want.

Working with a Longer Program

For more practice using the program editor, type the following program. The program asks for your name and displays it around the screen in various ways. As with the last program, do not worry about the language, but concentrate on using the program editor. Getting used to the editor now enables you to concentrate on the language later in the book.

```
CLS
INPUT "What is your first name"; f$
CLS
```

```
REM Print the name randomly on the screen
FOR i = 1 TO 15
   row = INT(RND * 24) + 1
   col = INT(RND * (81 - LEN(f$))) + 1
      LOCATE row, col
   PRINT f$
   FOR t = 1 TO 500                    'Short timing loop
   NEXT t
   LOCATE row, col
   PRINT STRING$(LEN(f$), 32);        'Blank the name
NEXT i
CLS

REM Print name in columns
FOR row = 1 TO 24
   LOCATE row, 1
   PRINT f$, f$, f$, f$, f$
NEXT row
FOR t = 1 TO 5000     'Short timing loop
NEXT t
CLS

REM Print message in the middle of the screen
LOCATE 12, 30
PRINT "That's all, "; f$
END
```

As the text scrolls, practice using the arrow keys (if you use the keyboard) and the scroll bar (if you have a mouse). When you finish typing the program, select **S**tart (F5) from the **R**un menu to see the results of the program.

Advanced Editing

Typing, scrolling, inserting, and deleting are all you need in order to write and modify QBasic programs. There are some advanced editing features that even beginners can master with a little practice. You can work with *blocks* of text instead of individual characters. You can move or copy those blocks of text throughout your program. You can set *bookmarks* that, as with regular books, help you find your way back to certain places within a long program.

You also can view your program from two different windows, which enables you to see two different parts of your program at the same time.

Working with Blocks of Text

Before moving or copying a block of text, you must *select* (or mark) it. As you select text, QBasic highlights the text so that you always know which text you are marking. The previous example printed your name randomly around the screen, then printed it in five columns down the screen. If you want to reverse that order by printing the columns first, you can delete the last half of the program and type this piece into the first half; however, that requires much typing. By selecting the text that prints the columns first, you can move the entire block of text with only a few keystrokes.

Example

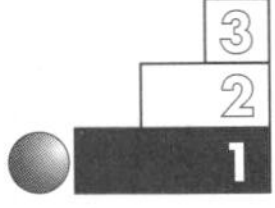

1. To help you practice working with blocks of text, the following example shows you how to rearrange the screen printing program.

   Select the section of text that begins with the blank line before `REM Print name in columns`. Move the cursor to this line; then press the Shift key and the down arrow until the line with `CLS` (seven lines later) is highlighted (see Figure 3.5).

   To move the text, you must delete the text and copy it to QBasic's *clipboard*. The clipboard is a section of memory reserved for blocks of text. The clipboard holds only one block of text at a time. You cannot copy or delete more than one block of text to the clipboard. The clipboard is the in-between location for blocks of text; you cannot see text you send to the clipboard, but you can insert it in your program. Now that you have selected the text, display the Edit pull-down menu. The top section of the menu shows you the commands that work on clipboard text. (These and other commands are in Table 3.2 at the end of the chapter.)

```
 File  Edit  View  Search  Run  Debug  Options                              Help
                                   Untitled
   PRINT STRING$(LEN(f$), 32);     ' Blank the name
NEXT i
CLS

REM Print name in columns
FOR row = 1 TO 24
   LOCATE row, 1
   PRINT f$, f$, f$, f$, f$
NEXT row
FOR t = 1 TO 5000      ' Short timing loop
NEXT t
CLS

REM Print message in the middle of the screen
LOCATE 12, 30
PRINT "That's all, "; f$
END

                                   Immediate
<Shift+F1=Help> <F6=Window> <F2=Subs> <F5=Run> <F8=Step>          N 00025:004
```

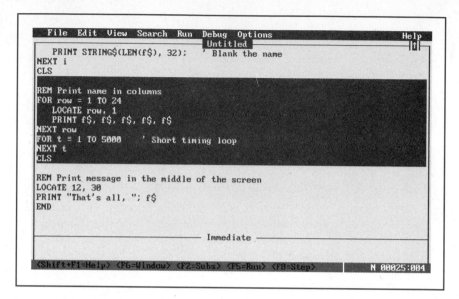

Figure 3.5. Selecting a block of text.

Delete (Cu**t**) the selected text from the program by selecting Cu**t** (Shift+Del). The entire block of text disappears from the program and goes to the clipboard. Move the cursor until it rests on the blank line before `REM Print your name randomly on the screen` early in the program. Select **P**aste (Shift+Ins) from the **E**dit pull-down menu. QBasic places the clipboard text in the program. **P**aste always inserts clipboard text wherever the cursor is when you select this command.

Run the program again to see the new order of its code.

TIP: The text is still in the clipboard, although you pasted it into your text. By pasting clipboard program text throughout a program, you can put several copies of the text in several places within the same program. This keeps you from typing the same thing more than once. If you do not want the text moved from its original spot when you first move it to the clipboard, select **C**opy (Ctrl+Ins), instead of Cu**t**, from the **E**dit menu.

If you want to remove a block of selected text completely without destroying the contents of the clipboard, select Cl**e**ar (Del) from the **E**dit menu. This removes the selected text from the program. The program closes up to fill the gap left by the deleted text.

Using Blocks of Help Code

After mastering more of QBasic, you can begin to use the on-line help feature often. The examples supplied for each command can be more helpful than the descriptions of the commands. If you see a QBasic command in the on-line help program that is used in the same way you want to use the command, you can select and copy text from the help screen directly to your program. This is faster than retyping the example.

Example

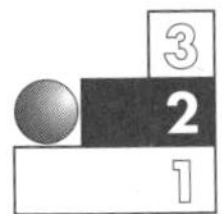

1. Display the help screen for the `PLAY` statement. To do this, select **I**ndex from the **H**elp menu. When the list of commands appears, press **P** to scroll to the commands starting with the letter *P*. Click on `PLAY (Music) Statement` (keyboard users can move the cursor there and press Enter) to see the first of three help screen descriptions of the `PLAY` command.

   Press PgDn twice. You see a sample QBasic program that uses the `PLAY` statement. You do not have to understand anything about this program now. Select all the lines of the program as though it were a block of text in your own program editing window (see Figure 3.6).

   After you select the entire program, select **E**dit **C**opy to copy the program to the clipboard. Press Esc to get rid of the on-line help screen. You now can select **E**dit **P**aste. The entire program from Help is copied to your program editing window.

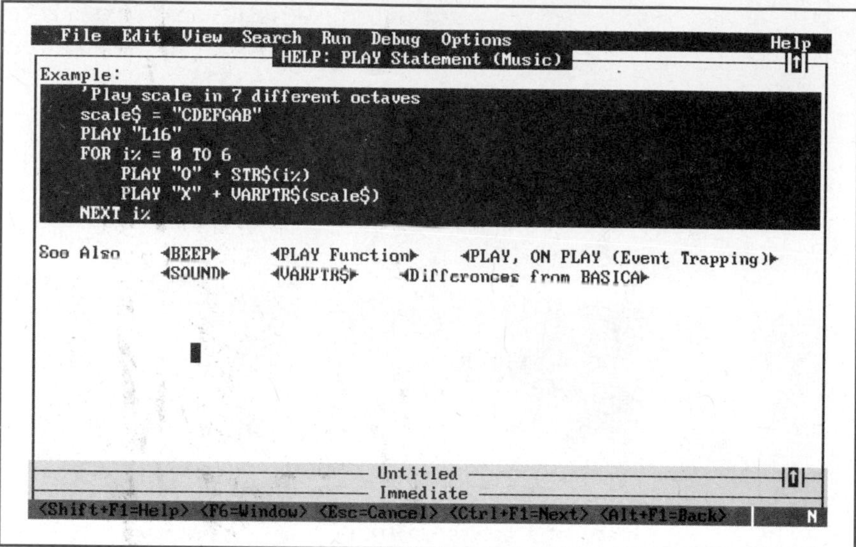

Figure 3.6. Selecting Help's PLAY statement program code.

Using Bookmarks

In programs that are several screens long, you might want to mark a line or two with bookmarks. Marking lines enables you to edit other parts of the program and then jump back to any of the bookmarks quickly, without having to scroll the entire program to find them.

NOTE: You can set up to four bookmarks in a program.

To set a bookmark, follow these steps:

1. Using the scrolling keys, move the cursor to the position at which you want the bookmark.
2. Press Ctrl+K, followed by a number *0, 1, 2,* or *3*. Each number represents a different bookmark. You can see nothing on the screen to let you know the bookmark was set.

To move the cursor to any bookmark you have set, press Ctrl+Q followed by the number of the bookmark to which you want to go.

Window Editing

By using the QBasic windowing feature, you can view two different parts of your program at the same time. By creating two windows, you essentially are creating two program editing windows, one on top of the other. Figure 3.7 shows the name-printing program displayed in two windows. Notice that the first few lines are in the top window and the last few are in the bottom window. On an extremely long program, using two windows enables you to see two different (but related) parts of a program at the same time.

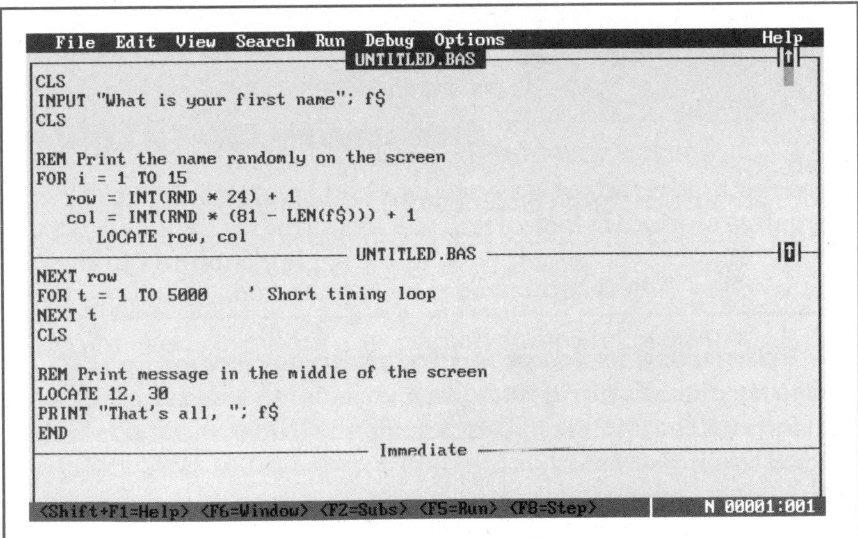

Figure 3.7. Viewing two editing windows at the same time.

Example

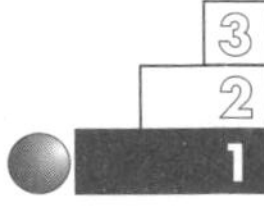

1. To create the two windows in Figure 3.7, move the cursor to the center of the screen and select **V**iew S**p**lit. The window is split horizontally into two windows at the cursor's position.

You then can scroll the two windows independently of each other. To move the cursor to the other window, press F6. You can close the second window by selecting **View Split** again.

Even when you are using two windows, there is still only one clipboard. When you copy or cut text to the clipboard from one window, you can move the cursor to the other window and insert that same clipboard text there.

If you want to see more of the text in one of the windows, but you still want the split screen, press Ctrl+F10 to zoom out the current window (the window the cursor is in) so that it fills the entire program editing area as if it were the only active window. Pressing Ctrl+F10 again zooms the window back to its original size so that the split screen appears again.

Pressing Alt+PLUS and Alt+MINUS zooms the current window one row at a time. This enables you to fine-tune the size of each window.

Table 3.2. The QBasic editing keys.

Description	*Keystroke*	*WordStar Equivalent*
Cursor Movement		
Character left	Left arrow	Ctrl+S
Character right	Right arrow	Ctrl+D
To one word left	Ctrl+Left arrow	Ctrl+A
To one word right	Ctrl+Right arrow	Ctrl+F
One line up	Up arrow	Ctrl+E
One line down	Down arrow	Ctrl+X
Beginning of line	Home	Ctrl+Q, S
Start of next line	Ctrl+Enter	Ctrl+J
End of line	End	Ctrl+Q, D
Top of window		Ctrl+Q, E
Bottom of window		Ctrl+Q, X
Move to next window	F6	
Insert and overstrike	Ins	Ctrl+V

Description	*Keystroke*	*WordStar Equivalent*
Text-Scrolling Keys		
One line up	Ctrl+Up arrow	Ctrl+W
One line down	Ctrl+Down arrow	Ctrl+Z
One page up	PgUp	Ctrl+R
One page down	PgDn	Ctrl+C
Text-Selection Keys		
Character left	Shift+Left arrow	
Character right	Shift+Right arrow	
Word left	Shift+Ctrl+Left arrow	
Word right	Shift+Ctrl+Right arrow	
Current line	Shift+Down arrow	
Line above	Shift+Up arrow	
Screen up	Shift+PgUp	
Screen down	Shift+PgDn	
To the beginning of the file	Shift+Ctrl+Home	
To the end of the file	Shift+Ctrl+End	
To Insert, Copy, and Delete		
Copy selected text to the clipboard	Ctrl+Ins	
Delete selected text and copy it to the clipboard	Shift+Del	
Delete the current line and copy it to the clipboard	Ctrl+Y	
Delete to end of line and copy it to the clipboard	Ctrl+Q, Y	
Paste the contents of the clipboard	Shift+Ins	
Insert a blank line below the cursor position	End, Enter	
Insert a blank line above the cursor position	Home, Ctrl+N	
Insert special characters	Ctrl+P, Ctrl+key	

continues

Table 3.2. continued

Description	*Keystroke*	*WordStar Equivalent*
Delete one character to the left of the cursor	Backspace	Ctrl+H
Delete one character at the cursor	Del	Ctrl+G
Delete the rest of the word the cursor is on		Ctrl+T
Delete selected text	Del	Ctrl+G
Delete leading spaces from selected lines	Shift+Tab	
Bookmark Keys		
Set up to four bookmarks	Ctrl+K, 0-3	
Go to a specific bookmark	Ctrl+Q, 0-3	
Window Commands		
Increase the size of the active window	Alt+PLUS	
Decrease the size of the active window	Alt+MINUS	
Zoom in or out of the active window	Ctrl+F10	
Move left one window	Ctrl+PgUp	
Move right one window	Ctrl+PgDn	

Summary

After reading this chapter, you should understand the steps necessary to write a QBasic program. You know that advanced planning makes writing programs much easier and that the program's instructions produce output only after you run the program.

You also have the tools you need to type the program with the QBasic editor. The editor is as powerful as some word processors. Now that you know how to type programs in QBasic, it is time to look at Chapter 4, "Working with Your Program File," to see how to save your programs to disk so that you can reuse them without typing them again.

Review Questions

Answers to the Review Questions are in Appendix B.

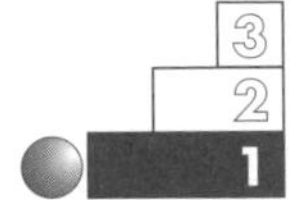

1. What is a program?
2. What are the two ways to obtain a program you want?
3. TRUE or FALSE: Computers can think.
4. What is the difference between a program and its resulting output?
5. What do you use to type QBasic programs into the computer?

6. What file name extension do all QBasic programs have?
7. Why is typing the program one of the *last* steps in the programming process?
8. TRUE or FALSE: You can use the left arrow and Backspace keys interchangeably.
9. What is the area of memory in which you temporarily store blocks of text called?
10. What is the maximum number of bookmarks you can put into a QBasic program?

4

Working with Your Program File

Chapter 3, "What Is a Program?" showed you how to enter and edit a QBasic program. After you type the program, you want to save it to disk for future use. You need to understand the File menu's options for saving and loading QBasic programs from a disk. Before you learn the language elements, it helps to see the format of a QBasic program and how to search and replace text in your programs. This chapter introduces the following concepts:

- Loading saved program files in the program editor.
- Saving QBasic program files to disk.
- Erasing a program from memory.
- Printing a program on the printer.
- Understanding the format of a QBasic program.
- Searching for text in a QBasic program.
- Replacing text in a QBasic program.

This chapter finishes Part I, "Introduction to QBasic." When you master the concepts in this chapter, you will be ready to begin your journey into QBasic programming.

Loading Program Files from the Disk

In Chapter 3 you ran the GORILLA.BAS program by loading it from the disk to memory. The **File** **O**pen... command loads program files, a process that will become second nature to you. Remember that a program you type is erased when you power-off the computer unless you save that program to a nonvolatile disk, such as a floppy disk or a hard disk.

Figure 4.1 shows the **File** **O**pen... dialog box. You can type a file name in the File Name box or select one from the list in the Files box. Remember that Tab takes you between the parts of a dialog box, and so does clicking with the mouse. If you want to look at a different disk or subdirectory, you can select another from within the Dirs/Drives list. When you finish entering the file information in the dialog box, press Enter or click OK.

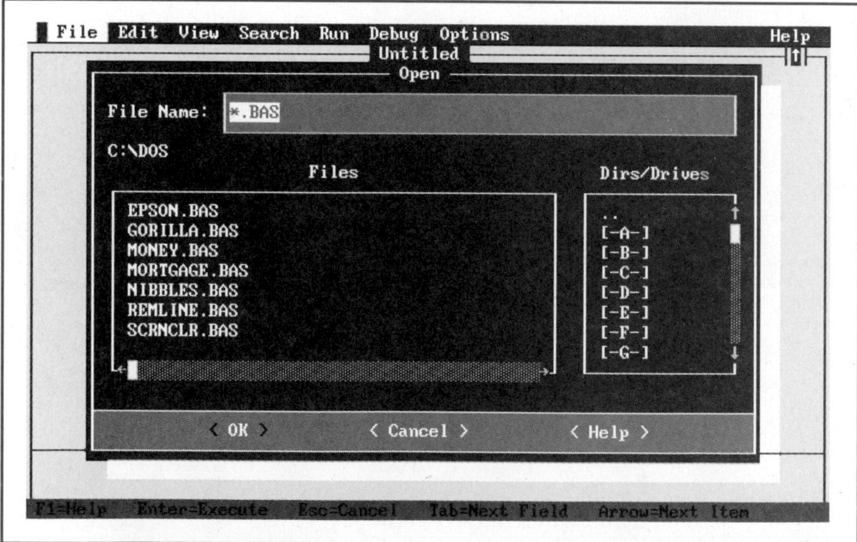

Figure 4.1. The **File** **O**pen... dialog box.

QBasic holds only one program in memory at a time. If you attempt to load a program file in memory and have not saved the program that is already in the program editing window, QBasic

reminds you to save the file. QBasic gives you a chance to do so before loading the other program over the one in the program editing window. When you load a program in memory, it completely replaces the program already there before loading the disk's program.

Saving Programs to Disk

When you save a file, you must choose a file name. QBasic appends .BAS to the end of the file name, but you must supply the first part. Save programs with the **F**ile Save **A**s... command. After choosing **F**ile Save **A**s..., you see the dialog box shown in Figure 4.2. You can type a new file name or you can type the name of a file that already exists. If you choose the latter, QBasic overwrites that file with the program in memory. You have the option also of selecting a different disk drive or directory by selecting the Dirs/Drives box.

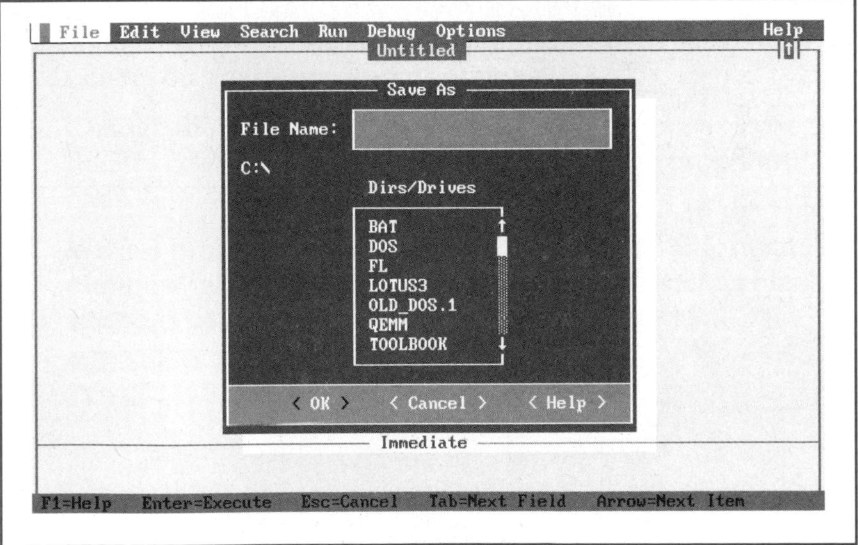

Figure 4.2. The **F**ile Save **A**s... dialog box.

When typing the file name, you can use one to eight characters. The file name can contain letters, numbers, the underscore character (_), and a few other special characters such as the exclamation point (!) and the pound sign (#).

TIP: Many special characters cannot be included in a file name. It is not easy to remember which you can and cannot use, so it is best to stay away from all special characters except letters, numbers, and the underscore. Use the underscore as a separating character, as in ACT_PAY.BAS, because you cannot put spaces in a file name.

The **F**ile **S**ave command saves the current program to disk under the most recent file name. For instance, if you load a file called MYFILE.BAS from disk and then make changes to it, **F**ile **S**ave saves it under the name MYFILE.BAS. This process is quicker than selecting **F**ile Save **A**s... and typing or selecting the same name it was saved under. If you previously used **F**ile Save **A**s... but are still working on the program, **F**ile **S**ave uses the same name that you formerly saved it under.

While working on a long program, you would be wise to save a program often (about every 10 minutes) in case you have a power failure. Otherwise, you could recover only what is on the disk—not what was in memory when the power went out. You might consider also saving to a diskette periodically to guard against hard disk failure.

Erasing the Program Editing Window

Sometimes you want to clear the program editing window without saving the program on which you are working. To start over with a clear program editing window, select **F**ile **N**ew. QBasic warns you that you have not saved the program and gives you a chance to do so with the dialog box shown in Figure 4.3. You can select No to tell QBasic that you intend to erase the program without saving it first. The screen's program editing window clears also.

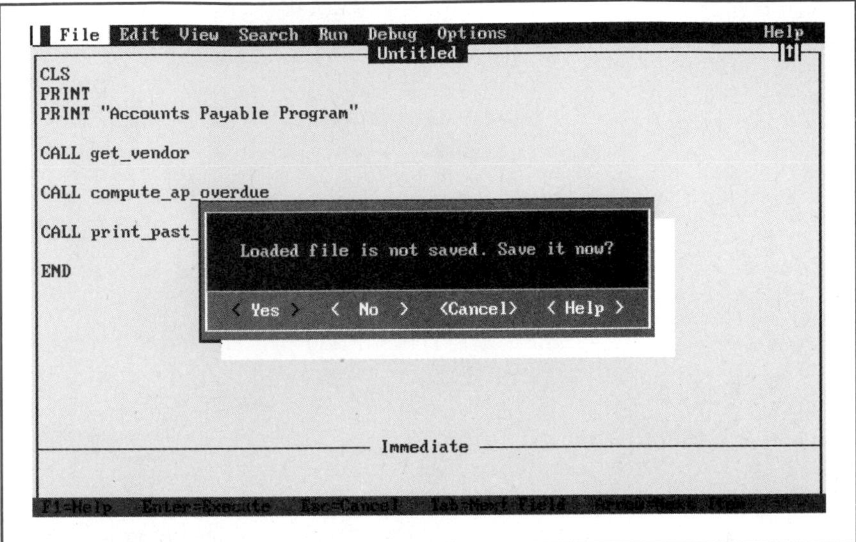

Figure 4.3. A dialog box warning that you have not saved the program.

Printing a Program

Sometimes you want to send your program to the printer. Having a printout helps when you are working with a large program because it is easier to look for errors on paper than on the screen. The printout is also a safe backup copy (called a *hard copy*) for the program in case the disk is erased.

To print your program, select the **File** **P**rint... command, which triggers the dialog box shown in Figure 4.4. The three options enable you to print selected text (if you selected any), the current window (whatever window you were editing in when you selected **F**ile **P**rint), and the entire program. Make sure your printer is on and has paper before accepting this dialog box. If you want to cancel the **F**ile **P**rint command, press Esc or click Cancel.

> **CAUTION:** You will get a `Device Fault` error if you attempt to print to a printer that is off or out of paper. If this occurs, correct the problem and reissue the command.

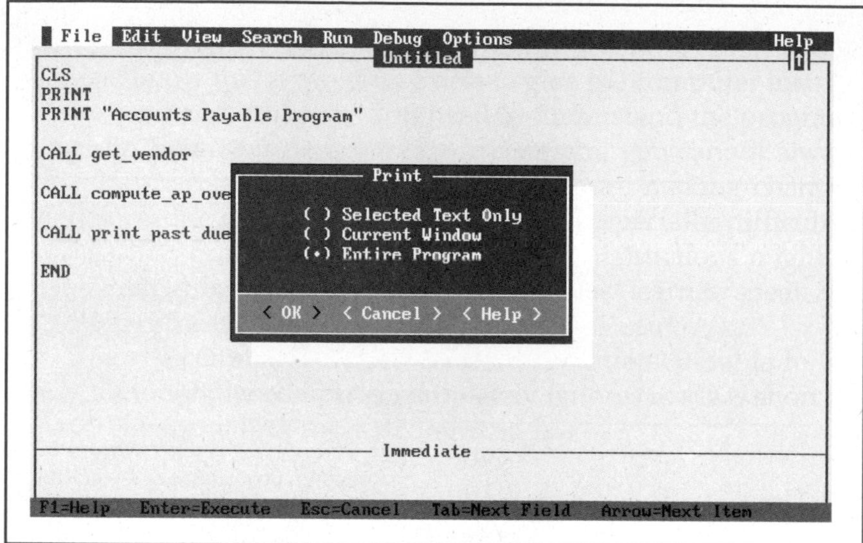

Figure 4.4. The **File** **P**rint... dialog box.

Writing a QBasic Program

Before learning the QBasic language, recall that a program is a set of instructions that tells the computer what to do and the steps in which to do it. You write a program to solve a problem.

QBasic programs execute one instruction after the other in a top-to-bottom order. To override an order you can *branch* to another part of the program by using certain QBasic commands. The QBasic instructions are for the computer and must be precise.

Spacing in Programs

QBasic programs, however, can be typed *free-form,* which means that you can add spacing and blank lines to make the program more readable. For example, Figure 4.5 shows the short program you typed in Chapter 3, with no spacing or blank lines. Your computer does not care about blank lines and spacing. You put those in to break up the program and make it more readable to you, the programmer.

Figure 4.6 shows the program with spacing and blank lines. Although it all might be cryptic to you now, you can see how QBasic's free-form style is nice to have. Remember also that when you run (execute) the program, the computer looks at the first instruction (the CLS statement) and interprets it first, followed by the second one, and so on.

```
 File  Edit  View  Search  Run  Debug  Options                     Help
                              UNTITLED.BAS
CLS
INPUT "What is your first name"; f$
CLS
REMPrint the name randomly on the screen
FOR i = 1 TO 15
row = INT(RND * 24) + 1
col = INT(RND * (81 - LEN(f$))) + 1
LOCATE row, col
PRINT f$
FOR t = 1 TO 500 'Short timimg loop
NEXT t
LOCATE row, col
PRINT STRING$(LEN(f$), 32); 'Blank the name
NEXT i
CLS
REMPrint name in columns
FOR row = 1 TO 24
LOCATE row, 1
PRINT f$,f$,f$,f$,f$
                              Immediate
<Shift+F1=Help> <F6=Window> <F2=Subs> <F5=Run> <F8=Step>     N 00019:021
```

Figure 4.5. A program with no extra spaces or blank lines.

As you write your QBasic programs, remember the difference between Figure 4.5 and Figure 4.6 and use as much spacing and as many blank lines as you want. Notice that white space is not required in a QBasic line (except for one space between words), although the line is more readable if you put spaces between symbols and numbers as well.

Example

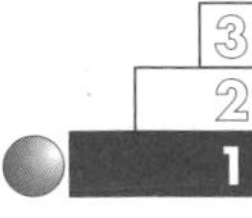

1. To put all this together, type the program in Figure 4.6 in your QBasic program editing window if it's not still there from the previous chapter. Save the program to disk under the file name PROG1.BAS by selecting **F**ile Save **A**s... and filling in the dialog box with the file name.

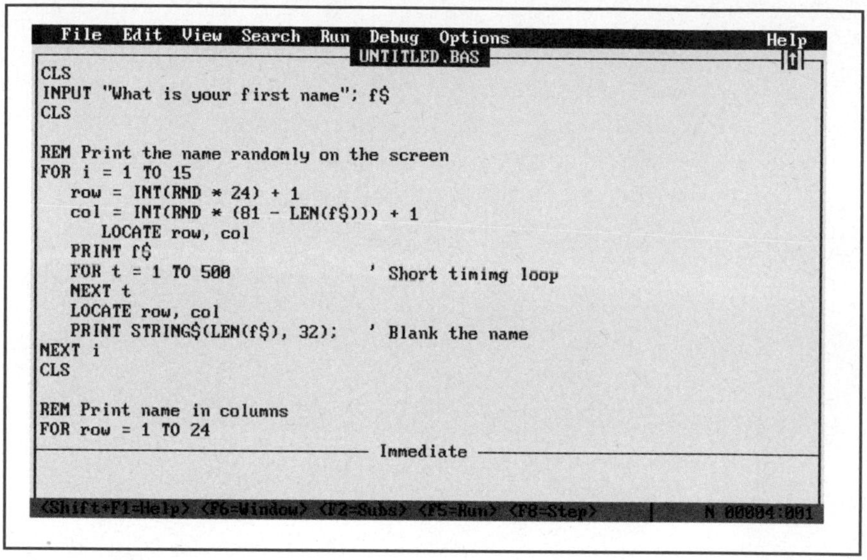

```
 File  Edit  View  Search  Run  Debug  Options                        Help
                                UNTITLED.BAS
CLS
INPUT "What is your first name"; f$
CLS

REM Print the name randomly on the screen
FOR i = 1 TO 15
   row = INT(RND * 24) + 1
   col = INT(RND * (81 - LEN(f$))) + 1
      LOCATE row, col
   PRINT f$
   FOR t = 1 TO 500                ' Short timing loop
   NEXT t
   LOCATE row, col
   PRINT STRING$(LEN(f$), 32);     ' Blank the name
NEXT i
CLS

REM Print name in columns
FOR row = 1 TO 24
                               Immediate

<Shift+F1=Help> <F6=Window> <F2=Subs> <F5=Run> <F8=Step>     N 00004:001
```

Figure 4.6. A more readable program with white spaces and blank lines.

Print the program after you type and save it. Before printing with **F**ile **P**rint..., make sure your printer is on and has paper. After the program is printed, erase your program editing window with **F**ile **N**ew. Your program is now on disk (but not on your screen or in memory) in case you want to load it again later.

Searching for Text in Your Programs

QBasic has a helpful menu command that is typically found on word processors. It is the **F**ind option from the **S**earch pull-down menu. The **S**earch **F**ind command searches for any character, word, or phrase in your QBasic program's editing window.

The **S**earch menu is helpful when you work with long programs. When you edit a short, 10-line program, you can visually find text almost as easily as you can using the **S**earch command. Most programs, however, especially those used in many business applications, span many screens of text. If you need to find the line that a specific command or phrase is on, the **S**earch command makes it easy.

When you display the **S**earch pull-down menu, you see three options: **F**ind..., **R**epeat Last Find, and **C**hange.... Suppose you wanted to find the following command:

```
INPUT "Please enter the amount"; amt
```

(This is a valid QBasic command that you learn in a later chapter.) To find this command line, display the **S**earch menu and select **F**ind... to display the dialog box shown in Figure 4.7. Next to the Find What: message, type enough of the line you are looking for so that QBasic can distinguish it from the rest of the program's lines. For instance, any of the following values for the Find What: prompt would find this command line if it were in your program:

```
INPUT "Please enter the amount"; am
INPUT "Please enter
the amount";
"; am
```

Notice that it really doesn't matter what part of the line you search for. You can search for text at the beginning, middle, or end of the line. You must realize, however, that if there is another line *anywhere* in the program that contains matching text, QBasic finds the first match, whether or not it is the line you really want. You do not have to match the uppercase and lowercase letters in the line unless you tab (or point with the mouse) to Match Upper/Lowercase and select it by pressing the space bar (or clicking with the mouse). Typically, you shouldn't waste time matching uppercase and lowercase characters unless that is critical for finding the right item.

Select the Whole Word option only if you want to search for a full word. For example, to find the line shown earlier you could search for *am*, but you likely would find lines other than the one you were looking for. For instance, if you searched for the letters *am*, QBasic would find all the following lines:

```
PRINT "The extra amount, "; extra.amt; "is zero."
title.str$ = "American Anthem"
```

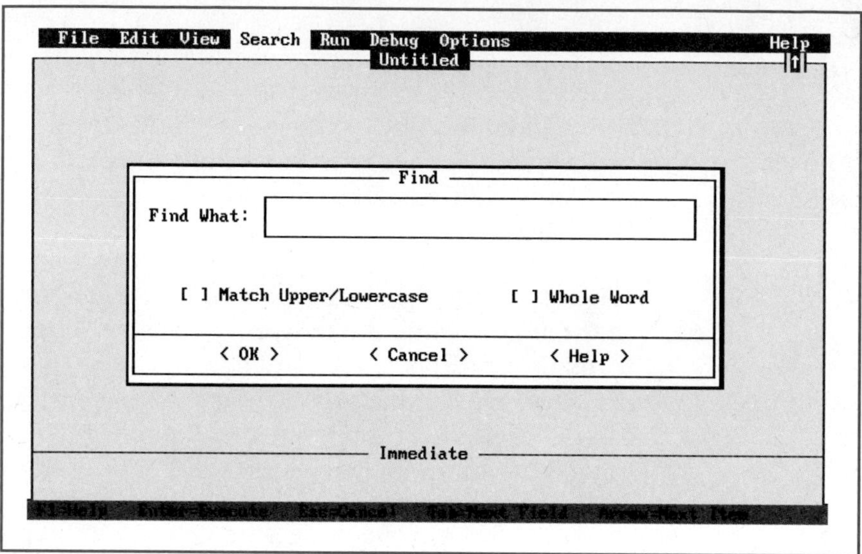

Figure 4.7. The **S**earch **F**ind... dialog box.

If you don't want to find words that contain the letters *am*, but only those lines that contain the word *am*, you have to select Whole Word.

When you finish answering the prompts on the **S**earch **F**ind screen, QBasic looks for the first line that contains matching text. If QBasic does not find a match, it displays a `Match not found` message. If it finds a match, however, it scrolls the screen to the found line and highlights the matching text. You then can edit the text or press F3 (the speed key for the **S**earch **R**epeat Last Find command) to look for the next line that contains the same match.

Replacing Text in Your Programs

After mastering the **S**earch **F**ind... command, it's easy to replace text in your programs. Suppose you printed a customer's last name as *MacMasters* throughout several lines of the program, but you found out later that the name is correctly spelled *McMasters*. You could use the cursor-movement keys to scroll through the text and change each occurrence of the error. QBasic does the work for you with the **S**earch **C**hange... menu option. If you select **S**earch **C**hange..., you see the dialog box in Figure 4.8.

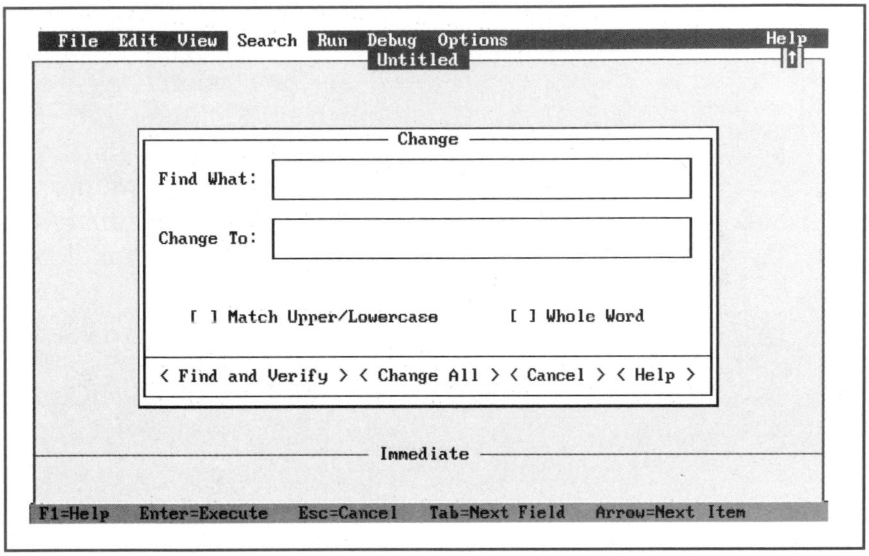

```
 File  Edit  View  Search  Run  Debug  Options                        Help
                              Untitled
                                Change
       Find What:  [                                        ]

       Change To:  [                                        ]

          [ ] Match Upper/Lowercase          [ ] Whole Word

       < Find and Verify > < Change All > < Cancel > < Help >
                              Immediate
 F1=Help  Enter=Execute  Esc=Cancel  Tab=Next Field  Arrow=Next Item
```

Figure 4.8. The **S**earch **C**hange... dialog box.

Type the text you want changed after the Find What: prompt and the change you want QBasic to make after the Change To: prompt. For this example, you would type `MacMasters` after Find What: and `McMasters` after the Change To: prompt.

The Match Upper/Lowercase and Whole Word options work as they did with the **F**ind command. There are two new options at the bottom of the Change dialog box. If you select the first one, Find and Verify, QBasic finds the text and asks your permission before changing it. This is a safeguard in case you do not want every match changed. If you select Change All instead, QBasic quickly finds every match and changes each one.

Summary

This is a short chapter, but it prepares you for managing program files and searching and replacing text within those program files. You are now ready to write programs from scratch by starting Part II, "Primary QBasic Language Elements."

Review Questions

Answers to the Review Questions are in Appendix B.

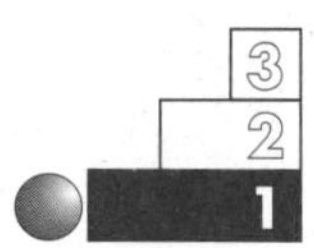

1. What menu command loads a QBasic program file from disk to memory?
2. Why is it important to save your QBasic programs to disk?
3. How many letters can you use for the first part of a file name?
4. TRUE or FALSE: The following are valid file names for QBasic programs:

   PGM 1.BAS   EMPLOYEES.BAS   PAYROLL.PGM
5. How many QBasic programs can be in memory at the same time?

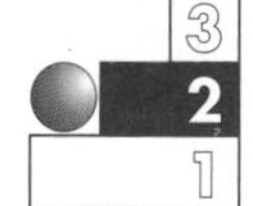

6. TRUE or FALSE: Erasing the program editing window with **F**ile **N**ew erases the program from disk as well.
7. What does the term *free-form* mean?

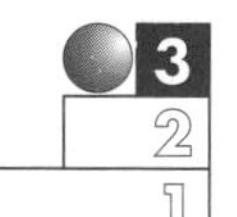

8. Why is it a good idea to save your programs every few minutes as you enter them?

Part II

Primary QBasic Language Elements

Understanding Numeric Variables and Constants

To understand data processing with QBasic, you must understand how QBasic creates, stores, and manipulates data. This chapter covers the following topics:

- What variables and constants are
- Naming and using numeric variables
- The types of numeric variables
- The LET assignment command
- The types of numeric constants
- The PRINT and CLS commands
- The optional END statement

You have mastered the QBasic screen and program files. Before you finish this chapter, you should be able to write your own QBasic programs. You will have fun seeing how easy it is.

QBasic Data

A QBasic program takes data and processes it into meaningful results. You have seen a few programs. Within those programs are

- Commands
- Data

VARIABLE: Data that can change as a program runs.

CONSTANT: Data that remains the same during program execution.

The data is made of *variables* and *constants*. As the name implies, a variable is data that can change as the program runs. A constant is data that remains the same during a program run. In real life, a variable might be your age or your salary. Both increase over time (if you're lucky). A constant might be your first name or your social security number, which remain with you throughout your life.

This chapter focuses on numeric variables and constants. If you are not a "numbers person," don't fret. Working with numbers is the computer's job. You only have to understand how to tell the computer what you want it to do.

Variables

A variable is like a box inside your computer that holds something. That something can be a number, a special character, a word, a sentence, or an entire paragraph of text. You can have as many variables as your program requires to hold data that changes. When you are ready for a variable, simply refer to a new variable and QBasic makes sure you get it.

Variables have characteristics. Because you are responsible for making up your own variables, you must understand each of the possible characteristics of variables so that you can choose one that fits the data. The characteristics of variables are

- Each variable has a name.
- Each variable has a type.
- Each variable holds your specified value.

To help you understand these characteristics, the following sections explain each of them.

Variable Names

Because you can have many variables in one program, you must assign a name to each variable so that you can keep track of them. Variable names are unique, like house addresses. If two variables were allowed to have the same name, QBasic wouldn't know which variable you wanted when you requested the name.

Variable names can be as short as one letter, or they can be a maximum of 40 characters long. Variable names must begin with a letter of the alphabet; after the first letter, however, they can contain letters, numbers, or a period.

> **TIP:** A period helps separate parts of the variable name because you cannot use spaces in the name.

The following variable names are valid:

```
Salary      Aug91.Sales      I      index      AGE
```

You can use uppercase or lowercase letters in a variable name. `Sales`, `SALES`, and `sales` all refer to the same variable. Variables cannot have the same name as a QBasic command or function. Appendix C lists all QBasic commands and function names so that you can avoid them when you name variables.

The following variable names are *invalid:*

```
81_SALES      Aug91+Sales      MY AGE      PRINT
```

Use Meaningful Variable Names

Although you can call a variable any name that fits the naming rules (as long as it is not being used by another variable in the program), you always should use meaningful variable names. Give your variables names that describe the values they hold.

For example, keeping track of total payroll in a variable called `total.payroll` is much more descriptive than using the variable name `XYZ34`. Although both names are valid, `total.payroll` is easier to remember, and later you will have a good idea of what the variable holds by looking at its name.

Variable Types

Variables can hold different *types* of numbers. For example, when a variable holds an integer, QBasic assumes that no decimal point or fractional part (the part to the right of the decimal point) exists for the variable's value. Table 5.1 lists the different numeric types QBasic recognizes.

Table 5.1. QBasic numeric variable types.

Type	*Variable Suffix*	*Examples*
Integer	%	12, 0, -765, 21843
Long integer	&	32768, 99876
Single-precision	!	1.0, 34.32345
Double-precision	#	-0.99999987654

Basically, an integer is a number without a decimal place (its content is a whole number). Single-precision and double-precision variables are *real* numbers. They have decimal points and a fractional part to the right of the decimal. Single-precision variables can accurately keep six decimal places, whereas double-precision variables keep accuracy to 14 places. Unless you specify otherwise, QBasic assumes that all variables are single-precision. If you put an integer into a variable without overriding the default, QBasic converts that integer to a single-precision number.

The variable suffix goes at the end of the variable's name if you want QBasic to assume the variable is a specific type. For example, if you want to store a distance in miles between two cities in a variable called `distance`, QBasic assumes that the variable holds a single-precision number. If you want the mileage stored as an integer, however, refer to the variable by the name `distance%`. The percent sign (`%`) is not considered part of the name; it is a suffix you add to indicate which type of value the variable holds.

When you use a suffix to indicate the type of a particular variable, you must continue to use that variable suffix every time you reference the variable. To QBasic, `N!`, `N%`, `N&`, and `N#` are different variables.

You might wonder why it is important to have so many types. After all, a number is just a number. It turns out that the type of the variable is critical, but it is not as difficult to use as it might first appear. Table 5.2 lists the *ranges* of values each variable type can hold. A variable cannot hold just any value; it can hold only values that fall within its own type and range of values. You cannot, for instance, put a number larger than 32,767 into a variable that is defined as an integer. Only long integers can hold numbers larger than 32,767. Most of the time, integers and single-precision numbers are sufficient. If you are working with very large or very small numbers or are doing scientific work, however, you might need the extra precision the other types of numbers give you.

Table 5.2. Ranges of each variable type.

Type	*Range of Value*
Integer	-32,768 to +32,767
Long integer	-2,147,483,648 to +2,147,483,647
Single-precision	
Positive numbers	3.402823×10^{38} to 2.802597×10^{-45}
Negative numbers	$-2.802597 \times 10^{-45}$ to -3.402823×10^{38}
Double-precision	
Positive numbers	$1.79769313486231 \times 10^{308}$ to $4.940656458412465 \times 10^{-324}$
Negative numbers	$-4.940656458412465 \times 10^{-324}$ to $-1.79769313486231 \times 10^{308}$

All variables used in this book are integer or single-precision unless otherwise noted. You can put an integer number into a single-precision variable (remember, QBasic always assumes the variable is single-precision unless you specify another variable suffix) because the range of regular integers falls within the range of single-precision numbers.

NOTE: The variables mentioned in this chapter are all *numeric* and hold only numbers. In later chapters, this book discusses how to hold other types of data.

The Lengths of Data

Because double-precision variables can hold such large numbers, you might be tempted to make all variables double-precision by appending the # to the ends of their names. At first glance, this seems like a good solution because you wouldn't have to worry whether your variables were large enough to hold the data. This would not be prudent, however, because your programs slow down considerably when you use double-precision variables.

Eight bytes of memory are required to store a double-precision variable, as opposed to four for single-precision variables, four for long integers, and only two for regular integers. Therefore, when you do not need the extra precision, you use more memory than necessary.

This extra memory usage takes extra CPU time. Every time you use a double-precision variable when a single-precision variable or an integer would do, QBasic has to retrieve eight bytes of memory—two to four times as much as for the other types. Therefore, be conscious of your data lengths and variable requirements, and do not use an "extra-precision" variable when an integer would be sufficient.

The Assignment of Values to Variables

Now that you know about variables, you probably wonder how to put values in them. You do so with the *assignment statement*. The format of the assignment statement is

assign value of expression to variable

```
[LET] variable = expression
```

Notice that the LET command name is in brackets, meaning it is optional. (You never type the brackets.) Because assigning values to variables is common in QBasic programs, the designers of the language decided to make LET optional. The *variable* is any valid variable name you make up. The equal sign is required and must go after the variable name. The *expression* is a value or an expression that equates to a value (you learn more about expressions in the next chapter). Because a variable contains a value, you can assign variables to each other.

> **TIP:** Think of the equal sign as a left-pointing arrow. Loosely, the equal sign means you want to take whatever number, variable, or expression that is on the right side of the equal sign and put it into the variable on the left side of the equal sign.

Examples

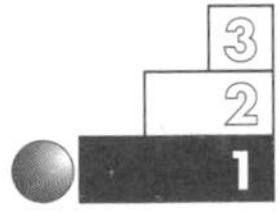

1. If you want to keep track of your current age, salary, and dependents, you can store these values in three variables and include them in your program. These values might change later in the program, for example, when the program calculates a pay increase for you.

   Good variable names might be `age`, `salary`, and `dependents`. To assign values to these three variables, your program would look something like this:

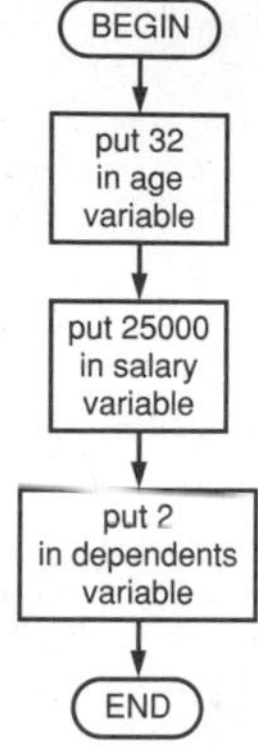


```
LET age = 32
LET salary = 25000
LET dependents = 2
```

You do not need to put a decimal point in the value of the salary because QBasic assumes single-precision variables (unless you override the type). Although you are putting an integer value into these variables, QBasic changes them to single-precision (by adding a decimal point) for you. This conversion from an integer to a single-precision number usually does not cause any problems for you.

Do not put commas in values you assign to variables. The following statement is *invalid:*

```
LET salary = 25,000
```

2. Because the `LET` is optional, you can rewrite this three-line program like this:

```
age = 32
salary = 25000
dependents = 2
```

3. To see how to assign one variable to another, suppose you stored your tax rate in a variable earlier in the program and you decide to use your tax rate for your spouse's tax rate as well. You can code the following:

```
spouse.tax.rate = tax.rate
```

The value you assigned to `tax.rate` would at this point in the program be *copied* to a new variable named `spouse.tax.rate`. The value in `tax.rate` is still there after this line finishes.

4. Remember that a variable can hold only one number at a time. Therefore, you cannot put two values in the same variable. For example, the following program assigns `mileage` one value, then assigns `gallons` a value, and then reassigns `mileage` another value. Because a variable holds only one value at a time, the original value is replaced in the third line.

```
mileage = 100
gallons = 20
mileage = 150
```

The ability to change variables is important, but this example stretches it. There is no good reason to put the 100 in `mileage` when you do not use `mileage` for anything before putting another value into it two lines later. When you print and use variables for more powerful programs, you can see that sometimes it makes more sense to overwrite a variable after using its previous value for something else.

5. Suppose you want to keep your age in an integer variable, your salary in a single-precision variable, and the number of your dependents in an integer variable. You can add the type suffix to the end of the variable name to do this, as follows:

```
age% = 32
salary! = 25000.00
dependents% = 2
```

QBasic's Default Values

If you do not put values in variables, QBasic does it for you. QBasic always puts a zero in each variable you use in a program. As soon as you assign that variable a value, you replace the default zero that was there.

Although QBasic initializes variables to zero, you should not depend on this in your programs; if you want a zero in a variable, put one there with LET. This might seem redundant, but it makes better programs. A person looking at your program later knows that you intended for the zero to be in there and won't have to wonder whether you forgot to initialize the variable.

Using QBasic Constants

Unlike a variable, a *constant* does not change. You already have used constants in this chapter. The values you put into the variables were constants. Numbers are always constant. The number 7 always has the value of 7, and you cannot change it. You can change a variable, however, by putting another value into it.

Numeric constants can be positive or negative. Constants have types just as variables do. Table 5.3 shows the types that are available as constants.

Table 5.3. Types of numeric constants.

Type	*Suffix*	*Examples*
Integer	none	158, 0, -86
Long integer	none	21233343, -32889
Fixed-point	none	4.67, -0.08
Floating-point		
Single-precision	!	1.08E+8
Double-precision	#	-1.8765456D-09

Numeric constants also have ranges. Table 5.4 lists the ranges possible for each type of constant. It is important for you to be aware of those ranges. Unlike with variables, however, QBasic interprets the constants in your programs and makes a good judgment on how to store them. You generally do not have to worry about putting a suffix on a constant.

Remember, do *not* put commas in constants when you put them in your programs.

Scientific Notation

You might find it easier to use *scientific notation* when typing extremely small or large numbers. Scientific notation is a shortcut method of representing numbers of extreme values. Many people program in BASIC for years without using scientific notation. By understanding it, however, you can feel at home with many language reference manuals, and you won't be surprised if QBasic prints a number on your screen in scientific notation.

Table 5.4. Numeric constants and their ranges.

Type	*Range*
Integer	-32,768 to 32,767
Long integer	-2,147,483,648 to 2,147,483,647
Fixed-point	Positive or negative numbers that have decimal points
Floating-point	
Single-precision	-3.37×10^{38} to 3.37×10^{38} (scientific notation)
Double-precision	-1.67×10^{308} to 1.67×10^{308} (scientific notation)

It is easiest to learn scientific notation by looking at a few examples. Basically, you can represent any number in scientific notation, but this representation usually is limited to extremely large or extremely small numbers. All scientific notation numbers are floating-point number constants. Table 5.5 shows some scientific notation numbers, their equivalents, and their types.

Table 5.5. Looking at scientific notation numbers.

Scientific Notation	*Equivalent*	*Type*
3.08E+12	3,080,000,000,000	Single-precision
-9.7587E+02	-97,587	Single-precision
+5.164D-4	0.0005164	Double-precision
-4.6545D-9	-0.0000000046545	Double-precision
1.654D+302	1.654×10^{302}	Double-precision

Notice it is easy to see whether a floating-point number is single- or double-precision. Single-precision scientific notation numbers contain a letter *E*, whereas double-precision numbers contain a *D*.

Positive scientific notation numbers begin with a plus sign or have no sign. Negative scientific numbers begin with a minus sign.

To figure out the rest, take the portion of the number at the left and multiply it by 10 raised to the number on the right. Thus, +2.164D+3 means to take 2.164 and multiply it by 1,000 (1,000 is 10 raised to the third power, or 10^3). Also, -5.432D-2 is negative 5.432 times .01 (10 raised to the -2 power, or 10^{-2}).

Examples

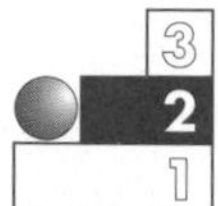

1. Light travels 186,000 miles per second. To store 186,000 as a variable in single-precision scientific notation, type

```
light.speed = 1.86E+5
```

When you use QBasic to perform calculations, QBasic might choose to output a calculated value in scientific notation, although the calculations used numbers that were not in scientific notation.

2. The sun is 93,000,000 miles from the earth. (You're learning space trivia while practicing programming!) The moon is only about 268,000 miles from the earth. To store these two distances in scientific notation, code them as shown:

```
sun.dist = 9.3D+7
moon.dist = 2.68E+5
```

Hexadecimal and Octal Constants

You can express QBasic integer constants in both the hexadecimal (base 16) and octal (base 8) numbering systems. This is helpful if you want to access internal memory locations or other advanced QBasic programs.

To express a constant in hexadecimal, add the prefix `&H` to the number. Any valid hexadecimal constant can follow the prefix. For instance, `32` is a decimal (base 10) integer constant, but `&H20` is that same hexadecimal constant. `&HCD3` is the hexadecimal representation for `3,283`. You can type either upper- or lowercase letters in the hexadecimal constant. For instance, `&HFF00` is the same as `&hff00` and `&Hff00`.

You can express octal constants by prefixing the integer with `&O`, `&o`, or just `&` by itself. For example, `&14` is the octal constant for a decimal `12`, and `&o10` is the octal constant for a decimal `8`. Octal notation is not used much these days, but hexadecimal notation is still common.

If you do not add a hexadecimal or an octal prefix, QBasic assumes the constant is decimal.

Viewing Output

Now that you understand variables and constants, you need to know how to look at that data on the screen. This section introduces one of the most important commands in the QBasic language: `PRINT`.

The `PRINT` Statement

The `PRINT` statement takes whatever is to the right of the word `PRINT` and sends it to the screen. The first format of the `PRINT` statement you should understand is

PRINT expression

```
PRINT expression
```

The *`expression`* you print can be a variable or a constant. If you use a variable name as the *`expression`*, `PRINT` prints the *contents* of that variable on the screen. If you put a constant after `PRINT`, that constant is printed. `PRINT` is a complex command with more options. But for now, you should learn just this fundamental format.

CAUTION: Despite its name, `PRINT` sends the output of variables and constants to the screen and *not* to the printer. Other commands send output to the printer; you can read about them later.

If you put `PRINT` on a line by itself, QBasic prints a blank line. This is a good way to separate lines of screen output from each other.

Examples

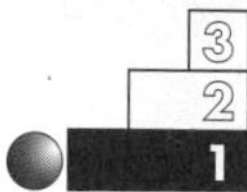

1. You can print the three variables you typed in an earlier example (`age`, `salary`, and `dependents`) by adding three `PRINT` statements after you initialize them. For example:

```
LET age = 32
LET salary = 25000
LET dependents = 2

PRINT age
PRINT salary
PRINT dependents
```

Notice the blank line before the group of `PRINT` statements that separates them from the variable assignments. The blank line is not required, but it helps break the program into logical parts. If you type this program into the QBasic editor and run it (with **R**un **S**tart), you see the output in Figure 5.1.

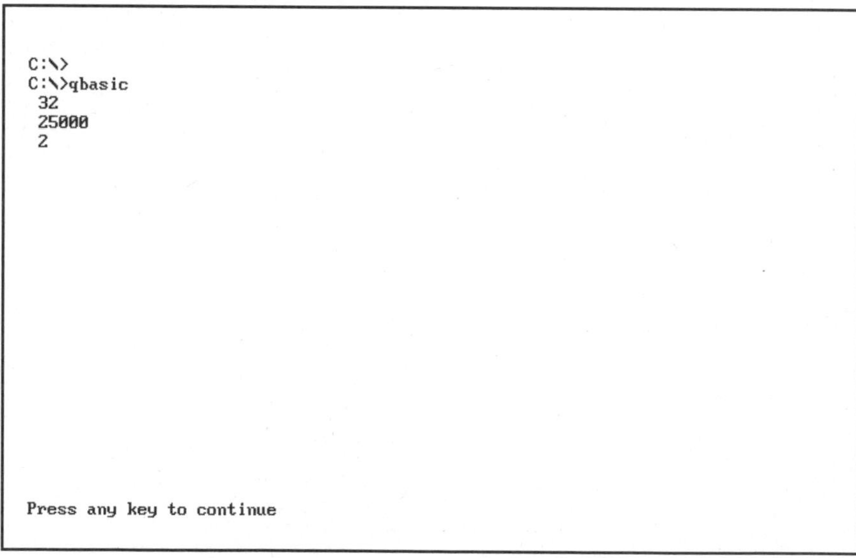

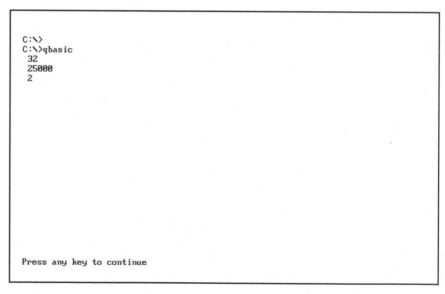

Figure 5.1. The results of running your first `PRINT` program.

Notice that QBasic prints each of the variable's values on a separate line.

2. The order of statements in a program is up to the programmer. As long as your program follows a logical order and produces the output you desire, you decide how to order the statements. You can rewrite the last program as follows:

```
LET age = 32
PRINT age

LET salary = 25000
PRINT salary

LET dependents = 2
PRINT dependents
```

Again, the blank lines are optional. You might want to review the QBasic editor by changing the program to match the previous one and then running it. You can see that the results from both runs are the same.

3. You can put constants also to the right of a PRINT statement. These numbers print exactly as you type them. For example, QBasic prints the first three odd numbers followed by the first three even numbers when you type and run the following program. The odd numbers are stored in variables, and the even numbers are printed from constants.

```
odd1 = 3
odd2 = 5
odd3 = 7

PRINT odd1
PRINT odd2
PRINT odd3
PRINT 2
PRINT 4
PRINT 6
```

This program produces six lines of output, which are shown in Figure 5.2.

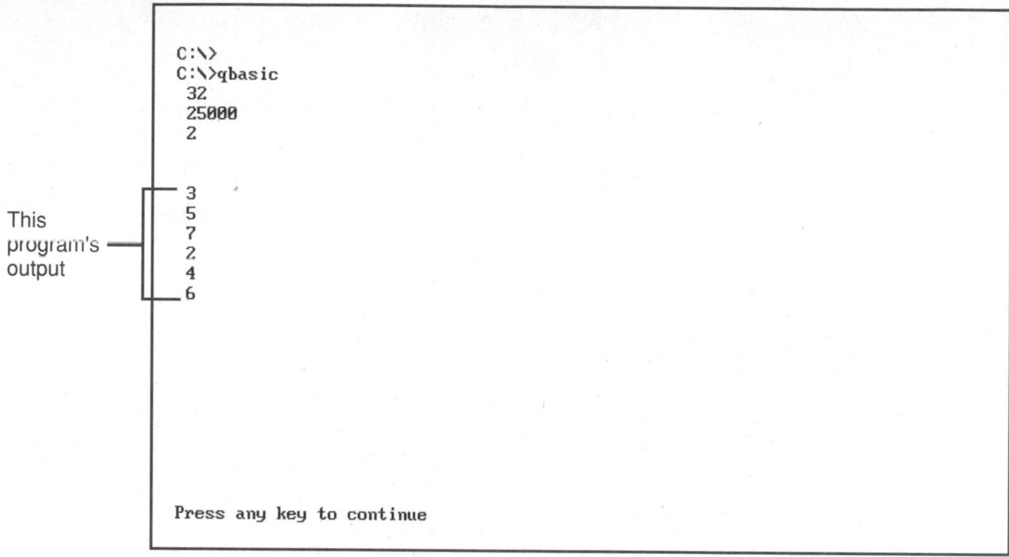

Figure 5.2. The results of running the PRINT constants program.

4. If you want blank lines between lines of output, use blank PRINT statements, as the following program shows:

```
PRINT 2
PRINT
PRINT 4
PRINT

PRINT 6
PRINT
PRINT 8
PRINT
PRINT 10
```

When you run this program, you see the output in Figure 5.3. Notice that the blank line in the middle of the program did not add an extra blank line to the output; there is still only one blank line between the numbers when you run the program. You put blank lines in a program to separate lines of the program's listing. The program's output is affected only by PRINT statements.

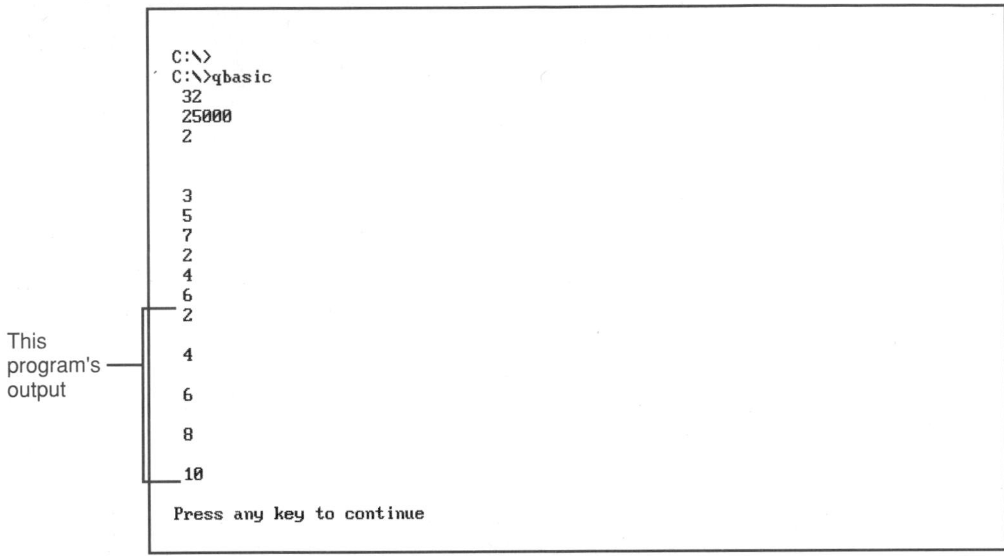

Figure 5.3. The output after you put blank lines in a program.

Clearing the Screen

If you have been running the examples so far in this chapter, you might notice an annoying problem with the output: The results of the previous output are still on the screen when you run another QBasic program. To eliminate this, use the CLS command.

The CLS Command

CLS is an easy command. Whenever QBasic runs a program and gets to a line with CLS on it, it erases the output screen. The format for the CLS command is

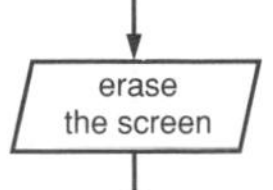


```
CLS
```

Most QBasic programmers use CLS as the first line of every program so that their screen clears when the program runs. This eliminates output from previous runs of the program so that the current program starts with a fresh screen.

Example

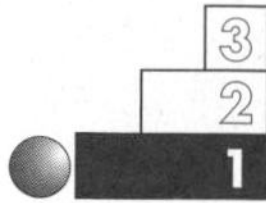

1. To clear the screen before printing, insert a CLS statement, as in this example:

```
CLS

LET age = 32
PRINT age

LET salary = 25000
PRINT salary

LET dependents = 2
PRINT dependents
```

If you run this program several times in succession, your screen clears before each run.

The CLS statement can go anywhere in a program. Many programs have several CLS statements. Whenever you need the program to erase the screen, insert a CLS statement.

Using the END Command

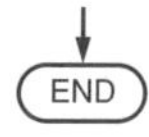

You can add the END command to the end of QBasic programs. END was required in earlier versions of BASIC. This command is now *optional.* Your computer knows when it gets to the end of a program, so END is there for compatibility with older versions of BASIC.

Some people always use an END statement. As a result, people reading the program listing know that they are at the end of the program. They do not have to worry about the possibility of a missing page. This helps eliminate ambiguity. Although the computer does not require END, this statement clarifies the true end of the program for people.

Examples

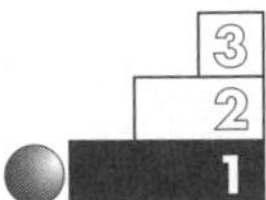

1. The following program is the same as the previous example except for the `END` statement. (Also, the extra blank lines were removed from between the `PRINT` statements.)

```
CLS

LET age = 32
PRINT age
LET salary = 25000
PRINT salary
LET dependents = 2
PRINT dependents

END
```

In programs throughout this book, the `END` is not shown for small programs. When you reach the subroutines and much longer program sections, I use the `END` statement more because `END` makes the stopping point of each program or routine more obvious to QBasic.

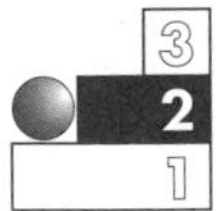

2. Although `END` is optional, you cannot put it just anywhere in your program because execution ends with `END`. Its purpose is to go at the end of the program. Therefore, despite its optional nature, `END` makes the following rewrite of the previous example's program invalid:

```
END
CLS

LET age = 32
PRINT age
LET salary = 25000
PRINT salary
LET dependents = 2
PRINT dependents
```

Summary

Congratulations! You now are writing QBasic programs. In this chapter you learned about variables and constants, which are the fundamental building blocks for the rest of QBasic.

You are now ready to learn how to document your programs and make them more readable. You can expand on your knowledge of the `PRINT` statement by adding more options to it, such as printing more than one value on the same line.

Review Questions

Answers to the Review Questions are in Appendix B.

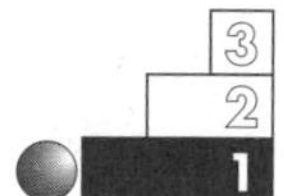

1. What are the two parts of a QBasic program?
2. What is a variable?
3. Which of the following variable names are valid?

```
81QTR      QTR.1.SALES     data file     DataFile
```

4. TRUE or FALSE: A variable can be any of three types of integers: integer, single integer, or double integer.
5. TRUE or FALSE: A variable can be any of two types of floating points: single-precision or double-precision.
6. How many values can a variable hold at the same time?
7. What command writes output to the screen?

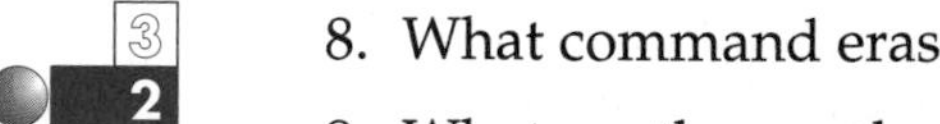

8. What command erases the screen?
9. What are the regular number equivalents of the following scientific notation numbers? What are their types?

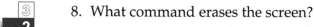

```
-3.0E+2     4.541D+12     1.9D-03
```

10. Rewrite the following numbers in scientific notation format (assume single-precision):

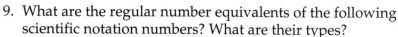

```
15     -0.000043     -54,543     531234.9
```

Review Exercises

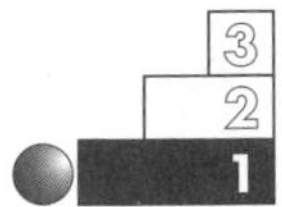

1. Write a program to store your weight (you can fib), height in feet, and shoe size in three variables. Use the LET statement.

2. Rewrite the program in the preceding exercise without using the word LET.

3. Write a program that clears the screen and then prints the temperature on the screen. (You might have to look at a thermometer or the Weather Channel to get the correct temperature.)

4. Write a program that stores your two favorite television channels in two variables and prints them. Clear the screen first.

5. Write a program that stores and prints each type of variable you have learned about in this chapter. Make up any valid variable names you want. Because you know four types, you should have four variables. Use the suffixes of the values when you are storing and printing values.

6. Change the program you wrote in the preceding exercise so that it is clear from the code exactly where the program ends.

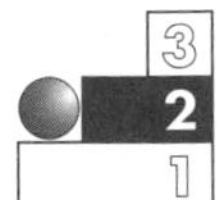

7. Write a program that stores the following scientific notation numbers in three variables and then prints them to a blank screen. Make sure you use the right type of variable by appending the correct suffix to its name.

```
-3.43E-9      +5.43345D+20      +5.43345D-20
```

REMarks and Additional PRINT Options

Now that you understand programs and data, it's time to expand on those fundamentals by exploring ways to improve your programs and their output. This chapter covers the following topics:

- The REM command
- Printing string constants
- How to print more than one value on a line
- Printing with tabs
- Printing to the printer

By mastering these new concepts and commands, you can be prepared to write longer programs that do more than store and print values.

Program REMarks

You know that a program exists to give the computer instructions to read and interpret. You need to understand the programs you write, however. After writing a program, you cannot always remember parts of the program when you are making changes. When someone else writes a program, it is especially difficult to work on that program. Someday computer instructions might be written in regular English. Until then, you must learn to speak and understand the computer's language.

The REM command makes code more understandable to humans, although the computer completely ignores it. REM is short for *remark.* The format for the REM command is:

```
REM any message you choose
```

You can have as many remarks in your program as you want. Many programmers scatter remarks throughout a program. The computer completely ignores the command; it produces no output, stores no variables, and requires no constants as a result of the REM command.

Examples

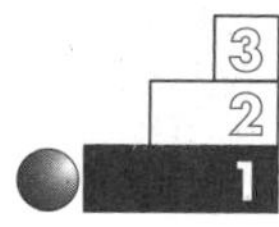

If a computer completely ignores remarks, you probably wonder why you should bother to use them. REM statements are there for people to use so that they can understand programs better. For example, a QBasic program that produces a fancy colored box with flashing lights around it and your name inside (like a marquee) would take some cryptic QBasic commands. Before those commands, you might put a comment like this:

```
REM The next few lines draw a colorful fancy boxed name
```

This remark does not tell QBasic to do anything, but it makes the next few lines of code more understandable to you and others; this statement explains in English exactly what the program is going to do.

REM statements are helpful for putting the programmer's name at the top of the program. In a large company with several programmers, it's helpful to know who to contact if you need help changing the programmer's original code. Remember that REM does not print that name when you run the program (printing is done with PRINT statements, not with REM statements), but the name is there for anyone looking at the program's listing.

You might consider also putting the file name of the program in an early REM statement. For example, the statement

```
REM Programmer: Pat Johnston, Filename: PAYROL81.BAS
```

tells who the programmer is, as well as the program's file name on disk. When you are looking through many printed program listings, you quickly can load the one you want to change with the program editor by looking at the REM's file name at the top of the program. Throughout this book, programs have REM statements that include possible file names under which you can store the programs. The names have the format C*x*, in which *x* is the chapter number (for example, C6REM1.BAS is a program from Chapter 6, and C10COLOR.BAS is from Chapter 10).

A REM by Any Other Name

Through the years, programmers have used REM for some humorous program remarks. Some have little to do with the programs, but add some humor to an otherwise frustrating programming problem.

Do not be surprised if you are looking through a QBasic program someday and run across REM statements that look something like:

```
REM ember the Alamo!

REM arkable program by Michael Stapp

REM iniscent of another program I wrote years ago!
```

These witty comments and any others you can think of are possible because the computer ignores everything after REM.

The REM Shortcut

Because REM statements appear so often in programs, the authors of QBasic supplied an abbreviation for the statement. Instead of typing REM, you can type an apostrophe.

Unlike REM, apostrophe remarks can appear to the right of program lines to help explain each line. REM statements, however, have to go on separate lines.

Examples

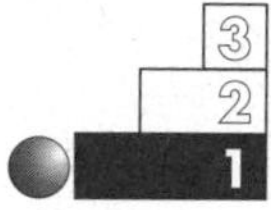

1. Suppose you wanted to put remarks in the variable print program from the last chapter. You can put REM statements anywhere you want and also use the apostrophe remark for side comments. The following example shows one way to put remarks in the program.

```
REM Filename: C6REM1.BAS
REM Blank REMarks like the following one help separate
REM the remark's comments from surrounding code.
REM
REM This program puts a few values in variables
REM and then prints those values to the screen.
REM
CLS
LET age = 32                 ' Stores the age
LET salary = 25000           ' Yearly salary
LET dependents = 2           ' Number of dependents

' Print the results

PRINT age
PRINT salary
PRINT dependents
```

Because a QBasic program can contain blank lines, you do not need to use a remark to separate sections of the program. Pressing Enter to add an extra blank line is permissible.

2. To help find the program on disk, you could take the extra remarks out of the exercise in the preceding example and replace them with the more usable file name under which the program is stored.

```
' Filename: C6VRPRN1.BAS
'
' This program puts a few values in variables
' and then prints those values to the screen.
'
CLS
LET age = 32                ' Stores the age
LET salary = 25000          ' Yearly salary
LET dependents = 2          ' Number of dependents

' Print the results

PRINT age
PRINT salary
PRINT dependents
```

Without the REM or apostrophes, QBasic would think you were typing incorrect program commands when you typed the remarks.

Use Helpful REMarks

Although a program without remarks can be difficult to understand, you should use only helpful remarks. Remarks are there to explain what the program code is doing. Therefore, the following remark is not helpful:

```
REM Put the value 3 into the variable called NUM.KIDS
LET NUM.KIDS = 3
```

Although the previous remark is lengthy, it does not explain why the value 3 is placed in the statement. Consider the following improved example:

```
REM Save the number of kids for dependent calculations
LET NUM.KIDS = 3
```

This REM gives a better idea of what the program's next statement is used for. Someone trying to figure out the program would appreciate the second remark more than the first.

This was a simple example. Many QBasic statements do not require remarks. For example, including a remark to explain CLS would be useless because there is no ambiguity about what is going on; the screen is cleared.

Put remarks in your programs as you write them. You are most familiar with your program logic when you are typing your program in the editor. Some people put off including remarks in their program until after the program is written. As a result, the remarks never are included or the programmer makes only a half-hearted attempt to include them.

The rest of this book's examples include remarks that explain how they are used in programs.

More with PRINT

After reading the previous chapter, you understand the following features of the PRINT statement:

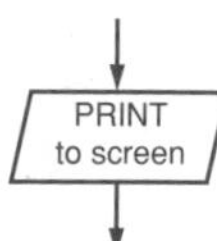

- PRINT prints output to the screen.
- PRINT prints any constant that is to the right of PRINT.
- PRINT prints any contents of any variable that is listed to the right of PRINT.

PRINT can do many other things. To write more helpful programs, you should learn how to access more of PRINT's options.

PRINTing String Constants

In QBasic, a *string constant* is one or more groups of characters inside quotation marks (" "). For example, here are five string constants:

```
"This is a string constant."
"ABC 123 $#@ --- +=][ x"
"X"
```

```
"QBasic is fun!"
"123.45"
```

Notice that even one character, when it is inside quotation marks, is a string constant. (String constants are sometimes called *string literals.*) The only member of this list you might find questionable is the number `"123.45"`.

`"123.45"` fulfills the definition of a string constant: one or more characters enclosed within quotation marks. `"123.45"` is *not* a number, a numeric constant, or a variable. The quotation marks always designate string constants. You cannot use `"123.45"` in mathematical calculations because QBasic does not view this string constant as a number.

String constants are helpful for printing names, titles, addresses, and messages on the screen and printer. When you want your QBasic program to print a title or a word, put that title or word after the word `PRINT`.

Examples

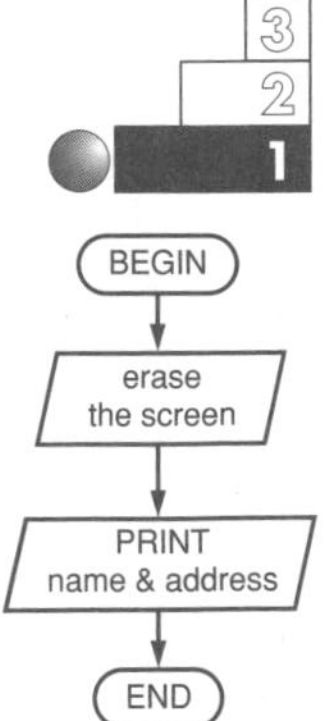

1. To print the name and address of a company called Widgets, Inc. on the screen, you can put the following section of code in the program:

```
' Filename: C6TITLE.BAS

' Prints a company's name and address on the screen.
CLS
PRINT "Widgets, Inc."
PRINT "307 E. Midway"
PRINT "Jackson, MI    03882"
```

After running this program, your screen should look like Figure 6.1.

2. The primary reason for using string constants is to label your output. When you ran the C6VRPRN1.BAS program earlier, three numbers appeared on the screen. The problem is that anyone who did not write the program might not know what each number meant. You can modify the program to describe its output, as in:

```
' Filename: C6VRPRN2.BAS
'
' This program puts a few values in variables
' and then prints those values to the screen.
'
CLS
LET age = 32                ' Stores the age
LET salary = 25000          ' Yearly salary
LET dependents = 2          ' Number of dependents

' Print the results
PRINT "age"
PRINT age
PRINT "salary"
PRINT salary
PRINT "dependents"
PRINT dependents
```

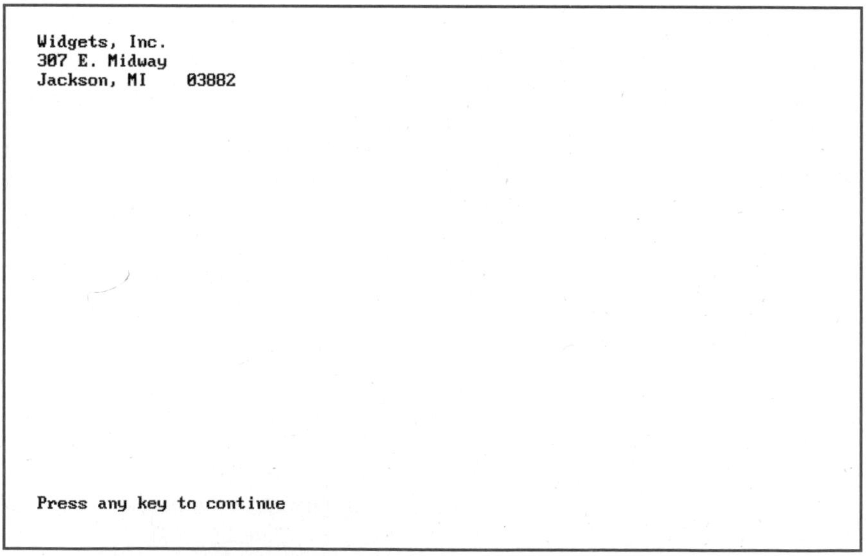

```
Widgets, Inc.
307 E. Midway
Jackson, MI    03882




Press any key to continue
```

Figure 6.1. The results of TITLE.BAS.

The output of this program is shown in Figure 6.2. Look closely at the last six lines of the program. The word *age* is printed followed by the value of the variable `age`, because you first printed the string constant `"age"` followed by the variable `age`. The same is true for the rest of the `PRINT` statements.

```
age
 32
salary
 25000
dependents
 2




Press any key to continue
```

Figure 6.2. After adding descriptive `PRINT` statements.

The following rule of thumb is helpful to remember:

NOTE: Whenever you print string constants, everything inside the quotation marks prints exactly as it appears. This includes any spaces you typed between the quotation marks. The quotation marks, however, never print.

The following four `PRINT` statements all produce different output because the data inside the quotation marks is different for each.

```
PRINT "The Amount is"; amt
PRINT "The Amount is  "; amt
PRINT " The  Amount is"; amt
PRINT "T h e  A m o u n t  i s";amt
```

The C6VRPRN2.BAS program illustrates why quotation marks are required around string constants. Without the quotation marks, the previous example's program would not know when to print the *word* age and when to print the *contents* of the variable age.

Printing More Than One Value on a Line

You now know several ways to use PRINT, but you can do more with this statement. The PRINT statements you have seen printed one value per line (a numeric constant, a variable, or a string constant). You also can print several values on a line in one statement. When printing more than one value on a line, you must separate each value with a semicolon or a comma. The choice depends on how closely you want the values printed.

PRINT with Semicolons

To print two or more values next to each other, separate the values by using the semicolon in the PRINT statement. When you use the semicolon, the format of PRINT looks like this:

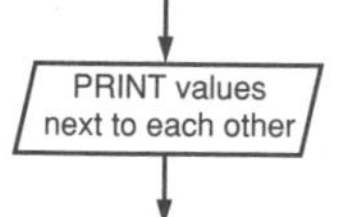


```
PRINT value1;value2[;value3][;value#]...
```

In other words, if you put more than one value (they can be variables or constants or a combination of both) after PRINT and separate them with semicolons, QBasic prints those values next to each other instead of on two separate lines.

PRINT with Commas

To print more than one value separated by several spaces, you might want to use commas between the values. The comma is helpful in a PRINT statement when you want to print columns of output. The format of PRINT with commas is

PRINT values in print zones

```
PRINT value1,value2[,value3][,value#]...
```

In other words, when you put more than one value (variables, constants, or a combination of both) after PRINT and separate them with commas, QBasic prints those values and separates them with a few spaces.

Before seeing examples, you must understand how QBasic determines the spacing between two printed values separated by commas. QBasic assumes there are five *print zones* on your screen. A new print zone occurs every 14 columns. Figure 6.3 shows how QBasic determines the print zones.

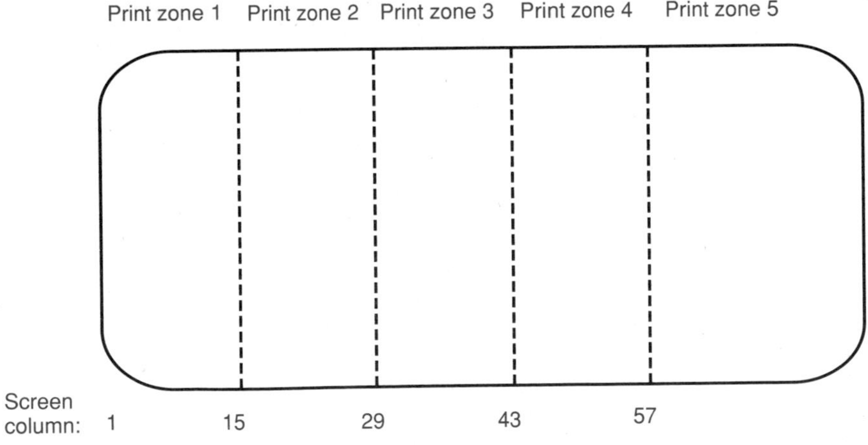

Figure 6.3. The QBasic screen print zones.

A comma separating PRINT values tells QBasic to print the next value in the next print zone. Therefore, the following PRINT statement prints QBasic in the fourth print zone:

```
PRINT ,,,"QBasic"
```

> **CAUTION:** If your data is longer than a print zone, the next value prints one print zone over. For example, if you printed a name that had 20 letters and then followed the name with a comma and another name, the second name would print in the third print zone (column 28), even though the name was the second one printed.

Examples

1. You can change the C6VRPRN2.BAS program to use the screen more efficiently by printing the values of each variable *after* its description. The following program produces a more readable output screen:

```
' Filename: C6VRPRN3.BAS
'
' This program puts a few values in variables
' and then prints those values to the screen
' using semicolons for better-looking output.
'
CLS
LET age = 32                  ' Stores the age
LET salary = 25000            ' Yearly salary
LET dependents = 2            ' Number of dependents

' Print the results
PRINT "The age is";age
PRINT
PRINT "The salary is";salary
PRINT
PRINT "The number of dependents is";dependents
```

Figure 6.4 shows the previous program's screen output. One peculiar feature of printing numbers shows up in this example. Notice that a space is printed before each variable, although you did not type the spaces in the program listing. This is how QBasic prints positive numbers.

```
The age is 32

The salary is 25000

The number of dependents is 2




Press any key to continue
```

Figure 6.4. Improving the output.

QBasic always inserts a space after each printed number. The last program, however, has a space before each number. The extra space can be explained.

QBasic knows that every number is either positive or negative. When QBasic prints a negative number, it prints the negative sign in front of the number. QBasic has to print the negative sign so that you know the number is negative. QBasic does not print a plus sign in front of all positive numbers. QBasic does, however, print a space for the plus sign. You cannot override this imaginary plus sign, and you should expect a positive number to print with an extra blank before it.

2. The second blank does not appear in front of string constants or negative numbers. The blank before positive numbers is the space left by the imaginary plus sign.

   To see another example, run the following program. It prints three string constants, three negative numbers, and three positive numbers separated by semicolons.

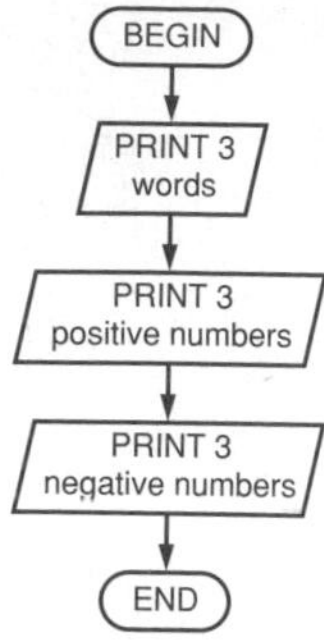


```
' Filename: C6SMPRNT.BAS
'
' This program prints three sets of values showing
' how QBasic handles the spacing between them.
'
CLS
' Three string constants
PRINT "Books"; "Movies"; "Theatre"
' Three positive numbers
PRINT 123; 456; 789
' Three negative numbers
PRINT -123; -456; -789
```

When you run this program, you see the screen shown in Figure 6.5. Although this example illustrates the way QBasic prints positive numbers, you can see that you must be careful when printing string constants with the semicolon. If you wanted the three string constants printed with a space between them, you would have to code the PRINT in the following way:

```
PRINT "Books "; "Movies "; "Theatre"
```

To ensure that the space is printed, you must insert the space inside the string constant's quotation marks. The space after the semicolon makes the line more readable and does not affect the output.

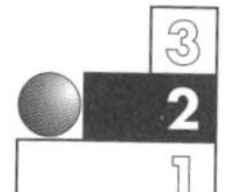

3. So far, every PRINT statement has caused the output to start on a new line. This is because QBasic automatically prints a carriage return–line feed sequence after each PRINT.

   You can suppress the carriage return–line feed sequence by putting a semicolon at the end of a PRINT statement. This ensures that the next PRINT statement continues at the same location on the screen at which the last one finished. For example, the following short section of code prints all three names on the same line:

```
' Filename: C6SUPPCR.BAS
'
' This program suppresses the automatic carriage
```

```
' return-line feed by leaving a trailing semicolon at
' the end of each PRINT statement.
'
CLS
PRINT "Heath ";
PRINT "Jarrod ";
PRINT "Nick"
```

```
BooksMoviesTheatre
 123  456  789
-123 -456 -789





Press any key to continue
```

Figure 6.5. An example of printing with the semicolon between values.

Figure 6.6 shows the output of this program. If the spaces were not at the end of the first two names, the names would have printed next to each other without being separated.

At first, you might think that you never need the trailing semicolon. After all, you could have accomplished this same output with the following statement:

```
PRINT "Heath ";"Jarrod ";"Nick"
```

As you program more in QBasic, you might have to *build* your output line. That is, you print some of the line, make some computations, and then finish printing the rest of the line. Leaving off the trailing semicolon enables you to finish the PRINT later in the program.

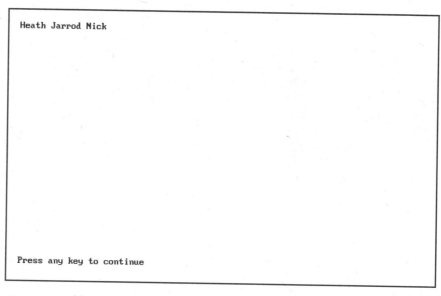

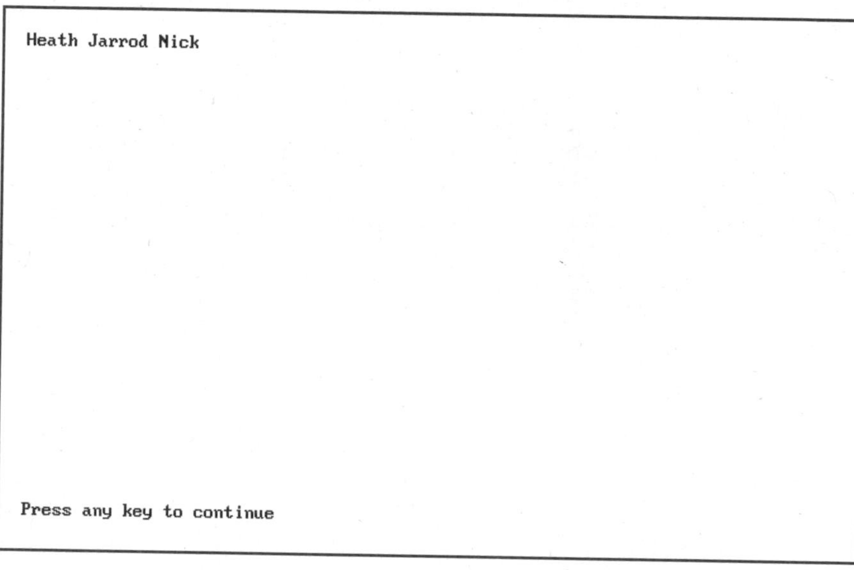

Figure 6.6. Using the trailing semicolon to keep PRINTs on the same output line.

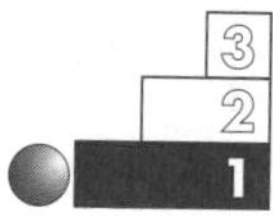

4. The following program illustrates the comma between PRINT values. The three lines print the animals' names in four columns. Although the names are different lengths, they begin in the same print zone. The comma means that the next animal name is printed in the next print zone.

```
' Filename: C6CMAPRN.BAS
'
' Uses the comma between printed values. Each comma
' forces the next animal name into a new print zone.
'
CLS
PRINT "Lion", "Whale", "Monkey", "Fish"
PRINT "Alligator", "Bat", "Seal", "Tiger"
PRINT "Dog", "Lizard", "Cat", "Bear"
```

Figure 6.7 shows the preceding program's output. Only string constants are printed in this example, but you can print also variables and numeric constants in print zones. Remember that all positive numbers print with at least one space preceding them. QBasic prints positive numbers with an extra blank for the imaginary plus sign. Therefore, when you print a positive number, whether it is in a variable or a numeric constant, an extra space appears before the value at the beginning of the next print zone.

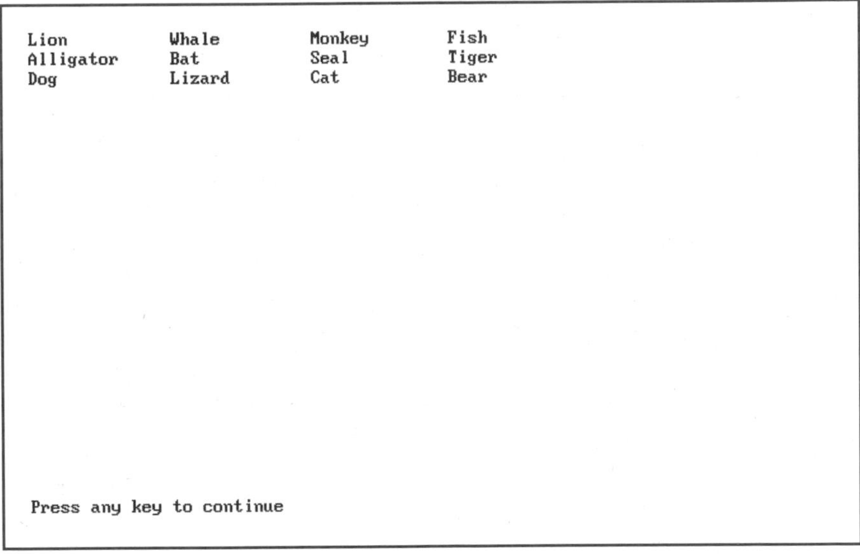

Figure 6.7. Printing in the print zones with commas.

Printing with TAB

Printing with commas is similar to using tabs. The commas act like a tab by moving the next value to the next print zone. A print zone, however, is not a real tab because you cannot change its location. Print zones always occur every 14 spaces. You might want to print a table of values that print in locations different from the print zones. When you do, use the TAB command in your PRINT statement. The format of the TAB command is

```
TAB(tab value)
```

The *tab value* is the number of characters to tab over from the beginning of the screen before printing the next value. The tab value always goes in parentheses after the word TAB. Never use TAB by itself; always combine it with a PRINT statement. The format of the combined PRINT TAB command is

```
PRINT TAB(tab value1);data1[;TAB(tab value2);data2;...]
```

Notice that you can have several TAB commands in one PRINT statement.

TIP: Although QBasic does not require semicolons, you almost always see them on both sides of a TAB, telling you that the tab occurs immediately after the last value is printed. Never use commas on either side of the TAB; the commas force the cursor over to the next print zone, and then the TAB occurs. The next print zone might be past the column you wanted. TABs immediately following PRINT statements do not have semicolons in front of them.

Examples

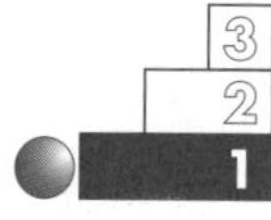

1. The following program prints the first column of animal names in screen position 1, the second column in position 20, the third in screen position 40, and the fourth in screen position 60.

```
' Filename: C6TBPRN1.BAS
'
' Uses the TAB between printed values. Each TAB's
' value pushed the next animal name over to that tab stop.
'
CLS
PRINT "Lion"; TAB(20); "Whale"; TAB(40); "Monkey";
PRINT TAB(60); "Fish"
PRINT "Alligator"; TAB(20); "Bat"; TAB(40);"Seal";

PRINT TAB(60); "Tiger"
```

```
PRINT "Dog"; TAB(20); "Lizard"; TAB(40); "Cat";
PRINT TAB(60); "Bear"
```

You do not have to put the spaces before TAB in the program, but these spaces make the program more readable. Figure 6.8 shows the result of running this program. The TAB is required because print zones are located in fixed positions on the screen. With TAB, you have more freedom to place data exactly where you want it.

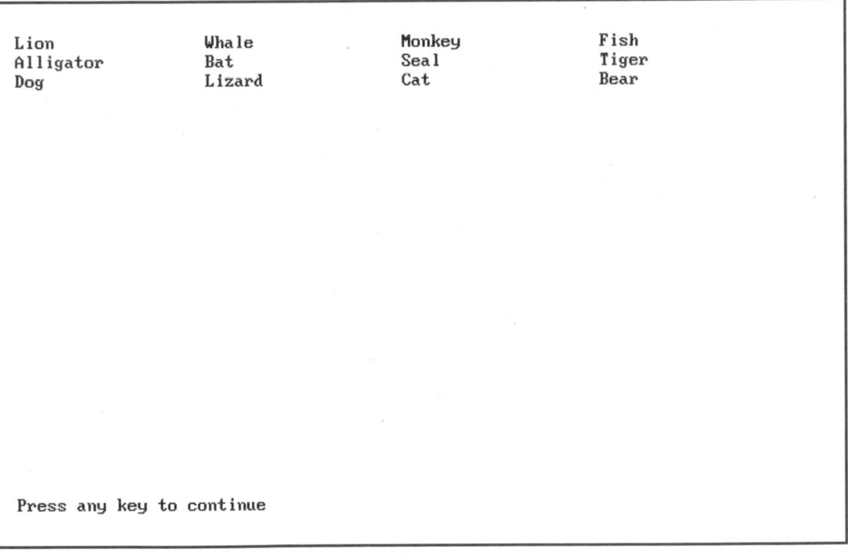

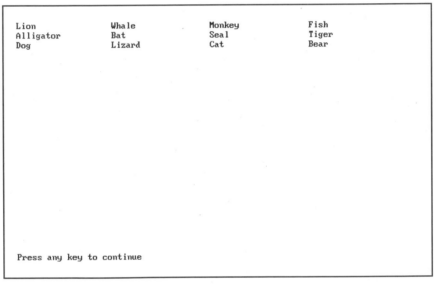

Figure 6.8. Printing in specific columns with the PRINT TAB option.

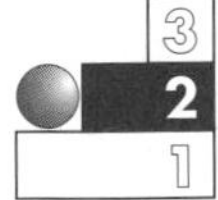

2. The TAB option is especially helpful for tables of data. Although words and values do not always take the same width on the screen (Alligator is longer than Dog), you might want the data to begin printing in the same column.

   The following program prints a list of names and addresses on the screen. The PRINT commands are lengthy, but if you insert TABs between the data, the output lines up in columns. Because some of the data is longer than the 14-character print zones, you could not print this output in print zones separated by commas.

```
' Filename: C6TBPRN2.BAS
'
' Uses TABs to print a name and address report.
'
CLS
' Print underlined report titles
PRINT TAB(69); "Zip"
PRINT TAB(5); "Name"; TAB(25); "Address"; TAB(48); "City";
PRINT TAB(60); "State"; TAB(69); "Code"

PRINT TAB(5); "----"; TAB(25); "-------"; TAB(48); "----";
PRINT TAB(60); "-----"; TAB(69); "----"

' Print the data values
PRINT TAB(5); "Michael Stapp"; TAB(25); "6104 E. 6th";
PRINT TAB(48); "Tulsa"; TAB(60); "Okla."; TAB(69); "74135"

PRINT TAB(5); "Jayne M. Wiseman"; TAB(25);
PRINT "Elm and Broadway"; TAB(48); "Cleveland"; TAB(60);
PRINT "Ohio"; TAB(69); "19332"

PRINT TAB(5); "Lou Horn"; TAB(25); "12 East Sheridan Ave.";
PRINT TAB(48); "Carmel"; TAB(60); "Indi."; TAB(69); "46332"

PRINT TAB(5); "Luke Ben Tanner"; TAB(25);
PRINT "5706 S. Indianapolis"; TAB(48); "Salem"; TAB(60);
PRINT "Mass."; TAB(69); "23337"
```

In this example, `TAB` enabled the headings to print directly over the data in the columns. Notice that a `PRINT TAB` was required to print the heading `Zip` on a line by itself so that it sits on top of `Code` on the next line.

The dashes help underline each title to separate the title from the data. The output of the program is shown in Figure 6.9.

```
                                                                    Zip
Name                    Address                    City         State      Code
----                    -------                    ----         -----      ----
Michael Stapp           6104 E. 6th                Tulsa        Okla.      74135
Jayne M. Wiseman        Elm and Broadway           Cleveland    Ohio       19332
Lou Horn                12 East Sheridan Ave.      Carmel       Indi.      46332
Luke Ben Tanner         5706 S. Indianapolis       Salem        Mass.      23337




Press any key to continue
```

Figure 6.9. Printing a report with titles using the PRINT TAB option.

Printing to Paper

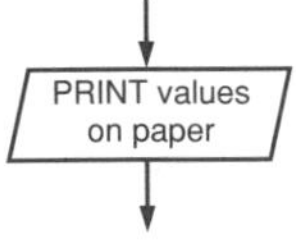

You have made much progress toward producing nice-looking output. Printing to the screen, however, is not always the best method. If you want a permanent record of something, you should send the output to the printer. Printing with the printer is easy to do with the LPRINT command.

The LPRINT Command

LPRINT is identical to PRINT, except that its output goes to the printer rather than the screen. Any program that uses PRINT statements can be redirected to the printer by substituting an LPRINT for each PRINT.

Your printer sometimes is called a *line printer.* LPRINT got its name from the line printer to which it sends output.

Example

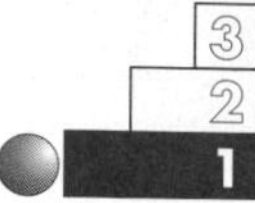

1. The following program is identical to C6TBPRN1.BAS, which printed the names of the animals to the screen. All the PRINTs in the original program, however, are changed to LPRINTs. CLS still clears the screen, but it does nothing to the printer.

```
' Filename: C6TBPRN3.BAS
'
' Uses the TAB between printed values. Each TAB's
' value pushes the next animal over to that tab stop.
'
' All output goes to the printer.

CLS
LPRINT "Lion"; TAB(20); "Whale"; TAB(40); "Monkey";
LPRINT TAB(60); "Fish"
LPRINT "Alligator"; TAB(20); "Bat"; TAB(40);"Seal";
LPRINT TAB(60); "Tiger"
LPRINT "Dog"; TAB(20); "Lizard"; TAB(40); "Cat";
LPRINT TAB(60); "Bear"
```

If your printer isn't on or doesn't have paper, you get the following error message:

```
Device fault
```

Correct the problem and run the program again if you get this error.

Summary

In this chapter you learned how to document your programs by adding REM statements. You should scatter remarks throughout your programs, telling the name of the file and the program's author, and describing (in English) the program's logic. As you write longer programs, remarks become even more important.

You learned also the many ways to print several values with PRINT and LPRINT. You now can send multiple values, variables, and

string constants to the screen or printer. The next chapter, "QBasic's Math Operators," discusses the math operators in QBasic and how QBasic can do calculations for you instead of you doing the math yourself.

Review Questions

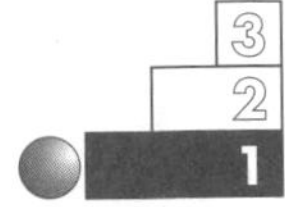

Answers to the Review Questions are in Appendix B.

1. What does REM stand for?
2. What does the computer do when it finds a REM statement?
3. TRUE or FALSE: The following section of a program puts a *4* in the variable called R, a *5* in ME, and a *6* in REM.

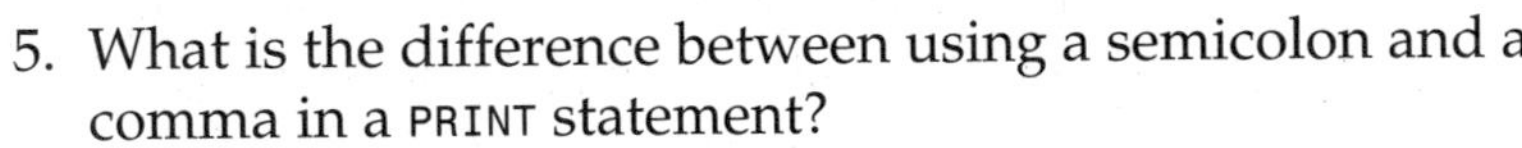

```
R = 4
ME = 5
REM = 6
```

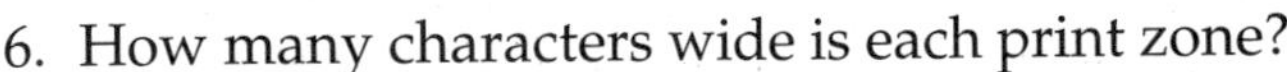

4. TRUE or FALSE: PRINT sends output to the screen.

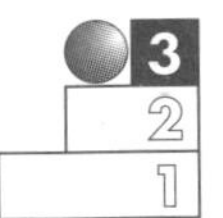

5. What is the difference between using a semicolon and a comma in a PRINT statement?
6. How many characters wide is each print zone?
7. Why would you put a semicolon at the end of a PRINT statement?
8. In what column would the word Computer start, given the following LPRINT command?

```
LPRINT TAB(20), "Computer"
```

9. In what column would the number 765 start, given the following LPRINT command?

```
LPRINT -21; 21, 0; TAB(30); 765
```

10. List three ways to print Hello in column 28.
11. What is the output of the following program?

```
REM -------------------
REM     SECRET AGENTS
```

```
REM -------------------
PRINT 86;
PRINT " and";
PRINT 99;
PRINT " are secret agents."
```

Review Exercises

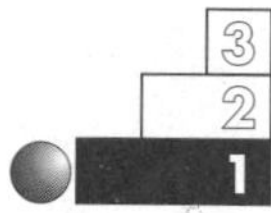

1. Write a program to store your weight (you can fib), height in feet, and shoe size in three different variables. Print the values with descriptions on three separate lines. Then print the values next to each other on the same line. Use appropriate REM statements to document the program.

2. Modify the previous program to print your weight in column 15, your height in column 25, and your shoe size in column 35.

3. Write a program that prints (on the printer) the names and phone numbers of your three best friends. Add appropriate REM statements to document the program. Make sure you print nicely underlined titles over the names and phone numbers. The report's columns also should line up. You can use print zones or TAB.

NOTE: Using TAB is usually preferred to using print zones. If one of the names took more than one print zone, the report would be out of alignment for that line if you used commas.

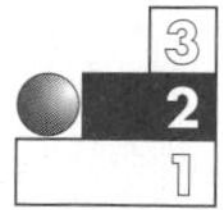

4. Look in your newspaper's financial section and find a table of figures. Try to duplicate the table on your screen or printer, making sure the columns of data line up under nice headings. Use TAB, semicolons, and commas appropriately. Try to match the newspaper as closely as possible. The newspaper's characters are not always the same size, so you might have to guess and not use the same number of spaces

the paper uses. The more printing you do (practicing all three ways of aligning columns), the faster you can produce any screen output required by any program you ever want to write.

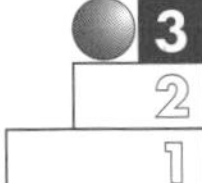

5. Find and correct the three errors in the following program:

```
REM This program prints payroll information
pay = 2,102.32
dependents = 3
tax.rate = .35     REM This is the percentage tax rate
PRINT
PRINT "The pay is:"; pay
PRINT "The number of dependents is:"; dependents
CLS
PRINT "The tax rate percentage is:"; tax.rate
```

6. You can use LPRINT to print pictures on the printer. Use a series of LPRINT statements to produce the following house and rocket:

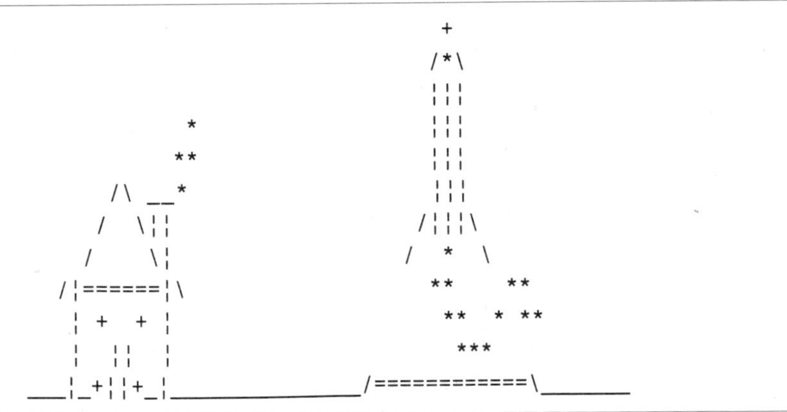

7

QBasic's Math Operators

If you are dreading this chapter because you do not like math, relax. QBasic does all your math for you. It is a misconception that you have to be good at math to understand how to program computers. The opposite is true. The computer follows your instructions and does all the calculations for you. This chapter explains how QBasic computes by introducing

- ♦ QBasic math operators
- ♦ The order of operators
- ♦ How to store the results of calculations in variables
- ♦ How to print the results of calculations

Many people who dislike math actually enjoy learning how the computer does the calculations. After learning the operators and a few simple ways QBasic uses them, you will feel comfortable putting calculations in your programs. Computers can perform math operations many times faster than people can.

The Math Operators

A *math operator* is a symbol used for addition, subtraction, multiplication, division, or other calculations. The operators are similar to the ones you use when you do arithmetic. Table 7.1 lists every QBasic operator and its meaning.

Table 7.1. The QBasic math operators and their meanings.

Symbol	*Meaning*
*	Multiplication
/	Division
+	Addition
-	Subtraction
^	Exponentiation
\	Integer division
MOD	Modulus

The Four Primary Operators

The four primary QBasic operators, *, /, +, and -, operate in the way you are used to. Multiplication, division, addition, and subtraction produce the same results as when you do these math functions with a calculator. Table 7.2 contains four samples that illustrate each of these simple operators.

Table 7.2. The results of calculations done with the primary operators.

Formula	*Result*
4 * 2	8
95 / 2	47.5
80 - 15	65
12 + 9	21

For multiplication you must use an asterisk rather than an *x*, as you normally write it by hand. You cannot use an *x* because QBasic would confuse it with a variable called x; QBasic wouldn't know whether you wanted to multiply or use the value of x.

You can use the addition and subtraction operators by themselves, in which case they are called *unary* operators. (The addition operator is optional because QBasic assumes a positive value unless you tell it otherwise.) For instance, you can assign a variable a positive or negative number or assign it a positive or negative variable by using the unary plus or minus, as the following shows:

```
a = -25
b = +25
c = -a
d = +b
```

Integer Division, Modulus, and Exponentiation

The three remaining operators, integer division (\), MOD, and exponentiation (^), may be new to you. They are as easy to use as the four operators you saw in the previous section.

Use integer division to produce the integer (or whole number) result of a division. Integer division always produces an integer result and discards any remainder. You do not have to put integers on both sides of the \; you can use floating-point numbers, integers, or a combination of both on each side of the \. Table 7.3 shows the results of some sample integer division programs.

Table 7.3. Integer division results.

Formula	*Result*
8 \ 2	4
95 \ 2	47
95.0 \ 2	47
95 \ 2.0	47
95.0 \ 2.0	47

Math Inside the Computer

Internally, your computer can perform addition only. This seems strange because people use computers for all kinds of powerful mathematical solutions. Addition, however, is all your computer needs to know.

At the binary level, your computer can add two binary numbers. Your computer has no problem with adding 6 + 7. To subtract 6 from 7, however, your computer has to use modified *addition.*

To subtract 6 from 7, your computer actually adds a *negative* 6 to 7. When your program stores the result of 7 - 6 in a variable, your computer interprets it as 7 + -6. The result is *1*.

Your computer can add, and it can take the negative of any number (called the *two's complement*). These two things are all the computer requires to simulate subtraction.

Multiplication is simply repeated addition. Therefore, 6 * 7 is interpreted as 6 added to itself seven times, or 6 + 6 + 6 + 6 + 6 + 6 + 6.

Division is repeated subtraction. When you calculate 42 / 6, the computer repeatedly subtracts 6 from 42 until it gets to zero and then adds the number of times it did that. This becomes 42 - 6 - 6 - 6 - 6 - 6 - 6 - 6 = 0. Reaching 0 takes seven subtractions of 6 (or actually the addition of seven negative 6s). Thus, the result of 42 / 6 is 7. Depending on the numbers, division does not always result in an even number. If the repeated subtraction results in a negative number, the computer uses it to produce the remainder.

When your computer is able to add and simulate subtraction, multiplication, and division, it has the tools required for every other math function as well.

The MOD operator is the only QBasic operator that does not use a symbol. It produces the *modulus,* or integer remainder, of division. Table 7.4 shows the results of some simple MOD operations.

Table 7.4. MOD operation results.

Formula	*Result*
8 MOD 2	0
8 MOD 3	2
8 MOD 7	1

Use the exponentiation symbol (^) when you want to raise a number to a power. The number to the left of the ^ is the base, and the number to the right is the power. You can put integers, floating-point, or a combination of both on each side of the ^. Table 7.5 shows the results of sample exponentiation calculations.

Table 7.5. Exponentiation results.

Formula	*Description*	*Result*
2^4	2 raised to the fourth power (2^4)	16
16^2	16 raised to the second power (16^2)	256
5.6^3	5.6 raised to the third power (5.6^3)	175.616
144^0.5	144 raised to the .5 power ($144^{1/2}$)	12

The Assignment of Formulas to Variables

Most of your programs use variables to store the results of these calculations. You already have seen how to assign values and variables to other variables. The true power of variables appears when you assign results of formulas to them.

Examples

1. The following program illustrates a payroll computation. The program assigns to three variables the hours worked, the pay per hour (the `rate`), and the tax rate. It then creates three new variables from calculations using these variables: the gross pay, the taxes, and the net pay.

```
' Filename: C7PAY.BAS
'
' Computes three payroll variables.

hours.worked = 40             ' Total hours worked
rate = 7.80                   ' Pay per hours
tax.rate = .40                ' Tax rate percentage

gross.pay = hours.worked * rate
taxes = tax.rate * gross.pay
net.pay = gross.pay - taxes

CLS                           ' Print the results
PRINT "The Gross Pay is"; gross.pay
PRINT "The Taxes are"; taxes
PRINT "The Net Pay is"; net.pay
```

   Figure 7.1 shows the result of running C7PAY.BAS. Be sure you understand the answers before reading further.

2. The following program takes the value in the variable `inches` and converts it to feet.

```
' Filename: C7CNVTIF.BAS
'
' Converts inches to feet.

inches = 72

CLS

feet = inches / 12
PRINT "The number of feet in";inches;" are";feet
```

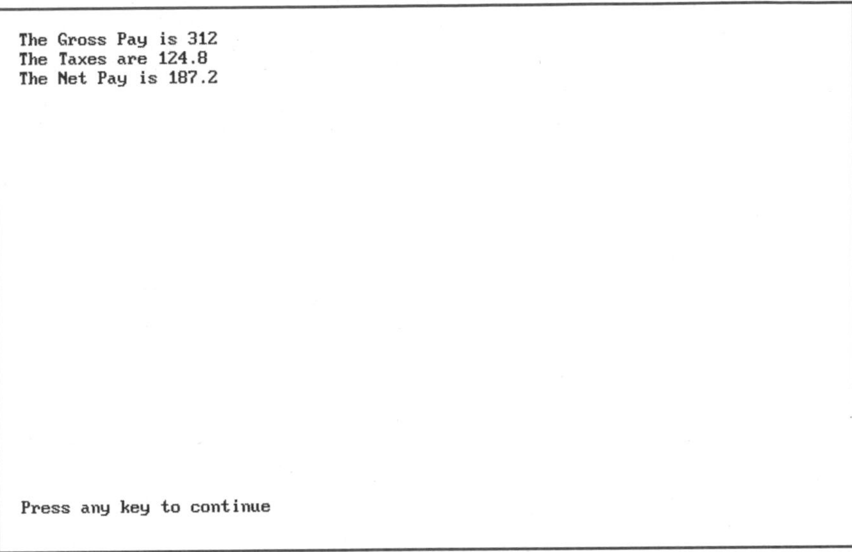

```
The Gross Pay is 312
The Taxes are 124.8
The Net Pay is 187.2

Press any key to continue
```

Figure 7.1. Results of the C7PAY.BAS payroll program.

The Order of Operators

Knowing the meaning of the math operators is the first of two steps toward understanding QBasic calculations. You must understand also the *order of operators.* The order of operators (sometimes called the *hierarchy of operators* or the *precedence of operators*) determines exactly how QBasic computes formulas. The order of operators is exactly the same as that used in high school algebra. To see how the order of operators works, try to determine the result of the following calculation:

```
2 + 3 * 2
```

Many people would say the answer is 10. However, 10 is correct only if you interpret the formula from left to right. But what if you calculated the multiplication first? If you took the value of *3 * 2,* got an answer of *6,* and then added the 2 to it, you would end up with the answer *8.* That is the answer QBasic would compute.

QBasic performs any exponentiation first, then multiplication and division. Finally, it performs addition and subtraction. Table 7.6 shows this order of operators.

Table 7.6. The order of operators.

Order	*Operator*
1	Exponentiation (^)
2	Unary addition and subtraction
3	Multiplication, division, integer division (*, /, \), MOD
4	Addition, subtraction (+, -)

Examples

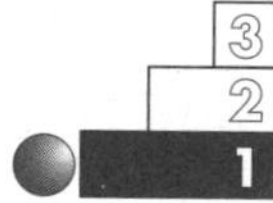

1. It is easy to follow QBasic's order of operators if you follow the intermediate results one at a time. The three complex calculations in Figure 7.2 show you how to do this.

2. Looking back at Table 7.6, notice that multiplication, division, integer division, and MOD are on the same level. This implies that there is no hierarchy on that level. If more than one of these operators appear in a calculation, QBasic performs the math from left to right. The same is true of addition and subtraction; the leftmost operation is done first.

   Figure 7.3 shows an example of left-to-right division and multiplication.

   Because the division appears to the left of the multiplication (and because division and multiplication are on the same level), the division is computed first.

You should understand the order of operators so that you know how to structure your calculations. Now that you have mastered the order, you can see how to override the order of operators with parentheses.

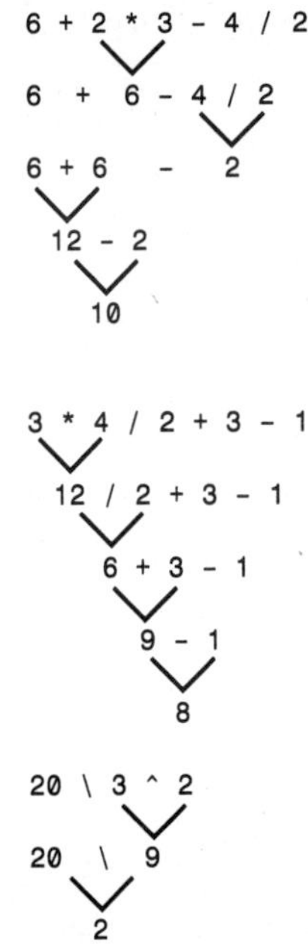

Figure 7.2. Three complex calculations showing how to follow QBasic's order of operators.

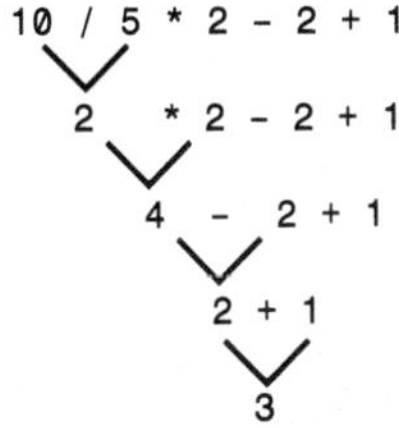

Figure 7.3. Operators on the same precedence level calculate from left to right.

Parentheses

If you want to override the order of operators, put parentheses in the calculation. In other words, anything in parentheses, whether it is addition, subtraction, division, or whatever, always is calculated before the rest of the line. The rest of the calculations are performed in the normal order.

> **TIP:** If there are expressions with parentheses inside other parentheses, such as ((5 + 2) - 7 + (8 + 9 - (5 + 2))), calculate the innermost expression first.

The formula *2 + 3 * 2* produced an *8* because multiplication is performed before addition. If you add parentheses around the addition, as in *(2 + 3) * 2,* the answer becomes *10.*

Examples

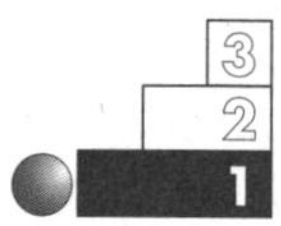

1. The calculations in Figure 7.4 illustrate how parentheses override the regular order of operators. These are the same three formulas shown in Figure 7.3, except their calculations are different because the parentheses override the order of operators.

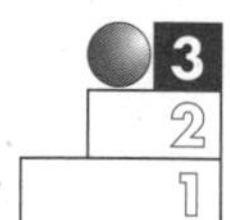

2. The following program produces an incorrect result, although it looks as though it should work. See whether you can spot the error.

```
' Compute the average of three grades
LET grade1 = 86
LET grade2 = 98
LET grade3 = 72

LET avg = grade1 + grade2 + grade3 / 3
PRINT "The average is"; avg
```

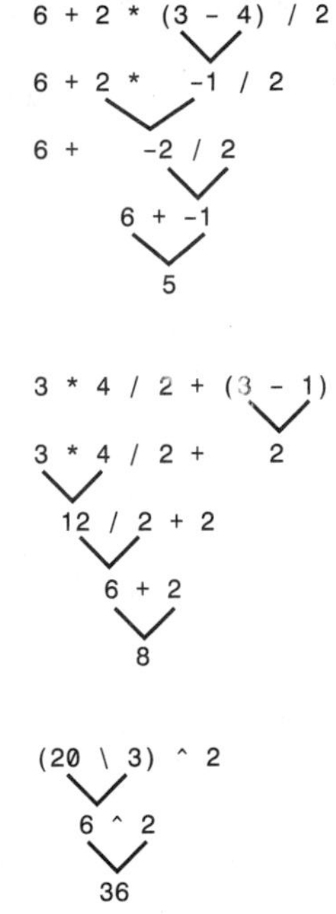

Figure 7.4. Overriding the order of operators with parentheses.

The problem is that division is performed first. Therefore, the third grade is divided by three, and then the other two grades are added to that result. To fix the problem, you would have to add one set of parentheses, as shown in the following code:

```
' Fix the Computation of the average of three grades
LET grade1 = 86
LET grade2 = 98
LET grade3 = 72

LET avg = (grade1 + grade2 + grade3) / 3
PRINT "The average is"; avg
```

TIP: Use plenty of parentheses in your programs to make the order of operators clearer, even if you don't override the order of operators. The parentheses make the calculations easier to understand if you modify the program later.

Printing Calculations

You have seen how PRINT and LPRINT print variables and constants. These two statements can print also the values of expressions. As long as the expression results in a valid constant, you can put the expression to the right of PRINT or LPRINT.

Do not confuse PRINT and LPRINT with the assignment statement. The following PRINT statement is *invalid:*

```
PRINT sales = "are the sales"
```

Running this line in a program would result in a syntax error. PRINT and LPRINT require an expression to the right of PRINT or LPRINT. The equal sign is reserved for the LET assignment statement. You would first have to assign sales a value and then print that value, as in the following program:

```
sales = 18750.43
PRINT sales; " are the sales."
```

Examples

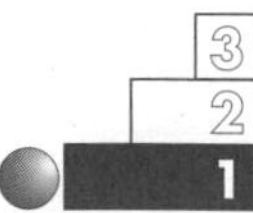

1. You can compute and print payroll amounts at the same time. The following program, a rewritten version of C7PAY.BAS, prints the results of the three payroll expressions without storing the results in variables.

```
' Filename: C7PAY2.BAS
'
' Computes and prints three payroll values.

hours.worked = 40        ' Total hours worked
```

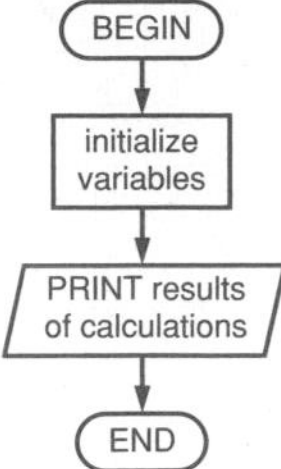

```
rate = 7.80              ' Pay per hour
tax.rate = .40           ' Tax rate percentage

CLS                      ' Print the results
PRINT "The Gross Pay is"; hours.worked * rate
PRINT "The Taxes are"; tax.rate * hours.worked * rate
PRINT "The Net Pay is";
PRINT (hours.worked * rate)-(hours.worked * rate * tax.rate)
```

The output of this program is in Figure 7.5. Notice that it is identical to the output of Figure 7.1, although the programs are very different.

```
The Gross Pay is 312
The Taxes are 124.8
The Net Pay is 187.2









Press any key to continue
```

Figure 7.5. Results of running C7PAY2.BAS.

This program is not necessarily better than the original, but it does illustrate that you can print variables, constants, *and* expressions. Notice that the parentheses are not required in the last expression, but they make the meaning of the formula clearer: You must compute the gross pay before subtracting the taxes.

Although this program is shorter than C7PAY.BAS, a shorter program is not always better. A more readable program is generally the best kind. Being able to store the three values lets you use them later in the program without recalculating their results. The last expression is much less complicated if you first calculate and store the `gross.pay` and `taxes`, as you did in PAY.BAS.

Shorter Is Not Always Better

If you program computers for the company you work for, it is much more important to write programs that are easy to understand than programs that are short or include a tricky calculation.

Maintainability is the computer industry's word for the ability to change and update programs that were written in a simple style. The business world is changing rapidly, and the programs that companies have used for years must be updated to reflect the changing environment. Businesses do not always have the resources to write programs from scratch, so they must modify the ones they have.

Years ago, when computer hardware was much more expensive and when computer memories were much smaller, it was important to write small programs, despite the problems these programs caused when they needed to be changed. These problems were aggravated when the original programmers left and someone else had to step in and modify the code.

Companies are realizing the importance of spending time to write programs that are easy to modify and that do not rely on tricks or "quick and dirty" routines that are hard to follow. You are a much more valuable programmer if you write clean programs with ample white space, plentiful remarks, and straightforward code. Put parentheses around formulas if doing so makes them clearer, and use variables for storing results in case you need the same answer later in the program. Break long calculations into several smaller ones.

2. You can write simple programs to illustrate the operators in QBasic. Suppose you want to write a tutorial program that shows how each operator works. The following program computes and prints the results of simple calculations using each operator.

```
' Filename: C7OPRTR.BAS
'
' This program shows the result of each operator.

num1 = 7              ' The variables to compute with
num2 = 4

CLS
PRINT "+num1 is"; num1
PRINT "+num2 is"; num2
ans = -num1           ' Unary minus
PRINT "-num1 is "; ans
ans = num1 - num2     ' Subtraction
PRINT "num1 - num2 is"; ans
ans = num1 + num2     ' Addition
PRINT "num1 + num2 is"; ans
ans = num1 * num2     ' Multiplication
PRINT "num1 * num2 is"; ans
ans = num1 / num2       ' Division
PRINT "num1 / num2 is"; ans
ans = num1 \ num2       ' Integer Division
PRINT "num1 \ num2 is"; ans
ans = num1 MOD num2 ' Modulus remainder
PRINT "num1 MOD num2 is"; ans
ans = num1 ^ num2     ' Exponentiation
PRINT "num1 ^ num2 is"; ans
```

Figure 7.6 shows the output of this program. Make sure you understand how the program produces the output. The results don't have to be stored in `ans` before being printed; if they are, however, the code is easier to change later. You can modify the `PRINT`s without affecting the calculations.

```
+num1 is 7
+num2 is 4
-num1 is-7
num1 - num2 is 3
num1 + num2 is 11
num1 * num2 is 28
num1 / num2 is 1.75
num1 \ num2 is 1
num1 MOD num2 is 3
num1 ^ num2 is 2401






Press any key to continue
```

Figure 7.6. Printing answers to expressions with descriptions of each.

Summary

You now can perform almost any math function you'll ever need. By understanding the order of operators, you know how to structure your formulas so that QBasic computes the answers the way you prefer them. You always can override the order of operators by using parentheses.

There is much more to computers than math. The next chapter shows how you can store letters, words, and sentences in variables, and thus store names and addresses. When you learn how to store character string data in variables, you will have mastered most of the data types of QBasic and you will be ready to process that data with more powerful QBasic commands.

Review Questions

Answers to the Review Questions are in Appendix B.

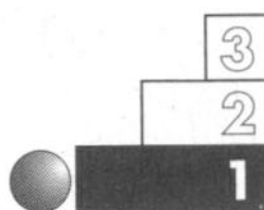

1. What are the results of the following expressions?

   A. 1 + 2 * 4 / 2
   B. (1 + 2) * 4 / 2
   C. 1 + 2 * (4 / 2)

2. What are the results of the following expressions?

   A. 9 \ 2 + 1
   B. (1 + (10 - (2 + 2)))

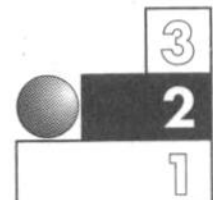

3. What output does the following program produce?

```
LET a = 6
LET b = 10
PRINT "a, b"
PRINT "a; b"
```

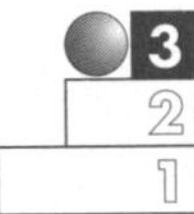

4. Convert each of the formulas in Figure 7.7 to its QBasic assignment equivalent.

5. Write a line of code that prints the area of a circle with a radius of 4. Pi is equal to 3.14159 on the screen. (The area of a circle is equal to Pi * radius^2.)

6. Write a `PRINT` statement that prints only the remainder of 100 / 4.

Review Exercises

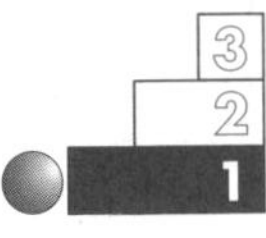

1. Write a program that prints each of the first eight powers of 2 (in other words, 2^1, 2^2, 2^3,...2^8). Use remarks to include your name at the top of the program. Clear the screen before printing anything. Print string constants that describe each printed answer. The first two lines of your output should look like this:

```
2 raised to the first power is 2
2 raised to the second power is 4
```

$$a = \frac{3 + 3}{4 + 4}$$

$$x = (a - b) * (a - c)^2$$

$$f = \frac{a^{1/2}}{b^{1/3}}$$

$$d = \frac{(8 - x^2)}{(x - 9)} - \frac{(4 * 2 - 1)}{x^3}$$

Figure 7.7. **Formulas to be converted to QBasic assignment equivalents.**

2. Change C7PAY.BAS so that it computes and prints a bonus of 15 percent of the gross pay. Don't take taxes out of the bonus. After printing the four variables, `gross.pay`, `taxes`, `bonus`, and `net.pay`, print a paycheck to the printer. Add string constants so that the check includes the name of the payee. Print your name as the payor at the bottom of the check.

TIP: Use `PRINT` for the screen prompts and `LPRINT` for the check.

3. Store the weights and ages of three people in variables. Print a table (with titles) of the weights and ages. At the bottom of the table print the average of the weights and heights, and their totals.

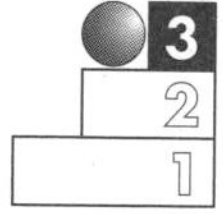

4. Assume that a video store employee works 50 hours in a pay period. The employee is paid $4.50 for the first 40 hours. She gets time-and-a-half pay (1.5 times the regular pay rate) for the first five hours over 40. She gets double-time pay for hours over 45. Assuming a 28 percent tax rate, write a program that prints her gross pay, taxes, and net pay to the screen. Label each amount with appropriate titles (using string constants), and add appropriate remarks in the program.

8

String Variables

Chapter 5, "Understanding Numeric Variables and Constants," explained how to use string constants. Without string constants you would not be able to print messages to the screen or printer. You are ready to see how to store string data in variables. A *string variable* can hold string data, just as integer variables hold integers and double-precision variables hold double-precision numbers. By storing strings of characters in variables, you can change the strings. This is useful if you keep track of names and addresses; when a person moves to another city, simply change the string variable that holds that person's city.

Learning about string variables completes Part II of this book. After this chapter, you will know almost everything there is to know about the fundamental data types and variables in QBasic. Part III, "Input/Output," shows you how to manipulate, control, and process that data into meaningful results.

This chapter introduces the following topics:

- Creating string variables
- Printing string variables
- String concatenation
- Ensuring proper types with variables
- A summary of advanced string uses

By storing string data in string variables, you have to type your string data only once, even if you need to print it several times. After you store the string data in a string variable, you simply print the string variable from then on.

Creating String Variables

If computers worked only with numbers, they would be little more than calculators. True data processing occurs when you can process any type of data, including character string data. String variables can hold any character, word, or phrase that your PC can produce. There are two types of string variables: *variable-length string variables* and *fixed-length string variables.*

Most strings are variable-length strings, which means that the string data stored in the variable can be any length. If you put a short word in a variable-length string variable and then replace it with a longer word or phrase, the string variable grows to hold the new, longer data. This is different from the numeric variables you have been using; they have fixed lengths, or ranges of values, and you cannot exceed those stated ranges of numbers.

Fixed-length string variables can hold only strings that are shorter than or equal to the length you define. These strings are not as flexible as variable-length strings. Chapter 23, "Variable Scope," addresses fixed-length strings and explains their uses.

CAUTION: String variables can hold strings as long as 32,767 characters. This should be more than ample for virtually every application, but you should keep this limit in the back of your mind while you work with string-intensive data.

Naming String Variables

As with numeric variables, it is up to you to give names to your string variables. String variable names are easy to spot; they follow the same naming rules as numeric variables (must begin with a

letter, cannot contain spaces, and so on), except they always end with a dollar sign ($). Whenever you see a variable with a name ending in a dollar sign, it is a string variable. The following are valid string variable names:

```
MY.NAME$      month$      Customer.city$      X$      address$
```

To store a name, an address, or any other character, word, or phrase in a variable, make up a name for the variable and end it with the `$` suffix.

As with string constants, QBasic does not recognize the variable as numeric just because you put a string of numbers in a string variable. The dollar sign suffix informs QBasic that no math is to be done with the variable's data, so QBasic looks at the string of numbers only as individual characters and not as one number.

> **CAUTION:** Although it may be tempting, do not name a string variable `DATE$` or `NAME$`. These are both reserved command names in QBasic (as are `PRINT`, `LET`, and so on), and you cannot use command names for variable names. You will see the uses for these two commands later. You can find a complete list of QBasic reserved words in Appendix C.

Examples

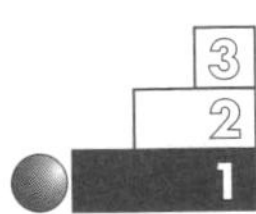

1. If you want to keep track of a customer's name, address, city, state, ZIP code, and age in variables, you might make up the following variable names:

```
cust.name$
cust.address$
cust.city$
cust.state$
cust.zip$
cust.age
```

Notice that the customer's age is numeric, so it is stored in a numeric variable (the name does not end with a $). You should store data in numeric variables only if you might do math with it. This generally excludes data such as phone numbers, social security numbers, customer numbers, and so on. For instance, although ZIP codes consist of numbers, you never add or subtract ZIP codes. They are best stored in string variables. You might use age in an average age calculation, so it is best to leave it in a numeric variable.

2. If you want to keep track of an employee's salary, age, name, employee number, and number of dependents, you might use the following variable names:

```
emp.salary!
emp.age%
emp.name$
emp.number$
emp.dependents
```

Only the name and employee number should be stored in string variables. The salary should be stored in a numeric variable. I use a single-precision variable here (due to the ! suffix), although if the salary is extremely large, a double-precision variable might be better. The age is stored in an integer variable, and the number of dependents is stored in a single-precision variable (the default variable type if you do not specify a suffix).

Storing Data in String Variables

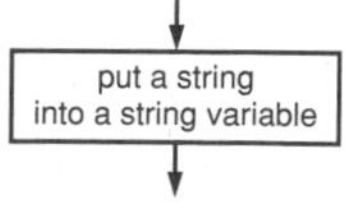
put a string
into a string variable

You put string data in string variables with the LET assignment statement just as you do with numeric data and variables. You can put either a string constant or another string variable in a string variable with LET. The format of the LET string assignment statement is

```
[LET] varname$ = "String"

or

[LET] varname1$ = varname2$
```

As with all LET statements, the word LET is optional. Each variable (varname$, varname1$, and varname2$) can be any valid string variable name (make sure its name ends with a dollar sign). The equal sign is required. Any string constant or another string variable name can follow the equal sign.

Notice that if you put a string constant in a string variable name, you must enclose the string constant in quotation marks. The quotation marks are not stored in the string; only the data between the quotation marks are.

You can put an empty string, called a *null string,* in a string variable by putting two quotation marks with no space between them after the equal sign. For instance, the assignment statement

```
LET E$ = ""
```

puts an empty string, with zero length, in the string variable named E$. QBasic initializes all string variables to null strings before you use them. You might want to start with a null string if you build strings one character at a time—for instance, if you were receiving data sequentially from a modem.

Examples

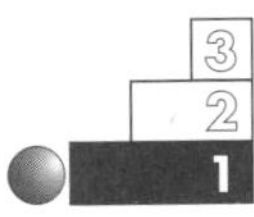

1. Appendix E, "The Complete Application," contains a complete sample application that manages a book inventory for a library, collector, or bookstore. Throughout this text you see portions of the book management program in examples.

   To keep track of a book's title, author, and edition, you might store the data in three string variables as shown:

   ```
   LET book.title$ = "In Pursuit of Life"
   LET book.author$ = "Francis Scott Key"
   LET book.edition = "2nd"
   ```

2. Because LET is always optional in assignment statements, these three book string variables could be assigned:

```
book.title$ = "In Pursuit of Life"
book.author$ = "Francis Scott Key"
book.edition = "2nd"
```

3. You can assign a string variable's value to another string variable, as the second line in the next example shows.

```
LET emp.last.name$ = "Payton"
LET spouse.last.name$ = emp.last.name$
```

Printing String Variables

To print the data stored inside a string variable, put the string variable after PRINT or LPRINT, just as you did for numeric variables. You can combine numeric variables, string variables, string constants, semicolons, commas, and TABs in PRINT and LPRINT statements if the output warrants it.

TIP: If you have to print a string constant several times in a program, it is easiest to store that string constant in a string variable and then print the string variable name. For instance, if you have to print your company's full legal name at the top of several checks and reports, store that name in a string variable, such as co.name$, and print co.name$ to keep from having to type (and risk mistyping) the entire company name throughout the program.

Separating Spaces

When printing a string variable next to another string variable or a string constant using the semicolon, QBasic does not automatically print a separating space between them. Therefore, if you need to print a description before a string variable, be sure to add a space inside the description's closing double quotation marks, as shown in the following line:

```
PRINT "The highest-paid executive is: "; max.exe$
```

You have to include a separating space surrounded by two quotation marks if you want to print two string variables next to each other. If you store the names of three automobile makers in three string variables and want to print them, you would want to print them separated by a space, as in

```
PRINT auto1$; " "; auto2$; " "; auto3$
```

This would place a blank space between the names of the automobile makers, as in

```
GM Ford Chrysler
```

Otherwise, you get run-on string output, like

```
GMFordChrysler
```

which is harder to read.

Examples

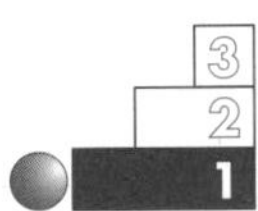

1. The following program stores and prints the three book-related string variables mentioned in a previous example.

```
' Filename: C8BKSTR1.BAS
'
' Stores and prints three book-related variables.

book.title$ = "In Pursuit of Life"
book.author$ = "Francis Scott Key"
book.edition$ = "2nd"

' Now, print them to the screen

CLS
PRINT book.title$
PRINT book.author$
PRINT book.edition$
```

2. You know by now that printing the contents of variables without first describing them produces confusing output. To improve on the previous program, you could add a header and descriptive titles, and TAB the data over so that it begins in the same column, as the following program shows:

```
' Filename: C8BKSTR2.BAS
'
' Stores and prints three book-related variables with a title.

book.title$ = "In Pursuit of Life"
book.author$ = "Francis Scott Key"
book.edition$ = "2nd"

' Print a title
CLS
PRINT TAB(30);"Book Listing"
PRINT TAB(30);"---- -------"
PRINT                                   ' Print two
PRINT                                   ' blank lines

' Now, print the book data to the screen
PRINT "The book's title is:"; TAB(24); book.title$
PRINT "The book's author is:"; TAB(24); book.author$
PRINT "The book's edition is:"; TAB(24); book.edition$
END
```

Figure 8.1 shows the screen output from this program. Although the descriptions are three different lengths, the book's data are aligned in column 24 because of the TAB values. The END statement is optional.

If you want the book data to go to the printer rather than the screen, change the PRINT statements to LPRINT statements.

```
                              Book Listing
                              ---- -------


The book's title is:   In Pursuit of Life
The book's author is:  Francis Scott Key
The book's edition is: 2nd













Press any key to continue
```

Figure 8.1. Results of printing the strings with descriptions.

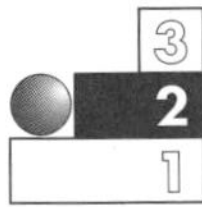

3. The following program adapts the payroll example programs shown in earlier chapters to print a paycheck. Before running the program, make sure your printer is on and has paper in it.

```
' Filename: C8PAY.BAS
'
' Computes and prints a payroll check.

' Initialize data variables
emp.name$ = "Larry Payton"
pay.date$ = "01/09/92"
hours.worked = 40            ' Total hours worked
rate = 7.50                  ' Pay per hour
tax.rate = .40               ' Tax rate percentage

' Compute the pay
```

```
gross.pay = hours.worked * rate
taxes = tax.rate * gross.pay
net.pay = gross.pay - taxes

' Print the results on the format of a check
LPRINT TAB(40);"Date: "; pay.date$
LPRINT                                  ' Print a blank line
LPRINT "Pay to the Order of: "; emp.name$
LPRINT
LPRINT "Pay the full amount of:";gross.pay
LPRINT TAB(25);"---"                    ' Underline the amount
LPRINT
LPRINT TAB(40);"----------------------"
LPRINT TAB(40);"Dan Chambers, Treasurer"
```

Figure 8.2 shows the result of running this program. (Granted, this check does not have the amount written out in words as well as in numbers.) You are learning some of the different ways to print string variables and numeric data together in the same program.

At this point you might think it would be easier to type the check in a typewriter than to write the program to compute and print it. Do not despair. You are learning the solid groundwork required to make QBasic do your tedious work for you. As you learn more of the language, you will see how writing the program becomes much faster than typing the data by hand, especially when you are using large data files.

String Concatenation

You cannot perform math on string variables, even if they contain numbers. You can perform another type of operation on string variables: *concatenation.* Concatenation is attaching one string to the end of another or combining two or more strings into a longer string. You can concatenate string variables, string constants, or a combination of both and assign the concatenated strings to a string variable.

```
                                Date: 01/09/92

Pay to the Order of: Larry Payton

Pay the full amount of: 300
                        ---


                                ------------------------
                                Dan Chambers, Treasurer
```

Figure 8.2. The check printed to the printer.

The string concatenation operator is the plus sign. QBasic knows not to confuse the concatenation symbol with the addition symbol because of its context; if it sees string data on either side of the plus sign, it knows to concatenate the strings.

> **CAUTION:** You can concatenate as many strings (variables and constants) as you like, as long as you do not exceed QBasic's 32,767 string variable limit.

Examples

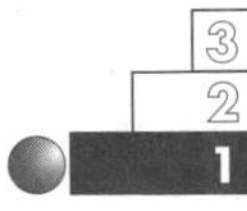

1. If you store an employee's first name in one string variable and his last name in a second string variable, you can print his full name by printing the two string variables next to each other, as the following example shows:

```
LET first.name$ = "Bill"
LET last.name$ = "Cole"
PRINT first.name$;" ";last.name$
```

The problem with printing the two variables is that you always have to print both of them together with a separating space between them. It would be easier to concatenate the two names into another string variable, as shown in the following code:

```
LET first.name$ = "Bill"
LET last.name$ = "Cole"
LET full.name$ = first.name$ + " " + last.name$
PRINT full.name$
```

The extra space is a string constant you concatenate between the two strings. If you didn't include it, the names would run together.

Running this short section of code produces

```
Bill Cole
```

on the screen.

This may seem like extra typing because you have to include the line that concatenates the two variables. Nevertheless, this process makes printing the full name much easier later in the program, especially if you have to print it several times.

2. If you want to print the previous example's full name with the last name first, you can do so by concatenating a comma between the names, as in

```
LET first.name$ = "Bill"
LET last.name$ = "Cole"
LET full.name$ = last.name$ + ", " + first.name$
PRINT full.name$
```

Running this section of code produces

```
Cole, Bill
```

on your screen. The space after the comma is there because it was concatenated in the string constant that contained the comma in the third line of code.

3. The book management database program in Appendix E saves the book data in a file specified by the user. If you do not type a file extension, the program automatically concatenates one to the file name you typed, in code similar to the following code:

```
file.name$ = user.file.name$ + ".DAT"
```

You then could append a disk drive name, which is stored in another string variable, as follows:

```
file.name$ = disk.drive$ + file.name$
```

Notice that you are adding to the length of the string variable on the left side of the equal sign.

Do Not Mix Types

You have seen many examples of programs that use each of these variables and constants:

Integer

Single-precision

Double-precision

String

You must be careful when you use the assignment statement. You never can put string data in a numeric variable or numeric data in a string variable. The following rule is critical:

> **CAUTION:** In an assignment statement, always be sure that both sides of the equal sign contain the same type of data and variables.

For instance, Table 8.1 shows several assignment statements. You have seen many like them. There is nothing wrong with them because the variable on the left side of the equal sign is the same type as the expression, variable, or constant on the right side. Make sure you understand why the statements in this table are valid before reading on.

The assignment statements in the second column of the table are arbitrary assignment statements that have the same type of variable, constant, or expression on both sides of the equal sign.

Table 8.1. Valid assignment statements.

Variable = Expression	*Assignment Statement*
integer = integer	`distance% = 175`
integer = integer	`distance2% = distance%`
integer = integer	`diff% = distance% / 2`
single-precision = single-precision	`salary = 45023.92`
single-precision = single-precision	`length! = range`
single-precision = single-precision	`month.pay = salary! / 12`
double-precision = double-precision	`temp# = -123.43337689`
double-precision = double-precision	`high.temp# = temp#`
double-precision = double-precision	`avg.rain# = inches# / 8`
string = string	`a$ = "Candy"`
string = string	`b$ = a$`
string = string	`full.name$ = first$ + last$`

If you follow some precautions, you can mix certain types of numeric data types in the same expression. Typically, you can assign a smaller variable type to a larger one. For example, you can assign an integer to a single- or double-precision variable. QBasic will convert the integer to single or double precision when it assigns the integer to the variable. In a like manner, you can assign a single-precision number, variable, or expression to a double-precision variable without any loss of accuracy.

Table 8.2 is very different. It shows many combinations of assignments that do not work because the type on one side of the equal sign does not match the type on the other side.

Table 8.2. Invalid assignment statements with nonmatching types.

Assignment	*Problem Description*
`greet$ = hello`	No quotation marks around `"hello"`.
`salary = "43234.54"`	Do not put string constants in numeric variables.
`avg.age$ = "100" / 2`	You cannot perform math with string constants.
`full.name$ = first + last`	No dollar sign after `first` and `last` (QBasic thinks these are two numeric variables called `first` and `last`).
`weight% = pounds# + kilos#`	You cannot put a double-precision number in an integer with accuracy (QBasic will round improperly).
`month = month.name$`	You cannot put a string variable in a numeric variable.

If you attempt to mix strings and numeric variables in an assignment statement, you get a `type mismatch` error like the one in Figure 8.3.

Other String Features

You can perform many more operations on string variables and string constants. Storing and printing them are only the first steps in learning about QBasic strings. Future chapters address the string functions that enable you to move, copy, and delete parts of a string variable while keeping the remaining characters intact.

When you learn about writing disk files, you see also how to create fixed-length strings. So far, you have seen variable-length strings. Most QBasic strings can shrink or grow to hold whatever string constant you assign to them. For instance, the following eight lines of code show how you can print the same string variable with many different lengths of data in it:

```
LET a$ = "QBasic is fun!"
PRINT a$
a$ = "Actually, QBasic is challenging, but VERY, VERY fun!"
PRINT a$
a$ = "Yes"
PRINT a$
a$ = "This variable holds many different lengths of data!"
PRINT a$
```

Variable-length strings are much more flexible than fixed-length strings because they do not dictate the length of the data they hold (as long as you do not exceed the 32,767 limit). Fixed-length strings are important when you work with disk data files. By limiting the size of the string variables, you can avoid wasting disk space.

Through the rest of this book, you will learn these additional string features and see how to tackle their advanced programming requirements.

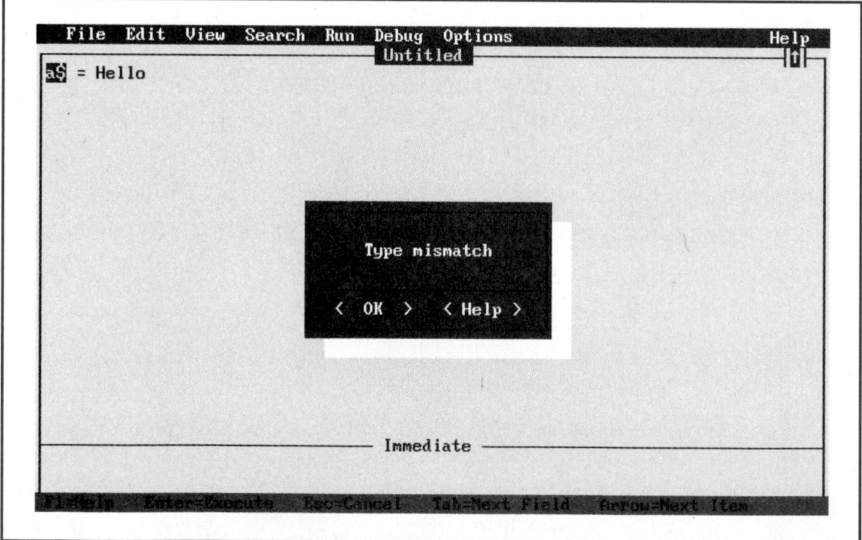

Figure 8.3. The error that occurs when you mix types in an assignment statement.

Summary

This chapter showed you the basics for working with string variables. By storing strings in variables, you can print and change them throughout a program. You also can concatenate them to build longer string variables.

This chapter concludes Part II, "Primary QBasic Elements." You have learned how to store and print the different types of QBasic variables and constants. Most of the printing has been limited. Although `PRINT` and `LPRINT` have many options, QBasic offers additional commands that format your output to print exactly the way you want it, such as in dollar amounts with two decimal places for the cents. The next section shows you ways to produce color printing on your screen, and how to input data to your programs from the keyboard.

Review Questions

Answers to the Review Questions are in Appendix B.

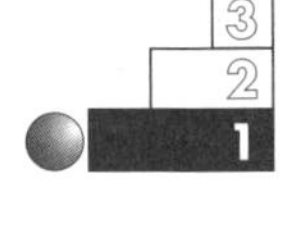

1. How many characters of data can a string variable hold?
2. What character is *always* part of a string variable name?
3. What are the two most common types of string variables, and which is most flexible to use?
4. What is the string concatenation operator?
5. Which of the following assignment statements are valid?

   A. `LET f$ = g$ + h$`
   B. `LET name$ = "Michael"`
   C. `LET last.name = "Harrison"`
   D. `LET emp.name$ = first.name$ + last.name$`

6. State the type (integer, single-precision, double-precision, or string) of each of the following variables:

```
a#
a
a$
a%
a!
```

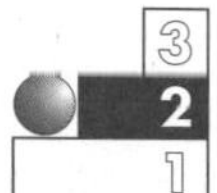

7. Why can't you give a string variable the name NAME$?
8. TRUE or FALSE: When calculating payroll taxes, the following statement would work:

   ```
   LET taxes = gross.pay * "40%"
   ```

9. Write a statement to print city$ and state$ with a comma and space between them.

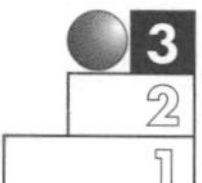

10. Given the assignment statement

    ```
    LET filename$ = "AugSales"
    ```

    how would you, in one statement, add the disk drive C:\ to the front of the file name, and the extension .DAT to the end of it?

Review Exercises

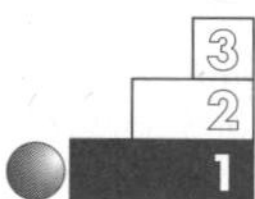

1. Write a program to store your first, middle, and last names in three string variables. Print the names on the screen and the printer with appropriate descriptions.
2. Modify the program in the preceding exercise to print your name in reverse order, with your last name first. Print the names in the following ways: next to each other, one in a different print zone, and in columns 10, 20, and 30. (Hint: Use the TAB feature to print every 10 columns.)

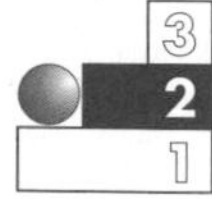

3. Write a program to store your first, middle, and last name in three separate string variables. Concatenate them so that they are stored in one string variable called full.name$. Be sure there is at least one space between the three names when you concatenate them. Print full.name$ on the screen after clearing it first.

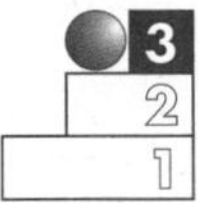

4. Change the C8PAY.BAS payroll program presented earlier in this chapter. Print a string of asterisks around the check to mark the check's border. Change the name on the check so that the check pays to you. Give yourself a raise by increasing the hourly rate.

Part III

Input/Output

9

Inputting Values

You now understand data and variables in QBasic. You also have seen several methods for outputting data with the PRINT and LPRINT statements. Nevertheless, you have not seen one critical part of programming: inputting data to your programs.

Every program you have seen so far has had no data input. All data you worked with was assigned to variables within the program. This is not the best way, however, to get the data that your programs process; you rarely know what the data will be when you write your programs. The data values are known only when the user runs the programs.

To give you a sampling of some ways to get input in QBasic, this chapter introduces

- The INPUT statement
- The LINE INPUT statement

This chapter shows you ways to program the complete data processing cycle: *input →process → output*. Starting with this chapter, the programs you write work on different data depending on what the *user* (the person who runs the program) types at the keyboard.

The INPUT Statement

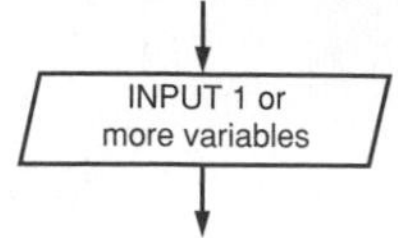

Here is the INPUT statement in its simplest form:

```
INPUT var1 [, var2][, var3][, ..., varN]
```

INPUT goes on a line by itself and is followed by one or more variables, each separated by commas. The sole purpose of INPUT is to get one or more values from the person at the keyboard.

When your program reaches the INPUT statement, it displays a question mark and waits for the user to type one or more values. If one variable follows INPUT, the program expects only one value. If more than one variable follows INPUT, the user must type values separated by commas until each of the variables is filled. Pressing Enter after typing values in response to INPUT informs QBasic that the user is finished typing values into the INPUT variables.

INPUT Fills Variables with Values

There is a major difference between INPUT and the assignment statements you have seen. Both fill variables with values. An assignment statement, however, assigns specific values to variables *at programming time.* When you run a program with assignment statements, you know from the program listing exactly what values go in the variables because you wrote the program to store those values there. The results are the same every time you run the program, because the same values go in the same variables.

When you write programs that use INPUT, you have no idea what values go in the INPUT variables because their values are not known until the program is run. This makes for more flexible programs that a variety of people can use. Every time the user runs the program, different results are output depending on what the user types at the INPUT prompts.

Examples

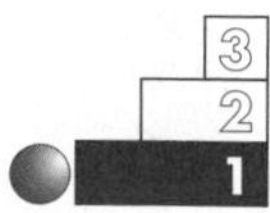

1. If you want a program that computes a 7 percent sales tax, use the INPUT statement to get the sales, compute the tax, and then print the results, as the following program shows:

```
' Filename: C9SLSTX.BAS
'
CLS

' Get the total sales
INPUT total.sales

' Calculate sales tax
stax = total.sales * .07

' Print the results
PRINT "The sales tax on"; total.sales; " is: "; stax
PRINT "Bringing the total needed to:"; (total.sales + stax)
```

When you run this program, the screen clears and you see a question mark. This signals that QBasic got to the `INPUT` statement and is waiting for you to type a value. This value is stored in `total.sales` when you type it. You always must press Enter when you finish typing values for `INPUT`.

The program then computes the sales tax, prints the tax, and prints the total for the sale, including the sales tax.

2. Suppose you want to write a program that computes the average of three numbers. In Chapter 5, you saw a program that used the `LET` assignment statement to store three numbers and print their average.

   A much more helpful program first would ask the person running the program which three numbers to average. Then the program would print the average of those three numbers. The following code does that:

```
' Filename: C9INPAV1.BAS
'
CLS
' Get three numbers from user
INPUT num1, num2, num3

' Calculate the average
avg = (num1 + num2 + num3) / 3
```

```
' Print the results
PRINT "The average of your three numbers is:"; avg
```

When you run this program, a question mark appears on the screen when QBasic gets to the INPUT statement. The program halts until you type three values, each separated by a comma. After you type three values and press Enter, the program continues from the INPUT statement, calculates the average, and prints the results. Figure 9.1 shows the output screen if you run this program and enter three numbers.

```
? 19, 43, 56
The average of your three numbers is: 39.33333













Press any key to continue
```

Figure 9.1. The output after you enter three values in the INPUT variables.

As you can see, only one question mark appears on the screen when you use INPUT, even if more than one variable appears after INPUT.

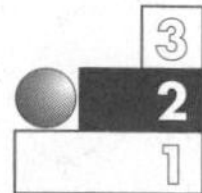

3. The following program asks the user to input a name in two separate variables. The program then prints the name as it would appear in a phone book: It prints the last name, a comma, and then the first name.

```
' Filename: C9PHONE1.BAS
'
' Program that gets the user's name and prints it
' to the screen as it would appear in a phone book.

CLS
INPUT first.name$
INPUT last.name$

PRINT "In a phone book, your name would look like this:"
PRINT last.name$; ", "; first.name$
```

Figure 9.2 shows the result of running this program. Run it yourself and see the results on your screen. Run it a second time and type a completely different pair of names. See how INPUT makes the output of your programs change, although the actual programs do not change.

```
? George
? Harris
In a phone book, your name would look like this:
Harris, George










Press any key to continue
```

Figure 9.2. Printing the INPUT names as they might appear in a phone book.

This example illustrates two more aspects of INPUT. You can input any value to any kind of variable, even string variables, as long as the values you type at the keyboard match the type of variable listed after INPUT. Also, two question marks appear on the screen, each of which appears when the next INPUT statement is reached. If you combine the two INPUT statements into one, as in the INPUT statement

```
INPUT first.name$, last.name$
```

you see only one question mark because there is only one INPUT statement. You would have to type both names separated by a comma, because that is the format of this particular INPUT.

CAUTION: Your keyboard input values must match in number and type the variables that follow the INPUT statement.

Improving the Use of INPUT

The preceding programs have flaws. These flaws are not exactly program bugs, but the programs contain logic that is not appropriate for the users. The problem is that when users run the programs, they see only one question mark. They have no idea what kind or how many values to type.

You always should *prompt* users for values that they have to type in response to INPUT. For example, do not simply let the INPUT's question mark tell the users that values are required. PRINT a message telling the users exactly what they are to type in response to the INPUT's question mark.

The following examples build on previous examples to illustrate the importance of using prompts before INPUT statements.

Examples

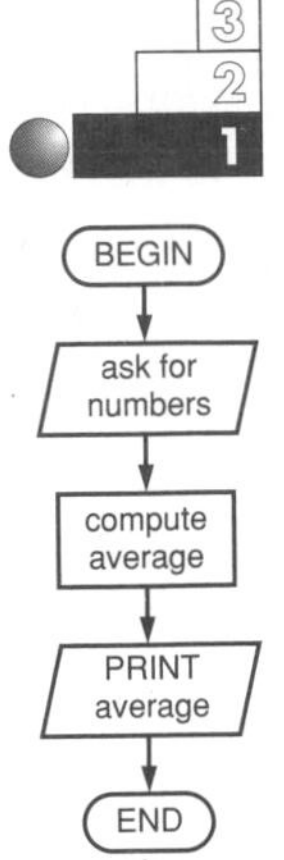

1. The following program is a rewritten version of the program that averages three numbers. The addition of a PRINT statement greatly improves the program.

```
' Filename: C9INPAV2.BAS
'
CLS

' Prompt the user at the keyboard
PRINT "Please ENTER three numbers, separated by commas"

' Get the three numbers from user
INPUT num1, num2, num3

' Calculate the average
avg = (num1 + num2 + num3) / 3

' Print the results
PRINT "The average of your three numbers is:"; avg
```

Figure 9.3 shows how the output screen looks if you run this program. Notice that the users know exactly what to type. There is no ambiguity and little chance that they will type input in the wrong format.

Some programmers prefer to print an example INPUT response to further ensure that the user knows exactly what to type. You could do this by adding a second PRINT statement.

```
PRINT "Please type three numbers, separated by commas"
PRINT "(for example, 4, 25, 70), and press Enter when done."
```

2. The following program adds prompts to the phone book listing. The program also prompts for the address and telephone number. Without the prompts, the user has no idea what to type next.

```
' Filename: C9PHONE2.BAS
'
' Gets the user's telephone information and prints
' it to the screen as it would appear in a phone book.
CLS

' Prompt for each value before inputting them
PRINT "Please enter your first name"
INPUT first.name$
PRINT "Please enter your last name"
INPUT last.name$
PRINT "Please enter your address"
INPUT address$
PRINT "Please enter your telephone number"
INPUT phone$

PRINT "In a phone book, your listing would look like this:"
PRINT last.name$; ", "; first.name$; " "; address$;
".....";  phone$
END
```

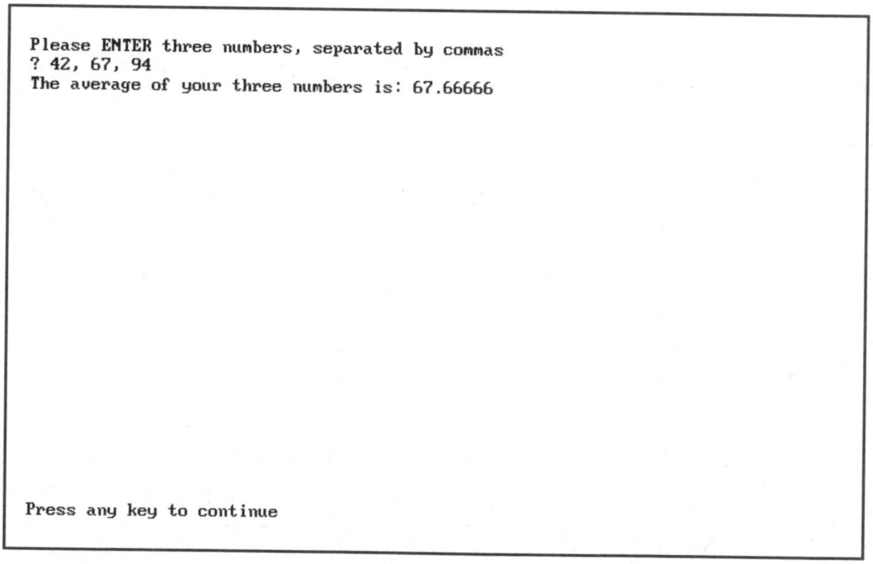

```
Please ENTER three numbers, separated by commas
? 42, 67, 94
The average of your three numbers is: 67.66666









Press any key to continue
```

Figure 9.3. The averaging program with a prompt for the user.

Figure 9.4 shows a result of running this program.

```
Please enter your first name
? Mary
Please enter your last name
? Carter
Please enter your address
? 3234 East Maple Dr.
Please enter your telephone number
? 555-6543
In a phone book, your listing would look like this:
Carter, Mary 3234 East Maple Dr......555-6543









Press any key to continue
```

Figure 9.4. Prompting for the phone book information.

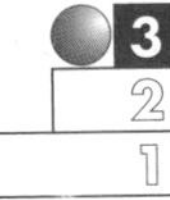

3. The INPUT programs you have seen so far display a question mark when the INPUT is executed. This is to be expected. The question mark appears on the line following the prompt it goes with. If you want a user to answer a question inside the prompt, two question marks appear. Therefore, the section of code

```
PRINT "What is your name?"
INPUT full.name$
```

produces the following output:

```
What is your name?
?
```

If you omit the question mark in the printed prompt, the INPUT question mark still appears on the next line. This makes answering questions with INPUT awkward.

You already have the tools you need to fix this problem. Remember the trailing semicolon? It forces the cursor to remain on the line on which the PRINT prints. If you put a semicolon at the end of a prompt message, the next INPUT prints its question mark directly to the right of the question.

Consider the following child's addition program. Notice how you can ask a question directly, and the question marks fall where they naturally would—at the end of the question.

```
' Filename: C9MATH2.BAS
'
' Program to help children with simple addition.
'
' Prompt child for 2 values, after printing a title message
CLSPRINT "*** Math Practice ***"
PRINT            ' Print 2 blank lines
PRINT
PRINT "What is the first number";    ' Force question
INPUT num1                           ' mark to appear
PRINT "What is the second number";   ' directly after
INPUT num2                           ' each prompt.
' Compute answer and give child a chance to wait for it
ans = num1 + num2
PRINT
PRINT "Press ENTER when you want to see the answer..."
INPUT ent$             ' Nothing gets entered here

' Print answer after a blank line
PRINT
PRINT num1; " plus"; num2; " is:"; ans
PRINT
PRINT "I hope you got it right!"
END
```

Figure 9.5 shows the result of running this addition program. When you add trailing semicolons to each prompt, the program's questions are smoother and sound more appropriate.

```
*** Math Practice ***


What is the first number? 6
What is the second number? 3

Press ENTER when you want to see the answer...
?

 6  plus 3  is: 9

I hope you got it right!









Press any key to continue
```

Figure 9.5. Running the revised addition program with improved prompts.

Prompting with INPUT

You've seen the importance of prompting for input. If the program tells the users exactly how to type the input, they will be more likely to match the INPUT's expected variables in type and number.

The designers of QBasic also knew this. They understood that every INPUT should be preceded with a PRINT statement to prompt the user. They added a shortcut to the typical PRINT-INPUT pair of statements by designing INPUT so that you can print the prompt directly in the INPUT statement without a stand-alone PRINT before it. This format of INPUT looks like this:

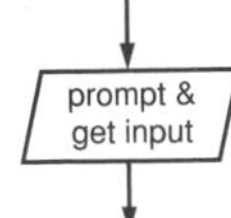


```
INPUT "prompt message"; var1[, var2][, var3][, ..., varN]
```

The *prompt message* is where the prompt goes. This considerably shortens programs that use INPUT. By putting the prompt message directly inside INPUT, no PRINT is required before INPUT.

Examples

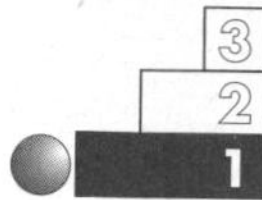

1. The following program is a revised version of the program that averages three numbers. Its `INPUT` statements contain the prompt message previously printed by `PRINT` statements.

```
' Filename: C9INPAV3.BAS
'
CLS

' Prompt the user at the keyboard and input numbers

INPUT "Enter 3 numbers, separated by commas";num1,num2,num3

' Calculate the average
avg = (num1 + num2 + num3) / 3

' Print the result
PRINT "The average of your three numbers is:"; avg
```

Running this program produces the same results as before. The prompting `INPUT` string streamlines it and all other programs that prompt before `INPUT` statements.

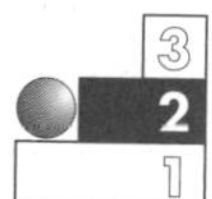

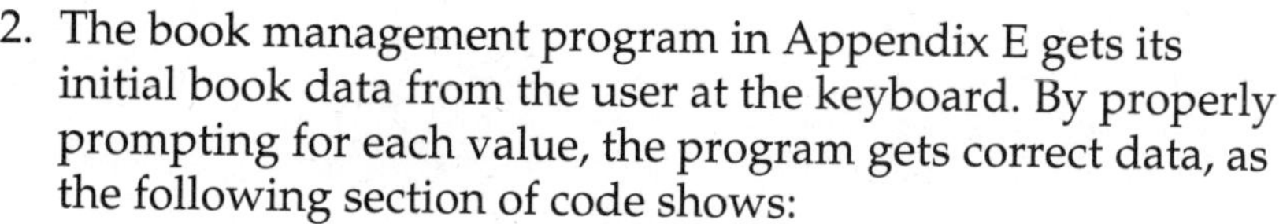

2. The book management program in Appendix E gets its initial book data from the user at the keyboard. By properly prompting for each value, the program gets correct data, as the following section of code shows:

```
' Section of book data input routine
INPUT "What is the book's title"; book.title$
INPUT "What is the book's author"; author$
INPUT "What is the publication date"; pub.date$
INPUT "What edition is it (1, 2, 3, etc.)"; edition
```

Notice that the last prompt explains how to type the book edition. If the user types a value such as `2nd`, an error occurs because a numeric variable cannot hold the last two characters of `2nd`.

Inputting Strings

Although you might not have realized it, there is a character on the keyboard that you cannot input with the INPUT statement. It is the comma. The comma is the delimiter that separates values from each other in the INPUT list of values.

Many times, however, you need to enter information that contains commas. For example, if you enter a full name, last name first, you cannot put a comma between the two names; INPUT would think you entered two values.

To fix this problem, put quotation marks around INPUT strings that contain commas. The quotation marks are not part of the input value; they serve to enclose the full string, including the commas.

Examples

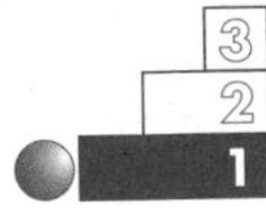

1. The following program asks the user for a book title and prints the title on the screen.

```
' Filename: C9BOOKT1.BAS
'
' Gets a book title and prints it on the printer.

CLS
PRINT "Type a book's title and enclose it ";
PRINT "inside double quotes."
INPUT "What is the name of the book"; book.title$

PRINT "The title you entered is: "; book.title$
```

Notice that only one string variable, book.title$, is INPUT, and only one is printed. If the book title contains a comma, the user has to enter that title enclosed in quotation marks, as the prompt indicates. Figure 9.6 shows a sample run. The user types quotation marks around the book title because the title includes a comma.

```
Type a book's title and enclose it inside double quotes.
What is the name of the book? "To Err, To Live"
The title you entered is: To Err, To Live




Press any key to continue
```

Figure 9.6. Entering a comma as part of an INPUT value.

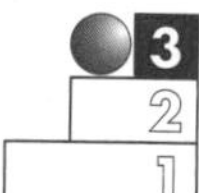

2. The following program requests three city and state combinations. Figure 9.7 shows the results of running the program and entering the three cities. Notice that only three variables are entered, but more than three words are entered. Be sure to study the input values to see exactly how the city-state combinations are entered in three different variables.

```
' Filename: C9CITST1.BAS
'
' Request three city-state pairs in a single INPUT
' statement. The user must enclose each in quotes.

CLS
PRINT "At the question mark, please enter three city and"
PRINT "state pairs.  Enclose each city-state combination"
PRINT "in double quotes, and separate them with commas."
INPUT city1$, city2$, city3$

PRINT "You entered the following:"
PRINT city1$, city2$, city3$  ' Prints in 3 different zones
END
```

You might wonder why no prompt message was included in the INPUT statement. Because no direct question was asked, there was not a good reason to put the question mark at the end of the prompt message. It took so many lines (four) to prompt correctly for the values that putting the prompt inside INPUT offered no advantage over using PRINT statements followed by an INPUT.

```
At the question mark, please enter three city and
state pairs.  Enclose each city-state combination
in double quotes, and separate them with commas.
? "Joplin, MO", "New York, NY", "San Diego, CA"
You entered the following:
Joplin, MO    New York, NY  San Diego, CA









Press any key to continue
```

Figure 9.7. Entering city-state pairs in individual variables.

Match the INPUT Variables

This chapter has stressed the need for good prompts for your INPUT statements. There is a one-to-one correlation between the number and types of your INPUT variables and the values you type at the keyboard. Nevertheless, there will be a time when a user does not enter enough values, enters too many values, or enters the wrong type of values for the variables being INPUT.

Suppose your program required the user to type three values. If the INPUT statement looked like

```
INPUT num1, num2, num3
```

but the user entered only two numbers, QBasic would realize that there were not enough values typed for the INPUT statement. It would display the error message

```
Redo from start
```

and prompt for the entire INPUT again.

The same error occurs if the user types too many values for the variables specified, or if the user enters values with the wrong type. This is most commonly due to the lack of quotation marks around the input strings. The `Redo from start` error message continues to appear until the user types values that match the variables.

Eliminating the Question Mark

Although you almost always want the INPUT question mark, QBasic offers a way for you to eliminate it when asking for keyboard values. If you follow the prompt string in the INPUT statement with a comma instead of a semicolon, no question mark appears. For example, the INPUT statement

```
INPUT "Please type your first name here -->", first.name$
```

does not produce a question mark. A question mark after the arrow (-->) would not look correct. The comma suppresses the question mark, and the value entered appears directly to the right of the prompt message.

The LINE INPUT Statement

Your application dictates the kind of string data your program requires. The book management program in Appendix E requests book titles. Book titles often have commas in them. Earlier in this chapter you saw that to input commas, the user must enclose the input string in quotation marks.

The less your users have to remember, the more likely they will be to type valid input. Another command, the LINE INPUT statement, lets your users input strings that contain commas without having to enclose the strings in quotation marks.

LINE INPUT even allows input that contains quotation marks *as part of the string*. The format of LINE INPUT is

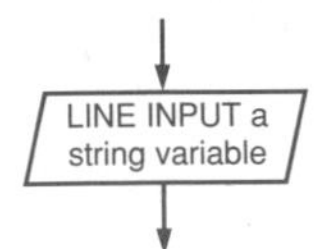


```
LINE INPUT [prompt message;] stringvariable
```

Differences Between LINE INPUT and INPUT

This format of LINE INPUT differs from INPUT in several ways. It accepts only a string variable, not numeric variables, as input. It lets you enter only one string variable; you cannot list several variables after LINE INPUT and separate them with commas.

LINE INPUT also does not automatically display a question mark. If you ask a question with LINE INPUT's prompt message, you must put a question mark at the end of your prompt message.

LINE INPUT is best used for strings that may contain the characters that INPUT does not handle well. LINE INPUT accepts commas and quotation marks as part of the input string.

Examples

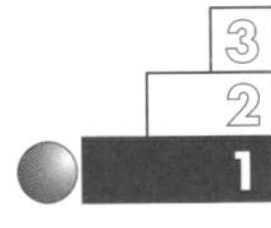

1. Suppose you want your program to ask for a list of favorite quotes and their authors. LINE INPUT is the only way to input those quotes to string variables because they probably contain commas and quotation marks. The following program clears the screen, then requests three of the user's favorite quotes. It then prints the quotes back to the screen.

```
' Filename: C9QUOTE.BAS
'
' Requests and displays the user's favorite quotes.

CLS
LINE INPUT "What is your 1st favorite quote? "; q1$
PRINT
LINE INPUT "What is the second? "; q2$
PRINT
LINE INPUT "What is the third? "; q3$
```

```
PRINT
PRINT
PRINT "Quote 1:"
PRINT q1$
PRINT
PRINT "Quote 2:"
PRINT q2$
PRINT
PRINT "Quote 3:"
PRINT q3$
```

As you can see from the run shown in Figure 9.8, each quote includes quotation marks and commas. `LINE INPUT` stored every character typed by the user in the three variables: `q1$`, `q2$`, and `q3$`.

```
What is your 1st favorite quote? "Early to bed...", Franklin

What is the second? "You can have freedom or peace, but not both at once", Long

What is the third? "I did it MY way!", Sinatra


Quote 1:
 "Early to bed...", Franklin

Quote 2:
 "You can have freedom or peace, but not both at once", Long

Quote 3:
 "I did it MY way!", Sinatra








Press any key to continue
```

Figure 9.8. Entering quotes with `LINE INPUT`.

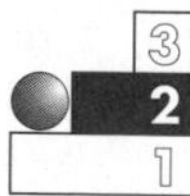

2. When do you use `INPUT` and when do you use `LINE INPUT`? Only you can decide that. The answer depends on the potential input data. For instance, the following program contains a combination of `INPUT` and `LINE INPUT` statements. It is a simple program that gets name and address information

from the user and prints it to the printer. INPUT is fine for the first and last names. The address, however, might contain commas, so you should use LINE INPUT for the address. The city and state could be entered with INPUT. (If you asked the user to enter the city and state with one prompt, however, LINE INPUT would be required because the user would type a comma between the city and the state.)

Notice that the LINE INPUT prompts must contain question marks, whereas INPUT displays the question marks for you.

```
' Filename: C9NMADR1.BAS
'
' Program to request name and address information
' and print it to the printer.

' Get the input data
CLS
INPUT "What is the first name"; first.name$
INPUT "What is the last name"; last.name$
LINE INPUT "What is the address?"; address$
INPUT "What is the city"; city$
INPUT "What is the state"; state$
INPUT "What is the zip code"; zip$

' Print the results
LPRINT first.name$; " "; last.name$
LPRINT address$
LPRINT city$; ", "; state$; "   "; zip$
END
```

INPUT and LINE INPUT Cursor Control

One last option is available when you use INPUT and LINE INPUT. If you put a semicolon immediately after INPUT or LINE INPUT, the cursor remains on the same line as the input prompt. For example, here are the complete formats of INPUT and LINE INPUT statements:

```
INPUT [;] [prompt message][;][,]var1 [, var2][, var3][,.., varN]

LINE INPUT [;] [prompt message][;][,] stringvariable
```

Notice the optional semicolons after the command names. These semicolons tell QBasic to keep the cursor where it ends up after the user inputs the data. In other words, if you answer the INPUT statement

```
INPUT "What is your name"; full.name$
```

by typing `Steve Austin` and pressing Enter, QBasic places the cursor on the next line. Subsequent INPUT and PRINT statements would begin on the next line. If the INPUT statement included the semicolon, as in

```
INPUT ; "What is your name"; full.name$
```

subsequent INPUT or PRINT statements would begin immediately after the n in `Steve Austin`. This sometimes makes for more appropriate INPUT and LINE INPUT prompts, as the following examples show.

Examples

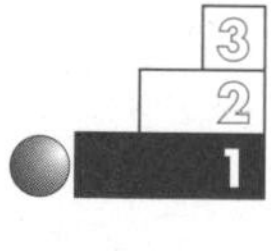
3
2
1

1. The following program is a variation on many you have seen so far. It asks for a first name and a last name and prints them back to the screen. Because of the semicolon after INPUT, both input prompts appear on the same line.

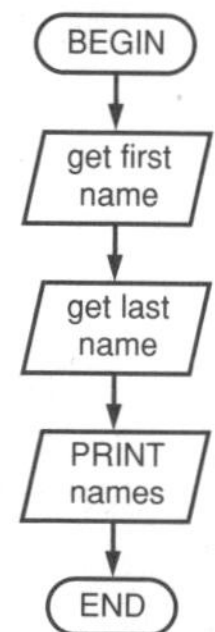
BEGIN
get first name
get last name
PRINT names
END

```
' Filename: C9NMADR2.BAS
'
' Program to demonstrate the extra semicolon in INPUTs.
'
CLS
INPUT ; "What is your first name"; first.name$
INPUT " What is your last name"; last.name$
PRINT first.name$; " "; last.name$
```

Figure 9.9 shows the results of the program. For the first time, you can see a second INPUT statement directly to the right of the preceding one. The extra space at the beginning

of the second INPUT's prompt is needed. Without it, the second prompt prints next to the input string from the first INPUT.

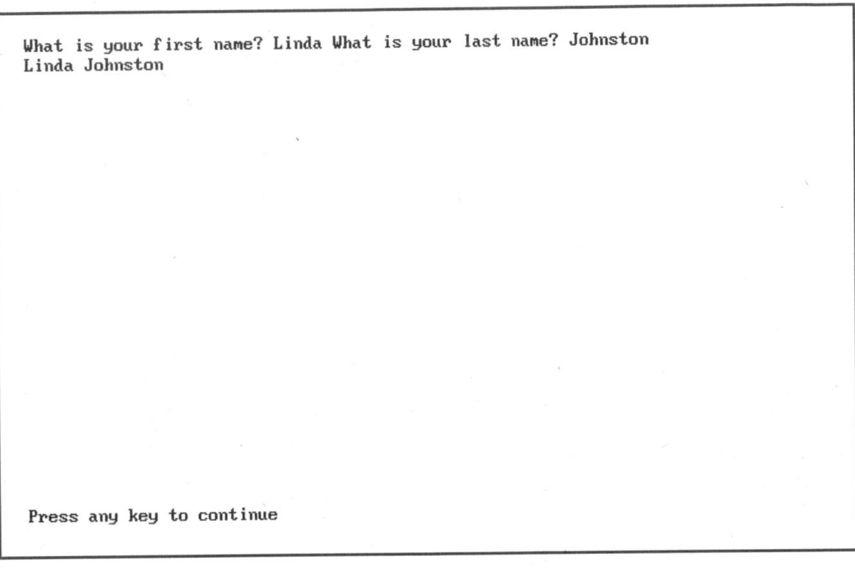

What is your first name? Linda What is your last name? Johnston
Linda Johnston
Press any key to continue

Figure 9.9. Keeping the cursor for the next INPUT.

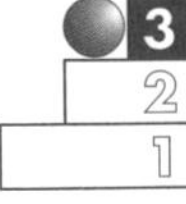

2. The book management program in Appendix E requests much book information. Many of the prompts use combinations of INPUT and LINE INPUT with and without the cursor-controlling semicolon. By using the appropriate semicolons and printing blank lines, you can create your own data-entry input screens with titles and INPUT prompts that make you feel as though you are entering data on a blank form or an index card, as you might do with a manual book file system.

   The following program illustrates the beginnings of such an input data-entry screen.

```
' Filename: C9DATENT.BAS
'
' Program that builds a data-entry screen as the
' user enters data for a book management system.
```

```
' Print a title at the top of the screen
CLS
PRINT TAB(15); "*** Book Data-Entry Screen ***"
PRINT TAB(15); "    ---------------------"
PRINT                              ' Print 2 blank lines
PRINT

' Request the data
LINE INPUT "Book title? "; book.title$
PRINT
INPUT "Author"; author$
PRINT
INPUT ; "Edition"; edition$  ' Keep the cursor on this line
INPUT ; "   Price"; price$
INPUT "   Date of Publication"; pub.date$
PRINT
LINE INPUT "Type any notes here -> "; notes$
PRINT
PRINT

' Print the results when the user is ready
PRINT "Press Enter to see the book's data on the printer"
INPUT ent$

LPRINT TAB(20); "*** Book Data ***"
LPRINT TAB(20); "    ---------"
LPRINT
LPRINT
LPRINT "Title: "; book.title$
LPRINT
LPRINT "Author: "; author$
LPRINT
LPRINT "Edition: "; edition$; "  Price: "; price$;
LPRINT "Publication date: "; pub.date$
LPRINT
LPRINT "Notes: "; notes
```

This is the longest program you have seen so far. It is only the first step toward inputting data in ways the user best understands. Because the prompts for edition and price are so short, it makes sense to input these on the same line instead of one per line, as you saw in previous program examples.

It is worth the time for you to study this program to find where the semicolons are and where they are not. Notice that no cursor-control semicolon was placed in the publication date prompt. If it were, the subsequent `PRINT` would print on that line, and the `notes` input value would not be separated from the previous line with a blank line.

`LINE INPUT` is required for the notes field because the user might want to keep track of free-form notes, as shown in the output in Figure 9.10.

Data-Entry Fields

Each input value in a data-entry form is called a *field*. There are six fields in the last program: title, author, edition, price, publication date, and notes.

When you write programs that require much input, consider building data-entry forms such as the one in the previous example. Later chapters in the book show you how to generate even better forms with colors and lines around them.

Make data-entry screens look like forms you would see on paper. This adds to the *user-friendliness* of a program.

A program is user-friendly if it makes the user comfortable and simulates what the user is already familiar with. The term *user-friendly* has been overused these past few boom years of computers; nevertheless, always keep the user in mind when you design your programs. Keep input screens simple, add blank space so that the screens do not appear too "busy," and prompt the user for data in a logical order.

```
                  *** Book Data-Entry Screen ***
                  ------------------------------

Book title? It's not Friday, but It'll Do!

Author? Billy Bob

Edition? 4th   Price? 3.95   Date of Publication? 1987

Type any notes here -> This is one of Billy Bob's classics.  It is a signed, and
limited edition!
```

Figure 9.10. Building a book data-entry screen.

Summary

In this chapter you learned to write a program that can accept input from the keyboard. Before this chapter, you had to assign values to variables when you wrote the program. The variables can be filled in by prompting the users for values when the users run the program. Depending on the required data, you can use `INPUT`, `LINE INPUT`, or a combination of both.

This chapter focused on input; the next chapter, however, builds on your knowledge of output. You will learn commands that produce color, move the cursor, and print numeric data exactly the way you want it printed.

Review Questions

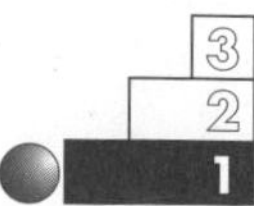

Answers to the Review Questions are in Appendix B.

1. Which of the following statements always produces a question mark?

A. LINE INPUT
B. PRINT
C. LET
D. INPUT

2. Why is the prompt message important when you use INPUT and LINE INPUT?

3. TRUE or FALSE: You can enter more than one variable value with INPUT.

4. TRUE or FALSE: You can enter more than one variable value with LINE INPUT.

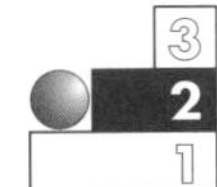

5. How many question marks are produced by the following two lines of code?

```
INPUT "How old are you?"; age
INPUT "What is your name?", full.name$
```

6. How many values does the following INPUT statement require? What are their types?

```
INPUT a, b$, c, d$
```

7. What, if anything, is wrong with the following LINE INPUT statement?

```
LINE INPUT "Please enter your city and state"; city$, st$
```

8. How could you enter the address

```
8109 East 15th St., Apt. 6
```

with the following INPUT statement?

```
INPUT address$
```

9. What error message appears if you enter three numbers for the following INPUT?

```
INPUT "Enter your sales and net sales"; sal, net.sal
```

10. What error message appears if you enter two numbers for the following INPUT?

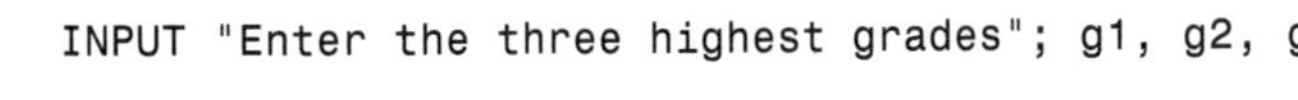

```
INPUT "Enter the three highest grades"; g1, g2, g3
```

Review Exercises

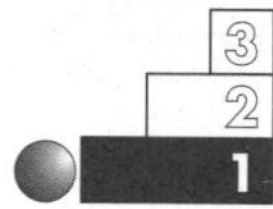

1. Write an INPUT statement that prompts users for their name and weight, stores the name and weight in appropriate variables, and keeps the cursor on the same line.

2. Assume you are a college professor needing to average grades for 10 students. Write a program that prompts you for 10 different grades and then displays an average of them.

3. Modify the program in the preceding exercise to ask for each student's name as well as the grade the student is in. Print the grade list to the printer, with each student's name and grade in two columns. At the bottom of the report, print the average of the grades. (Hint: Store the 10 names and 10 grades in different variables, such as `name1$`, `grade1`, `name2$`, `grade2`, and so on.) This program is easy, but it takes almost 30 lines of code, plus appropriate remarks. Later, you will learn ways to streamline this program.

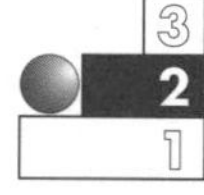

4. Write a program that prompts the user for the number of hours worked, the hourly rate, and the tax rate, then displays the taxes and net pay.

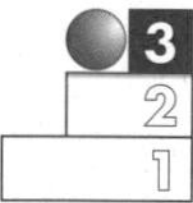

5. Write a program to prompt a user for a full name, hours worked, hourly rate, and tax rate. Compute the taxes and net pay, and print a check to the user on the printer.

6. Modify the child's math program shown earlier in this chapter so that the child can practice subtraction, multiplication, and division after finishing the addition.

10

Producing Better Output

This chapter shows you ways to add pizazz to your program's output. QBasic gives you many tools in addition to PRINT and LPRINT that improve the appearance of your program's output. For instance, programs with color screens appeal to users. Another way to improve your output's appearance is to format the output so that two decimal places always appear, which is great for printing dollars and cents.

To give you a sampling of some ways to get better output from QBasic, this chapter introduces

- The PRINT USING statement
- Printing with SPC
- The BEEP statement
- The ASCII table and CHR$
- Printing with color
- The GOTO statement
- The LOCATE statement

After learning the material in this chapter, you will be able to print much more appealing output. Many of the later chapters include programs that use many of these powerful output statements.

The PRINT USING Statement

PRINT USING is a statement similar to PRINT that sends output to the screen. The corresponding LPRINT USING statement is identical to PRINT USING, except that its output goes to the printer. PRINT USING is especially helpful for printing numbers. You can print dollars and cents, a plus or minus sign in front of or at the end of a number, and so on. These are controlled by a *format string* inside the PRINT USING statement. The formats of PRINT USING and LPRINT USING are

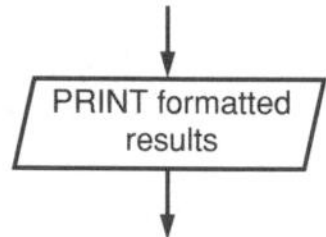


```
PRINT USING format string; expression [; expr2] [...; exprN]
```

and

```
LPRINT USING format string; expression [; expr2] [...; exprN]
```

The *format string* is a string constant or string variable that controls the appearance of the output. It is in the *format string* that you specify output control information such as the decimal places. The rest of the statements are like regular PRINT and LPRINT statements. The *expressions* are one or more variables or constants separated by semicolons.

NOTE: You can use commas in place of the semicolons. Most programmers do not do this, however, because the commas are misleading; they do not force the variables over to the next print zone because a PRINT USING's output is controlled solely by the format string.

Printing Strings with PRINT USING

Although you use PRINT USING primarily for numbers, there are four string control codes you can place inside the format string. Each of these codes prints the characters in the string differently. Until now, you could print strings and string constants only exactly as they appear in memory. With the format string control codes in Table 10.1, you can print strings in more than one way. (Any character not listed in the control code table prints exactly as you type it.)

Table 10.1. `PRINT USING` **string control codes.**

Control Code	*Explanation of Its Use*
`!`	Requests that only the first character of the string constant or variable prints.
`\ \`	Prints at least two characters of the string constant or variable: one character for each backslash and blank. If you insert one blank between the backslashes, the first three characters print. Two blanks print the first four characters, and so on.
`&`	Prints the string as it would appear in a regular `PRINT` or `LPRINT` statement.
`_`	Literally prints whatever character follows the underscore. `__`, `_!`, `_\`, and `_&` are the only ways to print `_`, `!`, `\`, and `&` inside a format string.

You cannot include more than 24 characters in a format string. If you do, you get an `Illegal function call` error message.

Examples

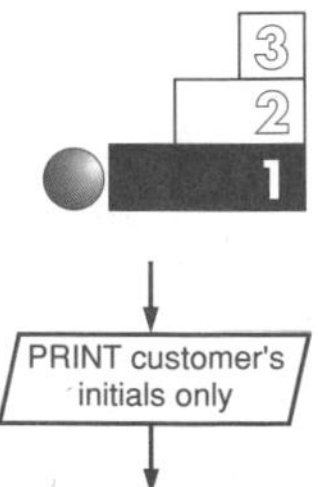

1. Assume a customer's first and last names are stored in two variables called `first.name$` and `last.name$`. You could print the customer's initials with the following `PRINT USING` statement:

```
PRINT USING "!!"; first.name$; last.name$
```

If you want a space between the names, you have to add one to the format string as follows:

```
PRINT USING "! !"; first.name$; last.name$
```

You do *not* put blanks between the actual variables. All control of printing is done by the format string. You could print periods after each initial with

```
PRINT USING "!. !."; first.name$; last.name$
```

Because spaces, periods, and most other characters are not control codes for strings (see Table 10.1), they print exactly as they appear in the format string without controlling output as do the `!`, `\`, and `&`.

2. You can put a format string in a string variable, as the following example shows:

```
LET fs$ = "!. !."
PRINT USING fs$; first.name$; last.name$
```

TIP: If you find yourself repeating the same format string throughout a program, put it in a variable, as in the previous example. You then can use the variable name in subsequent `PRINT USING` statements instead of typing the same format string repeatedly.

3. Assume you are printing the customer's first and last names on mailing labels. You don't have room to print a long name. Therefore, you can limit the customer's first name to eight characters, regardless of how many characters are in the name, with the following `LPRINT USING`:

```
LPRINT USING "\      \ &"; first.name$; last.name$
```

Limit the first name to eight characters using the two backslashes and the six spaces between them (making a total of eight control codes).

As a result, the program prints a blank between the two names. The blank comes from the blank following the format string's slashes. Without the format string's blank, the two names print next to each other.

The ampersand (&) lets the last.name$ print as it appears, regardless of its length. Without the ampersand, the last name is limited to eight characters because QBasic repeats control codes if there are more variables than control codes.

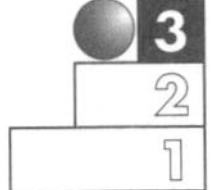

4. If you want to print an exclamation point or any of the other control codes, precede it with the underscore. To print an exclamation point after the first letter of each name, you would use the following PRINT USING:

```
PRINT USING "!_! !_!"; first.name$; last.name$
```

This would create output such as

```
G! P!
```

The leading underscores before the second and fourth exclamation points instruct QBasic to print the exclamation points literally without interpreting them as control codes.

Printing Numbers with PRINT USING

There are more PRINT USING control codes for numeric constants and variables than there are for strings. You rarely want numeric data to print exactly as it appears in memory, because it might contain more decimal places than you want printed. You probably want control over the placement of the number's sign, decimal places, commas, and so forth.

Table 10.2 presents every PRINT USING format control code for numbers, along with their descriptions. As with strings, any character you include in the format string that is not a control code prints exactly as you type it. This lets you output words and symbols around formatted numbers.

If QBasic cannot fit the number inside your designated format string, a percent sign (%) prints to the left of the number. Even though the number is larger than the format string, it prints (with the leading %) in its entirety.

Table 10.2. `PRINT USING` numeric control codes.

Control Code	*Explanation of Its Use*
#	One number is printed for every pound sign in the format string. If the number contains fewer digits than the total number of pound signs, QBasic right-justifies the number and pads it with spaces to the left.
.	Ensures that QBasic prints a decimal point, even for whole numbers. QBasic rounds if needed.
+	Forces the sign (+ or -) of the number to print, even if the number is positive. If you put the + at the beginning of the format string, the sign is printed at the beginning of the number. Putting the + at the end of the format string forces the sign to print at the end of the number.
-	To print negative numbers with trailing minus signs (and no sign for positives), put the - at the end of the format string.
**	Prints asterisks to the left of the number. If the number does not take as many spaces as the total number of pound signs and asterisks, asterisks fill the extra spaces. This is called a *floating asterisk* because it prints one or more asterisks immediately to the left of the number, regardless of how many digits the number has.
$$	Prints dollar signs to the left of the number. This is called a *floating dollar sign* because it prints immediately to the left of the number, regardless of how many digits the number has.
**$	Designed for printing check amounts. These three print positions force asterisks to fill from the left, followed by a dollar sign. If the number is negative, the minus sign prints directly to the left of the dollar sign.

Control Code	Explanation of Its Use
,	You can put the comma in one of two places in a format string. A comma to the left of the decimal point (if there is one in the format) causes commas to print every third digit of the number. No commas print in the decimal portion of the number. Putting the comma at the end of the format string prints a comma at the end of the number if the number contains a decimal point.
^^^^	Prints the number in scientific notation, in the `E+`*xx* format.
^^^^^	Prints the number in expanded scientific notation, in the `E+`*xxx* format.

Examples

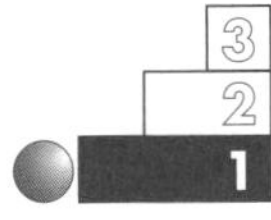

1. The next program is a rewrite of the payroll programs you have seen throughout this book. Now that you understand `PRINT USING` format strings, you can print each dollar amount with a dollar sign and two decimal places.

```
' Filename: C10PAY1.BAS
'
' Computes and prints payroll data.

' Initialize data variables
emp.name$ = "Larry Payton"
pay.date$ = "01/09/92"
hours.worked = 40              ' Total hours worked
rate = 7.5                     ' Pay per hour
tax.rate = .4                  ' Tax rate percentage

' Compute the pay
gross.pay = hours.worked * rate
taxes = tax.rate * gross.pay
net.pay = gross.pay - taxes

' Print the results on the screen
CLS
```

```
PRINT "As of: "; pay.date$
PRINT emp.name$; " worked"; hours.worked; "hours"
PRINT USING "and got paid $$##.##."; gross.pay
PRINT USING "After taxes of: $$##.##,"; taxes
PRINT USING "his take-home pay was: $$##.##."; net.pay
```

Figure 10.1 shows the result of running this program. There is much to this program's simple-looking output. By mastering it, you are well on your way to understanding formatted output and QBasic.

```
As of: 01/09/92
Larry Payton worked 40 hours
and got paid $300.00.
After taxes of: $120.00,
his take-home pay was: $180.00.




Press any key to continue
```

Figure 10.1. A payroll program with dollars and cents.

Printing the date and the hours worked does not require a `PRINT USING` statement; there are no fixed decimal points to worry about. The last three lines of the program print dollar amounts, so they require format strings. The words inside the strings print literally as they appear in the format string because they are not control codes. The double dollar signs, pound signs, and periods, however, *are* control codes. They affect the way the variables print.

The gross.pay and net.pay variables can be as large as $999.99, because a total of seven places are reserved for the dollar sign, amount, and decimal point. If the pay happened to be more than $999.99, QBasic would print the number preceded by a percent sign to warn you that the number could not fit in the specified format.

> **TIP:** To expand the field to hold a larger number, add a pound sign and a comma (before the decimal point) so that the field can hold an amount as large as $9,999.99 and print it with the comma.

The commas and periods at the end of the format strings are not control codes. Because they appear at the end, QBasic prints them literally.

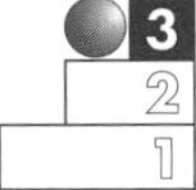

2. The following program illustrates each of the various numeric format strings available with PRINT USING. The output is shown in Figure 10.2.

```
' Filename: C10PUSG2.BAS
'
' Program to demonstrate printing numbers with PRINT USING.
'
CLS
PRINT USING "¦######¦"; 9146   ' Numbers print right-
                               ' justified
PRINT USING "¦######¦"; 21
PRINT
PRINT USING "#####.##"; 2652.2 ' Always prints two
                                ' decimal places
PRINT USING "#####.##"; 2652.212  ' Rounds if needed
PRINT USING "#####.##"; 2652.215
PRINT
PRINT USING "+###"; 45      ' Always prints plus or minus
PRINT USING "+###"; -45
PRINT USING "###+"; 45      ' Prints the sign at the end
PRINT USING "###-"; 45      ' Only prints sign at end if
                            ' negative
```

```
PRINT USING "###-"; -45
PRINT
PRINT USING "**####.##"; 2.5   ' Left AND right fills with
                               ' asterisks
PRINT USING "$$####.##"; 2.5   ' Floating dollar sign
PRINT USING "**$###.##"; 2.5   ' Combine the two for checks
PRINT
PRINT USING "######,.##"; 3234.54        ' A comma before
                                         ' decimal
PRINT USING "####,.##, "; 3234, 7832; 4326  ' Repeating
                                            ' format string
PRINT
PRINT USING "#.##^^^^"; 0.00012    ' Scientific notation
PRINT USING "#.##^^^^^"; 0.00012   ' More precision
PRINT
PRINT USING "###"; 43567.54    ' Not enough control codes
                               ' specified
PRINT USING "##.##"; 43567.54
PRINT
PRINT USING "_#_###.##_#_#"; 32.45   ' Illustrates printing of
                                     ' literals
END
```

Printing with SPC

Like TAB, SPC goes inside a PRINT statement or an LPRINT statement. SPC specifies how many spaces to skip. This keeps you from having to type many string constants filled with only spaces in your output. The format of SPC is

```
SPC(space value)
```

The *space value* is the number of characters to skip before printing the next value. The space value always goes in parentheses after SPC. Never use SPC by itself; always combine it with a PRINT statement or an LPRINT statement. The format of the combined PRINT and SPC commands is

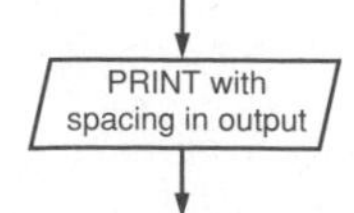


```
PRINT SPC(space value1);data1[;SPC(space value2);data2;...]
```

```
|  9146|
|    21|
 2652.20
 2652.21
 2652.22
 +45
 -45
 45+
 45
 45-
*****2.50
    $2.50
****$2.50
  3,234.54
3,234.00, 7,832.00, 4,326.00,
0.12E-03
0.12E-003
%43568
%43567.54
##32.45##



Press any key to continue
```

Figure 10.2. A program that illustrates printing numbers with PRINT USING.

As you can see, you can put more than one SPC inside a PRINT (or an LPRINT). You can combine SPC with TAB, semicolons, and commas as well. The following rule of thumb explains the difference between TAB and SPC:

NOTE: When you use TAB, the cursor always skips to a fixed position, the column number inside the TAB's parentheses. When you use SPC, the cursor skips over the number of spaces inside the SPC command's parentheses.

Examples

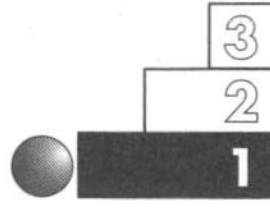

1. If you always want a fixed number of spaces between numeric or string variables when you print them, use SPC instead of TAB. TAB forces the cursor to a fixed location regardless of how wide the data is. The following program shows you the difference.

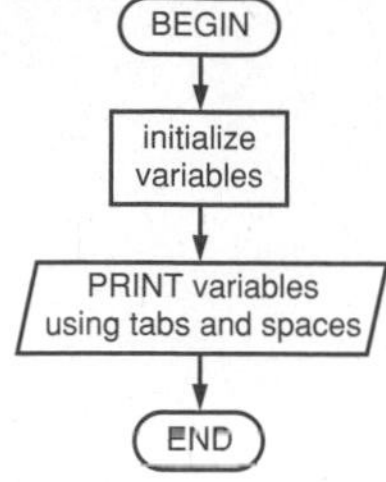


```
' Filename: C10SPC.BAS
'
' Program that compares TAB and SPC.
'
CLS
a = 7865
b = 1
c = 6543.2
PRINT "Printing with TAB:"
PRINT a; TAB(7); b; TAB(14); c   ' The numbers are not
                                 ' uniformly spaced
PRINT
PRINT "Printing with SPC:"
PRINT a; SPC(7); b; SPC(7); c    ' There are 7 spaces
                                 ' between each
```

Figure 10.3 shows the result of running this program. Notice that with TAB the numbers are not uniformly separated, because they are different lengths. SPC solves this by spacing over an equal number of spaces.

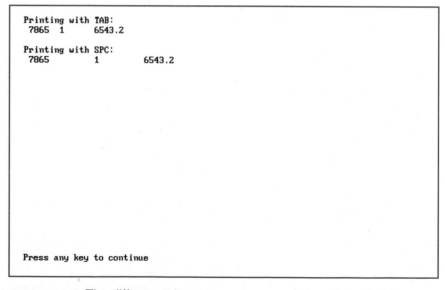

```
Printing with TAB:
 7865  1      6543.2

Printing with SPC:
 7865         1         6543.2










Press any key to continue
```

Figure 10.3. The difference between using TAB and SPC to separate numbers.

Using BEEP

The BEEP command is a fun command that sounds the system unit's speaker. It has an easy format; put BEEP on a line by itself whenever you want to beep (or buzz) the user. The format of the BEEP command is

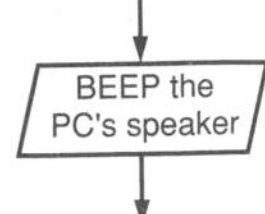


```
BEEP
```

There are no more parameters to BEEP. You use BEEP to warn the user, to signal the user for input, or to tell the user that an operation is finished. The BEEP lasts for about one-half second. You cannot modify the tone or duration of BEEP. If you want the BEEP to last longer than one-half second, put two or three together in the program.

> **TIP:** Do not overuse BEEP. Users get tired of hearing the signal too often.

Example

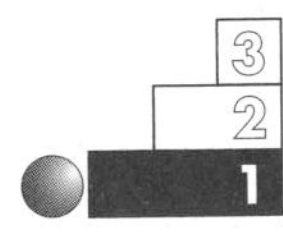

1. Before printing is to be done, it might be good to BEEP and warn the user to check the printer for ample paper before the printing begins. The following section of code would do that.

```
CLS
BEEP         ' Get the user's attention
PRINT
PRINT "The checks are ready to be printed."
PRINT "Make sure the printer is turned on and has paper..."
INPUT ent$   ' Pause until the user presses Enter
```

Printing Special Characters

You know how to print and store characters that are on the keyboard. You can type string constants and store them in string variables and print them on the screen and printer. There are several more characters that do not appear on the keyboard that you might want to type as well. They include foreign characters, math symbols, line-drawing characters, and more.

Your computer uses a table that includes every character your computer can represent. This table is called the *ASCII table.* The complete ASCII (pronounced *ask-ee*) table is located in Appendix A. Turn to Appendix A and glance at the table. You see many special characters, only some of which are on the keyboard.

Your computer internally represents these ASCII characters by their ASCII numbers. A different number is assigned to each character. These number assignments were arbitrarily designed similarly to the Morse code table. A unique number represents each character.

When you press a letter on the keyboard, your keyboard does not actually send that character to the computer. Instead, it sends the ASCII number equivalent of that character. Your computer stores that number. When you see characters on the screen or printer, your screen or printer has converted the number sent to it by the computer to its character representation.

ASCII Representations

Your computer stores characters in binary format. There are 256 ASCII codes (0-255). The numbers 0 through 255 are represented in eight *bits* (00000000 through 11111111), with a bit being a 1 or a 0 (*bits* comes from the words *BInary digiTS*).

Eight bits make a byte. Because you can represent every possible PC character in eight bits, eight bits are required to represent a byte or a character. This is the intrinsic reason why a byte is the same thing as a character. In Chapter 1, "Welcome to QBasic," you learned that if your computer has 640K of RAM, it has 640K bytes or 640K characters of memory. It takes a total of eight bits (one byte) to represent a character from the ASCII table.

By having the ASCII table available, you can print any character by referring to its ASCII number. For instance, the capital letter *A* is number 65. The lowercase *a* is 96. A space is ASCII 32 (the space is a character to your computer, just as the other characters are).

Because you can type letters, numbers, and some special characters on your keyboard, the ASCII table is not needed much for these. You cannot, however, use the keyboard to type the Spanish Ñ or the cent sign (¢) under normal circumstances. You need a way to tell QBasic to print these special characters that do not appear on the keyboard. You do this with the `CHR$` function.

The format of `CHR$` is

```
CHR$(ASCII number)
```

The *`ASCII number`* can be a numeric constant or a numeric variable. `CHR$` is not a command, but a *function*. You have already seen two functions, the `TAB` and the `SPC`. Chapters 19 and 20, "Numeric Functions" and "String Functions," are devoted exclusively to string and numeric functions. You can begin to use string and numeric functions without understanding their intricacies, as you have been doing with `TAB` and `SPC`.

As with `TAB` and `SPC`, you do not use `CHR$` by itself. It is combined with other statements. If you combine `CHR$` with a `PRINT` or an `LPRINT`, the character matching the ASCII number in the parentheses prints. The following statement prints an up arrow on the screen:

```
PRINT CHR$(24)
```

Without the `CHR$(24)`, you could not type the up arrow from a key on the keyboard. Pressing the up arrow key controls the cursor by moving it upward; it does not display an up arrow.

You can use the `CHR$` function also to store special characters in string variables. The concatenation character (+) also lets you insert a special character inside another string and store the complete string in a variable, as in

```
msg$="One-half is ";+CHR$(171);+" and one-fourth is ";+CHR$(172)
```

If you then print `msg$` on the screen, you see the following result:

```
One-half is ½ and one-fourth is ¼
```

The first 31 ASCII codes represent *nonprinting* characters. Nonprinting characters cause an action to be performed, instead of producing characters. For instance, ASCII 7 is the *bell* character. If you print it with

```
PRINT CHR$(7)
```

the computer's speaker beeps. You might think you don't need this; after all, the BEEP command does this same thing. If you have a dot-matrix printer, however, you can cause your printer to beep by sending it an ASCII 7, as in

```
LPRINT CHR$(7)
```

You can cause the printer to *form feed* (ASCII 12) by sending it the form feed ASCII code:

```
LPRINT CHR$(12)
```

This ensures that the next LPRINT begins printing at the top of the page. If the previous program left the print head in the middle of the page, printing CHR$(12) ejects the rest of the page so that the next LPRINT begins at the top of the next page. Conversely, if your program has been printing several lines of text to the printer, one of the last things you could do is print a CHR$(12) to eject the page you were working on. The next program then would print on a fresh piece of paper.

The higher ASCII codes are line-drawing characters. With practice, you can combine them to form shapes and boxes that enclose text on the screen.

Examples

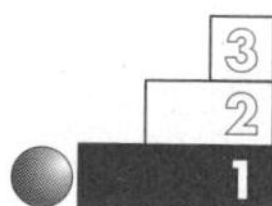

1. You can use the ASCII table to produce some uncommon characters.

```
' Filename: C10ASC1.BAS
'
' Program that illustrates printing of special characters.
'
CLS
PRINT "Some common Greek characters are:"
```

```
PRINT CHR$(224), CHR$(225), CHR$(226), CHR$(227), CHR$(228)
END
```

The output of this program is shown in Figure 10.4.

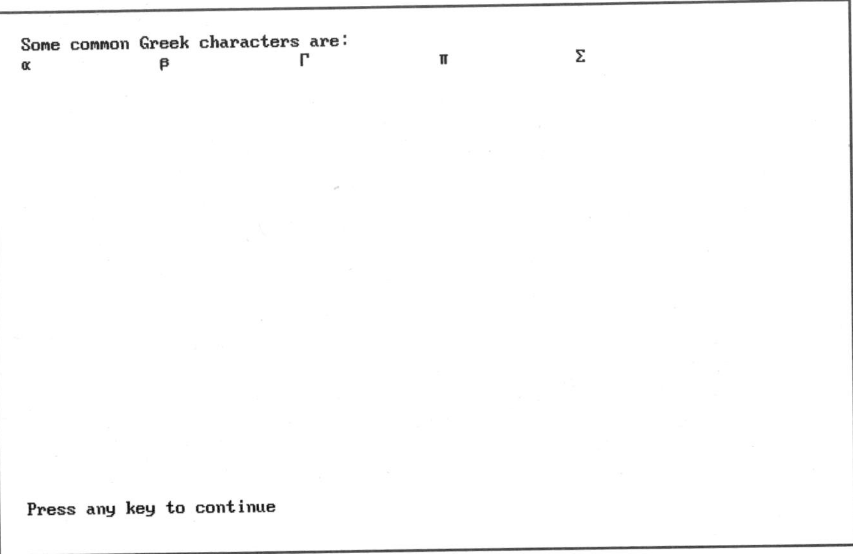
Some common Greek characters are:
α β Γ π Σ
Press any key to continue

Figure 10.4. Using the ASCII table to print special characters.

Printing with Color

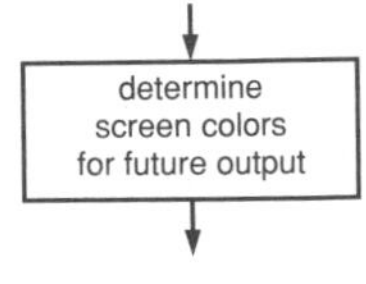
determine screen colors for future output

If you have a color monitor, you can add colors to output with the COLOR statement. The format of the COLOR statement is

```
COLOR [foreground #] [, background #] [, border #]
```

The *foreground #* is a number from 0 to 31 that represents the color of the characters on the screen. The *background #* is a number from 0 to 7 that represents the color of the screen behind the characters. (In this book, the foreground color is black and the background is white.) The *border #* is a number from 0 to 15 that represents the border drawn around the screen's edges.

Each of these is optional, although the foreground and background colors are almost always specified. The border only works for CGA (Color Graphics Adapter) monitors and is not supported for EGA, VGA, or MCGA monitors. If you do not specify a parameter, the current color does not change. In other words, if you change only the foreground color, the background color does not change.

The `COLOR` statement does not affect any text on the screen that was printed before the `COLOR` statement. `COLOR` affects only future `PRINT` statements.

Table 10.3 shows colors and their corresponding numbers. Although monochrome (one-color) monitors do not produce colors, you can specify special screen attributes (such as underlining and blinking) on monochrome monitors.

Table 10.3. Color numbers for the `COLOR` statement.

Color Monitors		*Monochrome Monitors*	
Number	*Color*	*Number*	*Color*
0	Black	0	Black
1	Blue	1	Underline if foreground Black if background
2	Green	2	Standard foreground color Black if background
3	Cyan	3	Standard foreground color Black if background
4	Red	4	Standard foreground color Black if background
5	Magenta	5	Standard foreground color Black if background
6	Brown	6	Standard foreground color Black if background
7	White	7	Standard foreground color, even if used for background
8	Gray*	8	Highlighted character
9	Light Blue*	9	Highlighted character

Color Monitors		Monochrome Monitors	
Number	*Color*	*Number*	*Color*
10	Light Green*	10	Highlighted character
11	Light Cyan*	11	Highlighted character
12	Light Red*	12	Highlighted character
13	Light Magenta*	13	Highlighted character
14	Yellow*	14	Highlighted character
15	Bright White*	15	Highlighted character

* denotes foreground only

If you add 16 to the color number, the characters blink in the color of that number, less 16. In other words, setting the foreground color to 28 (12 + 16) produces blinking light red text with the next `PRINT` statement.

If the foreground and background numbers are the same, QBasic prints the text, but you will not be able to see it.

TIP: Do not overuse colors. Too many colors make the screen look too "busy" and not as readable.

Example

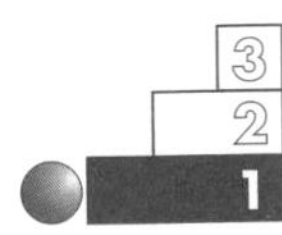

1. To illustrate the effects of different color combinations, the following program prints several lines of text, each with a different color. This program illustrates the `COLOR` statement well but shows you that too much color is too much to look at for normal applications.

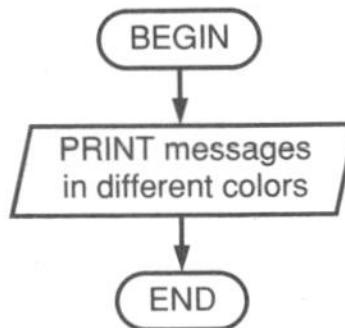


```
' Filename: C10COLOR.BAS
'
' Prints several lines of text in different colors.
'
CLS
COLOR 15, 1
PRINT "Bright white characters on blue"
```

```
COLOR 1, 7
PRINT "Blue characters on white"
COLOR 4, 2
PRINT "Red characters on green"
COLOR 30, 2
PRINT "Blinking yellow characters on green"
COLOR 13, 0
PRINT "Light magenta on black"
```

The GOTO Statement

The next few examples require more program control than you have seen to this point. The GOTO statement gives you that extra control. GOTO lets your program jump to a different location. Each program you have seen executes sequentially; the statements execute one line after another, in a sequential order. GOTO lets you override that default execution. With GOTO, you can make the last line (or any other line) in the program execute before execution would normally get there. GOTO lets you execute the same line (or lines) repeatedly.

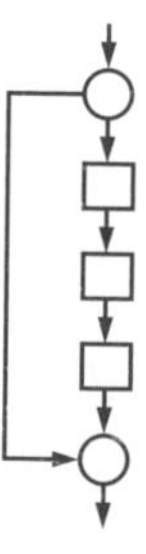

The format of the GOTO statement is

```
GOTO statement label
```

The *statement label* is a line number or a line label. You have not seen statement labels in the QBasic programs so far, because none of the programs required them. Statement labels are usually optional, although if you have a GOTO, you need to include a statement label in your program.

Each of the four following lines of code has a statement label. These four lines are not a program, but they are instead individual lines that might be included in a program. Notice that statement labels go to the left of their lines. Separate line number statement labels from the rest of the line with at least one space. If you use a word label, separate it from the rest of the line with a colon. Name non-numeric labels according to the same rules you would use to name variables. (See Chapter 5, "Understanding Numeric Variables and Constants," for a review of naming variables and other identifiers.)

```
PAY: PRINT "Place checks in the printer"
Again: INPUT "What is the next employee's name"; emp.name$
20 CLS
Set.Colors: COLOR 15, 1
```

Statement labels are not intended to replace REMarks, although the labels should reflect the code that follows. Statement labels give GOTO statements a place to go to. When your program gets to the GOTO, it branches to the statement labeled by the statement label. The program then continues to execute sequentially until the next GOTO changes the order again (or until the program ends).

TIP: The use of line numbers for statement labels is a carryover from older versions of BASIC and is included in QBasic for compatibility. Use identifying line labels rather than line numbers unless you are working on a QBasic program that might be executed in an older version of BASIC.

Use GOTOs Judiciously

GOTO is not a good programming statement if it is overused. Programmers, especially beginners, tend to include too many GOTOs in a program. If a program branches all over the place, it is difficult to follow. Some people call programs with many GOTOs *spaghetti code.*

Using a few GOTOs here and there is not necessarily a bad practice. Usually, however, you can substitute better, more thought-out code. To eliminate GOTOs and write programs with more structure, you must learn a few more control concepts. The next few chapters in this book address alternatives to GOTO.

For now, become familiar with GOTO so that you can continue to build on your knowledge of QBasic.

Examples

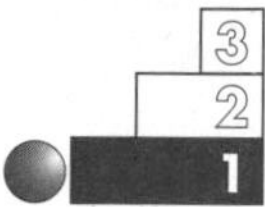

1. The following program has a problem that is the direct result of the GOTO. This program, however, is one of the best illustrations of the GOTO statement. The program consists of an *endless loop* (sometimes called an *infinite loop*). The first three lines after the remarks execute. Then the fourth line (the GOTO) causes execution to loop back to the beginning and repeat the first three lines. The program continues to loop until you press the Ctrl+Break key combination.

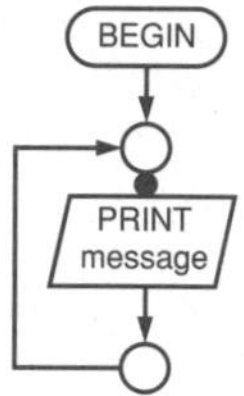


```
' Filename: C10GOTO1.BAS
'
' Program to show use of GOTO.
' (This program ends only when user presses CTRL+BREAK.)
'
Again: PRINT "This message"
PRINT TAB(14); "keeps repeating"
PRINT TAB(30); "over and over"
GOTO Again      ' Repeat continuously
```

Notice that the statement label has a colon to separate it from the rest of the line, but you never put the colon on the label at the GOTO statement that branches to it.

Figure 10.5 shows the result of running this program. To stop the program, press Ctrl+Break.

2. The following poorly written program is the epitome of spaghetti code. Nevertheless, do your best to follow it and understand its output. By understanding the flow of the output, you hone your understanding of the GOTO. You will appreciate the fact that the rest of this book uses the GOTO only when it is required to make the program clearer.

```
' Filename: C10GOTO3.BAS
'
' Program demonstrates overuse of GOTO.
'
CLS
GOTO Here
First:
```

```
PRINT "A"
GOTO Final
There:
PRINT "B"
GOTO First
Here:
PRINT "C"
GOTO There
Final:
END
```

```
             keeps repeating
                              over and over
This message
             keeps repeating
                              over and over
This message
             keeps repeating
                              over and over
This message
             keeps repeating
                              over and over
This message
             keeps repeating
                              over and over
This message
             keeps repeating
                              over and over
This message
             keeps repeating
                              over and over
This message
             keeps repeating
                              over and over
```

Figure 10.5. A repeating printing program.

At first glance, this program appears to print the first three letters of the alphabet; however, the `GOTO`s make them print in the reverse order: `C`, `B`, `A`. Although the program is not a well-designed program, indenting the lines that don't have statement labels would make it more readable. This indention lets you quickly distinguish the statement labels from the rest of the code, as you can see from the next program.

```
' Filename: C10GOTO4.BAS
'
' Program demonstrates overuse of GOTO.
' (Indentions separate labels from the other statements.)
   CLS
   GOTO Here
First:
   PRINT "A"
   GOTO Final
There:
   PRINT "B"
   GOTO First
Here:
   PRINT "C"
   GOTO There
Final:
   END
```

This program's listing is slightly easier to follow than the preceding program's listing, although the programs do the same thing. The rest of the programs in this book that use statement labels also use indentions.

The `GOTO` warning is worth repeating: Use `GOTO` sparingly and only when its use makes the program more readable and maintainable. Usually, there are better commands you can use.

The LOCATE Statement

The screen is divided into 25 rows and 80 columns. You can place the cursor at the screen position at which you want to print with the `LOCATE` statement. The format of `LOCATE` is

position cursor's next location

```
LOCATE [row #] [, column #]
```

The *row #* has to be a number from 1 to 25. The *column #* must be a number from 1 to 80. `LOCATE` places the cursor at the row and column you specify. The next `PRINT` statement begins printing at the cursor's new location.

If you do not specify a row number, the cursor moves to the column number you indicate without changing rows. For instance, the LOCATE command

```
LOCATE , 40
```

moves the cursor to column 40 and does not change the row the cursor is on.

Example

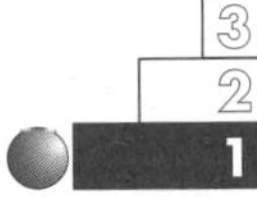

1. The following program prints QBasic in four different locations on the screen after setting the colors:

```
' Filename: C10LOC1.BAS
'
' Prints QBasic in four screen locations.

COLOR 15, 1     ' Bright white on blue screen
CLS
LOCATE 22, 60
PRINT "QBasic"
LOCATE 2, 5
PRINT "QBasic"
LOCATE 17, 25
PRINT "QBasic"
LOCATE 3, 40
PRINT "QBasic"
```

Figure 10.6 shows the result of this program. Notice that the row and column numbers of the LOCATE statements placed the message at the specified locations.

Summary

Although the PRINT USING command is easy to understand, it has more options than any command you have seen so far. PRINT USING lets you format your output of strings and numbers so that screens and printed results look the way you want them to. Combining PRINT

USING with COLOR, BEEP, the ASCII table, and the SPC function lets you control your screen and produce eye-catching displays. By using GOTO judiciously, you can repeat sections of your code.

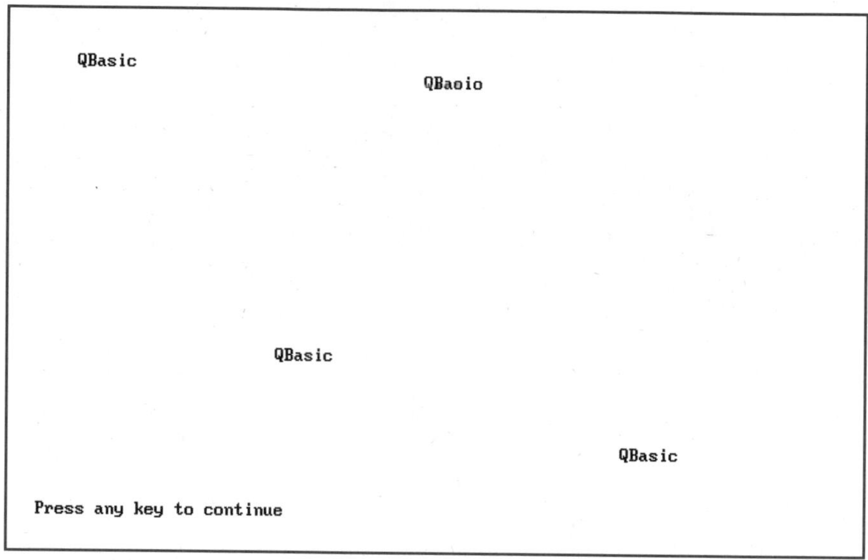

Figure 10.6. Printing at four different places on the screen.

One problem with using GOTO is its inability to stop. GOTO is an *unconditional branching* instruction that always occurs. To control GOTO better, the next chapter introduces a fundamental concept in every computer programming language: comparing data. By learning the ways to test for certain results, you can begin to limit the use of GOTO as you learn more powerful ways to program in QBasic.

Review Questions

Answers to the Review Questions are in Appendix B.

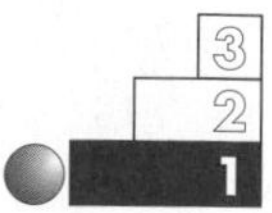

1. What statement produces formatted output on the printer?
2. TRUE or FALSE: You can use either a string variable or a string constant as a format string.

3. What are the ASCII numbers for the following characters?

   M $ £ z

4. The GOTO statement causes the computer to:
   A. Execute the next statement in sequence.
   B. Execute the next INPUT statement.
   C. Execute the statement having the label that follows the GOTO.
   D. Execute the last PRINT statement in the program.

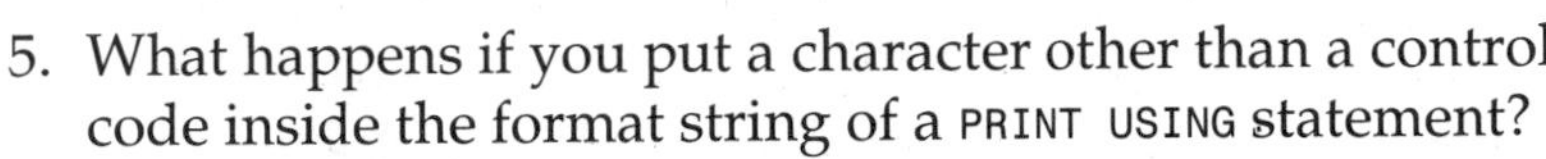

5. What happens if you put a character other than a control code inside the format string of a PRINT USING statement?

6. What is the largest number that accurately prints with the following format string?

   ####,.##

7. How does GOTO change the order in which a program would normally execute statements?

8. TRUE or FALSE: The following two statements do exactly the same thing:

```
BEEP
LPRINT CHR$(7)
```

9. What output occurs given the following PRINT USING statement?

```
PRINT USING "####"; 34543.21
```

10. What colors and attributes are set by the following COLOR statement?

```
COLOR 27, 5
```

11. What output is produced by the following LOCATE statement?

```
LOCATE 12, 40
```

Review Exercises

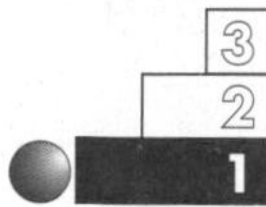

1. Write a program that prompts for three grades (with INPUT) to be put into three variables. Compute the average of the grades. Print the average on the screen with two decimal places.

2. Write a program to ask for the user's favorite month. Change the screen colors, clear the screen, and use LOCATE and PRINT USING to print the month's first three letters on the screen in five different places.

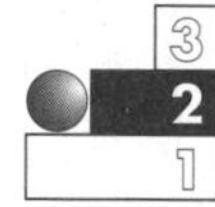

3. Write a program that asks the user for an ASCII number from 32 to 255. (ASCII codes below 31 cannot be printed.) Print the ASCII character that matches the number the user entered. Continue to ask the user for the number until the user presses Ctrl+Break.

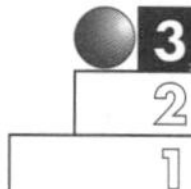

4. Produce a report showing the user's business expenses. Ask the user for a description of each expense and the dollar amount, one expense at a time. After printing an appropriate title at the top of the paper, print the expenses and their descriptions down the page. Make sure you print them with dollar signs and two decimal places. Because of the user's accounting requirement, all negative amounts (prior expenses that were reimbursed) should have *trailing* negative signs. (Because a GOTO is required to keep asking the user for the next expense, the user can stop the program only by pressing Ctrl+Break.) Prompt the users to press Ctrl+Break when they want to end.

5. Rewrite the program that draws the picture in exercise 6 of Chapter 6, "REMarks and Additional PRINT Options." Use as many of the line-drawing characters from the ASCII table as possible in place of the dashes and plus signs used previously. Use LOCATE to move the cursor. Make the computer BEEP to get the user's attention when the drawing is complete.

11

Comparing Data

Believe it or not, not every statement in your QBasic programs should execute every time you run the program. Your programs operate on data. They are known as *data-driven* programs. In other words, the data should dictate what the program does. For example, you would not want the computer to print a paycheck for every employee who works for you every pay period; some of them might have taken a leave of absence, or some might be on a sales commission and might not have made a sale that pay period. Printing paychecks for no money would be ridiculous. You want the computer to print checks only to the employees who have pay coming to them.

This chapter shows you how to create data-driven programs. These programs do not execute the same way every time you run them. Rather, they look at the constants and variables in the program and operate based on what they find. This might sound difficult, but it is straightforward and intuitive.

This chapter shows you ways to compare data and run programs according to those comparisons. It introduces

- Comparison operators
- IF-THEN logic
- String comparisons

- Compound logical operators
- The complete order of operators
- Counters and totals

Not only does this chapter introduce these comparison commands, but it also prepares you for the READ-DATA pair of statements in Chapter 12, "READ and DATA Statements."

Comparison Operators

In addition to the math operators you learned earlier, there are operators that you use for data comparison. These are called *relational operators.* Relational operators compare data; they tell how two variables or constants relate to each other. They tell you whether two variables are equal or not equal, or which one is less than or more than the other. Table 11.1 lists each relational operator and its description.

Table 11.1. The relational operators.

Operator	*Description*
=	Equal to
>	Greater than
<	Less than
>=	Greater than or equal to
<=	Less than or equal to
<>	Not equal to

These six operators form the foundation of comparing data in QBasic. They always appear with two constants, variables, or expressions, or a combination of the three, on each side. Many of these relational operators might already be familiar to you. You should learn them as well as you know the +, -, *, and / mathematical operators.

Examples

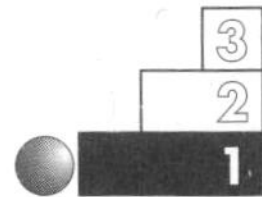

1. Assume that a program initializes four variables as follows:

```
LET A = 5
LET B = 10
LET C = 15
LET D = 5
```

The following statements are true:

A is equal to D	so	A = D
B is less than C		B < C
C is greater than A		C > A
B is greater than or equal to A		B >= A
D is less than or equal to B		D <= B
B is not equal to C		B <> C

These are not QBasic statements, but they are instead statements of relational fact about the values in the variables. Relational logic is not difficult. Relational logic always produces a *true* or *false* result. Each of the preceding statements is true.

2. Assuming the values in the previous example's four variables, each of the following statements about the values is false:

```
A = B
B > C
D < A
D > A
A <> D
B >= C
C <= B
```

You should study these statements to see why each is false. A and D are equal to the same value (5), so neither is greater than or less than the other.

You deal with relational logic in everyday life. Think of the following statements you might make:

"The generic butter costs less than the name brand."

"My child is younger than Johnny."

"Our salaries are equal."

"The dogs are not the same age."

Each of these statements can be only true or false. There is no other possible outcome.

Watch the Signs!

Many people say they are not "math-inclined" or "logical," and you might be one of them. As mentioned earlier, you do not have to be good in math to be a good computer programmer. You should not be frightened by the term "relational logic"; you just saw that you use relational logic everyday. Nevertheless, some people see the relational operators and get confused about their meanings.

The two primary relational operators, less than (<) and greater than (>), are easy to remember. You might have been taught which is which in school but forgotten them. Actually, their symbols tell you exactly what each means.

The arrow of the < or > points to the smaller of the two values. Notice that in the true examples (in example 1) the small part of the operator, or the point of the < and >, always points to the smaller number. The large, open part of the operator points to the larger value.

The relation is false if the arrow points in the wrong direction. In other words, *4 > 9* is *false* because the small part of the operator is pointing to the *9*. In English, "*4 is greater than 9* is false because *4* is less than *9*."

The `IF` Statement

You incorporate relational operators in QBasic programs with the `IF` statement. `IF` (sometimes referred to as an `IF-THEN` *statement*) is called a *decision statement*. It tests a relationship using the relational operators and makes a decision about which statement to execute next based on the result of that decision.

`IF` has several formats. The first one is

```
IF condition THEN QBasic statement
```

`IF` is the first QBasic statement you have seen with two keywords: `IF` and `THEN`. The *`condition`* is any relational comparison. You saw several relational comparisons earlier, such as `A=B`, `C<D`, and so on. The *`QBasic statement`* is any possible QBasic statement, such as `LET`, `PRINT`, or `GOTO`. That statement executes only if the condition is *true.* If the condition is false, QBasic ignores the statement and simply executes the next physical statement in the program following the `IF`.

In the first few examples of `IF`, the statement is a `GOTO` followed by a statement label. You probably can already guess that the `IF-THEN-GOTO` *should be limited.* For now, get acquainted with this one, and you will see other formats shortly as your programs become more sophisticated. The `IF-THEN-GOTO` will be helpful in introducing the next chapter's statements.

Basically, you can read an `IF-THEN-GOTO` in the following way:

If the condition is true, go to the statement labeled to the right of `GOTO`*. Otherwise, the condition must be false, so do NOT go to the statement, but continue execution as though the* `IF` *did not exist.*

`IF` is used to make a decision. The `GOTO` (or whatever statement follows `THEN`) occurs if the decision (the result of the relation) is true; the `GOTO` does not occur otherwise. As with relational logic, you use `IF` logic in everyday life. Consider the following statements:

"If the day is warm, then I will go swimming."

"If I make enough money, then we will build a new house."

"If the light is green, then go."

"If the light is red, then stop."

Each of these statements is *conditional.* That is, if and only if the condition is true do you complete the statement.

Examples

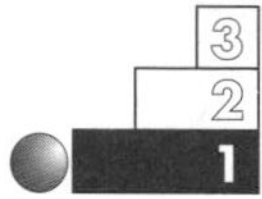

1. The following is a valid QBasic IF statement:

```
IF sales > 5000 THEN GOTO Bonus
```

Assuming this statement is part of a QBasic program, the value inside the variable sales determines what happens next. If sales contains more than 5000, the next statement that executes is the one following the statement label Bonus. If sales is 5,000 or less, however, the GOTO does not occur, and the line following the IF executes.

It usually is helpful to enclose the relational test in parentheses. This makes the IF more readable. You could rewrite the preceding line as follows:

```
IF (sales > 5000) THEN GOTO Bonus
```

Using the parentheses does not change the meaning of the statement, but it does help you spot the relational test more easily.

```
IF (age <= 21) THEN GOTO Minor
```

If the value in age is less than or equal to 21, the line at the label Minor executes next.

```
IF (balance <> low.balance) THEN GOTO Act.Pay
```

If the balance is not equal to low.balance, whether it is higher or lower, execution of the program continues at Act.Pay. You can compare two variables (as in this example), a variable to a constant (as in the previous example), a constant to a constant (although that is rarely done), or an expression in place of any variable or constant. The following IF statement shows an expression included in the IF:

```
IF (pay * tax.rate < minimum) THEN GOTO Low.Salary
IF (i/j = q^6) THEN GOTO Valid.Num
```

You can make expressions such as these much more readable by using parentheses around the them, although parentheses are not required. Here is a rewrite of these two IF statements with ample parentheses:

```
IF ((pay * tax.rate) < minimum) THEN GOTO Low.Salary
IF ((i/j) = (q^6)) THEN GOTO Valid.Num
```

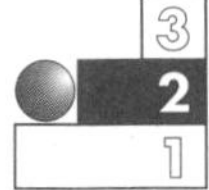

2. When getting input from users, it is often wise to perform *data validation* on the values they type. If users enter bad values (for instance, a negative number when you know the input cannot be negative), you can inform them of the problem and ask them to re-enter the input.

   Not all data can be validated, but most of it can be checked for reasonableness. For example, if you write a record-keeping program to track each student's name, address, age, and other pertinent data, you can check to see whether the given age falls within a reasonable range. If the user enters 213 for the age, you know the value is incorrect. If the user enters -4 for the age, you know the input value is incorrect also. If the student is 21 and the user types 22, however, your program would have no way of knowing whether the age is correct, because 22 falls within a reasonable range.

   The following program section is a routine that requests an age and checks to make sure it is less than 100 and more than 14. This is certainly not a foolproof test, because the user can still enter an incorrect age. The program can, however, detect an unreasonable age.

```
' Filename: C11AGE1.BAS
'
' Program that helps ensure age values are reasonable.

CLS
Start:
   PRINT
   INPUT "What is the student's age"; age

   IF (age > 14) THEN GOTO Over14   ' Age is at least 14
   BEEP
```

```
   PRINT "*** The age cannot be less than 14 ***"
   PRINT "Try again..."
   GOTO Start

Over14:
   IF (age < 100) THEN GOTO OkAge     ' Age is also less than
                                      ' 100
   BEEP
   PRINT "*** The age cannot be more than 100 ***"
   PRINT "Try again..."
   GOTO Start

OkAge:
   PRINT "You entered a valid age."
```

This routine could be a section of a longer program. This program uses the BEEP statement to warn users that they entered an incorrect age.

If the entered age is less than 14, users get an error message. The same is true if the age is too large (over 100). The program continues to beep and warn users about the incorrect age until they enter a more reasonable age.

Figure 11.1 shows the result of running this program. Notice that the program knows, because of the IF statement, whether the age falls between 14 and 100.

String Comparisons

In addition to comparing numeric data with the IF, you can use the IF to compare character string data. This is useful for alphabetizing, testing answers, comparing names, and much more.

When comparing string data, you should always refer to the ASCII table to see how characters relate to each other. Sometimes the ASCII table is known as the *collating* sequence of QBasic; it tells the order of characters.

You know that *A* comes before *B*. Therefore, it is true that *A* is less than *B*. The ASCII numbers determine the order of the characters. The ASCII table is handy also when you are comparing nonalphabetic data. For instance, the ASCII table shows that a question mark is less than an exclamation point. You can see also that lowercase letters are higher than uppercase letters. Therefore, an uppercase *P* is less than the lowercase *p*.

```
What is the student's age? 2
*** The age cannot be less than 14 ***
Try again...

What is the student's age? 24
You entered a valid age.




Press any key to continue
```

Figure 11.1. Checking to ensure that the user enters valid input data.

When comparing more than one character at a time, QBasic scans each character of each string being compared until it finds a difference. For instance, `"Adam"` and `"Adam"` are exactly equal. `"Jody"` is less than `"Judy"`, however, because the *o* is less than the *u* according to the ASCII table. Also, a longer string such as `"Shopping"` is greater than `"Shop"` because of the extra characters.

TIP: An empty string, called a *null string*, is always less than any other string except another null string. A null string can occur when you press Enter in response to an `INPUT` without typing a value first.

Examples

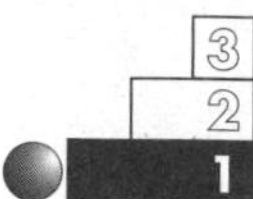

1. The following string comparisons are all true. If you are unsure about some of them, check the ASCII table in Appendix A to see for yourself why they compare to true.

```
"abcdef" > "ABCDEF"
"Yes!" < "Yes?"
"Computers are fun!" = "Computers are fun!"
"PC" <> "pc"
"Books, Books, Books" >= "Books, Books"
```

   Notice there are always quotation marks around the strings. This is consistent with the string constants you have seen so far.

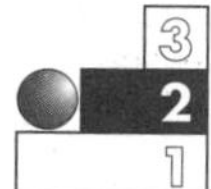

2. You can use string comparisons to determine whether users type correct passwords. After typing a password, compare it to an internal password to check its validity.

   This program requests a password. It then checks the entered password against one stored in a variable. If the passwords match, the program beeps once and a secret message appears. If they do not match, the program clears the screen and asks the user again. Only when a correct password is entered does the secret message appear.

```
' Filename: C11PASS1.BAS
'
' Program to prompt for a password and
' check it against an internal one.

stored.pass$ = "XYZ123"

COLOR 15, 1    ' Bright white on blue

GetPass:
   CLS
   PRINT "What is the password";
   COLOR 1, 1     ' Blue on Blue to hide the user input
```

```
   INPUT user.pass$
   COLOR 15, 1    ' Change the colors back

IF (user.pass$ <> stored.pass$) THEN GOTO GetPass

' Control falls here if the user entered proper password
BEEP
CLS   ' Print the secret message for the valid user
   PRINT "You entered the correct password."
   PRINT "The cash safe is behind the picture of the ship."
   END
```

If users know the password, they see the secret message. Of course, users can press Ctrl+Break to stop the program and look at the listing to find the password and secret message. After learning how programs work with data files, you will see how to encrypt the passwords so that users cannot find them as easily.

Password routines are good for front-end sections of programs with confidential data, such as payroll or banking systems.

Intelligent Passwords

Throughout your use of computers, you will have to choose passwords. Please take this responsibility seriously. Computer crime is serious and illegal.

It is wise to change your password every few weeks. This keeps someone from using it for long if they do determine it. Do not write your password down, and do not make it so long that you forget it.

Make up passwords that are not English words, even though they might be more difficult to remember. Foreign words and letter-number combinations make good passwords. Passwords like `X1Y2Z6`, `Giorno`, and `MY912AB` are good candidates.

Compound Logical Operators

There might be times when you need to test more than one set of variables. You can combine more than one relational test into a *compound relational test* by using the following logical operators:

```
AND    OR    XOR    NOT
```

These might not seem like typical operators. The operators you have learned so far have been symbols, such as +, <>, and *. These logical operators are, however, operators of QBasic, and they go between two or more relational tests.

Tables 11.2, 11.3, 11.4, and 11.5 show how each of the logical operators works. These tables are called *truth tables,* because they show how to achieve true results from an IF test that uses them. Take a minute to study the tables.

Table 11.2. The AND truth table—both sides must be true.

True	AND	True	= True
True	AND	False	= False
False	AND	True	= False
False	AND	False	= False

Table 11.3. The OR truth table—one side or the other must be true.

True	OR	True	= True
True	OR	False	= True
False	OR	True	= True
False	OR	False	= False

Table 11.4. The XOR truth table—one or the other must be true, but not both.

True	XOR	True	= False
True	XOR	False	= True
False	XOR	True	= True
False	XOR	False	= False

Table 11.5. The NOT truth table—causes an opposite relation.

NOT True	= False
NOT False	= True

Examples

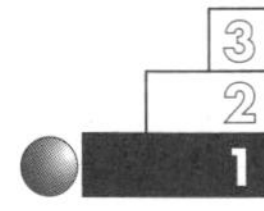

1. The True and False on each side of the operators represent a relational IF test. For instance, the following are valid IF tests that use logical operators (sometimes called *compound relational operators*):

A must be less than B, and C must be greater than D for the CalcIt routine to execute.

```
IF ((A < B) AND (C > D)) THEN GOTO CalcIt
```

The sales must be more than 5000 or the hrs.worked must be more than 81 before the OverPay routine executes.

```
IF ((sales > 5000) OR (hrs.worked > 81)) THEN GOTO OverPay
```

The variable called bit2 must be equal to 0 or bit3 must not be equal to 1 before Error is printed. If they both are true, however, the test fails (because XOR is used), the PRINT is ignored, and the next instruction in sequence executes.

```
If ((bit2 = 0) XOR (bit3 <> 1)) THEN PRINT "Error"
```

If the sales are not less than 2500, the bonus is initialized.

```
IF (NOT(sales < 2500)) THEN bonus = 500
```

This illustrates an important programming tip: Use `NOT` sparingly. (As some wisely state: Do not use `NOT` or your programs will not be `NOT(unclear)`.) It would be much clearer to rewrite this previous example by turning it into a positive relational test as in

```
IF (sales >= 2500) THEN bonus 500
```

Notice that the overall format of the `IF` statement is retained, but the relational test has been expanded to include more than one relation. You can even have three or more, as in

```
IF ((A = B) AND (D = F) OR (L = m) XOR (K <> 2)) ...
```

This is a little too much. Good programming practice dictates using only two relational tests inside one `IF`. If you need to combine more than two, use more than one `IF` statement.

As with other relational operators, you use these in everyday conversation, as in these examples:

"If my pay is high *and* my vacation time is long, we can go to Italy this summer."

"If you take the trash out *or* clean your room, you can watch television tonight."

"I can go to the grocery *or* go to the flower shop, but *not* both."

The first two examples are straightforward. The last example illustrates the `XOR` operator. Notice from the `XOR` truth table that one side of the `XOR` or the other side of the `XOR` can be true for the final result to be true, but not both sides. This is known as the *exclusive or* operator. It is sometimes called the *mutually exclusive* operator. There are many times when you are faced with two choices, but you can do only one or the other; you do not have the time or resources to do both.

The same is true sometimes with computer relational tests. You might need to print an exception report if a customer's payment is late or if the customer's debt is forgiven, but not if both happen.

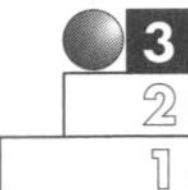

Internal Truths

The true or false results of relational tests occur internally at the bit level. For example, look at the following `IF` test:

```
IF (A = 6) THEN ...
```

To determine the truth of the relation `(A = 6)`, the computer takes a binary 6, or 00000110, and compares it bit-by-bit to the variable `A`. If `A` contains 7, a binary 00000111, the result of the equal test is false because the right bit (called the *least-significant bit*) is different.

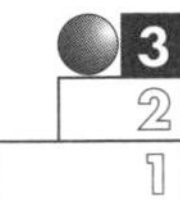

2. The following program gets three numbers from the user. Regardless of the order in which the user types the numbers, the program prints the smallest and the largest of the three. The program uses several compound `IF` statements.

```
' Filename: C11MNMAX.BAS
'
' Program to print largest and smallest of three input values.
'
CLS
PRINT "Please type 3 different numbers,"
INPUT "and separate them with commas"; num1, num2, num3

' Test for the highest
IF ((num1>num2)AND(num1>num3)) THEN PRINT num1;"is highest"
IF ((num2>num1)AND(num2>num3)) THEN PRINT num2;"is highest"
IF ((num3>num1)AND(num3>num2)) THEN PRINT num3;"is highest"

' Test for the smallest
IF ((num1<num2)AND(num1<num3)) THEN PRINT num1;"is smallest"
IF ((num2<num1)AND(num2<num3)) THEN PRINT num2;"is smallest"
IF ((num3<num1)AND(num3<num2)) THEN PRINT num3;"is smallest"
END
```

Future chapters show you even better ways to produce results like these.

The Complete Order of Operators

The order of math operators you saw in Chapter 5, "Understanding Numeric Variables and Constants," did not include the relational operators you are learning in this chapter. You should be familiar with the entire order, which is presented in Table 11.6. As you can see, the math operators take precedence over the relational operators, and parentheses override any of these defaults.

Table 11.6. The entire order of operators.

Order	*Operator*
1	Parentheses
2	Exponentiation (^)
3	Negation (the unary -)
4	Multiplication, division, integer division (*, /, \), MOD
5	Addition, subtraction (+, -)
6	Relational operators (=, <, >, <=, >=, <>)
7	`NOT` logical operator
8	`AND`
9	`OR`
10	`XOR`

You might wonder why the relational and logical operators are included. The following statement helps show why:

```
IF (sales < min.sal * 2 AND yrs.emp > 10 * sub) ...
```

Without the complete order of operators, it would be impossible to determine how such a statement would execute. According to the operator order, this `IF` statement would execute as follows:

```
IF ((sales < (min.sal * 2)) AND (yrs.emp > (10 * sub))) ...
```

This statement is still confusing, but it is less confusing than the previous statement. The two multiplications would be performed first, followed by the relations < and >. The AND is performed last because it is lowest in the order of operators.

To avoid such problems, use ample parentheses, even if you want the actions to be performed in the default order. In addition, do not combine too many expressions inside one IF relational test.

Counters and Totals

Now you are ready to learn how to program two powerful routines: *counters* and *totals.* Computers do not think, but they do lightning-fast calculations, and they do not get bored. This makes them perfect for counting and adding totals.

There are no commands inside QBasic to count occurrences or total a list of numbers; with the IF statement, however, you can write these routines yourself. Almost every program in use today has some sort of counter or totaling algorithm, or a combination of both.

Counting with QBasic

Counting is important for many applications. You might want to know how many customers you have. You might want to know how many people scored over a certain average in a class. You might want to count how many checks you wrote last month with your computerized checkbook system.

To begin developing a QBasic routine to count occurrences, think of how you count in your own mind. When you add the total number of something (such as the stamps in your stamp collection or the number of wedding invitations you sent), you follow this procedure:

Start at 0 and add 1 for each item you are counting. When you finish, you have the total number (the total count) of the items.

This is all you do when you count with QBasic. Put 0 in a variable and add 1 to it every time you process another data value.

Examples

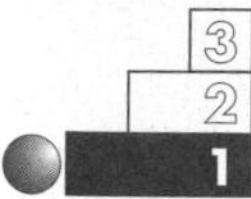

1. Using a counter, you can create a *conditional loop.* A conditional loop occurs a fixed number of times. Remember the endless loop problem that sometimes plagues the `GOTO` statement? By counting and stopping on the total count, you can loop a specified number of times.

   To illustrate the conditional loop, the following program prints `Computers are fun!` on the screen 10 times. You could write a program that had 10 `PRINT` statements, but that wouldn't be very elegant. It would also be too cumbersome to have 5,000 `PRINT` statements if you want to print that same message 5,000 times.

   By adding a loop and counter that stops after a certain total is reached, you can control a `GOTO` much better, as the following program shows:

```
' Filename: C11CNT1.BAS
'
' Program to print a message 10 times.

' Initialize the counting variable to 0
ctr = 0

CLS
PrAgain:
   PRINT "Computers are fun!"
   ctr = ctr + 1      ' Add one to the count, after each PRINT
   if (ctr < 10) THEN GOTO PrAgain   ' Print again if fewer
                                     ' than 10 times

END  ' The program is through
```

   Figure 11.2 shows the output from this program. Notice that the message was printed exactly 10 times.

   The heart of the counting process in this program is the following statement:

```
ctr = ctr + 1
```

```
Computers are fun!
Computers are fun!
Computers are fun!
Computers are fun!
Computers are fun!
Computers are fun!
Computers are fun!
Computers are fun!
Computers are fun!
Computers are fun!

Press any key to continue
```

Figure 11.2. Controlling output with a counter.

In algebra, this would not be a valid statement because nothing is ever equal to itself plus 1. In QBasic, however, the equal sign means assignment; the right side of the equal sign is computed, 1 is added to whatever is in `ctr` at the time, and that value is stored back in `ctr`, in effect replacing the old value of `ctr`.

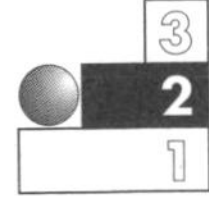

2. Notice that the previous program not only added to the counter variable, but also tested for a value. This is a common method of conditionally executing parts of a program a fixed number of times.

   The following program is a revised password program. Instead of allowing an unlimited number of tries, it lets the user attempt only three passwords. If the user does not type the correct password in three tries, the program ends. This is a common method that dial-up computers use; they let the person calling try the password a fixed number of times and then hang up the phone if the caller exceeds that limit. This helps deter people from trying hundreds of different passwords in one sitting.

```
' Filename: C11PASS2.BAS
'
' Program to prompt for a password and
' check it against an internal one.

stored.pass$ = "XYZ123"
num.tries = 0   ' The counter for password attempts

COLOR 15, 1   ' Bright white on blue

GetPass:
   IF (num.tries >= 3) THEN GOTO NoGood  ' Don't let them
                                         ' past three tries
   CLS
   PRINT "What is the password (You get 3 tries...)";
   COLOR 1, 1    ' Blue on Blue to hide the user input
   INPUT user.pass$
   COLOR 15, 1   ' Change the colors back
   num.tries = num.tries + 1   ' Add to the counter
   IF (user.pass$ <> stored.pass$) THEN GOTO GetPass

' Control falls here if the user entered proper password
BEEP
CLS
PRINT "You entered the correct password."
PRINT "The cash safe is behind the picture of the ship."
GOTO Finished   ' Stop the program

' Control falls here if user ran out of tries
NoGood:
   BEEP
   BEEP
   PRINT "*** Warning -- You did not know the password ***"

Finished:
   END
```

The program gives the user three chances, just in case a typing mistake or two occurs. After three attempts, however, the program refuses to let the user see the secret message.

Producing Totals

Writing a routine to add values is as easy as counting. Instead of adding 1 to the counter variable, you add a value to the total variable. For instance, if you want to find the total dollar amount of checks you wrote in December, start at 0 (nothing) and add to that each check written in December. Instead of building a count, you are building a total.

When you want QBasic to add values, initialize a total variable to 0 and add each value to the total until you have gone through all the values.

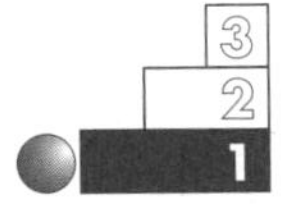

1. Suppose you want to write a program to add your grades for a class you are taking. The teacher has informed you that if you earn more than 450 points, you will receive an A.

   The following program continues to ask for values until you type `-1`. The `-1` is a signal that you are finished entering grades and now you want to see their total. The program also prints a congratulations message if you get an A.

```
' Filename: C11GRAD1.BAS
'
' Adds up grades and determines if an A was made.

' Initialize total variable and screen
total.grade = 0
COLOR 15, 1    ' Bright white letters on blue background
CLS

NextGrade:
   INPUT "What is your grade"; grade
   IF (grade = -1) THEN GOTO Done     ' User signaled no more
                                      ' grades
   total.grade = total.grade + grade    ' Add to total
   GOTO NextGrade      ' Get another grade to add

' Control begins here if no more grades
Done:
   PRINT "You made a total of"; total.grade; " points."
   IF (total.grade >= 450) THEN PRINT "** You made an A!!"
```

Notice that the *-1* response is not added into the total grade. The program checks for the *-1* before adding to `total.grade`.

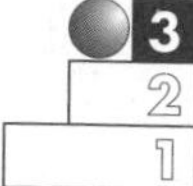

2. The following program is an extension of the grade calculation program. It not only totals the grades, but also computes an average.

   The average calculation must know how many grades were entered before it works. This is a subtle problem; the number of grades entered is unknown in advance. Therefore, every time the user enters a valid grade (not *-1*), the program must add 1 to a counter, as well as add that grade to the total variable. This is a combination of a counter and a totaling routine, which is common to many programs.

```
' Filename: C11GRAD2.BAS
'
' Adds up grades, computes average,
' and determines if an A was made.

' Initialize total variable, counter, and screen
total.grade = 0
grade.ctr = 0
COLOR 15, 1    ' Bright white letters on blue background
CLS

NextGrade:
   INPUT "What is your grade"; grade
   IF (grade = -1) THEN GOTO Done    ' User signaled no more
                                     ' grades
   total.grade = total.grade + grade   ' Add to total
   grade.ctr = grade.ctr + 1    ' Only add 1 to counting
                                ' variables
   GOTO NextGrade     ' Get another grade to add
' Control begins here if no more grades
Done:
   grade.avg = total.grade / grade.ctr    ' Compute average
   PRINT "You made a total of"; total.grade; "points."
   PRINT "Your average was"; grade.avg
   IF (total.grade >= 450) THEN PRINT "** You made an A!!"
```

Figure 11.3 shows the result of running this program.

```
What is your grade? 90
What is your grade? 86
What is your grade? 93
What is your grade? 95
What is your grade? 88
What is your grade? 90
What is your grade? -1
You made a total of 542 points.
Your average was 90.33334
** You made an A!!




Press any key to continue
```

Figure 11.3. Adding grades and computing the average.

Summary

This chapter showed you how to compare data. By testing constants and variables, your program can behave differently depending on its input data. Computers should be data-driven. When programmers write the programs, they do not know what data will be input. Therefore, they should write the programs to conditionally execute certain statements depending on the data given.

This chapter is the basis of many programs you will write. Programs that test results and conditionally execute accordingly make computers flexible by enabling them to react to given data.

Review Questions

Answers to the Review Questions are in Appendix B.

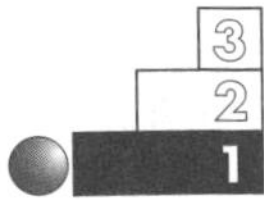

1. Please state whether these relational tests are true or false.

   A. 4 >= 5
   B. 4 >= 4

C. 165 = 165
D. 0 <> 25

2. TRUE or FALSE: `"QBasic is fun"` prints on the screen when the following statement is executed:

```
IF (54 <= 50) THEN PRINT "QBasic is fun"
```

3. Using the ASCII table, please state whether these string relational tests are true or false.

A. `"Que" < "QUE"`
B. `"" < "0"`
C. `"?" > "}"`
D. `"yES" < "Yes"`

4. What is the result of executing the following program lines?

```
LET N1 = 0
LET N1 = N1 + 5
```

A. The value of N1 is 0.
B. The value of N1 is 6.
C. The value of N1 is 5.
D. The value of N1 cannot be determined.

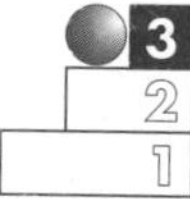

5. The following compound relational tests compare true and false values. Determine whether each of them is true or false.

A. NOT (TRUE OR FALSE)
B. (TRUE AND FALSE) AND (FALSE XOR TRUE)
C. NOT (TRUE XOR TRUE)
D. TRUE OR (FALSE AND FALSE) OR FALSE

6. Which of the following is not a valid comparison?

A. `IF S$ = T$ THEN PRINT "Okay"`
B. `IF dir$ = "dos" THEN LET dv = 1`
C. `IF co.name = "XYZ" THEN GOTO CalcIt`
D. `IF x = y THEN INPUT extra1, extra2`

7. Determine whether the following statements produce a true or false result. Use the complete order of operators table to help. (After determining the result, you will appreciate the use of extra parentheses.)

A. `5 = 4 + 1 OR 7 * 2 <> 12 - 1 AND 5 = 8 \ 2`

B. `8 + 9 <> 6 - 1 XOR 10 \ 2 <> 5 + 0`

C. `17 - 1 > 15 + 1 AND 0 + 2 = 1 + 1 OR 4 <> 1`

D. `409 * 0 <> 1 * 409 + 0 XOR 1 + 8 * 2 >= 17`

Review Exercises

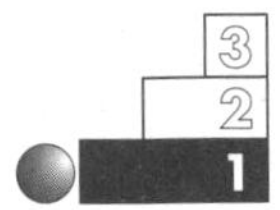

1. Write a weather-calculator program that asks for a list of the temperatures from the previous 10 days, computes the average, and prints the results. You have to compute a total as the input occurs, then divide that total by 10 to find the average.

2. Write a program that asks for the user's age. If the age is under 21, print the following message:

```
Have a lemonade!
```

If, however, the age is 21 or more, print the following message instead:

```
Have a scotch and soda!
```

3. Write a program similar to the weather-calculator in exercise 1, but make it general-purpose so that it computes the average of any number of days. You have to count the number of temperatures entered so that you have it when you compute the final average.

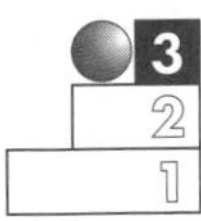

4. Write a program to produce your own ASCII table on the printer. Do not print the first 31 codes because they are nonprintable. Print the codes numbered 32 through 255, using the `CHR$` function explained in Chapter 10. To do this, start the counter at 32 instead of 0. Print the ASCII value of the number, increment the count by 1, and go back and print again. Make sure the program stops after printing `CHR$(255)`. (This requires an `IF-THEN-GOTO`.)

5. Write a payroll program that asks for the weekly hours worked and the pay per hour. Compute the pay, assuming the firm pays regular pay (rate * hours worked) for all hours less than or equal to 40, time and a half (1.5) for any hours more than 40 and less than 50, and double pay for any hours 50 or more. Run it several times, trying different values for the hours worked to ensure that the calculations are correct. Your program probably will have at least two or three `IF` statements to handle the various types of overtime pay. Do not worry about taxes or other deductions.

READ **and** DATA **Statements**

You have seen two ways to put data values into variables: the assignment (LET) statement and the INPUT statement. This chapter addresses another way QBasic offers to assign values to variables that your program uses: READ and DATA statements. The following concepts are introduced:

- The READ statement
- The DATA statement
- The RESTORE statement

READ and DATA statements are good to use when you know the data values in advance. Not all programs can use READ and DATA statements, however, because there is much data you do not know until the user runs the program. That is why you learned INPUT—so that the user can type the data at run time.

Because of the dual nature of the READ and DATA statements, this chapter focuses on both of them at the same time. READ and DATA are used so much in QBasic programs that this chapter is devoted to their use.

READ **and** DATA **Overview**

The two statements READ and DATA never operate by themselves; you never see one without the other. A program that contains one or more READ statements must contain at least one DATA statement. These two statements do not necessarily appear close together in a program.

The format of the READ statement is

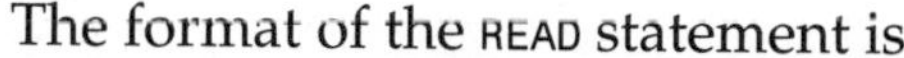


```
READ var1 [, var2] [, var3] [, ..., varN]
```

in which *var1* is a numeric or string variable name. Optionally, you can list more than one variable name after READ by separating the variable names with commas.

The format of the DATA statement is

```
DATA value1 [, value2] [, value3] [, ..., valueN]
```

in which *value1* is a numeric or string constant. Optionally, you can list more than one value after DATA by separating the values with commas.

You probably are starting to see a resemblance between READ and DATA statements. These statements typically have a one-to-one correspondence to each other. Usually, if a READ statement has three variable names after it, the DATA statement (or statements) has three values after it.

> **NOTE:** The most important thing to remember is that READ is followed always by one or more variable names and never by constants.
>
> DATA is followed always by one or more constants and never by variable names.

Examples

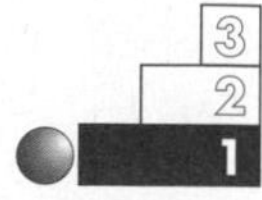

1. The following are four valid READ statements. They are not related, but they are examples of typical READ statements.

```
READ grade
READ first.name$, last.name$
READ full.name$, age, weight, home.town$
READ diameter, circum, radius
```

Notice that one or more numeric variables, string variables, or a combination of both can appear after READ.

2. The following are four valid DATA statements. They are not related to each other, but each might correspond to the preceding READ statements, respectively.

```
DATA 87.5
DATA "Jim", "Nickles"
DATA "Bettye Horn", 38, 117, "St. Louis"
DATA 4, 12.6, 2
```

As with any string constant, be sure to enclose string data values in quotation marks. A line of DATA is often called a *data record.*

Using READ and DATA

One of the easiest methods of learning how READ and DATA work is to see their statements compared to assignment (LET) statements. Remember that the READ and DATA statements are just another pair of statements that put data values into variables. To be more specific:

NOTE: READ reads DATA values into variables.

Consider the following assignment statement:

```
sales = 50000
```

By now, you fully understand this simple statement.

50,000 is assigned to the variable called `sales`.

The following READ and DATA statements do the same thing as the preceding assignment statement:

```
READ sales
DATA 50000
```

The data value of 50,000 is placed into `sales` *when the* `READ` *executes.*

Of the two statements, `READ` is active and `DATA` is passive. `DATA` statements really do not execute. QBasic ignores `DATA` statements, regardless of where they fall in a program, until a `READ` statement is reached. When QBasic runs across `READ`, it carries out the following steps:

1. Looks for the next unread `DATA` statement.
2. Assigns the value(s) in the `DATA` statement to the `READ` variable(s).
3. Remembers that the `DATA` was used, so it does not reuse it again.

Therefore, when QBasic sees the preceding `READ sales` statement, it looks through the program starting from the top until it finds a `DATA` statement it has not used. Assuming that these `READ` and `DATA` statements are the only `READ` and `DATA` statements in the program, the data value of 50,000 is placed into `sales` when the `READ` executes.

Because `DATA` statements are passive, they can go anywhere in the program without affecting the program's execution, even at the beginning. Therefore, the following two statements do the same thing as the last two:

```
DATA 50000
READ sales
```

NOTE: Remember that nothing happens to a `DATA` statement until a `READ` is executed.

Multiple READ-DATA Values

To continue the comparison of `READ`, `DATA`, and assignment statements, the assignment statements

```
emp.name1$ = "Dent"
emp.name2$ = "Robeson"
```

are equivalent to the following READ and DATA statements:

```
READ emp.name1$, emp.name2$
DATA "Dent", "Robeson"
```

Notice that the DATA statement values must match in data type and number to the variables at the READ. Because emp.name1$ and emp.name2$ are string variables, the DATA statement must have string constants.

You might wonder why you would use this READ-DATA pair of statements and the one in the earlier example rather than the shorter assignment statements. When only one or two variables are being assigned, an assignment statement is much easier to use and understand. However, what if you had to assign 25 values to 25 variables? If you write a program to keep track of the previous 25 daily temperatures in your city, you can put these 25 values into 25 variables, as in

```
temp1 = 87
temp2 = 92
temp3 = 89.5
     :
     :
temp24 = 76
temp25 = 81.5
```

It would be easier, however, to read the 25 values into 25 variables using READ and DATA statements:

```
READ temp1, temp2, temp3, temp4, temp5, temp6, temp7, temp8
READ temp9, temp10, temp11, temp12, temp13, temp14, temp15
READ temp16, temp17, temp18, temp19, temp20, temp21, temp22
READ temp23, temp24, temp25
DATA 87, 92, 89.5, 85, 80, 79.5, 76, 78, 77, 77, 80, 83, 85
DATA 86, 86.5, 86, 88. 91. 90.5, 93, 90, 89, 89.5, 76, 81.5
```

This still might seem like a messy way of assigning 25 values to 25 variables, but it's better than using 25 lines of code for individual assignment statements. This example shows you also that the number of READ and DATA statements do not have to match. There must be enough DATA values in the program somewhere, however, to fill the variables being read.

QBasic does not read the same DATA values twice. Once QBasic assigns the first DATA value (87) into the first READ variable (temp1) it does not use that 87 again in another READ.

NOTE: The commas in the READ and DATA statements have nothing to do with the print zones. Commas inside PRINT and LPRINT statements are there to space output values, whereas the commas in READ and DATA are there to separate the values from each other.

Match READ and DATA Types

If a READ statement has a mixture of numeric and string variables after it, the DATA values being read into those variables also must be the same mixture of type. It is up to you as the programmer to ensure this compatibility because you type DATA values into the program when you write it.

TIP: If QBasic gives you a Syntax Error on a READ statement and the READ statement seems to be correct, check your data types. You probably are reading the wrong type of value, such as a string constant, into the wrong type of variable, such as a numeric variable.

The following groups of READ and DATA statements match in number and type:

```
READ emp.name$, phone$, age, weight, salary
DATA "Bill Brown", "555-3212", 27, 188, 23500

READ x, y, desc$
DATA 1.2, 3.4, "Coordinates of the point"
```

```
READ a, b, c
DATA 4
DATA 13
DATA 64
```

The preceding example illustrates how QBasic treats DATA it has already read. Although there is only one value listed after the first DATA statement, QBasic continues to search through your program for another DATA statement until it can fill all the READ's variables. In this example, it didn't have to look far.

The converse is possible as well. The following example shows how several READ statements can read data from only one DATA statement:

```
READ student.id$
READ student.avg
READ student.age
DATA "JONE554", 92.75, 20
```

When QBasic executes the first READ, it looks for DATA it hasn't used yet. It finds the DATA statement and reads "JONE554" into student.id$. When it runs into the next READ, it knows it already read "JONE554", so it puts 92.75 into student.avg. Then when QBasic reaches the third READ, it knows that the 20 is the only value that has not previously been read.

> **TIP:** Although the number of READ variables and DATA values on each line do not have to match, you should make them match if at all possible. This makes for easier debugging.

Example

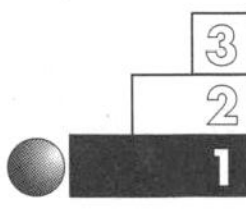

1. The following program reads three student names and their three grades one student at a time. Then the program prints the names and grades on the screen.

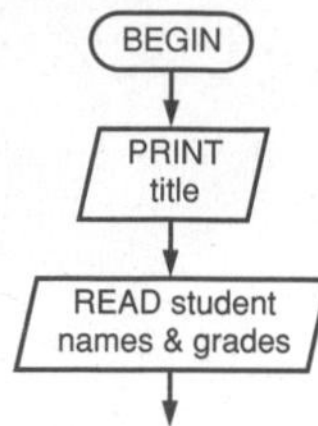


```
' Filename: C12STD1.BAS
'
' Reads each student name and three grades
' and prints them to the screen.

' Clear the screen and print a title
CLS
PRINT "Grades for students"
PRINT

NextStd:
   READ s.name$, grade1, grade2, grade3      ' Get the next
                                             ' data values
   PRINT s.name$, grade1, grade2, grade3     ' Print values
                                             ' just read
   GOTO NextStd            ' Get another set to print

' The data to be printed
DATA "Michael", 87, 62, 52
DATA "Mary", 62, 91, 90
DATA "Sam", 81, 76, 90
```

This program is not quite complete. If you type and run it, you get the error message `Out of DATA` when it ends. Study the program and see whether you can determine why you would get that error message.

One of the advantages of READ and DATA over regular assignment statements is the ease of adding and deleting data they enable. Say that the class size grows considerably to 12 students. No change has to be made to the program's logic. The only change required is to type nine additional DATA statements for the additional students at the bottom of the program.

The problem with the program has to do with the GOTO causing the READ to execute repeatedly. There is no more DATA to read, however, after the third time READ executes. Remember that READ does not reread data it has already read.

CAUTION: Do not put a remark to the right of a DATA statement's values. Not knowing whether that text is data or a remark, QBasic tries to read it (incorrectly).

The Trailer DATA Statement

To fix the error described in the previous example, you must add a *trailer data record.* A trailer data record is simply a special DATA statement that contains specified data values for which to check. Commonly, a trailer data record contains a -99 for each numeric position of data and a "-99" for each string position.

For instance, a trailer data record that would work in the previous program would be

```
DATA "-99", -99, -99, -99
```

There is nothing magic about this data. Because "-99" will never be a student's name and -99 will never be a student's grade, this trailer data record works in this program.

The trailing data record is always the last line of DATA. Your program should check for these special values after each READ. If the program finds these trailer data record values, it knows that it is at the end of the DATA and that it can quit. This ensures that the End of DATA error message does not appear.

Examples

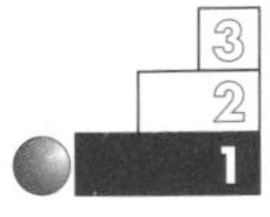

1. The following program fixes the preceding program by adding a conditional GOTO. The GOTO NextStd *does not* execute if the READ reads trailer record values. (Remember that a conditional statement is triggered by an IF statement.)

```
' Filename: C12STD2.BAS
'
' Reads each student name and three grades
' and prints them to the screen.
```

```
' Clear the screen and print a title
CLS
PRINT "Grades for students"
PRINT

NextStd:
   READ s.name$, grade1, grade2, grade3    ' Get the next
                                           ' data values
   IF (s.name$ = "-99") THEN GOTO NoMore   ' Stop if you
                                           ' just read trailer
   PRINT s.name$, grade1, grade2, grade3   ' Print values just
                                           ' read
   GOTO NextStd                     ' Get another set to print

' The data to be printed
DATA "Michael", 87, 62, 52
DATA "Mary", 62, 91, 90
DATA "Sam", 81, 76, 90
DATA "-99", -99, -99, -99

NoMore:
   END     ' This executes if the trailer was just read
```

Three changes were made to this program. The following three changes always fix an `Out of DATA` error:

1. Add a trailer data record that matches in type and number the surrounding DATA statements.
2. Test to see whether that trailer data record was read immediately following the READ.
3. Add a statement label at the bottom of the program to GOTO if the trailer was just read.

Figure 12.1 shows the result of this run. It might seem like a long program to simply display three students' information on the screen. Remember that if many more students are added later, however, the program's logic does not have to change. You only have to insert the additional DATA before the trailing data record.

```
Grades for students

Michael        87          62          52
Mary           62          91          90
Sam            81          76          90










Press any key to continue
```

Figure 12.1. Running the READ and DATA program.

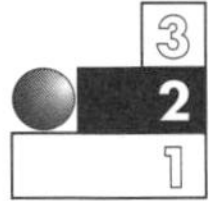

2. The following program is similar to the preceding program, except that the following program has more DATA. The inventory for a sporting goods company is stored in DATA statements. This program produces a report of the inventory. Notice that it prints the inventory in a different order than it read it from the DATA. The order of the READ-DATA values has nothing to do with what you do with those values. When READ and DATA finish filling variables, you can print and change the variables any way you prefer.

```
' Filename: C12INV1.BAS
'
' Program to produce an inventory listing on the printer
CLS
' Print titles on the printer
PRINT "Inventory Listing"
PRINT
PRINT "Part No.", "Quantity", "Price", "Description"
PRINT "--------", "--------", "-----", "-----------"
```

```
' Read the inventory, one DATA line at a time
ReadIt:
   READ part.no$, price, quantity, desc$
   IF (price = -99) THEN GOTO NoMore     ' If just read last
                                          ' record, quit
   PRINT part.no$, quantity, price, desc$
   GOTO ReadIt      ' Get another inventory record

DATA "10112", 10.95, 13, "Widget"
DATA "21943", 14.78, 2, "Metal Wire #4"
DATA "38745", 10.91, 10, "Bolt Clip"
DATA "44335", 17.64, 43, "Fastener"
DATA "44336", 17.64, 56, "Long Fastener"
DATA "-99", -99, -99, "-99"

NoMore:
   END
```

Notice that the test for the trailer data record did not test for the first READ variable, `part.no$`, but it tested for the price. This helps show the reason for the trailing data record. It doesn't matter which value you test for, as long as it is a possible trailer record value. You could just as easily test the program for `part.no$ = "-99"` or any of the other variables.

Figure 12.2 shows the result of this program. You must always print titles before the READ-GOTO loop begins; otherwise, the title prints before each data record prints. If the inventory changes, you only have to change the DATA statements in the program—not the program's logic.

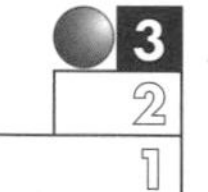

3. The following example builds on the inventory program from the previous example. It not only prints the inventory report, but also totals the value of the inventory. This requires that the price be multiplied by the total number of items for each part and that the extended total be added into the final valuation.

```
' Filename: C12INV2.BAS
'
' Program to produce an inventory listing on the printer
' and print the total value of the inventory.
```

```
total.inv = 0     ' Initialize the total variable

' Print titles on the printer
LPRINT "Inventory Listing"
LPRINT
LPRINT "Part No.", "Quantity", "Price", "Description"
LPRINT "--------", "--------", "-----", "-----------"

' Read the inventory, one DATA line at a time
ReadIt:
   READ part.no$, price, quantity, desc$
   IF (price = -99) THEN GOTO NoMore    ' If just read last
                                         ' record, quit
   LPRINT part.no$, quantity, price, desc$
   total.inv = total.inv + (price * quantity)
   GOTO ReadIt      ' Get another inventory record

DATA "10112", 10.95, 13, "Widget"
DATA "21943", 14.78, 2, "Metal Wire #4"
DATA "38745", 10.91, 10, "Bolt Clip"
DATA "44335", 17.64, 43, "Fastener"
DATA "44336", 17.64, 56, "Long Fastener"
DATA "-99", -99, -99, "-99"

NoMore:
   ' Print the total and stop
   LPRINT
   LPRINT USING "& $$###,.##"; "Total inventory value is",
   LPRINT total.inv
   END
```

Sophisticated business inventory programs are not much more intricate than the preceding example. If you understand the example, you are becoming an excellent QBasic programmer.

The DATA statements are no longer at the end of the program. They fall before the final LPRINTs in the example. Remember that DATA statements are passive. They can go anywhere in the program, even at the beginning, and the program's execution does not change at all.

```
Inventory Listing

Part No.        Quantity        Price           Description
--------        --------        -----           -----------
10112            13              10.95          Widget
21943            2               14.78          Metal Wire #4
38745            10              10.91          Bolt Clip
44335            43              17.64          Fastener
44336            56              17.64          Long Fastener








Press any key to continue
```

Figure 12.2. Viewing an inventory listing from the DATA statements.

4. The following example program keeps track of scientific measurements from a measuring instrument. The program simply reads all the data one value at a time; adds the values together; counts the values; and prints the total, count, and average.

```
' Filename: C12MEAS.BAS
'
' Produces statistics on the measurement data.

' Initialize the screen, total, and count variables
CLS
total = 0
count = 0

ReadAgain:
   READ meas.num  ' Get next measurement value from the DATA
   IF (meas.num = 9999) THEN GOTO NoMore  ' Hit trailer value
   total = total + meas.num  ' Add measurement just read
                             ' to total
```

```
   count = count + 1          ' Add 1 to count
   GOTO ReadAgain     ' Read another value

NoMore:      ' Execution gets here if no more data
   avg = total / count      ' Compute average
   PRINT "The total of the measurements is"; total
   PRINT "The average measurement is"; avg
   PRINT "There were"; count; "measurements"

DATA 9, -344, 66, -87, 101, -145, -44, -21, 11
DATA 23, -56, -98, 123, 34, -25, 112, -32, -102
DATA 27, 32, -65, -157
DATA 9999

END
```

This example seems to violate the rules of a trailer data record. The value on the trailer data record is neither -99 nor "-99". (Of course, of the two, "-99" would not be allowed because it is a string constant and the READ is reading a numeric variable.)

The trailer value of 9999 is consistent with the goal of a trailer data record. If you look through the measurement data, you see wide fluctuations. The typical data value -99 is a possible measurement value. Just because it happens not to be one of the DATA values now does not mean that it couldn't be one as more measurements are added.

Therefore, you have to find a trailer value that is out of the range of possible data values. Because this particular measuring instrument goes only as high as 500, it is safe to use 9999 as the trailer value; under ordinary circumstances, 9999 never appears in the actual temperature data to trigger the end of the data condition early.

The RESTORE Statement

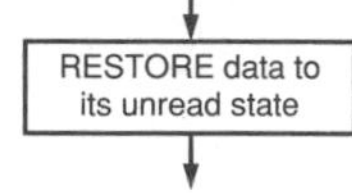

Although use of the RESTORE statement is limited, it lets you override the way READ and DATA work. The format of the RESTORE statement is

```
RESTORE [statement label]
```

Notice that the *statement label* is optional. If you do not include one, RESTORE goes on a program line by itself.

When QBasic executes a RESTORE, QBasic resets all the internal DATA checking. A subsequent READ statement starts over at the first DATA value again. RESTORE makes the program think it has never read any of the data, so it begins again from the starting DATA value.

If you include a statement label, QBasic starts reading data from that DATA statement.

Examples

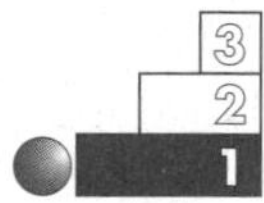

1. The following program illustrates the RESTORE statement. This program reads and prints three data values. After a RESTORE, the program passes control back to the top so that the program can read the values again. The program continues to do this until the user presses Ctrl+Break.

   Due to the endless loop, this program has a major problem. Because there is no conditional check (as there should be in such a program), the program quits rereading the same data repeatedly. However, this program is for illustrative purposes only. Without the RESTORE, the program displays an Out of DATA error.

```
' Filename: C12REST1.BAS
'
' Program to help show the RESTORE statement.

CLS

Again:
   READ emp.name$, age, salary
   PRINT emp.name$, age, salary
```

```
   READ emp.name$, age, salary    ' Get another...
   PRINT emp.name$, age, salary

   READ emp.name$, age, salary    ' and another
   PRINT emp.name$, age, salary

   RESTORE       ' Reset the READ-DATA checker
   GOTO Again ' Start reading and printing from the beginning

DATA "Jones", 34, 23500
DATA "Smith", 54, 46554
DATA "Brown", 42, 34995
```

The READ-RESTORE combination continues until you stop it with Ctrl+Break.

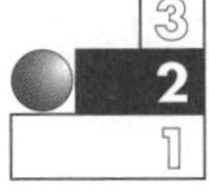

2. The following revised inventory program shows a better use of RESTORE. The only difference between this version and the one shown in C12INV1.BAS is that this program asks users whether they want to see the printed inventory report again. If so, the program sends a form feed to the printer, and a second report appears. This is possible because the RESTORE resets the READ-DATA and enables the data to be read again.

```
' Filename: C12INV3.BAS
'
' Program to produce an inventory listing on the printer.

' Print titles on the printer
PrintRep:
   LPRINT "Inventory Listing"
   LPRINT
   LPRINT "Part No.", "Quantity", "Price", "Description"
   LPRINT "--------", "--------", "-----", "-----------"

' Read the inventory, one DATA line at a time
ReadIt:
   READ part.no$, price, quantity, desc$
   IF (price = -99) THEN GOTO NoMore    ' If just read last
                                        ' record, quit
```

```
   LPRINT part.no$, quantity, price, desc$
   GOTO ReadIt      ' Get another inventory record

DATA "10112", 10.95, 13, "Widget"
DATA "21943", 14.78, 2, "Metal Wire #4"
DATA "38745", 10.91, 10, "Bolt Clip"
DATA "44335", 17.64, 43, "Fastener"
DATA "44336", 17.64, 56, "Long Fastener"
DATA "-99", -99, -99, "-99"

NoMore:
   INPUT "Do you want another copy (Y/N)"; ans$
   IF (ans$ = "N") THEN GOTO EndIt    ' User wants to quit

' Control gets to here only if user wants to see another
' report
RESTORE
LPRINT CHR$(12)   ' Print a form feed to ready a blank page in
                  ' printer
GOTO PrintRep   ' Re-do entire report
EndIt:
   END
```

Summary

READ and DATA statements are not good for extremely large amounts of data. You will eventually store large amounts of data in data files on the disk. You will also learn to read a line of data from a file rather than from DATA statements.

In many programs, you find READ and DATA statements that initialize several variables toward the top of the code. Instead of typing several assignment statements, QBasic programmers usually prefer to initialize variables with READ and DATA because the variable initialization takes up fewer lines of code than assignment statements do. The book management system in Appendix E uses this method to initialize some variables.

This chapter completes Part III, "Input/Output." Now that you know several ways to get values into variables, you are ready to add more power to your programs with Part IV, "Control Statements."

Review Questions

Answers to the Review Questions are in Appendix B.

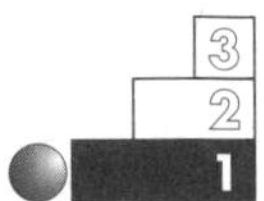

1. TRUE or FALSE: You must list one or more variable names after the word DATA in a DATA statement.

2. Write two QBasic statements to read a customer number, store it in cust.num$, and read a customer balance into cust.balance.

3. Are the following pairs of statements equivalent?

```
READ amt, charge
DATA 13.45, 10.00
```

```
amt = 13.45
LET charge = 10.00
```

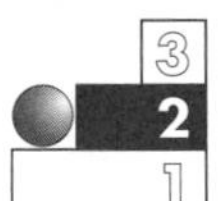

4. What is the purpose of the trailer data record?

5. Write a trailer data record for the following DATA statements:

```
DATA "Barney", "Male", 16
DATA "Julia", "Female, 18
DATA "Mary", "Female, 19
DATA "Joseph", "Male", 17
```

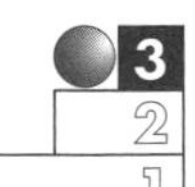

6. When the following section of a QBasic program finishes, what value will be in S?

```
READ Q
READ R, S
READ T, U, V
DATA 13, 43, 6
DATA 73, 2
DATA 25
```

7. How can you force QBasic to reread DATA statements?

8. What is the error in the following section of code?

```
READ emp.name$, emp.id, emp.salary
DATA "Larry Hannah", "10221", 32454.50
```

9. What error occurs in the following program?

```
Again:
   READ a, b, c
   PRINT a, b, c
   DATA 10, 20, 30
   GOTO Again
```

10. In an effort to fix the program in the preceding exercise, a programmer changed it to this:

```
Again:
   READ a, b, c
   PRINT a, b, c
   DATA 10, 20, 30
   RESTORE
   GOTO Again
```

Does the program still have a problem? If so, what is it?

Review Exercises

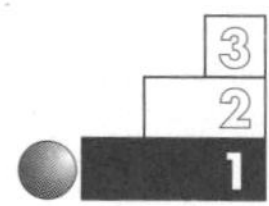

1. Write a READ and DATA statement that reads two names, two ages, and two weights into six variables. Print the data. Be sure the data types of the variables match the data.

2. Write a program for a coin collector that reads data for ten rare coins and prints it out. Keep track of the name, nationality, date, and value of each coin. Make sure you include a trailer data record in case the user wants to add more coins to this small collection.

3. Add to the program in Exercise 2 so that it prints a report to the printer and totals up the amount of the denominations of each coin.

4. Keep track of a health club's member information in DATA statements. Read each member's name, sex, and age into variables, and print them either to the screen or to the printer depending on what the user requests. When finished, ask the user whether he or she wants to see the data again. If so, RESTORE the DATA statements and repeat the reading and printing.

Part IV

Control Statements

13

FOR-NEXT **Loops**

The repetitive ability of the computer makes it a good tool for processing large amounts of information. The GOTO provided one method of repeating a group of statements, but you saw that endless loops can occur if you don't use the GOTO with care. GOTO can also make programs difficult to follow. For these reasons, there are better ways to repeat sections of your programs than using GOTO statements.

LOOP: A repeated circular execution of one or more statements.

The FOR and NEXT statements offer a way to repeat sections of your program conditionally. They create a *loop,* which is the repeated circular execution of one or more statements. The FOR-NEXT loop is a control structure that repeats a section of code a certain number of times. When that number is reached, execution continues to the next statement in sequence. This chapter focuses on the FOR-NEXT loop construct by introducing

- The FOR statement
- The NEXT statement
- Nested FOR-NEXT loops
- The EXIT FOR statement

The FOR-NEXT loop is just one of the many ways to loop through sections of code. Chapter 14, "The WHILE-WEND Loop, the DO Loop, and the EXIT DO Statement," introduces you to other looping commands.

The FOR and NEXT Statements

The FOR and NEXT statements always appear in pairs. If your program has one or more FOR statements, it will have the same number of NEXT statements. FOR and NEXT enclose one or more QBasic statements that form the loop; the statements between FOR and NEXT repeat a certain number of times. The programmer controls the number of times the loop repeats.

The format of the FOR statement is

```
FOR counter = start TO end [STEP increment]
```

The *counter* is a numeric variable that you supply. This variable is important to the FOR loop. It helps control the body of the loop (the statements between FOR and NEXT). The *counter* variable is initialized to the value of *start* before the first iteration of the loop. The *start* value typically is 1, but it can be any numeric value (or variable) you specify. Every time the body of the loop repeats, the *counter* variable increments or decrements by the value of the *increment*. If you do not specify a STEP value, the FOR statement assumes an *increment* of 1.

The value of *end* is a number (or variable) that controls the end of the looping process. When *counter* is equal to or greater than *end*, QBasic does not repeat the loop, but instead continues at the statement following NEXT.

The NEXT statement is QBasic's way of ending the loop. The NEXT statement is the signal to QBasic that the body of the FOR loop is finished. If the *counter* variable is less than the *end* variable, QBasic increments the *counter* variable by the value of *increment*, and the body of the loop repeats again.

The format of the NEXT statement is

```
NEXT [counter] [, counter2] [, counterN]
```

Although the *counter* variable is optional, most programmers specify one. The *counter* variable is the same *counter* variable used at the top of the loop in the FOR statement.

To give you a better feel for the FOR-NEXT loop, the following lines show the combined format of both statements as they might appear in a program with statements between them:

```
FOR counter = start TO end [STEP increment]

   One or more QBasic statements go here

NEXT [counter] [, counter2] [, counterN]
```

The Concept of FOR Loops

You use the concept of FOR loops in your daily life. Any time you have to repeat a certain procedure a specified number of times, the procedure is a good candidate for a computerized FOR loop.

To further illustrate the concept of a FOR loop, suppose you are putting 10 new shutters on your house.

For each shutter, you must complete the following steps:

Move the ladder to the location of the next shutter.
Take a shutter, a hammer, and nails up the ladder.
Nail the shutter to the side of the house.
Climb down the ladder.

You must perform each of these four steps exactly 10 times because you have 10 shutters. After 10 times, you don't put up another shutter because the job is finished. You are looping through a procedure that has four steps. These four steps are the body of the loop. It is certainly not an endless loop, because there are a fixed number of shutters; you run out of shutters after 10.

For a less physical example that might be more easily computerized, suppose you have to complete a tax return for each of your three teenage children. (If you have three teenage children, you probably need more than a computer to help you get through the day!)

For each child, you must complete the following steps:

Add the total income.
Add the total deductions.
Complete a tax return.
Put it in an envelope.
Mail it.

You must repeat this procedure two more times.

Notice that the sentence before these steps began like this: "For each child...." This signals a structure similar to the FOR loop.

Examples

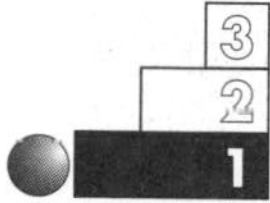

1. To give you a glimpse of the FOR-NEXT loop's capabilities, listings 13.1 and 13.2 show you programs that do and do not contain FOR-NEXT loops. The first one is a counting program. Before reading the description of its contents, look at the program and its output in Figure 13.1. The results speak for themselves and illustrate the FOR-NEXT loop well.

Listing 13.1. Program with FOR-NEXT statements.

```
FOR ctr = 1 to 10
   PRINT ctr
NEXT ctr
```

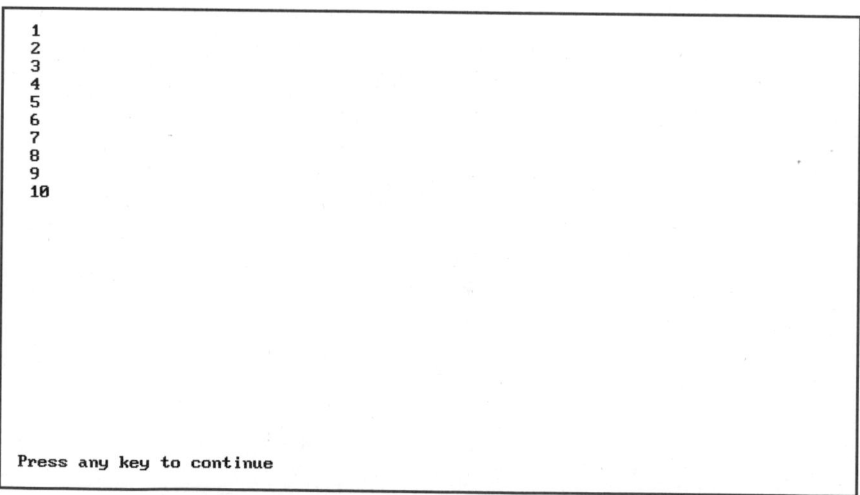

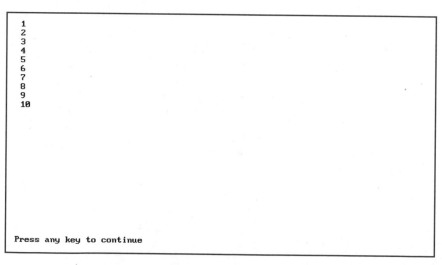

Figure 13.1. A counting routine using FOR and NEXT.

Listing 13.2. The same program without FOR-NEXT statements.

```
ctr = 1
Again:
   IF (ctr > 10) THEN GOTO EndIt
   PRINT ctr
   ctr = ctr + 1      ; Add 1 to count
   GOTO Again
EndIt:
   END
```

Notice that the FOR-NEXT loop is a much cleaner way of controlling the looping process than an IF and GOTO. The FOR-NEXT statements do several things that you used to have to write extra statements to do. The FOR statement initializes ctr to 1 (because 1 was the starting value). Everything in the body of the loop (in this case, just the PRINT statement) executes. Finally, the counter variable ctr gets incremented by 1 automatically. As long as ctr is not more than 10 (the end value), the body of the loop repeats again.

Without FOR-NEXT, not only do you have to write extra code that is more difficult to follow, but you are forced to use the GOTO statement. FOR-NEXT enables you to control the looping much more cleanly and eliminates the messy GOTO.

2. The example programs in listings 13.3 and 13.4 add the numbers from 100 to 200. Listing 13.3 uses a FOR-NEXT loop, whereas Listing 13.4 does not. The first example shows how adding a start value other than 1 starts the loop with a bigger counter variable.

Listing 13.3. A program with FOR-NEXT statements.

```
total = 0
FOR ctr = 100 to 200       ' Loop goes 100, 101, 102, ..., 200
  total = total + ctr      ' Add value of ctr each iteration
NEXT ctr
PRINT "The total is"; total
```

Listing 13.4. The same program without FOR-NEXT statements.

```
total = 0           ' Initialize total
num = 100           ' Starting value
AddIt:
   total = total + num
   num = num + 1    ' Increment num
   IF (num<=200) THEN GOTO AddIt    ' Keep looking while num<=200
```

Although the FOR loop (and the equivalent program) adds the numbers through 200, the body of the loop in both programs executes only 100 times. The starting value is 100, not 1 as in the previous example.

Notice how the body of the FOR-NEXT loop is indented. Indenting is a good habit to develop; it makes the beginning of the loop (the FOR) and the end of the loop (the NEXT) easier to find. The indentation has no effect on the loop's execution.

This is the last example that compares a program with a FOR-NEXT loop to an equivalent program without FOR-NEXT statements.

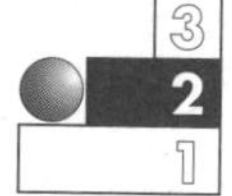

3. The body of the FOR-NEXT loop certainly can have more than one statement. The following example reads and prints the five pairs of data values. Notice that no trailer data record is required. Because there are five pairs of data values, the FOR-NEXT loop ensures that the READ does not read past the last data value.

```
' Filename: C13DATAF.BAS
'
' Program that reads and prints data values inside a loop.

CLS
PRINT "Name", "Age"
FOR ctr = 1 to 5          ' ctr is not used, except to control
                          ' the number of iterations
   READ child.name$
   READ child.age
```

```
   PRINT child.name$, child.age
NEXT

DATA "Susie", 6, "Bob", 8, "Jane", 10, "Tim", 7, "Joe", 9
```

Reading and printing this data within a FOR-NEXT loop makes for a much more readable program.

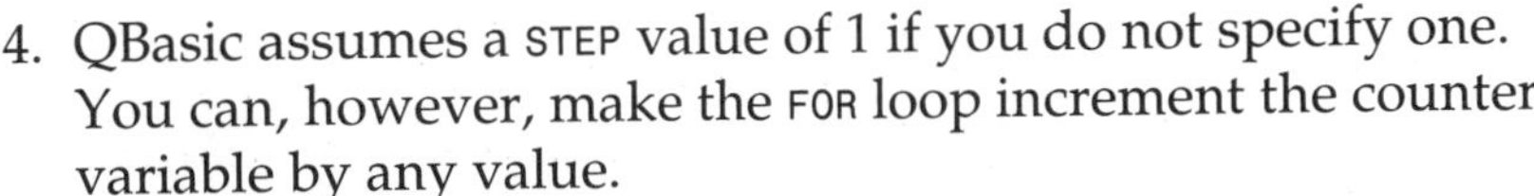

4. QBasic assumes a STEP value of 1 if you do not specify one. You can, however, make the FOR loop increment the counter variable by any value.

   The following program prints the even numbers from 1 to 20. It then prints the odd numbers from 1 to 20. To do this, a STEP value of 2 is specified. This ensures that the program adds 2 to the counter variable each time the loop executes, rather than the default of 1 in the previous examples.

```
' Filename: C13EVOD1.BAS
'
' Prints the first few odd and even numbers.

CLS
PRINT "Even numbers below 20"
FOR num = 2 to 20 STEP 2     ' Start at 2 since it's the
                             ' first even number
   PRINT num
NEXT num

PRINT "Odd numbers below 20"
FOR num = 1 to 20 STEP 2
   PRINT num
NEXT num
```

   The first section's start value is 2 rather than 1. If it were 1, the number 1 would print first as it does in the odd number section. There are two loops in this program. The body of each consists of one PRINT statement.

   The CLS and the first PRINT are not part of either loop. If they were, the screen would clear and the title would print before each number printed. Figure 13.2 shows the result of running this program.

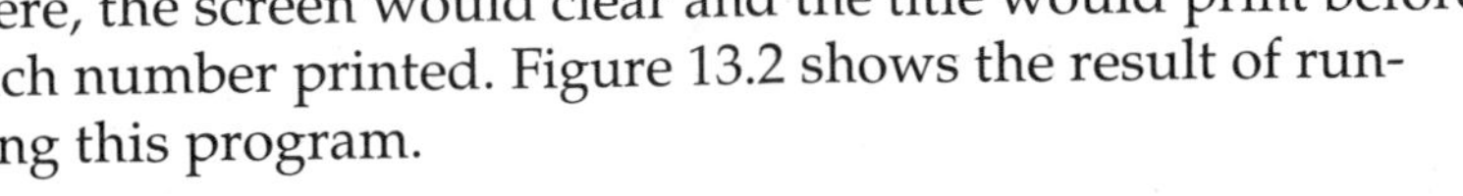

```
Even numbers below 20
 2
 4
 6
 8
 10
 12
 14
 16
 18
 20
Odd numbers below 20
 1
 3
 5
 7
 9
 11
 13
 15
 17
 19


Press any key to continue
```

Figure 13.2. Printing even and odd numbers.

NOTE: The STEP value can also be negative. If it is, that value is subtracted from the counter variable each time through the loop.

6. You can combine a FOR-NEXT loop with READ-DATA statements and eliminate the trailer data record. This adds to the flexibility of READ-DATA in some cases.

   All you have to do is make sure the first DATA value is the total number of DATA values that follow. For instance, if you were summing up eight students' grades in preparation for finding an average class grade, the DATA statement could look like this:

   ```
   DATA 8, 97, 93.5, 88, 100, 74, 83.5, 63, 90
   ```

   The first DATA value, 8, is the number of DATA values that follow. Many programmers prefer to put the count of DATA values on a line by itself, as in

```
DATA 8
DATA 97, 93.5, 88, 100, 74, 83.5, 63, 90
```

Putting the count on a line by itself makes the value easier to change if you add or remove data from the program. The following program shows how the count can be used. It first reads the number of DATA values, then stores this in a variable used to control the end of the FOR-NEXT loop. You then do not have to check for a trailer record; the READ and DATA quit when the FOR-NEXT loop finishes.

```
' Filename: C13RDFOR.BAS
'
' Processes the number of DATA values specified by the
' first READ.

total.grade = 0          ' Initialize a total grade variable
CLS
READ total.data          ' Read the total number of DATA values
                         ' that follow
FOR ctr = 1 TO total.data     ' Process total.data times
                              ' through loop
   READ stud.grade
   total.grade = total.grade + stud.grade
NEXT ctr

' Compute average
class.avg = total.grade / total.data
PRINT "The class average is"; class.avg

DATA 8
DATA 97, 93.5, 88, 100, 74, 83.5, 63, 90
```

Neither the total nor the average calculations has to be changed if the data changes. If more students join the class, you simply add their DATA values (their scores) to the end of the list of DATA and increase the `total.data` value (the first DATA value) by the number of extra students.

Other FOR-NEXT Options

A couple of other options are available with the FOR-NEXT loop. The variable name after NEXT is optional; you do not have to specify it. QBasic realizes that every FOR statement in your program requires a NEXT statement. Therefore, whenever QBasic encounters a NEXT without a variable, it already knows that the NEXT is the conclusion to the loop started with the last FOR statement. A few programs in the "Examples" section later in this chapter show this.

TIP: Although the NEXT variable is optional, good programmers always specify one. QBasic does not require the variable; however, using it makes your program clearer to those who have to make changes to the program later (including you).

Another feature of FOR-NEXT loops is the ability to change the counter, start, end, or increment value within the body of the loop. As you saw in the previous examples, the execution of the FOR-NEXT loop automatically changes the counter variable, but you can do this also within the loop. Some people set up a FOR-NEXT loop and then insert an IF statement within the body of the loop. Depending on the result of the IF, they might change one or more of the controlling variables of the FOR-NEXT loop.

The FOR-NEXT loop also changes these variables. In other words, if you change the counter variable within the loop, QBasic still adds the increment to that variable's new value on the next iteration of the loop. This makes for some awful debugging sessions if you do not change the variables properly. It sounds complicated, and it is. Here's a general rule to remember:

TIP: Never change the counter, start, stop, or increment values within the body of a FOR-NEXT loop. Let the FOR-NEXT take care of them. Use separate variables inside the loop.

Examples

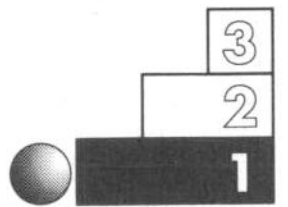

1. The following programs are rewritten versions of two you saw previously. The first program is a revision of the program that printed the numbers from 1 to 10; the second is a revision of the odd and even program. The only difference between these programs and their counterparts is that no variable is specified after the `NEXT` statement. QBasic knows to match each `NEXT` with its preceding `FOR` counter variable.

   ```
   FOR ctr = 1 to 10
      PRINT ctr
   NEXT                        ' No variable specified
   ```

   The last line of this program could have read

   ```
   NEXT ctr
   ```

   instead.

   ```
   ' Filename: C13EVOD2.BAS
   '
   ' Prints the first few odd and even numbers.

   CLS
   PRINT "Even numbers below 20"
   FOR num = 2 to 20 STEP 2     ' Start at 2 since it's the
                                ' first even number
      PRINT num
   NEXT       ' No variable specified

   PRINT "Odd numbers below 20"
   FOR num = 1 to 20 STEP 2
      PRINT num
   NEXT       ' No variable specified
   ```

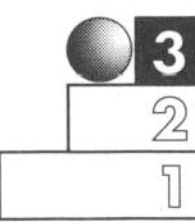

2. The following program does nothing except show how the `FOR` loop control variables can be changed in the body of the loop. Trace the result of the program, which is shown in Figure 13.3, to see how the results generate. The program is difficult to follow, so be cautious about changing any of the control variables in the body of the loop.

```
' Filename: C13FORVR.BAS
'
' Program that changes the FOR loop control variables.

start.var = 15
end.var = 30
step.var = 2

CLS
FOR ctr = start.var TO end.var STEP step.var
   PRINT ctr
   ctr = ctr + 1    ' Even though STEP value is 2, add 1 to
                    ' make ctr increment
   end.var = end.var - 1      ' Each time through the loop,
                              ' change the ending
NEXT ctr
```

There are a couple of points to note. The loop's controlling values are all variables: `start.var`, `end.var`, and `step.var`. The previous examples had constants for these values.

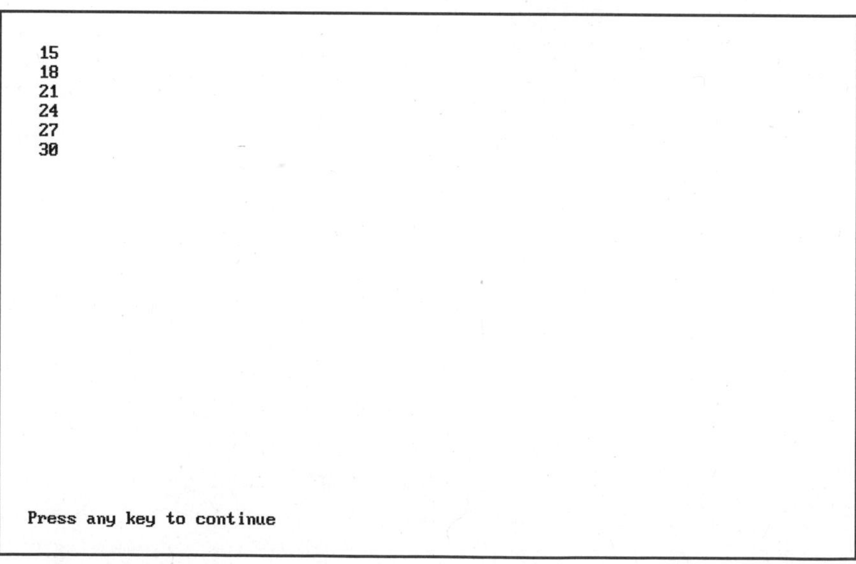

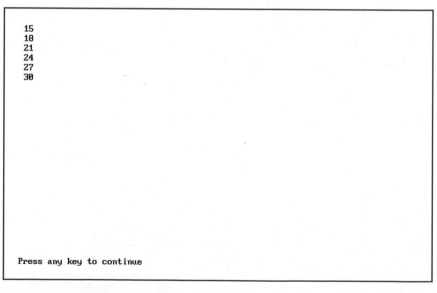

Figure 13.3. The program output when you change control values within the body of the loop.

The programming task dictates whether you use variables or constants or a mixture of both. This program does not have any "real world" application; if you were asking the user how many checks to process or how many grades to average, however, you would want to use variables in the FOR statement so that it loops only as many times as the user requests.

If you try to follow the output, you realize that the program appears to decrease the end.var each time through the loop. The loop starts out as 30. Because the loop decrements each time through the loop, you would think the FOR statement would finish long before ctr got the 30; however, it does not.

NOTE: QBasic looks at the start, end, and step values only *once.* If you change the values of these variables in the loop, the loop acts as though the original values are in effect.

The only variable you can change within a FOR loop that actually changes the execution of the FOR loop is the counter variable. Changing a FOR loop's variables can lead to so many confusing programs that you should stay away from modifying any of the FOR loop variables within the body of the loop.

Nested FOR-NEXT Loops

NESTED LOOP: A loop within a loop.

Any QBasic statement can go inside the body of a FOR-NEXT loop—even another FOR-NEXT loop. When you put a loop within a loop, you create *nested loops.* The clock in a sporting event works like a nested loop. The clock at a football game counts down from 15 minutes to 0 minutes for each of four quarters. The first countdown is a loop from 15 to 0 (for each minute). That loop is nested within another loop that counts from 1 to 4 (for each of the four quarters).

Any program that needs to repeat a loop more than once is a good candidate for a nested loop. Figure 13.4 shows the outlines of two nested loops. You can think of the inside loop as looping "faster" than the outside loop. In the first example, the FOR loop that counts from 1 to 5 is the inside loop. It loops fastest because the variable inner goes from 1 to 5 before the outside loop, the variable outer, finishes its first iteration. Because the outside loop does not repeat until the NEXT outer statement, the inside FOR loop has a chance to finish in its entirety. When the outside loop finally iterates a second time, the inside loop starts all over again.

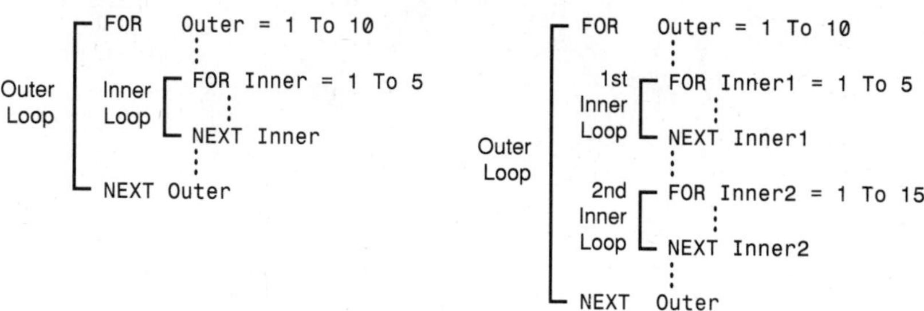

Figure 13.4. Outlines of two nested loops.

The second nested loop outline shows two loops within an outside loop. Both of these inner loops execute in their entirety before the outside loop finishes its first iteration. When the outside loop starts its second iteration, the two inside loops repeat again.

Notice the order of the NEXT variables in each example. The inside loop *always* finishes, and therefore its NEXT has to come before the outside loop's NEXT variable. Figure 13.5 shows the incorrect order of NEXT statements. The "outside" loop in each example finishes before either of the "inside" loops. This does not fit the description of nested loops.

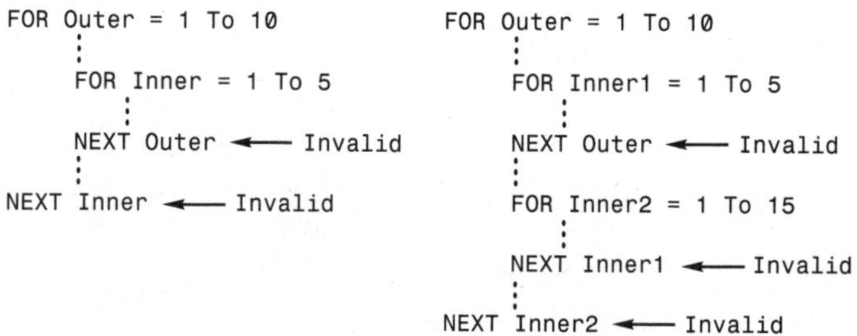

Figure 13.5. Two incorrect nested loops.

> **NOTE:** To sum up nested loops, follow this rule of thumb: In nested loops, the order of the NEXT variables should be the opposite of the order of the FOR variables. This gives the inside loop (or loops) a chance to complete before the outside loop's next iteration.

Nested loops become important later when you use them for array and matrix processing, described later in the book.

Examples

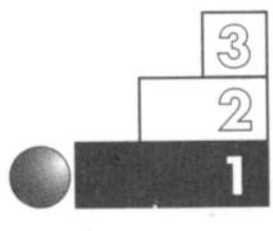

1. The following program contains a loop within a loop—a nested loop.

   The inside loop counts and prints from 1 to 5. The outside loop counts from 1 to 3. Therefore, the inside loop repeats in its entirety three times. In other words, this program prints the values 1 to 5 and does so three times.

```
' Filename: C13NEST1.BAS
'
' Prints numbers from 1 to 10 five times using a nested
' loop.

CLS
FOR times = 1 TO 3          ' Outside loop
   FOR num = 1 TO 5         ' Inside loop
      PRINT num
   NEXT num
NEXT times
```

   Notice that the inside loop that prints from 1 to 5 repeats three times. Figure 13.6 shows the result of running this program. The indention also maintains the standard for FOR loops; every statement in each loop is indented three spaces. Because the inside loop is already indented, its body is indented three more spaces.

```
1
2
3
4
5
1
2
3
4
5
1
2
3
4
5





Press any key to continue
```

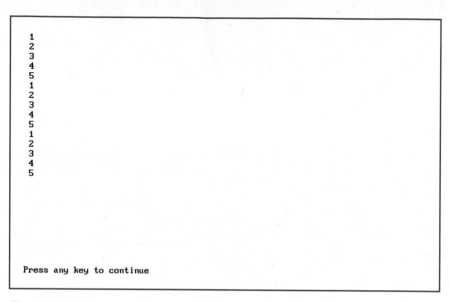

Figure 13.6. Running the nested loop.

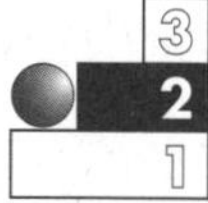

2. The outside loop's counter variable changes each time through the loop. If one of the inside loop's control variables is the outside loop's counter variable, you see an effect such as that shown in the following program.

```
' Filename: C13NEST2.BAS
'
' An inside loop controlled by the outer loop's counter
' variable.

CLS
FOR outer = 5 TO 1 STEP -1
   FOR in = 1 TO outer
      PRINT in;       ' The semicolon forces the next
                      ' number next to this one
   NEXT in
   PRINT         ' Print a blank line--this forces cursor to
                 ' next line
NEXT outer
```

Figure 13.7 shows the output from this program. The inside loop repeats five times (as `outer` counts down from 5 to 1) and prints the numbers from 5 to 1.

```
1  2  3  4  5
1  2  3  4
1  2  3
1  2
1

Press any key to continue
```

Figure 13.7. An inside loop controlled by an outside loop's counter variable.

Table 13.1 shows the two variables being traced through the program. Sometimes you have to "play computer" when you are learning a new concept such as nested loops. By executing one line at a time and recording each variable's contents, you produce a table like Table 13.1.

Table 13.1. Tracing C13NEST2.BAS' output.

Variable `outer`	*Values* `in`
5	1
5	2
5	3
5	4
5	5
4	1
4	2
4	3

continues

Table 13.1. continued

Variable `outer`	*Values* `in`
4	4
3	1
3	2
3	3
2	1
2	2
1	1

> **Tip for Mathematicians**
>
> The `FOR` statement is similar to the mathematical summation symbol. Actually, when you write programs to simulate the summation symbol, the `FOR` statement is an excellent candidate. A nested `FOR` statement is good for double summations.
>
> For example, the summation
>
> $$\sum_{i=1}^{i=30} (i / i * 2)$$
>
> can be rewritten as:
>
> ```
> total = 0
> FOR i = 1 TO 30
>    total = total + (i / i * 2)
> NEXT i
> ```

The EXIT FOR Statement

The `FOR-NEXT` loop was designed to execute a loop a specified number of times. There might be rare instances, however, when the `FOR-NEXT` loop should quit before the `FOR`'s counter variable has reached its end value. You can use the EXIT FOR statement to quit a FOR loop early.

The format of EXIT FOR is

```
EXIT FOR
```

Notice that there are no extra parameters; the command consists of the two command names EXIT FOR. Although EXIT FOR can go on a line by itself, it generally does not.

The EXIT FOR statement goes in the body of a FOR loop. EXIT FOR almost always follows the true condition of an IF test. If the EXIT FOR is on a line by itself, the loop quits early, defeating the purpose of the FOR-NEXT statements.

Examples

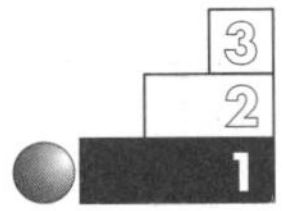

1. The following program shows what can happen if QBasic encounters an unconditional EXIT FOR statement (in other words, one that is not preceded by an IF statement).

```
' Filename: C13EXIT1.BAS
'
' A FOR-NEXT loop defeated by the EXIT FOR statement.

CLS
PRINT "Here are the numbers from 1 to 20"
FOR num = 1 TO 20
   PRINT num
   EXIT FOR      ' Will exit the FOR loop immediately
NEXT num         ' Never gets looked at

PRINT "That's all, folks!"
```

Figure 13.8 shows the result of running this program. Notice that the EXIT FOR immediately terminates the FOR loop before it has gone though one cycle. The FOR-NEXT loop might as well not be in this program.

```
Here are the numbers from 1 to 20
 1
That's all, folks!




Press any key to continue
```

Figure 13.8. A poor use of the EXIT FOR statement.

2. The following program is an improved version of the previous example. It asks users whether they want to see another number. If so, the FOR-NEXT loop continues its next iteration. If not, the EXIT FOR statement terminates the FOR loop.

```
' Filename: C13EXIT2.BAS
'
' A FOR-NEXT loop running at the user's request.

CLS
PRINT "Here are the numbers from 1 to 20"
FOR num = 1 TO 20
   PRINT num
   INPUT "Do you want to see another (Y/N)"; ans$
   IF (ans$ = "N") THEN EXIT FOR    ' Will exit the FOR loop
                                    ' if user wishes
NEXT num         ' Never gets looked at

PRINT "That's all, folks!"
```

Figure 13.9 shows a sample run of this version. The FOR-NEXT loop prints 20 numbers as long as the user types *Y*. Otherwise the EXIT FOR takes over and terminates the FOR loop early. The statement after NEXT always executes next if the EXIT FOR occurs.

```
Here are the numbers from 1 to 20
 1
Do you want to see another (Y/N)? Y
 2
Do you want to see another (Y/N)? Y
 3
Do you want to see another (Y/N)? Y
 4
Do you want to see another (Y/N)? Y
 5
Do you want to see another (Y/N)? Y
 6
Do you want to see another (Y/N)? Y
 7
Do you want to see another (Y/N)? N
That's all, folks!




Press any key to continue
```

Figure 13.9. A better use of the EXIT FOR statement.

If you nest one loop inside another, the EXIT FOR terminates the "most active" loop. In other words, it terminates the innermost loop in which the EXIT FOR resides.

The *conditional* EXIT FOR (an IF followed by an EXIT FOR) is sometimes good for missing data. When you start processing data files or large amounts of user data-entry, you might expect 100 input numbers and get only 95. If this happens, you could use an EXIT FOR to terminate the FOR-NEXT loop before it cycles through its 96th iteration.

Summary

This chapter taught you how to control loops. As opposed to the tendency of GOTO loops to get out of hand, the FOR-NEXT loop enables you to control the number of iterations made. All FOR-NEXT loops contain three parts: a starting value, an ending value, and the step value.

Several other types of loops are possible in QBasic. Chapter 14 shows you other ways to control a loop, primarily with the DO loop.

Review Questions

Answers to the Review Questions are in Appendix B.

1. What is a loop?
2. What statement must always appear with the FOR statement in a program?
3. What is a nested loop?

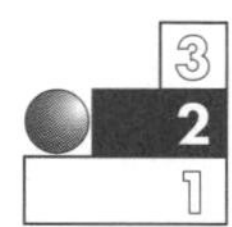

4. If you do not specify a STEP value, what value does QBasic assume?
5. Which loop "moves fastest": the inner loop or the outer loop?
6. What is the output from the following program?

```
FOR ctr = 10 TO 1 STEP -3
   PRINT ctr
NEXT
```

7. TRUE or FALSE: A FOR-NEXT loop is good to use when you know in advance exactly how many iterations a loop requires.

8. What happens when the counter variable becomes larger than the end variable in a FOR-NEXT statement?
9. TRUE or FALSE: The following program contains a valid nested loop:

```
FOR i = 1 TO 10
   FOR j = 1 to 5
      PRINT i, j
   NEXT i
NEXT j
```

10. What is the output of the following program?

```
start.val = 1
end.val = 5
step.val = 1

FOR i = start.val TO end.val STEP step.val
   PRINT i
   end.val = end.val - 1
   step.val = step.val + 1
NEXT i
```

Review Exercises

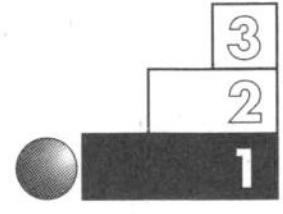

1. Write a program that prints the numbers from 1 to 15 on the screen. Use a FOR-NEXT loop to control the printing.
2. Write a program to print the values from 15 to 1 on the screen. Use a FOR-NEXT loop to control the printing.

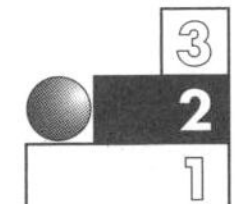

3. Write a program that uses a FOR-NEXT loop to print every odd number from 1 to 100.
4. Write a program that asks users for their age. Use a FOR-NEXT loop to print "Happy Birthday!" for every year of the age.
5. Change the program in the preceding exercise to ask users whether they want to see the message again. (Some people don't like to be reminded of their birthdays.) Use an EXIT FOR to do this.

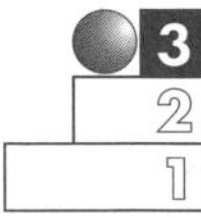

6. Write a program that uses a FOR-NEXT loop to print the ASCII characters from 32 to 255 on the screen. Hint: Use the CHR$ function with the FOR loop's counter variable inside the CHR$'s parentheses.

7. Using the ASCII table in Appendix A and the CHR$ function, write a program to print the following output using a nested FOR-NEXT loop:

```
A
AB
ABC
ABCD
ABCDE
```

Hint: The outside loop should loop from 1 to 5. The inside loop's start variable should be 65 (the value of ASCII *A*).

14

The WHILE-WEND Loop, the DO Loop, and the EXIT DO Statement

The combined FOR and NEXT statements are only one way to control a loop. Although a FOR-NEXT loop is great for loops that must execute a specific number of times, the WHILE-WEND and DO loops let your program execute a loop as long as (or until) a certain true-false condition is met.

This chapter shows you several ways to program a loop by introducing

- The WHILE-WEND loop
- The DO WHILE-LOOP loop
- The DO-LOOP WHILE loop
- The DO UNTIL-LOOP loop
- The DO-LOOP UNTIL loop
- The EXIT DO statement

After completing this chapter, you will know every command QBasic offers to control the execution of a loop. This chapter is relatively short; when you understand the nature of loops, the DO loops are easy.

The WHILE-WEND Loop

The WHILE and WEND statements operate in pairs, just as the FOR and NEXT statements do. You never see a WHILE statement in a program without a WEND following it somewhere later. The WHILE and WEND statements enclose a repeating loop, just as the FOR and NEXT statements do. Unlike the FOR-NEXT loop, however, the WHILE-WEND loop is controlled by a relational test and not by a specified number of iterations.

The format of the WHILE-WEND is

```
WHILE relational test

   One or more QBasic statements

WEND
```

You can put one or more statements between WHILE and WEND. Because WHILE and WEND enclose a loop, indent the body of the loop as you did with the FOR-NEXT loop.

The body of the WHILE-WEND loop executes repeatedly as long as the relational test is true.

The *relational test* is any relational or compound relational test. You can use the same types of tests you used with the IF statement. As long as the relational test is *true,* the WHILE-WEND loop repeats (the body of the loop executes).

This implies that the body of the loop *must* modify one of the variables being tested in the *relational test;* otherwise, the loop will repeat indefinitely. Also, the loop does not execute even once if the relational test is false to begin with. Later in this chapter, you will see a loop that always executes at least once. As with most statements, examples should help clarify the WHILE-WEND loop considerably.

Examples

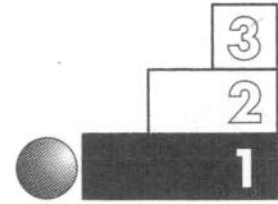

1. The following program checks the user's input to make sure Y or N was entered. Unlike a FOR-NEXT loop, the WHILE loops as long as the *relational test* is true.

```
' Filename: C14WHIL1.BAS
'
' Input routine used to ensure user types a correct
' response.
' This routine might be part of a larger program.

CLS
INPUT "Do you want to continue (Y/N)"; ans$
WHILE ((ans$ <> "Y") AND (ans$ <> "N"))
   BEEP
   PRINT "You must type a Y or an N"
   PRINT
   INPUT "Do you want to continue (Y/N)"; ans$
WEND   ' The input routine quits when user types Y or N
```

Notice that there are two INPUT statements that do the same thing. An initial INPUT outside the WHILE loop must be done to get an answer that the WHILE loop can check for. If the user types something other than Y or N, the program prints an error message, asks for another answer, and loops back to check the answer again. This method of data-entry validation is preferred to the IF-THEN-GOTO process.

The WHILE-WEND loop tests for the relational condition at the top of the loop. That is why the loop might never execute; if the test is initially false, the loop does not execute even once. Figure 14.1 shows the output from this program. The program repeats indefinitely until the relational test is true (until the user types either a Y or an N).

Because the WHILE-WEND executes until the test is true, it is known as an *indeterminate loop* because you do not know in advance how many cycles of the loop will be made (unlike with the FOR-NEXT loop).

```
Do you want to continue (Y/N)? h
You must type a Y or an N

Do you want to continue (Y/N)? no
You must type a Y or an N

Do you want to continue (Y/N)? N




Press any key to continue
```

Figure 14.1. Checking user input with WHILE-WEND.

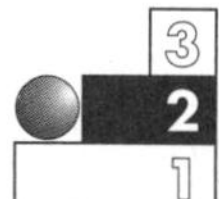

2. The following program is an example of an *invalid* WHILE loop. See whether you can find the problem.

```
A = 10
B = 20
WHILE (A > 5)
   PRINT A, B
   B = B - 1
WEND
```

This WHILE loop is an endless loop. At least one of the statements inside the WHILE statement must change the control variable or the condition will always be true and the WHILE will always loop. Because A does not change inside the WHILE-WEND loop, the program never ends without the user's Ctrl+Break intervention.

The DO Loop

A much more flexible loop is available in QBasic. It is called the DO loop. The DO loop is much like the WHILE-WEND loop except that it allows the relational test to be either true or false; you can loop on either condition. The DO loop can test the relation at the top *or* the bottom of the loop, ensuring that the loop always executes at least once if you want it to.

There are actually several forms of the DO loop. To help illustrate them better, the next sections describe each of four different forms.

The DO WHILE-LOOP

The body of DO WHILE-LOOP might not execute at all.

The DO WHILE-LOOP is similar to the WHILE-WEND. It tests at the top of the loop (implying that the loop might not execute at all), and it tests for a positive relational test. As long as the test is true, the loop executes.

The format of the DO WHILE-LOOP is

```
DO WHILE relational test

   One or more QBasic statements

LOOP
```

As with all the other loops in this chapter, the *relational test* does not have to go in parentheses, but programmers generally put parentheses around the tests. Notice that this is identical to the way the WHILE-WEND works. You should become familiar with the DO WHILE-LOOP because it is similar to the remaining three types of DO loops.

Example

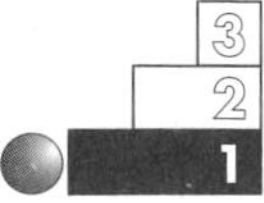

1. The following program is just like the first one you saw for WHILE-WEND, except that it uses a DO WHILE-LOOP set of statements instead. The DO WHILE-LOOP is more flexible than WHILE-WEND, and you should probably get used to using it. QBasic retains the WHILE-WEND only for compatibility with previous versions of BASIC.

```
' Filename: C14WHIL2.BAS
'
' Input routine used to ensure user types a correct
' response.
' This routine might be part of a larger program.

CLS
INPUT "Do you want to continue (Y/N)"; ans$
DO WHILE ((ans$ <> "Y") AND (ans$ <> "N"))
   BEEP
   PRINT "You must type a Y or an N"
   PRINT
   INPUT "Do you want to continue (Y/N)"; ans$
LOOP    ' The input routine quits when user types either
        ' Y or N
```

The DO-LOOP WHILE

The body of DO-LOOP WHILE always executes at least once.

The DO-LOOP WHILE is similar to the DO WHILE-LOOP, except the relational test occurs at the *bottom* of the loop. This ensures that the body of the loop executes at least once. It tests for a positive relational test. As long as the test is true, the body of the loop continues to execute.

The format of the DO-LOOP WHILE is

```
DO

   One or more QBasic statements

LOOP WHILE relational test
```

Checking at the bottom of the loop has its advantages at times. The following examples show this loop in use.

Examples

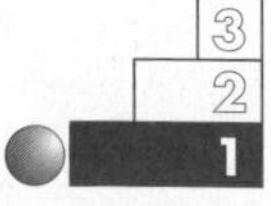

1. The DO-LOOP WHILE lets you make the input-checking routine that was shown earlier a little clearer. Because the body of the loop always executes at least once, you need only one INPUT statement to accomplish the same thing.

```
' Filename: C14WHIL3.BAS
'
' Input routine used to ensure user types a correct response.
' This routine might be part of a larger program.

CLS
INPUT "Do you want to continue (Y/N)"; ans$
IF ((and$ <> "Y") AND (ans$ <> "N")) THEN
   DO
      INPUT "Do you want to continue (Y/N)"; ans$
      BEEP
      PRINT "You must type a Y or an N"
      PRINT
      INPUT "Do you want to continue (Y/N)"; ans$
   LOOP WHILE ((ans$ <> "Y") AND (ans$ <> "N"))
END IF
' The input routine continues until user types Y or N
```

The `INPUT` is not required before the loop starts because it is the first statement in the loop and it always executes at least once. This gives the user a chance to enter the answer. If the answer to the prompt is either `Y` or `N`, the `LOOP` relational test fails (at the bottom of the loop), and the rest of the program continues from there.

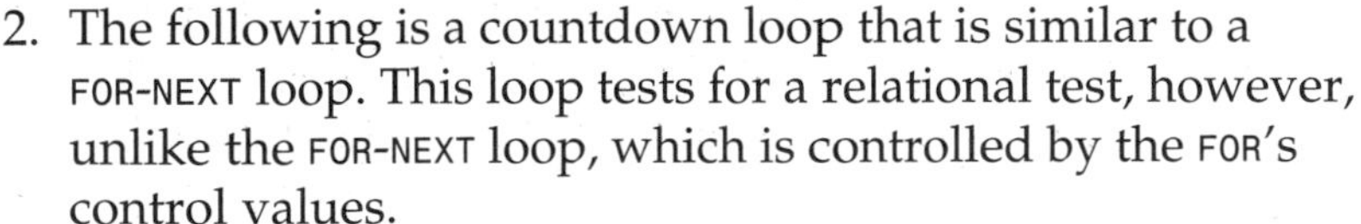

2. The following is a countdown loop that is similar to a `FOR-NEXT` loop. This loop tests for a relational test, however, unlike the `FOR-NEXT` loop, which is controlled by the `FOR`'s control values.

```
' Filename: C14DOCD1.BAS
'
' Countdown program to illustrate DO-LOOP WHILE.

value = 100
CLS
DO
   PRINT value     ' Print each value in the body of the loop
   value = value - 3   ' Decrement value by 3 each time
                       ' through loop
LOOP WHILE (value >= 0)
```

The DO UNTIL-LOOP

The body of the DO UNTIL-LOOP might not execute at all.

The DO UNTIL-LOOP is the first loop statement that cycles through the body of the loop, repeating those statements until the relational test is false.

The format of the DO UNTIL-LOOP is

```
DO UNTIL relational test

   One or more QBasic statements

LOOP
```

The DO UNTIL-LOOP statements check the relational test (for falseness) at the top of the loop. This means that if the condition is false to begin with, the loop never executes.

Examples

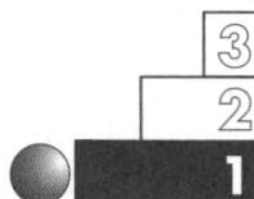

1. Being able to check for a false relational test actually makes the data-validation routine even easier. You can change the "not equal to" symbols to "equal" symbols, making the relational test easier to read, as shown here:

```
' Filename: C14DOUN1.BAS
'
' Input routine used to ensure user types a correct
' response.
' This routine might be part of a larger program.

CLS
INPUT "Do you want to continue (Y/N)"; ans$
DO UNTIL ((ans$ = "Y") OR (ans$ = "N"))
   BEEP
   PRINT "You must type a Y or an N"
   PRINT
   INPUT "Do you want to continue (Y/N)"; ans$
LOOP   ' The input routine quits when user types either Y or N
```

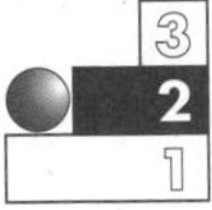

2. The following program requests a list of numbers. As the list of numbers is input, the program adds them to a total and counts them. When the user enters a *0*, the program computes the final total and average. The *0* is not part of the list. It signals the end of input.

   A DO UNTIL-LOOP is used to test the input for the *0*.

```
'Filename: C14DOUN2.BAS
'
' Program that accepts a list of numbers, counts, and
' averages them.
'
total = 0      ' Initialize total and count variables
count = 0

' Get input until a 0 is entered
CLS
INPUT "What is your number (0 will end the input)"; num
DO UNTIL (num = 0)
   total = total + num
   count = count + 1
   INPUT "What is your number (0 will end the input)"; num
LOOP

' Control gets here when user has entered last number
PRINT
PRINT "The total is"; total
PRINT "The average is"; (total / count)
```

   Notice that the program works even if *0* is entered as the first number. The check at the top of the loop, right after the initial INPUT, makes this possible. The INPUT statement also informs the user of the way to end the input. Figure 14.2 shows a sample run of the program.

```
What is your number (0 will end the input)? 45
What is your number (0 will end the input)? 43
What is your number (0 will end the input)? 22
What is your number (0 will end the input)? 56
What is your number (0 will end the input)? 76
What is your number (0 will end the input)? 5
What is your number (0 will end the input)? 0

The total is 247
The average is 41.16667











Press any key to continue
```

Figure 14.2. Using a `DO UNTIL-LOOP` to get user input.

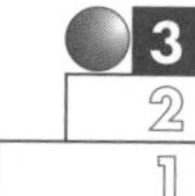

3. The `DO UNTIL-LOOP` can be used also to process `READ-DATA` statements. You previously saw the `IF-THEN` used to test for the trailer data record. The following program reads city names and their average temperatures in the summer. It then prints only those cities with temperatures that average more than 90 degrees.

```
' Filename: C14TEMP1.BAS
'
' Reads city names and temperatures and prints high temp
' cities only.
'
' Initialize screen with titles
CLS
PRINT "List of high temperature cities:"
PRINT
PRINT "City Name"; TAB(20); "Temperature"

READ city$, temp      ' Initial READ to start data checking
DO UNTIL (city$ = "-99")   ' or (temp = -99) would work too!
```

```
   IF (temp > 90) THEN PRINT city$; TAB(20); temp
   READ city$, temp
LOOP   ' The bottom of the cycle

DATA "Memphis", 90, "Miami", 94, "Salem", 86
DATA "Tulsa", 97, "San Francisco", 83, "Dallas", 98
DATA "Bangor", 76, "Juno", 65, "Chicago", 89
DATA "-99", -99
```

Although the DO UNTIL-LOOP reads every data value, only selected values are printed. Figure 14.3 shows the resulting run. If you want to add more city-temperature combinations, put them before the trailer data record. The IF-THEN ensures that only the high-temperature cities are printed. It filters out low-temperature cities from the output.

```
List of high temperature cities:

City Name          Temperature
Miami               94
Tulsa               97
Dallas              98



Press any key to continue
```

Figure 14.3. Displaying only those temperatures over 90 degrees.

The use of DO loops or FOR-NEXT loops to process data values is up to you. Which one you choose to use depends on which one best suits the application. The more comfortable you are with your code, the cleaner it will be, and the easier it will be to maintain in the future.

The DO-LOOP UNTIL

The body of the DO-LOOP UNTIL always executes at least once.

The DO-LOOP UNTIL is another loop statement that cycles through the body of a loop, repeating those statements until the relational test is false. The difference between the DO-LOOP UNTIL and the DO UNTIL-LOOP is the position of the relational test. The DO-LOOP UNTIL tests at the *bottom* of the loop, which means that the loop always executes at least once.

The format of the DO-LOOP UNTIL is

```
DO

   One or more QBasic statements

LOOP UNTIL relational test
```

Examples

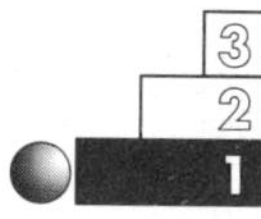

1. The following program is a brief, familiar example of the DO-LOOP UNTIL. It is a revisited version of the blast-off program.

```
' Filename: C14CTDN.BAS
'
' Program to count down to a blast-off using DO-LOOP UNTIL.
'
CLS
count = 10      ' Begin the count...
DO
   PRINT count
   count = count - 1
LOOP UNTIL (count = 0)    ' Do not loop past 1
PRINT "*** Blast off! ***"
```

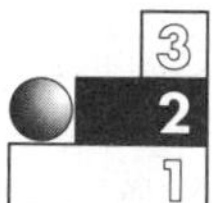

2. The following program is a "poor man's word processor." It accepts lines of input from the keyboard and sends that input to the printer. You can use this simple text-to-printer program to turn your computer into a typewriter.

   Because the lines of input text might contain quotation marks and commas, the LINE INPUT statement is used to capture the input. When the user presses Enter without typing anything, the DO-LOOP UNTIL check fails and the program ends.

```
' Filename: C14TYPE.BAS
'
' Program that loops to get input lines and sends them to
' the printer.
'
CLS
PRINT "Typewriter program."
PRINT "(Make sure your printer is on and has paper.)"

PRINT "Please type your text"
LINE INPUT "?"; text$
DO
   LPRINT text$
   LINE INPUT "?"; text$
LOOP UNTIL (text$ = "") ' Loop stops when user presses Enter
```

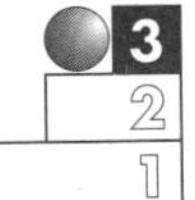

3. A mathematician once found an easy way to approximate the square root of any number. Subtract in succession the odd numbers (1, 3, 5, and so on) from any number. When you reach 0 or less, the square root is the number of subtractions it took to reach 0.

   For example, to find the square root of 49, start subtracting odd numbers until you reach (or go past) 0, as in

   49 - 1 = 48

   48 - 3 = 45

   45 - 5 = 40

   40 - 7 = 33

   33 - 9 = 24

   24 - 11 = 13

   13 - 13 = 0

It took subtracting the first seven odd numbers (1 to 7) to find the square root of *49*. It was *7*.

The following program computes the root of the number specified, using this odd-number subtraction method. Notice the program's use of the `DO-LOOP UNTIL` to count through the odd numbers as it subtracts.

```
' Filename: C14SQRT.BAS
'
' Program to approximate square root by subtracting
' consecutive odd numbers.
'
count = 0     ' Will count the odd numbers used
odd = 1       ' Starting point of odd numbers
CLS
INPUT "What number do you want the square root of"; num
num.save = num    ' You will subtract from entered number,
                  ' so keep a copy
DO
   num = num - odd            ' Subtract next odd number
   odd = odd + 2              ' Get next odd number
   count = count + 1          ' Count number of odd numbers
                              ' used
LOOP UNTIL (num <= 0)         ' Quit when reach zero

IF (num < 0) THEN count = count - 1 ' Went 1 too far if < 0
PRINT "The square root of";num.save;"is approximately"; count
```

The `EXIT DO` Statement

As with the `FOR` loop, there is a way to exit a `DO` loop early; it is with the `EXIT DO` statement. The format of `EXIT DO` is

```
EXIT DO
```

EXIT DO goes inside the body of any of the DO loops. It is usually preceded by the IF statement. As with the EXIT FOR, putting EXIT DO on a line by itself makes the loop unconditionally exit the DO loop, which defeats the purpose of the DO loop.

Example

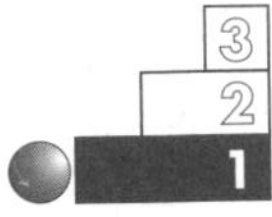

Here is the city high-temperature program, changed to print the values to the printer. Only the first five of the cities with temperatures over 90 degrees are printed. If five are printed, the EXIT DO takes control and forces the end of the DO loop. If the end of the data is reached before five values are printed, the DO loop ends naturally at the DO UNTIL.

```
' Filename: C14TEMP2.BAS
'
' Reads city names and temperatures and prints high temp
' cities only.
'
city.count = 0

' Initialize screen with titles
CLS
PRINT "List of high temperature cities:"
PRINT
PRINT "City Name"; TAB(20); "Temperature"

READ city$, temp      ' Initial READ to start data checking
DO UNTIL (city$ = "-99")  ' or (temp = -99) would work too!
   IF (temp > 90) THEN PRINT city$; TAB(20); temp
   IF (temp > 90) THEN city.count = city.count + 1
   IF (city.count > 4) THEN EXIT DO      ' Quit if five have
                                         ' been printed

   READ city$, temp
LOOP   ' The bottom of the cycle

DATA "Memphis", 90, "Miami", 94, "Salem", 86
DATA "Tulsa", 97, "San Francisco", 83, "Dallas", 98
DATA "Bangor", 76, "Juno", 65, "Chicago", 89
```

```
DATA "New York", 88, "Atlanta", 95, "Burbank", 79
DATA "New Orleans", 93, "Boston", 84, "Phoenix", 98
DATA "-99", -99
```

Figure 14.4 shows that although six cities have temperatures over 90, the program prints only the first five.

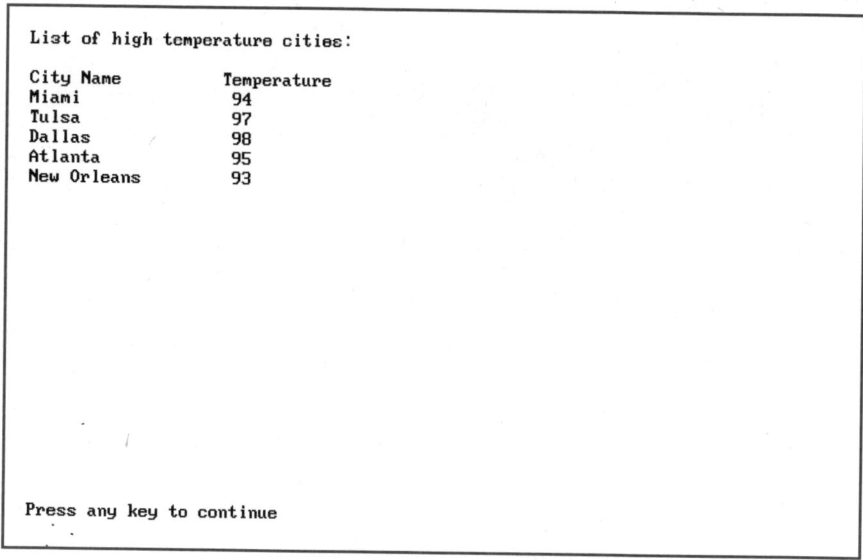

List of high temperature cities:
City Name   Temperature
Miami   94
Tulsa   97
Dallas   98
Atlanta   95
New Orleans   93
Press any key to continue

Figure 14.4. Displaying only the first five temperatures over 90 degrees.

This example also introduces a problem with the IF-THEN statement. Notice that *two* statements (the one that prints the city name and the one that increments the city count) occur every time a city with a high temperature is read. It would be nice if an IF-THEN would let you execute more than one statement if the IF test is true. There is a way to do this. Chapter 15, "The Block IF-THEN-ELSE," shows you how.

Summary

This chapter shows you five more ways to produce a QBasic loop: the WHILE-WEND, DO WHILE-LOOP, DO-LOOP WHILE, DO UNTIL-LOOP, and DO-LOOP UNTIL. The variations of DO loops are more flexible than the

WHILE-WEND because they allow for the testing of different conditions (either true *or* false) and at different places (at the top *or* bottom) of the DO loop. If you ever need to exit early from any of the DO loops, use the EXIT DO.

Chapter 15 expands on the IF-THEN statement.

Review Questions

Answers to the Review Questions are in Appendix B.

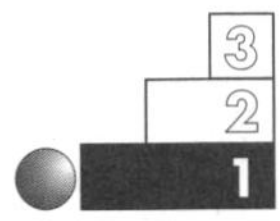

1. TRUE or FALSE: More than one statement can appear in the body of a WHILE-WEND loop.

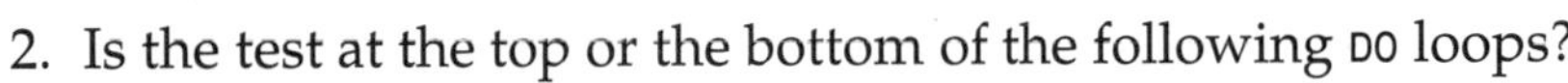

2. Is the test at the top or the bottom of the following DO loops?

   A. DO-LOOP UNTIL
   B. DO UNTIL-LOOP
   C. DO-LOOP WHILE
   D. DO WHILE-LOOP

3. How do the following DO loops determine when to loop, on *True* or *False* conditions?

   A. DO-LOOP UNTIL
   B. DO UNTIL-LOOP
   C. DO-LOOP WHILE
   D. DO WHILE-LOOP

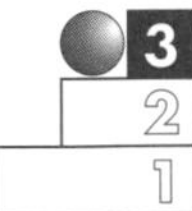

4. How does the test of a DO loop differ from that of a FOR loop?

5. How many times does the body of this loop occur?

```
A = 0
DO WHILE (A > 5)
   PRINT "Careful!"
LOOP
```

6. What is the output of the following program?

```
A = 10
PRINT "Here's the loop:"
DO WHILE (A < 10)
   PRINT "QBasic"
LOOP
```

Review Exercises

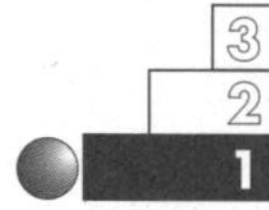

1. Write a program with a WHILE-WEND loop that prints the numbers from 10 to 20 with a blank line between each number.

2. Rewrite the program in the preceding exercise using each of the other four DO loops. Run each of them to ensure that they do not quit one number too early or too late.

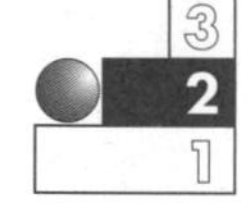

3. Write a program to ask the user for a number from 1 to 10. BEEP the user that many times, using each of the four DO loops.

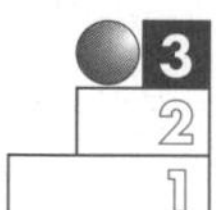

4. Write a program using the DO-LOOP UNTIL that prints the ASCII characters from number 65 to number 90 (these are the uppercase letters A through Z). Immediately following that loop, print the characters backward using a DO WHILE-LOOP statement.

5. Use any of the four DO loops to produce the following pattern of letters:

```
A
AB
ABC
ABCD
ABCDE
```

15

The Block IF-THEN-ELSE

This chapter is one of the most important chapters in the book. It actually teaches you few new statements; however, it shows how you can build on the conditional IF statement to create truly well-written, structured programs. When you sit down to write a program, you should always think about how easy it should be to follow, how little it should jump from place to place, and how well-documented (with ample REM statements) it should be.

This chapter introduces

- Multiple statements on a line
- The ELSE statement
- The block IF-THEN-ELSE
- The ELSEIF statement

Here you learn how to create powerful, but readable, conditional logic that performs complicated decision-making with little effort from you or your program.

Multiple Statements on a Line

You can put more than one QBasic statement on a line by separating the statements with a colon. This has limited use; however, you can use it for variable initializations or for a couple of statements after an IF. Do not overuse the colon. Putting too many statements on one line makes the program unreadable.

Examples

1. The following simple program takes only one statement.

   Print "Hello" on the screen. For 20 times, Print "QBasic".

   ```
   PRINT "Hello" : FOR ctr = 1 TO 20 : PRINT "QBasic" : NEXT ctr
   ```

   This line is a complete program. It is identical to the following four-line program:

   ```
   PRINT "Hello"
   FOR ctr = 1 TO 20
      PRINT "QBasic"
   NEXT ctr
   ```

   Even without remarks, the second version is clearer than the first.

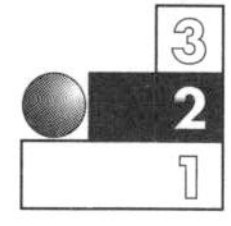

2. The colon statement separator is not always a poor structure and is not necessarily bad to use at times. One common place you might use and see the multiple-line separator is after an IF-THEN statement. The following program shows two QBasic statements being executed after an IF, rather than the single statements you saw in earlier examples.

```
' Filename: C15IF1.BAS
'
' Program that reads and prints high football
' teams and scores (those over 21 points) and
' prints the average of those high scores.

' Initialize total and count variables for average
ac = 0          ' Will hold the number of high scores
total = 0
READ count      ' The first DATA value is the number of
                ' values that follow

' Read one at a time, print them, and add to total
CLS
FOR ctr = 1 TO count

READ team$, score
' Test for high score and use only those over 21
IF (score > 21) THEN PRINT team$:total=total+score:ac=ac+1

NEXT ctr

PRINT
PRINT "The average of the high scores is"; total / ac

DATA 9
DATA "Tigers", 32, "Cyclones", 3, "Centurions", 21
DATA "Pintos", 14, "Stars", 20, "Thunder", 24
DATA "Okies", 56, "Surfers", 7, "Elks", 31
```

Figure 15.1 shows the output from this program. Pay special attention to the IF statement that has three statements following it, separated by colons.

```
Tigers
Thunder
Okies
Elks

The average of the high scores is 35.75









Press any key to continue
```

Figure 15.1. Using the separating colon after an IF.

Styles Come and Go...

When PCs were first gaining popularity in the early 1980s, several magazines and books were written describing these new machines and how to program them. Memory and disk space were at a premium. Compared to today, RAM and disk memory were small and expensive.

Programmers learned to make the most of the small memory by writing compact, tight code that did much in little space. Eventually, such programmers were praised for their wit and insight when magazines started offering prizes for *one-liners,* which are complete programs that do many things in one statement.

To write these one-liners, programmers used the separating colon to its fullest extent. Graphics screens, music, and math puzzles were programmed in a single line. Variable names were kept to single letters, and programmers avoided large constants for the sake of saving space.

> Today, the tide has turned. Programmers have much more room in which to work. The short, quick, and tight one-liners have been replaced by well-documented programs with ample white space and better development. Programs are not constants. The world is forever changing, and programs must be modified to take advantage of those changes. To ensure your future as a programmer, stay away from one-liners and produce well-documented code that does its job well and clearly.

The ELSE Statement

The ELSE statement is always combined with the IF-THEN. This section introduces the ELSE statement by showing you the IF-THEN-ELSE compound statement in its simplest format:

```
IF relational test THEN QBasic statmnt(s) ELSE QBasic statmnt(s)
```

The first part of this statement is identical to the IF-THEN you saw earlier. If the *relational test* is true, the QBasic statement (or statements, if they are separated by colons) following the THEN executes. If the *relational test* is false, however, the QBasic statement (or statements, if they are separated by the semicolon) following the ELSE executes instead.

The simple IF-THEN determines only what happens when the *relational test* is true. The IF-THEN-ELSE determines what happens if the *relational test* is true as well as what happens if the *relational test* is false. Regardless of the outcome, the statement following the IF-THEN-ELSE executes next, unless one of the results of the *relational test* is a GOTO.

The following sidebar describes the nature of the IF-THEN-ELSE.

relational test = true, statement following THEN executes.

relational test = false, statement following ELSE executes.

> **NOTE:** When the relational test is true, the statement following THEN executes.
>
> When the relational test is false, the statement following the ELSE executes.

Examples

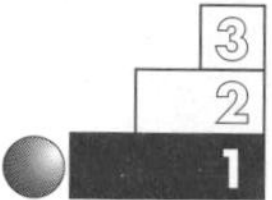

1. The following program asks the user for a number. It then prints a message indicating whether the number is greater than zero, using the IF-THEN-ELSE statement.

```
' Filename: C15IFEL1.BAS
'
' Program demonstrates IF-THEN-ELSE by printing whether
' or not an input value is greater than zero.

CLS
INPUT "What is your number"; num
IF(num>0)THEN PRINT"More than 0"ELSE PRINT"Less or equal to 0"

' No matter what the number was, the following is executed
PRINT : PRINT "Thanks for your time!"
```

The IF-THEN-ELSE can make for long statements, especially if you use the colon to execute more than one statement after THEN, ELSE, or both THEN and ELSE. This is one reason why the IF-THEN-ELSE is best used for simple comparisons.

The last line is an acceptable use of the colon. It separates a blank line PRINT from another PRINT that prints a short closing message. Because this is a simple pair of statements, the colon does not take away from the readability of the line.

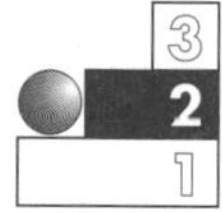

2. The following program is an example of using string variables to determine the way a message gets printed. The program asks for a name. If the name is in the list of club members, a message prints saying so. Otherwise, a message prints saying the person is not a member.

The IF-THEN-ELSE helps build the message string as shown here:

```
' Filename: C15CLUB.BAS
'
' Determines if the input name is a member of the club.
```

```
CLS
INPUT "What is the person's name"; nam$

' Test it against all club members in the DATA
READ members$
DO

IF (nam$ = members$) THEN mess$="is":EXIT DO ELSE mess$="isn't"
   READ members$
LOOP UNTIL (members$ = "-99")

' Build the message string from the result of the IF-THEN-ELSE
message$ = nam$ + " " + mess$ + " " + "in club."
PRINT message$

' Club members' last names
DATA "Johnson", "Smith", "Brown", "Jones", "Murphy", "Wilson"
DATA "Burgess", "Hill", "Grady", "Moore", "Nickles", "Kray"
DATA "-99"
```

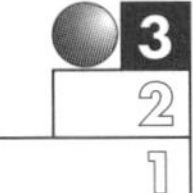

3. The following program uses LOCATE, COLOR, and the IF-THEN-ELSE to print a message on the screen in several colors and at several locations. The IF-THEN-ELSE controls the location of the cursor to keep it within the screen's boundaries.

```
' Filename: C15SCRN.BAS
'
' Fancy screen printing program.

fg = 7             ' Initial foreground color
bg = 0             ' Initial background color
row = 1            ' Initial row to print message
col = 1            ' Initial column to print message
num.prints = 0     ' Number of times message prints
mess$ = "QBasic"   ' The message to print

' Initialize first screen
COLOR fg, bg
CLS
```

```
DO
   LOCATE row, col
   PRINT mess$
   ' Add 1 to col, row, fg, bg, unless they are out of
   ' bounds
   IF (row < 24) THEN row = row + 1 ELSE row = 1
   IF (col < 75) THEN col = col + 1 ELSE col = 1
   IF (fg < 13) THEN fg = fg + 1 ELSE fg = 7
   IF (bg < 6) THEN bg = bg + 1 ELSE bg = 0
   num.prints = num.prints + 1
   COLOR fg, bg                         ' Next color to use
                                        ' for message
LOOP UNTIL (num.prints = 2000)          ' Print for a while
                                        ' and then quit
```

This program knows that the screen has only 25 rows and 80 columns. It makes sure that the row and column being printed to do not go past these boundaries. As long as the row and column values are within this range, the program adds 1 to both of them to ensure that `QBasic` is printed in a different location each time through the loop.

`IF-THEN-ELSE` logic controls the row and column values, as well as the foreground and background colors.

The Block IF-THEN-ELSE

Often you will want to perform several statements if the `IF` test is true. There may also be several statements you want performed if the `ELSE` portion is true. The one-line `IF-THEN-ELSE` statement you just saw was too limiting. Too much code on one line can look squeezed. QBasic offers the block `IF-THEN-ELSE` to get around this problem.

BLOCK: One or more statements treated as though they are a single statement.

In computer terminology, a *block* is generally one or more statements treated as though they are a single statement. The block `IF` is similar. Here is the format of the block `IF-THEN-ELSE`:

```
IF relational test THEN

  A block of one or more QBasic statements
```

```
[ELSE

  A block of one or more QBasic statements]

END IF
```

Notice that the block IF-THEN-ELSE spans more than one line. The QBasic statements between the IF and the ELSE make up the block. The ELSE portion is optional; if you include the ELSE, ELSE also can be followed by one or more QBasic statements.

The following rules hold:

NOTE: If the relational test is true, the block of statements following IF is performed.

If the relational test is false, the block of statements following ELSE is performed.

The block IF-THEN-ELSE statement enables you to create well-structured programs. Instead of a true IF result branching off to a large section of code (with GOTO), you can keep the code near the IF.

Examples

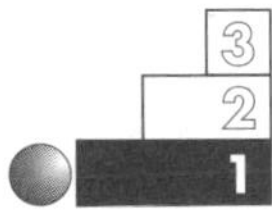

1. The following program is an improvement over some of the input routines you have seen so far. It uses the block IF to test the user's response to a yes-or-no question. You could incorporate this into your own programs just as the book-management database program in the back of the book does.

   If the user answers the yes-or-no question with a *Y* or an *N*, the program completes normally. (You would typically execute certain code depending on the answer.) If, however, the user does not type a *Y* or an *N*, the program prompts for a correct response inside the block.

```
' Filename: C15YN.BAS
'
' Checks the input using the block IF.
```

```
'
CLS

' The following ensures that a proper input was typed
DO
   INPUT "What is your answer (Y/N)"; ans$
   IF ((ans$ <> "Y") AND (ans$ <> "N")) THEN
      BEEP
      PRINT
      PRINT "You must enter a Y or an N!"
      PRINT "Please try again..."
      PRINT
   ELSE
      PRINT "Thank you."
      PRINT
   END IF
LOOP UNTIL ((ans$ = "Y") OR (ans$ = "N"))

' Rest of program would go here
```

Figure 15.2 shows the result of running this program. The user is taking a while to type an *N* or a *Y*. The program keeps looping until the user succeeds in typing a valid response.

Notice the END IF statement. Without it, QBasic would have no idea where the block of statements ends. It knows where the true result's block is because of the ELSE. The false result is not known, however, until the END IF statement.

The indention makes this program very readable without affecting the program's operation. Each time a new block begins, it is preceded by another set of three spaces.

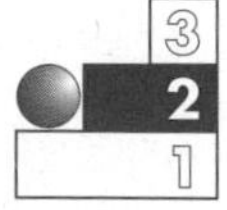

2. Get in the habit of using the block IF-THEN-ELSE, even in situations in which a single-line IF statement would work. Good programmers understand that the block IF-THEN-ELSE adds readability to programs.

   The following program shows this. An earlier program, C15IFEL1.BAS, showed a long, single-line IF-THEN-ELSE statement that told whether an input value was above 0. It was difficult to read because the IF-THEN was squeezed on one line.

```
What is your answer (Y/N)? s

You must enter a Y or an N!
Please try again...

What is your answer (Y/N)? Y
Thank you.











Press any key to continue
```

Figure 15.2. Validating `INPUT` with the block `IF-THEN-ELSE`.

This program simply breaks that line into a block `IF` and adds the `END IF` statement to signal the end of the block. With these two simple changes, the program is already easier to follow.

```
' Filename: C15IFEL2.BAS
'
' Program demonstrates block IF-THEN-ELSE by printing
' whether or not an input value is greater than 0.

CLS
INPUT "What is your number"; num
IF (num > 0) THEN
   PRINT "More than 0"
ELSE
   PRINT "Less or equal to 0"
END IF

' No matter what the number was, the following is executed
PRINT : PRINT "Thanks for your time!"
```

The ELSEIF Statement

The statements following the block IF can be anything. Even another IF statement can go inside the block IF. You also might need to perform another IF statement after the ELSE portion of the block IF. To do this, use an ELSEIF statement.

ELSEIF is actually an extension of the block IF-THEN statement. The format of the complete block IF-THEN-ELSEIF statement is

```
IF relational test THEN

  A block of one or more QBasic statements

[ELSEIF relational test THEN

  A block of one or more QBasic statements]
   [ELSE
     A block of one or more QBasic statements]

END IF
```

The ELSEIF is useful for a number of reasons. A decision can have more than two choices. For instance, you might ask for a *yes, no,* or *maybe* answer to a question. Depending on the outcome, you might want to perform any of three sections of code. As the following examples show, the ELSEIF is just an extension of the block IF statement that simply adds power to an already powerful QBasic command.

TIP: Be sure to type ELSEIF as one word rather than two, as in: ELSE IF. QBasic would think you were starting another block IF-THEN without matching END IF statements.

Examples

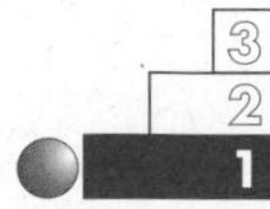

1. Suppose you want to give an annual award to employees based on years of service to your company. You are giving a

gold watch to those with more than 20 years, a paperweight to those with more than 10 years, and a pat on the back to everyone else.

One way to print these messages is with three separate IF statements. Here is one way:

```
' Filename: C15SERV1.BAS
'
' Program to print a message depending on years of service.
'
CLS
INPUT "How many years of service"; yrs

' Test for length of time and print matching message
IF (yrs > 20) THEN
   PRINT "Give a gold watch"
END IF

IF ((yrs > 10) AND (yrs <= 20)) THEN
   PRINT "Give a paperweight"
END IF

IF (yrs <= 10) THEN
   PRINT "Give a pat on the back"
END IF
```

Although these IF statements could have been single-line IFs, the block IF makes the program easier to read and maintain because it breaks the program into sections that are easily separated from the surrounding code.

There is, however, no IF-THEN-ELSEIF in this program. By rewriting the program to take advantage of this new command, you can see that the readability is improved again, as shown here:

```
' Filename: C15SERV2.BAS
'
' Improved program to print a message depending on
' years of service using the block
' IF-THEN-ELSEIF.
'
```

```
CLS
INPUT "How many years of service"; yrs

' Test for length of time and print matching message
IF (yrs > 20) THEN
   PRINT "Give a gold watch"
ELSEIF ((yrs > 10) AND (yrs <= 20)) THEN
   PRINT "Give a paperweight"
ELSEIF (yrs <= 10) THEN
   PRINT "Give a pat on the back"
END IF
```

The ELSEIF dictates what occurs in such a way that more than one decision can be made inside one block IF statement without losing the meaning and ease of readability.

You probably should not rely on the block IF-THEN-ELSEIF to take care of too many conditions, because more than three or four conditions start to get confusing again. (You can get into messy logic, such as *If this is true, and then if this is true, then do something, else if this is true do something, else if this is true do something,* and so on.) The SELECT CASE statement in Chapter 16 handles these types of multiple IF selections better than a long IF-THEN-ELSEIF.

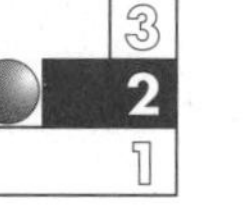

2. The following routine could be used by the book management database application in Appendix E. It asks for an edition of the book and prints an appropriate message to a label on the printer.

```
' Filename: C15BOOK.BAS
'
' Program to print a label for a book's edition.
'
CLS
INPUT "What is the book's edition (1, 2, 3, ...)"; ed

' Print a label based on that number
IF (ed = 1) THEN
   LPRINT "1st Edition"
```

```
ELSEIF (ed = 2) THEN
   LPRINT "2nd Edition"
ELSEIF (ed = 3) THEN
   LPRINT "3rd Edition"
ELSEIF (ed = 4) THEN
   LPRINT "4th Edition"
ELSEIF (ed = 5) THEN
   LPRINT "5th Edition"
ELSE
   LPRINT "Older edition"    ' All other cases
END IF
```

This program helps to show that a long multiple-case IF can be confusing if it is overused.

Summary

You now have the tools to write powerful programming constructions. This chapter showed how you can use the separating colon to put more than one statement on a single line. You then learned the ELSE statement, which gives the IF statement another option for its relational test.

The block IF-THEN-ELSE puts all this together. Instead of branching to another place in the program with a GOTO, you now can perform several statements depending on the IF relational test. Chapter 16 introduces the SELECT CASE statement, which adds readability to your multiple-decision IF statements.

Review Questions

Answers to the Review Questions are in Appendix B.

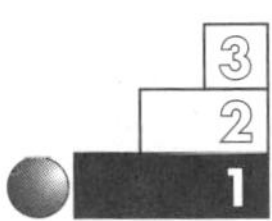

1. What character separates multiple QBasic statements on one line?
2. TRUE or FALSE: The ELSE statement can go on a line by itself.

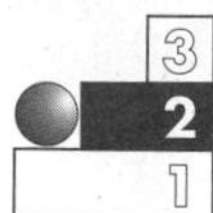

3. Why is it sometimes not preferred to put several statements on one line in a QBasic program?

4. TRUE or FALSE: If a decision has more than one branch, an `IF-THEN-ELSEIF` can be used.

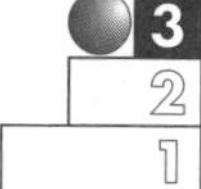

5. What is the error in the following program?

```
a = 6
IF (a > 6) THEN
   PRINT "George"
ELSE IF (a = 6) THEN
   PRINT "Henry"
ELSE IF (a < 6) THEN
   PRINT "James"
END IF
```

6. Why does QBasic require an `END IF` statement?

7. Rewrite the following code using a block `IF-THEN-ELSE`:

```
IF (A < 2) THEN PRINT "Yes" : GOTO Here ELSE PRINT "No" :
GOTO There
```

Review Exercises

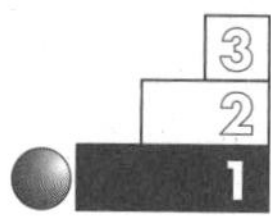

1. Write a program that uses a single-line `IF-THEN` statement that asks for a number and prints the square and cube (the number raised to the second power and the third power, respectively) of the input number, as long as the number is greater than 1. Otherwise, do not print anything.

2. Ask the user for three test scores. Print the largest of the three scores.

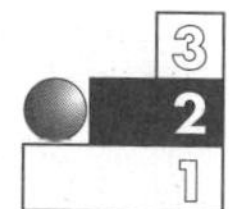

3. Ask the user for two numbers. Print a message telling how the first number compares to the second. In other words, if the user enters *5* and *7*, the program prints "5 is less than 7."

4. Ask the user for an employee's annual salary before taxes. Print the employee's salary and taxes. The taxes are 10 percent of the salary if the employee made less than $10,000,

15 percent if the employee earned between $10,000 and $20,000, and 20 percent if the employee earned more than $20,000.

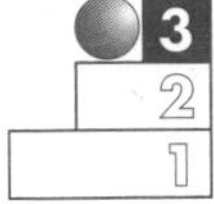

5. Ask the user for three numbers. Print a message telling the user whether any two of the numbers add up to the third.

6. Write a program to ask users for their first and last names. Then give them a choice from the following selection:

   1. Print your first and last name on the screen.
   2. Print your first and last name on the printer.
   3. Print your name, last name first, on the screen.
   4. Print your name, last name first, on the printer.

   Ask the users which option they choose, and then give them a chance to input that value. Depending on their response, perform that option. (This is called a *menu* program, because it gives users a chance to order what they want, similar to ordering food from a restaurant menu.)

16

The SELECT CASE Statement

This chapter focuses on the SELECT CASE statement, which improves on the block IF-THEN-ELSEIF by streamlining the "IF within an IF" construction.

This chapter introduces

- The SELECT CASE statement
- The STOP statement

The SELECT CASE statement is similar to an IF that has multiple selections. If you have mastered the block IF-THEN-ELSE, you should have little trouble with SELECT CASE. By learning the SELECT CASE statement, you will be able to write menus and multiple-choice user data-entry programs with ease.

Introducing SELECT CASE

This chapter develops the SELECT CASE by starting with a simple form and then adding options. The format of SELECT CASE is a little longer than the statements you have seen so far. The format of the primary SELECT CASE statement is

```
SELECT CASE expression

CASE expression1

   Block of one or more QBasic statements

CASE expression2

   Block of one or more QBasic statements

  :
  :
  :

[CASE ELSE

   Block of one or more QBasic statements]

END SELECT
```

Your application determines the number of CASE expressions that follow the SELECT CASE line. The *expressions* can be either text or numeric expressions. They can be constants or variables. The *block of one or more QBasic statements* is similar to the block of statements you saw for the block IF; you can type one or more statements following each other to make up that block. The CASE ELSE is optional; not all CASE SELECT statements have it. You must put the END SELECT line at the end of every CASE SELECT statement; otherwise, QBasic has no way of knowing where the last block of statements ends.

The use of the SELECT CASE is easier than its format might lead you to believe. You can use a SELECT CASE anywhere that you can use a block IF-THEN-ELSE. Furthermore, SELECT CASE is usually easier to follow than a block IF-THEN-ELSE.

Do not hesitate to use the block IF-THEN-ELSE, however. It is not a bad statement, nor is it difficult to follow. When the relational test that determines the choice is complex and contains many AND and OR operators, the block IF is the better alternative. The SELECT CASE statement is preferred when there are multiple-choice possibilities based on one decision.

QBasic Improves with Age

The `SELECT CASE` statement is an improvement over the `ON GOTO` statement. `ON GOTO` is an older statement that was part of previous versions of BASIC. QBasic still recognizes the `ON GOTO` statement, but the authors of QBasic realize how superior the `SELECT CASE` is.

Here is an example of the `ON GOTO`:

```
ON n GOTO Pay1, Pay2, Pay3, Pay4, Pay5, Pay6
```

When QBasic gets to this `ON GOTO` statement, it looks at the value of the variable *n*. If *n* is equal to 1, QBasic branches to the statements starting at the label `Pay1`. If *n* is equal to 2, the program branches to the `Pay2` label, and so on.

There are several problems with the `ON GOTO`. The value of the control variable (*n* in this example) must be an integer from 1 to the number of statement labels after `GOTO`. You cannot use a string variable or constant to control the execution.

The biggest problem with the `ON GOTO` is that it makes your program branch to too many places. Following an `ON GOTO` is difficult at best and is especially terrible when more than four or five statement labels are used.

Do yourself (and others who may be looking at your programs) a favor: Use the `SELECT CASE` to keep control and readability in your QBasic programs.

The following set of examples clarifies the `SELECT CASE` statement. They compare the `SELECT CASE` to the block `IF-THEN-ELSE`.

Examples

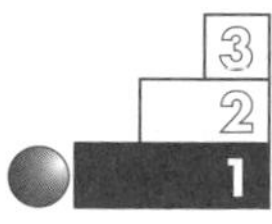

1. Suppose you are writing a program to teach your child how to count. Your program should ask the child for a number. The program then beeps that many times.

The program can assume that the child presses a number from 1 to 5. The following program uses the block IF-THEN-ELSEIF to accomplish the beeping counting program.

```
' Filename: C16BEEP1.BAS
'
' Beeps a certain number of times.
'
' Get a number from the child (you may have to help)
CLS
INPUT "Please enter a number"; num

IF (num = 1) THEN
   BEEP        ' 1 time
ELSEIF (num = 2) THEN
   BEEP : BEEP               ' 2 times
ELSEIF (num = 3) THEN
   BEEP : BEEP : BEEP        ' 3 times
ELSEIF (num = 4) THEN
   BEEP : BEEP : BEEP : BEEP ' 4 times
ELSE           ' You know here they must have entered a 5
   BEEP : BEEP : BEEP : BEEP : BEEP
END IF
```

The next program improves on the previous one by substituting a SELECT CASE statement for the block IF-THEN-ELSEIF.

```
' Filename: C16BEEP2.BAS
'
' Beeps a certain number of times.
'
' Get a number from the child (you may have to help)
CLS
INPUT "Please enter a number"; num

SELECT CASE num
   CASE 1
      BEEP                            ' 1 time
   CASE 2
      BEEP : BEEP                     ' 2 times
   CASE 3
      BEEP : BEEP : BEEP              ' 3 times
```

```
   CASE 4
      BEEP : BEEP : BEEP : BEEP        ' 4 times
   CASE 5
      BEEP : BEEP : BEEP : BEEP : BEEP ' 5 times
END SELECT
```

Notice how much easier this multiple-choice program is to follow. It is obvious that the value of the variable num controls the execution. Only the CASE that matches num executes. The indention helps separate the CASEs from each other.

The SELECT CASE has another advantage: If none of the cases matches the input value, nothing happens. The program continues to the statement following END SELECT without performing any of the cases. Therefore, if the child types a *7*, no beeps occur.

The BEEP statement is so short that it is OK to put more than one BEEP statement on one line, separated by the colon, as shown in this program. This is not a requirement, however, and the block of statements following a CASE selection can be more than one statement long.

If more than one of the CASE expressions are the same, only the first expression executes.

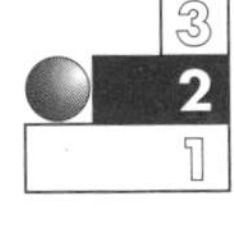

2. If the child did not type a *1*, *2*, *3*, *4*, or *5*, nothing happened in the previous program. Here is the same program modified to take advantage of the CASE ELSE option. The CASE ELSE block of statements executes if none of the previous cases was true.

```
' Filename: C16BEEP3.BAS
'
' Beeps a certain number of times.
'
' Get a number from the child (you may have to help)
CLS
INPUT "Please enter a number"; num

SELECT CASE num
   CASE 1
      BEEP                             ' 1 time
```

```
    CASE 2
       BEEP : BEEP                           ' 2 times
    CASE 3
       BEEP : BEEP : BEEP                    ' 3 times
    CASE 4
       BEEP : BEEP : BEEP : BEEP             ' 4 times
    CASE 5
       BEEP : BEEP : BEEP : BEEP : BEEP ' 5 times
    CASE ELSE    ' The default if the other cases did not occur
       PRINT "You must enter a number 1, 2, 3, 4, or 5!"
END SELECT
```

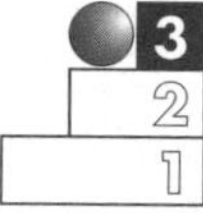

3. The expression that controls the SELECT CASE can also be a string variable. The following program prints a message to the users depending on their department.

```
' Filename: C16DEPT.BAS
'
' Print a meeting message to certain people.
' Their department determines the message printed.

CLS
PRINT "*** Message Center ***"
PRINT
INPUT "What department are you in"; dept$

SELECT CASE dept$
CASE "Sales"
   PRINT "Your meeting is at 9:00 this morning."
CASE "Accounting"
   PRINT "Your meeting is at 10:00 this morning."
CASE "Engineering"
   PRINT "You have no meetings this week."
CASE "Marketing"
   PRINT "You have three meetings on Tuesday at 1, 2, and 3."
CASE "Computer"
   PRINT "You have no meetings this week."
CASE ELSE
   PRINT "I do not recognize your department."
END SELECT
```

Figure 16.1 shows the result of running this program. It could be part of a larger program used by office employees to get messages. They have to type their department name exactly, making sure the first letter is an uppercase letter; otherwise, the message does not display. If they do not type the department name correctly, the error message prints. Later, another form of SELECT CASE takes care of these kinds of typing errors.

```
*** Message Center ***

What department are you in? Marketing
You have three meetings on Tuesday at 1, 2, and 3.









Press any key to continue
```

Figure 16.1. Viewing a message based on a certain department.

4. The SELECT CASE is great for handling a menu. As explained in Chapter 15, a menu is simply a selection of options the user can order the computer to perform. Instead of your users having to remember many commands, they can simply look at a menu of choices that you display and select one of the choices from the menu. The book management program in Appendix E uses the SELECT CASE statement in all its menus.

The following program is an adaptation of the math tutorial program shown earlier in this book. It asks for two numbers and then asks the users which type of math they want to perform. This program lets users check their math accuracy.

Although it seems like a lengthy program, most of it is made up of PRINT statements. The SELECT CASE makes choosing from the menu straightforward.

```
' Filename: C16MATH1.BAS
'
' Program to practice math accuracy.

COLOR 7, 1      ' White characters on a blue background
CLS
PRINT "Please type two numbers, separated by a comma"
PRINT "(For example, 8, 5) and press ENTER"
INPUT num1, num2
PRINT

DO      ' Display the menu, and ensure that they enter a
        ' correct option
   PRINT "Choose your option:"
   PRINT "1. Add"; num1; "to"; num2
   PRINT "2. Subtract"; num2; "from"; num1
   PRINT "3. Multiply"; num1; "and"; num2
   PRINT "4. Divide"; num1; "by"; num2
   PRINT
   INPUT choice
LOOP UNTIL ((choice >= 1) AND (choice <= 4))

' Execute the appropriate math operation and print its result
SELECT CASE (choice)
   CASE 1
      PRINT num1; "plus"; num2; "is:"; (num1 + num2)
   CASE 2
      PRINT num1; "minus"; num2; "is:"; (num1 - num2)
   CASE 3
      PRINT num1; "times"; num2; "is:"; (num1 * num2)
```

```
   CASE 4
      PRINT num1; "divided by"; num2; "is:"; (num1 / num2)
END SELECT      ' Done
```

Figure 16.2 shows a sample run of this program. The program is *bullet proof,* which means that all input is checked to ensure it is within bounds (the user cannot cause the program to stop working by entering a strange value, like an *8,* for the menu option). Because the program keeps looping until the user chooses a proper menu option (1 through 4), no CASE ELSE is required.

```
Please type two numbers, separated by a comma
(For example, 8, 5) and press ENTER
? 3, 6

Choose your option:
1. Add 3 to 6
2. Subtract 6 from 3
3. Multiply 3 and 6
4. Divide 3 by 6

? 3
 3 times 6 is: 18



Press any key to continue
```

Figure 16.2. Using SELECT CASE to choose from a menu.

The CASE control value does not have to have parentheses around it, but the parentheses sometimes help differentiate the value and make it easier to find.

Relational SELECT CASE Choices

As with the IF statement, the expression tested for by SELECT CASE can be relational. A specific CASE executes only if the result of its relational expression is true. When using relational CASEs, the format of the SELECT CASE is

```
SELECT CASE expression
CASE IS relational expression1
   Block of one or more QBasic statements
CASE IS relational expression2
   Block of one or more QBasic statements
   :
   :
   :
[CASE ELSE
   Block of one or more QBasic statements]
END SELECT
```

Because you can put a relational test after one or more of the CASEs, you can test for a broader range of values. The single constant or variable check is simply too limiting and is useful only for certain applications, such as a menu program. The keyword IS is required if you use a relational test in a CASE.

> **TIP:** You cannot combine CASE IS *relational expressions* with AND, OR, or NOT. If you need to make a compound relational test, you must use a block IF-THEN-ELSEIF.

Examples

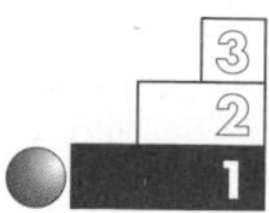

1. The following program asks users for their ages and prints appropriate messages. Without the relational CASE testing, it would take too many individual CASEs testing for each possible age to make the SELECT CASE useful here.

The Department of Motor Vehicles could use this program to inform young motorists of what vehicle they can legally drive. It asks for the user's age and then prints the vehicle the user can legally drive.

```
' Filename: C16AGE1.BAS
'
' Program to tell legal vehicles based on age.
CLS
INPUT "How old are you"; age

SELECT CASE age
   CASE IS < 14
      PRINT "You can only ride a bike"
   CASE IS < 16
      PRINT "You can ride a motorcycle"
   CASE ELSE
      PRINT "You can drive a car"
END SELECT
```

The default `CASE ELSE` executes for only those ages over 16.

Notice that unlike `IF` relational tests, the relational expression for the `CASE`s does not repeat the control variable. In other words, the second `CASE` would be incorrect if it read:

```
CASE IS age < 16
```

or

```
CASE age IS < 16
```

2. If you have an extensive record collection and want an easy way to locate a record, you can start with the following program. It asks for the name of a record and then tells you which cabinet the record is in. All records with titles that begin with *A* through *G* are in cabinet 1. Records with titles that begin with *H* through *P* are in cabinet 2, and those that begin with *Q* through *Z* are in cabinet 3. This program shows the use of the ASCII table when `CASE IS` comparisons are made. All string comparisons are made in the `SELECT CASE` statement, just as they are in `IF` relational tests.

```
' Filename: C16REC.BAS
'
' Determines which cabinet a record is located in.
CLS
LINE INPUT "What is the name of the record? "; rec.name$

PRINT
SELECT CASE rec.name$
   CASE IS < "H"
      PRINT "The record is in cabinet 1."
   CASE IS < "Q"
      PRINT "The record is in cabinet 2."
   CASE ELSE
      PRINT "The record is in cabinet 3."
END SELECT
```

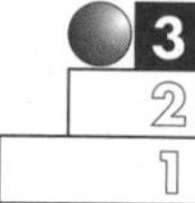

3. Use the CASE ELSE liberally to take care of user input that is not correct. For instance, the following program asks retail customers for their purchase codes and tells them where to pick up packages bought that day. If a user enters a bad code, an appropriate message is displayed.

```
' Filename: C16CUST.BAS
'
' Tells customers where their packages are.

CLS
INPUT "What is your customer code"; cc$

SELECT CASE cc$
   CASE IS = "A1"
      PRINT "Your packages will be taken to your car."
      PRINT "Please drive to our pick-up dock."
   CASE IS = "B2"
      PRINT "Please go to the second floor for your packages."
   CASE IS = "C3"
      PRINT "You must come back tomorrow for your packages."
   CASE ELSE
      PRINT "You typed a bad customer code."
      PRINT "Please ask for assistance."
END SELECT
```

This program shows that you can include more than one statement with the CASE options.

You might notice that this program is not as efficient as it should be. The relation CASE IS test is wasted. Because each CASE (except for the CASE ELSE, of course) tests for equality, it would have been better to eliminate the IS = on each of the CASE lines.

The Range of SELECT CASE Choices

The last option of a SELECT CASE shows that you can test for a range of values on each line of CASE. The format of this last SELECT CASE statement is

```
SELECT CASE expression
CASE expression TO expression1
   Block of one or more QBasic statements
CASE expression TO expression2
   Block of one or more QBasic statements
  :
  :
  :
[CASE ELSE
   Block of one or more QBasic statements]
END SELECT
```

The *expression* TO *expressionN* format of the CASE lets you specify a range of values that QBasic checks to determine which CASE executes. This is useful when possibilities are ordered sequentially and you want to perform certain actions if one of the sets of values is chosen.

The first expression (the one to the right of TO) must be lower numerically, or as determined by the ASCII table if it is character data, than the second expression. The following examples make this clear.

> **TIP:** Put the most likely case at the top of the CASE list. QBasic mandates no particular order, but this order improves your program's speed. If you are testing for cases 1 through 6 and the fifth case is the most likely, put it at the top of the list. The only CASE that must go last is the CASE ELSE.

Examples

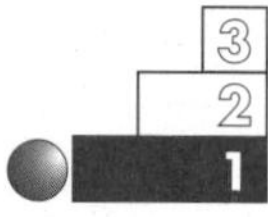

1. The following program is a rewritten version of the driving program from an earlier CASE example (C16AGE1.BAS). The previous program tested for the user's age and printed an appropriate driving message. This program looks at a range of age values instead of using a relational test. Because ages of people are always sequential (that is, a person gets exactly one year older every birthday), using the CASE range may be a better way to program this problem.

```
' Filename: C16AGE2.BAS
'
' Program to tell legal vehicles based on age.
CLS
INPUT "How old are you"; age

SELECT CASE age
   CASE 1 TO 13       ' Covers everyone under 14
      PRINT "You can only ride a bike"
   CASE 14 TO 15      ' Covers everyone under 16
      PRINT "You can ride a motorcycle"
   CASE ELSE
      PRINT "You can drive a car"
END SELECT
```

2. You might at times want to combine one or more of the CASE options. For instance, you might want to use a range for one CASE and a relational test for another within the same SELECT CASE statement.

   The previous program has one subtle bug. It appears to work, but if the user enters a bad age value, such as 0 or –43, the program tells the user to drive a car. This is not a good example of data validation. You can add a range check to print a message if the age is not valid, as the following program shows.

```
' Filename: C16AGE3.BAS
'
' Program to tell legal vehicles based on age.
CLS
INPUT "How old are you"; age

SELECT CASE age
   CASE 1 TO 13        ' Covers everyone under 14
      PRINT "You can only ride a bike"
   CASE 14 TO 15       ' Covers everyone under 16
      PRINT "You can ride a motorcycle"
   CASE 16 TO 99
      PRINT "You can drive a car"
   CASE ELSE
      PRINT "You typed a bad age. Please ask for assistance."
END SELECT
```

   The range check ensures that anyone aged 16 or older will be told that they can drive a car. Any age *not* checked for, however, such as 0 and negative ages, will trigger the CASE ELSE error message.

The STOP Statement

STOP quits execution of a program before the regular end-of-program is reached.

The STOP statement ends a program's execution. It is sometimes confused with the END statement, but it is used for a different purpose. Remember from Chapter 5, "Understanding Numeric Variables and Constants," that the END statement often goes at the end of a program. It is optional; without an END statement, QBasic still knows where your program ends, so many QBasic programmers choose not to include an END statement.

The STOP statement, on the other hand, can go anywhere in a program, and it immediately stops the execution of the program. When QBasic encounters a STOP statement, it quits execution of the current program and returns to the program editing window.

Because STOP is unconditional, you usually see it as an option of the IF or SELECT CASE statements. A menu program is a good use of STOP. When you display a menu, give the users an extra option to stop the program. If the users display the menu and then decide that they do not want to perform any of the options on it, they can choose the stop option. The IF or SELECT CASE statement controlling the menu can then execute STOP without performing any of the other options.

Examples

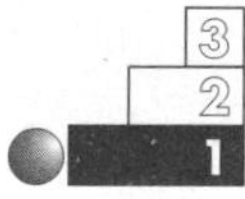

1. Here is the math program with a menu that was presented earlier. This time it has an extra option that lets the user stop the program without seeing any math performed.

```
' Filename: C16MATH2.BAS
'
' Program to practice math accuracy.

COLOR 7, 1      ' White characters on a blue background
CLS
PRINT "Please type two numbers, separated by a comma"
PRINT "(For example, 8, 5) and press ENTER"
INPUT num1, num2
PRINT

DO      ' Display the menu, and ensure that they enter a
        ' correct option
```

```
      PRINT "Choose your option:"
      PRINT "1. Add"; num1; "to"; num2
      PRINT "2. Subtract"; num2; "from"; num1
      PRINT "3. Multiply"; num1; "and"; num2
      PRINT "4. Divide"; num1; "by"; num2
      PRINT "5. Stop the program"
      PRINT
      INPUT choice
   LOOP UNTIL ((choice >= 1) AND (choice <= 5))

   ' Execute the appropriate math operation and print its result
   SELECT CASE (choice)
      CASE 1
         PRINT num1; "plus"; num2; "is:"; (num1 + num2)
      CASE 2
         PRINT num1; "minus"; num2; "is:"; (num1 - num2)
      CASE 3
         PRINT num1; "times"; num2; "is:"; (num1 * num2)
      CASE 4
         PRINT num1; "divided by"; num2; "is:"; (num1 / num2)
      CASE 5
         STOP
   END SELECT      ' Done
```

This example stretches the point a bit because the program stops immediately after doing any of the math anyway. You can, however, get an idea of how STOP works; it quits execution of a program before the regular end-of-program is reached. You can have more than one STOP in a program if several places require the ability to end execution depending on certain situations.

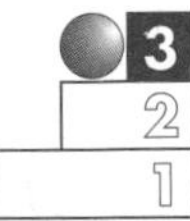

2. The following program is simple, but it illustrates two concepts you haven't seen before. The first of these concepts is the IF within a SELECT CASE statement. The program asks the user for a number and then prints the square of that number (the number raised to the second power) and the square root of the number (the number raised to the one-half power). Because negative numbers cannot have a square root (nothing multiplied by itself equals a negative number), the program does not print the square root of a negative number.

A LOOP controls the SELECT CASE so that the user can keep seeing the program execute with different INPUT values. The program does, however, offer a chance to STOP. Notice that this is a conditional STOP; the program stops only if the user requests that it stop.

```
' Filename: C16SQRT.BAS
'
' Program that finds squares and roots of input values.

CLS
PRINT "Prints the square and square root of any number"
DO
   INPUT "What number would you like to use"; num
   SELECT CASE num
      CASE >= 0
         PRINT num; "squared is"; (num ^ 2)
         PRINT "The root of"; num; "is"; (num ^ (1 / 2))
      CASE ELSE              ' Handles all negative values
         PRINT num; "squared is"; (num ^ 2)
         PRINT "There is no square root for "; num
   END SELECT
   PRINT
   INPUT "Do you want to see another (Y/N)"; ans$
   IF (ans$ = "N") THEN STOP    ' Quit program
LOOP WHILE (ans$ = "Y")
```

Summary

You have seen the SELECT CASE statement and all its related options. It can improve the readability of a complex IF-THEN-ELSEIF selection. The SELECT CASE is especially good when several outcomes are possible based on a certain choice. You can use the STOP statement also inside a SELECT CASE to end a program earlier than its physical conclusion if the user desires.

This ends Part IV, "Control Statements." Part V, "Data Structures: Arrays," introduces advanced data types. Now that you can control the execution of your programs, you are ready to store more complex (but not complicated) data values in formats that will improve your ability to represent real-world data.

Review Questions

Answers to the Review Questions are in Appendix B.

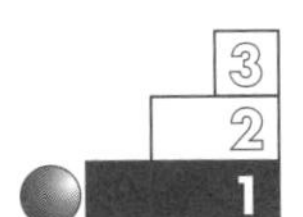

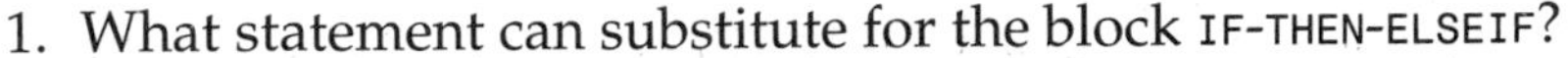

1. What statement can substitute for the block IF-THEN-ELSEIF?

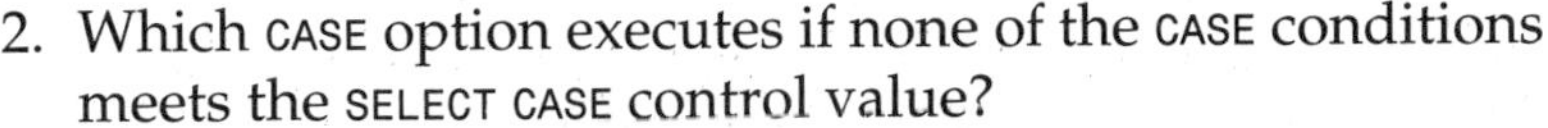

2. Which CASE option executes if none of the CASE conditions meets the SELECT CASE control value?
3. TRUE or FALSE: The STOP statement performs the same function as the END statement.

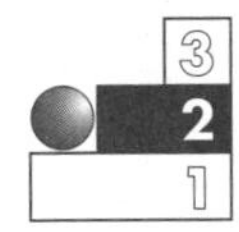

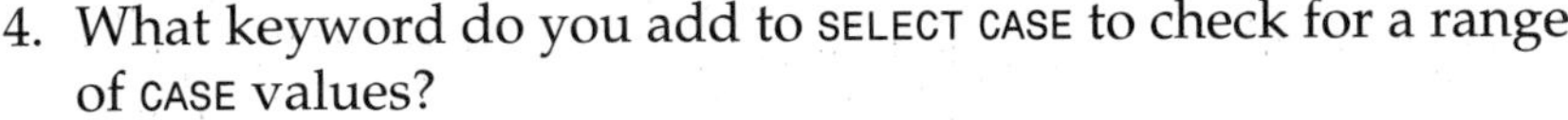

4. What keyword do you add to SELECT CASE to check for a range of CASE values?
5. What keyword do you add to SELECT CASE to check for a relational set of CASE values?

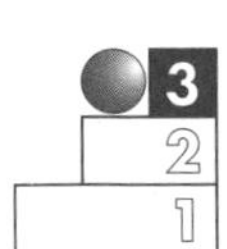

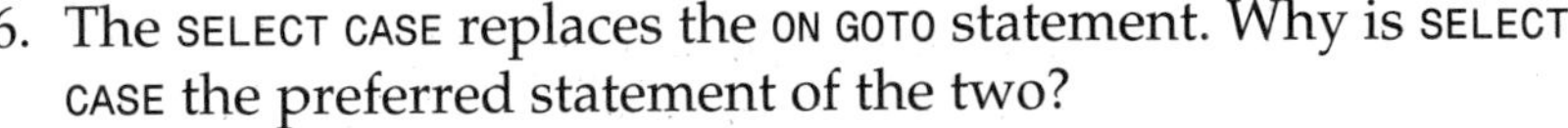

6. The SELECT CASE replaces the ON GOTO statement. Why is SELECT CASE the preferred statement of the two?
7. TRUE or FALSE: The order of the CASE options has no bearing on the efficiency of your program.
8. Rewrite the following program, replacing the IF-THEN-ELSEIF with a SELECT CASE.

```
IF (num = 1) THEN
   PRINT "Alpha"
ELSEIF (num = 2) THEN
   PRINT "Beta"
ELSEIF (num = 3) THEN
   PRINT "Gamma"
ELSE
   PRINT "Other"
END IF
```

9. Rewrite the following program, replacing the IF-THEN-ELSE with a SELECT CASE.

```
IF ((code$ >= "A") and (code$ <= "Z")) THEN
   PRINT "Code is within range"
ELSE
   PRINT "Code is out of range"
END IF
```

10. Rewrite the following program, replacing the IF-THEN-ELSEIF with a SELECT CASE.

```
IF (sales > 5000) THEN
   bonus = 50
ELSEIF (sales > 2500) THEN
   bonus = 25
ELSE
   bonus = 0
ENDIF
```

Review Exercises

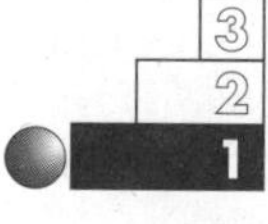

1. Write a program using the SELECT CASE to ask users for their ages. Print a message saying `Drink a cola` if the age is less than 21, and one that says `Drink a martini` otherwise.

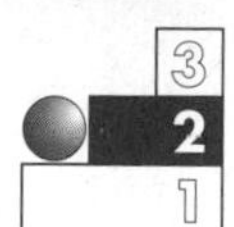

2. Write a program that your local cable television company can use to compute charges. Here is how your cable company charges: If you live within 20 miles of the city limits, you pay $12 per month. If you live within 30 miles of the city limits, you pay $23 per month. You pay $34 per month if you live within 50 miles of the city limits.

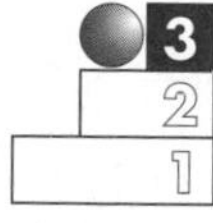

3. Write a program that calculates parking fees for a multilevel parking garage. Ask whether the driver is in a car or a truck. Charge the driver $2 for the first hour, $3 for the second hour, and $5 for parking more than two hours. If the driver is in a truck, add an extra $1 to the total fee. (Hint: Use one SELECT CASE and an IF statement.)

4. Modify the parking problem to charge depending on the time of day the car is parked. If the car is parked before 8 a.m., charge the fees in the preceding exercise. If the car is parked after 8 a.m. and before 5 p.m., charge an extra usage fee of 50 cents. If the car is parked after 5 p.m., deduct 50 cents from the computed price. You have to prompt the user for the starting time in a menu, as shown here:

   1. Before 8 a.m.
   2. Before 5 p.m.
   3. After 5 p.m.

Part V

Data Structures: Arrays

Introduction to Arrays

This chapter begins a new approach to an old concept: storing data in variables. The difference is that you will now store data in *array* variables. An array is a list of variables, sometimes called a *table* of variables.

This chapter introduces

- Storing data in arrays
- The DIM statement
- The OPTION BASE statement
- Finding the highest and lowest values in an array
- Searching arrays for values
- The SWAP statement
- Sorting arrays
- Advanced DIM subscripts
- The ERASE statement

Conquering arrays is your next step toward understanding advanced uses of QBasic. This chapter's examples are some of the longest programs you have seen in the book. Arrays are not difficult, but their power lends them to be used with advanced programs.

What Is an Array?

An array is a list of more than one variable with the same name. Not every list of variables is an array. The following list of four variables is *not* an array:

```
sales      bonus.92      first.name$      ctr
```

These four variables do not define an array because they each have different names. You might wonder how more than one variable can have the same name; this seems to violate the rules of variables. If two variables had the same name, how would QBasic know which one you wanted when you used the name of one of them?

Array variables are distinguished from each other by a *subscript.* A subscript is the number inside brackets that differentiates one *element* of an array from another. Elements are the individual variables in an array.

Before you hear too much more about definitions, an illustration may help.

Good Array Candidates

Suppose you want to keep track of 35 people in your neighborhood association. You might want to track their names and their monthly dues. Their dues are fixed and are different for each person because the people joined the association at different times and bought houses with different prices.

Without arrays, you would have to store the 35 names in 35 different variables. You would also have to store the amount each person pays in dues in 35 different variables. Both of these factors would make for a complex and lengthy program. To enter the data, you would do something like this:

```
INPUT "What is the 1st family member's name"; family1$
INPUT "What are their dues"; dues1
INPUT "What is the 2nd family member's name"; family2$
INPUT "What are their dues"; dues2
INPUT "What is the 3rd family member's name"; family3$
INPUT "What are their dues"; dues3
                    :
                    :
INPUT "What is the 35th family member's name"; family35$
INPUT "What are their dues"; dues35
```

Every time you have to print a list of members, calculate average dues, or use any of this data, you have to scan at least 35 different variable names. You would get tired of doing this. This is why arrays were developed; it is too cumbersome for similar data to have different variable names. The time and typing required to process more than a handful of variables with different names is too much. Not only that, but imagine if the neighborhood grew to 500 residents!

Arrays let you store similar data, such as the neighborhood data, in one variable. In effect, each of the data values has the same name. You distinguish the values (the elements in the array) from each other by a numeric subscript. For instance, instead of using a different variable name (`family1$`, `dues1`, `family2$`, `dues2`, and so on), give the similar data the same variable name (`family$` and `dues`) and differentiate the variables with subscripts, as shown in Table 17.1.

Table 17.1. Using arrays to store similar data.

Old Names	*Array Names*
`family1$, dues1`	`family$(1), dues(1)`
`family2$, dues2`	`family$(2), dues(2)`
`family3$, dues3`	`family$(3), dues(3)`
: :	: :
: :	: :
`family35$, dues35`	`family$(35), dues(35)`

The column of array names has a major advantage over the old variable names. The number inside parentheses is the *subscript number* of the array. Subscript numbers are never part of an array name; they are always enclosed in parentheses and serve to distinguish one array element from another.

How many arrays are listed in Table 17.1? If you said *two,* you are correct. There are 35 elements in each array. How many elements are there in Table 17.1? There are 70 (35 family name elements and 35 dues elements). The difference is very important when you consider how you can process them.

> **TIP:** Because the subscript number (the only thing that differentiates one array element from another) is not part of the array name, you can use a `FOR-NEXT` loop or any other counter variable to input, process, and output all elements of arrays.

For instance, to input every family name and the family's dues into the two arrays, you do not need 70 statements as you did when each variable had a different name. You would need only *four* statements, as shown here:

initialize family$ and dues$ arrays

```
FOR ctr = 1 to 35
   INPUT "What is the 1st family member's name"; family$(ctr)
   INPUT "What are their dues"; dues$(ctr)
NEXT ctr
```

This is a major advantage. Notice that the `FOR-NEXT` loop keeps incrementing `ctr` throughout the data input of all 70 values. The first time through the loop, the user enters a value in `family$(1)` and in `dues(1)` (because `ctr` is equal to 1). The loop then increments `ctr` to 2, and the input process starts again for the next two variables. These four lines of code are much easier to write and maintain than the previous 70 lines were, and they do exactly the same thing: They use only two arrays of 35 elements rather than two groups of 35 different variable names. You could not use the `FOR-NEXT` loop to process a group of differently named variables, even if they had numbers in their names as the first method showed.

When you are working with a list of data with similar meanings, an array works best. Arrays make your input, process, and output routines much easier to write. QBasic always initializes all array elements to 0 (and string arrays to null strings) when it dimensions them.

Using `DIM` to Set Up Arrays

Unlike when you use nonarray variables, you must tell QBasic that you are going to use a specific number of array elements. You use the `DIM` (which means *dimension*) statement to do this. To reserve enough array elements for the 35 families, you would dimension 35 string array elements called `family$` and 35 single-precision array elements called `dues`. Here is the format of the `DIM` statement:

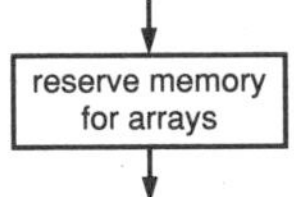


```
DIM arrayname(maximum number of elements used by your program)
     [ arrayname2(#) ] [ , ...,arraynameN(#)]
```

If you want to declare a data type for an array, make sure you put the proper symbol after its name and before the opening parenthesis. For example, to dimension the `family$` and `dues` arrays, you would type the following line:

```
DIM family$(35), dues(35)
```

The dollar sign follows `family` because it must be a character string array. Nothing follows `dues` because it defaults to become a single-precision array. You must remember the following rule:

> **NOTE:** All array elements must be the same type (string, integer, and so on). That type is determined when you dimension the array. You must dimension an array before using it.

Typically, programmers dimension all arrays as early in the program as possible. A good place to dimension the arrays is after the opening remarks. The first subscript is normally *0* (although later you will see a way to override this), and the maximum number of elements in the array (the highest subscript) is determined by the

DIM statement. Because each element in an array has the same type, you might see the elements being used in calculations, just as nonarray variables are, as in

```
dues(5) = dues(4) * 1.5
```

Table 17.2 consolidates this information in a meaningful format. Study the table before going further. If you have forgotten the variable type symbols for single-precision, double-precision, and integers, review Chapter 5, "Understanding Numeric Variables and Constants."

> **NOTE:** All arrays contain one more element than the DIM statement reserves, because the first usable subscript in an array is 0. Most QBasic programmers ignore this 0 element and begin their subscripting at 1. The choice to start subscripting at 0 is up to you.

Table 17.2. Array declarations and the subscripts.

DIM *Statement*	*Type*	*Array Name*	*First Element*	*Last Element*
DIM months(12)	single	months	months(0)	months(12)
DIM names$(5)	string	names	names$(0)	names$(5)
DIM temp#(300)	double	temps	temps#(0)	temps#(300)
DIM sales!(20)	single	sales	sales(0)	sales(20)
DIM ages%(10)	integer	ages	ages%(0)	ages%(10)
DIM amt&(15)	long	amt	amt&(0)	amt&(15)

You can dimension a maximum of 32,767 elements in an array. This should be more than enough for most purposes.

> **TIP:** If you need more than 32,767 elements, dimension two or more arrays. It makes your work a little more cumbersome, but it circumvents the 32,767-element limit. Be careful, however; you can easily run out of RAM and not have room to hold all your data. If this happens, QBasic tells you when it processes the DIM statement.

To further illustrate the way an array works, suppose you dimensioned an array called ages to nine elements with the following DIM statement:

```
DIM ages(8)
```

Its elements would be numbered ages(0) through ages(8), as shown in Figure 17.1. The values of each element are filled in when the program runs with INPUT, assignment, or READ-DATA statements.

AGES(8)

AGES(0)	AGES(1)	AGES(2)	AGES(3)	AGES(4)	AGES(5)	AGES(6)	AGES(7)	AGES(8)

Figure 17.1. The nine elements and their subscripts in the ages array.

Although the following examples show array elements being filled by INPUT and READ-DATA statements, most programs get their input data from disk files. Because arrays can store large amounts of data, you don't want to have to type that data into the variables every time you run a program. Also, READ-DATA statements do not always suffice, either, because they are not good statements to use for extremely large amounts of data. For now, concentrate on the arrays and how they operate. In Chapter 25, "Sequential Disk Processing," you will see how arrays can be initialized from data on a disk drive.

> **Arrays and Storage**
>
> QBasic wants to know the maximum number of array elements your program will use because it has to reserve that many elements of memory. Arrays can take up much memory. For instance, it takes more than 32,000 characters of memory to hold the array created by the following `DIM` statement:
>
> ```
> DIM measurements#(4000)
> ```
>
> Because array memory adds up fast, QBasic needs to ensure there is enough to handle the highest array element your program will ever use. This is an advantage to programmers; QBasic will not wait until you have data in several array elements before it knows whether it has enough memory to store that data. If there is not enough room to create the array when it is dimensioned, QBasic tells you then.
>
> QBasic does not need to know about arrays with fewer than 11 elements, but dimensioning them is a good practice. In other words, you could use the array elements `grades(0)` through `grades(10)` without needing a `DIM grades(10)` statement first. If you try to store more than 10 elements in an array without dimensioning it first, however, QBasic refuses to run your program and displays a `Subscript out of range` error on the screen.

Examples

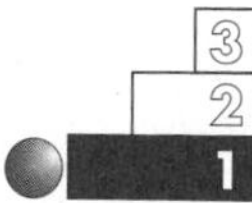

1. Here is the full program that dimensions two arrays for the neighborhood association's 35 family names and their dues. It prompts for input and then prints the names and dues. If you type this program, you might want to change the number from 35 to 5 to avoid having to type so much input.

   Notice that the program can input and print all these names and dues with simple routines. The input routine uses a `FOR-NEXT` loop, and the printing routine uses a `DO` loop. The method you use to control the loop is not critical. The important thing to see at this point is that you can input and print a large amount of data without having to write much code. The array subscripts make this possible.

```
' Filename: C17FAM1.BAS
'
' Program to gather and print 35 names and dues.
DIM family$(35)    ' Reserve the array elements
DIM dues(35)

CLS
FOR subsc = 1 TO 35
   INPUT "What is the next family's name"; family$(subsc)
   INPUT "What are their dues"; dues(subsc)
NEXT subsc

subsc = 1      ' Initialize the first subscript
DO
   PRINT "Family"; subsc; "is "; family$(subsc)
   PRINT "Their dues are"; dues(subsc)
   subsc = subsc + 1
LOOP UNTIL (subsc > 35)     ' Prints all the input data
```

TIP: You can combine the dimensioning of more than one array in a single `DIM` statement. For instance, the preceding two `DIM` statements could be written as:

```
DIM family$(35), dues(35)
```

This is an example of *parallel arrays.* Two arrays are working side by side. Each element in each array corresponds to one in the other array.

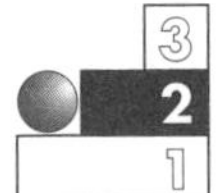

2. The neighborhood association program is fine for illustration, but it works only if there are exactly 35 families. But if the association grows, you have to change the program.

   Therefore, most programs do not have a fixed limit like the preceding example did. Most programmers dimension more than enough array elements to handle the largest array they could ever need. The program then lets the user control how many of those elements are really used.

The following program is similar to the preceding one, except that it dimensions 500 elements for each array. This reserves more than enough array elements for the association. The user then inputs only the actual number (from 1 to 500 maximum). Notice that the program is flexible, allowing a variable number of members to be input and printed each time it is run. It does, however, have to have an eventual limit, but that limit is reached only when there are 500 members.

```
' Filename: C17FAM2.BAS
'
' Program to gather and print up to 500 names and dues.

DIM family$(500), dues(500)   ' Reserve the array elements

CLS
subsc = 1     ' Initial subscript to get loop started
' The following loop asks for family names and dues until the
' user presses Enter without typing a name. Whenever a null
' input is given (just an Enter key press), the DO-LOOP exits
' early with subsc holding the number input to that point.

DO
   PRINT "Please type the next family's name"
   PRINT "(Press ENTER without typing a name if you are done)";
   INPUT family$(subsc)
   IF (family$(subsc) = "") THEN EXIT DO ' This triggers
                                         ' early exit
   INPUT "What are their dues"; dues(subsc)
   subsc = subsc + 1     ' Add one to the subscript variable
LOOP UNTIL (subsc > 500)

' When the last loop finishes, subsc holds the actual number input

FOR ctr = 1 to (subsc - 1) ' Loop through each family entered
   PRINT "Family"; ctr; "is "; family$(ctr)
   PRINT "Their dues are"; dues(ctr)
NEXT ctr                 ' Prints all the input data
```

Figure 17.2 shows the output from this program. Only a few of the maximum 500 families are entered in the figure. The empty Enter keypress is a good way to trigger the early exit of the loop. Just because 500 elements are reserved for each array does not mean that you have to use all 500 of them.

```
Please type the next family's name
(Press ENTER without typing a name if you are done)? Johnson
What are their dues? 18.55
Please type the next family's name
(Press ENTER without typing a name if you are done)? Underhill
What are their dues? 12.54
Please type the next family's name
(Press ENTER without typing a name if you are done)? Blackburn
What are their dues? 17.92
Please type the next family's name
(Press ENTER without typing a name if you are done)?
Family 1 is Johnson
Their dues are 18.55
Family 2 is Underhill
Their dues are 12.54
Family 3 is Blackburn
Their dues are 17.92





Press any key to continue
```

Figure 17.2. Entering and looking at names and dues.

Dimensioning more than enough array elements is common, but don't go overboard. Too many dimensioned array elements could cause your computer to run out of RAM space.

TIP: Alternatively, if users are familiar with the data, you could ask them how many values they want to enter. You then loop until that value is reached. Because the users rarely are familiar enough with their data to know how many values they will input, this is not as common as the previous method, which lets the user trigger the end of the input.

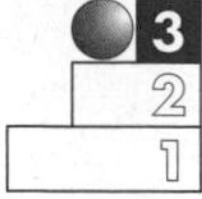

3. Many QBasic programmers use READ-DATA statements to fill an array when all data is known when the programmer writes the program. For example, the programmer knows the names of the 12 months in advance. Therefore, expert users use READ and DATA statements to fill arrays with month names, days of the week, and so on.

   The following program stores each month's name in a separate array element. Users can then see the month name next to the salary they requested.

```
' Filename: C17SAL2.BAS
'
' Stores 12 months of salaries and month names,
' printing selected ones at the user's request.
'
DIM sal(12)  ' Reserve enough elements for the 12 salaries
DIM months$(12)  ' and the 12 month names

' Fill up the month names
FOR ctr = 1 TO 12
   READ months$(ctr)    ' Save the next month name
NEXT ctr

' The DATA can go at the bottom of program if you desire
DATA "January", "February", "March", "April", "May", "June"
DATA "July", "August", "September", "October", "November"
DATA "December"

CLS
FOR subsc = 1 TO 12
   PRINT "What is the salary for "; months$(subsc);
   INPUT sal(subsc)    ' The previous trailing semicolon keeps
                       ' the question mark after the month name
NEXT subsc

' Clear the screen, and wait for a requested month
CLS
PRINT "*** Salary Printing Program ***"
PRINT "Prints any salary from the last 12 months"
PRINT
' Request the month number
```

```
DO
   INPUT "What month (1-12) do you want to see"; month.num
   PRINT
   PRINT "The salary for "; months$(month.num); " is";
   PRINT sal(month.num)
   PRINT
   INPUT "Do you want to see another (Y/N)"; ans$
LOOP WHILE ((ans$ = "Y") OR (ans$ = "y"))
```

Figure 17.3 shows the input screen for the preceding program. Because the program stores each month name in an array, you get prompts that use the month name, as in

```
What is the salary for April?
```

```
What is the salary for January? 43445.54
What is the salary for February? 40332.34
What is the salary for March? 43556.76
What is the salary for April? 48776.70
What is the salary for May? 39763.12
What is the salary for June? 54665.73
What is the salary for July? 39459.02
What is the salary for August? 54776.43
What is the salary for September? 32345.78
What is the salary for October? 50009.87
What is the salary for November? 43345.43
What is the salary for December? 34553.21
```

Figure 17.3. Printing month names with requests for salary input.

You can ask users whether they want to change any of the data in the array. You can do more than print an array to the screen or printer. If the users see that one of the salaries was typed incorrectly, it would be easy to add an INPUT statement that asked for the month number to change (in this case, 4). You then could replace the array element that matches that month number with the new value the users input.

The OPTION BASE Statement

Until now, every array's first element was 0. This is the QBasic default. There is a statement that lets you change this to 1. It is the OPTION BASE statement, which has the following format:

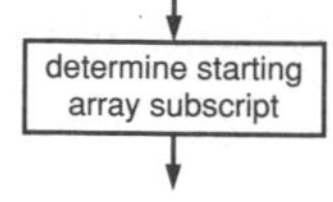


```
OPTION BASE 0 or 1
```

As you can see, a *0* or a *1* must follow OPTION BASE. If your program contains an OPTION BASE statement, that statement must precede all DIM statements.

The first subscript of any array is 0, unless you change it to 1 with OPTION BASE 1. As mentioned earlier, most QBasic programmers ignore the 0 subscript. If you precede the DIM statement with OPTION BASE 1, however, QBasic does not use the 0 subscript and reserves only enough storage locations for subscript 1 through the dimensioned number.

The OPTION BASE statement is not used much, because the space that is "wasted" by the 0 subscript element rarely makes a difference and is usually ignored.

Examples

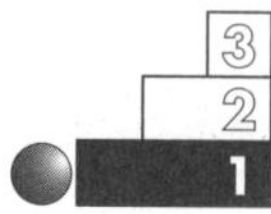

1. The following program reads day names into seven variables. The program has no OPTION BASE. As a result, you have to dimension only six elements, because QBasic lets you use subscript 0.

```
' Filename: C17DAYS1.BAS
'
DIM days$(6)       ' For elements days(0) through days(6)
FOR ctr = 0 TO 6
   READ days$(ctr)
NEXT ctr
DATA "Sunday", "Monday", "Tuesday", "Wednesday", "Thursday"
DATA "Friday", "Saturday"

' Print them out
FOR ctr = 0 to 6
   PRINT "Day"; ctr; "is "; days$(ctr)
NEXT ctr
```

Putting an OPTION BASE 0 statement in this program would be redundant; QBasic assumes zero-based arrays.

2. The following program is just like the previous one, except that it includes an OPTION BASE statement. The statement informs QBasic that the base subscript (the first one) is to be 1. Therefore, the programmer must reserve seven elements.

```
' Filename: C17DAYS2.BAS
'
OPTION BASE 1
DIM days$(7)     ' For elements days(1) through days(7)
FOR ctr = 1 TO 7
   READ days$(ctr)
NEXT ctr
DATA "Sunday", "Monday", "Tuesday", "Wednesday", "Thursday"
DATA "Friday", "Saturday"

' Print them out
FOR ctr = 1 to 7
   PRINT "Day"; ctr; "is "; days$(ctr)
NEXT ctr
```

Searching and Sorting Arrays

Arrays are the primary means by which data is stored in QBasic programs. As mentioned earlier, array data is usually read from a disk. Chapter 25 explains disk processing. For now, you should understand how to manipulate arrays so that you see the data exactly the way you want to see it.

In the previous examples, you saw arrays printed in the same order in which you entered the data. This is sometimes done, but it is not always the most appropriate method of looking at data. For instance, suppose that a high school uses QBasic programs for its enrollment. As each student enrolls, the clerk at the computer types the student's name. When the next student walks up, his or her name is entered, and so on until the names of the entire student body are in the computer, stored in a string array.

What if the school wants a listing of each student's name in alphabetical order? You would not be able to write a FOR-NEXT loop to print the elements from 1 to the total number of students; because the students did not enroll in alphabetical order, the list is out of sequence.

You need a method of putting arrays in a specific order, even if that order is not the same order in which the elements were entered. This is called *sorting* an array. When you sort an array, you put that array in a specific order, such as alphabetical order or numerical order. A dictionary is in sorted order, and so is a telephone book.

You can also reverse the order of a sort, which is called a *descending sort*. For instance, if you want to look at a list of all employees in descending salary order, the highest-paid employees are printed first.

Before learning to sort, it is helpful to learn how to search an array for a value. This is a preliminary step in learning to sort. What if one of those students gets married and wants her record to reflect her name change? Neither the student nor the clerk knows under which element the student's name is stored. As the following section shows, however, the computer can search for the name.

Searching for Values

You do not need to know any new commands to search an array for a value. The IF-THEN and FOR-LOOP statements are all you need. To search an array for a value, simply compare each element in that array with the IF-THEN statement to see whether they match. If they do, you have found the value. If they do not, keep searching down the array. If you run out of array elements before finding the value, it is not in the array.

There are several different kinds of searches you can perform. You might need to find the highest or lowest value in a list (array) of numbers. This is informative when you have much data and want to know the extremes of the data (such as the highest and lowest sales region in your division).

The following example program illustrates one of these array-searching techniques. It prints the highest sales of a company's sales staff.

Example

1. To find the highest number in an array, you compare each element to the first one. If you find a higher value, it becomes the basis for the rest of the array. Continue until you reach the end of the array and you will have the highest value, as the following program shows.

```
' Filename: C17HIGH.BAS
'
' Finds the highest sales total in the data.

' Reserve room for up to 25 sales values
DIM sales(25)
' Read all data into the array
subsc = 1    ' Array subscript
DO
   READ sales(subsc)
   subsc = subsc + 1
LOOP UNTIL (sales(subsc - 1) = -99)
subsc = subsc - 2
high.sales = sales(1)    ' Store first sales value
FOR ctr = 2 TO subsc     ' and compare all others to it
' Store current sales if it is higher than high sales so far
   IF sales(ctr) > high.sales THEN
      high.sales = sales(ctr)
   END IF
NEXT ctr
PRINT "The highest sales were"; high.sales
DATA 2900, 5400, 3429, 3744, 7678, 4585, -99
```

Notice that no ELSE or ELSEIF is needed, because you have to save the high sales information only if you find a higher value than the one you are comparing. Finding the smallest value in an array is just as easy. However, make sure you compare to see whether each succeeding array element is less than the lowest value found so far.

Sorting Arrays

Many times you need to sort one or more arrays. Suppose you take a list of names, write each name on a separate piece of paper, and throw the pieces in the air. The steps you would take to alphabetize the names (shuffling and changing the order of the pieces of paper) would be similar to what your computer has to go through to put numbers or character data into a sorted form.

Because sorting arrays requires exchanging values of elements, it helps to learn a new command in QBasic called the SWAP command. Here is the format of SWAP:

```
SWAP var1, var2
```

This command exchanges the values of the two variables that follow SWAP. You ought to be able to see that the following does not exchange the values of a and b:

```
a = b
b = a
```

This doesn't work because in the first line, the value of a is replaced with b's value. When the first line finishes, both a and b contain the same value. Therefore, the second line cannot work.

To swap these variables with the SWAP statement, you would type

```
SWAP a, b
```

This exchanges the values in the two variables.

There are several ways to sort arrays. These methods include the *bubble sort,* the *quick sort,* and the *shell sort.* The goal of each method is to compare each array element to another array element and swap them if needed to put them in order.

The theory behind these sorts is beyond the scope of this book; however, the bubble sort is one of the easiest sorting methods to follow. Values in an array are compared to each other, a pair at a time, and swapped if they are not in correct order. The lowest value eventually "floats" to the top of the list, like a bubble in a glass of water.

The following programs show the bubble sort in action.

Examples

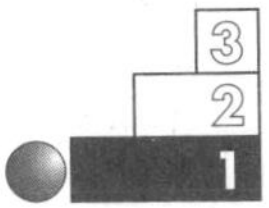

1. The following program reads 15 random numbers into an array and prints them in sorted order.

```
' Filename: C17SORT1.BAS
'
' Sorts and prints a list of numbers.
DIM number(15)
CLS
PRINT "Here are the unsorted numbers:"
FOR ctr = 0 TO 14
   READ number(ctr)
   PRINT number(ctr);
NEXT ctr

DATA 4, 3, 17, 5, 23, 44, 54, 8, 7, 54, 33, 22, 42, 48
DATA 90

FOR ctr1 = 0 TO 14
   FOR ctr2 = ctr1 + 1 TO 14  ' Each element will be
                              ' compared to its predecessor
      IF number(ctr1) > number(ctr2) THEN
         SWAP number(ctr1), number(ctr2)  ' "Float" the
                                          '  lowest to the top
      END IF
   NEXT ctr2
NEXT ctr1

' Print them to show that they are sorted
PRINT
LINE INPUT "Press ENTER to see the sorted numbers:"; ans$
FOR ctr = 0 TO 14
   PRINT number(ctr);

NEXT ctr
```

Figure 17.4 shows the output from this program. Notice that even the two numbers that are the same (54) sort next to each other as they should.

```
Here are the unsorted numbers:
 4  3  17  5  23  44  54  8  7  54  33  22  42  48  90
Press ENTER to see the sorted numbers:
 3  4  5  7  8  17  22  23  33  42  44  48  54  54  90





Press any key to continue
```

Figure 17.4. Demonstrating the bubble sort.

TIP: To sort in reverse order, from high to low, use a less-than-or-equal sign (<=) in place of the greater-than-or-equal sign (>=).

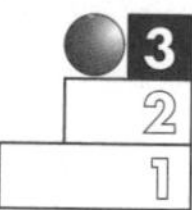

2. You can also sort character data. The computer uses the ASCII table to decide how the characters sort. Here is a program that is similar to the first one in this section (C17SORT1.BAS), but it reads and sorts a list of people's names.

```
' Filename: C17SORT3.BAS
'
' Sorts and prints a list of names.

DIM names$(15)
CLS
PRINT "Here are the unsorted names:"
FOR ctr = 0 TO 14
```

```
   READ names$(ctr)
   PRINT names$(ctr); " ";
NEXT ctr

DATA "Jim", "Larry", "Julie", "Kimberly", "John", "Mark"
DATA "Mary", "Terry"
DATA "Rhonda", "Jane", "Adam", "Richard", "Hans", "Ada"
DATA "Robert", "-99"

FOR ctr1 = 0 TO 14
   FOR ctr2 = ctr1 + 1 TO 14
      IF names$(ctr1) > names$(ctr2) THEN
         SWAP names$(ctr1), names$(ctr2)
      END IF
   NEXT ctr2
NEXT ctr1

' Print them to show that they are sorted
PRINT
LINE INPUT "Press Enter to see the sorted names:"; ans$
FOR ctr = 0 TO 14
   PRINT names$(ctr); " ";
NEXT ctr
```

Notice that `Ada` sorts before `Adam`, as it should. Remember that the goal of a sort is to reorder the array, but not to change any of the array's contents.

Advanced DIM Options

The `DIM` statement is actually more complex than shown earlier. For instance, although the `OPTION BASE` statement lets you change the first subscript in your arrays to 1, the `DIM` statement has options to make the starting subscript any number, even a negative number.

A more complete format of `DIM` is

```
DIM arrayname(bottom subscript TO highest subscript)
```

The *bottom* and *highest subscripts* can be from -32,768 to 32,767. The bottom subscript must be less than the highest. The total number of elements reserved is computed as follows:

```
(highest subscript - bottom subscript + 1)
```

Therefore, if the DIM statement looks like

```
DIM ara(4 TO 10)
```

there are seven total elements (10 minus 4 plus 1), and they are

```
ara(4)    ara(5)    ara(6)    ara(7)
ara(8)    ara(9)    ara(10)
```

If the DIM statement read

```
DIM scores(-45 TO -1)
```

there would be 45 total subscripts (-1 minus -45 plus 1 is 45), and they would be

```
scores(-45)    scores(-44)    scores(-43)
...
scores(-3)     scores(-2)     scores(-1)
```

Programmers do not often change these subscript boundaries from their original base of 0, but there are times when it might be a little clearer if they did. For example, suppose you have to write a QBasic program to keep track of the internal value of a bank's safety deposit boxes. The bank's boxes are numbered 101 through 504. You could store the values in an array based at 0 or 1, as seen earlier.

It is much easier, however, to reserve the storage for this array with the following DIM statement:

```
DIM boxes(101 TO 504)
```

The subscripts are then very meaningful, and they make it easier to reference a specific box's value.

The ERASE Statement

ERASE erases the contents of arrays. It does this by zeroing all elements of numeric arrays and putting null strings into each element of character string arrays. The format of ERASE is

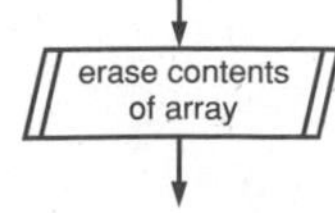


```
ERASE array1 [, array2] [, array3] [,..., arrayN]
```

ERASE can be followed by one or more array names (separated by commas if there is more than one array).

There is no reason to use ERASE immediately after dimensioning an array because QBasic automatically clears all elements when an array is dimensioned. If you have been using an array for values and need to use the same array for a different set of values, however, ERASE is a quick way to clear the array. This beats the old BASIC method of writing a loop to clear each array.

Example

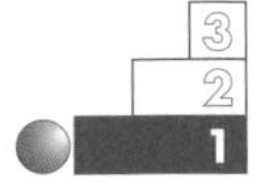

1. The following program loads numbers into an array and prints them. The program then erases that array and prints it again.

```
' Filename: C17ERAS1.BAS
'
' Program to demonstrate ERASE statement.

DIM a(5), b$(5)
CLS

FOR ctr = 1 to 5
   READ a(ctr), b$(ctr)
NEXT ctr

PRINT "Here are the arrays:"
PRINT "a:", "b$:"
FOR ctr = 1 to 5
   PRINT a(ctr), b$(ctr)
NEXT ctr

ERASE a, b$

PRINT
PRINT "After erasing them, they hold:"
PRINT "a:", "b$:"
FOR ctr = 1 to 5
   PRINT a(ctr), b$(ctr)
NEXT ctr

DATA 10, "Joy", 20, "Happy", 30, "Glad", 40, "Nice", 50
DATA "OK"
```

Figure 17.5 shows what happens if you run this program. Nothing prints under the b$: column because null strings (sometimes called *empty strings*) never appear on the screen.

```
Here are the arrays:
a:            b$:
 10           Joy
 20           Happy
 30           Glad
 40           Nice
 50           OK

After erasing them, they hold:
a:            b$:
 0
 0
 0
 0
 0




Press any key to continue
```

Figure 17.5. Demonstrating the ERASE statement.

Summary

This chapter covered a lot of ground. You learned about arrays, which are a more powerful way to store lists of data. By stepping through the array subscript, your program can quickly scan, print, sort, and calculate a list of values or names. You have the tools to sort lists of names and numbers, as well as search for values in a list.

When you have mastered this chapter, Chapter 18, "Multidimensional Arrays," will be easy. It is relatively short. It shows how you can keep track of arrays in a different format, called a *multidimensional array.* Not all lists of data lend themselves to matrices, but you should be prepared for them when you do need them.

Review Questions

Answers to the Review Questions are in Appendix B.

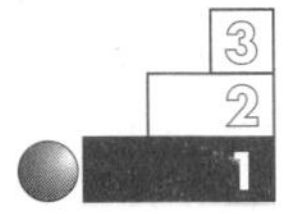

1. TRUE or FALSE: Arrays hold more than one variable with the same name.
2. How do QBasic programs tell one array element (value) from another if the elements have identical names?
3. Can array elements be different types?
4. How can you quickly erase the contents of an array?

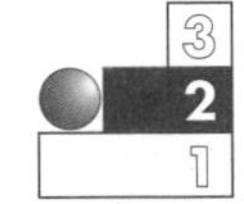

5. How many elements are reserved in the following dimension statement? (Assume an `OPTION BASE` of 0.)

```
DIM ara(78)
```

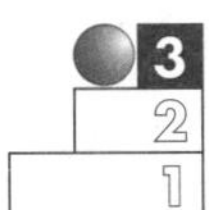

6. Which statement(s) lets you change the beginning 0 subscript to another number?
7. How would you exchange the values of two variables?
8. Why is it redundant to use an `ERASE` statement immediately after a `DIM` statement?
9. How many elements are reserved in the following dimension statement?

```
DIM staff(-18 TO 4)
```

Review Exercises

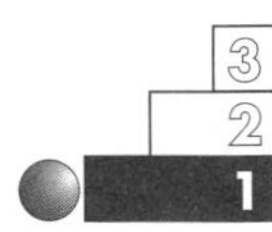

1. Write a program to store six of your friends' names in a single string array. Use `INPUT` to initialize the arrays with the names. Print the names on the screen.
2. Modify the program in the preceding exercise, and print the names backward after using `READ` and `DATA` to initialize the arrays (do not use `INPUT`).

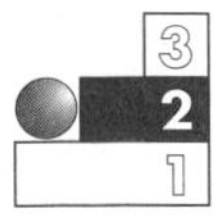

3. Write a simple database program to track the names of a radio station's top 10 hits. After storing the array, print the songs in reverse order (to get the top 10 countdown).

4. Write a program that uses READ and DATA to initialize an array that holds the names of the top 10 graduating seniors from a local high school. Make sure QBasic assumes a starting subscript of 1 instead of its default of 0. After reading in the values, ask the principal which number (1 through 10) he or she wants to see, and print that name.

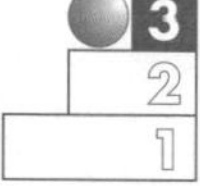

5. Write a program that small business owners could use to track their customers. Assign each customer a number, starting at 1001. When customers come in, store their last names in the element numbers that match their new customer numbers (the next, unused array element). When the owner signals the end of the day by pressing Enter without entering a name, print a report of each customer's number and name information for that day. Make sure you start the subscripts at 1001 instead of at 0 or 1. (Hint: Use the TO option of the DIM statement.)

6. Change the program assigned in #5 to sort and print the report in alphabetical order by customer name. After each name, print the customer's account number as well (his or her corresponding subscript).

18

Multidimensional Arrays

Some data fits in lists like those you saw in Chapter 17; other data is better suited to a table of information. This chapter expands on arrays. The previous chapter introduced *single-dimensional* arrays, which are arrays that have only one subscript. Single-dimensional arrays represent a list of values.

This chapter introduces arrays of more than one dimension, called *multidimensional arrays*. Multidimensional arrays, sometimes called *tables* or *matrices*, have rows and columns. This chapter explains the following concepts and procedures:

- ♦ What multidimensional arrays are
- ♦ Putting data in multidimensional arrays
- ♦ Using nested FOR-NEXT loops to process multidimensional arrays

If you understand single-dimensional arrays, you should have no trouble understanding arrays with more than one dimension.

What Multidimensional Arrays Are

A multidimensional array is an array with more than one subscript. A single-dimensional array is a list of values, whereas a multidimensional array simulates a table of values, or even multiple tables of values. The most commonly used table is a two-dimensional table (an array with two subscripts).

Suppose a softball team wants to keep track of its players' hits. The team played 10 games, and there are 15 players on the team. Table 18.1 shows the team's hit record.

Table 18.1. A softball team's hit record.

Player Name	*Game 1*	*Game 2*	*Game 3*	*Game 4*	*Game 5*	*Game 6*	*Game 7*	*Game 8*	*Game 9*	*Game 10*
Adams	2	1	0	0	2	3	3	1	1	2
Berryhill	1	0	3	2	5	1	2	2	1	0
Downing	1	0	2	1	0	0	0	0	2	0
Edwards	0	3	6	4	6	4	5	3	6	3
Franks	2	2	3	2	1	0	2	3	1	0
Grady	1	3	2	0	1	5	2	1	2	1
Howard	3	1	1	1	2	0	1	0	4	3
Jones	2	2	1	2	4	1	0	7	1	0
Martin	5	4	5	1	1	0	2	4	1	5
Powers	2	2	3	1	0	2	1	3	1	2
Smith	1	1	2	1	3	4	1	0	3	2
Smithtown	1	0	1	2	1	0	3	4	1	2
Townsend	0	0	0	0	0	0	1	0	0	0
Ulmer	2	2	2	2	2	1	1	3	1	3
Williams	2	3	1	0	1	2	1	2	0	3

Do you see that the softball table is a two-dimensional table? It has rows (one of the dimensions) and columns (the second dimension). Therefore, you would call this a two-dimensional table with 15 rows and 10 columns. (Generally, the number of rows is specified first.)

Each row has a player's name, and each column has a game number associated with it, but these are not part of the data. The data consists only of 150 values (15 rows times 10 columns equals 150 data values). The data in a table, like the data in an array, always is the same type of data (in this case, every value is an integer). If the table contained names, it would be a string table, and so on.

The number of dimensions, in this case two, corresponds to the dimensions in the physical world. The first dimension represents a line. The single-dimensional array is a line, or list, of values. Two dimensions represent both length and width. You write on a piece of paper in two dimensions; two dimensions represent a flat surface. Three dimensions represent width, length, and depth. You have seen three-dimensional movies. Not only do the images have width and height, but they also (appear to) have depth.

It is difficult for us to visualize more than three dimensions. You can, however, think of each dimension after three as another occurrence. In other words, a list of one player's season hit record could be stored in an array. The team's hit record (as shown previously) is two-dimensional. The league, made of up several team's hit records, would represent a three-dimensional table. Each team (the depth of the table) would have rows and columns of hit data. If there is more than one league, leagues could be considered another dimension.

QBasic gives you the capability of storing up to 60 dimensions, although "real world" data rarely requires more than two or three dimensions.

Dimensioning Multidimensional Arrays

Use the `DIM` statement to reserve multidimensional tables. Rather than putting one value in the parentheses, you put a value for each dimension in the table. The basic syntax of the `DIM` statement for multidimensional arrays is

```
DIM variable(row [, col] [, depth] [, ...])
```

For example, to reserve the team data from Table 18.1, you would use the following DIM statement:

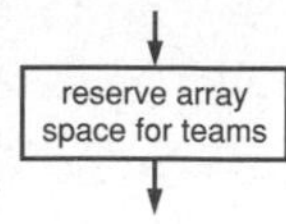


```
DIM teams(15, 10)
```

This reserves a two-dimensional table with 150 elements. Each element's subscript looks like those in Figure 18.1 (assuming an OPTION BASE of 1).

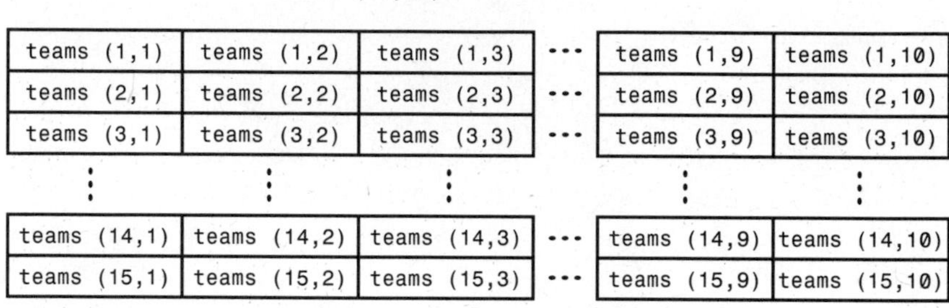

Figure 18.1. Subscripts for the softball team table.

If there were three teams that you needed to track, and each team had 15 players and played 10 games, you could dimension the table as:

```
DIM teams(15, 10, 3)
```

This dimensions three occurrences of the team table shown in Figure 18.1.

When dimensioning a table, always put the maximum number of rows first and the maximum number of columns second. Because QBasic always assumes a starting subscript of 0 unless you override it with the OPTION BASE command, the two-dimensional DIM statement shown earlier actually stores up to 16 rows (numbered 0 through 15) and 11 columns (numbered 0 through 10). Most programmers, however, ignore the 0 subscript. To be totally correct, if you want to keep the total number of rows and columns the same as that in the DIM statement, be sure to use the OPTION BASE statement to set the starting subscript to 1, as in

```
OPTION BASE 1
DIM teams(15, 10)
```

OPTION BASE sets the starting value for both subscripts to 1 or 0. You cannot set only one of them with OPTION BASE.

If, however, you are keeping track of complex subscripted data, you can use the TO option of the DIM statement to dimension a table with different starting and ending subscripts. The following statement dimensions a three-dimensional table. The first dimension (the number of rows) subscripts from -5 to 6. The second dimension (the number of columns) subscripts from 200 to 300. The third dimension (the number of depth values, or the number of sets of rows and columns) is subscripted from 5 to 10.

```
DIM ara1(-5 TO 6, 200 TO 300, 5 TO 10)
```

This can be confusing, and it's not always much more useful than simply using the default subscript values. Therefore, you rarely see this complex kind of DIM statement used for multidimensional arrays.

If you need to, you can combine several DIM statements into one. For instance, the following line reserves storage for three multidimensional arrays:

```
DIM ara1(10, 20), ara2(4,5,5), ara3(6, 10, 20, 30)
```

Assuming an OPTION BASE of 1, the first multidimensional array, ara1, reserves 200 elements. The second array reserves 100 elements (4 times 5 times 5). The third reserves 36,000 elements (6 times 10 times 20 times 30). As you can see, the number of elements adds up quickly. Be careful that you do not reserve so many array elements that you run out of memory in which to store them. If you run out of memory, you receive the following error message:

```
Subscript out of range
```

As with single-dimensional arrays, QBasic always initializes numeric table values to 0 and string table values to null strings.

Tables and FOR-NEXT Loops

As you will see in the examples, nested FOR-NEXT loops are good candidates for looping through every element of a multidimensional table. For instance, the section of code

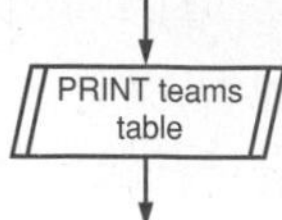


```
FOR row = 1 TO 2
   FOR col = 1 TO 3
      PRINT row, col
   NEXT col
NEXT row
```

produces the following output:

```
1    1
1    2
1    3
2    1
2    2
2    3
```

These are exactly the subscripts, in row order, for a two-row by three-column table that is dimensioned in

```
DIM table(2, 3)
```

Notice that there are as many FOR-NEXT statements as there are subscripts in the DIM statement (two). The outside loop represents the first subscript (the rows), and the inside loop represents the second subscript (the columns).

You can use INPUT statements to fill a table, although this is rarely done. Most multidimensional array data comes from READ and DATA statements, or more often, from data files from the disk. Regardless of what method actually stores values in multidimensional arrays, nested FOR-NEXT loops are excellent control statements to step through the subscripts. The following examples illustrate how nested FOR-NEXT loops work with multidimensional arrays.

Examples

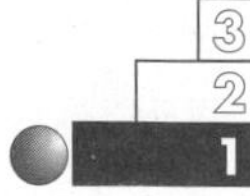

1. The following statements reserve enough memory elements for a television station's shows for one week:

```
OPTION BASE 1
DIM shows$(7, 48)
```

These statements reserve enough elements to hold seven days (the rows) of 30-minute shows (because there are 24 hours in a day, this table holds up to 48 30-minute shows).

Every element in a table is always the same type. In this case, each element is a string variable. Some of them could be initialized with the following assignment statements:

```
shows$(3, 12) = "Sally's Shoreline"
shows$(1, 5) = "Guessing Game Show"
shows$(7, 20) = "As the Hospital Turns"
```

2. A computer company sells two sizes of diskettes: 3½-inch and 5¼-inch. Each diskette comes in one of four capacities: single-sided double-density, double-sided double-density, single-sided high-density, and double-sided high-density.

   The diskette inventory is well-suited for a two-dimensional table. The company determined that the diskettes have the following retail prices:

	Single-sided Double-density	*Double-sided Double-density*	*Single-sided High-density*	*Double-sided High-density*
3½-inch	2.30	2.75	3.20	3.50
5¼-inch	1.75	2.10	2.60	2.95

   The company wants to store the price of each diskette in a table for easy access. The following program does that with assignment statements.

```
' Filename: C18DISK1.BAS
'
' Assigns diskette prices to a table.

OPTION BASE 1
DIM disks(2, 4)

disks(1, 1) = 2.30      ' Row 1, Column 1
disks(1, 2) = 2.75      ' Row 1, Column 2
disks(1, 3) = 3.20      ' Row 1, Column 3
disks(1, 4) = 3.50      ' Row 1, Column 4
disks(2, 1) = 1.75      ' Row 2, Column 1
disks(2, 2) = 2.10      ' Row 2, Column 2
```

```
disks(2, 3) = 2.60      ' Row 2, Column 3
disks(2, 4) = 2.95      ' Row 2, Column 4

CLS
' Print the prices
FOR row = 1 TO 2
   FOR col = 1 TO 4
      PRINT USING "##.##"; disks(row, col)
   NEXT col
NEXT row
```

This program displays the prices, as shown in Figure 18.2. It prints them one line at a time without any descriptive titles. Although the output is not extremely helpful, it illustrates how you can use assignment statements to initialize a table, and how nested FOR-NEXT loops can print the elements.

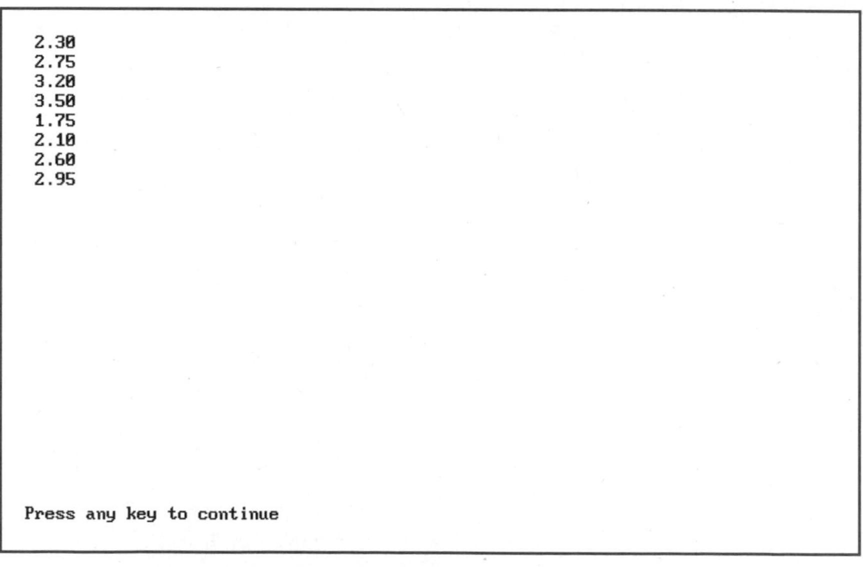

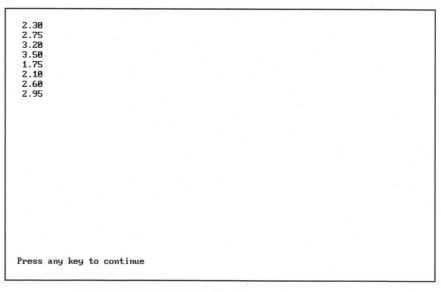

Figure 18.2. Viewing the diskette pricing values.

3. Filling table elements with values is cumbersome if you use assignment statements like those shown previously. When a table has more than eight values (as most probably do), such assignment statements are especially difficult to follow.

Therefore, most tables are filled with either READ-DATA statements or INPUT statements (or else they are filled from a disk file, as you will see later). The following program fills the disk inventory pricing table with READ-DATA statements.

```
' Filename: C18DISK2.BAS
'
' Reads diskette prices into a table.

OPTION BASE 1
DIM disks(2, 4)

FOR row = 1 TO 2
   FOR col = 1 TO 4
      READ disks(row, col)
   NEXT col
NEXT row

DATA 2.30, 2.75, 3.20, 3.50
DATA 1.75, 2.10, 2.60, 2.95

CLS
' Print the prices
FOR row = 1 TO 2
   FOR col = 1 TO 4
      PRINT USING "##.##"; disks(row, col)
   NEXT col
NEXT row
```

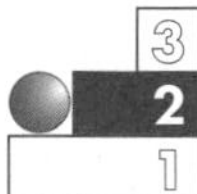

4. The preceding diskette inventory would be displayed better if the output had descriptive titles. Before you add titles, it is helpful for you to see how to print a table in its native row and column format.

   Typically, a nested FOR-NEXT loop such as the one in the previous example is used. If you put a semicolon at the end of the PRINT statement, however, the values do not print one number per line; rather, they print next to each other on one line. (Remember, the trailing semicolon keeps a carriage return from happening at the end of a PRINT or an LPRINT statement.)

You do not want to see every diskette price on one line, but you want each row of the table printed on a separate line. A blank `PRINT` statement without a trailing semicolon sends the cursor to the next line, so insert a `PRINT` statement before the row number changes (immediately before the `NEXT row` statement). Doing so prints the table in its row and column format, as shown here.

```
' Filename: C18DISK3.BAS
'
' Assigns diskette prices to a table.

OPTION BASE 1
DIM disks(2, 4)

FOR row = 1 TO 2
   FOR col = 1 TO 4
      READ disks(row, col)
   NEXT col
NEXT row

DATA 2.30, 2.75, 3.20, 3.50
DATA 1.75, 2.10, 2.60, 2.95

CLS
' Print the prices in table format
' Print the numbers with a few spaces before
' them to separate them from each other when printed
FOR row = 1 TO 2
   FOR col = 1 TO 4
      PRINT USING "   ##.##"; disks(row, col);
   NEXT col
   PRINT     ' Forces the cursor to the next row
NEXT row
```

Figure 18.3 shows the result of a run of this program. The only things missing are the titles.

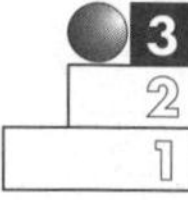

5. To add the titles, simply print a row of titles before the first row of values, and then print a new column title (with a trailing semicolon) before each column, as shown in the following program.

```
  2.30   2.75   3.20   3.50
  1.75   2.10   2.60   2.95









Press any key to continue
```

Figure 18.3. Printing in a table format.

```
' Filename: C18DISK4.BAS
'
' Assigns diskette prices to a table.

OPTION BASE 1
DIM disks(2, 4)

FOR row = 1 TO 2
   FOR col = 1 TO 4
      READ disks(row, col)
   NEXT col
NEXT row

DATA 2.30, 2.75, 3.20, 3.50
DATA 1.75, 2.10, 2.60, 2.95

CLS
' Print the prices in table format
' Print the numbers with a few spaces before
' them to separate them from each other when printed
' Add spaces to PRINT USING to center numbers under titles
```

```
PRINT TAB(9); "Single-sided,    Double-sided,    ";
PRINT "Single-sided,   Double-sided"
PRINT TAB(9); "Double-density   Double-density   ";
PRINT "High-density    High-density"
  FOR row = 1 TO 2
     IF row = 1 THEN PRINT "3-1/2 inch"; ELSE PRINT "5-1/4 inch";
     FOR col = 1 TO 4
        PRINT USING "  ##.##          "; disks(row, col);
     NEXT col
     PRINT      ' Forces the cursor to the next row
  NEXT row
```

Figure 18.4 shows the output from this program.

```
        Single-sided,   Double-sided,   Single-sided,   Double-sided
        Double-density  Double-density  High-density    High-density
3-1/2 inch   2.30            2.75            3.20            3.50
5-1/4 inch   1.75            2.10            2.60            2.95

Press any key to continue
```

Figure 18.4. Printing in a table format.

6. The following program is a comprehensive program that reads in the softball team hits table shown earlier in the chapter. The values are read from DATA statements.

   This example shows the usefulness of such tables. Instead of simply printing the complete table, it actually processes the table's raw data into meaningful information by supplying the following information:

- A list showing each player's total hits for the season
- The name of the player with the most hits
- The name of the player with the fewest hits
- The game with the most hits
- The game with the fewest hits

The player names cannot be stored in the table with the hit data because the names are string data and the hits are stored as integers. Therefore, a separate array (single-dimensional) that holds the player names is read. When the numbers of the rows with the most and fewest hits are known, those two players' names are printed from the player name array using the row number.

```
' Filename: C18HITS.BAS
'
' Program to display stats from the team's softball league.

' Reserve storage for hits and player names
OPTION BASE 1
DIM hits(15, 10), player$(15)

CLS
' Read the data into a table
FOR row = 1 TO 15       ' First read the hits
   FOR col = 1 TO 10
      READ hits(row, col)
   NEXT col
NEXT row

FOR ctr = 1 TO 15       ' Now read the player names
   READ player$(ctr)
NEXT ctr

'  Find and print each player's total hits, and find highest
'  and lowest
highest = 0        ' Ensure that first player's hits are more
                   ' than highest
lowest = 999       ' and less than lowest to start the ball
                   ' rolling
```

```
PRINT "Name", "Total Hits"
FOR row = 1 TO 15
   total = 0         ' Initialize before each player's hit
                     ' total begins
     FOR col = 1 TO 10
        total = total + hits(row, col)
     NEXT col
     PRINT player$(row), total
     IF (total > highest) THEN high.row = row: highest = total
     IF (total < lowest) THEN low.row = row: lowest = total
  NEXT row
  PRINT
  PRINT player$(high.row); " had the highest number of hits ";
  PRINT "at"; highest
  PRINT player$(low.row); " had the lowest number of hits ";
  PRINT "at"; lowest
  highest = 0  ' Ensure first game's hits are more than highest
  lowest = 999 ' and less than lowest to start the ball rolling
  FOR col = 1 TO 10       ' This time step through columns 1st
                          ' to add game totals
     total = 0            ' Initialize before each game's hit
                          ' totals begin
     FOR row = 1 TO 15
        total = total + hits(row, col)
     NEXT row
     IF (total > highest) THEN high.game = col: highest = total
     IF (total < lowest) THEN low.game = col: lowest = total
  NEXT col
  PRINT
  PRINT "Game number"; high.game; "had the highest number of ";
  PRINT "hits at"; highest
  PRINT "Game number"; low.game; "had the lowest number of ";
  PRINT "hits at"; lowest
  ' Two teams worth of hits per line for most of these DATA
  ' statements
  DATA 2, 1, 0, 0, 2, 3, 3, 1, 1, 2, 1, 0, 3, 2, 5, 1, 2, 2, 1, 0
  DATA 1, 0, 2, 1, 0, 0, 0, 0, 2, 0, 0, 3, 6, 4, 6, 4, 5, 3, 6, 3
  DATA 2, 2, 3, 2, 1, 0, 2, 3, 1, 0, 1, 3, 2, 0, 1, 5, 2, 1, 2, 1
  DATA 3, 1, 1, 1, 2, 0, 1, 0, 4, 3, 2, 2, 1, 2, 4, 1, 0, 7, 1, 0
  DATA 5, 4, 5, 1, 1, 0, 2, 4, 1, 5, 2, 2, 3, 1, 0, 2, 1, 3, 1, 2
  DATA 1, 1, 2, 1, 3, 4, 1, 0, 3, 2, 1, 0, 1, 2, 1, 0, 3, 4, 1, 2
  DATA 0, 0, 0, 0, 0, 0, 1, 0, 0, 0, 2, 2, 2, 2, 2, 1, 1, 3, 1, 3
```

```
DATA 2, 3, 1, 0, 1, 2, 1, 2, 0, 3
DATA Adams, Berryhill, Downing, Edwards, Franks, Grady
DATA Howard, Jones, Martin, Powers, Smith, Smithtown
DATA Townsend, Ulmer, Williams
```

Figure 18.5 shows the result of this program's table computations.

```
Name          Total Hits
Adams          15
Berryhill      17
Downing        6
Edwards        40
Franks         16
Grady          18
Howard         16
Jones          20
Martin         28
Powers         17
Smith          18
Smithtown      15
Townsend       1
Ulmer          19
Williams       15

Edwards had the highest number of hits at 40
Townsend had the lowest number of hits at 1

Game number 8 had the highest number of hits at 33
Game number 4 had the lowest number of hits at 19


Press any key to continue
```

Figure 18.5. Printing table data and computations.

Summary

You know how to create, initialize, and process multidimensional arrays. Although not all data fits in the compact format of tables, much does. Using nested FOR-NEXT loops makes stepping through a multidimensional array straightforward.

One of the limitations of a multidimensional array is that each element must be the same data type. This keeps you from being able to store several kinds of data in tables.

In the next chapter you will learn about built-in routines that work with numbers.

Review Questions

Answers to the Review Questions are in Appendix B.

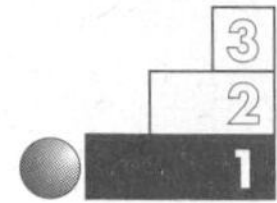

1. What statement reserves a two-dimensional table of integers called `scores` with five rows and six columns? Assume an `OPTION BASE` of 1.

2. What statement reserves a three-dimensional table of string variables called `names` with two sets of 10 rows and 20 columns? Assume an `OPTION BASE` of 1.

3. Given the `DIM` statement

```
DIM names$(5, 10)
```

which subscript (first or second) represents rows and which represents columns?

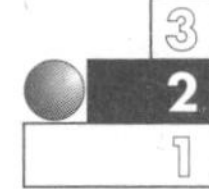

4. How many elements are reserved with the following statements:

```
OPTION BASE 1
DIM ara(5, 6)
```

5. Given the following table of integers in the matrix called `ara`

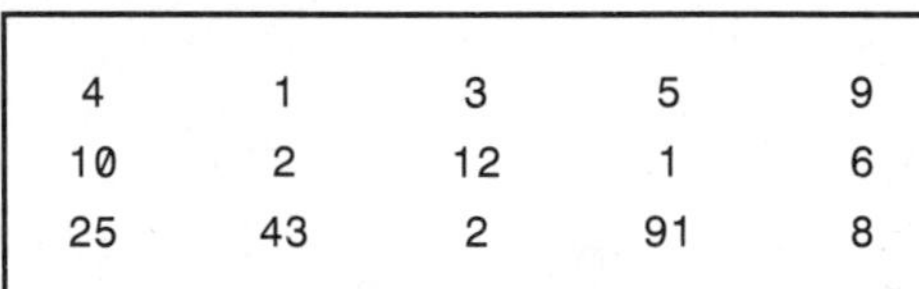

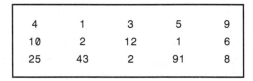

4	1	3	5	9
10	2	12	1	6
25	43	2	91	8

what values do the following elements contain? Assume an `OPTION BASE` of 1.

A. `ara(2, 2)`
B. `ara(1, 2)`
C. `ara(3, 4)`
D. `ara(3, 5)`

6. Given the program

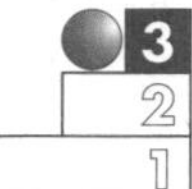

```
OPTION BASE 1
DIM grades(3, 5)
FOR row = 1 TO 3
   FOR col = 1 TO 5
      READ grades(row, col)
   NEXT col
NEXT row

DATA 80, 90, 96, 73, 65, 67, 90, 68
DATA 92, 84, 70, 55, 95, 78, 100
```

what are the values of

A. `grades(2, 3)`
B. `grades(3, 5)`
C. `grades(1, 1)`

7. What control statement is best used for "stepping" through multidimensional arrays?

8. How many elements do the following statements reserve?

```
OPTION BASE 1
DIM  accounts(-10 TO 12, 30 TO 35, -1 TO 2)
```

Review Exercises

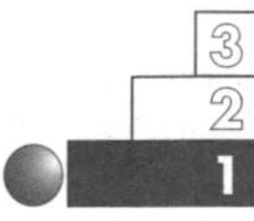

1. Write a program that reserves storage for three years of sales data for five salespeople. Use assignment statements to fill the matrix with data and print it one value per line. (Hint: Use columns for the years and rows for the salespeople.)

2. Rather than assignment statements, use READ and DATA statements to fill the salespeople data from the preceding exercise.

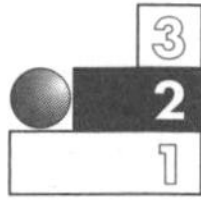

3. Write a program that tracks the grades for five classes that have 10 students each. Read the data from DATA statements, and print the table in its native row and column format.

4. Add appropriate titles to the table you printed in the preceding exercise.

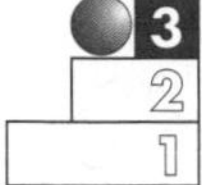

5. Read the softball team hits into a table. Compute and print the average number of hits per game and the average number of hits per player. (Hint: This requires that you step through the rows and columns twice, which is similar to the C18HITS.BAS example that printed the maximum and minimum values earlier.)

6. Given the following table of distances between cities

	Tulsa	*Okla. City*	*Joplin*	*Dallas*
Tulsa	0	101	89	400
Okla. City	101	0	178	420
Joplin	89	178	0	532
Dallas	400	420	532	0

write a program to read this data into a table of mileage and print the following:

- ◆ The city closest to Tulsa (not including Tulsa)
- ◆ The city farthest from Dallas
- ◆ The average mileage of surrounding towns (not including itself) to Joplin
- ◆ The two cities closest together

Although it is easy to look at the table and see the answers, your program should search the table to find this data. If you add many more cities to the table, your program does not change except for a few subscripts and DATA values.

Part VI

Subroutines and Functions

19

Numeric Functions

You have already seen several methods of writing routines that make your computer work for you. This chapter is the first of a series of chapters designed to show you ways to increase QBasic's productivity on your computer. This chapter shows you ways to use many built-in routines that work with numbers. These are called *numeric functions.* By learning the QBasic numeric functions, you can let QBasic manipulate your mathematical data.

This chapter introduces you to

- ♦ Integer functions
- ♦ Common mathematical functions
- ♦ Noninteger precision functions
- ♦ Trigonometric functions
- ♦ Logarithm and *e* functions
- ♦ The LEN function
- ♦ The TIMER function
- ♦ Random-number processing

Although some of these functions are highly technical, many of them are used daily by QBasic programmers who do not use much math in their programs. Most of these functions are useful for reducing your programming time. Instead of having to "reinvent the wheel" every time you need QBasic to perform a numeric operation, you might be able to use one of the many built-in functions to do the job for you.

Overview of Functions

Functions are built-in routines that manipulate numbers, strings, and output. You have already seen two functions that manipulate output: the `TAB` and `SPC` functions inside the `PRINT` and `LPRINT` statements.

You have already seen a string function, the `CHR$()` function. By putting a number inside the parentheses, you can print the character that corresponds to that number on the ASCII table. The statement

```
PRINT CHR$(65); CHR$(66); CHR$(67); CHR$(7)
```

prints the letters *A*, *B*, and *C*, and then rings the bell (ASCII value 7 is the bell character).

Each of these functions illustrates what all functions (numeric, string, and output) have in common: The function name is always followed by parentheses. The value in the parentheses determines what the function does. It is called an *argument*. The `TAB()` output function in the statement

```
PRINT TAB(23); "Hi!"
```

contains one argument, `23`, and that argument is sent to the function. Without the argument, the function would have nothing on which to work.

The format of a *function call* (using a function anywhere in your program) is

```
FunctionName [( arg 1 )] [, arg 2 )] [, ..., arg N )]
```

A function never stands by itself on a line.

Notice that a function can have no arguments, one argument, or more than one argument, depending on how it is defined. A function never stands by itself on a line; you always combine functions with other statements (assignment statements, output statements, and so on).

A function always returns a value.

A function always *returns* a value as well. The output functions always perform a cursor movement. The numeric and string functions return either a number or a string based on the argument you send to it. When a numeric function returns a value, you must do something with that value: Either print it, assign it to a variable, or use it in an expression. Because the purpose of a function is to return a value, you cannot put a function on the left side of an equal sign in an assignment statement.

NOTE: A function name always has parentheses following it if it requires an argument, as most of them do.

Integer Functions

Several functions are related to integers:

- `INT()`
- `FIX()`
- `CINT()`
- `CLNG()`

One of the most common integer functions is the `INT()` function. It returns the integer value of the number you put in the parentheses. If you put a single-precision or double-precision number inside the parentheses, `INT()` converts it to an integer. For example:

```
PRINT INT(8.93)
```

prints an `8` (the return value) on the screen.

NOTE: `INT()` returns a whole number that is equal to or less than the argument in the parentheses. `INT()` does not round numbers up.

You can use a variable or expression as the numeric function argument, as shown here:

```
num = 8.93
PRINT INT(num)
```

The preceding lines and the lines

```
num = 8
PRINT INT(num + 0.93)
```

as well as the lines

```
num1 = 8.93
num2 = INT(num1)
PRINT num2
```

all produce the same output: `8`.

`INT()` works for negative arguments as well. The following section of code

```
PRINT INT(-7.6)
```

prints `-8`. This might surprise you until you look back at the definition of `INT()`. It returns the highest integer that is less than or equal to the argument in the parentheses. The highest integer less than or equal to -7.6 is -8.

Notice that calling `INT()` does not change its argument. This is true of all function calls. If you put a variable inside a function's argument list, that variable is used by the function, but it is not changed. Only an assignment statement changes an argument's value.

> **NOTE:** `FIX()` returns the *truncated* whole number value of the argument.

Truncation means that the fractional part of the argument (the part of the number to the right of the decimal point) is taken off the number. `FIX()` always returns an integer value. The line

```
PRINT FIX(8.93)
```

prints the value of `8`. For positive numbers, `FIX()` and `INT()` work identically.

For negative numbers, `FIX()` and `INT()` return very different return values. `FIX()` simply drops the fractional part of the number, whether it is positive or negative, from the argument. Therefore,

```
PRINT FIX(-8.93), FIX(-8.02)
```

prints the following two numbers

```
-8   -8
```

whereas `INT()` would return *-9* in both examples because `INT()` does not truncate, but returns the closest integer less than or equal to the argument.

`INT()` and `FIX()` both return whole numbers, but they return the whole numbers in single-precision format. In other words, although `INT()` and `FIX()` eliminate their arguments' fractional portions and leave only the whole-number portions, their return values are still single-precision numbers (with *0* as the fractional part).

For practical purposes, you can assume that `INT()` and `FIX()` return integers, because it appears that they do. Because they actually return whole-number, single-precision values, however, you can use them for arguments that are much larger or smaller than those the integer data type can hold.

NOTE: `CINT()` returns the closest rounded integer to the value of the argument.

Therefore, the statement

```
PRINT CINT(8.1), CINT(8.5), CINT(8.5001), CINT(8.8)
```

produces the following output:

```
8     8     9     9
```

Notice how `CINT()` (for *convert integer*) handles the rounding. For positive numbers, if the fractional portion of the argument is less than or equal to one-half (.5), `CINT()` rounds downward. Otherwise, it rounds upward. For negative numbers, `CINT()` rounds to the closest negative integer. For instance:

```
PRINT CINT(-8.1), CINT(-8.5), CINT(-8.5001), CINT(-8.8)
```

produces the following output:

```
 -8    -8    -9    -9
```

CINT() has a limitation: It is limited to return values that fall within the range of *-32,768* to *32,767* because it returns only the integer data type. Unlike with INT() and FIX(), you must use a different function if you want to round values outside these two extremes.

Use the CLNG() (for *convert long integer*) if you need to round numbers outside CINT()'s extremes. For example:

```
PRINT CLNG(-44034.1), CLNG(985465.6)
```

produces the following output:

```
-44034    985466
```

If you attempt to use CINT() to round numbers larger or smaller than its extreme values, you get an error message that says Overflow.

CLNG() rounds integers within the range of *-2,147,483,648* to *2,147,483,647.*

Example

1. The following program summarizes each of the four integer functions. It prints the return values of each integer function using several different arguments. Pay attention to how each function differs for both positive and negative numbers.

```
' Filename: C19INTF.BAS
'
' Illustrates the way the four integer functions compare.
CLS

PRINT "Argument", "INT()", "FIX()", "CINT()", "CLNG()"
PRINT "--------", "-----", "-----", "------", "------"
num = 10    ' 1st use an integer argument
PRINT num, INT(num), FIX(num), CINT(num), CLNG(num)
num = 10.5
PRINT num, INT(num), FIX(num), CINT(num), CLNG(num)
num = 10.51
```

```
PRINT num, INT(num), FIX(num), CINT(num), CLNG(num)
num = 0.1
PRINT num, INT(num), FIX(num), CINT(num), CLNG(num)
num = 0.5
PRINT num, INT(num), FIX(num), CINT(num), CLNG(num)
num = 0.51
PRINT num, INT(num), FIX(num), CINT(num), CLNG(num)
num = -0.1
PRINT num, INT(num), FIX(num), CINT(num), CLNG(num)
num = -0.5
PRINT num, INT(num), FIX(num), CINT(num), CLNG(num)
num = -0.51
PRINT num, INT(num), FIX(num), CINT(num), CLNG(num)
num = -10
PRINT num, INT(num), FIX(num), CINT(num), CLNG(num)
num = -10.5
PRINT num, INT(num), FIX(num), CINT(num), CLNG(num)
num = -10.51
PRINT num, INT(num), FIX(num), CINT(num), CLNG(num)
```

Figure 19.1 shows the output of this program.

```
Argument     INT()       FIX()       CINT()      CLNG()
--------     -----       -----       ------      ------
 10          10          10          10          10
 10.5        10          10          10          10
 10.51       10          10          11          11
 .1          0           0           0           0
 .5          0           0           0           0
 .51         0           0           1           1
-.1          -1          0           0           0
-.5          -1          0           0           0
-.51         -1          0           -1          -1
-10          -10         -10         -10         -10
-10.5        -11         -10         -10         -10
-10.51       -11         -10         -11         -11

Press any key to continue
```

Figure 19.1. Comparing each of the four integer functions.

Common Mathematical Functions

You don't have to be an expert in math to use many of the mathematical functions that come with QBasic. Often, even in business applications, the following functions come in handy:

- `SQR()`
- `ABS()`
- `SGN()`

Each function takes a numeric argument (of any data type) and returns a value.

NOTE: `SQR()` returns the square root of its argument.

The argument can be any positive data type. The square root is not defined for negative numbers. If you use a negative value as an argument to `SQR()`, you get an `Illegal function call` error. The section of code

```
PRINT SQR(4), SQR(64), SQR(4096)
```

produces the following output:

```
2       8       64
```

The *n*th Root

There are no functions to return the *n*th root of a number; there are only functions to return the square root. In other words, you cannot call a function that gives you the fourth root of 65,536.

(By the way, *16* is the fourth root of 65,536, because 16 times 16 times 16 times 16 is 65,536.)

You can use a mathematical trick to simulate the *n*th root, however. Because QBasic lets you raise a number to a fractional power, you can raise a number to the *n*th root by raising it to the (1/*n*) power. For example, to find the fourth root of 65,526, you

would type something like

```
PRINT 65536 ^ (1/4)
```

To store the 7th root of 78,125 in a variable called `root`, you would type

```
root = 78125 ^ (1 / 7)
```

This would store a 5 in `root` because 5 ^ 7 equals 78,125.

Knowing how to compute the *n*th root comes in handy in scientific programs and also in financial applications, such as time value of money problems.

The `ABS()` function, called the *absolute value* function, can be used in many programs as well.

NOTE: `ABS()` returns the absolute value of its argument.

The absolute value of a number is simply the positive representation of a positive or negative number. Whatever argument you pass to `ABS()`, its positive value is returned. For example, the section of code

```
PRINT ABS(-5), ABS(-5.76), ABS(0), ABS(5), ABS(5.76)
```

produces the following output:

```
5      5.76      0      5      5.76
```

Absolute value is used for distances (which are always positive), accuracy measurements, age differences, and other calculations that require a positive result.

NOTE: The `SGN()` function returns the following:

-1 if the argument is negative

0 if the argument is zero

+1 if the argument is positive

The SGN() function (the *sign* function) determines the sign of its argument. This might be used to determine whether a balance is more than 0 or a temperature is below 0. The following sections of code are identical:

```
IF (balance < 0) THEN
   PRINT -1
ELSEIF (balance = 0) THEN
   PRINT 0
ELSE PRINT +1
END IF
```

and

```
PRINT SGN(balance)
```

Notice that the SGN() function is a quick way to determine the sign of a number. The following PRINT statement shows the SGN() function when three separate arguments are passed to it:

```
PRINT SGN(-86.5), SGN(0), SGN(301)
```

This PRINT statement produces the following output:

```
-1      0      1
```

TIP: If you want the positive sign printed when you use SGN(), be sure to use PRINT USING with the + control character.

Examples

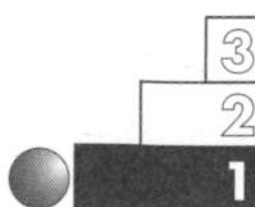

1. This program uses the ABS() function to tell the difference between two ages.

```
' Filename: C19ABS.BAS
'
' Prints the differences between two ages.
CLS
INPUT "What is the first child's age"; age1
```

```
INPUT "What is the second child's age"; age2

PRINT "They are"; ABS(age1 - age2); "years apart."
```

2. The following program asks for a number and prints the square root of it. Notice that it tests whether the number is greater than or equal to 0 to ensure that the square root function works properly.

```
' Filename: C19SQR.BAS
'
' Program to compute square roots.
CLS

DO
   PRINT "What number do you want to see the"
   INPUT "square root of (it cannot be negative)"; num
LOOP UNTIL (num >= 0)

PRINT
PRINT "The square root of"; num; "is"; SQR(num)
```

You should always be aware of the limits of function arguments and make sure the program does not exceed those limits by performing input validation checking, as this example program does.

Noninteger Precision Functions

The following two functions convert their arguments to either single-precision or double-precision numbers:

- `CSNG()`
- `CDBL()`

These functions are similar to the integer `CINT()` and `CLNG()` functions.

> **NOTE:** `CSNG()` converts its argument to the single-precision data type. `CDBL()` converts its argument to the double-precision data type.

When you compute long expressions in QBasic, it is best to ensure that every variable and constant is the same data type, unlike in the following section of code:

```
age% = 30                   ' An integer variable
factor# = .05676732         ' A double-precision variable
multiplier = 6.5            ' A single-precision variable
answer = age% * factor# * multiplier
```

Although this example might be more extreme than everyday calculations, it shows a calculation with three different data types being multiplied together and stored in a single-precision variable.

You should convert the variables or constants to the same data type before using them in the same calculation. Long-precision calculations, however, lose accuracy quickly. It is better to convert an integer or a single-precision number to a double-precision number than to convert a double-precision number to one of the smaller-precision data types; you lose much of the fractional parts. Nevertheless, `CSNG()` and `CDBL()` give you the ability to convert both.

The following sections of code show these two functions being used:

```
num.doub# = 3234.54384567
PRINT num.doub#             ' Prints correctly
PRINT CSNG(num.doub#)       ' Prints as a single-precision number
```

The preceding code produces the following output:

```
3234.54384567
3234.544
```

Notice that `CSNG()` rounds down the double-precision number so that it fits within the single-precision range. The code

```
num.sing! = 3234.544
PRINT num.sing!          ' Prints correctly
PRINT CDBL(num.sing!)    ' Prints incorrectly in the fractional
                         ' portion
```

produces the following output:

```
3234.544
3234.5439453125
```

Notice that when QBasic goes from a lower-precision number to a higher-precision number, it cannot simply extend the precision; it also adds extra digits that are incorrect. The extra digits might be too small for you to worry about unless you are performing critical scientific calculations. These functions are rarely used in business.

Trigonometric Functions

The following four functions are available for trigonometric applications:

- `ATN()`
- `COS()`
- `SIN()`
- `TAN()`

These are probably the least-used functions in QBasic. This is not to belittle the work of scientific and mathematical programmers who need them; thank goodness QBasic supplies these functions! Otherwise, programmers would have to write their own routines to perform these four basic trigonometric functions.

NOTE: The `ATN()` function returns the arctangent of the argument in radians. The argument is assumed to be an expression representing an angle of a right triangle.

The result of `ATN()` always falls between *-pi/2* and *+pi/2*.

For example, the following statement prints the arctangent of the angle stored in the variable `ang`:

```
PRINT ATN(ang)
```

TIP: If you need to pass an angle expressed in degrees to these functions, convert the angle to radians by multiplying it by (pi/180). (Pi is approximately 3.141592654.)

NOTE: The `COS()` function returns the cosine of the angle, expressed in radians, of the argument.

For example, the following statement prints the cosine of an angle with the approximate value of pi:

```
PRINT COS(3.14159)
```

The output is `-1`.

NOTE: The `SIN()` function returns the sine of the angle, expressed in radians, of the argument.

For example, the following statement prints the sine of an angle with the approximate value of pi divided by two:

```
PRINT SIN(3.14159 / 2)
```

The output is `1`.

NOTE: The `TAN()` function returns the tangent of the angle, expressed in radians, of the argument.

For example, the following statement prints the tangent of an angle with the approximate value of pi divided by four:

```
PRINT TAN(3.14159 / 4)
```

The output is `.9999987` (approximately `1`).

Logarithm and *e* Functions

Two highly mathematical functions are sometimes used in business and mathematics:

- `EXP()`
- `LOG()`

If you understand the trigonometric functions, you should have no trouble with these. You use them the same way. (If you do not understand these mathematical functions, that's OK. Some people program in QBasic for years and never need them.)

> **NOTE:** `EXP()` returns the base of natural logarithm (*e*) raised to a specified power.

The argument to `EXP()` can be any constant, variable, or expression less than or equal to 88.02969. *e* is the mathematical expression for the value 2.718282.

The following program shows the `EXP()` function in use:

```
FOR num = 1 TO 5
   PRINT EXP(num)
NEXT num
```

This produces the following output:

```
2.718282
7.389056
20.08554
54.59815
148.4132
```

Notice the first number. *e* raised to the first power does indeed equal itself.

> **NOTE:** `LOG()` returns the natural logarithm of the argument.

The argument to `LOG()` can be any positive constant, variable, or expression. The following program shows the `LOG()` function in use:

```
FOR num = 1 TO 5
   PRINT LOG(num)
NEXT num
```

This produces the following output:

```
0
.6931472
1.098612
1.386294
1.609438
```

The natural logarithm of *e* is *1*. If you type

```
PRINT LOG(2.718282)
```

you get `1` as the result.

The LEN Function

The `LEN()` function (which stands for *length*) is one of the few functions that can take numbers or strings as arguments.

NOTE: `LEN()` returns the number of bytes needed to hold a variable.

The variable can be any data type. `LEN()` returns the length of the integer variable, single-precision variable, or double-precision variable. You can use this function later when you work with data files. Most programmers do not care what internal size each variable takes. If you are getting ready to dimension a single-precision array of 200 elements and you want to see how much internal memory the array will take, however, you can code this program:

```
test! = 0   ' A sample single-precision variable
PRINT "The 200-element single-precision array will take"
PRINT (LEN(test!) * 200); "bytes of storage."
```

This program prints the following:

```
800
```

Each single-precision number takes four bytes of internal storage. You will see how to apply this function to string data in the next chapter.

The TIMER Function

TIMER is a time function. It behaves differently than any of the other functions you have seen. It requires no arguments; therefore, no parentheses are used with it.

> **NOTE:** TIMER returns the number of seconds since midnight.

Midnight to your computer is exactly 00:00:00 o'clock (in other words, 0 hours, 0 minutes, and 0 seconds). When your computer's internal clock gets to 00:00:00, it starts a new day on its internal calendar. Because most computers have a built-in clock so that the date and time are not erased when you power-off (turn off) the machine, you should ensure that your computer's internal clock is set properly so that functions such as TIMER work properly.

A function that tells the number of seconds since midnight might not seem like a useful function, but it can be. You can use TIMER to time routines, such as a user's input. This timing capability can be useful when writing game programs in which players' scores are dependent on how fast they answer a question.

> **NOTE:** Actually, the return value of TIMER is a single-precision number. It not only returns the number of seconds, but it does so to six decimal places. Therefore, TIMER can be an extremely accurate measure of time.

Example

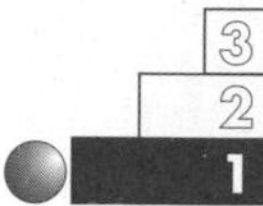

1. The following program illustrates the TIMER function. Depending on the time of day you run this program, you get different results. It simply asks the user to press Enter and then displays the number of seconds since midnight at the moment the user pressed the Enter key.

```
' Filename: C19TIME1.BAS
'
' Demonstrates TIMER.
CLS
PRINT "At the press of the ENTER key, I will tell you"
PRINT "how much time has elapsed since midnight..."
LINE INPUT ans$      ' Wait for user to press key

num.secs = TIMER     ' Store number of seconds since midnight
PRINT num.secs; "seconds have elapsed since midnight."
PRINT (num.secs / 60); "minutes have elapsed since midnight."
PRINT (num.secs/60/60); "hours have elapsed since midnight."
BEEP                 ' Makes it sound more official!
```

Figure 19.2 shows the result of running this program. Depending on the time of day, the results will be different.

Random-Number Processing

Random events happen every day of your life. It might be rainy or sunny when you wake up. You might have a good day or a bad day. You might get a phone call or you might not. Your stock portfolio might go up in value or down in value. Random events are especially important in games. Part of the fun of games is the luck involved with the roll of a die or the draw of a card when it is combined with your playing skills.

Simulating random events is important for a computer to do also. Computers, however, are *finite* machines; that is, given the same input, they always produce the same output. This consistency makes for boring game programs.

```
At the press of the ENTER key, I will tell you
how much time has elapsed since midnight...

 49543.67 seconds have elapsed since midnight.
 825.7278 minutes have elapsed since midnight.
 13.76213 hours have elapsed since midnight.




Press any key to continue
```

Figure 19.2. Using TIMER to inform the user of relative time.

The designers of QBasic knew this and found a way to overcome it. They wrote a function that generates random numbers. With it, you can get a random number to compute a die roll or a draw of a card. The format of the RND function is

```
RND [(n)]
```

Using RND

RND is the first function you have seen that might or might not require an argument. RND always returns a random number between 0 and 1. For instance, the section of code

```
PRINT RND, RND, RND, RND
```

might produce the following output:

```
.7055475    .533424     .5795186     .2895625
```

Depending on your computer, you might get different results. Try this PRINT statement on your machine to see the results. Each of these numbers is between 0 and 1, which is the definition of the RND function's output.

If you write a program with this one PRINT statement and run it repeatedly, you get the same four random numbers.

The argument inside the RND function's parentheses determines how the random number is generated. The sign of the argument determines how it affects the next random number that is generated. If you put a positive number inside the parentheses, it has no effect on RND.

Therefore, the section of code

```
PRINT RND(1), RND(848.5), RND(100), RND(19)
```

also produces the output

```
.7055475    .533424     .5795186     .2895625
```

(or whatever four numbers you got earlier when you used RND without any arguments).

> **NOTE:** RND with no argument and RND with a positive argument produce the same results.

Using 0 or a negative value causes RND to behave differently. For example, if you use 0 as the RND argument, RND returns the last random number generated. Therefore, the following code:

```
PRINT RND, RND(0), RND, RND(0)
```

might produce the following result:

```
.7055475     .7055475     .533424     .533424
```

The second and fourth numbers are the same as the first and third numbers because RND(0) tells QBasic to repeat the previous RND-generated number. RND(0) obviously makes the random-number generator less random, but it is sometimes useful when you want to duplicate an event such as the roll of a die.

NOTE: `RND(0)` repeats the last random number generated.

Using a negative number as the argument to `RND` lets you *reseed* the QBasic random-number generator. When you reseed the random-number generator, you force QBasic to use a different random-number calculation. For example, the section of code

```
PRINT RND(-1), RND, RND, RND
```

might produce the following random numbers:

```
.224007     .0035845     .00863523     .1642639
```

Again, on your computer, the four numbers might be different. These numbers differ from the previous four numbers you got when you used `RND` with no argument. The negative value starts (reseeds) the random-number generator at a different point to ensure that the numbers differ from their usual pattern.

NOTE: `RND` with a negative argument reseeds the random-number generator to a different starting value.

If you use a different negative number, `RND` starts with a new seeded value. Therefore, the program

```
INPUT "Please type a number"; r.num
IF (r.num > 0) THEN r.num = -r.num      ' Negate the number
PRINT RND(r.num), RND, RND, RND
```

produces a different output every time you run it, as long as you enter a different number when prompted. This helps "get the ball rolling" and makes the random-number generator produce a different set of numbers every time you run the program.

The RANDOMIZE Statement

The RANDOMIZE statement is another way to reseed the random-number generator. In almost every program that uses the RND function, you see the RANDOMIZE statement toward the beginning of the code. The format of RANDOMIZE is

```
RANDOMIZE [ (seed) ]
```

in which *seed* is an optional numeric value. If you supply RANDOMIZE with an argument, you will seed all random numbers from that point in the program to the number (*seed*) you supply.

Putting RANDOMIZE at the top of a program that uses RND helps make the program more "random." If you run the program repeatedly using the same RANDOMIZE seed value, you get the same RND results throughout the program. If you run the program using a different RANDOMIZE seed each time, however, the program's RND functions return different values.

If you do not specify a seed, the RANDOMIZE statement causes QBasic to stop and prompt you for a seed with the following message:

```
Random-number seed (-32768 to 32767)?
```

This lets you seed with a different random number every time you run the program without going to the program to change the RANDOMIZE statement's value.

Using the Random-Number Generator for Applications

So far, the random-number generation of QBasic might seem like a mixed blessing. The ability to generate random numbers is nice, but the numbers don't seem truly random; you have to keep entering a different seed every time you run the program. It would take away from a great game if the players had to answer this prompt every time they ran the game.

```
Random-number seed (-32768 to 32767)?
```

Yet without the prompt, the players would get the same random numbers every time they played the game. That would make for a boring game.

Another seemingly limited result of the RND function is its ability to produce random numbers only between 0 and 1. If you want the computer to simulate rolling a die with six sides, how can a number from 0 to 1 help? There are some programming techniques that address (and solve) these dilemmas.

You have already seen one function that is basically random every time you run a program. It is the TIMER function. Your computer's internal clock keeps ticking away every second, and TIMER returns whatever number of seconds have ticked off since midnight. Because there are 86,400 seconds in a day, the odds of running the same program at exactly the same second twice in a row are slim.

Therefore, why not put the following RANDOMIZE statement at the beginning of any program that uses the RND function?

```
RANDOMIZE TIMER
```

This assures you that you will get different random results every time you run the program (there is only a 1 out of 86,400 chance that TIMER will return a given value in any given day).

Why Do They Make Us *Do* This?

There is much debate among QBasic programmers concerning the random-number generator. Many of them feel that the random numbers should be truly random, and that programmers should not have to seed the generator themselves or resort to using the TIMER function. They feel that QBasic should do its own internal TIMER when you ask for a random number, to take the burden of *randomness* off the programmer's back.

Many applications, however, would no longer work if the random-number generator were randomized for you. Computer simulations are used all the time in business, engineering, and research to simulate the pattern of real-world events. Researchers need to be able to duplicate these simulations repeatedly. Although the events inside the simulations might be random from each other, the running of the simulations cannot be random if researchers are to study several different effects.

Mathematicians and statisticians also need to repeat random-number patterns for their analysis, especially when they are working with risk, probability, and gaming theory.

Because so many computer users need to repeat their random-number patterns, the designers of QBasic have wisely chosen to give you, the programmer, the option of keeping the same random patterns or changing them. The advantages far outweigh the trouble of including an extra `RANDOMIZE TIMER` statement.

The "limitation" of returning random numbers between 0 and 1 does not turn out to be a limitation, either. There is a simple formula you can use to return a random number between any two numbers. This lets you get random numbers for whatever range you desire.

To produce a random number from 1 to *N*, use this formula:

```
INT(RND * N) + 1
```

Therefore, if you write a program to simulate the drawing of a card from a deck of 52 cards, you can use the following statement:

```
next.card = INT(RND * 52) + 1
```

Assuming that you stored the 52 cards in a string array, this would choose the subscript of the next card.

Examples

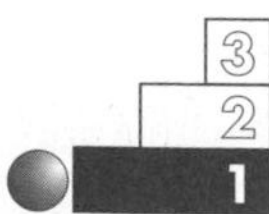

1. The following program prints 10 random numbers from 0 to 1 on the screen. Run this program on your computer to look at the results. Run it several times. The output is always the same because the random-number seed never changes.

```
' Filename: C19RAN1.BAS
'
' Demonstrates unseeded random numbers.
```

```
CLS
FOR ctr = 1 TO 10
   PRINT RND
NEXT ctr
```

2. The next example improves on the preceding one by asking for a random-number seed each time the program runs. Run the program several times. If you enter the same random-number seed, the results are the same. If you enter a different seed, however, you see a new group of 10 random numbers.

```
' Filename: C19RAN2.BAS
'
' Seeds a new random-number generator.
CLS

INPUT "Please type a random-number seed"; seed
RANDOMIZE seed    ' Initialize the random-number generator
FOR ctr = 1 TO 10
   PRINT RND
NEXT ctr
```

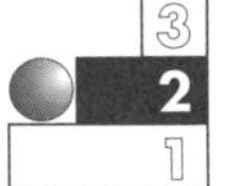

3. If you do not specify a seed for RANDOMIZE, QBasic prompts you for one. The following program is basically the same as the preceding one, except that it leaves the seed to QBasic and not to the program.

```
' Filename: C19RAN3.BAS
'
' Lets QBasic seed the random-number.
CLS

RANDOMIZE    ' Initialize the random-number generator
FOR ctr = 1 TO 10
   PRINT RND
NEXT ctr
```

As you can see from the output in Figure 19.3, QBasic prompts for the RANDOMIZE seed. If you enter the same seed, the program produces the same 10 random numbers every time you run it.

```
Random-number seed (-32768 to 32767)? 4345
 .7058679
 .1105877
 .1136525
 .8902857
 .8904032
 .8374995
 .3413644
 .2318082
 4.186124E-02
 .1050493

Press any key to continue
```

Figure 19.3. QBasic prompts for a random-number seed.

4. The following program prints random numbers based on the user's INPUT value. It prints them in the range of 1 to the number the user enters.

```
' Filename: C19RAN4.BAS
'
' Program to print several random-numbers
' from 1 to whatever value typed by the user.
CLS
DO
   INPUT "Please enter a positive number"; num
LOOP UNTIL (num >= 1)    ' Ensure number is a good one

FOR ctr = 1 TO 20
   PRINT INT(RND * num) + 1   ' Put number in range
NEXT ctr
```

Summary

This chapter showed you QBasic's many built-in numeric functions. Functions save you programming time because they perform some of the computing tasks for you, leaving you time to concentrate on your program. There are functions that convert numbers from one data type to another, round numbers, perform advanced mathematical operations, and generate random numbers.

Along with the numeric functions, there are several string functions that work on character string data. With the string functions, you are able to write better input routines and manipulate string data in ways you were not able to before. The next chapter discusses string functions.

Review Questions

Answers to the Review Questions are in Appendix B.

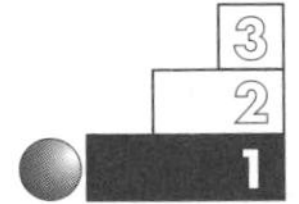

1. What advantage does using built-in functions have over writing your own routines?
2. What is a function argument?
3. What is the difference between `ABS()`, `SGN()`, and `SQR()`?

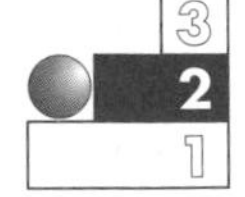

4. What is the output of the following program:

```
RANDOMIZE TIMER
PRINT RND, RND(2), RND(-7), RND
```

(Hint: Be careful, this is a trick question!)

5. What are the four functions that convert one data type to another?

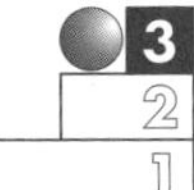

6. What is the output of the following program?

```
num = -5.6
PRINT INT(num), FIX(num), CINT(num)
```

7. Assuming that the statement

```
PRINT RND
```

prints the number `.054456`, what does the following statement produce?

```
PRINT RND(+8)
```

8. TRUE or FALSE: The following two statements are equivalent:

```
PRINT 64 ^ (1/2)
PRINT SQR(64)
```

Review Exercises

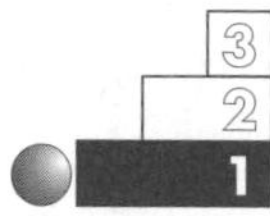

1. Write a program that rounds the numbers *-10.5*, *-5.75*, and *2.75* three different ways.
2. Write a program that computes the number of minutes since midnight. (Hint: There are 60 seconds in one minute, or 1/60 minute in a second.)

3. Write a program to compute the square root, cube root, and fourth root of the numbers from 10 to 25.
4. Write a program to ask for two children's ages. Print the positive difference between the ages without using an `IF-THEN` statement.

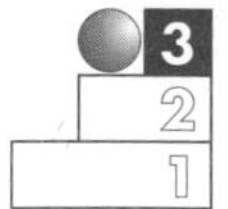

5. Change the number-guessing game to time the user's input and add the total number of seconds the user takes to guess the right answer. If it takes less than 15 seconds to guess the answer, `BEEP` and print a congratulatory message. (Hint: Use the `TIMER` function.)
6. Write a program that simulates the rolling of two dice. Print the random dice values, from 1 to 6 for each die, for five separate rolls.
7. Modify the card-drawing routine so that it uses two decks of cards. This is an easy modification requiring only a few extra `FOR-LOOPS` and a `RESTORE` statement, but it tests your grasp of the routine and random numbers.

20

String Functions

This chapter shows you QBasic's string functions. They work in a manner similar to numeric functions: When you pass them an argument, they return a value you can store or print. String functions enable you to print strings in ways you never could before, as well as look at individual characters from a string.

This chapter introduces you to the following functions and statements:

- ASCII string and output functions
- String conversion functions
- String character functions
- Justified string statements
- The `MID$()` statement
- Date and time functions
- The `INKEY$` string input function

The string-handling functions are what make QBasic excel over other computer languages. Few languages offer the string manipulation that QBasic does. After completing this chapter, you will know all the built-in functions of QBasic, and you will be ready to write your own functions in the next chapter.

ASCII String Functions

You have already seen one of the ASCII string functions, the `CHR$()` function. When you enclose an ASCII number inside the `CHR$()` parentheses (the argument), QBasic substitutes the character which matches that ASCII value. Two additional string functions work with the ASCII table:

- `ASC()`

and

- `STRING$()`

The `ASC()` string function is the opposite of `CHR$()`. Instead of returning the character of the ASCII number in parentheses (as `CHR$()` does), it returns the ASCII number of the character argument you give it.

> **NOTE:** `ASC()` returns the ASCII number of the character argument you give it. The argument must be a string of one or more characters. If you pass `ASC()` a string of more than one character, it returns the ASCII number of the first character in the string.

For example, the statement

```
PRINT ASC("A"), "ASC("B"), ASC("C")
```

produces the following output:

```
65      66      67
```

You can look at the ASCII table in Appendix A to see that these three numbers are the ASCII values for `A`, `B`, and `C`. You can also use string variables as arguments:

```
letter1$ = "A"
letter2$ = "B"
letter3$ = "C"
PRINT ASC(letter1$), ASC(letter2$), ASC(letter3$)
```

This produces the same output as the previous example.

If you pass a string with more than one character to `ASC()`, it returns the ASCII value of only the first character. Therefore, the statement

```
PRINT "Hello"
```

prints `72` (the ASCII value of `H`).

This is a better method of testing for input than you have seen so far. Look at the following example:

```
INPUT "Do you want to see the name"; ans$
IF ((ASC(ans$) = 89) OR (ASC(ans$) = 121)) THEN
   PRINT "The name is: "; a.name$
ENDIF
```

The user can answer the prompt with `y`, `Y`, `Yes`, `yes`, or `YES`. The `IF-THEN` test works for any of those input values, because *89* is the ASCII value for `Y` and *121* is the ASCII value of `y`.

Any string can go inside the `ASC()` parentheses, even a string returned from another string function. The section of code

```
PRINT ASC(CHR$(75))
PRINT CHR$(ASC("g"))
```

prints the following output:

```
75
g
```

In the first `PRINT` statement, the `CHR$(75)` returned a letter `K`, which was then used as the argument to `ASC()`. `ASC()` used the `K` to return its ASCII value of *75*. In the second `PRINT` statement, the `ASC("g")` returned the ASCII value of the letter `g`, which was *103*. The *103* was then passed to the `CHR$()` function to produce the matching ASCII character `g`.

The `STRING$()` function also uses the ASCII table to do its job. This function is generally used to create strings for output and storage.

> **NOTE:** The `STRING$()` function requires two arguments: an integer followed by a character, a character string, or another integer. `STRING$()` replicates its second argument.

The best way to learn the `STRING$()` function is to see it used. Consider the following statement:

```
PRINT STRING$(15, "a")
```

This prints the lowercase letter `a` 15 times, as in

```
aaaaaaaaaaaaaaa
```

If you use a string of characters (or a string variable) as the second argument, `STRING$()` replicates only the first character of the string. If the second argument is an ASCII number (from 0 to 255), `STRING$()` replicates the matching ASCII character. The following section of code illustrates this:

```
PRINT STRING$(60, 43)
```

The preceding line produces the following row of 60 plus signs:

```
++++++++++++++++++++++++++++++++++++++++++++++++++++++++++++
```

`STRING$()` is useful for drawing boxes around text, or for underlining words on the screen. You can also assign the return result of `STRING$()` to a string variable, as in

```
underlines$ = STRING$(30, "-")
```

Using `STRING$()` is quicker (and easier to change) than using the following assignment statement:

```
underlines$ = "------------------------------"
```

You can use `STRING$()` in output to insert spaces:

```
PRINT "Apples"; STRING$(10, " "); "Oranges"
```

This line prints the following:

```
Apples          Oranges
```

You saw another function in an earlier chapter that produced spaces: the `SPC()` function. There is a third function in QBasic that also produces spaces: the `SPACE$()` function.

> **NOTE:** `SPACE$()` returns the number of spaces specified by its integer argument.

Because a row of spaces is commonly required to space apart output, QBasic includes this function. `SPACE$()` is nothing more than a specific `STRING$()` function. The following `PRINT` statements do exactly the same thing:

```
sp$ = STRING$(40, " ")
sp$ = SPACE$(40)
```

Examples

1. You can use the `ASC()` and `CHR$()` functions to find a person's initials, given the first and last name. The following program asks users for their first and last names. It then uses the `ASC()` function to store the ASCII value of the first letter of each name. This is possible because `ASC()` works only on the first letter of any string.

   Those two ASCII values are then used in `CHR$()` to get the original characters back and then store them in initial string variables.

```
' Filename: C20INIT.BAS
'
' Program to "strip" the user's initials.
CLS
INPUT "What is your first name"; first.name$
INPUT "What is your last name"; last.name$
PRINT

' Find the ASCII number of each initial
first.init.num = ASC(first.name$)   ' ASC() ignores all
last.init.num = ASC(last.name$)     ' but 1st letter

' Convert the numbers to single characters
first.init$ = CHR$(first.init.num)
```

```
last.init$ = CHR$(last.init.num)

PRINT "Your initials are: "; first.init$; ". "; last.init$; "."
```

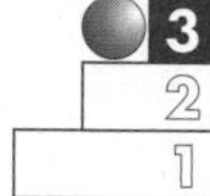

2. The following program reads a list of children's ages. It then uses the `STRING$()` function to print a graph showing their ages. The `STRING$()` function prints as many asterisks as there are years in their ages.

```
' Filename: C20AGEGR.BAS
'
' Prints a graph showing children's ages.
'
' Reserve storage for their names and ages
DIM names$(10), ages(10)
CLS

FOR ctr = 1 TO 10
   READ names$(ctr), ages(ctr)
NEXT ctr

DATA "Jim", 16, "Nancy", 12, "Terry", 9, "Michael", 19
DATA "Jane", 14, "Paula", 8, "Richard", 13, "Christine", 18
DATA "Glen", 12, "Adam", 15

PRINT "Name"; TAB(12); "Age Graph"
PRINT STRING$(4, "-"); TAB(12); STRING$(9, "-")
FOR ctr = 1 TO 10    ' Run through the children, building
                     ' the graph
   PRINT names$(ctr); TAB(12); STRING$(ages(ctr), "*")
NEXT ctr
```

Figure 20.1 shows the graph that results from this program. The output is impressive, considering how little code is necessary to produce it.

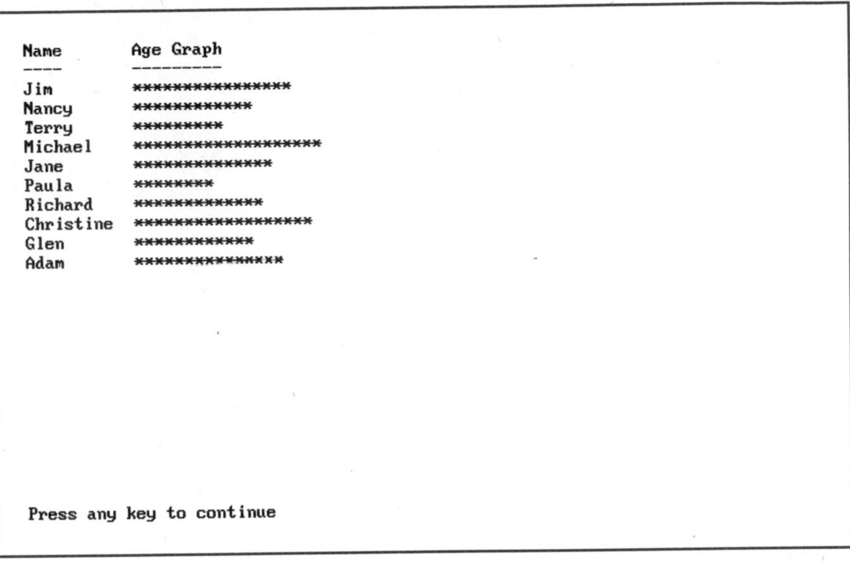

Name Age Graph
---- ---------
Jim *****************
Nancy *************
Terry **********
Michael ********************
Jane ***************
Paula *********
Richard **************
Christine *******************
Glen *************
Adam ****************
Press any key to continue

Figure 20.1. Using the STRING$() function to produce a graph.

String Conversion Functions

As with numeric functions, there are several string functions that convert string data from one form to another. There are two functions that convert data from numeric to string and back again. The string conversion functions are

- LCASE$()
- UCASE$()
- STR$()
- VAL()

The first two string functions convert strings to and from their native cases.

NOTE: `LCASE$()` converts its string argument to lowercase letters. If the argument contains only lowercase letters, no conversion is done.

`UCASE$()` converts its string argument to uppercase letters. If the argument contains only uppercase letters, no conversion is done.

These functions are straightforward. Each can take a string variable, constant, or expression (such as two strings concatenated together) and convert it to the indicated case.

The following section of code explains both functions nicely:

```
up$ = "HELLO"
lc$ = "goodbye"
mixed$ = "Hello, Goodbye"
PRINT LCASE$(up$), LCASE$(lc$), LCASE$(mixed$)
PRINT UCASE$(up$), UCASE$(lc$), UCASE$(mixed$)
```

If you run this program, you get the following output:

```
hello     goodbye     hello, goodbye
HELLO     GOODBYE     HELLO, GOODBYE
```

There are many uses for these two string functions. When asking your user a question, such as a yes-or-no question, you can ensure that the answer is in lowercase (or uppercase) and perform an `IF-THEN`. For example:

```
IF (UCASE$(ans$) = "YES)) THEN ...
```

Without the `UCASE$()` function, you would have to test for each of the following possible answers:

```
YES   YEs   YeS   Yes   yES   yEs   yeS   yes
```

A later example builds on this.

The `STR$()` and `VAL()` functions are mirror-image functions. These two functions convert string data to numeric data and numeric data to string data.

> **NOTE:** `STR$()` converts the numeric variable, constant, or expression inside the parentheses to a string. If the number is positive, the string will have a leading space.

The following statement is not a valid statement because you cannot put a number in a string variable:

```
LET s$ = 54.6    ' This is invalid
```

You can avoid the `Type Mismatch` error by first using `STR$()` to convert the number to a string before assigning it to a string variable, as in

```
LET s$ = STR$(54.6)    ' This works
```

If you print `s$`, you see `54.6` (with a space before it where the imaginary plus sign is). You must realize, however, that this is not a number; it is simply a string of characters with a period in the middle that looks like a number when it is printed. You cannot perform any math with `s$` because it is not a number.

There might be times when you want to combine numbers and words into a string. You can enclose the number inside the `STR$()` function and concatenate it with other strings to build the longer string.

> **NOTE:** `VAL()` converts the string variable, constant, or expression inside the parentheses to a number. The argument (the string in the parentheses) must start with a string of characters that looks like a valid number (integer, single-precision, or any other data type).

`VAL()` ignores any spaces that might be at the beginning of the string (called *leading blanks*). If there is no valid number at the beginning of the string (not including the leading zeros), `VAL()` converts the string to the number `0`.

The following section of code illustrates the `VAL()` function:

```
s1$ = "44 bottles"
n1 = VAL(s1$)        ' Ignores everything after the number
PRINT n1
```

```
s2$ = "00012.5"
n2 = VAL(s2$) ' Converts the string to a single-precision number
PRINT n2
s3$ = "Sam is 68 years old"     ' No valid number at beginning of
                                ' string
PRINT s3$
```

The following output is produced by these lines of code:

```
44
12.5
0
```

As with all positive numbers, a space is left where the imaginary plus sign goes.

String Character Functions

There are several more string functions that manipulate strings in many ways. They let you break one string into several smaller strings by removing portions of it. You can trim the leading spaces from strings and change the middle of a string without changing the rest of the string. The string character functions explained in this section are

- `LEN()`
- `LEFT$()`
- `RIGHT$()`
- `MID$()`
- `LTRIM$()`
- `RTRIM$()`
- `INSTR()`

The `LEN()` function is good to use when you want to know the length of a string. You saw it used in the preceding chapter with numeric values. `LEN()` can be used also with strings.

NOTE: `LEN()` returns the length (number of characters) of the string variable, constant, or expression inside its parentheses.

`LEN()` counts the number of characters inside its argument. The `PRINT` statement

```
PRINT LEN("abcdef")
```

produces `6` as its output. `LEN()` is usually combined with other string functions when a string length is required. If the string inside the parentheses is a null string (if it does not contain any data), `LEN()` returns a `0`. You can test to see whether a string variable has data (to see whether the user typed anything before pressing Enter) with the following section of code:

```
INPUT "Please type an answer"; ans$
IF LEN(ans$) = 0 THEN PRINT "You did not type anything..."
```

The `LEFT$()` and `RIGHT$()` functions are also useful mirror-image functions.

NOTE: `LEFT$()` requires two arguments: a string variable, a constant, or an expression followed by an integer constant or a variable. The integer determines how many characters are "stripped" from the left of the string and returned.

`RIGHT$()` requires two arguments: a string variable, a constant, or an expression, followed by an integer constant or a variable. The integer determines how many characters are "stripped" from the right of the string and returned.

The *arguments* of `LEFT$()` and `RIGHT$()` are never changed by the functions.

`LEFT$()` returns the leftmost characters from any string. This lets you take part of a string and assign it to another. The following section of code explains `LEFT$()`:

```
a$ = "abcdefg"
PRINT LEFT$(a$, 1)
PRINT LEFT$(a$, 3)
PRINT LEFT$(a$, 7)
PRINT LEFT$(a$, 20)
```

This produces the following output:

```
a
abc
abcdefg
abcdefg
```

Notice from the last `PRINT` statement that if you try to return more characters from the left of the string than exist, `LEFT$()` returns the entire string and not an error message.

`RIGHT$()` works in the same manner, except that it returns the rightmost characters from a string, as the following example shows:

```
a$ = "abcdefg"
PRINT RIGHT$(a$, 1)
PRINT RIGHT$(a$, 3)
PRINT RIGHT$(a$, 7)
PRINT RIGHT$(a$, 20)
```

This produces the following output:

```
g
efg
abcdefg
abcdefg
```

The `MID$()` function accomplishes what `LEFT$()` and `RIGHT$()` cannot: `MID$()` returns characters from the *middle* of a string.

> **NOTE:** `MID$()` uses three arguments: a string variable, a constant, or an expression followed by two integers. The first integer determines where `MID$()` begins stripping characters from the string (the position, starting at 1), and the second integer determines how many characters from that position to return. If you do not specify two integers, `MID$()` uses 1 as the starting position.

`MID$()` can pull any number of characters from anywhere in the string. The following example shows how the `MID$()` function works:

```
a$ = "QBasic FORTRAN COBOL C Pascal"
PRINT MID$(a$, 1, 6)
PRINT MID$(a$, 8, 7)
PRINT MID$(a$, 16, 5)
PRINT MID$(a$, 22, 1)
PRINT MID$(a$, 24, 6)
```

This produces a listing of these five programming languages, one per line, as shown in the following output:

```
QBasic
FORTRAN
COBOL
C
Pascal
```

Notice that the `MID$()` function can replace both the `LEFT$()` and `RIGHT$()` functions. The first and last `PRINT` statements from the previous examples could have used the `LEFT$()` and `RIGHT$()` functions to print the first and last programming languages. You might wonder why QBasic supplies the `LEFT$()` and `RIGHT$()` functions when `MID$()` can do their jobs, but `LEFT$()` and `RIGHT$()` are easier when only the left or right part of a string is required.

The `LTRIM$()` and `RTRIM$()` functions trim spaces from the beginning or end of a string.

NOTE: `LTRIM$()` returns the argument's string without any leading spaces. `RTRIM$()` returns the argument's string without any trailing spaces.

The `INSTR()` function is different from the others you've seen in this section. `INSTR()` is a string search function. You use it to find the starting location of a string inside another string.

NOTE: `INSTR()` returns the character position (an integer) at which one string starts within another string.

The format of `INSTR()` is different from most of the other string functions. It requires two or three arguments, depending on what you want it to do. The format of `INSTR()` is

```
INSTR( [start,] stringexpression1, stringexpression2 )
```

`INSTR()` looks to see whether *`stringexpression2`* exists within *`stringexpression1`*. (The *`stringexpression`*s can be string variables, constants, or expressions.) If the second string expression is in the first, `INSTR()` returns the starting position of the string within the first string. It assumes a beginning position of *1*.

`INSTR()` starts looking at position 1, the first position of the search string, unless you override it with a *`start`* value. If you give a *`start`* value of 5, `INSTR()` ignores the first four characters of the search string.

If `INSTR()` fails to find the first string within the second, it returns `0`. There is one exception to this: If the second string (the string to look for) is a null string, either `1` or the `start` value, if it is specified, is returned.

The following example makes `INSTR()`'s operation clear:

```
a$ = "QBasic FORTRAN COBOL C Pascal"
PRINT INSTR(a$, "FORTRAN")      ' Exists at position 8
PRINT INSTR(a$, "COBOL")        ' Exists at position 16
PRINT INSTR(a$, "C")            ' Exists at position 16 too!
PRINT INSTR(a$, "PL/I")         ' PL/I is not found
```

```
PRINT INSTR(16, a$, "FORTRAN") ' FORTRAN exists, but not past 16
PRINT INSTR(5, a$, "PL/I")     ' Does not exist
PRINT INSTR(a$, "")            ' NULL string always returns 1
PRINT INSTR(5, a$, "")         ' or start value
```

Study this example to see how it produces the following output:

```
8
16
16
0
0
0
1
5
```

The reason that the third `PRINT` statement does not return `22` (the position of the C denoting the C language) is that the C is also in `COBOL`. `INSTR()` returns only the first occurrence of the string.

Many times, these string functions are used together to search for and test for strings. One string function's return value can be a parameter to another function.

Examples

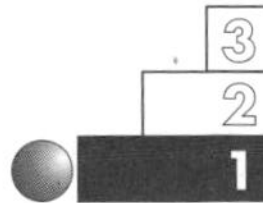

1. The following program uses `INSTR()` to see whether a name is included in the `DATA` statements.

```
' Filename: C20DATNM.BAS
'
' Check to see if user's name is in the data.
CLS
INPUT "What is your first name"; first$

' Check all data to see if name is there
DO
   READ data.name$
   IF (INSTR(data.name$, first$)) <> 0 THEN
```

```
         ' Name is in data so stop
         PRINT "Your name is already on record."
      END IF
   LOOP WHILE (data.name$ <> "-99")

   DATA "George", "Sam", "Mary", "Abby", "Carol", "Lou"
   DATA "Sally", "Martha", "James", "Kerry", "Luke"
   DATA "Judy", "Bill", "Mark", "John", "-99"
```

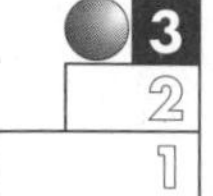

2. The book database program in Appendix E uses string functions for some of the book titles. If a book's title begins with *The...,* the book database program takes off the *The* from the front of the title and appends it to the end. Therefore, the title

```
The Rain in Spain
```

becomes

```
Rain in Spain, The
```

The following program asks for a book's title, saves all characters except for the leading *The,* and concatenates `", The"` to the end of the title. If the title does not begin with *The,* the program does not change the title.

```
' Filename: C20BOOKT.BAS
'
' Moves leading THE from the front of a book's title.
CLS
DO
   PRINT
   INPUT "What is the title of the book"; title$
   ' Only change it if "The " starts the title
   IF (LEFT$(title$, 4) = "The ") THEN
      ' Save all but the first four letters
      rtitle$ = RIGHT$(title$, (LEN(title$) - 4))
      ' Concatenate ", The" to the end of the title
      title$ = rtitle$ + ", The"
   END IF
   PRINT
   PRINT "Please file the book under:"
   PRINT title$
```

```
    PRINT
    INPUT "Do you want to enter another book title (Y/N)"; ans$
LOOP WHILE (LEFT$(UCASE$(ans$), 1) = "Y")
```

Notice how the program also uses an embedded `UCASE$()` function with the prompt. The user can enter *Y*, *y*, *yes*, or *YES*, and the program knows the user wants to loop again.

Justifying String Statements

The following statements left- or right-justify string data:

- The `LSET` statement
- The `RSET` statement

These two statements are similar to the `LTRIM$()` and `RTRIM$()` functions, except instead of trimming spaces from a string, these statements insert spaces at the beginning or end of a string. They can be used to build output strings and will be especially useful when you learn about disk files.

NOTE: `LSET` left-justifies one string within another. The format of `LSET` is

`LSET` *`string1`* `=` *`string2`*

`RSET` right-justifies one string within another. The format of `RSET` is

`RSET` *`string1`* `=` *`string2`*

The *`string1`* in each statement is assumed to already have a value. The length of that string value determines how many spaces have to be used to pad *`string2`*. For example:

```
string1$ = "1234567890"      ' 10 characters
LSET string1$ = "left"       ' LSET "left" in those 10 characters
PRINT "¦"; string1$; "¦"     ' Print between lines to see result
string2$ = "1234567890"      ' 10 characters
```

```
RSET string2$ = "right"     ' RSET "right" in those 10 characters
PRINT "¦"; string2$; "¦"    ' Print between lines to see result
```

This section of code produces the following output:

```
¦left      ¦
¦     right¦
```

Make sure that `string1$` and `string2$` both have an initial string value before using `LSET` or `RSET`. If they do not, QBasic assumes they are null strings (because they have nothing in them) and will not `LSET` or `RSET` `string1$` and `string2$` in them.

TIP: Remember that both `LSET` and `RSET` assign new strings to old strings but do not change the length of the target string from its previous value. Ordinarily, when you assign one string to another, the target string changes length to equal the string you are assigning it.

The `MID$()` Statement

`MID$()` is a QBasic *statement* as well as the function described earlier. When used as a function, `MID$()` cannot appear on the left side of an assignment statement. When you use `MID$()` as a statement, however, you must put it on the left side of an assignment statement.

The `MID$()` statement is similar to those of `LSET` and `RSET` in that it puts one string in another. Instead of the rest of the original string being overwritten with spaces (as with `LSET` and `RSET`), however, it remains unchanged. The format of `MID$()` is

```
MID$( string1, start [ , length ] ) = string2
```

The *string1* must be a string variable, although the *string2* can be a string variable, constant, or expression. Both *start* and *length* must be integer values. The length of *string2* is usually shorter than *string1*, although it does not have to be. The *string2* is placed inside *string1* starting at the position indicated by *start*. If the *length* is specified, it determines how many characters from *string2* are actually copied to *string1*. Regardless of how long *string2* is (or how large *length* is), the length of *string1* is never changed from its original length.

The `MID$()` statement lets you replace parts of a string without changing the rest of the string. For example, the following section of code replaces part of one string with another:

```
s1$ = "abc def ghi jkl"
MID$(s1$, 5) = "DEF"       ' Make the second group uppercase
PRINT s1$
MID$(s1$, 9, 3) = "G H I"  ' Only first three characters are
                           ' replaced
PRINT s1$
MID$(s1$, 1) = "abcdefghijklmnopqrstuvwxyz"
PRINT s1$
```

This produces the following output:

```
abc DEF ghi jkl
abc DEF G H jkl
abcdefghijklmno
```

Notice that the second `MID$()` statement's *string2* contained five characters, but the *length* indicated that only the first three characters were to be used. The third `MID$()` statement attempted to put 26 letters in `s1$`, but only the first 15 were replaced because `s1$`'s original value had only 15 characters.

Working with Date and Time Values

Most of today's microcomputers have a battery in them that keeps track of the system's date and time even when the computer is powered-off. If your computer does not have this feature, you should type the correct date and time every time you power-on your computer.

The date and time are important in programming. Many programmers like to put the date and time at the top of reports when they print them so that people reading the reports will know how old the reported data is.

You have already seen the TIMER function that returned the number of seconds that have elapsed since midnight. There are two more useful functions that return the date and time. They are

- DATE$

and

- TIME$

As with the MID$() function and statement, the date and time functions work also as statements.

The formats of the DATE$ and TIME$ functions are easy. They are

```
DATE$
TIME$
```

Neither the DATE$ function nor the TIME$ function requires parameters. They get their values from the computer's internal calendar and clock. Even if you have not properly set the date and clock, these functions return whatever values they find. Both DATE$ and TIME$ return string values that you can print, assign to another string, or use in a string expression.

When used as functions, DATE$ and TIME$ return only values, so you cannot use them on the left side of an equal sign. When your program calls the DATE$ function, it returns the currently set date in the format

mm-dd-yyyy

in which:

mm is a month number from 01 to 12.

dd is a day number from 01 to 31.

yyyy is a year number from 1980 to 2099.

The zeros in front of single-digit months and days are always returned.

The TIME$ function returns the currently set time in the format

hh:*mm*:*ss*

in which:

hh is the hour number from 00 to 23.

mm is the minute number from 00 to 59.

ss is the second number from 00 to 59.

Notice that TIME$ returns the time in a 24-hour format. To print the date and time, you would put the functions after PRINT, as in

```
PRINT DATE$
PRINT TIME$
```

> **TIP:** To convert a p.m. time to its 24-hour clock equivalent, add 12 to it. For example, 7:00 p.m. becomes 19:00 (7 + 12) on a 24-hour clock.

DATE$ and TIME$ are also statements. Instead of calling the functions and using their return values, you can put DATE$ and TIME$ to the left of the equal sign in assignment statements. This lets you set your computer's internal date and time settings.

When setting the date and time with these statements, use the format for the new date and time values that was shown earlier. The following statements set new date and time values:

```
DATE$ = "04/29/91"
TIME$ = "11:24:00"
```

Notice that you assign the DATE$ and TIME$ statement strings in the same format that their corresponding functions return.

Example

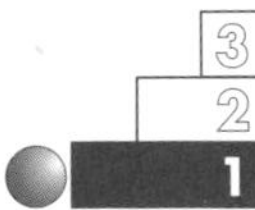

1. Users can run the following program when a time zone change occurs. It either adds or subtracts one hour from the clock, depending on the user's choice. It uses a combination of most of the string functions about which you have read. Use the MID$() statement to change the hour and store the updated hour in the TIME$ value.

```
' Filename: C20TIME.BAS
'
' Run this program to change the time value during a time
' change.
CLS
PRINT "This is a time changing program that you"
PRINT "should run when the time zone changes.
PRINT
PRINT "The current date is: "; DATE$    ' Calls the DATE$
                                        ' function
PRINT "The current time is: "; TIME$    ' Calls the TIME$
                                        ' function
PRINT
PRINT "Do you want to:"
PRINT
PRINT "1. Add an hour to the internal clock"
PRINT "2. Subtract an hour from the internal clock"
PRINT "3. Do nothing at this time and quit this program"
PRINT
PRINT "What is your choice";
DO
   INPUT choice
LOOP UNTIL ((choice >= 1) AND (choice <= 3))

SELECT CASE choice
   CASE 1: old.time$ = TIME$
      old.hour = VAL(LEFT$(old.time$, 2))  ' Convert hrs to
                                           ' number
      old.hour = old.hour + 1   ' Add 1 to the hour
      new.time$ = STR$(old.hour) + RIGHT$(TIME$, 6)
      new.time$ = RIGHT$(new.time$, 8)  ' Strip off leading
                                        ' blank
      TIME$ = new.time$
   CASE 2: old.time$ = TIME$
      old.hour = VAL(LEFT$(old.time$, 2))  ' Convert hrs to
                                           ' number
      old.hour = old.hour - 1   ' Add 1 to the hour
      new.time$ = STR$(old.hour) + RIGHT$(TIME$, 6)
      new.time$ = RIGHT$(new.time$, 8)  ' Strip off leading
                                        ' blank
      TIME$ = new.time$
```

```
    CASE 3:
        PRINT "No time change was done."
END SELECT
PRINT
PRINT "The time now is: "; TIME$
```

Figure 20.2 shows a sample run of this program.

```
This is a time changing program that you
should run when the time zone changes.

The current date is: 04-20-1992
The current time is: 14:27:52

Do you want to:

1. Add an hour to the internal clock
2. Subtract an hour from the internal clock
3. Do nothing at this time and quit this program

What is your choice? 1

The time now is: 15:27:55









Press any key to continue
```

Figure 20.2. Changing the computer's time because of a time zone change.

Because `TIME$` returns a string value, you must convert the hours to a number with `VAL()` before incrementing the hours. The hours then must be reconverted to a string variable to store it back in the `TIME$` statement. Because `TIME$` converts the hours to a number and then converts them back again, `TIME$` must strip off the space where the imaginary plus sign was.

The INKEY$ Input Function

There is a function that seems to be a distant relative of the INPUT statement. It is the INKEY$ function. As with INPUT, INKEY$ gets input from the keyboard. Unlike INPUT, however, INKEY$ can get only one character at a time from the keyboard, not an entire string of characters as INPUT can.

The format of the INKEY$ function is

```
INKEY$
```

Because you never pass an argument to INKEY$, it requires no parentheses. The return value of INKEY$ is the character typed at the keyboard.

Any character you type at the keyboard is returned from INKEY$, except the following keystrokes:

Shift

Ctrl

Alt

Ctrl+Break

Ctrl+Alt+Del

Ctrl+NumLock

PrintScreen

Shift+PrintScreen

The return value of INKEY$ is usually assigned to a string variable.

You might wonder why anyone would want to use INKEY$, because it can accept only one character at a time. However, it has one advantage over INPUT: It grabs the key you press and stores that character in the string variable without you having to press Enter. INPUT *requires* that you press Enter, whereas INKEY$ gets its character input and passes control to the next statement without waiting for an Enter keypress.

The INKEY$ function requires one other consideration. When you want to get a character with INKEY$, you must put the INKEY$ function in a loop. Otherwise, INKEY$ does not wait for the user to type anything. If a key is not being pressed at exactly the same time that the INKEY$ function executes, it returns a null character and moves on.

> **NOTE:** INKEY$ does not automatically print a question mark, and it also does not display the input character on the screen, unlike the INPUT statement.

Programs have a quicker feel to them if the user does not have to press Enter after a menu choice or a yes-or-no question. The following examples illustrate INKEY$.

Examples

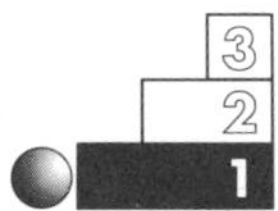

1. This program beeps at users when they press a *B* on the keyboard. If the user presses *Q*, the program quits. The program is simply a loop that gets the character with INKEY$. The program ignores characters other than *B* or *Q*. This shows you the quick response of INKEY$. Without INKEY$, the user would have to press Enter after the *B* or *Q*.

   Because the program converts the INKEY$ value to lowercase, it does not matter if the Caps Lock or Shift key is pressed.

```
' Filename: C20BEEP.BAS
'
' Beeps if user presses B; otherwise, quits when user press Q.
CLS
PRINT "I will beep if you press B"
PRINT "and I will quit if you press Q."
DO
   ans$ = INKEY$    ' Get a character if one is waiting
   IF (LCASE$(ans$) = "b") THEN BEEP
LOOP UNTIL (LCASE$(ans$) = "q")
```

2. You can use the following section of code to check for a user's answer to a yes-or-no question without the user's having to press Enter.

```
' Filename: C20YN1.BAS
'
' Routine to loop until the user enters Y or y or N or n.
CLS
PRINT "Do you want to continue (Y/N)? "
DO
   ans$ = INKEY$
LOOP UNTIL ((LCASE$(ans$) = "y") OR (LCASE$(ans$) = "n"))
```

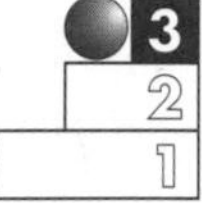

3. The following is a menu routine that uses INKEY$. It is only a portion of a larger program, but it is the basis of the menus used in the book-management application in Appendix E. As soon as the user presses one of the menu options, control leaves the menu routine.

```
' Filename: C20MENU.BAS
'
' Beginning of a menu routine.
CLS
PRINT "What do you want to do"
PRINT
PRINT "1. Print a report"
PRINT "2. Enter more data"
PRINT "3. Quit the program"
PRINT
PRINT "Please press the number of your choice...";
DO
   choice$ = INKEY$    ' Wait until user types 1, 2, or 3
LOOP UNTIL ((choice$="1") OR (choice$="2") OR (choice$="3"))
PRINT choice$          ' Echo types response back to user
```

Summary

You have seen the QBasic string functions. Many of them are often used in programs. QBasic is better at string handling than most programming languages, which is a direct result of these powerful string functions.

You have seen almost every built-in QBasic function. Although QBasic has many functions, there is not a function for everything you would ever need. That is why you need to learn how to program computers.

Not every routine needs to have a complete program, however. The next chapter shows you how to create your own functions. When you create a function, your program can call it and pass it parameters as though it were built-in.

Review Questions

Answers to the Review Questions are in Appendix B.

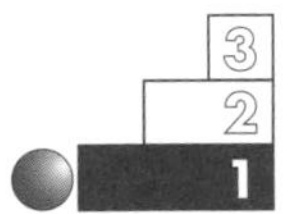

1. TRUE or FALSE: The `STRING$()` function returns a string containing one or more characters.
2. Which function would strip the two rightmost characters from the following string?

   ```
   Peoria, IL
   ```

3. What string function returns the length of a string?
4. Why is `ASC()` considered to be the mirror image of the `CHR$()` function?
5. TRUE or FALSE: `MID$()` is a statement and not a function if it appears on the left side of an equal sign.
6. When would you use the `INKEY$` function rather than the `INPUT` statement?

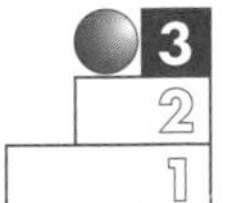

7. TRUE or FALSE: The following four statements do exactly the same thing:

   ```
   PRINT "a"; SPACE$(10); "b"
   PRINT "a"; STRING$(10, " "); "b"
   PRINT "a"; STRING$(10, 32); "b"
   PRINT "a"; STRING$(10, "   X   "); "b"
   ```

8. What does the following print statement do?

```
A$ = "QBasic is fun!"
b$ = LEFT$(RIGHT$(a$, 4), 3)
PRINT a$
```

9. What does the following statement produce?

```
PRINT ASC(CHR$(72))
```

10. Use PRINT with a combination of SPACE$ and LEN() to print the following title centered at the top of an 80-column screen (use only one statement):

```
QBasic by Example
```

Review Exercises

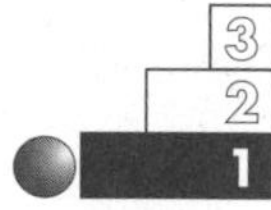

1. Write a program that prints the 26 letters of the alphabet down the screen, so that the *A*'s fill one 80-column line, the *B*'s fill the next 80-column line, and so on until all 26 letters are printed across the screen.

2. Write a program to ask users for their first and last names. Use LEFT$() to print only their initials.

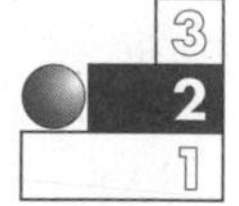

3. Write a program that asks users for their first, middle, and last names. Use INSTR() and MID$() to print only the middle names on the screen.

4. Write a program to ask users for their first names. Using LEN() and STRING$(), print the full names and underline them on the next line with a row of dashes exactly equal in number to the number of letters in the names.

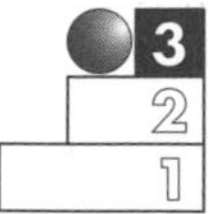

5. Study the fancy name-printing program toward the end of Chapter 3, "What Is a Program?" that lets you practice using the QBasic editor. It is full of string and number functions. Add a few more of your own routines to print the name in unique ways, such as across the screen diagonally.

21

User-Defined Functions

Now that you have seen QBasic's built-in functions, it's time to learn how to define your own. Although there are several built-in functions in QBasic, there is not a function to do everything that you would ever want to do with functions.

That's why QBasic lets you define your own functions. These are called *user-defined functions.* You can pass arguments to a user-defined function just as you did with the built-in functions. You can write string and numeric user-defined functions. As with some of QBasic's built-in functions, your user-defined functions do not have to require arguments.

This chapter introduces you to

- What user-defined functions are
- Single-line `DEF FN()` statements
- Multiple-line `DEF FN()` statements

This chapter contains several examples of user-defined functions that you might want to include in your own programs. The more routines you write that are user-defined functions, the less work you have to do in the future. You can reuse your user-defined functions instead of typing the same routine in every program you write.

Overview of User-Defined Functions

When you write a user-defined function, you are writing a miniprogram that will be called from your main program. In other words, a user-defined function is simply one or more QBasic statements that you write and assign a name to. After you write a user-defined function, you have only to type the function name, just as you did with `INT()` and `RIGHT$()`, plus any required arguments.

The next two chapters greatly expand on the concept of user-defined functions. Learning the single-line and multiple-line `DEF FN()` statements is a good introduction to the more advanced concept of subroutines and function procedures.

Over time, you will write a large number of user-defined functions. When you write a useful function, you cannot add it to the QBasic language. You can, however, save it in a program file. This file is called a *library of user-defined functions.* A library of user-defined functions is nothing more than a file with many of your functions in it. When you write a program that requires one or more functions from your library, you copy the functions you need (with the **E**dit menu's Cu**t**, **C**opy, and **P**aste options) to the new program you are writing. This saves you typing time and errors because you can later use the functions you have already written.

Mathematicians Like Functions!

If you have had some math courses, you probably know about the mathematical notation for functions, the *f(x)* symbol.

User-defined functions operate in the same way as mathematical *f(x)* functions, and you will notice the similarity.

Single-Line `DEF FN()` Statements

You must use the `DEF FN` statement to create a user-defined function. Most QBasic programmers put all their user-defined functions toward the top of the program that uses them. The `DEF FN()`

statement defines exactly what your user-defined function is to do. This statement should appear before any function calls that use the defined function. If you attempt to use a function before you have defined it, you get the following error message:

```
Function not defined
```

The format of the single-line `DEF FN()` statement is

```
DEF FNname [ ( parameter list ) ] = expression
```

The single-line `DEF FN()` statement requires a *name* that you make up. This name must conform to the same naming rules as variable names do. This is the name you will use when you call the function later. (You *must* precede a user-defined function name with `FN` when calling it, as later examples show.) The *name* has a data type, just as variables do. For instance, if the first part of a `DEF FN()` statement looks like

```
DEF FNcut$( ...
```

the full function name is `FNcut$`. You call that function (execute it) by referring to that name in the program. The function returns a string result because the `FNcut$` is a string.

The *parameter list* is a list of one or more variable names of any data type. The *parameter list* is optional. It defines the number and data type of each argument you pass to the user-defined function.

Parameters and Arguments

The preceding two chapters explained that functions require arguments, which are the values you pass to them. For example, in the statement

```
i = INT(8.45)
```

the `8.45` is an argument of the built-in `INT()` function.

Now, however, you are learning that user-defined functions require something called *parameters.* The difference between arguments and parameters can be confusing, but it doesn't have to be.

Many times, programmers say that "arguments are passed to functions, but functions receive parameters." In other words, the `8.45` in the preceding statement is an argument that you pass to the function `INT()`. It is said that the function `INT()` *receives a parameter.* In this case, the parameter that `INT()` receives is `8.45`.

The difference is basically semantics. Parameters and arguments are really the same things: the variables, constants, and expressions that go in the parentheses of a function call or function definition. These are "matched up" by QBasic when the function takes control. If a function requires no parameters, you will not pass any arguments to it.

The *`expression`* is the work you want the function to perform. It is also called the function's *return value.* Whatever *`expression`* you put after the equal sign (whether it is numeric or string) executes when the function is called. The *`expression`* can be any valid QBasic expression.

NOTE: A user-defined function can have more than one parameter passed to it, but it can have only one return value.

To get you started with the feel of functions, the first set of examples shows functions that require no parameters.

Examples

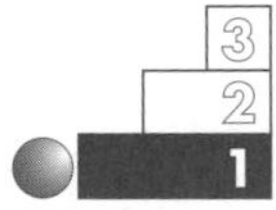

1. User-defined functions that have no parameters are fairly limited; however, you can perform some simple, timesaving operations with them. If you have a long name, you can define a function with the sole purpose of printing your name. Look at the following program.

```
' Filename: C21FNAME.BAS
'
' Defines a function that returns a long, full name.
CLS
```

```
DEF FNmyname$ = "Stephen Alonzo Jackson"

PRINT FNmyname$    ' Simply print the function's return value
PRINT FNmyname$    ' Print it a second time
PRINT LEFT$(FNmyname$, 7)   ' A function's return value is like
                            ' any other type
```

Figure 21.1 shows the output from this program. Notice that the return value is a string. You know that the return value is a string by looking at the data type of the `DEF FN()` variable, called `FNmyname$`.

```
Stephen Alonzo Jackson
Stephen Alonzo Jackson
Stephen







Press any key to continue
```

Figure 21.1. Printing the results of the user-defined function.

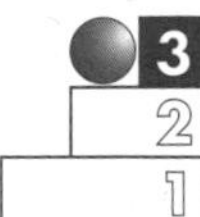

2. One good use of a user-defined function without parameters might be a multiple-character printing routine. For example, the following three user-defined functions save typing:

```
' Defines three multiple-character printing functions
DEF FNd80 = STRING$(80, "-")
DEF FNa80 = STRING$(80, "*")
DEF FNp80 = STRING$(80, "#")
```

```
' The rest of this program only has to print FNd80
' or FNa80 or FNp80 to print a string of 80 dashes,
' 80 asterisks, or 80 pound signs.
```

3. Single-line functions can work on variables around them. For example, the following program uses a user-defined function that calculates the area of a room. It assumes that the variables `rm.length` and `rm.width` are already defined with a value before they are used. Figure 21.2 shows the calculations of different areas.

```
' Filename: C21AREA1.BAS
'
' User-defined function to calculate area.
DEF FNarea = rm.length * rm.width

rm.width = 25                ' Have a fixed width
FOR rm.length = 10 TO 20     ' Loop through several length values
   PRINT "Width:"; rm.width; "Length"; rm.length; "Area:"; FNarea
NEXT rm.length
```

Adding Parameters to Single-Line Functions

As shown in the previous examples, using functions without parameters is not always better than simply writing the code without the functions. When you use parameters, however, this changes dramatically. Parameters let the expressions take on useful jobs by working on data passed to them. This means that the functions do not always perform the same function every time they are called; they are data-driven and return different values based on the parameters passed to them.

```
Width: 25 Length 10 Area: 250
Width: 25 Length 11 Area: 275
Width: 25 Length 12 Area: 300
Width: 25 Length 13 Area: 325
Width: 25 Length 14 Area: 350
Width: 25 Length 15 Area: 375
Width: 25 Length 16 Area: 400
Width: 25 Length 17 Area: 425
Width: 25 Length 18 Area: 450
Width: 25 Length 19 Area: 475
Width: 25 Length 20 Area: 500











Press any key to continue
```

Figure 21.2. Viewing different calculated areas.

The parameters you define in the `DEF FN()` statements do not have to be variables that are used in the rest of the program. They can simply be referred to in the function's *expression.* For example, the following user-defined function has a single parameter called `N`:

```
DEF FNdiv%(N) = N / 2
```

The function name is `FNdiv%`. The parameter is `N`. Because `N`'s default data type is single-precision (because there is no type suffix), the function expects to be passed a single-precision number. The function's expression is `N / 2`. The function returns an integer value based on that expression, because its name, `FNdiv%`, is an integer data type.

The program that uses this function does not have to have a variable called `N`. Actually, it is best that it does not. `N` is just a placeholder for the parameter. `N`'s primary job is to give the function the following message:

"Whatever value my programmer passes me, use that value in place of `N` *in my expression."*

This function's goal is to divide the number passed to it by 2 and return that result. You could call the function with the following line:

```
half.life = FNdiv%(84)
```

When this line of code executes, the function assumes that the `84` passed to it is to go everywhere the `N` was when the function was defined. The expression `N / 2` becomes `84 / 2` when `84` is passed to it.

Although it would have been easier to type the statement

```
half.life = 84 / 2
```

without a function, parameters give your functions much more flexibility, as the following examples show.

Examples

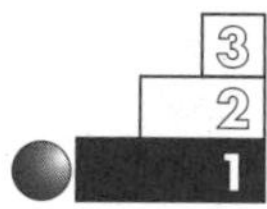

1. The following program uses the `RND` function. Instead of `RND` returning a random number from 0 to 1, this user-defined function called `FNrnd` returns a random number between 1 and the number the programmer passes to it. This keeps programmers from having to remember and retype the complete integer random-number formula every time they want a whole-number random number.

```
' Filename: C21RND.BAS
'
' Whole-number random-number generator.
CLS
DEF FNrnd(num) = INT (RND * num) + 1

' Print several random numbers between 1 and 6
FOR ctr = 1 TO 20
   PRINT FNrnd(6)    ' Return a number from 1 to 6
NEXT ctr
```

As you can see from Figure 21.3, only random numbers from 1 to 6 are generated when the program executes.

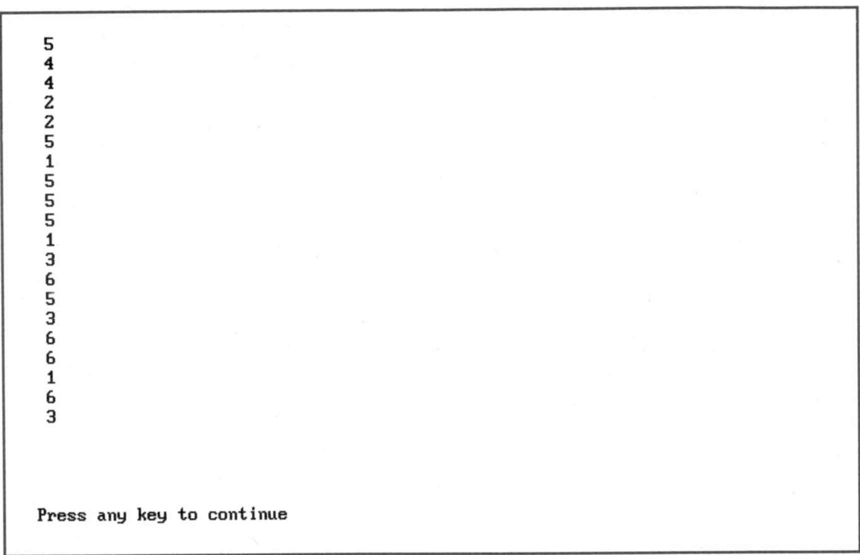

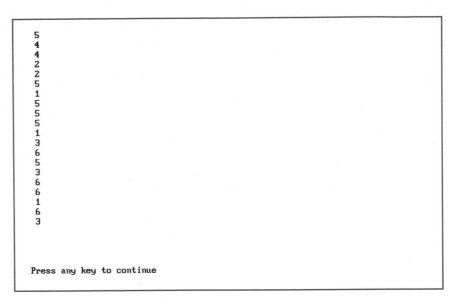

```
5
4
4
2
2
5
1
5
5
5
1
3
6
5
3
6
6
1
6
3

Press any key to continue
```

Figure 21.3. Looking at integer random numbers.

2. The following example shows two functions that many QBasic programmers think should have been included in the built-in numeric functions: *minimum and maximum functions.* These functions accept two values each. The maximum function returns the greater of the two values, and the minimum function returns the lesser of the two values. This saves you from having to write an IF-THEN-ELSE every time you want to know which of two numbers is bigger or smaller than the other.

```
' Filename: C21MINMX.BAS
'
' A minimum and maximum function.
DEF FNmin(n1, n2) = (n1 < n2) * n1 * -1 + (n2 <= n1) * n2 * -1
DEF FNmax(n1, n2) = (n1 > n2) * n1 * -1 + (n2 >= n1) * n2 * -1

CLS
INPUT "Please enter two values, separated by commas"; n1, n2
PRINT
PRINT "The highest value is:"; FNmax(n1, n2)
PRINT "The lowest value is:"; FNmin(n1, n2)
```

The arguments passed to `FNmax()` and `FNmin()` in the `PRINT` statements did not have to be named `n1` and `n2`. This program still would have worked if they were named `x` and `y` because the `n1` and `n2` in the user-defined functions are just placeholders for the expression. Figure 21.4 shows the result of this program.

```
Please enter two values, separated by oommas? 33, 54

The highest value is: 54
The lowest value is: 33










Press any key to continue
```

Figure 21.4. Using the maximum and minimum functions.

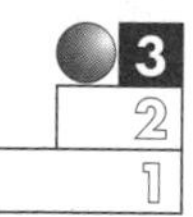

3. You can have more than one parameter in the parameter list. Earlier you saw how to compute the *n*th root of a number. By raising a number to a fractional power, you can simulate taking any root (called the *nth root*) of the number. The following function, called `FNnroot()`, does that. It raises the argument passed to it to the *n*th root. The value of *n* (the root) is sent as the second parameter.

```
' Filename: C21NROOT.BAS
'
' Function that computes nth root.
DEF FNnroot(num, n) = num ^ (1 / n)
```

```
FOR ctr = 100 TO 120        ' Computes and prints the 5th root
   PRINT FNnroot(ctr, 5)    ' of every number from 100 to 120
NEXT ctr
```

Multiple-Line DEF FN() Statements

You can write much more complex functions than the ones described previously by using extended multiple-line user-defined functions. They work in the same way single-line `DEF FN()` statements worked, except they are more flexible. Because you are not limited by one expression in the function, you can write powerful numeric and string functions that you can use later in other programs.

The simple format of the multiple-line `DEF FN()` statement is

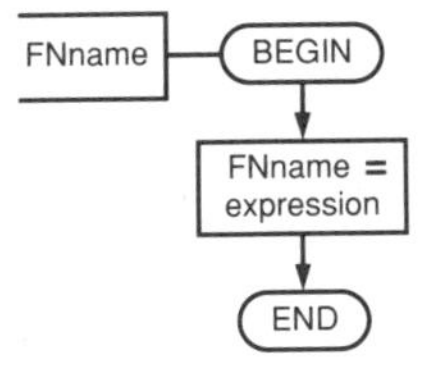


```
DEF FNname [ ( parameter list ) ]

      Block of one or more QBasic statements

   FNname = expression

END DEF
```

This is similar to the block `IF-THEN-ELSE` in that the body of the function can be a *`block of one or more QBasic statements`*. This adds much power to your function definitions because they can now be more than one line long.

After the body of the function definition, you must assign the function name to a final expression (which can be a variable, a constant, or a mixture of both). This is the multiple-line function's *return value.* When you write single-line functions, the functions have only one expression line in which to work. The result of that expression is the return value. To return a value (and every function in QBasic must return a value), you are required to assign the function name to the expression you want returned from the function.

TIP: The return value's data type must match the data type of the function name.

To know where the multiple-line function ends, you must also supply an END DEF statement to complete the function definition. To get a better understanding of the format, here is a multiple-line function that reverses the characters in a string:

```
DEF FNrev$ (s$)                  ' Reverse the characters in a string
      new$ = ""                  ' Initialize a null string
      FOR i = LEN(s$) TO 1 STEP -1
         new$ = new$ + MID$(s$, i, 1)  ' Build a new string
      NEXT i                  ' When loop finishes, string is reversed
   FNrev$ = new$                 ' The return value
END DEF
```

This is a multiple-line user-defined function because it begins with DEF FN and ends with END DEF. The parameter is s$. The function body (its block of code) begins with `new$ = ""` and ends with `FNrev$ = new$`. The function's return value is new$ because it is assigned to the function's name. Remember that all functions must return a value. In multiple-line functions, the return value is the value you assign to the function name.

To call this function (to execute it), you simply have to pass it a string value, just as you did with single-line functions. As long as you have defined the function before you use it, you can call it from anywhere in the program. The following line sends the function a string constant:

```
back.str$ = FNrev$ ("Larry")
```

Because FNrev$'s return value is a string, this line of code puts the reversed Larry in the variable called back.str$. If you then print back.str$, you see the following result:

```
yrraL
```

You might think that was a lot of work. You might be asking why you can't type the reverse string routine in the program when you need it without bothering with all the function definition code at the top of the program. The power of user-defined functions comes in when you need the same routine several times in one program (or several programs).

For instance, it is true that if you need to reverse only one string in a program, it would probably be easier to type the code that reverses it at the point in the program that requires it. If you have to reverse several strings in the same program, however, defining a function to do this makes your coding time much shorter. Now that you have defined the function, you can call it from several places in your program and pass it several different values without worrying about retyping the routine. Your program might have the following statements:

```
PRINT FNrev$("Larry")
back.name$ = FNrev$(first$) + FNrev$(last$)
mir$ = FNrev$("Look in a mirror to read this!")
PRINT mir$      ' Prints the reversed string
```

Although this might be a slightly exaggerated example, if you need to reverse more than one string, as this example code does four times, you have to write four sets of string-reversal routines in your program. Because you defined the function at the top of the program, however, you need only to call it from then on. Whatever string variable, constant, or string expression you pass to it from then on will be received in the function's parameter list and reversed.

Before you look at some multiple-line user-defined function examples, you should know about an additional way to code these functions. It is an extension of what you have seen. The complete format of the multiple-line user-defined function is

```
DEF FNname [ ( parameter list ) ]
      Block of one or more QBasic statements
   FNname = expression
      [Block of one or more QBasic statements
       FNname = expression
       EXIT DEF]
      [:
       :]
END DEF
```

Notice that a function can have more than one block of code. If it does, you must supply more than one return value. You can use the `EXIT DEF` statement (which usually follows an `IF-THEN`) to leave the function from the middle without executing any of the rest of the function's code.

This expanded version of user-defined functions lets the function pick from several return values. In other words, although the function can return only one value, it can have several `FN`*`name`* `=` *`expression`* statements. Only one of them executes, depending on the result of a relational test. A brief example makes this clear.

The following user-defined function is an expanded version of the string-reversal function you saw earlier. It simply returns the reversed parameter *unless* it is passed `"Don't reverse"` as a parameter. If it receives the `"Don't reverse"` string, it simply returns the string untouched.

```
DEF FNrev$ (s$)              ' Reverses the characters in a string
      IF (s$ = "Don't reverse") THEN
         FNrev$ = s$          ' Don't change string
         EXIT DEF
      END IF
      new$ = ""               ' Initialize a null string
      FOR i = LEN(s$) TO 1 STEP -1
         new$ = new$ + MID$(s$, i, 1)  ' Build a new string
      NEXT i              ' When loop finishes, string is reversed
   FNrev$ = new$              ' The return value
END DEF
```

Notice that the string is returned to the calling program untouched if it contains `"Don't reverse"`, but it is reversed otherwise. Although there are two `FNrev$ = ...` statements, only one of them executes because the `IF-THEN` conditionally controls them. The `EXIT DEF` is necessary to keep the string reversal from happening if the parameter equals `"Don't reverse"`.

You can put statements other than calculations inside a function. For instance, in the multiple-line function just shown, you could have included `PRINT` and `INPUT` statements. These types of statements, however, cloud the function. You should keep your functions as tight as possible and not include many input or output statements in them. In Chapter 22, "Subroutines and Function Procedures," you learn a better way to create extended sections of code called *subroutines,* which give you more freedom than functions do. Functions, however, are a great way to perform routine calculations and string manipulations on parameters you pass to them.

Examples

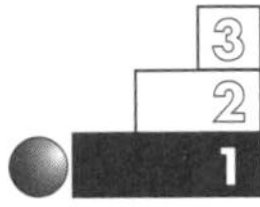

1. The following multiple-line user-defined function requires an integer parameter. When you pass it an integer, the function adds the numbers from 1 to that integer. In other words, if you pass the function a 6, it returns the result of the following calculation:

   1 + 2 + 3 + 4 + 5 + 6

   This is known as the *sum of the digits* calculation. It is sometimes used for depreciation in accounting.

```
' Filename: C21SUMD.BAS
'
' Function that computes the sum of the digits for its
' parameter.
DEF FNsumd(n)
   IF (n <= 0) THEN
      FNsumd = n  ' Return the parameter if it is too small
      EXIT DEF
   END IF
   sum = 0        ' Initialize total variable
   FOR ctr = 1 TO n
      sum = sum + ctr
   NEXT ctr
   FNsumd = sum   ' Return the result
END DEF

CLS
' Pass the function several values
n1 = FNsumd(6)
PRINT "The sum of the digits for 6 is"; n1
```

```
PRINT "The sum of the digits for 0 is"; FNsumd(0)
PRINT "The sum of the digits for 18 is";
PRINT FNsumd(18)

n2 = 25
n3 = FNsumd(n2)
PRINT "The sum of the digits for"; n2; "is"; n3
```

The output from this program is shown in Figure 21.5. The function is called four times. The second time, the argument is `0`, so the function simply returns it unchanged.

```
The sum of the digits for 6 is 21
The sum of the digits for 0 is 0
The sum of the digits for 18 is 171
The sum of the digits for 25 is 325








Press any key to continue
```

Figure 21.5. Computing the sum of the digits.

2. The following program includes two user-defined string functions. The first one is a single-line function, and the other is a multiple-line user-defined function. They perform the following actions:

   - ♦ Return the first word of the string.
   - ♦ Return the first word of the string in uppercase letters.

```
' Filename: C21STR2F.BAS
'
' Illustrates a single program with multiple user string
' functions.
DEF FNfword$ (s1$) = LEFT$(s1$, INSTR(s1$, " ") - 1)

DEF FNuword$ (s2$)
   first.word$ = LEFT$(s2$, INSTR(s2$, " ") - 1)
   first.word$ = UCASE$(first.word$)   ' Convert it to
                                       ' uppercase
   FNuword$ = first.word$
END DEF

CLS
test.st$ = "The rain in Spain"

PRINT FNfword$(test.st$)    ' Print results to show how each
                            ' is called
PRINT FNuword$(test.st$)
```

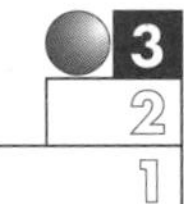

3. The following program includes a user-defined function that centers any string passed to it within 80 spaces. This builds an output line on the screen. Any time you need to center a string, simply pass it to this function. It returns the string so that you can print it centered on the screen.

```
' Filename: C21CENT.BAS
'
' Routine that returns a centered string.
DEF FNcentr$ (p.str$)
   IF (LEN(p.str$) > 80) THEN
      FNcentr$ = p.str$      ' Return the string if it is
                             ' too long
      EXIT DEF
   END IF
   st.len = LEN(p.str$)      ' Get length of parameter
   out.str$ = SPACE$(80)     ' Fill output string with 80
                             ' spaces
   MID$(out.str$, (80 - st.len) / 2) = p.str$   ' Center it
   FNcentr$ = out.str$    ' Return centered string
END DEF
```

```
' Show user how it works
CLS
PRINT "Please type a string, and I will print it"
PRINT "centered on the next line..."
LINE INPUT "? "; in.str$
PRINT FNcentr$(in.str$)    ' Print it centered
```

Figure 21.6 shows the output of a sample run. You can add this routine to your own library to use when you need to center a title on the screen.

```
Please type a string, and I will print it
centered on the next line...
? QBasic By Example
                               QBasic By Example







Press any key to continue
```

Figure 21.6. Centering a title.

Summary

You have seen how to build your own collection of user-defined functions. When you write a user-defined function, you save programming time later. Instead of writing the routine a second or third time, you only have to call the function by its name. Over time, you will develop a good library of your own functions to accent QBasic's built-in functions.

The next two chapters greatly expand on this concept by showing you how to write subroutines and functions that are more powerful and flexible than those shown here.

Review Questions

Answers to the Review Questions are in Appendix B.

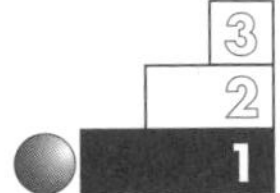

1. Why do you sometimes need to define your own functions?
2. TRUE or FALSE: A user-defined function can return more than one value.

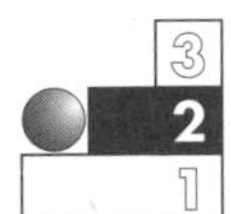

3. Given the user-defined function

```
DEF FNfun$(i%) = CHR$(i%) + CHR$(i%) + CHR$(i%)
```

A. What is the return data type?
B. How many parameters are passed to it?
C. What is the data type of the parameter(s)?

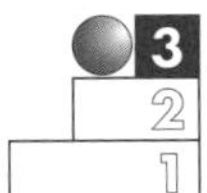

4. TRUE or FALSE: If a multiple-line function includes several `FNnam =` statements, it returns more than one value when it is called.
5. Which built-in numeric function does the following user-defined function simulate?

```
DEF FNa(x) = x ^ (1 / 2)
```

Review Exercises

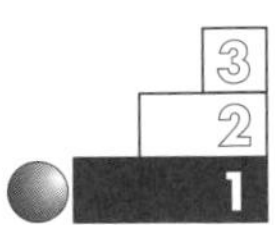

1. Write a single-line user-defined function to reverse a string of characters and convert them to uppercase.
2. Expand on the routine in the previous exercise by making it a multiple-line function. The body of the multiple-line function should be no more than two statements. This seems to add complexity to such a simple problem, but multiple-line functions can be changed much more easily than single-line functions.

3. Write a function that computes the double-precision area of a circle, given its double-precision radius. The formula to calculate the radius of a circle is

   area = 3.14159 * radius^2

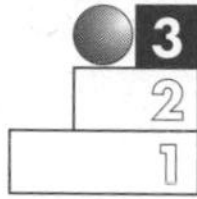

4. Write a multiple-line function to return the value of a polynomial (the answer), given this formula:

   $9x^4 + 15x^2 + x^1$

Subroutines and Function Procedures

The preceding three chapters taught you how to use QBasic's built-in functions and how to design your own. This chapter builds on that knowledge by extending the power of routines you write yourself.

Computers never get bored. They loop and perform the same input, output, and computations that your programs require as long as you want them to. You can take advantage of their repetitive nature by looking at your programs in a new way: as a series of small routines that execute when and as many times as you need them to execute.

Most of the material in this chapter and the next chapter improves on the function concept. This chapter covers

- An overview of subroutines
- Subroutine procedures
- The SUB statement
- The CALL statement

- The SHARED statement
- The DECLARE statement
- Function procedures
- The FUNCTION statement
- Building your own subroutine library

This chapter stresses the use of *modular programming.* QBasic was designed to make it easy for you to write your programs in several modules rather than as one long program. By breaking a program into several smaller program-line routines, you can isolate problems better, write correct programs faster, and produce programs that are much easier to maintain than if you wrote it as one long program.

An Overview of Subroutines

When you approach an application that needs to be programmed, it is best not to sit down at the keyboard and start typing. Rather, you should think about the program and what it is to do. One of the best ways to attack a program is to start with the overall program's goal and break it into several smaller modules. You should never lose sight of the overall goal of the program, but you should try to think of how the individual pieces fit together to accomplish that overall goal.

When you finally do sit down to start coding the problem, continue to think in terms of those pieces that fit together. Do not approach a program as if it is one giant program; rather, continue to write the small pieces individually.

This does not mean you should write separate programs to do everything. You can keep individual pieces of the overall program together if you write *subroutines.* Subroutines are sections of programs you can execute repeatedly. Many good programmers write programs that consist solely of subroutines, even if they are to execute one or more of the subroutines only once.

Look at Listing 22.1 to get a feel for the way subroutines work. It is not a QBasic program, but a preliminary outline for one. The listing shows an outline of a problem that needs to be programmed.

The program is to get a list of numbers from the keyboard, sort the numbers, and print them on the screen. You have seen examples of such programs in previous chapters.

Listing 22.1. An outline of a programming problem.

```
' Program to get a list of numbers, sort them, and print them.
'
   :
   QBasic statements to get a list of numbers into an array
   :
   QBasic statements to sort those numbers
   :
   QBasic statements to display those numbers to the screen
   :
```

It turns out that this is not a good way to approach this program. Until now, you were too busy concentrating on the individual language elements to worry about subroutines, but it is time for you to improve the way you think of programs. The problem with the approach shown in Listing 22.1 is that it is one long program with one QBasic statement after another, yet there are three distinct sections (or better yet, *sub*sections) in the program.

Because the overall program is obviously a collection of smaller routines, you can group these routines by making them QBasic subroutines. Listing 22.2 shows an outline of the same program, but it has broken the routines into distinct subroutines and added a new routine at the top of the program that controls the other subroutines.

Listing 22.2. An outline of a better approach to the same programming problem.

```
' Program with four routines.
' The main (first) one controls the execution of the others
' The next routine is a stand-alone routine that gets a list of
' numbers
' The next one sorts those numbers
' The last one prints them to the screen
   CALL GetNumbers
   CALL SortNumbers
```

```
   CALL DisplayNumbers
   END

' First Routine
GetNumbers Routine
   QBasic statements to get a list of numbers
   :
   RETURN to Main

' Second Routine
SortNumbers Routine
   QBasic statements to sort the numbers
   :
   RETURN to Main

' Third Routine
DisplayNumbers
   QBasic statements to display the numbers on the screen
   :
   RETURN to Main
```

This program outline is a much better way of writing the program. It is longer to type, but it is much more well-organized. The first routine simply controls, or *calls,* the other subroutines to do their work in the proper order. After all, it would be silly to sort the numbers before the user types them. Therefore, the first routine ensures that the other routines execute in the proper sequence.

The first routine is not really a subroutine. It is the main program. (QBasic calls this the *main module.*) This is where you previously would have typed the full program. Now, however, the program consists only of a group of subroutine calls. The primary program in all but the shortest of programs should be simply a series of subroutine-controlling statements.

Again, these listings are obviously not intended to be examples of code, but they are outlines of programs. From these types of outlines, it is easier to write the full program. Before going to the keyboard, you know there are four distinct sections of this program: a primary subroutine-calling routine, a keyboard data-entry subroutine, a sorting subroutine, and a printing subroutine.

Remember that you should never lose sight of the original programming problem. With the approach just described, you never do. Look at the main calling routine in Listing 22.2 again. Notice that you can glance at this routine and get a feel for the overall program without the entire program's statements getting in the way. This is a good example of modular programming. A large programming problem has been broken into distinct modules called subroutines. Each subroutine performs a primary job in a few QBasic statements.

The length of each subroutine varies depending on what the subroutine is to do. A good rule of thumb is that a subroutine's QBasic listing should not be more than one screen long. If it is, it will be more difficult to edit and maintain with the QBasic editor. Not only that, but if a subroutine is more than one screen long, it probably does too much and should be broken into two or more subroutines. This is not a requirement; you must make the final judgment on whether a subroutine is too long.

Notice that a subroutine is like a detour on a highway. You are traveling along in the primary program and then you run into a subroutine-calling statement. You must temporarily leave the main routine and go execute the subroutine's code. When that subroutine's code is finished, control of the program is passed back to the primary calling routine. (When you finish a detour, you end up back on your main route to continue your trip.) Control continues as the primary routine continues to call each subroutine one at a time and in the proper order.

Generally, the primary routine that controls subroutine calls and their order is called the *calling routine.* The subroutines controlled by the calling routine are called the *called subroutines.*

If Listing 22.2 were a complete QBasic program, where would the last executed statement be? The last statement executed is in the primary calling routine; it is an END or a STOP statement. (Without the END or STOP, execution would "fall through" to the first subroutine, execute it again, and get confused when it hits the RETURN.) By returning control to the primary routine after the last subroutine finishes, you make it easy for someone looking at the first page of your program to see the logic from the beginning to the end.

TIP: You used this calling pattern with the built-in and user-defined functions in the previous chapters. Control of your main program is temporarily suspended while the function executes. Control then returns to your program. As with functions, you can execute a subroutine call repeatedly in a loop without having to write the code more than once.

The SUB Subroutine Procedure

Subroutine procedures offer a much more convenient way of using subroutines. A subroutine procedure (the rest of this book usually refers to them simply as subroutines) is a completely separate section of code that you call from your primary calling routine. The primary calling routine is called the *main program* or *main procedure.*

When you designate that a section of code is to be a subroutine, QBasic isolates that routine from the rest of the program. When you look at your program, you see only the main program and not all the subroutines that go with it. This might seem confusing at first, but it makes programming much easier. When you want to look at a subroutine, you simply have to tell QBasic by selecting from a menu. QBasic displays that subroutine, which you can then edit. If you want to look at another subroutine or go back to the main program, QBasic easily does that as well. By using subroutines, you see only what you want to see. You are forced (thankfully) to think more in terms of modules because you can never see your entire program at once.

When you save a program that includes subroutine procedures, QBasic stores it as one complete program. When you load it in your QBasic editor, however, QBasic separates the subroutines from the main program for you.

To designate a subroutine as a subroutine procedure, you must use the SUB and END SUB statements. SUB defines the beginning of the subroutine, and END SUB tells QBasic when it is finished.

The format of SUB-END SUB is

```
SUB subroutine name
   A block of one or more QBasic statements
END SUB
```

You must give the subroutine a *subroutine name*. The *block of one or more QBasic statements* is one or more statements that make up the body of the subroutine. Unlike function names, the subroutine name should have no data type suffix (such as $, %, #, or !) because no value is returned from the subroutine. The name simply informs QBasic where to look when the main program calls it.

The following section of a program shows the SUB and END SUB statements enclosing statements that make up a subroutine:

```
SUB CalcInt          ' Interest rate calculation
   INPUT "What is the interest rate (i.e., .13)"; int.rate
   INPUT "How many years is the loan"; term
   INPUT "What is the original loan principal"; prin
   total.int = prin * ((1+rate) ^ term)  ' Interest calculation
END SUB
```

The subroutine procedure's name is CalcInt. It is common to indent the body of a subroutine procedure. Notice there is no RETURN statement at the end of this subroutine procedure. QBasic knows that it should always return from a subroutine procedure to the statement that called it. Therefore, the return from this procedure is automatic.

Never include a RETURN statement at the end of a subroutine procedure. If you need to exit a subroutine before its natural end, use an EXIT SUB statement. EXIT SUB is generally put after an IF-THEN to exit early on a special condition.

One way the main program calls the subroutine is with the CALL statement. (This is analogous to the way subroutines were called earlier with the GOSUB statement.) The format of the CALL statement is

```
[ CALL ] subroutine name
```

Notice that the CALL keyword is optional. For now, use it until you learn the DECLARE statement later in this chapter. To call the interest-calculation subroutine procedure shown earlier, you would use this statement:

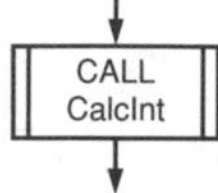


```
CALL CalcInt
```

This statement is located in the main program or in another subroutine procedure that needs to call CalcInt.

A Subroutine Procedure Example

This section is different from many of those you have seen earlier in this book. It is a complete walk-through example that takes you from the beginning of a programming problem to its conclusion. It is the application described when this chapter opened: Sort a list of numbers typed by the user and then print them.

This walk-through is important because the first time you use a subroutine procedure, the QBasic editor will take over when it can tell that you are starting the subroutine. For now, follow this example and see what happens.

The layout of this program is fairly obvious. As shown earlier, there is a main program that calls three subroutines. The first subroutine gets the list of numbers from the user. The second subroutine sorts those numbers. The third and last subroutines print the numbers on the screen. Therefore, the following code is a good main procedure:

```
' Filename: C22SRTSP.BAS
'
' Get a list of numbers, sort them,
' then print them on the screen.
DIM nums(100)   ' Reserve an array for the user's list of numbers
COLOR 7,1       ' White characters on blue background
CLS

PRINT "*** Number Sorting Program ***"
PRINT
```

```
CALL GetNums      ' Get the input
CALL SortNums     ' Sort them
CALL PrintNums    ' Print them

END
```

For now, type this program. Before working on the subroutine procedures, save it to disk under the file name in the comments: C22SRTSP.BAS (with the **F**ile **S**ave menu option). Your screen will look like the one in Figure 22.1.

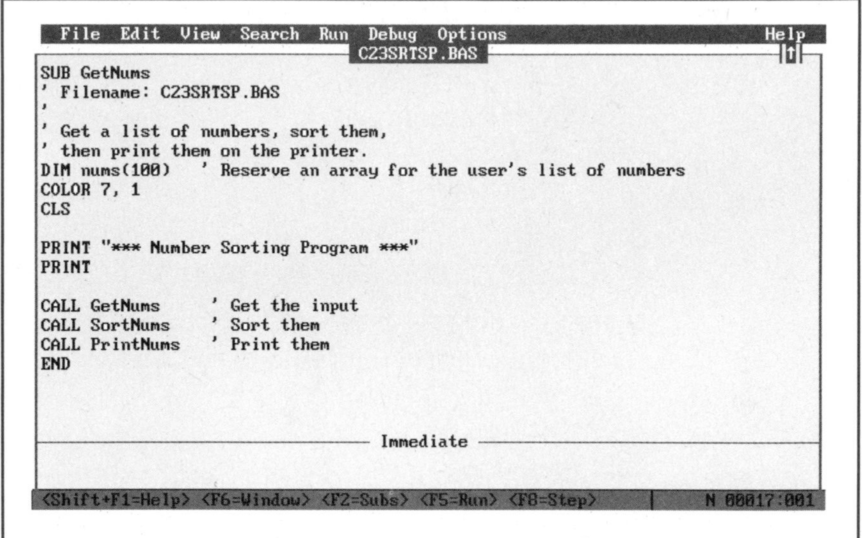

Figure 22.1. Your screen after typing and saving the main program.

You are ready for the first subroutine procedure, called `GetNums`. So far, you have typed subroutines after the last line of the main program (probably with a separating blank line or a row of asterisks), and this program should be no exception. The first line is the opening `SUB` statement of the subroutine. It looks like this:

```
SUB GetNums         ' Gets a list of user numbers
```

Type this line below the main program's `END` statement. As soon as you press Enter, QBasic pulls a "fast one" on you. Your screen now looks like the one in Figure 22.2. Although you did not scroll the screen or type an END SUB statement, QBasic erased the main program module from the screen and placed the cursor in the middle of the GetNums subroutine procedure.

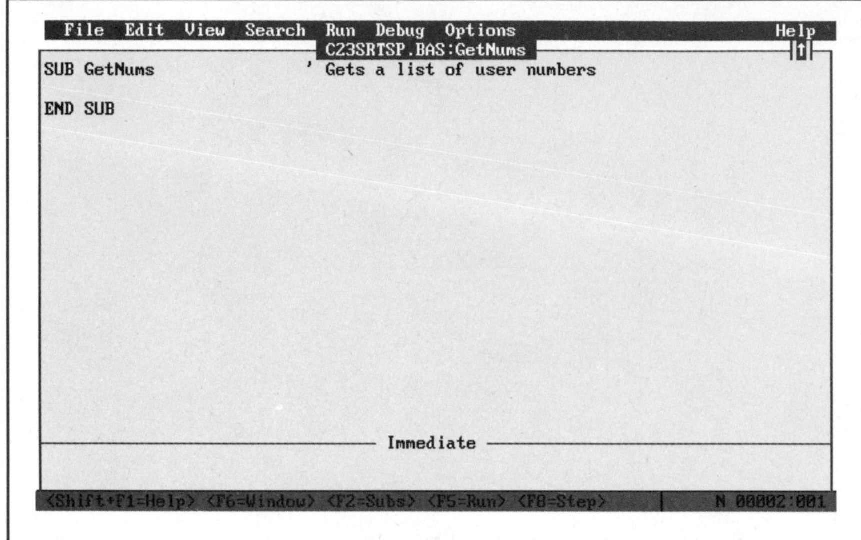

Figure 22.2. After typing the beginning SUB statement.

Regardless of how many times you press the up arrow key or the down arrow key, you will never be able to find the main program module. QBasic immediately isolated the subroutine from the rest of the program. Notice the title at the top of the editing window. It reads:

```
C22SRTSP.BAS:GetNums
```

This title is to remind you that you are working in the program with the file name C22SRTSP.BAS (you saved it earlier under this name), and that within this program you are editing the subroutine called GetNums. Because you are in the middle of the subroutine procedure anyway, type the body of the subroutine from the following code:

```
SHARED nums(), total.nums' Inform subroutine of shared variables

FOR total.nums = 1 TO 100  ' Maximum of 100 elements
   PRINT
   PRINT "Please type the next number in the list"
   INPUT "(type a -99 to quit)"; nums(total.nums)
   IF(nums(total.nums)=-99)THEN total.nums=total.nums-1: EXIT FOR
   ' Stop looping if user typed -99 or all 100 values
NEXT total.nums
```

Your screen should look like the one in Figure 22.3. You have typed the main program module and the first subroutine.

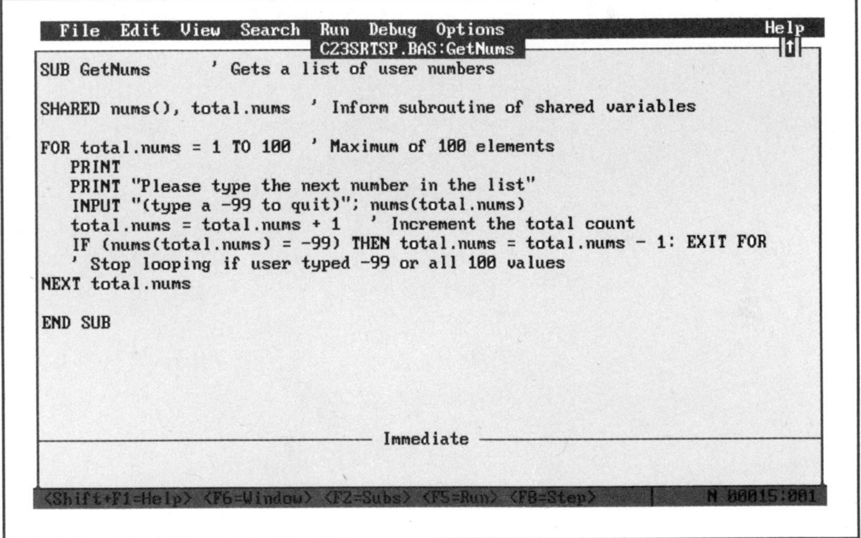

Figure 22.3. After typing the `GetNums` subroutine procedure.

The only surprise in this code is the SHARED statement. SHARED is required any time your subroutine procedure uses one or more variables from the main program module. Because QBasic isolates the subroutine module from the main module, it has no way of knowing that the array has been dimensioned yet, although the main program did so. The subroutine procedure does not care how many elements `nums()` has; you leave the array parentheses empty in a `SHARED` statement. The subroutine has to know only that the array is shared with one in the main program module. The main program needs to know also how many values were entered (for the sort and print), so `total.nums` must also be shared. (For now, type the subroutine as you see it. The `SHARED` statement will mean much more to you when you read about *variable scope* in Chapter 23.)

If a subroutine procedure will share a variable (or more than one variable) with the main program, you must add a `SHARED` statement to the top of each subroutine procedure. Type the variable name(s). If there is more than one variable, separate the variables with commas. If any of the shared variables is an array, add an empty set of parentheses to show the subroutine it's an array and not a regular variable.

You have to type the sorting and printing subroutine procedures. Move the cursor below the `GetNums END SUB` statement and type the following line:

```
SUB SortNums
```

QBasic again can tell that you are beginning a new subroutine procedure and opens a new subroutine function called `SortNums`, as shown in Figure 22.4.

Type the following sorting subroutine between the `SUB SortNums` and the `END SUB` statements:

```
SHARED nums(), total.nums' Inform subroutine of shared variables
FOR ctr1 = 1 TO total.nums  ' Start swapping pairs in bubble sort
   FOR ctr2 = ctr1 TO total.nums
      IF (nums(ctr1)>nums(ctr2)) THEN SWAP nums(ctr1),nums(ctr2)
   NEXT ctr2
NEXT ctr1
```

You need to type the last subroutine procedure, called `PrintNums`. As you know by now, you start the process by typing the following line *after* the `END SUB` statement:

```
SUB PrintNums     ' Print the sorted list of numbers
```

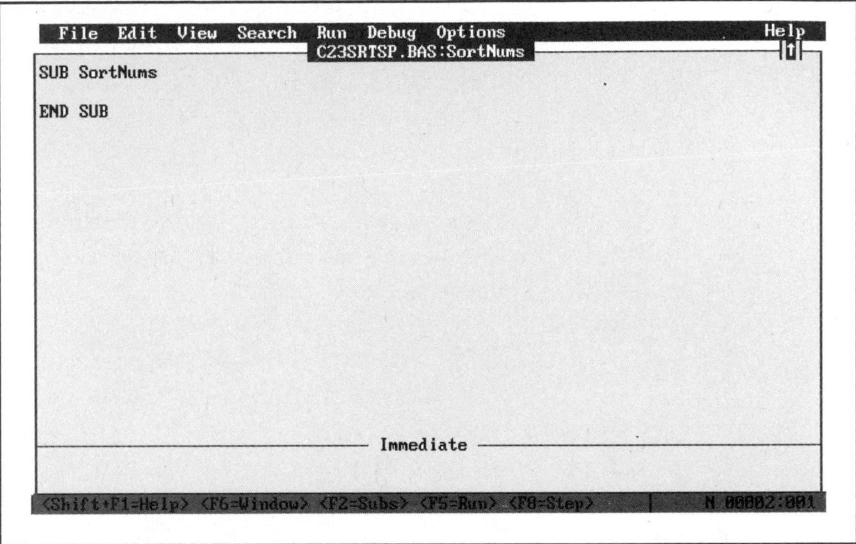

Figure 22.4. Getting ready to type the `SortNums` subroutine procedure.

When QBasic opens a new subroutine procedure block, type the following code:

```
SHARED nums(), total.nums' Inform subroutine of shared variables

PRINT
PRINT "Here are the sorted numbers"
PRINT "--------------------------"
PRINT

FOR ctr = 1 TO total.nums
   PRINT nums(ctr)    ' Print each sorted number
NEXT ctr
```

You have typed the complete program, including the subroutines. To run this program, you only have to select **R**un **S**tart from the menu (or press F5) as you have done with previous QBasic programs.

If you typed the program correctly, you should be able to run it, type several numbers, and see them printed. Everything in the program should work the way you are used to seeing it work.

You might wonder, however, how you can get back to the main module, or to one of the other subroutine procedures. After all, regardless of how careful you are, everybody makes typing mistakes, and you might have to go back and correct something. Even if you made no mistakes, you need to know how to edit different parts of the program.

QBasic makes moving between routines easy. It is easier to move between the main module and the subroutine procedures than it is to scroll and find them when you type single-module, long programs. The way to move between the modules is to select the **S**UBs... option from the **V**iew menu. F2 is the speed key for this. Press F2 now (or select **S**UBs...) and you are presented with the procedure-selection screen shown in Figure 22.5.

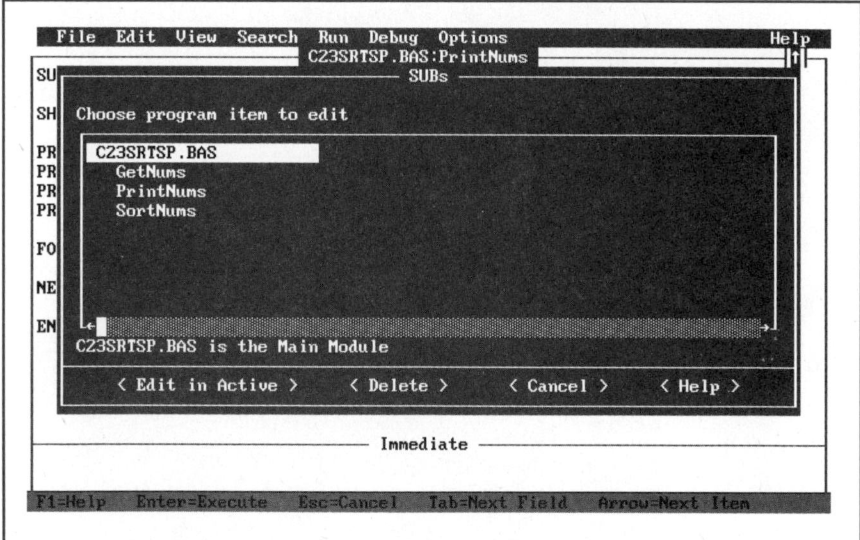

Figure 22.5. Viewing the procedure-selection screen.

You can probably figure out the rest. Press the down-arrow and up-arrow keys to see the highlight move from procedure to procedure. The message at the bottom of the window changes to tell you whether the highlighted procedure is the `Main Module` or a `SUB`. After highlighting a procedure, such as the `GetNums` procedure, press Enter.

(Mouse users can simply point and click with the mouse.) When you do, QBasic instantly displays that procedure. Press F2 again and select C22SRTSP.BAS (the `Main Module`, as shown at the bottom of the window). The main program module appears.

This is a unique and helpful method to isolate each module and still tie the modules together for ease of access. You can easily move from module to module from this screen. If you have edits to make or you just want to look at the code, you can jump between the modules. However, the goal of isolation has been maintained: QBasic takes care of the bookkeeping and lets you worry about writing the program.

> **TIP:** If you decide to delete a subroutine procedure, do so from the SUBS selection screen. The **D**elete option is at the bottom of the screen. If you want to delete a subroutine, highlight it and Tab (or point with the mouse) to the **D**elete option and press Enter. After a verifying message, QBasic erases the subroutine from your program.

Wrapping Up Subroutine Procedures

Save the completed example program to disk with **F**ile **S**ave. It is important to realize that when you save the program, the entire program is saved. On your disk it looks like one long program with a main procedure followed by three subroutine procedures enclosed by SUB and END SUB statements.

When it is saved, display the main module by pressing F2 and selecting it, if it is not already on the screen. A strange thing has happened. QBasic has inserted three new statements at the top of the program. Figure 22.6 shows your screen at this point.

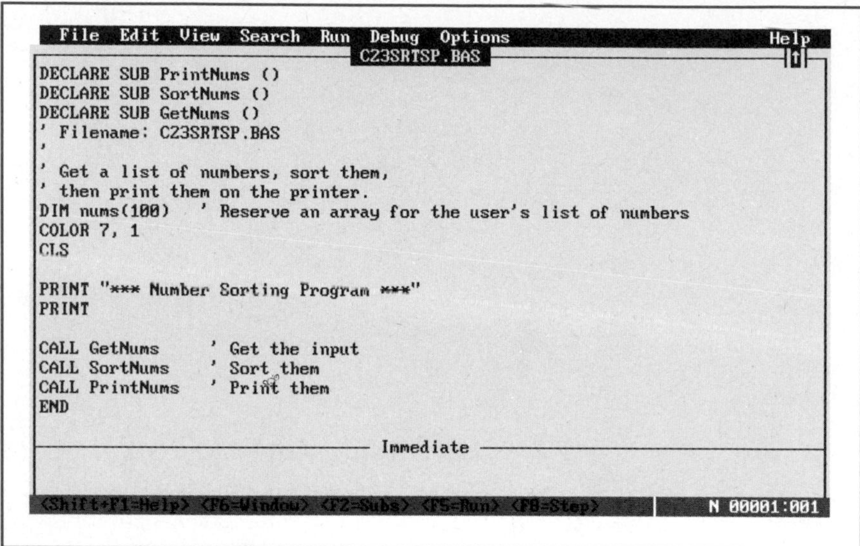

Figure 22.6. Three newly added DECLARE statements at the top of the program.

The DECLARE statements will be useful when you read about variable scope in Chapter 23. For now, they are optional. As you know, the program ran fine without the DECLARE statements. But when you saved the program to disk, QBasic added the statements. Notice that each DECLARE statement takes the following format:

```
DECLARE SUB subroutine name ()
```

The parentheses are required, and sometimes there are variables in them; however, this chapter's examples do not require variables. The purpose of the DECLARE statement is to inform the main module that three subroutine procedures are called from it.

As you saw, the main module really did not need to know anything before the DECLARE statements because everything worked fine. There are, however, some cases when the DECLARE statements are not optional. Because of this, QBasic ensures that every main module that calls subroutine procedures includes DECLARE statements, one for each procedure called.

You could have typed the DECLARE statements yourself, although for this example there was no reason to go to the effort because QBasic did it for you.

NOTE: You must place all DECLARE statements in your program before any executable statements. You can put remarks (REM or ') before DECLARE statements.

The DECLARE statement is required under several conditions. One of these is when you do not use the CALL keyword in a subroutine CALL statement. Remember that CALL is optional (just as LET is). The main program could have looked like this:

```
DECLARE SUB GetNums ()
DECLARE SUB SortNums ()
DECLARE SUB PrintNums ()
' Filename: C22SRTSP.BAS
'
' Get a list of numbers, sort them,
' then print them on the screen.
DIM nums(100)   ' Reserve an array for the user's list of numbers
COLOR 7,1       ' White characters on blue background
CLS

PRINT "*** Number Sorting Program ***"
PRINT

GetNums      ' Get the input
SortNums     ' Sort them
PrintNums    ' Print them

END
```

The CALL statement was not included in the subroutine procedure calls. Because of this, DECLARE is required. Most programmers do not like where QBasic inserts the DECLARE statements, either. They prefer to see them after the opening remarks, as in this program:

```
' Filename: C22SRTSP.BAS
'
' Get a list of numbers, sort them,
' then print them on the screen.

DECLARE SUB GetNums ()
DECLARE SUB SortNums ()
DECLARE SUB PrintNums ()
DIM nums(100)   ' Reserve an array for the user's list of numbers
COLOR 7,1       ' White characters on blue background
CLS

PRINT "*** Number Sorting Program ***"
PRINT

GetNums     ' Get the input
SortNums    ' Sort them
PrintNums   ' Print them

END
```

Because of this, all programs for the rest of this book include the DECLARE statements. They are inserted after the initial remarks so that QBasic does not add them before the remarks.

Getting back to the optional CALL, do you see any advantage to specifying CALL over not specifying it when you call subroutine procedures? Your programs are more readable without CALL. The body of the main program reads almost as though it were English. It looks like:

Get the numbers, sort the numbers, and then print the numbers.

This might be stretching things a bit, but the CALL does cloud things. By making up meaningful subroutine labels, you can make your programs more self-documenting by eliminating the CALL keyword from your subroutine calls.

Despite the isolation of the routines, you must understand that this is just one long program. Although you used several separate editing screens to write the program, it is saved on disk as one continuous program. QBasic keeps routines isolated for you, but if you print the program or save it to disk and look at it from DOS, the program looks like this (after moving the DECLARE statements):

```
' Filename: C22SRTSP.BAS
'
' Get a list of numbers, sort them,
' then print them on the printer.
DECLARE SUB PrintNums ()
DECLARE SUB SortNums ()
DECLARE SUB GetNums ()
DIM nums(100)  ' Reserve an array for the user's list of numbers
COLOR 7, 1
CLS

PRINT "*** Number Sorting Program ***"
PRINT

CALL GetNums     ' Get the input
CALL SortNums    ' Sort them
CALL PrintNums   ' Print them
END

SUB GetNums          ' Gets a list of user numbers
SHARED nums(), total.nums    ' Inform subroutine of shared
                             ' variables

FOR total.nums = 1 TO 100    ' Maximum of 100 elements
   PRINT
   PRINT "Please type the next number in the list"
   INPUT "(type a -99 to quit)"; nums(total.nums)
   IF(nums(total.nums)=-99)THEN total.nums=total.nums-1:EXIT FOR
   ' Stop looping if user typed -99 or all 100 values
NEXT total.nums

END SUB

SUB PrintNums      ' Print the sorted list of numbers

SHARED nums(), total.nums   ' Inform subroutine of shared
                            ' variables

PRINT
```

```
PRINT "Here are the sorted numbers"
PRINT "--------------------------"
PRINT

FOR ctr = 1 TO total.nums
   PRINT nums(ctr)    ' Print each sorted number
NEXT ctr

END SUB

SUB SortNums       ' Sort the user's list of numbers
SHARED nums(),total.nums ' Inform subroutine of shared variables

FOR ctr1 = 1 TO total.nums ' Start swapping pairs in bubble sort
   FOR ctr2 = ctr1 TO total.nums
      IF (nums(ctr1)>nums(ctr2)) THEN SWAP nums(ctr1),nums(ctr2)
   NEXT ctr2
NEXT ctr1

END SUB
```

For the rest of this book, all programs that include subroutine procedures will list them one after another, just like in this example. As you type the subroutine procedures (and function procedures seen next), however, you must remember that QBasic *isolates* them as you enter them in your programs.

FUNCTION **Procedures**

QBasic lets you create stand-alone, isolated user-defined function procedures as well as subroutine procedures. Function procedures always return a value, just as with user-defined functions. The data type of the return value is determined by the data type of the function name.

To specify a function procedure, you enclose it within a `FUNCTION-END FUNCTION` pair of statements. The format of the `FUNCTION` statement is

```
FUNCTION name [ ( parameter list ) ]
   Block of one or more QBasic statements
   name = expression
END FUNCTION
```

Basically, a FUNCTION procedure is set up just as a multiple-line user-defined function is, except the name does not have to begin with FN. QBasic isolates it in a separate editing window just as it does with subroutine procedures. You can pass a function procedure the parameters to work with, just as you did with user-defined functions. As with subroutines, any variables that the function procedure and another procedure use also must be declared with the SHARED statement or passed to the function procedure.

Never call a function procedure with a CALL statement. You must always remember that a function returns a value, and you must do something with that value. Therefore, you must assign a function call to a variable, use it in an expression, or print its results.

You can edit isolated function procedures using the F2 **S**UBs... menu option, just as you do with subroutine procedures. The **S**UBs... screen lists not only subroutine procedures, but function procedures as well. This lets you quickly change among the main program, subroutines, or functions, by highlighting the name.

A Function Procedure Example

As with the subroutine procedure example, here is an example of what you would do to enter a function procedure. It contains basically the same steps you took with the subroutine. As soon as you type the FUNCTION *name* statement, QBasic senses a new function definition and moves the cursor to an empty function editing area where you can type the rest of the function's code.

This program makes you feel good about your age *and* your weight! It contains a menu that controls the three things you might want to do. For now, type the main module of the program, which is listed here:

```
' Filename: C22AGEWT.BAS
'
' Program to compute age in dog years and weight on the moon
' to illustrate functions and subroutine calls.

DECLARE SUB ShowMoonWeight ()
DECLARE SUB ShowDogAge ()
DECLARE SUB DisplayMenu ()
DECLARE FUNCTION DogAgeCalc! (age!)
DECLARE FUNCTION MoonWeightCalc! (weight!)

COLOR 7, 1    ' White text on a blue background
CLS

DO
   DisplayMenu      ' Call subroutine that displays menu
   SELECT CASE choice
      CASE 1:    ' Compute dog age
         ShowDogAge       ' Call the dog age subroutine
      CASE 2:    ' Compute moon weight
         ShowMoonWeight   ' Call moon weight subroutine
   END SELECT
LOOP UNTIL (choice = 3)     ' Keep running menu until user wants
                            ' to quit
```

Notice that function procedures have to be declared, just as subroutine procedures do. Now that you have typed the main module, you are ready to begin on subroutines and functions. Start with the subroutines. To do so, type the following statement:

```
SUB DisplayMenu
```

QBasic switches to an isolated `DisplayMenu` screen where you can type the rest of the subroutine. It should look like this when you are through:

```
SHARED choice

PRINT
PRINT "Do you want to:"
PRINT
PRINT "1. Compute your age in dog years"
```

```
PRINT "2. Compute your weight on the moon"
PRINT "3. Quit this program"
PRINT
INPUT "What is your choice"; choice

END SUB
```

Before tackling the functions, type the second subroutine procedure after this one. It looks like this (and it appears in its own editing window as soon as you type the first line):

```
SUB ShowDogAge

PRINT
INPUT "How old are you"; age
dog.age = DogAgeCalc!(age!) ' Call dog age calculation procedure
PRINT
PRINT "Your age in dog years is only"; dog.age; "!"
PRINT "You're younger than you thought..."
PRINT

PRINT "Press any key to return to the main menu..."

DO
   a$ = INKEY$   ' Wait until they press a key
LOOP WHILE (a$ = "")    ' Keep looping until they press a key

END SUB
```

Following is one last subroutine that gets the moon weight information:

```
SUB ShowMoonWeight

PRINT
INPUT "How much do you weigh"; weight
moon.weight = MoonWeightCalc!(weight!) ' Call moon weight
                                       ' calculation procedure
PRINT
PRINT "Your weight on the moon is only"; moon.weight; "pounds!"
PRINT "You are light enough to fly! (on the moon...)"
```

```
PRINT

PRINT "Press any key to return to the main menu..."

DO
   a$ = INKEY$              ' Wait until they press a key
LOOP WHILE (a$ = "")      ' Keep looping until they press a key

END SUB
```

You are ready for the two calculating functions. Can you tell by the previous code what their names will be? They will be called `DogAgeCalc` and `MoonWeightCalc`. They both return values, and those values are stored in equations in the previous two subroutines. As soon as you type the first line of the first function procedure

```
FUNCTION DogAgeCalc! (age!)
```

QBasic switches to the isolated function procedure screen shown in Figure 22.7.

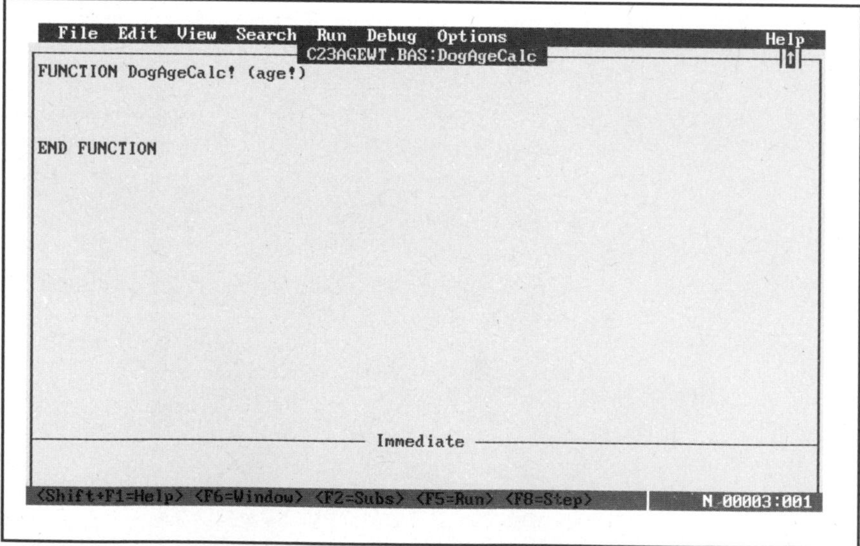

Figure 22.7. Getting ready to enter a new function.

Finish typing the rest of the function.

```
DogAgeCalc! = age / 7      ' A dog year is seven of yours

END FUNCTION
```

In the same manner, type the last function. It is:

```
FUNCTION MoonWeightCalc! (weight!)

   moon.factor = (1 / 6)      ' The moon is 1/6th earth's gravity
   MoonWeightCalc! = moon.factor * weight

END FUNCTION
```

To switch among functions, subroutines, and the main program, press F2. You see the screen shown in Figure 22.8. By pressing the down arrow and the up arrow, you can tell which module is a subroutine and which is a function from the message at the bottom of the screen.

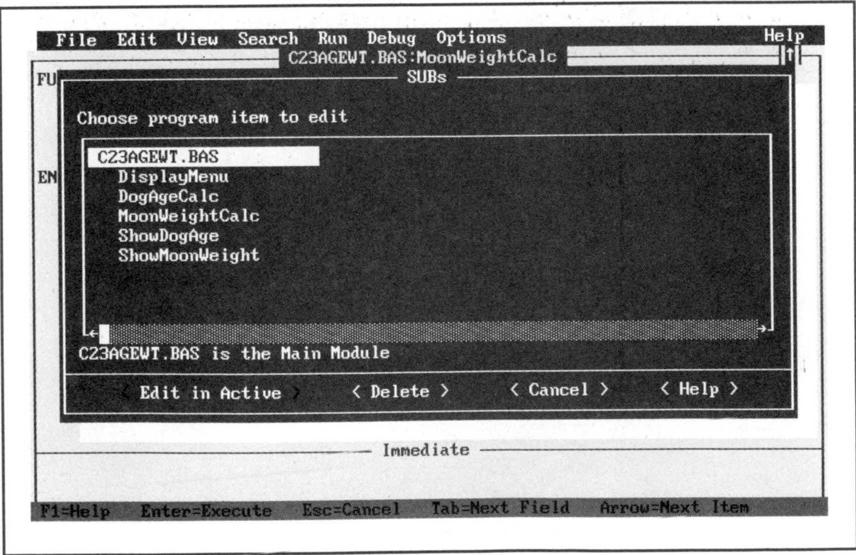

Figure 22.8. Selecting which routine to edit next.

The function procedures did not use the SHARED statements because you passed the parameter they needed within parentheses, just as you did with multiple-line functions. There are times when a function might need to share a variable. These times are discussed in Chapter 23.

Do you see any other way this program can be improved? There is one section of code repeated in both subroutines. It is the INKEY$ routine that simply displays a message and waits for the user to press a key. Because this code is duplicated, it is a good candidate for a subroutine procedure. If you put it in its own subroutine procedure (aptly named something meaningful such as WaitForKey), these two subroutines need only call it by name.

Building Your Own Library

Over time, you will develop several useful subroutines and functions that you might want to reuse in the future. Each time you write a new subroutine procedure, that's one routine you will never have to write again. Keep these routines in a file that is your library of subroutines and procedures. The **V**iew **S**UBs... menu option (the F2 speed key) lets you quickly search through these routines to find the one you need. When another program needs the routine, you can copy and paste it from your library file to your program.

By creating this library file, you invest in your programming future. These routines help you in future programs, and they help promote a structured, modular approach to QBasic programming.

Summary

You have been exposed to truly structured programs. Instead of typing long programs, you are able to break them into separate routines. This isolates your routines from each other so that surrounding code does not confuse things when you are concentrating on a section of your program.

There is only a little complexity introduced with procedures, and that concerns the SHARED variables concept. Because the routines are isolated so well, QBasic must have a way to link variables between the routines. The SHARED command is one way to do this.

The examples in this chapter were longer than previous examples. Even so, they showed that long programs are easy to manage and maintain when you break them into modules. Chapter 23, "Variable Scope," wraps up subroutines and functions by introducing the concepts of variable scope. Now that you have learned to isolate code, you must see how to isolate variables as well, to protect their values and write even better programs.

Review Questions

Answers to the Review Questions are in Appendix B.

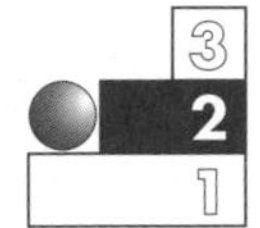

1. What happens when you type the following line of code?

```
SUB MySubroutine
```

2. TRUE or FALSE: A subroutine procedure should always include a RETURN statement as its last line.

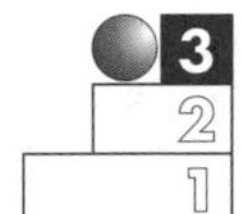

3. What key do you press to jump among subroutines, functions, and the main program module?
4. How does the function procedure know what data type to return?
5. When are you required to DECLARE function procedures and subroutine procedures?
6. TRUE or FALSE: All variables in subroutine procedures must be shared with the main program.
7. Without using SHARED, how does a function procedure get values from the calling procedure?

Review Exercises

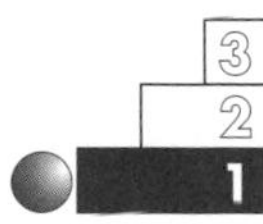

1. Write a program with two subroutine procedures. The first subroutine is to ask for a name, and the second is to print it randomly on the screen 10 times. Enclose the subroutines between two SUB-END SUB statements.

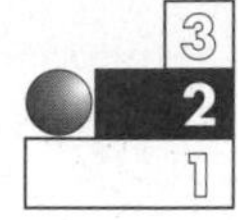

2. Rewrite the function procedure example program, shown earlier in this chapter, so that its two `INKEY$` routines are placed in a single separate subroutine procedure. `CALL` this subroutine from the two subroutines that need to use it.

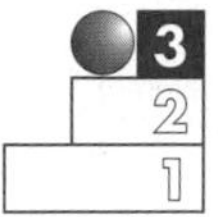

3. Load the REMLINE.BAS program in memory. This program comes with DOS and QBasic. If it is not on your hard disk, find the original DOS disks and transfer REMLINE.BAS to your computer. Look through its code. It is a great example that uses both subroutines and functions. It might have a few disk-related commands you are not familiar with yet, but it is full of procedures you can search for by pressing F2. Study the listings to glean as much insight from this well-structured program as you can. Can you find any area where an additional subroutine or function could be added? Do you think any of its functions or subroutines do too much? Pay special attention to the `IsDigit` function. How useful is this function? Could you write a similar function to check to see whether a character is a letter of the alphabet? (This is one of the first functions you have seen that returns a true or false value for the calling routine's relational testing.)

4. Write a simple in-memory database system to keep track of your compact disk and record collection. It can be similar to the student data-entry program described in this chapter in that it must be able to get the data, store the collection information in parallel arrays, and print a sorted listing by title. Add another print and sort routine to the program (and menu) that prints them by the artist's last name as well. Save this program. When you learn more about disk data files, you might actually want to use this program.

23

Variable Scope

The concept of *variable scope* is most important when you write subroutine and function procedures. Variable scope protects your variables. It protects variables in one routine from other routines. If a subroutine or function procedure does not need access to a variable located in another routine, that variable's scope keeps it protected. You were introduced to variable scope in Chapter 22 when you used the SHARED statement.

Most of this chapter discusses the concept of variable scope. To understand variable scope fully, you need to learn additional ways to declare data types for variables and constants. This chapter introduces

- The CONST statement
- Global variables
- Local variables
- The COMMON statement
- Passing parameters by value
- The LBOUND() and UBOUND() functions
- Passing parameters by address
- Automatic and STATIC variables

When you understand the concept of variable scope, the programs you write should run more reliably and should be easier to debug. Variable scope requires only a little more overhead and forethought in programming but rewards you with much more accurate code.

The CONST Statement

Before learning additional ways to declare data types for variables, you should see how to define constants in QBasic. Up to this point, a constant was an integer, single-precision, double-precision, or string, such as the following examples:

```
43      "A string"      32234!      545.6544432#      6.323E+102
```

With the CONST statement, you can give constants names. The format of CONST is

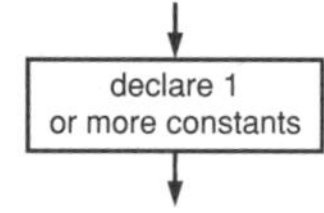


```
CONST constantname = expression [, constantname2 = expression2]...
```

The *constantname* follows the normal rules for variable names. You can append a data type character to it if you want to explicitly make it a certain type. The *expression* can be any numeric or string expression that contains the math operators, except the exponentiation (^) and concatenation (+) operators. You can declare more than one constant per line by separating them with commas.

If you do not specify a data-type suffix character after the *constantname*, QBasic interprets the *expression* to determine the data type. If the *expression* is a string expression, QBasic assumes that the constant is a string constant. If the expression is a numeric expression or constant, QBasic tries to find the simplest numeric data type (integer, single-precision, or double-precision) that can hold the entire expression.

The CONST *expression* can include constants and expressions that use most of the math and relational operators. It cannot include the exponentiation (^) or the string concatenation (+) operators, variables, user-defined functions, or built-in functions.

You must define a constant with CONST before using that constant in a program.

Examples

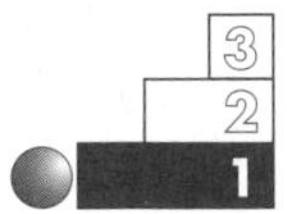

1. Many programmers prefer to use defined constants for extremes of data such as age limits or the maximum number of customers. If those extremes change, it is easy to change the CONST statement without having to change the constant everywhere it appears in a program. The following program shows a maximum and minimum employee age limit defined as a constant.

```
' Filename: C23CON1.BAS
'
' Defines constants.
CONST MinAge = 18, MaxAge = 67

INPUT "How old are you"; age
IF (age < MinAge) THEN
   PRINT "You are too young"
ELSEIF (age > MaxAge) THEN
   PRINT "You are too old"
END IF
```

   Because the defined constants do not have data type suffix characters, QBasic assumes they are integers because the integer data type is the simplest data type that can hold *18* and *67*.

   This is a simple example, but it illustrates the advantage of using defined constants. If the company changes its age limits, it has to change only one line (the CONST statement). If the constant is used several places in the program, it changes in those places as well.

2. By defining unchanging data as constants, you can ensure that you do not inadvertently change the constant. For example, the following program produces an error:

```
' Filename: C23BAD.BAS
'
' Shows incorrect use of a defined constant.
CONST PI = 3.141592#  ' Defines a double-precision constant
```

```
FOR radius = 1 TO 100
   area = PI * (radius ^ 2)    ' Compute area of a circle
   PI = PI + 1   ' **** ERROR - You cannot change a constant
NEXT radius
```

Because the value of PI should not be changed, this programming bug will be found quickly, whereas if PI were a variable, QBasic would let you add 1 to it each time through the loop, but the calculations would then be incorrect.

Without the double-precision data type suffix (#), QBasic would have assumed double-precision anyway, because double-precision would be required to hold the full expression (*3.141592*). QBasic tells you that you cannot change a constant by issuing a `Duplicate definition` error message.

Advanced Array Subscripting

You have seen several ways to dimension arrays so far. You know that you can control the starting and ending subscripts of arrays with the `OPTION BASE` command and with the `TO` keyword in the subscripts when you dimension the array. By now, you should be comfortable with statements like these:

```
DIM MyAra$(100) ' Reserves 101 string elements from MyAra$(0) to
                ' MyAra$(100)
OPTION BASE 1   ' Sets starting subscript to 1 for all DIMs in
                ' program
DIM MyAra$(100) ' Now reserves 100 elements with no MyAra$(0)
DIM MyAra$(4 TO 19) ' Reserves 16 elements from MyAra$(4) to
                    ' MyAra(19)
```

In each case, your array was reserved as a string array because the name ended with the `$` string suffix character.

There are several other possible array declarations. They come in handy when you are learning variable scope, so read the following sections to learn additional array characteristics.

Global and Local Variables

You are ready for a new concept that will improve your subroutine and function procedures. It deals with how procedures share variables between each other. You saw an example of one way data is shared when you learned the SHARED statement in Chapter 22.

Variable scope (sometimes called the *visibility of variables*) describes how variables are "seen" by your program. Some variables have *global* variable scope. A global variable can be seen from (and used by) every statement in the program. The programs you wrote before learning about subroutines and functions had global variable scope; a variable defined in the first statement could be used by (and is visible from) the last statement in the program.

Local scope is a new concept. It was because of local variables that you had to use the SHARED statement in Chapter 22. A local variable can be seen from (and used by) only the code in which it is defined.

If you use no subroutine procedures or function procedures, the concept of local and global variables is a moot point. You should, however, use subroutine and function procedures because it is best to write modular programs. When you include a subroutine or function procedure, you must understand how local and global variables work so that each routine can "see" the variables it requires.

To make a variable global, you must define it with the DIM SHARED or COMMON SHARED statement in the main program.

The DIM SHARED statement works just like its counterpart without the SHARED keyword. DIM and DIM SHARED allocate memory for variables and arrays, as well as define the variables' types. For example, the following statements define global variables using DIM SHARED:

```
DIM SHARED cnt.ara(100) AS INTEGER
DIM SHARED num.cars AS INTEGER
```

These statements say much about the data they define. Both of the variables cnt.ara and num.cars are global variables because of the SHARED keyword. The cnt.ara variable is not only global, but it is an integer array of 1,000 elements. The num.cars variable is a global integer (not an array). It is important that you understand these variables' definitions before going further. If you understand them, you will find that local and global variables are easy to understand.

The COMMON SHARED statement works in a similar manner, except it does not specify the maximum subscripts for arrays. Its purpose is to specify which variables in the main program are to be global for the rest of the program. If you put an array variable in a COMMON SHARED statement, you must still use DIM to declare the subscripts that the array will use.

The format of the COMMON SHARED statement is

```
COMMON SHARED var1[()] [ AS type ] [, var2[()] [AS type] ] ...
```

The following five lines are COMMON SHARED statements that define global variables:

```
COMMON SHARED x AS INTEGER, y AS SINGLE
COMMON SHARED ara()
COMMON SHARED i, j, k
COMMON SHARED ages() AS SINGLE, students() AS STRING
COMMON SHARED emp.names$(), cust.names() AS STRING * 25
```

The first COMMON SHARED defines x as a global integer variable and y as a single-precision variable. The second COMMON SHARED statement declares ara as a global array. The type and number of elements are to be determined in a later (or previous) DIM statement. (Never put subscripts in the parentheses of COMMON SHARED array variables.) The third COMMON SHARED declares i, j, and k as global variables. These variables are single-precision. The fourth COMMON SHARED statement declares two arrays as global arrays: the single-precision ages and the string students. The last COMMON SHARED also defines two arrays as global: the variable-length string array emp.name$ and the fixed-length string array cust.names.

If you put SHARED after each DIM, you do not need COMMON SHARED. Not all dimensioned arrays, however, are to be global, so you still need to use COMMON SHARED occasionally.

Think again about how to declare global variables: To make a variable global, you must define it with the DIM SHARED or COMMON SHARED statement in the main program. All other variables are local.

A variable is global only if it is defined in the *main* program's DIM SHARED or COMMON SHARED statements. Constants defined with the CONST statement in the main program are global as well. All other variables in a program are local.

Local and Global Variable Example

Given this rule, it should be obvious that loc1 and loc2 are local variables and glob1 and glob2 are global variables in the following program.

```
' Filename: C23LCGL1.BAS
'
' Shows local and global variables.
'
' loc1 and loc2 are local, glob1 and glob2 are global
DECLARE SUB subber ()      ' One subroutine procedure
DIM SHARED glob1 AS INTEGER
COMMON SHARED glob2 AS STRING

DIM loc1 AS INTEGER    ' NOT global since there is no SHARED

loc1 = 25
loc2 = 50

glob1 = 100
glob2 = "A global string"

PRINT loc1, loc2, glob1, glob2
' This prints: 25   50   100   A global string

CALL subber     ' Call the subroutine
END

SUB subber

   PRINT loc1, loc2, glob1, glob2
   ' This prints: 0   0   100   A global string
   ' Notice that loc1 and loc2 ARE NOT KNOWN HERE!!!
END SUB
```

The main program and the subroutine procedure both can see and modify the global variables. The global variables `glob1` and `glob2` have global scope, or they are visible globally from the entire program. The local variables are visible only from their own routines.

There are actually four local variables in this program: the two called `loc1` and `loc2` in the main program, and the two called `loc1` and `loc2` in the subroutine. The latter variables are local to the subroutine and have not been initialized, so their values are still 0. Although they have the same name as the two local variables in the main program, they are distinct local variables.

Try to avoid using *global* variables.

You might be wondering what to do with this new-found information. Here is the bottom line: Global variables can be dangerous because code can inadvertently overwrite a variable that was initialized in another place in the program. It is better to make every variable in your program *local* to the function that needs to access it.

Read the previous sentence once more. It means that although you know how to make variables global, you should not do so. Try to stay away from using global variables. It is easier to program using global variables at first. If you make every variable in your program global, including those in every subroutine and function procedure, you never have to worry about whether a variable is known. If you do this, however, even those subroutines that have no need for certain variables can change them.

The Need for Passing Variables

You saw the difference between local and global variables. You saw that by making your variables local, you protect their values because the subroutine or function that owns the local variable (the scope is visible from that routine only) is the only routine that can modify them.

What do you do, however, if you have a local variable that you want to use in two or more subroutines? In other words, you might have a need for a variable's value to be input from the keyboard in one subroutine, and that same variable is to be printed in another function. If the variable is local to the first subroutine, the second one can't print it because only the first sees it and knows its value.

There are two possible solutions. First, you could make the variable global. This is not good because you want only those two functions to see the variable. All functions could see it if it were global. The second, and much more acceptable, solution is to *pass* the variable from the first function to the other function. This has a big advantage: The variable is known only to those two functions.

When you pass a local variable from one routine to another, you are *passing an argument* from the first function to the next. You can pass more than one argument (variable) at a time if you want several local variables sent from one routine to another. The receiving routine *receives parameters* (variables) from the routine that sent them. You should not worry too much about whether to call them arguments or parameters. The important thing is that you are simply sending local variables from one function to another.

You have already passed arguments to parameters when you passed values (arguments) to a user-defined function (which received those arguments in its parameter list).

When a routine passes arguments, it is called the *passing routine*. The function that receives those arguments (which are called *parameters* when they are received) is called the *receiving routine*. The routines can consist of the main program, a subroutine procedure, a function procedure, or a combination of any two of them.

Figure 23.1 is a pictorial representation of what is going on.

To pass a local variable from one subroutine to another, you must place the local variable in parentheses in both the calling routine and the receiving routine. For example, the global and local variable program shown earlier did not pass the two local variables from the main program to the subroutine. That was why the subroutine could not print the local variable's values that were assigned in the main program. The following program is slightly changed from that one. The two local variables are passed to the subroutine. Because of this, the subroutine "knows" the values and can print them correctly.

TIP: When passing parameters, the calling routine's variable names do not have to match the receiving routine's variable names. They must, however, match in number and type.

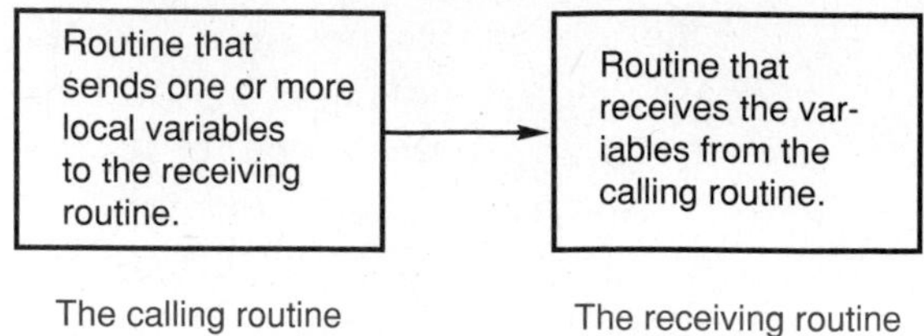

Figure 23.1. Overview of calling and receiving routines.

```
' Filename: C23LCGL2.BAS
'
' Shows passing of local variables.
'
' loc1 and loc2 are local, glob1 and glob2 are global

' Declare the subroutine and tell QBasic that it
' should expect passing of 2 locals
DECLARE SUB subber (loc1%, loc2)
DIM SHARED glob1 AS INTEGER
COMMON SHARED glob2 AS STRING

DIM loc1 AS INTEGER    ' NOT global since there is no SHARED

loc1 = 25
loc2 = 50

glob1 = 100
glob2 = "A global string"

PRINT loc1, loc2, glob1, glob2
' This prints: 25   50   100   A global string

CALL subber(loc1, loc2)  ' Call the subroutine and PASS local values
END

SUB subber (loc1%, loc2)  ' Receives the local values

   PRINT loc1%, loc2, glob1, glob2
   ' This prints: 25   50   100   A global string
   ' Notice that loc1 and loc2 print correctly now
END SUB
```

When you pass parameters, the subroutine has no idea what data types the incoming variables are. Therefore, the DECLARE statement must indicate the type by appending a data type character suffix to each parameter. That same parameter list in the subroutine must also be declared with the suffix.

The calling module does not need to indicate the variable types, although it doesn't hurt anything if it does. The main module already knows what type of variables they are because it defined them in the first place.

Passing by Address

By default, all QBasic variable arguments are passed *by address.* Sometimes this is called being passed *by reference.* When an argument (a local variable) is passed by address, the variable's *address in memory* is sent to, and is assigned to, the receiving routine's parameter list. (If more than one variable is passed by address, each of their addresses is sent to and assigned to the receiving function's parameters.)

All variables in memory (RAM) are stored at addresses of memory. Figure 23.2 shows addresses of memory.

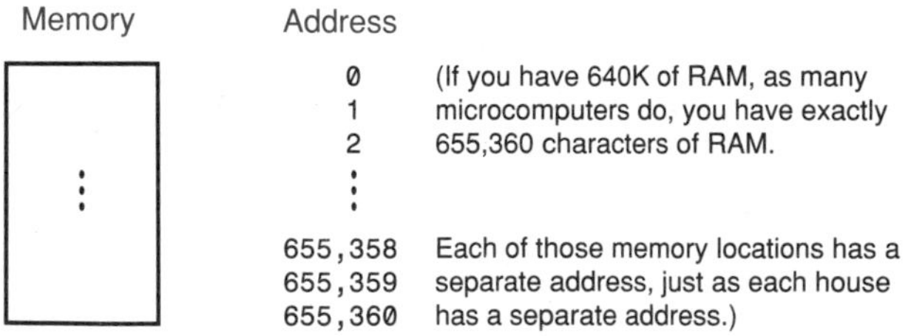

Memory	Address	
	0	(If you have 640K of RAM, as many
	1	microcomputers do, you have exactly
	2	655,360 characters of RAM.
⋮	⋮	
	655,358	Each of those memory locations has a
	655,359	separate address, just as each house
	655,360	has a separate address.)

Figure 23.2. Memory and its addresses.

When you instruct QBasic to define a variable, you are telling QBasic to find a blank place in memory and assign that memory's address to the variable name. When your program prints or uses the variable, QBasic knows to go to the variable's address and print what is there.

If you were to define seven variables as shown here

```
i% = 0
x! = 9.8
DIM ara$(2)
ara$(0) = "A"
ara$(1) = "B"
ara$(2) = "C"
j% = 8
k% = 3
```

QBasic might arbitrarily set them up in memory at the addresses shown in Figure 23.3.

NOTE: Actually, the integer, single-precision, and double-precision variables take more than one memory location each, but this figure illustrates the idea of how variables are stored at their addresses.

Variable Name	Memory	Address
		0
		1
		2
	⋮	⋮
i%	0	34,565
x	9.8	34,566
ara(0)	A	34,567
ara(1)	B	34,568
ara(2)	C	34,569
j%	8	34,570
k%	3	34,571
		34,572
	⋮	⋮
		355,359
		355,360

Figure 23.3. The variables in memory.

When a variable is passed by address, the address of the variable is copied to the receiving routine. Any time a variable is passed by address (as they all are in QBasic), if you change the local variable in the receiving routine, the variable is also changed in the calling routine.

Passing by Address Example

The following example is a sorting subroutine. You have seen several bubble sorting examples in this book. This one is a subroutine procedure, however, rather than a stand-alone program.

Before this sort subroutine is discussed further, take a look at it:

```
SUB sortit(s.array$(), ct%)
' This subroutine assumes it will be passed a character
' string array, and an integer count that includes the
' number of words in that array.
'
' This routine sorts the array using a bubble sort.
' Once sorted, control is passed back to the calling routine.
'
' This routine assumes the array will be passed by address.
' Therefore, when this routine sorts the array, it will also
' be sorted when the calling routine gets control again.

   FOR ctr1 = 0 TO (ct% - 2)    ' ctr1 are local ctr2
      FOR ctr2 = ctr1 + 1 TO ct% - 1
         IF (s.array$(ctr1) > s.array$(ctr2)) THEN
            SWAP s.array$(ctr1), s.array$(ctr2)
         END IF
      NEXT ctr2
   NEXT ctr1
END SUB
```

The first things to notice are the extensive remarks at the top. It is a good idea to tell what the subroutine does, what kind of values it expects (in this case, a character array and the integer count of the elements in that array, passed by address), and what it expects to happen when it finishes (the array is sorted when it gets back to the calling routine because it was passed by address).

This subroutine does not care what kind of program, subroutine, or function calls it. It is almost a stand-alone procedure, although it has to be passed some data. This is where the power of this subroutine comes into play. It can be used in any program that needs a string array sorted. All you have to do is copy this subroutine to that program. If the main program or any other subroutine or function wants a string array sorted, it only has to pass the string array to this subroutine, along with the number of elements in that array, as in

```
CALL sortit( name.array$(), 1200 )
```

or

```
sortit ( employees$(), num.of.emp )
```

CALL is optional as long as the calling procedure has a DECLARE statement declaring the sortit subroutine procedure.

This makes the sorting routine extremely flexible. sortit() does not care what the data is called that is passed to it. sortit() only knows it is getting a string array and count integer from some other routine.

This routine also has two local variables called ctr1 and ctr2. These variables are required only for subscripting, they do not need to be global, and they do not need to be passed back to the calling routine.

The LBOUND() and UBOUND() Functions

When you pass arrays such as in the preceding example, it might be helpful to know the smallest and largest subscripts defined for the array. This does not mean that the array has data in every element, but at least the subroutine or function procedure knows what the maximum and minimum subscripts can be. The LBOUND() and UBOUND() functions give the routines this information. Without them, you would have to pass two additional values telling the array's minimum and maximum subscripts.

The sortit example actually is flawed. It assumes that the array passed to it is a string array having 0 as its starting subscript. (The first FOR-NEXT loop indicates this.) Consider what would happen, however, if the calling program passed a string array that was defined as

```
DIM cust.names$(101 TO 500)
```

The `sortit` routine would not work properly. If it is passed this array and a total count of 25, `sortit` thinks the array begins at *0* and subscripts from *0* to *24* (making a total of 25). The true subscripts, however, should be *101* to *125* (the first 25 elements in an array defined this way).

`LBOUND()` and `UBOUND()` (for *lower bound* and *upper bound*) return the upper and lower limits of an array inside a subroutine or function procedure. A procedure has no idea otherwise what the dimensioned array subscripts are because the calling routine did that. The formats of `LBOUND()` and `UBOUND()` are

```
LBOUND( arrayname )
```

and

```
UBOUND( arrayname )
```

The `sortit` routine should be rewritten as

```
SUB sortit(s.array$(), ct%)
' This subroutine assumes it will be passed a character
' string array, and an integer count that includes the
' number of words in that array.
'
' This routine sorts the array using a bubble sort.
' Once sorted, control is passed back to the calling routine.
'
' This routine assumes the array will be passed by address.
' Therefore, when this routine sorts the array, it will also
' be sorted when the calling routine gets control again.

   ' Never go beyond UBOUND limit, or below LBOUND() limit
   FOR ctr1 = LBOUND(s.array$) TO (LBOUND(s.array$) + ct% - 2)
      FOR ctr2 = ctr1 + 1 TO (ct% + LBOUND(s.array$) - 1)
         IF (s.array$(ctr1) > s.array$(ctr2)) THEN
            SWAP s.array$(ctr1), s.array$(ctr2)
         END IF
      NEXT ctr2
   NEXT ctr1
END SUB
```

This version is much improved. You should ensure that every subroutine or function procedure you write that you also pass an array to uses `LBOUND()` to check for low-limit subscripts. Otherwise, the procedures will not be truly portable from one routine to another; they will assume a starting subscript that might well be incorrect.

Passing by Value

Although passing arguments by value is not common in QBasic, that is safer than passing them by address. Sometimes you hear passing by value called *passing by copy*. When you pass a value by address, the receiving subroutine or function can change it. If it does, however, the variable is *not* changed in the calling procedure.

For instance, if you pass an array to the `sort.it` routine by value, `sort.it` sorts the array. When control is returned to the calling procedure, however, that procedure's array is not sorted.

Any time you need to pass arguments to a function and return one value, you should consider passing the arguments by value. If the function needs to change the value in both the calling and the receiving functions, you need to stick with passing it by address.

To pass a variable by value, simply enclose it in parentheses inside the parameter list. For instance, the following call to the subroutine `Calc.Wages` passes each of its arguments by value because each appears in parentheses. `Calc.Wages` cannot change variables in the procedure that called `Calc.Wages`.

```
Calc.Wages( (hours), (rate), (tax.rate) )  ' Pass by value
```

All built-in functions such as `INT()` and `LEFT$()` assume that their values are passed by value, although you do not have to send them arguments individually enclosed in parentheses. For example, in the section of code

```
i = 5.2
new.i = INT(i)
```

the variable `i` is passed by value. It is not changed in the `INT()` function (remember that no built-in functions change their arguments, but instead they return a value based on that argument).

Passing by Value Example

The following subroutine procedures are similar to two routines you saw earlier in single-module programs. The first subroutine, `Moon.Weight`, calculates and prints the moon-equivalent of any weight passed to it. The second subroutine, `Dog.Years`, calculates and prints any age in dog years based on its passed value.

```
SUB Moon.Weight( weight )
   ' This routine calculates and prints the moon weight of
   ' any weight passed to it. Since it does not have to
   ' change any data passed to it, it is best called by value.

   moon.wt = (1 / 6) * weight   ' Moon is 1/6th earth's gravity
   PRINT "Your weight on the moon is:"; moon.wt

END SUB


SUB Dog.Years (years)
   ' This routine calculates and prints the dog years of
   ' any years passed to it. Since it does not have to
   ' change any data passed to it, it is best called by value.

   dog.years = years / 7   ' Dog years are seven times people's
   PRINT "You age in dog years is:"; dog.years

END SUB
```

No data passed to these procedures is changed. Therefore, pass them by value by enclosing each in an individual set of parentheses, such as:

```
INPUT "What is your weight"; user.weight
Moon.Weight( (user.weight) )  ' Passed by value

INPUT "How old are you"; age
Dos.Years ( (age) )           ' Passed by value
```

The choice between passing by value and by address might not appear as critical as it can be. If you are writing procedures that should never change the passed variables, pass them by address.

Later, if you (or someone else) make changes to the procedure and accidentally change one of the passed variables, at least the changed variable is not harmed in both routines (and hopefully the error will be easier to find) as it would be if you passed the variable by address.

Automatic and STATIC Variables

The terms *automatic* and STATIC describe what happens to local variables when a subroutine or function procedure returns to the calling procedure.

By default, all local variables are automatic. That means the variables are erased completely when the procedure ends. Consider the following program.

```
' Filename: C23STAT1.BAS
'
' Attempts to use STATIC variable without the STATIC statement.

CLS

FOR ctr = 1 TO 25
   triple.it(ctr)
NEXT ctr
END

SUB triple.it (num)
   ' Triples whatever value is passed to it
   ' and adds up the total

   num.by.3 = num * 3         ' Triple number passed
   total = total + num.by.3   ' Add up triple numbers as this is
                              ' called
   PRINT "The number,"; num; "multiplied by 3 is:"; num.by.3

   IF (total > 300) THEN
      PRINT "The total of the triple numbers is over 300"
   END IF

END SUB
```

This is a nonsense program that doesn't do much. Yet if you look at it, you might sense there is something wrong with it. The program passes numbers from 1 to 25 to the subroutine called `triple.it`. The subroutine triples the number and prints it.

The variable called `total` is automatically set to 0. Its purpose is to add the triple numbers and print a message when the total of the triples goes over 300. However, this `PRINT` statement never executes. Each of the 25 times this subroutine is called, `total` is set back to *0* again. `total` is an automatic variable; `total` is a local variable having a value that is erased and initialized each time their procedure is called.

If, however, you want `total` to retain its value even after the procedure ends, you have to make it a `STATIC` variable by using the `STATIC` statement. The format of `STATIC` is

```
STATIC variable [()] [ AS type ] ,...
```

Variables are automatic by default. The `STATIC` statement overrides the default and makes the variables `STATIC`. The variables' values are then retained each time the subroutine is called.

The following program corrects the intent of the previous one.

```
' Filename: C23STAT2.BAS
'
' Properly uses the STATIC variable with a STATIC statement.

CLS

FOR ctr = 1 TO 25
   triple.it(ctr)
NEXT ctr
END

SUB triple.it (num)
   ' Triples whatever value is passed to it
   ' and adds up the total

   STATIC total ' Makes total STATIC. It is 0 initially

   num.by.3 = num * 3            ' Triple number passed
   total = total + num.by.3      ' Add up triple numbers as this is
                                 ' called
```

```
    PRINT "The number,"; num; "multiplied by 3 is:"; num.by.3

    IF (total > 300) THEN
       PRINT "The total of the triple numbers is over 300"
       INPUT "Press any key to continue..."; ans$
    END IF

END SUB
```

Figure 23.4 shows the first part of this program's output. Notice that the subroutine's PRINT is triggered, although total is a local variable. Because total is STATIC, its value is not erased when the subroutine finishes. When the subroutine is called again, total's previous value (its value when you left the routine) is still there.

This does not mean that STATIC variables become global. The main program cannot refer, use, print, or change total because it is local to the subroutine. STATIC simply means that the local variable's value is still there if the program calls that function again.

```
The number, 1 multiplied by 3 is: 3
The number, 2 multiplied by 3 is: 6
The number, 3 multiplied by 3 is: 9
The number, 4 multiplied by 3 is: 12
The number, 5 multiplied by 3 is: 15
The number, 6 multiplied by 3 is: 18
The number, 7 multiplied by 3 is: 21
The number, 8 multiplied by 3 is: 24
The number, 9 multiplied by 3 is: 27
The number, 10 multiplied by 3 is: 30
The number, 11 multiplied by 3 is: 33
The number, 12 multiplied by 3 is: 36
The number, 13 multiplied by 3 is: 39
The number, 14 multiplied by 3 is: 42
The number, 15 multiplied by 3 is: 45
The number, 16 multiplied by 3 is: 48
The number, 17 multiplied by 3 is: 51
The number, 18 multiplied by 3 is: 54
The number, 19 multiplied by 3 is: 57
The number, 20 multiplied by 3 is: 60
The number, 21 multiplied by 3 is: 63
The number, 22 multiplied by 3 is: 66
The number, 23 multiplied by 3 is: 69
```

Figure 23.4. Using a STATIC variable.

STATIC can appear only in a SUB-END SUB, FUNCTION-END FUNCTION, or DEF FN statement.

Summary

This chapter has been unlike most in this book. It is much more theoretical in nature because there is so much to learn about passing parameters. The entire concept of parameter passing is required because local variables are better than global; they are protected in their own routines but must be shared between other routines. QBasic lets you pass by address or by value. If the receiving routine is to change the parameters in both places, you should pass by address.

Most of the information in this chapter will become more obvious as you use subroutines and function procedures in your own programs. Start using them right away; the longer your programs are, the more glad you will be that you wrote several small subroutines and functions rather than one long program. You can test and modify individual modules easier.

Chapter 24, "Reading and Writing to Disk," introduces a new section. It deals with disk processing. Your disks hold much more data than your RAM can hold. When you start using data files, you can begin to write powerful data-storing and tracking programs.

Review Questions

Answers to the Review Questions are in Appendix B.

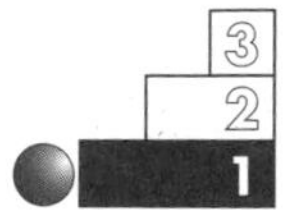

1. Why would you want to use the CONST statement to give a name to a constant, such as sales.minimum, instead of using the actual value, such as *20,000*, throughout your program?
2. TRUE or FALSE: A local variable is local only to the subroutine or function procedure in which it is declared, and the procedures that call that procedure.
3. What, if anything, is wrong with the following statement?

```
DIM my.name$ AS STRING
```

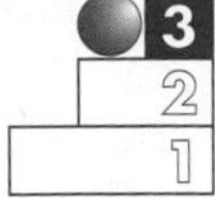

4. What is the output of the following section of code?

```
DIM emp.name AS STRING * 10
emp.name = "John L. Keating"
PRINT emp.name
```

5. When would you pass a global variable from one procedure to another? (Hint: Be careful, this is tricky!)

6. If a subroutine keeps track of a total or count of every time it is called, should the counting or totaling variable be automatic or `STATIC`?

7. If you want arguments to be changed in both the calling procedure and the receiving procedure, would you pass by address or pass by value?

8. Given the `DIM` statement

   ```
   DIM ara1(-5 TO 12), ara2(0 TO 20)
   ```

   if you pass `ara1` to a function that calls `LBOUND()`, what value is returned from `LBOUND()`? If you pass `ara2` to a function that calls `UBOUND()`, what value is returned from `UBOUND()`?

Review Exercises

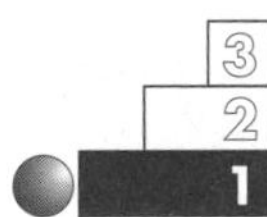

1. Write a function procedure that returns the total amount of money you have spent on diskettes in the past year. Assume it is passed two parameters: the number of diskettes bought and the average price per diskette. Do not print the price in the function; just compute and return it. Use only local variables.

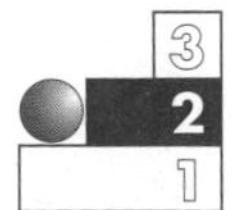

2. Write a subroutine procedure that simply counts the number of times it is called. Name the subroutine procedure `Count.it`. Assume that it will never be passed anything, but that it simply keeps track of every time you call it. Print the following message inside the procedure:

   ```
   The number of times this subroutine has been called is: xx
   ```

in which *xx* is the actual number. (Hint: Because the variable must be local, use the `STATIC` statement.)

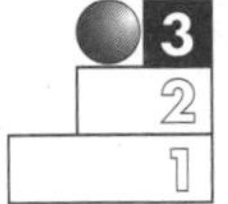

3. Write a subroutine procedure that draws a box on the screen using ASCII characters. Write the procedure so that it receives two parameters: the number of columns wide and the number of rows high that the box should be. (This would be a great subroutine procedure for drawing boxes around titles.)

4. Write a string-blanking routine that blanks whatever string is passed to it. Assume that the string is passed by address (or else the blank array could not be used in the calling procedure) and use `LBOUND()` and `UBOUND()` so that the procedure never exceeds the array boundaries.

5. Write a complete application program that keeps track of a holiday and birthday mailing list. The main program should consist of variable, subroutine, and function declarations; procedure calls; and an `END` statement. One of the procedures should let the user enter the data, and another should print the data. Before printing it, the print procedure should call another procedure to sort the list alphabetically (the main program does not call this sort routine or declare it). Include a function that returns the number of out-of-state names (make sure you use `CONST` for your home state name).

Part VII

Disk File Processing

Reading and Writing to Disk

So far, every example in this book has processed data that resides inside the program listing or comes from the keyboard. You learned about the DATA statement that holds numeric and string data. You assigned constants and variables to other variables and created new data values from existing ones. The programs also received input with INPUT and INKEY$ and processed the user's keystrokes.

The data created by the user with DATA statements is sufficient for some applications. With the large volumes of data that most real-world applications need to process, however, you need a better way of storing that data. For all but the smallest computer programs, the hard disk offers the solution.

By storing data on the disk, the computer helps you enter the data, find it, change it, and delete it. The computer and QBasic are simply tools to help you manage and process data.

This chapter focuses on disk and file theory before you get to numerous disk examples in the next chapter. Because disk processing takes some preliminary work to understand, it helps to cover some introductory explanations about disk files and their uses before looking at QBasic's specific disk file commands in Chapter 25, "Sequential Disk Processing."

This chapter introduces

- An overview of disks
- The types of files
- Processing data on the disk
- File names
- Types of disk file access

After this chapter, you will be ready to tackle the QBasic examples and specific disk file processing commands in Chapter 25. If you have programmed computerized data files with another programming language, you might want to skim this chapter and move on to the next to get the specific QBasic disk file commands. If you are new to disk file processing, study this chapter before delving into QBasic's file-related commands. The overview presented here rewards you with a deeper and better understanding of how QBasic and your disk work together.

Why Use a Disk?

The typical computer system has 640K of RAM and a 30- to 40-megabyte hard disk drive. (Chapter 1, "Welcome to QBasic," explained your computer's internal hardware and devices.) Figure 24.1 shows your RAM layout. The first part of conventional memory in most PCs is taken up by DOS and by some extra DOS information and memory-resident programs. DOS always resides in your computer's RAM. When you start QBasic, it shares memory with DOS. Whatever is left of the 640K is the room you have for your programs and data. There is not too much room left.

Your disk drive holds much more data than can fit in your computer's RAM. This is the primary reason for using the disk for your data. The disk memory, because it is nonvolatile, lasts longer. When you power-off your computer, the disk memory is not erased, whereas RAM is erased. Also, when your data changes, you (or more important, your *users*) do not have to edit the program and look for a set of DATA statements. Instead, the users run previously written programs that make changes to the disk data. This makes programming more difficult at first because programs have to be written to change the data on the disk. However, nonprogrammers can then use the programs and modify the data without knowing how to program.

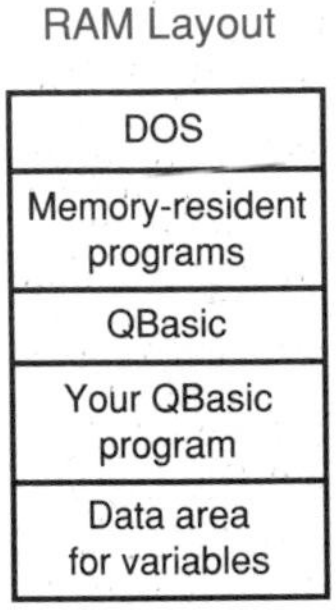

RAM Layout

DOS
Memory-resident programs
QBasic
Your QBasic program
Data area for variables

Figure 24.1. Your RAM and disk storage.

The capacity of your disk makes it a perfect place to store your data as well as your programs. Think about what would happen if all data had to be stored in a program's DATA statements. What if the Social Security office in Washington, D.C., asked you to write a QBasic program to compute, average, filter, sort, and print each person's name and address in their files? Would you want your program to include millions of DATA statements? Not only would you not want the program to hold that much data, but it could not do so because only relatively small amounts of data fit in a program before you run out of RAM.

By storing data on your disk, you are much less limited because you have more storage. Your disk can hold as much data as you have disk capacity. Also, if your disk requirements grow, you can usually increase your disk space, whereas you cannot always add more RAM to your computer. QBasic cannot access the special *extended* or *expanded* memory that some computers have.

QBasic does not have to access much RAM at once, however, because it can read data from your disk drive and process it. Not all your disk data has to reside in RAM for QBasic to process it. QBasic reads some data, processes it, and then reads some more. If QBasic requires disk data a second time, it rereads that place on the disk.

Data Files and File Names

You can store two types of files on your computer's disk drive. They are *program files* and *data files.* You are used to program files, which are the programs you write and store on the disk with the **F**ile **S**ave... command. Data files do not contain programs, but they contain the data that the programs process. For the rest of this book, *files* refers to data files unless *program file* is specifically mentioned.

A data file is a collection of related information stored on your disk.

To understand the computer's data files, you can think of files in a file cabinet. Files on your computer are treated just as files are in a file cabinet. You probably have a cabinet or box at home that contains several file folders. You might have a file of your insurance papers, a file of your automobile papers, a file of your home and mortgage information, and several other files. Do you see that these files fit the definition of computer data files? These files are sets of *related* information.

You would not (intentionally) mix your insurance and mortgage files. If you did, your file integrity would be lost. The files would no longer be related, so they would not be useful files.

Computer File Example

It helps to take the analogy of computer files and regular paper files one step further. Think about colleges 25 years ago before they computerized. How did they store their information about students, professors, and classes? They probably had three file cabinets. One of the cabinets probably held the student files.

As each student enrolled, the enrollment clerk completed a form similar to that in Figure 24.2, which includes the student's social security number, name, address, city, state, ZIP code, age, and so forth. The clerk would then file that piece of paper in the cabinet.

Later, if that student moved and needed his or her address changed, the student would tell the clerk. The clerk would have to go to the file cabinet, find the student's form, change the address, and then put the form back in the student file cabinet. The professor file and the class file would be handled similarly.

School Application

Social Security #: ____________

Name: ____________

Address: ____________

City: ______ State: ___ Zip: ____

Grade: ______ Sex: _____

GPA: ______ Age: _____

Figure 24.2. A college student's enrollment form that has to be filled out and filed in a manual data file.

Look forward in time about 25 years and think of how that same college handles students, professors, and classes with the help of computerized data files. Rather than three file cabinets, that college would have a huge disk drive with three files on it: the student file, the professor file, and the class file.

As students enroll, the clerk does not fill out a form. Instead, the clerk sits in front of a computer and answers questions on the screen. These questions, or prompts, might look like those in Figure 24.3. Do you notice anything familiar? The clerk is filling out the same information on the screen that might have been filled out on a piece of paper 25 years ago. When the information is complete, the clerk presses a key and the computer stores that information in the student file on the disk. If that student's information changes, the clerk displays the student's information on the screen again, changes it, and saves it back to the disk file.

The operations are the same in both the manual and the computerized filing systems, except the computer takes over much of the work required to get a blank form and manually file it in the proper location. The sooner you realize that computer files and files in cabinets are handled in the same way, the easier it is to learn how to use QBasic to create, modify, and delete disk information.

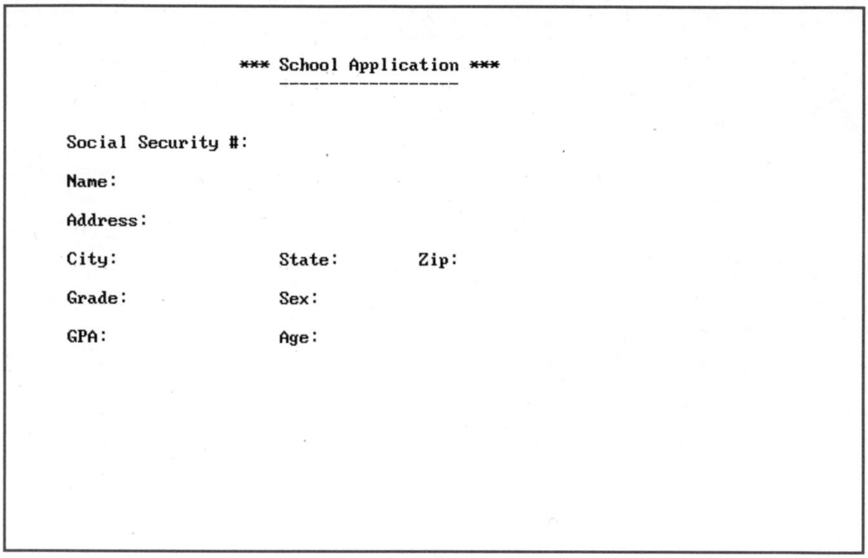

```
                    *** School Application ***
                        ------------------

Social Security #:

Name:

Address:

City:                  State:         Zip:

Grade:                 Sex:

GPA:                   Age:
```

Figure 24.3. The school's computerized data-entry screen.

Records and Fields

Before writing a program that creates a data file on disk, you must think through the data that will be stored in the file. The programmer decides exactly what information is stored and how it is stored. To make proper file decisions, you should understand exactly how data is stored on the disk.

The student data file described in the preceding section might look like the file in Table 24.1. The table shows data for four students. There is no specified order of the file; files are generally kept in the same physical order in which their data was entered (in this case, the order that the students enrolled in the school). This does not mean that file access can be made only in that order. QBasic programs can read this file and print a file listing in any order, including numerical order by social security number and alphabetical order.

Table 24.1. Sample student data.

Social Security	*Name*	*Age*	*Address*	*City*	*State*	*ZIP*
434-54-3223	Jones, Michael	21	9 W. Elm	Miami	FL	22332
231-34-5767	Brown, Larry	19	505 Baker	Tampa Bay	FL	23227
945-65-2344	Smith, Kim	20	14 Oak Rd.	Miami	FL	22331
294-78-9434	Lawton, Jerry	21	6 Main St.	Miami	FL	22356
:	:	:	:	:	:	
:	:	:	:	:	:	

Your computer files are broken into *records* and *fields*. A record is an individual occurrence in the file. In this case, the file is a collection of students, so each student's information is called a complete student record. If there are 12,000 students in the file, there will be 12,000 records in the file.

You can loosely view a record as a row from the file. This is not a technically accurate description because a record can span more than one row in a data file; however, for small data files (with relatively few columns of data), a record can be viewed as a row in the file.

The fields are the columns in the file. The student data file has seven columns: social security number, name, age, address, city, state, and ZIP. Even if 5,000 student records are added to the file, there will still be only seven fields because there will still be seven columns of data.

You can create files with *fixed-length records* or *variable-length records.* If the records are fixed-length, each field takes the same amount of disk space, even if that field's data value does not fill the field. Fixed strings are typically used for fixed-length records. For instance, most programmers create a data file table for their files such as the one shown in Table 24.2. This table lists each field name, the type of data in each field, and the length of each field.

Table 24.2. Student description table for a fixed-length data file.

Field Name	Length	Data Type
`soc.sec$`	9	character
`st.name$`	25	character
`st.age%`	2	integer
`st.addr$`	30	character
`st.city$`	10	character
`st.state$`	2	character
`st.zip$`	5	character
	—	
	83 total characters per record	

The total record length is 83 characters. Every record in this file takes exactly 83 characters of disk space. Just because a city takes only 5 characters of the 10-character field does not mean that 5 characters are all that are stored. Each field is padded with spaces to the right, if needed, to fill the complete 10 characters for each student's city. Using fixed-length fields has a major drawback: it wastes a lot of disk space. But each field is large enough to hold the largest possible data value.

A variable-length file, on the other hand, does not waste space like a fixed-length field does. As soon as a field's data value is saved to the file, the next field's data value is stored immediately after it. There is usually a special separating character between the fields so that your programs know where the fields begin and end.

Variable-length files save disk space, but it is not always as easy to write programs that process them as it is to write programs that process fixed-length files. If limited disk space is a consideration, there is more of a need for the space-saving variable-length records, even if the programs to process them are more difficult to write. The next two chapters discuss each of these types of files.

File Names

Each file in your file cabinet has a label on it. Without those labels, finding a certain file would be difficult, and the files would tend to get mixed up. You want your data to be as easy to find as possible, so you label the files as accurately as possible.

Files on a computer also have names. Each file on your disk has a unique file name. You cannot have two files on the same disk (or in the same directory on your hard drive) that have the same name. If that were possible, your computer would not know which file you wanted when you asked it to use one of them.

Some files are named for you. Others you must name. Just as QBasic variables have naming rules, and so do file names on the disk. A file name can be from one to eight characters long with an optional one-to-three-character *extension.* The file name and extension must be separated from each other with a period. For example, here are some valid file names:

sales89.dat	checks.apr	a.3	testdata
qbasic.exe	emp_name.ap	students	employee.q

Notice that some file names have an extension and some do not. No file name extension is longer than three characters. A file name can consist of letters, numbers, and the underscore (_) character. The underscore character is good to use when you want to separate parts of a name, as in emp_name.ap in the preceding list. Because spaces are not allowed in file names, the underscore helps to group parts of the name.

Although a few other special characters are allowed in file names, such as the pound sign and the exclamation point, many are not allowed, such as the asterisk and the question mark. To be safe, use just letters, numbers, and the underscore.

> **TIP:** Make your file names meaningful. Although you could call your December 1991 checkbook data file x_5.q, calling it checkdec.91 would make much more sense.

When you write a program to create a data file, you have to make up a name for that file, and it must conform to the file-naming rules listed previously. The file is created on the DOS default disk drive (the active drive at the DOS prompt when you started QBasic). If you want to override the default and save the file on another disk, you must precede the file name with a disk drive name, such as:

```
a:checkdec.91      B:SALES.DAT      D:myemps.nam
```

Types of Disk File Access

Your programs can access files two ways: through *sequential access* or through *random access.* Your application determines the method you should choose. The access mode of a file determines how you read, write, change, and delete data from the file. Some of your files can be accessed in both ways, sequentially and randomly.

A sequential file has to be accessed one record at a time in the same order that the records were written. This is analogous to cassette tapes: You play music in the same order it was recorded. (You can quickly fast-forward or rewind over songs that you do not want to listen to, but the order of the songs dictates what you do to play the song you want.) It is difficult, and sometimes impossible, to insert records in the middle of a sequential file. How easy is it to insert a new song in the middle of two other songs on a tape? The only way to truly add or delete records from the middle of a sequential file is to create a completely new file that combines both old and new files.

It may seem that sequential files are limiting, but it turns out that many applications lend themselves to sequential file processing. In Chapter 25, you will see several ways to best utilize sequential files.

You can access a random-access file in any order you want. Think of records in a random-access file as you would songs on a compact disc or record; you can go directly to any song you want without having to play or fast-forward over the other songs. If you want to play the first song, the sixth song, and then the fourth song, you can do so. The order of play has nothing to do with the order in which the songs were originally recorded.

Random file access takes more programming but rewards that effort with a more flexible file access method. Chapter 26 discusses how to program for random-access files.

Summary

This chapter introduced QBasic file processing. You have the tools you need to understand the statements that are covered by the next two chapters. You understand the difference between records and fields, and between sequential access and random file access modes.

When you learn how to write disk file programs, you rarely use DATA statements except to initialize program control variables such as age limits, month names, day of the week names, and other small groups of data required to control the incoming data on the disk and produce output.

Review Questions

Answers to the Review Questions are in Appendix B.

1. What are the two modes that access disk files?

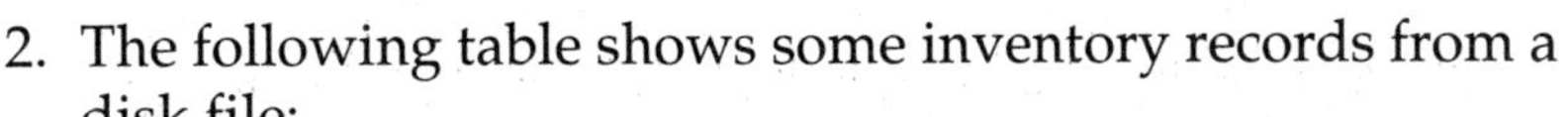

2. The following table shows some inventory records from a disk file:

Part No.	*Description*	*Quantity*	*Price*
43223	Bolt #45	12	0.45
52912	Long Widget	42	3.43
20328	Stress Clip	39	2.00
94552	Turn Mold	2	12.32
45357	#1 Roller	30	7.87

   A. How many records are in this file?
   B. How many fields are there?
   C. What are the field names?

3. What are the two types of disk access modes?

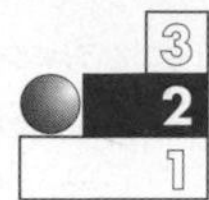

4. Name two drawbacks of keeping all your data in DATA statements.

5. Which are usually easier to program: fixed-length records or variable-length records?

6. The following three file names contain three months of video rental data for a video store. What, if anything, is wrong with the file names?

   0_0.0 bbbwws4.12a hatdata.apr

7. Of the following list of file names, which ones are *not* valid?

sales.89.may	employees.dec	userfile
pipe.dat	sales.txt	PROG1.BAS

25

Sequential Disk Processing

This chapter introduces QBasic sequential file processing commands. You will learn how to create, modify, and manage sequential files on the disk. Using the disk for your data storage dramatically increases the power of QBasic. You can process large amounts of data and store it for later use.

This chapter introduces

- The OPEN statement
- The FREEFILE and FILEATTR() functions
- The CLOSE statement
- Creating sequential files
- The PRINT # and WRITE # statements
- Reading sequential files
- The INPUT # statement
- The EOF() function
- Appending to sequential files

The concepts and commands you learn here are helpful for almost every QBasic application you write. Separating the data from the programs that process it makes your programs much more useful for long-term use and for real-world data processing.

The OPEN Statement

Chapter 24 described the analogy between files in cabinets and files on a disk. The designers of QBasic realized the importance of this analogy when they wrote the OPEN statement. Before you use a file from your file cabinet, you must open the file cabinet. Before creating, modifying, or printing a disk data file in QBasic, you must open the file with the OPEN statement.

There are several options of the OPEN statement that you can use for sequential files. The format of the OPEN statement is

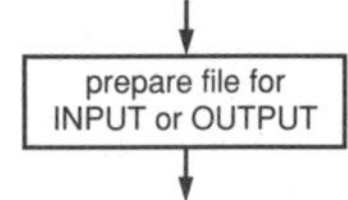


```
OPEN filename$ [FOR mode] AS [#]filenumber
```

The *filename$* must be a string variable or constant consisting of a valid file name. The *mode* can be any one of three values. It can be

```
APPEND

INPUT

OUTPUT
```

The *filenumber* must be an integer that links the file to a number used throughout the program. The *filenumber* can be in the range from *1* to *255*. You can open more than one file in one program (up to 255 of them). Instead of typing the complete file name every time you access a file, you refer to the *filenumber* you associated with that file when you opened it. You do not have to put the pound sign (#) before the *filenumber* because it is optional.

The *mode* refers to the way your program uses the file. If you want to create the file (or overwrite one that already exists), open the file in OUTPUT mode. If you want to read data from a file, open the file in INPUT mode. APPEND mode lets you add to the end of a file (or create it if it does not exist).

Examples

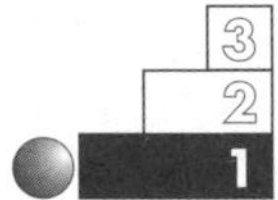

1. Suppose you need to create a sequential file containing an inventory of your household items. The following OPEN statement does that:

   ```
   OPEN "house.inv" FOR OUTPUT AS #1
   ```

   The file is ready to accept data from the program.

2. If you previously created the household inventory file and need to read values from it, you have to write a program that contains the following OPEN statement:

   ```
   OPEN "house.inv" FOR INPUT AS #1
   ```

3. After buying several items, you want to add to the household inventory file. To add to the end of the file, you would open it in the following way:

   ```
   OPEN "house.inv" FOR APPEND AS #1
   ```

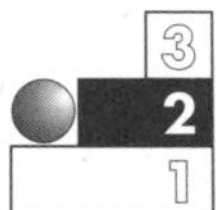

4. Suppose you want to make a back-up copy of the household inventory file. You have to create a new file from the old one. This involves opening the old file in INPUT mode and opening another in OUTPUT mode. The back-up file can even reside on another disk drive, as shown in the following OPEN statement pair:

   ```
   OPEN "c:house.inv" FOR INPUT AS #1    ' Old file
   OPEN "a:house.inv" FOR OUTPUT AS #2   ' New file
   ```

   If the file resides on the DOS default drive, you do not have to put a disk drive name before the file name. When you open more than one file in a program, make sure the files have different file numbers so that the rest of the program can keep them separated.

DOS Determines the Total Number of Open Files

The FILES= command resides in your DOS CONFIG.SYS file. It determines the number of open files you can have at any one time in QBasic. QBasic requires one of the files for its own use, and you can open additional files until the total equals the number set in the FILES= statement.

If you find that your programs need to open several files at the same time and you receive the following error message:

```
Too many files
```

you will have to increase the number following the FILES= statement in your CONFIG.SYS file.

The FREEFILE Function

The FREEFILE function returns the next unused file number. Before an OPEN statement, you can run FREEFILE to find a file number that has yet to be used in an earlier OPEN statement in the program. The format of FREEFILE is

find next available file number

```
FREEFILE
```

Because FREEFILE returns an integer file number, you must assign that file number to a variable.

In most programs, you do not need FREEFILE because you might have only one or two open files. If you write subroutine or function procedures to open files, however, you might want to call FREEFILE first. The calling program could have one or more files open. Without FREEFILE, the procedure would have no way of knowing how many are open.

Here is a section of code that opens three files. The first OPEN statement opens the file as file number 1. The second OPEN statement saves the return value of FREEFILE to a variable to be used in the next OPEN statement.

```
OPEN "sales89.DAT" AS #1 FOR INPUT
next.file% = FREEFILE                          ' Will return a 2
OPEN "sales90.DAT" AS next.file% FOR INPUT
```

Another useful function, especially in procedures, is the FILEATTR() function. It returns the mode in which the file was opened. The format of the FILEATTR() function is

```
FILEATTR(filenumber, attribute)
```

The *filenumber* must be an integer from 1 to 255 that represents the number of the open file about which you want information. Most of the time, you set the *attribute* to *1*. Because the FILEATTR() is a numeric function, you must assign the return value to a variable or print it (usually, you assign it and use it in an IF-THEN relational test).

If you type 1 as the *attribute*, the FILEATTR() function returns an integer value that indicates which mode the file was opened in. Table 25.1 shows a table of FILEATTR() return values. If you use an *attribute* of 2, the FILEATTR() function returns the DOS file handle, an internal number used by DOS in advanced systems programming.

Table 25.1. FILEATTR() return values with a 1 attribute.

Return Value	*Mode*
1	INPUT
2	OUTPUT
4	RANDOM
8	APPEND

The RANDOM mode is discussed in the next chapter.

An Alternative OPEN Statement

There is another, shorter form of the OPEN statement. Its format is as follows:

```
OPEN mode$, [#]filenumber, filename$
```

This format is more succinct than the previous one. The `mode$` can be one of the following letters:

`A` for append

`I` for input

`O` for output

The previous example's `OPEN` statements could be rewritten as:

```
OPEN "O", #1, "house.inv"
OPEN "I", #1, "house.inv"
OPEN "A", #1, "house.inv"
OPEN "I", #1, "c:house.inv"     ' Old file
OPEN "O", #2, "a:house.inv"     ' New file
```

The CLOSE Statement

After using a file, just as with a file cabinet, you must close the file with the `CLOSE` statement. You should close all files that are open in your program when you are through with them. By closing the files, QBasic frees the file number for use by other files that are opened later. DOS also does some closing bookkeeping on the file when you close it.

TIP: If you need a file open only for part of a program, close it immediately after you finish with it, rather than at the end of the program as some programmers do. In the event of a power failure, some of the data in open files might be lost.

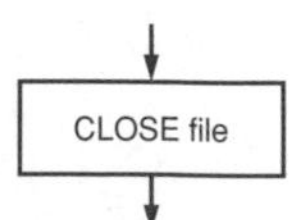

The format of the `CLOSE` statement is

```
CLOSE [[#]filenumber] [,[#]filenumber2] [,...]
```

You can close all files in a program by putting `CLOSE` on a line by itself. If you follow `CLOSE` with one or more integer *`filenumbers`* separated by commas, QBasic closes the files associated with those numbers. `CLOSE` does not care in which mode (`APPEND`, `INPUT`, or `OUTPUT`) you opened the file.

For example, to close an output file associated with file number 1, you would type

```
CLOSE #1
```

You could also type

```
CLOSE 1
```

because the pound sign is optional. To close files associated with file numbers 2 and 5, you would type

```
CLOSE #2, 5
```

To close all files in the program, you would type

```
CLOSE
```

Creating Sequential Files

Before creating a file, open it for OUTPUT. (The APPEND mode also creates a new file, but you should reserve it for adding data to the end of an existing file.) After you have opened the file, you need a way to write data to it. Most data going to a file comes from user input, calculations, DATA statements, or a combination of these. If you save your data in a disk file, it will be there the next time you need it, and you will not have to re-create it each time you run your program.

The PRINT # statement sends output data to a sequential file. The format of PRINT # is

```
PRINT #filenumber, expressionlist
```

The *#filenumber* must be the number of the opened file to which you want to print. The *expressionlist* is one or more variables, constants, expressions, or a combination of each separated by commas or semicolons. The only difference between PRINT and PRINT # is the *#filenumber*, which redirects the output to a file rather than to the screen.

It is important to remember that PRINT # prints data to a file *exactly* as that data would appear on the screen with the regular PRINT statement. This means that positive numbers have a space where the invisible plus sign is before the number, semicolons make the data print right next to each other, and the comma prints in the next print zone on the disk (each print zone is 14 characters wide, just as on the screen).

The following program prints three customer records to a file:

```
' Filename: C25CUST1.BAS
'
' Writes three customer records to a file.

CLS

OPEN "cust.dat" FOR OUTPUT AS #1    ' Open the file on the
                                    ' default drive
PRINT #1, "Johnson, Mike"; 34; "5th and Denver"; "Houston";
PRINT #1, "TX"; "74334"
PRINT #1, "Abel, Lea"; 28; "85 W. 123th"; "Miami"; "FL"; "39443"
PRINT #1, "Madison, Larry"; 32; "4 North Elm"; "Lakewood"; "IL";
PRINT #1, "93844"
CLOSE #1   ' Close open files when you are through with them
```

This program produces a file called cust.dat that looks like this:

```
Johnson, Mike 34 5th and DenverHoustonTX74334
Abel, Lea 28 85 W. 123thMiamiFL39443
Madison, Larry 32 4 North ElmLakewoodIL93844
```

This is an example of a variable-length file. Most sequential files contain variable-length records unless you write fixed-length strings to them.

As with the `PRINT` statement, you can also add a `USING` option to print formatted data to a disk file. This lets you format numbers and strings when you send them to disk files, just as when you send them to the screen and printer.

There is a major drawback to creating files with `PRINT #`. There is no easy method of reading the data back into memory. Notice in the preceding file that the data runs together in some places and is separated in other places. When you are ready to read this file, QBasic will have a difficult time distinguishing among the fields in each record.

Therefore, you should use `WRITE #` rather than `PRINT #` to create sequential files. The format of `WRITE #` is similar to that of the `PRINT #` statement.

```
WRITE #filenumber, expressionlist
```

The *filenumber* is any opened output file. The *expressionlist* is a list of one or more variables, constants, or expressions separated by commas (the semicolon is not used with WRITE #). WRITE # makes the variable-length data file much easier to process. You can later insert quotation marks around each string, and a separating comma between each field.

The following program is an improved version of the PRINT # program described earlier:

```
' Filename: C25CUST2.BAS
'
' Writes three customer records to a file.

CLS

OPEN "cust.dat" FOR OUTPUT AS #1     ' Open the file on the
                                     ' default drive
WRITE #1, "Johnson, Mike"; 34; "5th and Denver"; "Houston";
Write #1, "TX"; "74334"
WRITE #1, "Abel, Lea"; 28; "85 W. 123th"; "Miami"; "FL"; "39443"
WRITE #1, "Madison, Larry"; 32; "4 North Elm"; "Lakewood"; "IL";
WRITE #1, "93844"
CLOSE #1   'Close open files when you are through with them
```

Because the program uses WRITE # rather than PRINT #, the output file's fields are separated much better. Here is the output file called cust.dat created from this program:

```
"Johnson, Mike",34,"5th and Denver","Houston","TX","74334"
"Abel, Lea",28,"85 W. 123th","Miami","FL","39443"
"Madison, Larry",32,"4 North Elm","Lakewood","IL","93844"
```

When you use WRITE #, numbers are not enclosed in quotation marks, but each field containing strings is. This file can later be read by sequential input programs like those described in the next section. Although this is a variable-length file, the separating commas and quotation marks make it easy to input the fields later.

QBasic inserts a carriage return and a line feed character at the end of each record you write with PRINT # and WRITE #.

Examples

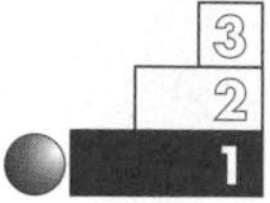

1. The following program creates a data file of books from a collection. This is similar to the way the book database program in Appendix E gets its data. It loops through prompts that ask the user for book information and writes that information to a file.

```
' Filename: C25BOOK1.BAS
'
' Gets book data and creates a file.

CLS

' Create the file
OPEN "book.dat" FOR OUTPUT AS #1
DO      ' Loop asking for data
   PRINT
   LINE INPUT "What is the next book title? "; book.title$
   LINE INPUT "Who is the author? "; author$
   INPUT "How many copies do you have"; copies
   INPUT "What edition (1st, 2nd, etc.) is the book"; edition$
   INPUT "What is the copyright date"; copy.date$
   ' Now write the data to the file
   WRITE #1,book.title$,author$,copies,edition$,copy.date$
   PRINT
   INPUT "Do you have another book to enter"; ans$
LOOP UNTIL (LEFT$(UCASE$(ans$), 1) = "N")    ' Loop until user
                                             ' wants to quit
CLOSE #1
```

`LINE INPUT` was used for the title and author because the user might enter commas as part of the input. The quotation marks produced by `WRITE #` enclose the entire string variable's value. Therefore, if the user types `Florence: Flowers, Art, and Food` for a title, the entire title, including the commas, is enclosed in quotation marks to make for easy input later.

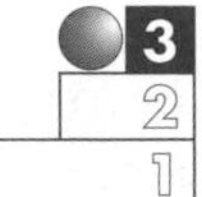

2. Many programmers remember that new computer users are used to filling out forms by hand when they are filing information. Therefore, they make their input screens look similar to a form. The LOCATE command is useful for this. The following program enters the same information in the book file that the previous one did. As you can see from the input screen shown in Figure 25.1, however, the user probably feels more at home with this screen than with a group of individual questions.

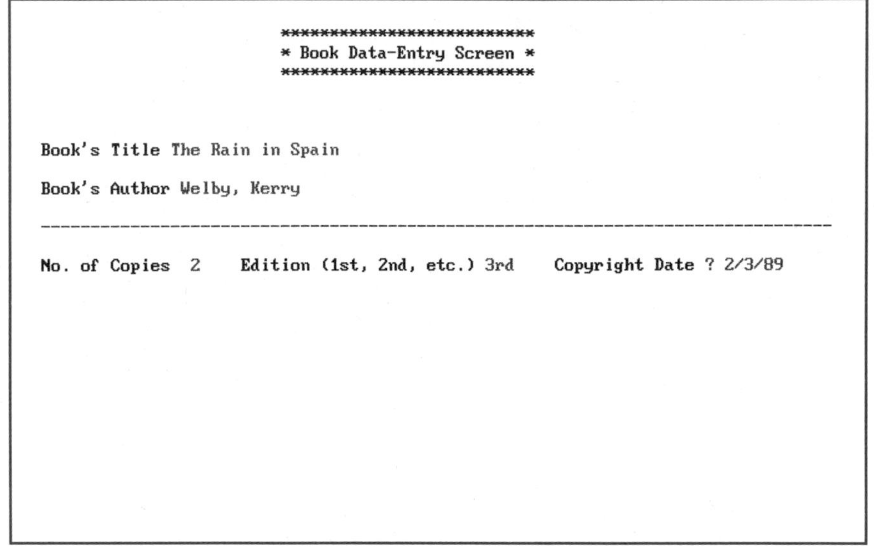

****
* Book Data-Entry Screen *
****
Book's Title The Rain in Spain
Book's Author Welby, Kerry
No. of Copies 2
Edition (1st, 2nd, etc.) 3rd
Copyright Date ? 2/3/89

Figure 25.1. A formlike data-entry screen.

The program displays the entire data-entry screen, then uses LOCATE to position the cursor after each prompt. Because of the modular nature of this program (and of most programs), subroutine procedures are called from the main program to perform their individual tasks, such as displaying titles and prompts and getting the input data. Only the input routine and data-saving routine require the values of the book data, so the data is local to those routines and is passed between them. Users are asked whether they want to enter another book in a function that returns their answer.

Due to space limitations, not all data-entry routines in this book are in a complete formlike program. You should, nevertheless, consider this for your applications that users will see.

```
' Filename: C25BOOK2.BAS
'
' Gets book data from a formlike data-entry screen and
' creates a file.
DECLARE SUB SaveBookData (book.title$, author$, copies!,
   edition$, copy.date$)
DECLARE FUNCTION AskAgain$ ()
DECLARE SUB GetBookData ()
DECLARE SUB DisplayTitle ()
DECLARE SUB DisplayScreen ()

CLS

' Create the file
OPEN "book.dat" FOR OUTPUT AS #1

DO      ' Loop asking for data

   DisplayTitle       ' Print title at the top of the screen
   DisplayScreen      ' Display the data-entry screen
   ' Get the user's input data
   GetBookData
   ans$ = AskAgain$    ' See if user wants to enter another book
LOOP UNTIL (ans$ = "N")

CLOSE #1
END

FUNCTION AskAgain$
' Ask if the user wants to enter another book,
' and return the uppercase answer
LOCATE 16, 10
INPUT "Do you want to enter another book"; ans$

' Return the user's answer
```

```
AskAgain$ = UCASE$(LEFT$(ans$, 1))

END FUNCTION

SUB DisplayScreen
' This subroutine places each data-entry prompt on various
' locations around the screen so the user gets a feel of a
' data-entry form.
LOCATE 7, 1
PRINT "Book's Title"

LOCATE 9, 1
PRINT "Book's Author"

LOCATE 11, 1
PRINT STRING$(80, "-")

LOCATE 13, 1
PRINT "No. of Copies"

LOCATE 13, 21
PRINT "Edition (1st, 2nd, etc.)"

LOCATE 13, 53
PRINT "Copyright Date"

END SUB

SUB DisplayTitle
' This subroutine simply displays the program's title on the
' screen

COLOR 7, 1
CLS

     PRINT TAB(25); STRING$(26, "*")
     PRINT TAB(25); "* Book Data-Entry Screen *"
     PRINT TAB(25); STRING$(26, "*")

END SUB

SUB GetBookData
```

```
' Change the color of the user's input values
COLOR 14, 1

' Place each data-input value after each prompt
LOCATE 7, 14
PRINT "? ";
LINE INPUT book.title$
' After each input, print the value left two places to
' get rid of question marks from the input prompt
LOCATE 7, 14
PRINT book.title$; "  "

LOCATE 9, 15
PRINT "? ";
LINE INPUT author$
LOCATE 9, 15
PRINT author$; "  "

LOCATE 13, 15
INPUT copies
LOCATE 13, 15
PRINT copies; "  "
LOCATE 13, 46
INPUT edition$
LOCATE 13, 46
PRINT edition$; "  "

LOCATE 13, 68
INPUT copy.date$
LOCATE 13, 68
PRINT copy.date$; "  "

' Write the input data to disk
CALL SaveBookData(book.title$, author$, copies, edition$,
   copy.date$)

END SUB

SUB SaveBookData (book.title$, author$, copies, edition$,
   copy.date$)
```

```
' This subroutine saves the entered data to the disk

WRITE #1, book.title$, author$, copies, edition$, copy.date$

END SUB
```

Reading Sequential Files

To read data files created with `WRITE #`, you need to use the `INPUT #` statement. `INPUT #` works with data files as `INPUT` works with the keyboard. As your program executes each `INPUT #`, another value or set of values is input from the disk file. The format of the `INPUT #` statement is

get input from disk file

```
INPUT #filenumber, variablelist
```

As with the `INPUT` statement, you must follow the `INPUT #` statement with one or more variables separated by commas. Each value in the comma-separated file is input to the `INPUT #` *`variablelist`*. You must have already opened the file referred to by the *`filenumber`* in `INPUT` mode.

The `INPUT #` reads any data sent to the file with `WRITE #`. If you use `PRINT #`, you have to supply your own commas and quotation marks around the strings before `INPUT #` can read the data. That is why `WRITE #` is preferred over `PRINT #`.

The following statement reads four variables from the input file opened as file `#3`. Two are numeric, and two arc string.

```
INPUT #3, group$, total%, city$, amount!
```

The data types of the variables must match the data file's data types.

TIP: You can also use the `LINE INPUT #` statement to read values from a file. `LINE INPUT #` reads an entire record at a time.

When you read data from an input file, one of two things always happens:

- The input values are read
- The end of the input file is reached

Most of the time, INPUT # returns whatever values were input from the file. When all the values are input, however, there will be no more data. If you try to INPUT # past the end of the file, you get the following error message:

```
Input past end of file
```

You saw a similar problem when you read data with READ-DATA statements. You needed to test for a trailer DATA record to find out whether the last record was read (otherwise, you had to know in advance exactly how many DATA values there were to read).

With file input, QBasic supplies a built-in function called EOF() that tells you whether you have just read the last record from the file. The format of EOF() is

```
EOF(filenumber)
```

EOF() returns a *-1* if you just input the last record from the file. EOF() returns *0* if there are more records to be input. This tells you whether you should continue looping to input more values.

Call the EOF() function after each INPUT # to see whether there are more values to input or whether you have just input the last one.

Examples

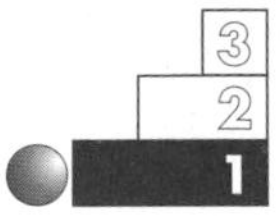

1. The following program reads the first three records from an inventory file. The program that created the file probably used a WRITE # statement that looked similar (in the number of variables and data types) to the INPUT # used here. Notice that the file must be opened in INPUT mode.

```
' Filename: C25INV.BAS
'
' Reads and prints the first three records from an input file.
CLS
OPEN "inv.dat" FOR INPUT AS #1

PRINT "Here are the first three records from the file:"
```

```
PRINT
PRINT "Part #", "Description", "Quantity", "Price"
' Get the first record
INPUT #1, part.no$, description$, quantity%, price!
PRINT part.no$, description$, quantity%, price!
' Get the second record
INPUT #1, part.no$, description$, quantity%, price!
PRINT part.no$, description$, quantity%, price!
' Get the third record
INPUT #1, part.no$, description$, quantity%, price!
PRINT part.no$, description$, quantity%, price!
CLOSE #1
```

2. The following program reads and prints the book data. The input is performed in a DO-LOOP UNTIL loop so that the end of the file can be tested for with EOF(). You want to keep reading records until you reach the end of the file.

```
' Filename: C25BOOK3.BAS
'
' Inputs book data from a file and prints it.

CLS

OPEN "book.dat" FOR INPUT AS #1

' Print headings
PRINT "Title"; TAB(28); "Author"; TAB(40); "Copies"; TAB(48);
PRINT "Edition"; TAB(60); "Date"
PRINT

' Read records until there are no more
DO
   INPUT #1,book.title$,author$,copies,edition$,copy.date$
   PRINT book.title$; TAB(28); author$; TAB(40); copies;
   PRINT TAB(48); edition$; TAB(60); copy.date$
LOOP UNTIL ( EOF(1) )
CLOSE #1
```

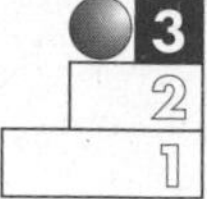

3. The following program counts the number of records in the file that the user enters. This program enables the user to find out how many students are in a student data file, how many customers are in a customer data file, or how many books are in a book data file.

```
' Filename: C25CNTRC.BAS
'
' Counts the number of records in a file.
CLS

PRINT "A Record Counting Program"
PRINT
PRINT "What is the name of the datafile you want to use for ";
INPUT "the count"; df$

count = 0     ' Initialize count
OPEN df$ FOR INPUT AS #1
DO
   LINE INPUT #1, rec$
   count = count + 1
LOOP UNTIL EOF(1)

PRINT
PRINT "The number of records in the file is:"; count
CLOSE #1
```

Figure 25.2 shows the result of running this program. The `LINE INPUT #` ignores the commas and quotation marks by reading the entire record into `rec$`. The user must know the name of the data file and type the complete file name and extension.

```
A Record Counting Program

What is the name of the datafile you want to use for the count? temp

The number of records in the file is: 34





Press any key to continue
```

Figure 25.2. A program that counts records in a file.

Appending to Sequential Files

After creating and reading files, you might want to add data to the end of a sequential file. This is easy when you open the file in APPEND mode. All subsequent writes to that file are added to the end of it. This lets users add data to a file over time.

The only difference between programs that create data files and those that append data to them is the OPEN statement's mode.

Examples

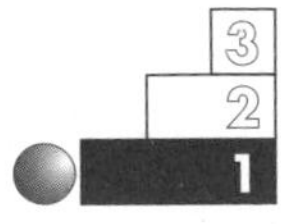

1. The following program adds to the book file you created in a previous program (C25BOOK1.BAS). It simply opens the file in APPEND mode and prompts the user through each input value to write to disk.

```
' Filename: C25BOOK4.BAS
'
' Appends to end of book data file.

CLS

' Open the file for append
PRINT "This program adds to the end of the book data file."
PRINT

OPEN "book.dat" FOR APPEND AS #1
DO      ' Loop asking for data
   PRINT
   LINE INPUT "What is the next book title? "; book.title$
   LINE INPUT "Who is the author? "; author$
   INPUT "How many copies do you have"; copies
   INPUT "What edition (1st, 2nd, etc.) is the book"; edition$
   INPUT "What is the copyright date"; copy.date$
   ' Now write the data to the file
   WRITE #1, book.title$, author$, copies, edition$, copy.date$
   PRINT
   INPUT "Do you have another book to enter"; ans$
LOOP UNTIL LEFT$(UCASE$(ans$), 1) = "N"    ' Loop until user
                                           ' wants to quit
CLOSE #1
```

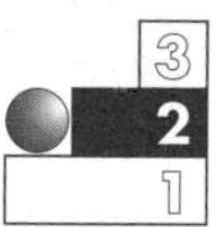

2. The following program appends two data files together. It asks users for the names of two files. It then adds the second file to the end of the first one. LINE INPUT # is used to read the entire records. Users must ensure that the two data files have the same type and number of fields if they later want to sequentially read the newly appended file.

```
' Filename: C25APND.BAS
'
' Appends one file to the end of the other.
CLS
INPUT "What is the name of the first file"; f1$
PRINT "What file do you want to append to the end of "; f1$;
INPUT f2$
```

```
OPEN f1$ FOR APPEND AS #1
OPEN f2$ FOR INPUT AS #2

DO
   LINE INPUT #2, rec$
   PRINT #1, rec$
LOOP UNTIL ( EOF(1) )
CLOSE      ' Close both files
```

Notice that a PRINT # statement is used because WRITE # could add more quotation marks to the file when it writes the records.

Summary

Now that you have been exposed to sequential data file processing, you will be able to keep permanent data on your disk and add to it or look at it when you need to without looking at the program code's DATA statements. Sequential file processing is fairly easy to do, but it is limited; you read the data in the same order it was stored on the disk.

Much data lends itself to sequential file processing. You can search sequential data files one record at a time looking for the record you desire (using the same concept as the parallel array key fields). But there is an even faster and more flexible way to search files for data. Using random files makes your data-processing programs true data-retrieval programs that can quickly find any data you need to find. Chapter 26, "Random-Access Disk Processing," introduces you to the concept of random file processing.

Review Questions

Answers to the Review Questions are in Appendix B.

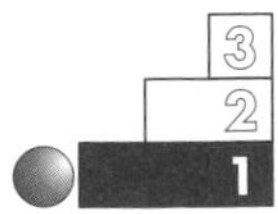

1. What statement must you always use before creating, reading, or appending to sequential files?

2. What are the three sequential access modes of the OPEN statement?

3. What command reads data from a sequential data file?

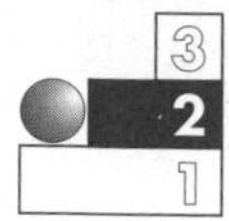

4. TRUE or FALSE: If you do not put a file number after a CLOSE statement, all open files are closed.
5. What function determines the next unused file number you can use?
6. What happens if you open a file in APPEND mode that does not exist?

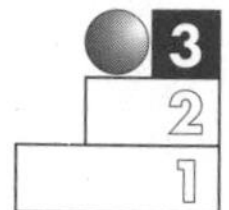

7. What is the difference between the PRINT # statement and the WRITE # statement?
8. What does the EOF() function do?
9. Which DOS statement determines how many files QBasic can open at once?
10. What statement reads an entire record at once into a string variable?

Review Exercises

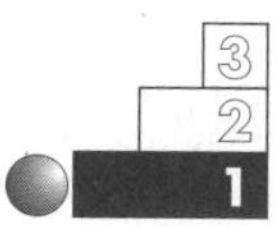

1. Write a program that stores your holiday mailing list in a data file.
2. Write a program that reads and prints the mailing list from the preceding example to the printer.

3. Add a menu to the holiday mailing list program to let the user add more data or see the data that already exists in the file.
4. Write a program to count the number of characters in a file. (Hint: Use LINE INPUT # combined with the LEN() function.)

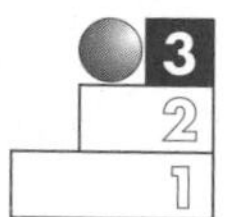

5. Write a program that makes a back-up copy of a file. The users are to enter the name of the file they want backed up. Your program is then to open that file with the extension BAK and make a copy of it by reading and writing (using PRINT #) one record at a time.

6. Add data-checking routines to the book data-entry program (C25BOOK2.BAS) to ensure that the user enters a proper date and edition. Check to make sure the data is within valid ranges.

7. Expand on the book database presented through this chapter to put the routines together in subroutine procedures and call them based on the user's menu choice. It does not have to be as complete as the one in Appendix E, but make sure it combines the concepts of creating the file, reading the file, and adding to it.

26

Random-Access Disk Processing

This chapter introduces the concept of random file access. Random file access lets you read or write any record in your data file without having to read or write every record before it. You can quickly search for, add, retrieve, change, and delete information in a random-access file. Although you need a few new commands to access files randomly, you will find that the extra effort pays off in flexibility, power, and speed of disk access.

This chapter introduces

- The random-access `OPEN` statement
- Random file access records
- The `TYPE` statement
- The `FIELD` statement
- The `MKtype$()` string functions
- The `CVtype()` numeric functions
- The `GET` and `PUT` statements
- The `LOF()` function

This chapter concludes Part VII, "Disk File Processing." With QBasic's sequential and random-access files, you can do everything you would ever want to do with data files.

Random File Records

Random files exemplify the power of data processing with QBasic. Sequential file processing is slow unless you read the entire file into parallel arrays and process them in memory. As explained in Chapter 25, however, you have much more disk space than RAM, and most disk data files do not even fit in your RAM at one time. Therefore, you need a way to quickly read individual records from a file in any order needed and process them one at a time.

Think about the data files of a large credit card organization. When you make a purchase, the store calls the credit card company to get an authorization. There are millions of people in the credit card company's files. Without fast computers, there would be no way that the credit card company could read every record from the disk that comes before yours in a timely manner. Sequential files do not lend themselves to quick access. It is not feasible in many situations to look up individual records in a data file with sequential access.

The credit card companies must use a random file access so that their computers can go directly to your record, just as you go directly to a song on a compact disk or record album. The file must be set up differently for random file access, but the power that results from the preparation is worth the effort.

All random file records must be fixed-length records. (Chapter 25 explained the difference between fixed-length and variable-length records.) The sequential files you read and wrote in the previous chapter were variable-length records. When you are reading or writing sequentially, there is no need for fixed-length records because you input each field one record at a time, looking for the data you want. With fixed-length records, your computer can better calculate exactly where the search record is located on the disk.

Although you waste some disk space with fixed-length records (because of the spaces that pad some of the fields), the advantages of random-file access make up for the "wasted" disk space.

> **TIP:** With random-access files, you can read or write records in any order. Therefore, even if you want to perform sequential reading or writing of the file, you can use random-access processing and "randomly" read or write the file in sequential record number order.

The Random-Access OPEN Statement

Just as with sequential files, you must open random-access files before reading or writing to them. The random-access OPEN statement is similar to the sequential file OPEN statement, except you do not have to include the mode; random-access files can be read *and* written to without your having to close and reopen the file as you would have to do with sequential-access files. The OPEN statement must also include the record length of the fixed-length file to access.

The format of the random-access file OPEN statement is

prepare file for random access

```
OPEN filename$ AS [#]filenumber LEN=recordlength
```

The *filenumber* (with the optional pound sign preceding it) is the file number used in the rest of the program to refer to this open file. The *recordlength* is the integer length of each record in the file. If you are creating a random-access file, you must know the record length before writing the program by deciding exactly which fields you will write to the file. If you do not specify a *recordlength*, QBasic assumes a 128-byte record length, although this length rarely is correct for your data files.

> **TIP:** You can optionally insert the words FOR RANDOM between the *filename$* and the keyword AS, but because the default mode is RANDOM, most programmers do not include this.

The following statement opens a file called ADDRESS.89, which has a record length of 62, on disk drive D:. Then the statement connects the file to file number 1.

```
OPEN "D:ADDRESS.89" AS #1 LEN=62
```

Just to be complete, there is a shortcut version of the random-access OPEN statement, just as there was for the sequential-access OPEN. QBasic includes this to be compatible with earlier versions of BASIC. The format of the shortened OPEN is

```
OPEN "R", [#]filenumber, filename$, recordlength
```

The previous OPEN statement could be rewritten as

```
OPEN "R", 1, "D:ADDRESS.89", 62
```

As with other file names, you can type the name in uppercase or lowercase letters.

The TYPE Statement

The TYPE statement describes a fixed-length record. The TYPE statement is new to QBasic; it did not exist in previous versions of BASIC that were supplied with DOS. Therefore, if you work with older programs, you will have to use the FIELD statement described in the next section.

TYPE is a big improvement over FIELD. With TYPE, you can describe your own records that contain any mixture of fields with any combination of data types you need. The format of TYPE is

define record layout

```
TYPE recordname
   fieldname AS datatype
   [fieldname2 AS datatype1]
        :
        :
   [fieldnameN AS datatypeN]
END TYPE
```

Think of the *recordname* as a record description. Its name can consist of one to 40 letters and numbers. Do not use any special characters such as a period or an underscore. For instance, if you want to create a record that contains the titles in your compact disk and record collection, you could use the following as a TYPE statement:

```
TYPE musicrec
```

The *recordname* has no data type suffix character. It is a new data type that you are creating. It is the name you refer to when you want to create variables that look like this record. The rest of the TYPE statement describes each field in the record. The *fieldname* can be any name you specify (also consisting of one to 40 letters and numbers), and the *datatype* is any QBasic defined data type from Table 26.1.

Table 26.1. The TYPE statement's possible field data types and their lengths.

Data Type	*Description*	*Length*
INTEGER	Integer	2
LONG	Long integer	4
SINGLE	Single-precision	4
DOUBLE	Double-precision	8
STRING * *N*	Fixed-length string	*N*

For example, to describe the rest of the record collection, you could use the following TYPE statement:

```
TYPE musicrec
   title     AS STRING * 20      ' Title of the album
   quantity  AS INTEGER          ' Number of them I have
   condition AS STRING * 5       ' GOOD, POOR, etc.
   numsongs  AS INTEGER          ' # of songs on album
   pricepd   AS SINGLE           ' Price I paid for it
END TYPE
```

Each field you define that contains a string must also include the string length. Because random-access records must be fixed-length records, you must declare each string length in advance. It helps to comment on your record descriptions with remarks after each field description, as done in this example.

The length of musicrec is 33. Table 26.1 described the length of each data type. The first field (title) takes 20 characters. The second field (quantity) is an integer that takes two characters. The third (condition) takes five characters, the fourth (numsongs) takes two characters, and the last (pricepd) takes four.

Figure 26.1 shows the format of the file being described by this record description's TYPE statement. In writing the TYPE statement, you prepare your program so that it can read and write records that look like the one described. The OPEN statement used for this file might be

```
OPEN "CDCOLLEC.DAT" AS #1 LEN=33
```

title	quantity	condition	numsongs	pricepd
1-20	21-22	23-27	28-29	30-33

Figure 26.1. The format of the CD collection record.

TIP: Instead of computing the total record length yourself, use the LEN() function. The previous OPEN statement could have been

```
OPEN "CDCOLLEC.DAT" AS #1 LEN=LEN(musicrec)
```

Declaring Record Variables from Your TYPE

The TYPE statement only describes your file records. It does not reserve any storage. Notice that no variables are listed in the TYPE statement's format; only field names are described. The TYPE statement only describes the record; you must then define one or more record variables for it. Your programs store data in variables. Therefore, you must create record variables just as you created integer, long integer, string, single-precision, and double-precision variables.

The following line shows the way you create record variables for the compact disc record:

```
DIM cd1 AS musicrec, cd2 AS musicrec, cd3 AS musicrec
```

This creates three variables: cd1, cd2, and cd3. Each of these variables has the type defined in the TYPE statement; in other words, cd1 consists of a 20-character string,

followed by an integer,

followed by a five-character string,

followed by an integer,

followed by a single-precision value (the "look" of the musicrec record)

These three variables are all local to the routine that creates them. If you want to make them global, you have to use the COMMON SHARED statement in the main program, such as

```
COMMON SHARED cd1 AS musicrec, cd2 AS musicrec, cd3 AS musicrec
```

The SHARED statement (without COMMON) lets the variables be local to the routines that contain the same SHARED statement, as in

```
SHARED cd1 AS musicrec, cd2 AS musicrec, cd3 AS musicrec
```

You can also create an array of record variables with

```
DIM cds(500) AS musicrec
```

The type of the array is not string or integer as you have seen in previous chapters; the array type is musicrec. Each element in the array looks like the record you defined with the TYPE statement.

If you pass a record created with the TYPE statement, the receiving function receives it with an AS ANY type in its parameter list. In other words, the following function receives a record called custrec that was passed to it from a calling function:

```
DisplayCust(custrec AS ANY)
```

For a review of local and global commands, refer to Chapter 23, "Variable Scope."

Accessing Fields in a Record

So far, you have learned how to open a random-access file, define a record, and create record variables. The following section of a program listing puts this all together.

```
OPEN "D:CDREC.DAT" AS #1 LEN=62
TYPE musicrec
   title     AS STRING * 20     ' Title of the album
   quantity  AS INTEGER         ' Number of them I have
   condition AS STRING * 5      ' GOOD, POOR, etc.
   numsongs  AS INTEGER         ' # of songs on album
   pricepd   AS SINGLE          ' Price I paid for it
END TYPE

DIM cd AS musicrec   ' Defines 1 record variable
```

Only one record variable, `cd`, was defined. Before saving this variable to a file, you need to put values in it. The names `title`, `quantity`, `condition`, `numsongs`, and `pricepd` are not variables; they are field names for the record `musicrec`.

The variable `cd` refers to a single variable in memory. To fill this variable, use the dot (.) operator. An example is worth a thousand words:

```
cd.title = "Bruno's Here Again!"
cd.quantity = 1
cd.condition = "GOOD"
cd.numsongs = 12
cd.pricepd = 9.75
```

Notice that to assign values to fields in a record variable, you only have to precede the field name with the record name and a period. (This is why record and field names cannot contain a period in their names.) The dot operator puts values in the record. The record is now ready to be written to disk. Figure 26.2 shows what the record looks like. Notice that some of the fields have been padded with spaces; this is how QBasic retains the fixed-length records it needs for random-access files.

These `recordname.fieldname` pairs combine to form individual values that you can print, assign, or pass to subroutines and functions. The first part of the name before the period specifies the record, and the last part specifies the field in that record.

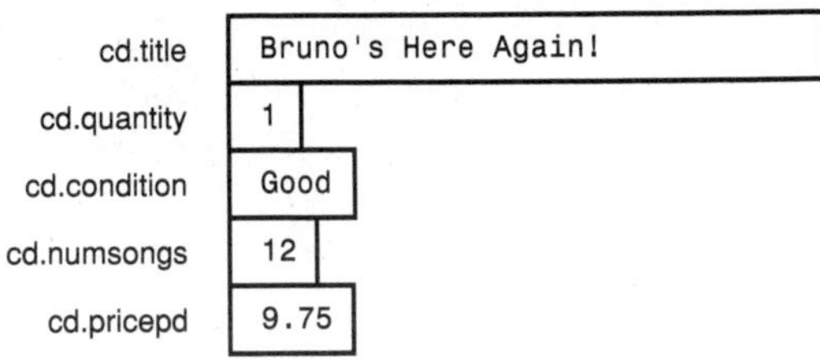

Figure 26.2. After putting values in the record variable.

Examples

The following examples prepare you for reading and writing random-access files. They illustrate the first part of the process: defining the record and its fields.

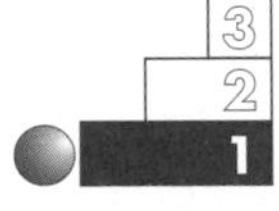

1. Suppose you want to save a list of friends' names to a random-access file. You must first decide how much storage per name your program requires. All random-access records must be fixed-length. Even if the records contain one field, the friend's name, that field must be a fixed-length field.

   You might quickly scan through your friends' names and try to determine who has the longest name. You can make the length of that name the length for all the names. Of course, you might meet someone with a longer name later and not have room for it, but you would waste too much space if you gave the field a length of 1,000 characters! Therefore, think of a good trade-off length, such as 20.

   Here are the first few lines of a program that sets up this simple random-access file:

```
OPEN "FRIEND.LST" AS #1 LEN=20

TYPE namerec
   firstname AS STRING * 10
   lastname  AS STRING * 10
END TYPE

DIM names(100) AS namerec
```

This gives you 100 elements, each 20 characters wide, that have the record format for the names. You could input values in this array with a FOR-NEXT loop such as

```
FOR ctr = 1 TO 100
   INPUT "What is the first name"; names(ctr).firstname
   INPUT "What is the last name"; names(ctr).lastname
NEXT ctr
```

Of course, if you do not have exactly 100 names, you need a way to exit this loop early. When the array is filled, you could then write it to a random-access file with the random-access statements explained in the next section.

This illustrates one consideration you might want to think about while planning your data file programs. There is really no good reason to store every name in the array of records before writing them to the disk file. When the user enters a name, the program can write that name to disk before asking for the next name. This procedure eliminates the need for an array of records. You need to define only one record variable in a line, such as this one:

```
DIM friendname AS namerec
```

2. The following section of code prepares an inventory record for random-access processing:

```
OPEN "d:INVEN.DAT" AS #1 LEN=21

TYPE invrec
   partno   AS STRING * 5
   descrip  AS STRING * 10
   quantity AS INTEGER
   price    AS SINGLE
END TYPE

DIM item AS invrec      ' A non-array variable of the record
```

The FIELD Statement

For completeness, you should understand the FIELD statement. Previous versions of BASIC used FIELD in place of the TYPE record definition statement. The FIELD statement defines a record you read and write in a random-access file, although it takes more effort to assign data to it. The format of FIELD is

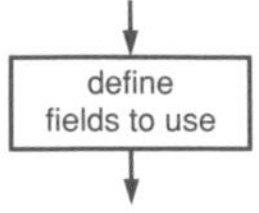


```
FIELD [#]filenumber, width AS stringvar$
          [, width2 AS stringvar2$ ]
                 :
                 :
          [, widthN AS stringvarN$ ]
```

FIELD is similar to TYPE except that each field defined in the record with FIELD must be a string. This does not mean that you can only have strings as fields, but it does mean that you have to convert each field to a string before saving it to the record.

Here is the compact disk collection record defined with a FIELD statement:

```
FIELD #1, 20 AS title$, 2 AS quantity$, 5 AS condition$,
          2 AS numsongs$, 4 AS pricepd$
```

This FIELD statement assumes that the compact disk collection file was opened as file number 1. Each field must be a string variable. You must reserve enough space to hold numeric data as integer (two bytes), long integer (four bytes), single-precision (four bytes), and double-precision (eight bytes) for each field that holds numeric data which you first convert to string.

You have seen a string function that converts numbers to strings. It is the STR$() function. STR$() works when you field numeric values, but there are additional numeric-to-string functions that work better for fielded values. The problem with STR$() is that it converts numbers to strings, but every digit, decimal point, and sign in the converted number gets converted to an individual string character. For instance, the STR$() functions

```
STR$(9.54345)   STR$(123456789)   STR$(-12.34)
```

convert the numbers to strings of eight characters (the leading imaginary plus sign, the six digits, and the decimal point), nine characters, and six characters, respectively. As you already know, however, numbers should not take this much space. That's because QBasic packs numbers in an internal format that does not require one byte of storage per digit in the number. If you had hundreds of numbers to store in a data file, you would waste much storage using `STR$()`.

The following `MKtype$()` (for `MaKe type`) numeric-conversion functions convert numbers to strings, but the resulting strings take no more storage than their native numbers:

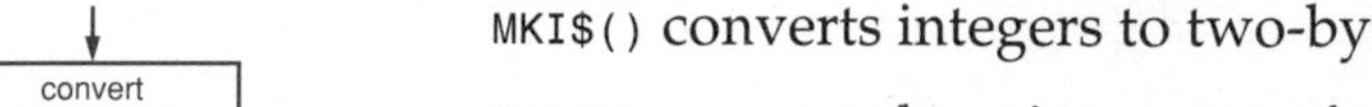

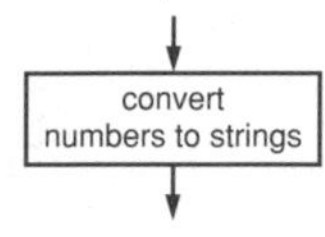

`MKI$()` converts integers to two-byte strings.

`MKL$()` converts long integers to four-byte strings.

`MKS$()` converts single-precision numbers to four-byte strings.

`MKD$()` converts double-precision numbers to eight-byte strings.

Table 26.2 shows you the range of values each type of number takes. For example, to store the previous three numbers in strings using the `MKtype$()` functions, you would use

```
MKS$(9.54345)    MKL$(123456789)    MKS$(-12.34)
```

You know to use `MKS$()` for *9.54345* because that number falls within the range of single-precision numbers, and so on. These three functions convert the three numbers to four-byte strings because single-precision numbers and long integers each take four bytes of storage. With a file of hundreds of numbers, saving two or three bytes per storage can add up quickly.

Table 26.2. Ranges of numeric data types.

Numeric Type	*Range of Possible Values*
Integer	-32,768 to 32,767
Long integer	-2,147,483,648 to 2,147,483,648

Numeric Type	Range of Possible Values
Single-precision	
Positive	2.802597E-45 to 3.402823E+38
Negative	-3.402823E+38 to -2.802597E-45
Double-precision	
Positive	4.940656458412465D-324 to 1.79769313486231D+308
Negative	-1.79769313486231D+308 to -4.940656458412465D-324

When reading from a file to a record created with `FIELD`, you have to convert all numeric string values back to numbers before using them in calculations. The following `CV`*`type`*`()` (for `ConVert` *`type`*) functions convert fielded input data from strings back to numbers:

`CVI()` converts two-byte string integers to integers.

`CVL()` converts four-byte string long integers to long integers.

`CVS()` converts four-byte single-precision numbers to single-precision numbers.

`CVD()` converts eight-byte double-precision numbers to double-precision numbers.

Getting back to the compact disk collection `FIELD` statement, the two numeric fields, `quantity` and `pricepd`, must be converted to strings before you can write the fielded record to disk. After they are converted, you cannot use the assignment statement to assign the strings values; you must use the left- and right-justifying statements `LSET` and `RSET`, such as

```
OPEN "CDCOLLEC.DAT" AS #1 LEN=33
FIELD #1, 20 AS title$, 2 AS quantity$, 5 AS condition$,
          2 AS numsongs$, 4 AS pricepd$
LSET title$ = "Songs to Sing By"    ' The title of the album
RSET quantity$ = MKI$(1)            ' I have 1 copy
LSET condition$ = "FAIR"            ' Some scratches
```

```
RSET numsongs$ = MKI$(12)          ' 12 songs on album
RSET pricepd$ = MKS$(8.95)         ' It was on sale
```

Typically, converted numbers are `RSET` (right-justified) into field variables, and strings are `LSET` (left-justified) into field variables.

If you need to assign one field variable to another, use only `LSET`. For example, suppose you create two fielded records: an employee record and a customer record. If an employee buys something, you might want to assign a customer record's variable to an employee record's variable, as in

```
LSET empname$ = custname$ ' Put employee's name in customer
                          ' record
```

> **TIP:** If you are creating new applications that will not interact with older versions of BASIC, use the `TYPE` statement to create record data. You will not have to spend time converting numbers to strings before writing them or converting strings to numbers after reading them.

The following examples are similar to those in the preceding section, except they use the `FIELD` statement rather than the `TYPE` statement. These examples are only partial programs. The next section explains how to read and write records to a random-access file.

Examples

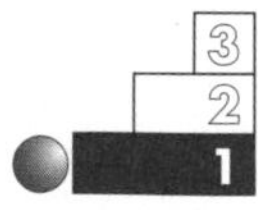

1. Here is the friend's name record setup and initialization using a `FIELD` statement:

```
OPEN "FRIEND.LST" AS #1 LEN=20
FIELD #1, 10 AS firstname$, 10 AS lastname$
```

If you store the names in two parallel arrays, `first$()` and `last$()`, you can dimension them, get the names from the user, and field them (create their record) with the following code:

```
DIM first$(100), last$(100)
FOR ctr = 1 TO 100
   INPUT "What is the first name"; first$(ctr)
   INPUT "What is the last name"; last$(ctr)
   LSET firstname$ = first$(ctr)    ' Put values in record
   LSET lastname$ = last$(ctr)
' Code goes here that writes the record to disk
'     :
'     :
NEXT ctr
```

Again, if you don't have exactly 100 names, you need a way to exit this loop early. Unless you are going to do some more processing with the names, there is really no good reason to store them in the arrays because you are writing them to the disk right after the user enters them.

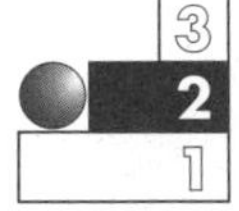

2. Here is the inventory file with its record created by the FIELD statement:

```
OPEN "d:INVEN.DAT" AS #1 LEN=21

FIELD #1,5 AS partno$,10 AS descrip$,2 AS quantity$,4 AS price$
```

Reading and Writing to Random-Access Files

After setting up your random-access record with TYPE or FIELD, it is easy to read or write that data to a file. The location of the record in the file becomes important when working with random-access files. The record number is the key to finding whatever record you want to write or read. To create or read files, you cannot use the sequential file INPUT # and PRINT # statements because they do not let you change the location of the next read or write.

Using the random-access reading and writing commands lets you specify which record in the file to read or write next.

Creating Random-Access File Data

You must use the PUT # statement to create a random-access file. After you define the record to write and initialize the fields in that record with data, PUT # writes that record to the disk. The format of PUT # is

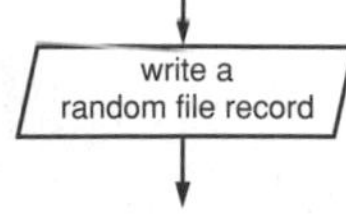


```
PUT [#] filenumber [ , recordnum] [, recordname ]
```

The *filenumber* is the open random-access file to write to. Notice that the pound sign is optional, although most programmers include it. The *recordnum* is an integer or a long integer which specifies the record number to write to. If you do not specify a *recordnum*, QBasic assumes the record following the last one written, but you must type the comma anyway if you specify a record name.

The *recordname* is the record's name created with a TYPE statement. If you use FIELD to define this *filenumber*'s record, you do not specify a *recordname* because QBasic uses the FIELD statement's record.

Examples

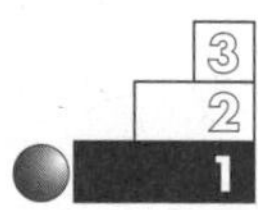

1. Here is the complete random-access friends' name program. This program creates the names in a random-access file using PUT #.

```
' Filename: C26FRND1.BAS
'
' Stores friends' names in a random-access file.
TYPE namerec
   firstname AS STRING * 10
   lastname  AS STRING * 10
END TYPE

DIM names AS namerec    ' A record variable

OPEN "FRIEND.LST" AS #1 LEN=20

recnum = 1      ' Initialize record number

DO
```

```
   PRINT
   PRINT "What is the first name"
   INPUT "(Press ENTER if no more)"; names.firstname
   IF (names.firstname = SPACE$(10)) THEN EXIT DO   ' Quit if no
                                                    ' more names
   INPUT "What is the last name"; names.lastname
   PUT #1, recnum, names   ' Write the next record
   recnum = recnum + 1
LOOP UNTIL (names.firstname = SPACE$(10))

CLOSE #1
```

The *recnum* is optional, because the next record is used anyway. Because each field must be a fixed-length string, the relational test must test for 10 spaces with the `SPACE$()` function, and not for a null string.

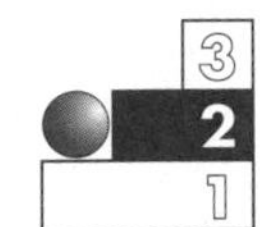

2. Here is the inventory program that creates the inventory file:

```
' Filename: C26INV1.BAS
'
' Creates an inventory random-access file.

CLS

TYPE invrec
   partno   AS STRING * 5
   descrip  AS STRING * 10
   quantity AS INTEGER
   price    AS SINGLE
END TYPE

DIM item AS invrec      ' A non-array variable of the record

OPEN "C:INVEN.DAT" AS #1 LEN=21

' Get the data from the user
DO
   PRINT
   INPUT "What is the part number"; item.partno
   INPUT "What is the description"; item.descrip
   INPUT "What is the quantity"; item.quantity
```

```
   INPUT "What is the price"; item.price
   INPUT "Is there another part (Y/N)"; ans$
   PUT #1,, item    ' No record number is needed. It
                    ' defaults to the next one
LOOP WHILE ( LEFT$(UCASE$(ans$),1) = "Y" )

CLOSE
```

This also shows that the record number is optional. If you do not specify a record number in the `PUT #` statement, QBasic inserts the next record after the last one written in the file. If you do not specify a record number, you must still type the comma where one would go to tell QBasic that `item` is a record and not a record number.

3. Here is the same program that uses the `FIELD` statement instead of the `TYPE` statement. It takes more work to use the `FIELD` statement because you have to `LSET` and `RSET` the field data before writing the record.

```
' Filename: C26INVF.BAS
'
' Creates an inventory random-access file using a FIELD
' statement.
OPEN "C:INVEN.DAT" AS #1 LEN=21

CLS

FIELD #1,5 AS partno$,10 AS descrip$,2 AS quantity$,4 AS price$

' Get the data from the user
DO
   PRINT
   INPUT "What is the part number"; part$
   INPUT "What is the description"; desc$
   INPUT "What is the quantity"; quant
   INPUT "What is the price"; price
   INPUT "Is there another part (Y/N)"; ans$
   LSET partno$ = part$          ' It takes LSET and RSET to
   LSET descrip$ = desc$         ' assign the input values
   RSET quantity$ = MKI$(quant)  ' to the field variables
```

```
   RSET price$ = MKS$(price)
   PUT #1   ' No record name is needed.  FIELD #1 is written
LOOP WHILE ( LEFT$(UCASE$(ans$),1) = "Y" )

CLOSE
```

The FIELD requires that you store input values in variables and then RSET and LSET them into additional field variables. This takes time and extra programming. With the TYPE statement, you did not have to do this because you could assign fields their values directly without using the MK*type*$() functions.

NOTE: Keep in mind that these are random-access files, although you create them in a sequential manner: the first record is followed by the second, and so on. Later, you can read these files randomly or sequentially using random-access commands.

Reading Random-Access Files

You must use the GET # statement to read from random-access files. GET # is the mirror image of PUT #. GET # reads records from the disk file to the record you define with TYPE or FIELD. The format of GET # is

READ record from random-access file

```
GET [#] filenumber [ , recordnum] [, recordname ]
```

The *filenumber* is the open random-access file to read from. Notice that the pound sign is optional, although most programmers include it. The *recordnum* is an integer or a long integer that specifies the record number to read. If you do not specify a *recordnum* , QBasic assumes it should read the record following the last one read, but you must type the comma anyway if you include the record name.

The *recordname* is the record's name created with a TYPE statement. If you use FIELD to define this *filenumber*'s record, you do not specify a *recordname* because QBasic uses the FIELD statement's record.

It might be helpful to use the LOF() function to determine how many bytes are in the file. The format of LOF() is

```
LOF( filenumber )
```

The *filenumber* must be an integer specifying the number under which you opened the file with the OPEN statement. LOF() always returns the total number of bytes written to the file. By dividing the LOF() value by the record length, you can determine exactly how many records there are in the file. Knowing this keeps you from reading past the end of the file. You can also append to the end of a random-access file by knowing the last record number.

Examples

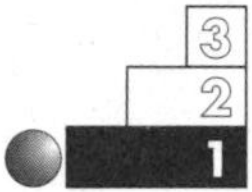

1. The following program reads the inventory file created earlier. It reads the file with GET #, but it reads from the first record to the last as if it were a sequential file.

```
' Filename: C26INV2.BAS
'
' Reads an inventory random-access file created earlier.

CLS
TYPE invrec
   partno   AS STRING * 5
   descrip  AS STRING * 10
   quantity AS INTEGER
   price    AS SINGLE
END TYPE

DIM item AS invrec      ' A non-array variable of the record

OPEN "C:INVEN.DAT" AS #1 LEN=21

num.recs = LOF(1) / 21  ' The total number of records

FOR recnum = 1 TO num.recs    ' Loop through the file
   GET #1, recnum, item    ' Get the next record
   PRINT
   PRINT "The part number: "; item.partno
   PRINT "The description: "; item.descrip
   PRINT "The quantity:"; item.quantity
   PRINT "The price:"; item.price
```

```
NEXT recnum

CLOSE
```

Figure 26.3 shows this program displaying an inventory listing. It prints the records in exactly the same order they were entered in the file.

```
The part number: 321
The description: Widgets
The quantity: 23
The price: 4.95

The part number: 190
The description: A-bolts
The quantity: 434
The price: 2

The part number: 662
The description: Crane top
The quantity: 4
The price: 544.54

The part number: 541
The description: Seal
The quantity: 32
The price: 5.66



Press any key to continue
```

Figure 26.3. Reading and printing the inventory data.

2. Here is the same program, except it reads and prints the inventory file in reverse order. You could not do this with sequential files.

   The record number starts at the last record in the file (gotten by dividing the `LOF()` function by the record length) and counts down. This should begin to give you an idea of what you can do with random-access files.

```
' Filename: C26INV3.BAS
'
' Reads an inventory random-access file created earlier
' and prints it backward.
```

```
CLS

TYPE invrec
   partno   AS STRING * 5
   descrip  AS STRING * 10
   quantity AS INTEGER
   price    AS SINGLE
END TYPE

DIM item AS invrec      ' A non-array variable of the record
OPEN "C:INVEN.DAT" AS #1 LEN=21

num.recs = LOF(1) / 21   ' The total number of records

FOR recnum = num.recs TO 1 STEP -1   ' Loop through the file
                                     ' backward
   GET #1, recnum, item    ' Get the next record
   PRINT
   PRINT "The part number: "; item.partno
   PRINT "The description: "; item.descrip
   PRINT "The quantity:"; item.quantity
   PRINT "The price:"; item.price
NEXT recnum

CLOSE
```

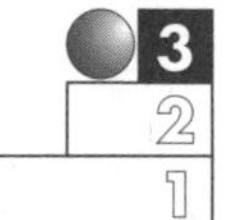

3. The following program asks users for the record number they want to see. The program then reads and prints only that record from the inventory file. This is true random-access. With sequential files, you have to read every record until you get to the one the users want to see.

```
' Filename: C26INV4.BAS
'
' Asks the user for a record number, and
' prints that record from the inventory file.

CLS

TYPE invrec
   partno   AS STRING * 5
```

```
   descrip  AS STRING * 10
   quantity AS INTEGER
   price    AS SINGLE
END TYPE

DIM item AS invrec      ' A non-array variable of the record

OPEN "C:INVEN.DAT" AS #1 LEN=21

num.recs = LOF(1) / 21   ' The total number of records

DO
   PRINT  "What inventory record number do you want to see";
   INPUT recnum
   IF ((recnum <= num.recs) AND (recnum > 0)) THEN
      GET #1, recnum, item    ' Get the record
      PRINT
      PRINT "The part number: "; item.partno
      PRINT "The description: "; item.descrip
      PRINT "The quantity:"; item.quantity
      PRINT "The price:"; item.price
   ELSE
      PRINT
      PRINT "You must enter a record number from 1 to";
      PRINT num.recs
   END IF
   PRINT "Do you want to enter another record number (Y/N)";
   INPUT ans$
LOOP UNTIL ( UCASE$(LEFT$(ans$, 1)) = "N")

CLOSE
```

4. Your users certainly might not know the record number of each customer. Therefore, you need to search random-access files, just as you had to do with sequential files. The following program asks the user for an inventory part number. It then reads the random-access file sequentially (using `GET #`). When it finds a matching part number, it prints that part's record information.

The next section shows you how to change record data in random-access files. One of the first steps needed to change a record is this search routine to find it, given a *key field* or a field value to look for. A key field usually contains unique data. Because no two inventory part numbers should have the same value, the inventory part number is a good field to search with (the unique key field).

```
' Filename: C26INV5.BAS
'
' Asks the user for an inventory part number, and
' prints that record from the inventory file.

CLS

TYPE invrec
   partno   AS STRING * 5
   descrip  AS STRING * 10
   quantity AS INTEGER
   price    AS SINGLE
END TYPE
DIM item AS invrec       ' A non-array variable of the record
DIM search.part AS STRING * 5  ' Must be a fixed string since
                               ' it will compare to the
                               ' record key
OPEN "C:INVEN.DAT" FOR RANDOM AS #1 LEN = 21

num.recs = LOF(1) / 21   ' The total number of records

PRINT "What part number do you want to see"
INPUT "(Type 0 to quit)"; search.part$

DO UNTIL (search.part$ = "0    ")
   found$ = "NO"   ' Will tell you if the part is in inventory
   FOR recnum = 1 TO num.recs
      GET #1, recnum, item    ' Get the next record
      IF (item.partno = search.part$) THEN ' Matched the file
         PRINT
         PRINT "The part number: "; item.partno
         PRINT "The description: "; item.descrip
         PRINT "The quantity:"; item.quantity
```

```
         PRINT "The price:"; item.price
         found$ = "YES"
         EXIT FOR
      END IF
   NEXT recnum    ' Get another record since the last one
                  ' did not match
   IF (found$ = "NO") THEN
      PRINT
      PRINT "That part is not in the inventory file"
      PRINT
   END IF
   PRINT
   PRINT "What part number do you want to see"
   INPUT "(Type 0 to quit)"; search.part$
LOOP

CLOSE
```

Notice that the key (`partno`) is a fixed string, so each string you compare to it must also be a fixed string. Figure 26.4 shows a user looking for an inventory item.

```
What part number do you want to see
(Type 0 to quit)? 812

That part is not in the inventory file


What part number do you want to see
(Type 0 to quit)? 321

The part number: 321
The description: Widgets
The quantity: 23
The price: 4.95

What part number do you want to see
(Type 0 to quit)?
```

Figure 26.4. The user requests an inventory record by entering the part number.

Changing a Random-Access File

When you find a random-access record, you can change it and write it back to the file. The advantage over sequential files is that the entire file does not have to be rewritten; only the record you want to change has to be rewritten.

When you find the record to change, you only have to perform a `PUT #`. QBasic remembers exactly where the record just read (with `GET #`) came from. After changing the record's field data (you can change any or all field data by assigning them other values), issue a `PUT #` to put the record back in its place.

Examples

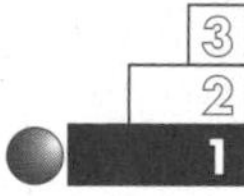

1. Suppose a company decides to add a letter *C* to each customer number stored in a customer file, and a *V* to each vendor number in a vendor file. (The company left enough room in these fields to add the prefix letter.) The following program opens the customer file and reads each customer record. It inserts a *C* before the customer number and writes each record back to the file. No other customer data is changed. Then the program does the same for the vendors.

```
' Filename: C26CV1.BAS
'
' Reads each record in a customer and vendor file and
' inserts a C or V in each file's customer and vendor number.
' No other fields in the files are changed.
'
TYPE custrec
   custnum  AS STRING * 8
   custname AS STRING * 15
   custaddr AS STRING * 20
   custcity AS STRING * 10
   custst   AS STRING * 2
   custzip  AS STRING * 5
   custbal  AS DOUBLE
END TYPE

TYPE vendrec
```

```
   vendnum  AS STRING * 10
   vendname AS STRING * 20
   vendaddr AS STRING * 20
   vendcity AS STRING * 10
   vendst   AS STRING * 2
   vendzip  AS STRING * 5
END TYPE

DIM customer AS custrec
DIM vendor   AS vendrec

OPEN "c:CUSTDATA.DAT" FOR RANDOM AS #1 LEN = LEN(customer)
cus.num.recs = LOF(1) / LEN(customer)    ' Total records in
                                         ' customer file
' Add the C to the customer number field
FOR rec = 1 TO cus.num.recs
   GET #1, rec, customer
   customer.custnum = LEFT$(("C" + customer.custnum), 8)
   ' Insert the C
   PUT #1, rec, customer' No other data needs to be changed
NEXT rec
CLOSE #1

' Add the V to the vendor number field
OPEN "c:VENDDATA.DAT" FOR RANDOM AS #2 LEN = LEN(vendor)
ven.num.recs = LOF(2) / LEN(vendor)    ' Total records in
                                       ' vendor file
FOR rec = 1 TO ven.num.recs
   GET #2, rec, vendor
   vendor.vendnum = LEFT$(("V" + vendor.vendnum), 10)
   ' Insert the V
   PUT #2, rec, vendor  ' No other data needs to be changed
NEXT rec
CLOSE #2
```

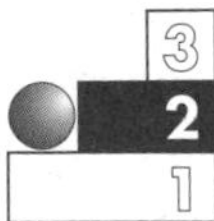

2. There is no need to explicitly define the entire record if you are changing only one field. For instance, the following program also adds the *C* and *V* to the customer and vendor files, but its TYPE statement defines a single string variable for all of the record except the field to change.

```
' Filename: C26CV2.BAS
'
' Reads each record in a customer and vendor file and
' inserts a C or V in each file's customer and vendor number.
' No other fields in the files are changed.
'
TYPE custrec
   custnum  AS STRING * 8
   other    AS STRING * 60 ' These fields will not be changed
END TYPE

TYPE vendrec
   vendnum  AS STRING * 10
   other    AS STRING * 57 ' These fields will not be changed
END TYPE

DIM customer AS custrec
DIM vendor   AS vendrec

OPEN "c:CUSTDATA.DAT" FOR RANDOM AS #1 LEN = LEN(customer)
cus.num.recs = LOF(1) / LEN(customer)    ' Total records in
                                         ' customer file
' Add the C to the customer number field
FOR rec = 1 TO cus.num.recs
   GET #1, rec, customer
   customer.custnum = LEFT$(("B" + customer.custnum), 8)
   ' Insert the C
   PUT #1, rec, customer  ' No other data needs to be changed
NEXT rec
CLOSE #1

' Add the V to the vendor number field
OPEN "c:VENDDATA.DAT" FOR RANDOM AS #2 LEN = LEN(vendor)
ven.num.recs = LOF(2) / LEN(vendor)    ' Total records in
                                       ' vendor file
FOR rec = 1 TO ven.num.recs
   GET #2, rec, vendor
   vendor.vendnum = LEFT$(("T" + vendor.vendnum), 10)
   ' Insert the V
   PUT #2, rec, vendor    ' No other data needs to be changed
NEXT rec
CLOSE #2
```

Consolidating the TYPE statement makes it easier to write the program because you do not have to specify each field in the TYPE statement.

Summary

You can now work with random-access files in QBasic. You saw that random-access files can still be read sequentially, but you can also read and write them in any order. You can also change a record in the middle of the file without affecting any surrounding records in the file. By ensuring that your random-access files have a unique field key, you can search the files for a record by using the key field; the first occurrence of that key field match will be the record the user wants.

This concludes the section on QBasic data files. You have the capability to store a large amount of data without relying on DATA statements to hold data. By using random-access files for your changing data, you ensure that you can easily update that data later.

Review Questions

Answers to the Review Questions are in Appendix B.

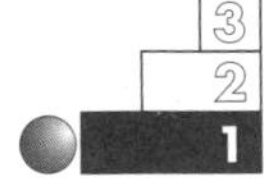

1. What is the advantage of random-access files over sequential files?
2. Which is preferred when you are defining a record:

   A. The TYPE statement
   B. The FIELD statement

3. Name the four functions that convert numeric data to string data for the FIELD statement.
4. Name the four functions that convert fielded string data back to its numeric equivalents.

5. TRUE or FALSE: Random-access records are fixed-length records.
6. What record is written if you do not specify a record number in the PUT # statement?

7. Why should a key field be unique?
8. What formula, using the `LOC()` function, returns the number of records in a file?
9. Why are the `MKtype$()` functions preferred over the `STR$()` function when you are converting numeric data to fielded string data?
10. How can a receiving function receive a passed record variable as a parameter?

Review Exercises

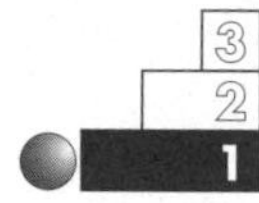

1. Write a `TYPE` statement that creates a record a hospital could use to track a patient's name and address information, the patient number, the doctor's name, and the patient's current balance.
2. Rewrite the record from the preceding exercise using a `FIELD` statement.
3. Write a simple data-entry program that fills the hospital file with patient data.

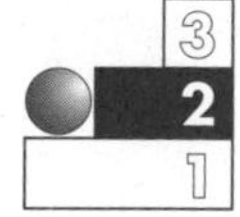

4. Combine exercise 1 and exercise 3 to produce a program the hospital's accounting department can use to print the name and number of every patient who owes more than $1,000.
5. Add a routine to the preceding exercise's program that lets the hospital change the current balance of a patient, given the patient number.

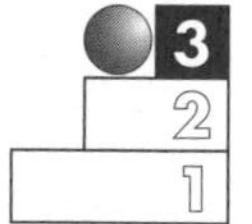

6. Add to the inventory program presented earlier so that the user can see a printed listing of every inventory part. Send the listing to the printer with appropriate titles.
7. Modify the student database program in Chapter 25, C25CNTRC.BAS, so that the students' names are stored in a random-access file rather than in a sequential file. Improve the add-student routine so that no two students can have the same student number. Also, let the user change a student's address and telephone number information if necessary.

Part VIII

Graphics and Sound

27

Drawing with QBasic

One of the most fun aspects of programming with QBasic is its graphics capabilities. You can draw lines and shapes, add color, and animate your art. Drawing is not only for playing; it is useful also for business graphics. It is said that a picture is worth a thousand words. Executives don't want to see a long list of numbers when a graph can show at a glance where the numbers are headed.

You must have a graphics adapter inside your computer and a graphics monitor attached to it before the drawing routines in this section will work. Available graphics adapters include the HGA (Hercules Graphics Adapter), CGA (Color Graphics Adapter), EGA (Enhanced Graphics Adapter), VGA (Video Graphics Array), and the MCGA (Memory Controller Gate Array) video cards.

There are many video graphics adapters on the market, and QBasic supports many of those. Sometimes the number of graphics adapters and possible colors confuses beginning programmers. Concentrate on those modes that match your graphics adapter. You can expand on the others as you get more accustomed to the options.

This chapter introduces

- ♦ Graphics and pixels
- ♦ The SCREEN statement
- ♦ The PSET and PRESET statements
- ♦ The LINE statement
- ♦ The CIRCLE statement
- ♦ The DRAW statement

Your Screen

The higher your screen's resolution, the sharper its picture is.

The difference in graphics adapters is measured by the number of colors each supports and the highest *resolution* possible. Resolution refers to the number of lines and columns on your screen. You already know that your PC screen can support 80 rows of 25 lines of text. In a graphics mode, the screen has more rows and columns. The intersection of a row and column represents a *picture element,* or a *pixel,* that is a dot on the screen. The more rows and columns of resolution (or the higher the resolution), the smaller each pixel is and the better picture you can draw; the lines are smoother and the image is crisper.

Several graphics modes are possible with most graphics adapters. When your program switches among modes, it selects a resolution and color combination. For instance, when you display graphics, your screen must be in a graphics mode. If there was text on the screen before the mode change, it is erased because changing to a graphics mode takes you out of the text mode.

TIP: The LOCATE command locates the next printed text at a row and column position but has no effect on locating pixels for graphics. You must use the graphics commands that are described later to locate and display pixels of graphics. If you are in a graphics mode, you can use LOCATE to print text.

All graphics on your computer are composed of many pixels. Lines, boxes, and circles are really just a group of pixels turned on while others are turned off (they are not displayed). Row and column combinations produce the pixel. Therefore, the higher the number of rows and columns, the more intersections there are and the better the graphics look.

The upper-left screen pixel is called the *home* location. It is located at column 0, row 0. This pixel is designated also with `(0, 0)`. This designation, in which the column number always comes first, is common. In other words, a pixel located at `(34, 50)` would be at graphics column *34* and graphics row *50.*

When you designate a pixel's location with its row and column intersection, it is known as a pixel *coordinate.* Obviously, the higher the resolution, the more coordinates possible, and the higher the row and column numbers can be. QBasic borrows from mathematics when it refers to its screen coordinates. The columns across the screen are known as the *x*-coordinates, whereas the rows down the screen are known as the *y*-coordinates. Therefore, the coordinate *(9, 56)* would refer to x-position *9* and y-position *56.*

The `SCREEN` statement sets your computer's graphics card to a certain resolution and color combination. The format of the `SCREEN` statement is

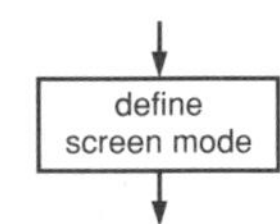


```
SCREEN mode [, colorswitch]
```

The *mode* can be any value in Table 27.1. Notice that in some modes, `SCREEN` supports several different resolutions of several different graphics adapters and monitors. One of these, mode *0*, supports only text modes. The rest support graphics and text modes. The modes that are most common and that pertain to true IBM-compatible graphics adapters are shown in Table 27.1.

Table 27.1. Graphics modes for the SCREEN statement.

SCREEN *Mode*	*Description*
0	The QBasic default for text resolution of 80 x 25. Supports up to 16 colors with CGA adapters and 16 out of 64 colors with EGA or VGA. This mode also supports up to eight video pages (numbered 0-7). This mode is for use with CGA, EGA, VGA, MCGA, and HGA.
1	320 x 200 graphics resolution. Also supports 40 x 25 text mode (all LOCATEs must be in this range). Supports 4 of 16 colors and one video page (0). For use with CGA, EGA, VGA, and MCGA.
2	640 x 200 graphics resolution. Also supports 80 x 25 text mode. Supports 2 of 16 colors (only one with CGA) and one video page (0). For use with CGA, EGA, VGA, and MCGA.
3	Requires the Hercules monochrome adapter (HGA). 728 x 348 graphics. Also supports 80 x 25 text and two video pages (0-1). For use only with HGA.
7	320 x 200 graphics resolution. Only supports 40 x 25 text mode (all LOCATEs must be in this range). Supports up to 16 colors and eight video pages (0-7) if the EGA has more than 64K RAM, otherwise two video pages (0-1). For use with EGA and VGA only.
8	640 x 200 graphics resolution. Also supports 80 x 25 text mode. Up to 16 colors and four video pages (0-3) if the EGA has more than 64K RAM, otherwise one video page (0). For use with EGA and VGA only.
9	640 x 350 graphics resolution. Also supports 80 x 25 text mode. Supports 16 of 64 colors and two video pages (0-1) if the adapter has more than 64K RAM, otherwise up to 16 colors and one video page (0). For use with EGA and VGA only.

SCREEN Mode	*Description*
10	640 x 350 monochrome graphics. Also supports 80 x 25 text mode. Supports four of nine shades and two video pages (0-1). For use with EGA and VGA with 256K and a monochrome monitor.
11	640 x 480 graphics resolution. Also supports 80 x 25 text mode. Supports 2 of 256K colors and one video page (0). For use with VGA and MCGA only.
12	640 x 480 graphics resolution. Also supports 80 x 30 text modes. Supports 16 of 256K colors and one video page (0). For use with VGA only.
13	320 x 200 graphics resolution. Also supports 40 x 25 text mode (all LOCATEs must be in this range). Supports 256 of 256K colors and one video page (0).

When you use a SCREEN statement to set a graphics mode, the rest of your graphics commands must be aware of the resolution you set with the SCREEN statement. In other words, if you type SCREEN 1 to initialize the screen to 320 x 200 resolution, no graphics commands can display a pixel past column 200. Many examples in this book use only SCREEN modes 0 (the default for text), 1, and 2 because these are so common and are available on almost every computer (from CGA adapters to VGA adapters).

It is a good idea to add the SCREEN 0 statement to the end of every program you write that uses graphics. This returns the video adapter to an 80-column text screen if you were in a graphics mode before.

Examples

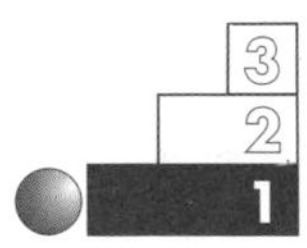

1. If you have a CGA adapter card and need to initialize a program for graphics, you can put the following statement at the top of your program:

```
SCREEN 1
```

This initializes your screen to 320 x 200 resolution.

2. If you want to display graphics in the highest possible resolution, you would type the following statement at the top of your program:

```
SCREEN 13
```

> **TIP:** You do not have to clear the screen (with CLS) before changing graphics modes. The SCREEN statement automatically clears the screen for you.

Drawing Pixels on the Screen

The most fundamental of all graphics statements turns pixels on and off. In Chapter 28, you will learn how to add color to your programs. For now, it is easiest to ignore colors and work with the default black and white (white pixels on a black background) colors that QBasic assumes. After you master the drawing commands, you can easily add colors.

The two commands that turn on and off pixels are PSET and PRESET. Their formats are

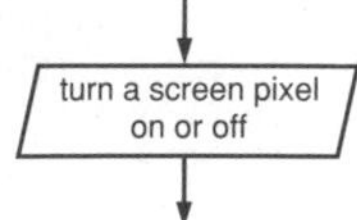


```
PSET [STEP] (x, y)
PRESET [STEP] (x, y)
```

The *x* and *y* values are integer numbers or variables representing the column and row intersections you want to turn on or off. The *x* and *y* values are absolute if you do not specify the STEP keyword. In other words, the statement

```
PSET (30, 67)
```

turns on the pixel at graphics x-position (column) 30 and y-position (row) 67. However, if you include the optional STEP keyword, as in

```
PSET STEP (30, 67)
```

QBasic turns on the pixel located at 30 and 67 positions *away* from the last PSET or PRESET statement. If there was not another graphics PSET or PRESET performed before the PSET STEP, QBasic turns on the pixel that is 30 and 67 positions away from the middle of the screen.

PRESET turns off any pixel located at its *row* and *col* (or relative to its *row* and *col* if you include STEP). If there is no pixel turned on at that location, PRESET does nothing.

PSET and PRESET are useful only when you need to do complex drawings. You can take advantage of the faster LINE and CIRCLE statements (described in the next section) for drawing lines and circles.

Examples

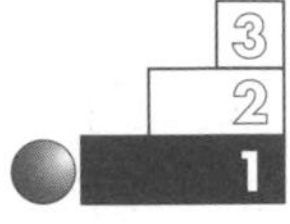

1. The following program puts the screen into a 640 x 200 pixel resolution and turns on several pixels on the screen.

```
' Filename: C27PIX1.BAS
'
' Turns on several pixels with PSET.
'
SCREEN 2    ' The 640 x 200 resolution

PSET (6, 10)    ' Turn on column 6, row 10
PSET (20, 20)   '           "      20    "     20
PSET (40, 50)   '  And so on
PSET (60, 90)
PSET (100, 101)   ' Draw a line of five pixels
PSET (100, 102)
PSET (100, 103)
PSET (100, 104)
PSET (100, 105)
PSET (200, 130)
PSET (250, 140)
PSET (300, 170)
PSET (400, 180)
PSET (500, 190)
PSET (639, 199)   ' The maximum coordinates for this mode
```

Because the screen's *x* and *y* numbers begin at (0, 0), the maximum values used in mode 2 are *639* and *199*. The SCREEN mode determines the maximum number of pixels you can turn on and off with PSET and PRESET.

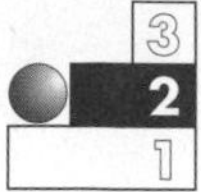

2. You can also add text using LOCATE and PRINT, as the following program shows.

```
' Filename: C27PIX2.BAS
'
' Turns on several pixels with PSET and prints a message.
'
SCREEN 2   ' The 640 x 200 resolution

PSET (6, 10)    ' Turn on row 6, column 10
PSET (20, 20)   '          "      20    "    20
PSET (40, 50)   '  And so on
PSET (60, 90)
PSET (100, 101)   ' Draw a line of five pixels
PSET (100, 102)
PSET (100, 103)
PSET (100, 104)
PSET (100, 105)
PSET (200, 130)
PSET (250, 140)
PSET (300, 170)
PSET (400, 180)
PSET (500, 190)
PSET (639, 199)   ' The maximum coordinates for this mode
LOCATE 12, 50     ' Locate a message
PRINT "Graphics are fun!"
```

Figure 27.1 shows the output from this program.

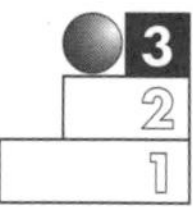

3. You can use FOR-NEXT loops to improve drawing with PSET. It gets to be cumbersome to have many PSET statements in a row when you want only to draw straight lines and dotted lines. The following program draws four diagonal lines on the screen. The first line is solid; the remaining lines have less "ink" because they are drawn with fewer pixels.

```
' Filename: C27PIX3.BAS
'
' Draws four diagonal lines on the screen.
'
' Draw the first solid line
SCREEN 2  ' 640 x 200 resolution
col = 1
```

```
FOR row = 1 TO 200
   PSET (col, row)
   col = col + 1   ' Move it over 1 column
NEXT

col = 20
FOR row = 1 TO 200
   PSET (col, row)
   col = col + 2   ' Move it over 2 columns
NEXT

col = 40
FOR row = 1 TO 200
   PSET (col, row)
   col = col + 3   ' Move it over 3 columns
NEXT

col = 60
FOR row = 1 TO 200
   PSET (col, row)
   col = col + 4   ' Move it over 4 columns
NEXT
```

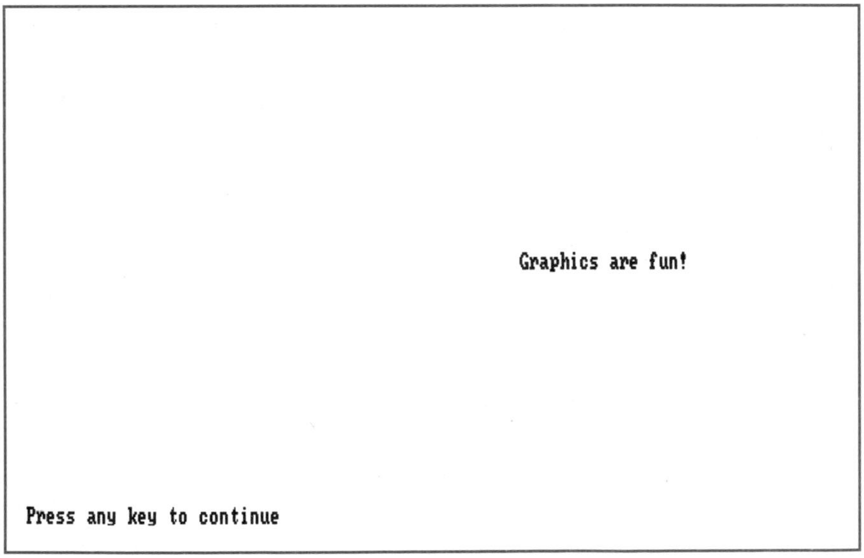

```
Graphics are fun!

Press any key to continue
```

Figure 27.1. Running a simple pixel program.

Figure 27.2 shows the output from this program.

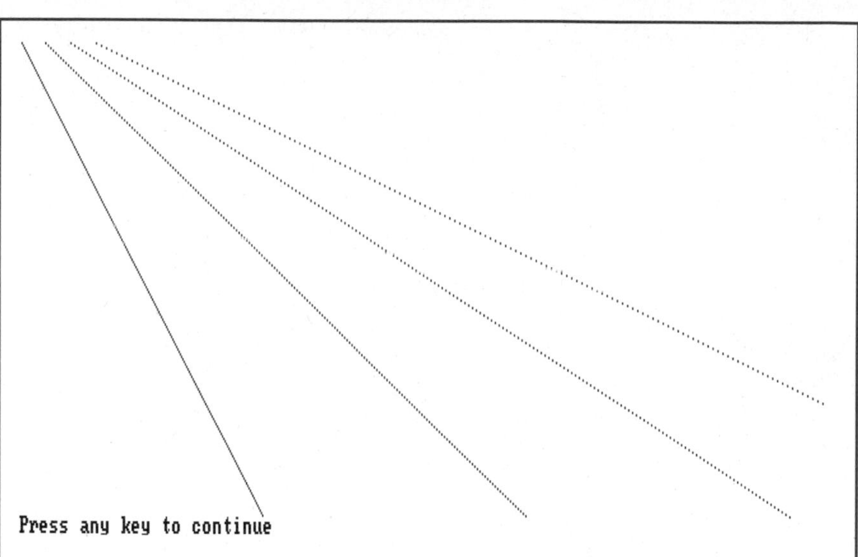
Press any key to continue

Figure 27.2. Drawing diagonal lines.

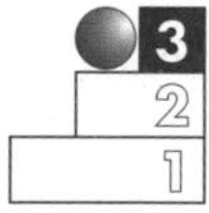

4. The following program is even fancier; it draws pixels randomly on the screen until the user presses any key. The `RND()` function determines the next screen coordinate to turn on or off. Each time through the loop, the program calculates a random value of *x* and *y* coordinate pairs to turn on and another to turn off. Eventually, the screen fills up with blinking lights.

```
' Filename: C27PIX4.BAS
'
' Randomly draws and turns off pixels until the user presses
' a key.
SCREEN 2    ' 640 x 200 resolution
LOCATE 12, 30
PRINT "Press any key to quit..."

RANDOMIZE TIMER  ' Reseed the random number generator
```

```
DO
   x = INT(RND * 640) + 1   ' Select a random coordinate
   y = INT(RND * 200) + 1
   PSET (x, y)     ' Turn it on

   x = INT(RND * 640) + 1
   y = INT(RND * 200) + 1
   PRESET (x, y)  ' Turn another one off

   key.press$ = INKEY$    ' Look for a keypress
LOOP UNTIL (key.press$ <> "")
```

Figure 27.3 shows the output from this program.

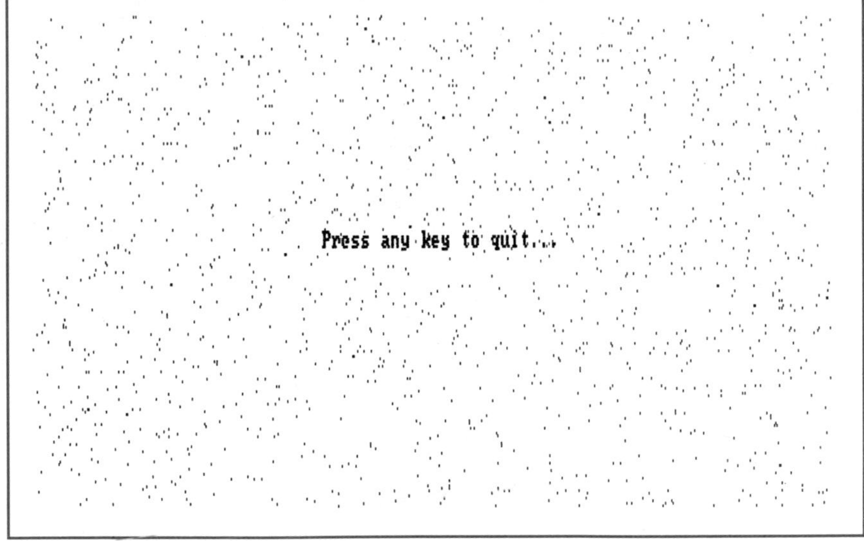

Figure 27.3. A screenful of on and off pixels appears.

Drawing Lines and Boxes

Although the PSET is good for individual pixels, it is slow for drawing lines and boxes. Because your program first has to calculate each pixel in the line or box, the results are fairly slow. QBasic offers the LINE statement to help make your line-drawing easier and faster. Instead of collecting a group of PSET statements to draw a line or box, the LINE does all the work at once.

The LINE statement draws both lines and boxes, depending on the format you use.

Drawing Straight Lines with LINE

The simplest format of LINE draws a line from one coordinate to another. The format of the LINE statement is

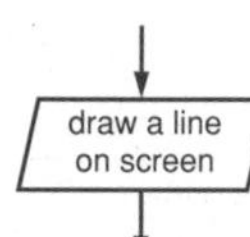


```
LINE [[STEP] (x1, y1)] - [STEP] (x2, y2)
```

The *x1* and *y1* values define the beginning point (coordinate) of the line, and the *x2* and *y2* coordinates define where the line ends. Of course, the coordinates cannot exceed the resolution of the screen mode set with the SCREEN statement. The following statement draws a line from pixel (100, 100) to pixel (150, 150):

```
LINE (100, 100) - (150, 150)
```

As with PSET and PRESET, the STEP option draws the line relative to the starting location (the last pixel drawn or turned off). You do not have to include the starting coordinate pair because it knows where to begin. Therefore, by using STEP, some of the coordinates may be negative, such as

```
LINE STEP (-15, 0)
```

(which means draw a line from the last pixel drawn to a point 15 pixels to the left of the last pixel drawn). If you have not drawn anything, STEP draws 15 pixels to the left of your screen's center pixel.

There is no mandatory order of LINE's parameters. You can draw up, down, to the left, or to the right.

Dotted Lines

You can draw dotted lines with DRAW if you are comfortable with binary and hexadecimal numbers. The format of LINE for dotted lines is

```
LINE [[STEP] (x1, y1)] - (x2, y2),,,style
```

(The three commas are required. You insert values between them when you use `LINE` to draw boxes and color lines.) The *`style`* must be a 16-bit integer. Typically, programmers use a hexadecimal integer (with the `&H` prefix) because it is easy to convert between binary and hexadecimal. The binary value of the integer determines the way the dotted line looks. For example, `&H5555` looks like `0101010101010101` binary. Therefore, if you use `&H5555` as the *`style`*, the line drawn is dotted (a dot for each `1` in the binary number).

Other values such as `&H3333` and `&HF0F0` are interesting as well. `&H3333` is `0011001100110011` in binary, which produces a dashed line, and `&HF0F0` is `1111111100000000`, which produces a more dramatic dashed line (with longer dashes).

Examples

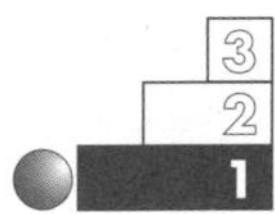

1. The following program draws three horizontal lines on the screen.

```
' Filename: C27LIN1.BAS
'
' Draws three straight lines.
SCREEN 1   ' Resolution of 320 x 200

LINE (10, 1) - (310, 1)
LINE (10, 100) - (310, 100)
LINE (10, 190) - (310, 190)
```

2. The `LINE` statement also draws diagonal lines, although they might not draw quite as smoothly as horizontal or vertical lines. The following program draws a diagonal line from the upper-left corner of the screen to the lower-right corner.

```
' Filename: C27LIN2.BAS
'
' Draws a diagonal line down the screen.
SCREEN 1 ' 320 x 200
LINE (0, 0)-(319, 199)    ' Draws the entire line
```

3. The following program uses some loops to draw lines that step down the screen. A short line is drawn, and then the FOR-NEXT loop changes the coordinates to draw the next one.

```
' Filename: C27LIN3.BAS
'
' Draws a diagonal stepping line down the screen.
SCREEN 1 ' 320 x 200

PSET (0, 0)    ' Set initial pixel starting location to 0, 0

FOR ctr = 1 TO 12
   LINE -STEP(25, 0)
   LINE -STEP(0, 15)
NEXT ctr
```

Figure 27.4 shows the output from this program.

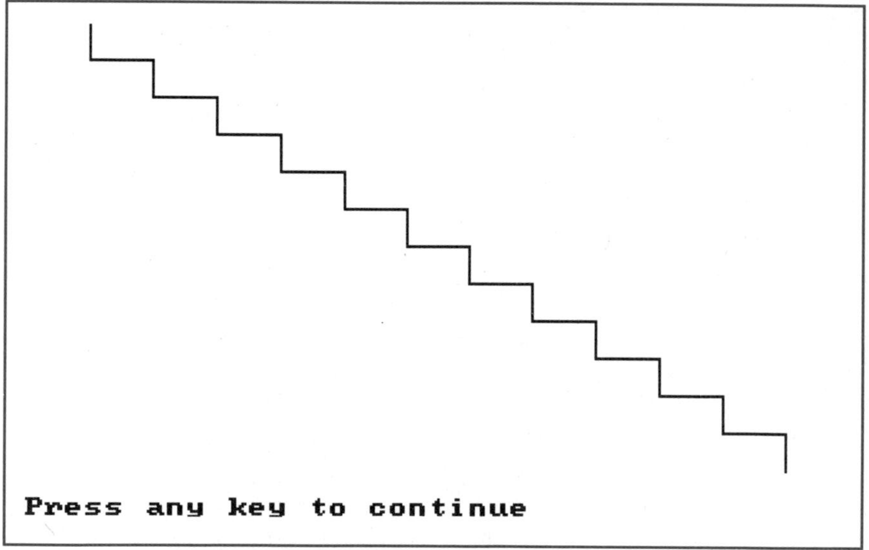
Press any key to continue

Figure 27.4. Drawing a staircase with LINE.

Drawing Boxes with LINE

The preceding example showed you how the LINE command draws boxes. When using LINE in this way, however, you have to draw the four sides of the box with four different LINE statements. There is an additional option you can add to LINE to draw a box or rectangle with a single LINE statement. The box-drawing LINE statement format is

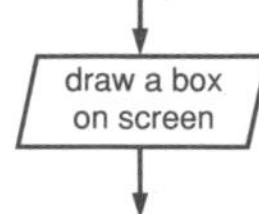


```
LINE (x1, y1) - (x2, y2) ,, B
```

A color attribute goes between the coordinates and the B. If you do not specify a color (which you will not learn to do until Chapter 28), you still need to include the empty comma before the B. The two coordinates specify the upper-left and the lower-right corners of the rectangle.

Examples

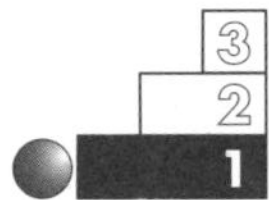

1. The following program draws a box in the middle of the screen. The upper-left corner is located at (20, 20), and the lower-left corner is located at (100, 100).

```
' Filename: C27BOX1.BAS
'
' Draws a single box on the screen.

SCREEN 2  ' 640 x 200

LINE (20, 20) - (100, 100),, B
```

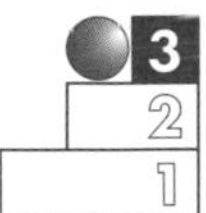

2. Here is a multiple box-drawing program (from the preceding section) that uses the box option of LINE rather than four separate LINE statements to draw a box.

```
' Filename: C27BOX2.BAS
'
' Draws boxes inside boxes with a single LINE statement.

SCREEN 1 ' 320 x 200
```

```
startx = 0      ' Defines the
starty = 0      ' four sides'
lastx = 319     ' starting and
lasty = 199     ' ending positions

FOR count = 1 TO 20

   LINE (startx, starty)-(lastx, lasty), , B ' Draw complete box

   startx = startx + 5      ' Prepare the next set of sides
   starty = starty + 5
   lastx = lastx - 5
   lasty = lasty - 5

NEXT count

DO
LOOP WHILE (INKEY$ = "")  ' Waits until the user presses a key
```

Drawing Circles and Ellipses

The CIRCLE statement lets you draw circles and ellipses (stretched circles). If you want to draw round circles, the format of CIRCLE is

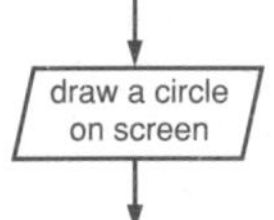


```
CIRCLE [STEP] (x, y), radius
```

The *x* and *y* values determine the center point of the circle, and the *radius* is the distance in pixels between the center point of the circle and its outer edge. If you include the STEP keyword, the *x* and *y* coordinates are relative (negative values are allowed) from the current (last-drawn) pixel.

To draw a stretched circle (an ellipse), you must also add an *aspect ratio* to the CIRCLE statement (after some commas that are placeholders for color commands you will learn later). The format of the ellipse CIRCLE statement is

```
CIRCLE [STEP] (x, y), radius,,,, aspect
```

The *aspect* value means two different things, depending on its value. If the value is less than *1*, it refers to the x-radius (the circle is stretched *widely* across the x coordinate). If the *aspect* is greater than or equal to *1*, it refers to the y-radius (the circle is stretched *lengthwise* up and down the y coordinate). Figure 27.5 shows an example of each type of radius.

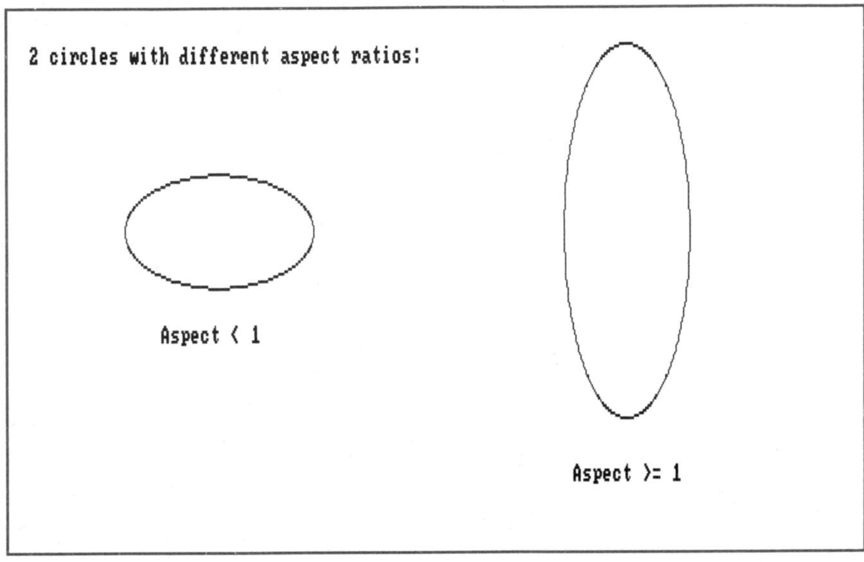

Figure 27.5. The x-radius and y-radius aspect ratios.

The aspect ratio acts as a multiplier of each radius. For example, an aspect of *4* means that the circle is vertically stretched four times the regular circle's height. An aspect ratio of *(4/10/2)* (or .2) means the circle is horizontally stretched five times its regular radius (one-half of 40 percent).

Examples

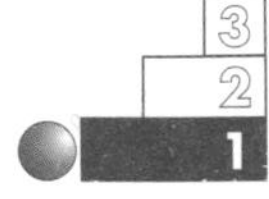

1. The following program simply draws a circle in the middle of the screen.

```
' Filename: C27CIR1.BAS
'
' Draws a circle in the center of the screen.
'
SCREEN 2  ' 640 x 200 resolution

CIRCLE (320, 100), 200
```

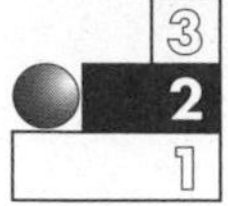

2. The following program draws two ellipses: one with a stretched x-radius and one with a stretched y-radius.

```
' Filename: C27CIR2.BAS
'
' Draws two ellipses on the screen.
'
SCREEN 2  ' 640 x 200 resolution

CIRCLE (150, 100), 50, , , , 4
CIRCLE (500, 100), 50, , , , (4 / 10 / 2)
```

This program produced the output previously shown in Figure 27.5.

Randomly Drawing with DRAW

There is a command called DRAW that includes its own built-in drawing language. There are many options to the DRAW statement, and some are covered here. The DRAW statement is similar to the Etch-a-Sketch you might have used as a child. DRAW leaves a trail as it draws, letting you draw lines without having to have a separate LINE statement for each.

The format for DRAW is

```
DRAW drawingstring
```

The language of the DRAW statement goes inside the *drawingstring*. There are many commands you can place in the *drawingstring* expression. You can have more than one of them. Table 27.2 lists the commands this book covers.

Table 27.2. The language commands of the DRAW statement.

Command	*Description*
B	Move without drawing.
N	Move and draw, but return to the original position when finished.
U*n*	Move up *n* pixels and draw while moving.
D*n*	Move down *n* pixels and draw while moving.
L*n*	Move left *n* pixels and draw while moving.
R*n*	Move right *n* pixels and draw while moving.
E*n*	Move diagonally up and to the right *n* pixels and draw while moving.
F*n*	Move diagonally down and to the right *n* pixels and draw while moving.
G*n*	Move diagonally down and to the left *n* pixels and draw while moving.
H*n*	Move diagonally up and to the left *n* pixels and draw while moving.
M*x,y*	Move to coordinate *x,y* and draw while moving.
M+*x,y*, M-*x,y*	Move to relative coordinates *x,y* places from the current pixel position and draw while moving.

Figure 27.6 shows eight of the most-used commands in another way. It illustrates the direction of the eight move and draw commands. By combining the move without drawing (B) commands, you can sketch your own lines as though you were drawing on a tablet with a pen.

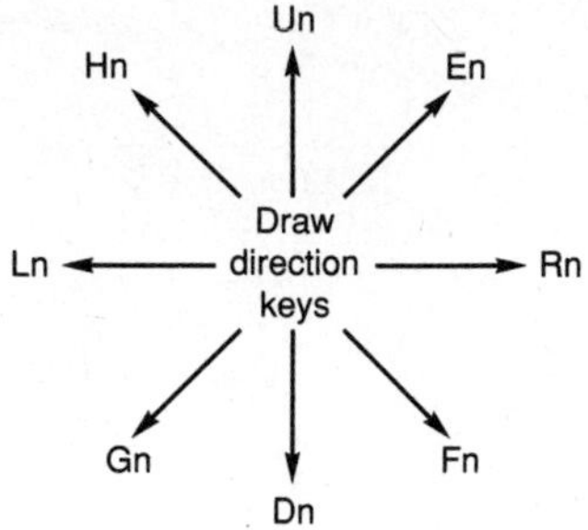

Figure 27.6. DRAW commands and their directions.

Examples

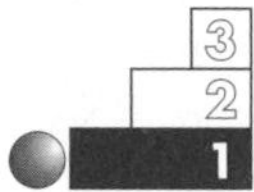

1. The following simple program draws a right angle by drawing up 50 units, then right 50 units.

```
' Filename: C27DRAW1.BAS
'
' Draws a right angle.
SCREEN 2    ' 640 x 200 resolution

DRAW "U 50"    ' Up 50 units
DRAW "R 50"    ' Right 50 units
```

The output is shown in Figure 27.7. Although both legs of the right angle are 50 units, the vertical (y-axis) of the angle is longer because there are fewer pixels on the y-axis (only 200 compared to 640 on the x-axis), so the pixels must be longer vertically than horizontally.

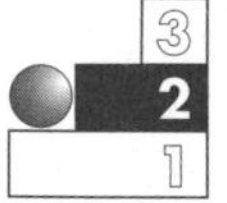

2. You can combine your drawing commands in a single string. The following program works exactly like the previous one.

```
' Filename: C27DRAW2.BAS
'
' Draws a right angle.
SCREEN 2          ' 640 x 200 resolution

DRAW "U50 R50"    ' Up and right 50 units
```

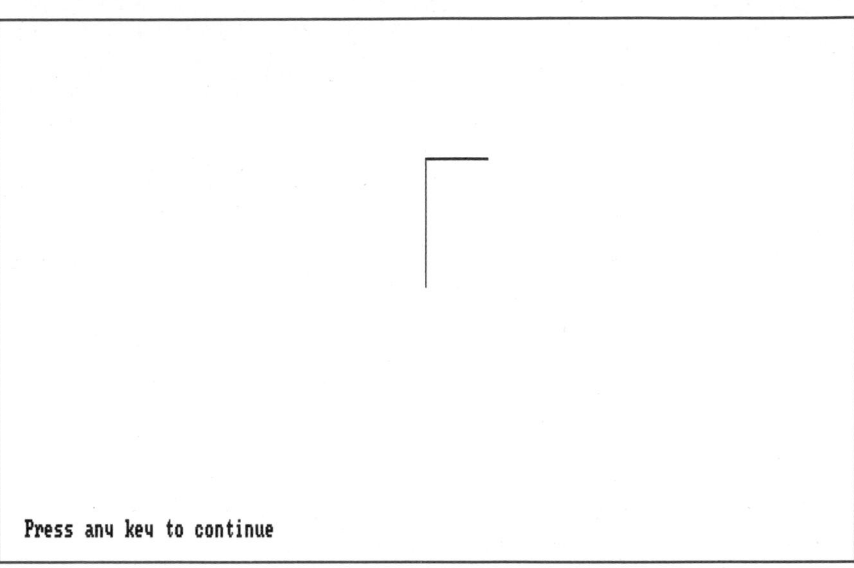
Press any key to continue

Figure 27.7. Drawing a simple right angle with DRAW.

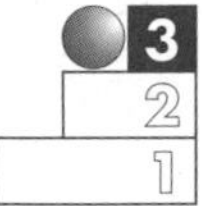

3. The following program draws two boxes on the screen. In this example, it might have been easier to use the LINE box-drawing command, but the example helps show what the DRAW can do and how it works.

```
' Filename: C27DRAW3.BAS
'
' Draws four boxes on the screen with DRAW.
SCREEN 2   ' 640 x 200 resolution

DRAW "BM100,50"    ' Move toward middle without drawing

DRAW "D50 R50 U50 L50"   ' Draw the box

DRAW "BM200,50"    ' Move to next box location without drawing

DRAW "D50 R50 U50 L50"   ' Draw another box

DRAW "BM300, 50"   ' Move to next box location without drawing

DRAW "D50 R50 U50 L50"   ' Draw another box
```

```
DRAW "BM400, 50"  ' Move to next box location without drawing

DRAW "D50 R50 U50 L50"
```

Figure 27.8 shows the result of running this program.

Press any key to continue

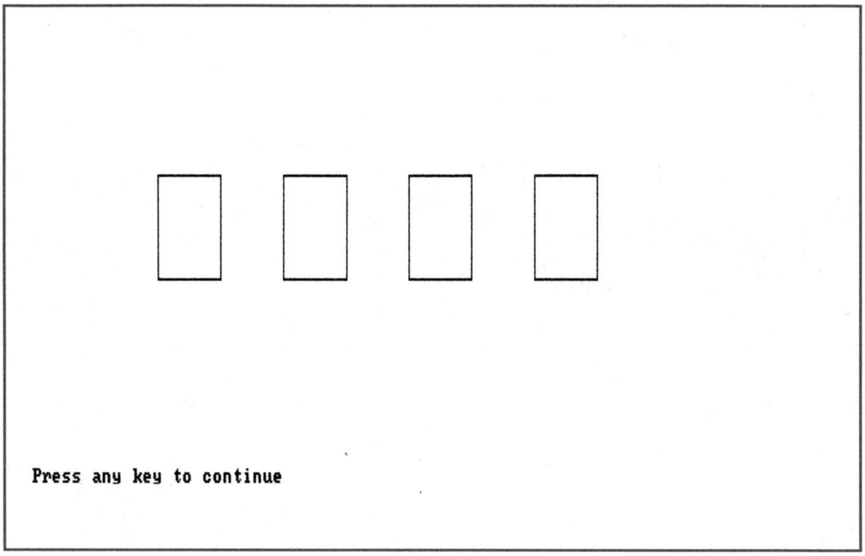

Figure 27.8. Using DRAW to draw four boxes.

Summary

This chapter introduced the world of drawing with QBasic. You should have seen that drawing is easy using QBasic's commands. You can draw a pixel or an entire figure at once, depending on the command you choose.

There is much more to these commands. There are additional commands that add colors and different types of shading to your art. The next chapter describes colors and their use with the graphics commands. Many of the commands you learned in this chapter have color options so that you can set the color when you draw a figure.

Review Questions

Answers to the Review Questions are in Appendix B.

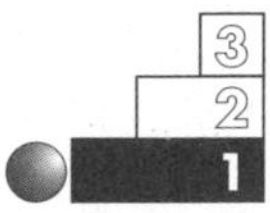

1. What type of video card must you have to display graphics?
2. What does *pixel* stand for?
3. What commands turn on and off individual pixels?

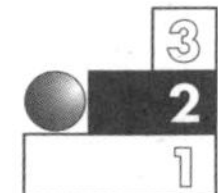

4. TRUE or FALSE: The `LOCATE` command positions you at the next pixel to display.
5. TRUE or FALSE: The `LOCATE` command locates your next `PRINT` command, even if you are in a graphics mode.

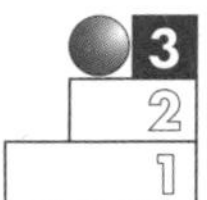

6. Which statement is easiest to use for drawing boxes?

   A. `PSET`
   B. `LINE`
   C. `BOX`
   D. `DRAW`

7. TRUE or FALSE: The `DRAW` command is good only for continuous drawings in which the entire picture is drawn with a connecting line.
8. What does the *`aspect ratio`* number of the `CIRCLE` command do?

Review Exercises

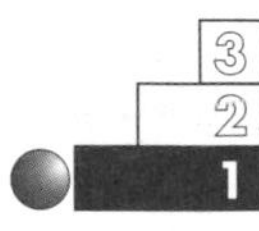

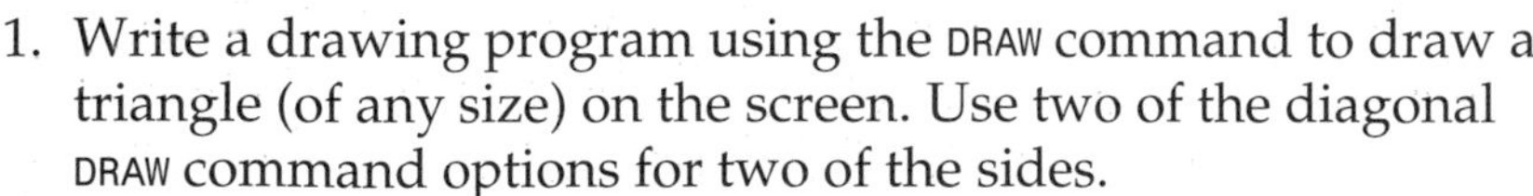

1. Write a drawing program using the `DRAW` command to draw a triangle (of any size) on the screen. Use two of the diagonal `DRAW` command options for two of the sides.

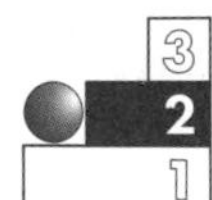

2. Write a program that asks the users what they want to see from a menu. Give them a choice of a box, a rectangle, a circle, or an ellipse.

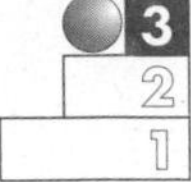

3. Rewrite the program in the preceding exercise so that it calls subroutine procedures for each type of graphics on the menu. Ask the user for sizes as needed. For instance, if the user wants to see a circle, you have to ask the user for the radius (always assume a starting position of the middle of the screen). If the user wants to see a square, ask the user how many pixels wide the square should be. Pass these values to the drawing procedures that need them as local variables.

4. Add to the sketching drawing program so that the user can draw diagonally in any of the four directions, as well as lift the pen up and down. If the pen is up, move the graphics cursor but do not draw anything. In the next chapter, you will learn how to color the parts of a picture to give your user a really nice drawing program.

28

Adding Colors to Graphics

This chapter expands on some of the graphics statements you learned in Chapter 27. Depending on your graphics adapter, you can add different colors to your drawings. Colors improve the enjoyment and ease of watching your programs.

This chapter introduces

- Colors in QBasic
- Adding colors to graphics statements
- Changing background colors
- Colors for CGA graphics adapters
- Colors for EGA and VGA graphics adapters
- The PALETTE statement
- The PAINT statement

There are so many color options available in QBasic that it would be difficult to cover them all here, especially in light of the fact that each graphics adapter handles colors in a different way. Instead of being an exhaustive walk-through of every possible color option for every possible graphics adapter and monitor, this chapter attempts to explore some of the common routines available for the majority of graphics adapters that most readers own. When you master the basic color concepts, you will find it easy to program the specific options available for your adapter.

QBasic and Color

The authors of QBasic chose to give you a wide variety of color programming tools, many of which you might never use. Color graphics add flair to almost any application. Suppose you decide to write a payroll program that you want to sell. A colorful opening graphics screen gets your customers' attention and makes your program look as though you put a lot of work into it (although graphics do not necessarily require much work).

To give you an idea of the range of possible colors, look at Table 28.1, which is the QBasic color attribute chart that shows possible colors for both color and monochrome video adapters in each of the SCREEN modes. Of course, no color is possible with monochrome adapters except the adapter's native two-color mode, but you can set attributes, such as underlining and high intensity, with a monochrome adapter. Table 28.1 explains those attributes. Most of the examples in this book stay with common color combinations possible for users with CGA, EGA, and VGA adapters. If your video adapter is VGA or MCGA, you might want to experiment with other color settings.

> **TIP:** Throughout this chapter, you might want to look at Table 27.1 from the previous chapter. It describes the possible resolutions.

Table 28.1. The range of possible color attributes for color and monochrome adapters.

Color Monitors		*Monochrome Monitors*	
Color Attribute	*Displayed Color*	*Default Color Value*	*Displayed Color*
SCREEN **Modes 0, 7, 8, 9(a), 12, and 13**			
0	Black	0**(b)**	Off
1	Blue		Underlined**(c)**
2	Green	1**(b)**	On**(c)**
3	Cyan	1**(b)**	On**(c)**
4	Red	1**(b)**	On**(c)**
5	Magenta	1**(b)**	On**(c)**
6	Brown	1**(b)**	On**(c)**
7	White	1**(b)**	On**(c)**
8	Gray	0**(b)**	Off
9	Light blue		High-intensity Underlined
10	Light green	2**(b)**	High-intensity
11	Light cyan	2**(b)**	High-intensity
12	Light red	2**(b)**	High-intensity
13	Light magenta	2**(b)**	High-intensity
14	Yellow	2**(b)**	High-intensity
15	High-intensity white	2**(b)**	High-intensity

continues

Table 28.1. continued

Color Monitors		*Monochrome Monitors*	
Color Attribute	*Displayed Color*	*Default Color Value*	*Displayed Color*
SCREEN **Modes 1 and 9(d)**			
0	Black	0	Off
1	Light cyan	2	High-intensity
2	Light magenta	2	High-intensity
3	High-intensity white	0	Off white

Notes:

(a) For VGA or EGA with video memory > 64K.

(b) Only for mode 0.

(c) Off when used for background.

(d) EGA with video memory <= 64K.

Not all the color resolutions you read about in the preceding chapter are covered here (for instance, SCREEN modes 10 and 11), because not all of them support colors.

Adding Colors to Graphics Statements

All the graphics statements you learned in the preceding chapter have optional color arguments. Their new formats with the color options are

```
PSET (x,y), color
PRESET (x,y), color
LINE (x1,y2) - (x2,y2), color
LINE (x1,y1) - (x2,y2), color, B
CIRCLE (x,y), radius, color
CIRCLE (x, y), radius, color,,, aspect
```

The *color* value is a number from Table 28.1 that is consistent with the SCREEN mode you are in. For example, if you have an EGA graphics adapter that has less than 64K of RAM and you set the SCREEN mode to 9, the *color* values can range from 0 to 3 to make the colors black, light cyan, light magenta, and high-intensity white, respectively.

The DRAW statement also has a color option as part of its miniature programming language. The command added to your DRAW statement's string draws a line of that number's color. As with all the graphics statements' color options, you must ensure that the number you use corresponds to the SCREEN mode's available colors.

Examples

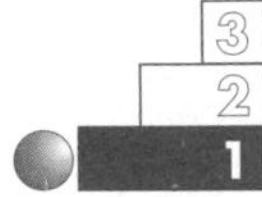

1. The following program draws a light cyan circle in the middle of the screen. The background is black, because that is the default color of the screen.

```
' Filename: C281.BAS
'
' Draws a light cyan circle in the center of the screen.
'
SCREEN 1   ' 320 x 200 resolution

CIRCLE (165, 100), 50, 1
```

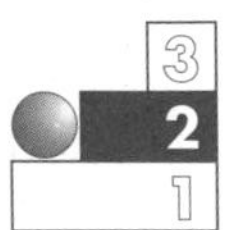

2. Here is a three-rectangle box-drawing program similar to one from the preceding chapter. It draws three rectangles, each with a different color. It uses SCREEN mode *1*, which limits the number of colors to three. There are four possible colors in SCREEN mode *1*, but the background is black, so a black rectangle would not be seen if it were drawn.

```
' Filename: C28LINE1.BAS
'
' Draws three rectangles in three different colors.

SCREEN 1    ' 320 x 200
```

```
' Draw the boxes of different colors
LINE (80, 50)-(120, 100), 1, B    ' Box of light cyan color
LINE (130, 50)-(170, 100), 2, B   ' Box of light magenta color
LINE (180, 50)-(220, 100), 3, B   ' Box of high-intensity
                                  ' white color
```

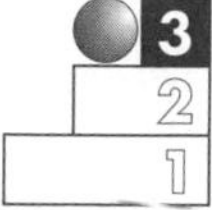

3. The following program draws random circles all over the screen in any of three random colors. It uses a SCREEN mode 1, which limits the number of colors to four. The color black (color number 0) is used, although the background is black, because the black circles eventually appear over the other colors and show up when the program draws them.

```
' Filename: C282.BAS
'
' Draws random circles in three colors on the screen.
'
SCREEN 1   ' 320 x 200 resolution

FOR count = 1 TO 350

   x = INT(RND * 640) + 1
   y = INT(RND * 200) + 1
   radius = INT(RND * 200) + 1
   s.color = INT(RND * 5)  ' Produces random color, 0 to 4
   CIRCLE (x, y), radius, s.color

NEXT count
```

When programming such a program, resist the temptation to call the color variable *color*. That is reserved for the QBasic COLOR statement.

4. Here is the sketching program rewritten for a color graphics adapter. It assumes a SCREEN mode of 7, which means that you must have an EGA or a VGA graphics adapter to run it. This mode was chosen because of its large number of colors.

   The standard drawing routine has been maintained. As the user presses U, D, L, and R, the screen draws up, down, left, and right. In addition, the user can press a number from 0 to

9 to see the next drawn line in one of 10 different colors. Although more colors are possible with the SCREEN mode 7, only 10 were used to keep the program simple.

```
' Filename: C28DRAW1.BAS
'
' Lets user sketch a continuous colorful line drawing on the
' screen.
'
SCREEN 7   ' 320 x 200 resolution

DO
   user.key$ = INKEY$
   SELECT CASE UCASE$(user.key$)
      CASE "U": DRAW "U"
      CASE "D": DRAW "D"
      CASE "L": DRAW "L"
      CASE "R": DRAW "R"
      CASE "Q": EXIT DO
      CASE "0" TO "9": DRAW "C" + user.key$   ' Append color
                                              ' number to string
  END SELECT
LOOP UNTIL (UCASE$(user.key$) = "Q")

SCREEN 0, 0  ' Restore the screen to 80 x 25 text
```

Example Color Setup Program

If you find yourself displaying colors in many programs, it might be worth your time to create a program similar to the following one that makes your coloring much easier. The program takes the color values for one of the SCREEN modes in Table 28.1 (in this case, for SCREEN mode 8) and assigns them to constants. If you assign these colors to constants using CONST, they cannot inadvertently be changed later in the program. You could put these defined colors at the top of a main program module that uses them. They will be global for the rest of the program, including all subroutines and functions that use them.

```
' Filename: C28.BAS
'
' Defines color constants for SCREEN mode 9.
'
' You can change these values for your own
' video adapter.

SCREEN 9   ' VGA and High-RAM EGA adapters, 640 x 350 resolution

CONST Black = 0
CONST Blue = 1
CONST Green = 2
CONST Cyan = 3
CONST Red = 4
CONST Magenta = 5
CONST Brown = 6
CONST White = 7
CONST Gray = 8
CONST H.Blue = 9
CONST H.Green = 10
CONST H.Cyan = 11
CONST H.Red = 12
CONST H.Magenta = 13
CONST Yellow = 14
CONST Hi.White = 15

' As an example, to draw three circles of three
' different colors, you could:

CIRCLE (165, 100), 50, Red
CIRCLE (165, 100), 60, Green
CIRCLE (165, 100), 70, Blue
CIRCLE (165, 100), 80, Brown
```

This keeps you from having to look up the table of color values for your adapter. The constant names are much easier to remember than the numbers associated with them.

Changing the Foreground and Background Colors

You saw one form of the COLOR statement in Chapter 10, "Producing Better Output," when you learned how to display text in different foreground and background colors. There are several extended formats of COLOR, depending on the SCREEN mode you use. All QBasic programs assume a SCREEN mode of 0 (the text mode). If you change the SCREEN mode, you can use one of the following COLOR statements:

```
COLOR [foreground][,[background][,border]]   ' For SCREEN 0
COLOR [background][, palette]                ' For SCREEN 1
COLOR [foreground][, background]             ' For SCREEN 7-9
COLOR [foreground]                           ' For SCREEN 12-13
```

NOTE: The *border* color is available only for CGA adapter cards.

The first COLOR statement, for SCREEN 0, is exactly like the one you read about in Chapter 10. It is reserved to change text colors and is not covered again here. Your adapter card determines the range of colors possible. If you own a CGA card that can display only four colors at a time, you cannot get more by using the COLOR statement. CGA users can display 16 colors in text mode.

To get an idea of possible COLOR modes and how to use them, read the section that pertains to your needs and graphics adapter.

CGA COLOR Mode Examples

Besides the text SCREEN mode 0, the CGA also supports SCREEN mode 1. The CGA adapter can display four colors at a time. (SCREEN mode 2 offers only two colors on the CGA: white or black.) The default colors, as shown in Table 28.1, are black, light cyan, light magenta, and high-intensity white. These are the colors on *palette* 1.

A QBasic palette is a collection of possible colors, just like an artist's palette of colors. If you specify the other palette, palette 0, you can choose another four colors. Table 28.2 shows these CGA palette colors.

Table 28.2. The CGA palette colors.

Palette Number	*Colors and Their Numbers*
0	0—Black, 1—Green, 2—Red, 3—Brown
1	0—Black, 1—Light cyan, 2—Light magenta, 3—High-intensity white

> **NOTE:** A PALETTE statement used for EGA, VGA, and MCGA color adapters is described later in this chapter. CGA users do not use the PALETTE statement.

Notice that the COLOR statement for SCREEN mode 1 specifies the background color as well as the palette. The palette must be 0 or 1 to specify which palette colors you want.

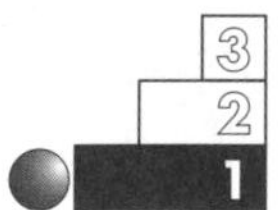

1. Suppose you want to draw a red box on a green screen. You must use the COLOR statement after specifying the SCREEN mode 1 (the CGA graphics mode) to set up the background color. The LINE statement takes care of the foreground color.

```
' Filename: C28CGA1.BAS
'
' Draws a red box on a green background (CGA only).

SCREEN 1    ' CGA's only color graphics mode, other than text
            ' mode 0
COLOR 2, 0

LINE (50, 50)-(100, 100), 2, B   ' Draw the box
```

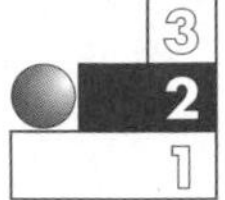

2. The following program draws three circles using one palette set, then changes the palette to the other set when the user presses a key. The two sets of colors cannot be on the screen at the same time. When you change the palette, the colors change as well.

```
' Filename: C28CGA2.BAS
'
' Draws colored circles (CGA only) and then changes palettes
' when the user presses a key.


SCREEN 1      ' CGA's only color graphics mode, other than
              ' text mode 0
COLOR 1, 0    ' The red, green, brown palette

CIRCLE (50, 50), 40, 1
CIRCLE (150, 100), 40, 2
CIRCLE (250, 150), 40, 3

PRINT "Press any key to change colors..."

DO
LOOP WHILE (INKEY$ = "")    ' Wait on a user keypress

COLOR 1, 1    ' The cyan, magenta, white palette
```

EGA and VGA COLOR Mode Examples

You have a lot more color options if you have an EGA or a VGA (see Table 28.1), especially if your EGA adapter has more than 64K of memory. The second and third formats of the COLOR statement set the background and foreground colors for graphics. The most critical color to set is the background color, because you determine the foreground color with each graphics statement (such as PSET, LINE, and so on).

If you have an EGA or a VGA, you might want to use the PALETTE command (described later in this chapter) to change your available colors.

Examples

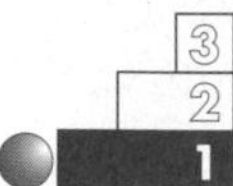

1. Here is a VGA program that draws a red circle on a green background. The green background comes from the COLOR statement, and the red circle results from the color attribute (number 4) after the CIRCLE statement.

```
' Filename: C28EVGA1.BAS
'
' Displays a red circle on a green background.
'
SCREEN 7    ' 320 x 200 EGA/VGA resolution
COLOR , 2   ' Green background

CIRCLE (150, 100), 50, 4    ' The 4 is the red color attribute
                            ' number
```

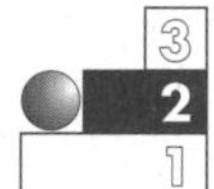

2. The preceding program used a low-resolution (320 x 200) SCREEN mode. The next program draws a crisper line because it uses the higher resolution (640 x 350) SCREEN mode 9.

```
' Filename: C28EVGA2.BAS
'
' Displays high-resolution red circle on a green background.
'
SCREEN 9    ' 640 x 350 EGA/VGA resolution
COLOR , 2   ' Green background

CIRCLE (320, 175), 150, 4   ' The 4 is the red color attribute
                            ' number
```

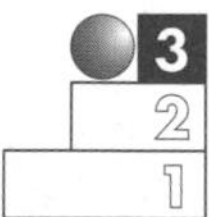

3. Here is the sketching program. The first number the user types changes the background color. After that, the user presses the U, D, L, and R keys to draw up, down, left, and right. The user also uses numbers to control the drawing color.

```
' Filename: C28EVGA3.BAS
'
' Lets user sketch a continuous colorful line drawing on the
' screen.
```

```
' The first value designates the background color.

SCREEN 9   ' 640 x 350 resolution

DO
   user.key$ = INKEY$       ' Get the background color
LOOP WHILE (user.key$ = "")

COLOR , VAL(user.key$)    ' Set the background color

DO
   user.key$ = INKEY$
   SELECT CASE UCASE$(user.key$)
      CASE "U": DRAW "U"
      CASE "D": DRAW "D"
      CASE "L": DRAW "L"
      CASE "R": DRAW "R"
      CASE "Q": EXIT DO
      CASE "0" TO "9": DRAW "C" + user.key$  ' Append color
                                             ' number to string
  END SELECT
LOOP UNTIL (UCASE$(user.key$) = "Q")

SCREEN 0  ' Restore the screen to 80 x 25 text
```

The PALETTE Statement

The EGA, VGA, and MCGA graphics adapters can produce many more colors than the 16 listed in Table 28.1. (The VGA and MCGA can display up to 262,143 colors.) The PALETTE statement maps different color values to the attributes numbered 0 to 15 in Table 28.1. When you then use a graphics statement (such as PSET or DRAW), the color value is the new color attribute you assigned with PALETTE. Any color value you do not map to a different value retains its default value.

The format of the PALETTE statement is

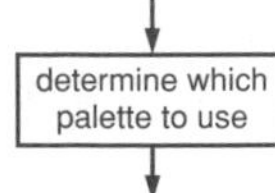
determine which palette to use

```
PALETTE [attribute, color]
```

The *attribute* is a number from 0 to 15, depending on your graphics adapter. The *color* value must be a long integer if you have a VGA or an EGA adapter (because VGA and EGA have so many possible colors, a regular integer will not hold all the colors). The *color* can be an integer *or* a long integer variable or value if you use an EGA card. It would be impossible to list all the possible colors for these adapters here. Check your video adapters' reference manuals for more information on their individual colors.

Using PALETTE without any attribute or color values changes the display palette back to its default colors.

The color value for 4 is usually red unless you map 4 to a different palette color. The following program displays a circle in red. It then maps 64 different VGA colors to 4. The VGA is capable of many shades of red, and this circle goes through each of those shades and back again.

```
' Filename: C28PAL1.BAS
'
' Draws a red circle in the center of the screen, then
' brightens and dims it by changing the palette color for red.
'
SCREEN 13   ' 640 x 480 resolution

DIM newattr AS LONG     ' Make the color a long integer

CIRCLE (165, 100), 50, 4    ' Red circle

FOR newattr = 0 TO 63               ' Cycle through each palette
                                    ' assignment
   PALETTE 4, newattr               ' Reassign the palette
   FOR time = 1 TO 400: NEXT time    ' Timer loop to slow it down
NEXT newattr

FOR newattr = 63 TO 0 STEP -1       ' Cycle backward
   PALETTE 4, newattr               ' Reassign the palette
   FOR time = 1 TO 400: NEXT time    ' Timer loop to slow it down
NEXT
```

With at least 64 combinations for each of the 16 colors, EGA, VGA, and MCGA give users many colors.

The PAINT Statement

The final color statement covered in this chapter does the most of any described so far. The PAINT statement fills an enclosed image with a color. After you draw an image on the screen, such as a circle or a box, you can "fill" that image with a color by painting it with the PAINT statement.

The format of the PAINT statement is

fill an enclosed drawing with color

```
PAINT [STEP] (x, y) [, [interior], [border]]
```

You should understand the first two parameters. The *x*- and *y*-values specify the screen coordinates. If you specify the STEP option, the painting is performed relative to the last-drawn pixel. The x- and *y*-coordinates must be inside an already-drawn shape on the screen, or else the entire screen is filled with the PAINT's *interior* color except for the figure itself. The *interior* is the color you want to fill a shape with, and the *border* is the color (optional) of the outline of the shape.

The *border* color must be the same as the outline of the shape, or else *PAINT* will not know where the figure's boundaries end and will paint the entire screen. If you do not specify a border color, QBasic assumes you want the same *border* as the *interior* color.

Examples

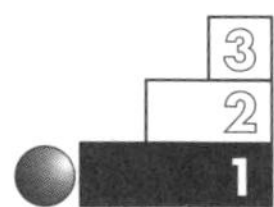

1. The following program simply draws a rectangle on the screen and then paints the rectangle red. Using the PAINT statement is much faster than setting all the pixels to red with the PSET statement.

```
' Filename: C28PAIN1.BAS
'
' Draws a rectangle and then paints it red.
'
SCREEN 7     ' 320 x 200 color mode

LINE (100, 50)-(200, 150), , B   ' Draw a box

PAINT (101, 51), 4, 15      ' Red inside the white border
```

2. The following program does the same as the preceding one, except it uses relative coordinates (the STEP option) to paint the figure. The coordinates (-1, -1) tell the PAINT statement to "back up" one *x*- and *y*-coordinate and fill the figure.

```
' Filename: C28PAIN2.BAS
'
' Draws a rectangle and then paints everything but it red.
'
SCREEN 7     ' 320 x 200 color mode

LINE (100, 50)-(200, 150), , B   ' Draw a box

PAINT STEP(-1, -1), 4, 15       ' Red inside the white border
```

3. The following program is like the preceding one, but everything *except* the box is painted red. This is because the PAINT coordinates lie outside the box.

```
' Filename: C28PAIN3.BAS
'
' Draws a rectangle and then paints everything but it red.
'
SCREEN 7     ' 320 x 200 color mode

LINE (100, 50)-(200, 150), , B   ' Draw a box

PAINT (0, 0), 4, 15            ' Red inside the white border
```

4. This program draws three circles and fills them with different colors.

```
' Filename: C28PAIN4.BAS
'
' Draws colored circles and fills them with three colors.

SCREEN 7      ' 320 x 200 resolution

CIRCLE (50, 50), 40, 1
CIRCLE (150, 100), 40, 2
CIRCLE (250, 150), 40, 3
PRINT "Press any key to fill with colors..."
```

```
DO
LOOP WHILE (INKEY$ = "")   ' Wait on a user keypress

PAINT (51, 51), 4, 1       ' Fill with colors. Make sure the
PAINT (151, 101), 5, 2     ' border colors are the same as the
PAINT (251, 151), 6, 3     ' the borders of the circles.
```

5. The following program shows what happens if you try to fill a shape that is not completely enclosed. The program draws a box and then draws four lines that almost make a box. When the PAINT statement attempts to fill the partially enclosed box, it fails and fills the entire screen (except for the first box) instead.

```
' Filename: C28PAIN5.BAS
'
' Draws 2 boxes, then attempts to color them.

SCREEN 7      ' 320 x 200 resolution

LINE (50, 50)-(125, 100), 2, B
' Almost draw another box...
LINE (150, 50)-(150, 100), 4    ' Draw one "side"
LINE (150, 50)-(225, 50), 4     ' and the other
LINE (150, 100)-(225, 100), 4   ' and the other
LINE (225, 100)-(225, 60), 4    ' ALMOST fill in rest of box

PRINT "Press any key to fill first one..."
DO
LOOP UNTIL (INKEY$ <> "")

PAINT (51, 51), 5, 2   ' Fill the first box

PRINT "Press any key to fill second one..."
DO
LOOP UNTIL (INKEY$ <> "")

PAINT (151, 51), 2, 4 ' Fill with colors. It actually "leaks"
                      ' out and fills the whole screen
```

Summary

You have learned the basics of using color in your programs. The `COLOR` statement's attributes are the foundation of adding color to your graphics commands. You will be working with Table 28.1 (in conjunction with Table 27.1 from the preceding chapter) to become familiar with your graphics adapter, its resolution, and its colors.

This chapter is only an introduction to colorful graphics. You can build on many of the statements used here. You can turn them into subroutine procedures to which you pass parameters that draw other shapes of various sizes. For instance, you might want to write a triangle procedure that uses `DRAW` and passes parameters to draw a triangle when it is called.

The next chapter adds another dimension to your senses: sound. QBasic offers simple commands that enable you to produce music and sounds to create games or interesting presentations.

Review Questions

Answers to the Review Questions are in Appendix B.

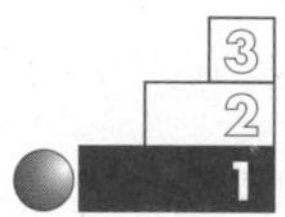

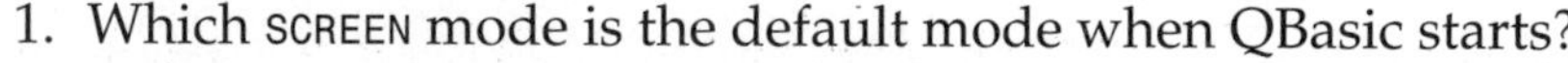

1. Which `SCREEN` mode is the default mode when QBasic starts?

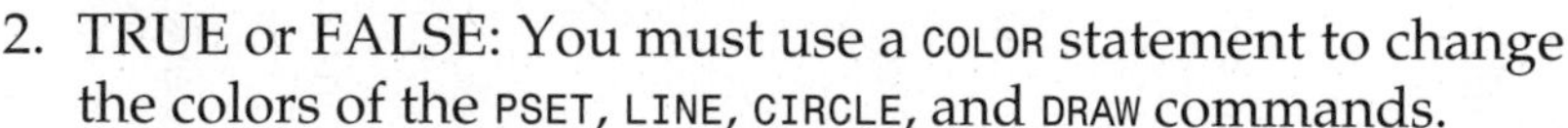

2. TRUE or FALSE: You must use a `COLOR` statement to change the colors of the `PSET`, `LINE`, `CIRCLE`, and `DRAW` commands.

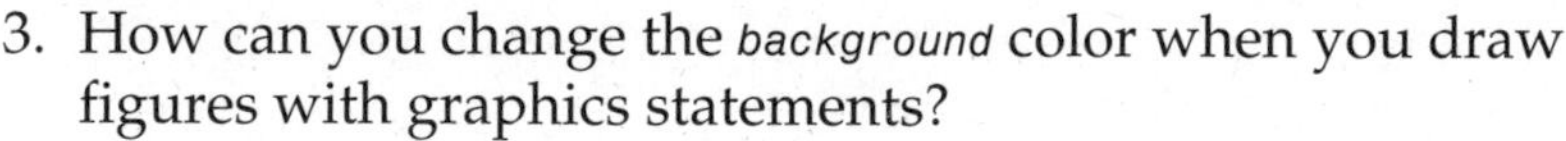

3. How can you change the *background* color when you draw figures with graphics statements?

4. Although the CGA displays seven different colors in screen mode 1, why do you have to display them in two sets?

5. TRUE or FALSE: The following PAINT statement fills the circle with a color.

```
CIRCLE (100,100), 50, 5
PAINT (101, 101), 4
```

Review Exercises

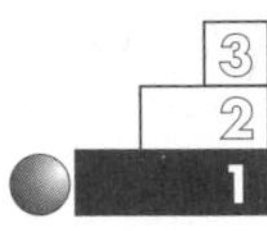

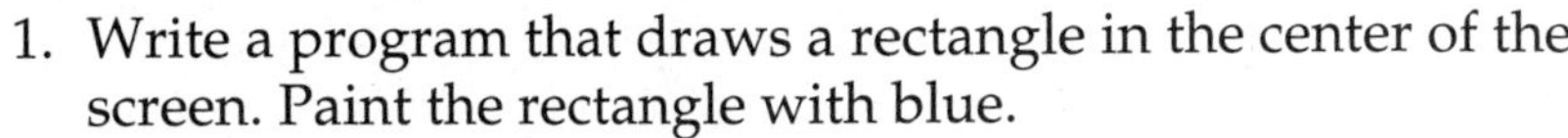

1. Write a program that draws a rectangle in the center of the screen. Paint the rectangle with blue.

2. Change the program in the preceding example so that it paints all of the screen blue *except* the rectangle.

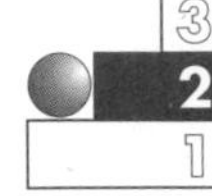

3. Write a program that displays a circle, a rectangle, and a triangle (use DRAW). Fill them all with different colors.

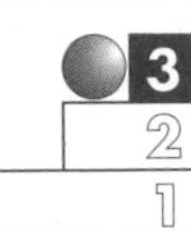

4. Modify the program in the preceding exercise so that it outlines each of the three shapes in different colors and fills them with different colors. (Hint: Use the COLOR statement.)

5. Type the color setup program (C28.BAS) listed in this chapter, and save it on disk as a SUB procedure file. Change the sketching program so that it uses this procedure's constants for its colors to make it more maintainable. (If you have a CGA adapter, you are limited to four different colors for each palette. You will have to take this into account when you write the procedure.)

29

Making Music and Special Sounds

Now that you can display graphics, you might want to stimulate your aural senses as well by producing music and sound effects with QBasic. This chapter explains the basics of generating sound through various sound-producing commands.

This chapter introduces

- ♦ The SOUND statement
- ♦ The PLAY statement
- ♦ The PLAY statement's musical language elements

The BEEP statement was your first introduction to the PC speaker. Rather than a single tone (as produced by BEEP), you can create your own top 40 hits.

The SOUND Statement

The SOUND statement is the foundation of music on your PC. Each sound statement produces a sound similar to that of a single piano key. You can produce any note for any duration. The format of the SOUND statement is

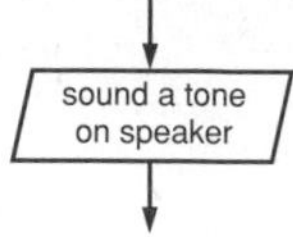
sound a tone
on speaker

```
SOUND frequency, duration
```

Although you do not need a degree in music theory to produce music with SOUND, understanding musical notation helps you understand the SOUND statement.

The *frequency* value (in hertz) must be a number from *37* to *32,767* (therefore, it can be an integer constant, integer expression, or integer variable). *Hertz* is the number of cycles per second the note "sings." On a piano, the A below middle C (the middle note of the 88 keys) has the frequency of 440 hertz. Therefore, a *frequency* of 440 produces the same note and key as pressing the A below middle C.

The *duration* must be a number from 0 through 65,536. It must be a constant, an expression, or a variable (any data type except an integer, because 65,536 is too large to fit in an integer variable). The *duration* measures the length of the note (how long it sounds) in *clock ticks.* A clock tick is based on the CPU's built-in timing clock. There are 18.2 ticks in one second. Therefore, if you want to produce middle C for one second, you would write the following statement:

```
SOUND 440, 18.2
```

The value of 440 hertz is important. It defines each octave available with sound. Each multiple of 440 (880, 1,320, 1,760, and so on) is the next octave A. Sound becomes inaudible at 28,160 hertz.

SOUND is not used as much as the more flexible and more musical PLAY statement, which is described in the next section. SOUND is good for producing gliding crescendos and sirens when matching a tone to a specific note is not as important as the actual sound.

Examples

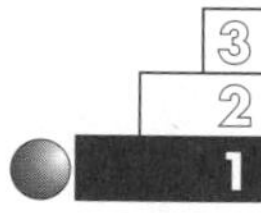
3
2
1

1. The following program simply uses SOUND to produce every possible A from its lowest frequency of 110 to its highest (and inaudible) frequency of 28,160. (Do not include commas in the numbers used with SOUND.)

```
' Filename: C29SND1.BAS
'
' Program that produces each octave of A's.
'
```

```
SOUND 110, 20      ' Two A's below middle C
SOUND 220, 20      ' One A below middle C
SOUND 440, 20      ' A below middle C
SOUND 880, 20      ' One A above middle C
SOUND 1760, 20     ' Two A's above middle C
SOUND 3520, 20     ' Three A's above middle C
SOUND 7040, 20     ' Four A's above middle C
SOUND 14080, 20    ' Five A's above middle C
SOUND 28160, 20    ' Six A's above middle C, not even audible
```

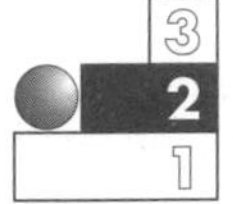

2. The following program uses a FOR-NEXT loop to cycle through every note that is possible with SOUND.

```
' Filename: C29SND2.BAS
'
' Program that cycles through every note of SOUND.
'

FOR n = 37 TO 32767
   SOUND n, 1   ' Sound each note for a very short duration
NEXT
```

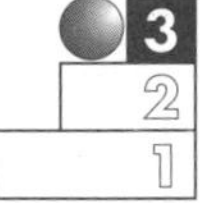

3. You can get rid of some of the static and long duration of these sounds by adding a larger STEP value to the FOR-NEXT loop. This makes the duration seem shorter. The following program demonstrates this.

```
' Filename: C29SND3.BAS
'
' Program that cycles through short notes of SOUND.
'

FOR n = 37 TO 32767 STEP 5
   SOUND n, 1   ' Sound notes
NEXT
```

4. The following program displays each note for an extremely short duration. This produces a strange warbling effect.

```
' Filename: C29SND4.BAS
'
' Program that cycles through short notes of SOUND.
'

FOR n = 37 TO 32767 STEP 5
   SOUND n, .1   ' Sound notes for an extremely short duration
NEXT
```

5. By playing with a few SOUND values, you can produce a rise-and-fall siren, as shown by the next program.

```
' Filename: C29SND5.BAS
'
' Program that sounds a siren.
'

FOR time = 1 TO 2

   FOR up = 1000 TO 1500 STEP 25
      SOUND up, 3
   NEXT up

   FOR down = 1500 TO 1000 STEP -25
      SOUND down, 3
   NEXT down

NEXT time   ' Repeat once
```

6. The following program uses the RND function to produce random "computer-like" sounds. You can use sounds like these if you write a space game and want to give the effect of being in a spaceship control room.

```
' Filename: C29SND6.BAS
'
' Program that produces random "computer-like" sounds.
'

FOR time = 1 TO 200
```

```
    note = INT(RND * 2735) + 500    ' Random note
    dur = INT(RND * 3) + 1          ' Random duration
    SOUND note, dur                 ' Sound the note

NEXT time   ' Repeat
```

The PLAY Statement

You do not need to use SOUND for many PC musical scores because the PLAY statement makes programming songs and melodies much easier. The PLAY command for sound is like the DRAW command for graphics; it includes its own miniature programming language. The musical programming language of PLAY is explained in the following paragraphs.

The format of the PLAY command is

play music defined by command string

```
PLAY commandstring
```

The *commandstring* is a string constant, string expression, or string variable that holds one or more commands from PLAY's musical programming language. The commands that appear in PLAY's *commandstring* are listed in Table 29.1.

PLAY can play notes from seven octaves (numbered 0 through 6). There are 84 notes in the seven octaves (because there are the notes A through G, and their flats and sharps, in each octave). The first octave (octave 0) begins at C.

Table 29.1. PLAY's commandstring musical commands and meanings.

Command	*Description*
Octave Commands	
>	Increases octave by *1*. The maximum possible is *6*.
<	Decreases octave by *1*. The minimum is *0*.
o *n*	Sets the current octave to one of the seven possible (*0* - *6*).

continues

Table 29.1. continued

Command	*Description*
Tone Commands	
A, B, C, D, E, F, G	Plays the note in the current octave.
A+, B+, C+, D+, E+, F+, G+	Plays the note in the current octave as a sharp.
A#, B#, C#, D#, E#, F#, G#	Plays the note in the current octave as a sharp.
A-, B-, C-, D-, E-, F-, G-	Plays the note in the current octave as a flat.
N *n*	Plays the note numbered *n*. The value for *n* must be from 0 to 84. A value of 0 indicates a rest.
Duration Commands	
L n	Sets the length for each note as follows: 4 is a quarter note, 3 is a half note, 2 is a dotted half note, and 1 is a whole note. If you want each note to be faster, you can continue the *n* value up to 64. When the length precedes a note, each note until the next *L* command changes the succeeding tempo. If you follow a note with the *n* value (without the *L*), only that note is set to that tempo, not the rest that follow.
.	The period (.) causes each note to play $1^1/_2$ times its *L n* length. This is identical to the musical notation's period (for dotted quarter notes, and so on). You can place multiple periods after each note to extend it even further.

Command	Description
MN	Turns on the *music normal* mode. This gives each note its fullest value.
ML	Turns on the *music legato* mode. Each note smoothly changes to the next.
MS	Turns on the *music staccato* mode. Each note is short and distinct from the next.
Tempo Commands	
P *n*	A pause, from 1 to 64. The time of the pause is measured just as the times listed in the *L* commands.
T *n*	Sets the tempo to the number of *L 4* quarter notes in one minute. This is a "metronome" measurement (the number of beats per minutes). The range for *n* is 32 to 255. The default is 120.
Operation Commands	
MF	Forces the PLAY *commandstring* to play in the foreground. No other QBasic statements execute until the PLAY statement's music finishes.
MB	Forces the PLAY *commandstring* to play in the background. Subsequent QBasic statements continue to execute while the PLAY is still finishing. This lets you draw or continue with a calculation while the user hears the music.

If you are familiar with music notation, you can already see that PLAY is much more powerful than the SOUND statement. You can look at a musical score and "write" the same music in QBasic using the PLAY statement's *commandstring* of commands and notes. For example, the two bars shown in Figure 29.1 can be played on the PC with the following PLAY command:

```
PLAY "L4 C2 E G < B. > L16 C D L2 C"
```

Figure 29.1. Two Bars to be played with the PLAY statement.

> **NOTE:** The PC speaker produces only one tone at a time, which means that chords are not possible. Any music playable with one finger on a piano is "playable" on the PC using PLAY.

Examples

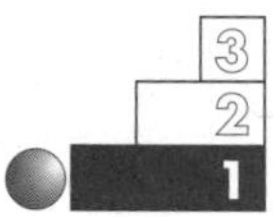

1. Suppose you want to use the PLAY command to play all seven octaves of the note A. The following program does that by setting the first octave (0), then playing A for a whole note (four beats at 120 quarter notes per minute, the default), then going up the octaves until it reaches octave 6 (the seventh octave).

```
' Filename: C29PLAY1.BAS
'
' Plays the note A at all 7 octaves.
'

FOR octave = 0 TO 6    ' Step through the 7 octaves
   oc$ = RIGHT$(STR$(octave), 1) ' Convert octave # to string
   PLAY "L1"     ' Set the length of each note to a whole note
   PLAY "o" + oc$  ' Set the octave
   PLAY "A"        ' Play the note

NEXT octave
```

2. The previous program could have been written with the PLAY statement combined on one line. It is separated in the preceding example to illustrate each of the parts (the length, the octave, and so forth). Here is the same program written in a more succinct style:

```
' Filename: C29PLAY2.BAS
'
' Plays the note A at all 7 octaves.
'

FOR octave = 0 TO 6    ' Step through the 7 octaves
   oc$ = RIGHT$(STR$(octave), 1) ' Convert octave # to string
                              ' and strip off leading plus sign
   PLAY "L1 o" + oc$ + "A"         ' Play the note

NEXT octave
```

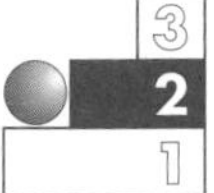

3. The following program plays every note possible at one-half beat (an eighth note) per note.

```
' Filename: C29PLAY3.BAS
'
' Plays all possible notes.
'
' Step each octave of the notes A through G

DIM note$(6)

FOR ctr = 0 TO 6
   READ note$(ctr)   ' Put note names in the array
NEXT

FOR octave = 0 TO 6
   PLAY "o" + RIGHT$(STR$(octave), 1)   ' Set the octave
   FOR ctr = 0 TO 6
      PLAY "L8" + note$(ctr)            ' Play the next note
   NEXT ctr
NEXT octave

DATA "C", "D", "E", "F", "G", "A", "B"
```

None of the flats and sharps is played in the preceding program. Because the first note played is a *C*, no flats or sharps are needed in the scales (the key of *C*).

4. The following program demonstrates the background music capabilities of QBasic. This program plays the same seven-octave scale as the previous one, only faster, using 16th notes. In addition, the last part of the program prints a repeated message randomly on the screen.

   The music does not have to finish before the message starts displaying because it plays in the background (as opposed to the default foreground mode). A limited number of notes can fit in the background, however. The scales must play several notes before the printing begins.

```
' Filename: C29PLAY4.BAS
'
' Plays all possible C-scale notes in background
' and prints a repeating musical message.
'
DIM note$(6)
CLS

FOR ctr = 0 TO 6
   READ note$(ctr)   ' Put note names in the array
NEXT

PLAY "MB"
FOR octave = 0 TO 6
   PLAY "o" + RIGHT$(STR$(octave), 1)   ' Set the octave
   FOR ctr = 0 TO 6
      PLAY "L16" + note$(ctr)        ' Play the next 16th note
   NEXT ctr
NEXT octave

DATA "C", "D", "E", "F", "G", "A", "B"

' Print a musical message randomly on the screen
FOR ctr = 1 TO 1000
   LOCATE INT(RND * 24) + 1, INT(RND * 60) + 1 ' Compute
                                               ' random row & column
   PRINT "Music has charms to tame the savage beast! ";
NEXT ctr
```

5. The following is a complete score of Mozart's Sonata in C (Theme from the First Movement). Run it to see the dramatic musical effects you can create with only one note at a time.

```
' Filename: C29PLAY5.BAS
'
' Plays Mozart's Sonata in C.
'
COLOR 7, 1
CLS
LOCATE 12, 30
PRINT "Mozart's Sonata in C"

PLAY "c2 L4 e g < b. > l16 c d l2 c"             ' 1st 2 bars
PLAY "> a l4 g > c < g l16 g f e f l2 e"         ' 2nd 2 bars
PLAY "< a8 l16 b > c d e f g a g f e d c < b a" ' And more...
PLAY "g8 a b > c d e f g f e d c < b a g f8 g a b > c d e"
PLAY "f e d c < b a g f e8 f g a b > c d e d c < b a g f e"
PLAY "d8 e f g a b > c# d <a b > c# d e f g"  ' Includes a C#
PLAY "a b > c < b a g f e f g a g f e d c"
PLAY "< L8 b MS > g e c ML d g MS e c"  ' Staccato & legato
PLAY "D4 g4 < g2 g2 > c4 e4 g2 "
PLAY "l16 a g f e f e d c e d e d e d e d e d e d e d c d"
PLAY "c4 c < g > c e g e c e f d < b > d"
PLAY "c4 <c < g > c e g e c e f d < b > d c4 > c4 c2"
```

Summary

Programming sound and music using QBasic is relatively easy, but it requires a fundamental background in music theory (reading notes, understanding tempo, and so on). You can use SOUND to produce special effects or learn the miniature programming language of PLAY for more advanced melodies.

Although music does not always have a place in business applications, it comes in handy as an opening theme song to a game or recreational program. Music also attracts attention if you want people to see a demonstration program running on your PC in a display window.

Review Questions

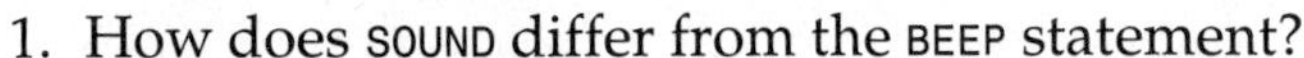

Answers to the Review Questions are in Appendix B.

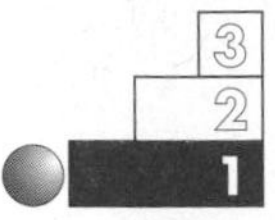

1. How does SOUND differ from the BEEP statement?
2. What SOUND statement would produce an A (below middle C) for two seconds?

3. How does PLAY differ from the SOUND statement?

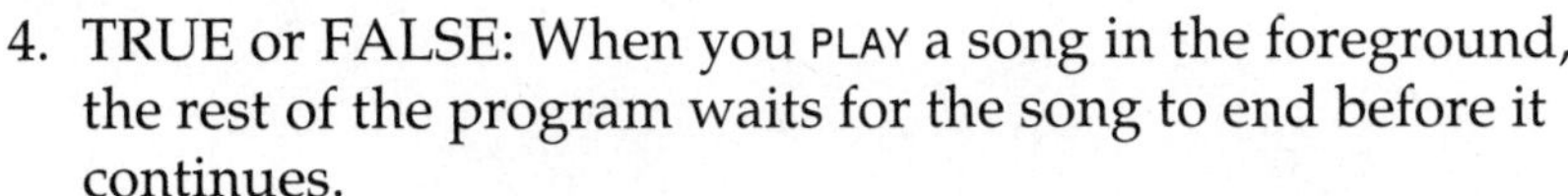

4. TRUE or FALSE: When you PLAY a song in the foreground, the rest of the program waits for the song to end before it continues.

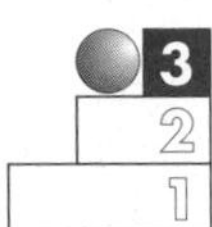

5. How many octaves are available on the PC using PLAY? What are their numbers?
6. What are the two symbols that represent a sharp when you are using the PLAY statement?
7. What does the following line do?

```
PLAY "o0 C > C > C > C > C > C"
```

Review Exercises

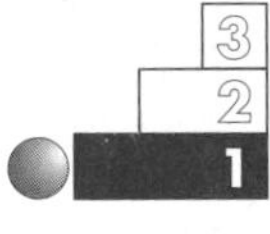

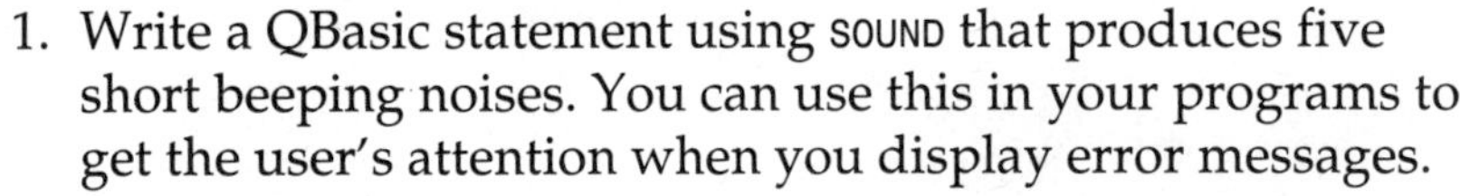

1. Write a QBasic statement using SOUND that produces five short beeping noises. You can use this in your programs to get the user's attention when you display error messages.

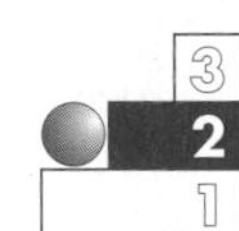

2. Write a program that produces a simple scale using SOUND. Then use PLAY. Notice how PLAY improves on the ease of programming sound. PLAY the scale twice as fast; then play the scale backward.

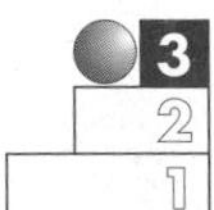

3. Write a birthday song to play for your users on their birthdays. Display a color birthday cake (using the graphics statements you learned in the previous chapters) while the song plays. (Hint: Play the song in the background so that it plays while the cake is drawn.)

4. Get the sheet music of your favorite song. Using Table 29.1, program the melody with the PLAY statement. Make sure you stick to the proper tempo and keep the keys accurate. After practicing this, you should quickly learn the ins and outs of the PLAY statement.

Part IX

Appendixes

ASCII Code Character Set

ASCII Dec	Value Hex	ASCII Character
000	00	null
001	01	☺
002	02	☻
003	03	♥
004	04	♦
005	05	♣
006	06	♠
007	07	•
008	08	◘
009	09	○
010	0A	◙
011	0B	♂
012	0C	♀
013	0D	♪
014	0E	♫
015	0F	¤
016	10	►
017	11	◄
018	12	↕
019	13	!!
020	14	¶
021	15	§
022	16	–
023	17	↨
024	18	↑
025	19	↓
026	1A	→
027	1B	←
028	1C	∟
029	1D	↔
030	1E	▲
031	1F	▼
032	20	SPACE
033	21	!
034	22	"
035	23	#

ASCII Dec	Value Hex	ASCII Character
036	24	$
037	25	%
038	26	&
039	27	’
040	28	(
041	29	)
042	2A	*
043	2B	+
044	2C	,
045	2D	–
046	2E	.
047	2F	/
048	30	0
049	31	1
050	32	2
051	33	3
052	34	4
053	35	5
054	36	6
055	37	7
056	38	8
057	39	9
058	3A	:
059	3B	;
060	3C	<
061	3D	=
062	3E	>
063	3F	?
064	40	@
065	41	A
066	42	B
067	43	C
068	44	D
069	45	E
070	46	F
071	47	G

ASCII Dec	Value Hex	ASCII Character
072	48	H
073	49	I
074	4A	J
075	4B	K
076	4C	L
077	4D	M
078	4E	N
079	4F	O
080	50	P
081	51	Q
082	52	R
083	53	S
084	54	T
085	55	U
086	56	V
087	57	W
088	58	X
089	59	Y
090	5A	Z
091	5B	[
092	5C	\
093	5D	]
094	5E	^
095	5F	_
096	60	`
097	61	a
098	62	b
099	63	c
100	64	d
101	65	e
102	66	f
103	67	g
104	68	h
105	69	i
106	6A	j
107	6B	k

ASCII Dec	Value Hex	ASCII Character
108	6C	l
109	6D	m
110	6E	n
111	6F	o
112	70	p
113	71	q
114	72	r
115	73	s
116	74	t
117	75	u
118	76	v
119	77	w
120	78	x
121	79	y
122	7A	z
123	7B	{
124	7C	¦
125	7D	}
126	7E	~
127	7F	Δ
128	80	Ç
129	81	ü
130	82	é
131	83	â
132	84	ä
133	85	à
134	86	å
135	87	ç
136	88	ê
137	89	ë
138	8A	è
139	8B	ï
140	8C	î
141	8D	ì
142	8E	Ä
143	8F	Å
144	90	É
145	91	æ
146	92	Æ
147	93	ô
148	94	ö
149	95	ò
150	96	û
151	97	ù
152	98	ÿ
153	99	Ö
154	9A	Ü
155	9B	¢
156	9C	£
157	9D	¥
158	9E	P_t
159	9F	ƒ
160	A0	á
161	A1	í
162	A2	ó
163	A3	ú
164	A4	ñ
165	A5	Ñ
166	A6	ª
167	A7	º
168	A8	¿
169	A9	⌐

ASCII Dec	Value Hex	ASCII Character	ASCII Dec	Value Hex	ASCII Character
170	AA	¬	201	C9	╔
171	AB	½	202	CA	╩
172	AC	¼	203	CB	╦
173	AD	¡	204	CC	╠
174	AE	«	205	CD	═
175	AF	»	206	CE	╬
176	B0	░	207	CF	╧
177	B1	▒	208	D0	╨
178	B2	▓	209	D1	╤
179	B3	│	210	D2	╥
180	B4	┤	211	D3	╙
181	B5	╡	212	D4	╘
182	B6	╢	213	D5	╒
183	B7	╖	214	D6	╓
184	B8	╕	215	D7	╫
185	B9	╣	216	D8	╪
186	BA	║	217	D9	┘
187	BB	╗	218	DA	┌
188	BC	╝	219	DB	█
189	BD	╜	220	DC	▄
190	BE	╛	221	DD	▌
191	BF	┐	222	DE	▐
192	C0	└	223	DF	▀
193	C1	┴	224	E0	α
194	C2	┬	225	E1	β
195	C3	├	226	E2	Γ
196	C4	─	227	E3	π
197	C5	┼	228	E4	Σ
198	C6	╞	229	E5	σ
199	C7	╟	230	E6	µ
200	C8	╚	231	E7	τ

ASCII Value Dec	Hex	ASCII Character
232	E8	Φ
233	E9	θ
234	EA	Ω
235	EB	δ
236	EC	∞
237	ED	ø
238	EE	∈
239	EF	∩
240	F0	≡
241	F1	±
242	F2	≥
243	F3	≤
244	F4	⌠
245	F5	⌡
246	F6	÷
247	F7	≈
248	F8	°
249	F9	•
250	FA	·
251	FB	√
252	FC	η
253	FD	2
254	FE	■
255	FF	

Answers to the Review Questions

Chapter 1 Answers

1. QBasic.
2. The 1950s.
3. FALSE. QBasic is an *extension* of BASIC and is more powerful than previous versions of BASIC.
4. The disk usually holds many times more bytes than RAM holds.
5. A modem.
6. B. The mouse acts like an input device. Remember that it can be used in place of the keyboard's arrow keys to move the cursor on the screen.
7. NumLock. Pressing it again turns on the numbers.
8. Beginner's All-Purpose Symbolic Instruction Code.
9. FORTRAN.

10. TRUE.
11. Because it is erased every time the power is turned off.
12. TRUE. The greater resolution means there are more dots that make up a graphics image.
13. 524,288 (512 times 1,024).
14. *Mo*dulate-*Dem*odulate.

Chapter 2 Answers

1. TRUE. When you install MS-DOS 5.0, the installation procedure ensures that QBasic goes to your DOS directory.
2. The program editing window.
3. Clicking means pressing and releasing the left mouse button; double-clicking means pressing and releasing the button twice in succession; and dragging means pressing a button and moving the mouse while still holding down the button.
4. The menus display every command you can request so that you do not have to remember commands.
5. Every time you start QBasic from DOS, the Help Survival Guide appears.
6. When you press F1, the QBasic Help shortcut key, QBasic displays a help message about what you are doing; it looks at the *context* of the help request.
7. It is important that you save your work and return to DOS before turning off your computer. QBasic properly ensures that you will not lose any work or changed QBasic environment settings.
8. You can get help from the Help Survival Guide when you start QBasic, you can display the **H**elp menu, and you can press F1, the Help shortcut key.
9. C. (The left arrow key does not erase, although it does move the cursor backward over the text.)

10. Command-line options change the QBasic environment so that the program starts the way you prefer.
11. You can execute many menu commands without displaying the menus by typing their keyboard-shortcut equivalents.

Chapter 3 Answers

1. A set of instructions that makes the computer do something.
2. Either buy it or write it yourself. Using QBasic can make the latter easy!
3. FALSE. They can do only exactly what *you* (the programmer) tell them to do.
4. The program is the instructions (like a recipe). The output is the results of executing those instructions (like the cake that is made by following a recipe).
5. The QBasic program editor.
6. BAS.
7. You must thoroughly plan the program before typing it. By thinking it out ahead of time, defining the problem to be solved, and breaking it into logical pieces, you will write the program faster than if you type it as you plan it.
8. FALSE. Backspace erases as the cursor moves to the left. The left arrow key does not erase.
9. The clipboard.
10. You can have up to four bookmarks in a QBasic program.

Chapter 4 Answers

1. **F**ile **O**pen...
2. Because a program in memory is erased if you power-off your computer.

3. You can use up to eight letters in a file name.

4. FALSE. You can have no spaces in a file name. A file name can have a maximum of eight letters, and it should end with the BAS extension.

5. Only one program at a time can be in memory, although you can have several on disk.

6. FALSE: You must use the `DEL` DOS command to erase files from the disk.

7. Free-form means that you can add a lot of white space and blank lines to make your programs more readable.

8. Save your programs often as you type them, in case of power failure or computer problems. Your work will be safe as of the last save to disk.

Chapter 5 Answers

1. Commands and data.

2. A storage location in your computer that holds values.

3. `QTR.1.SALES` and `DataFile`. Variable names cannot start with a number and cannot include spaces in their names.

4. FALSE. There is no such type as single integer or double integer.

5. TRUE.

6. One.

7. `PRINT`.

8. `CLS`.

9. -0.03 (single-precision)
   4,541,000,000,000 (double-precision)
   0.0019 (double-precision)

10. 1.5E+1 -4.3-05 -5.4543 5.312349+5

Chapter 6 Answers

1. `REM`ark.
2. The computer ignores the statement and goes to the next line in the program.
3. FALSE. The computer ignores the third line because it is a `REM` statement.
4. TRUE.
5. The semicolon tells `PRINT` to print the next value next to the last one printed. The comma forces the next value to print in the next print zone.
6. Fourteen columns wide.
7. So that a later `PRINT` would "finish" that printed line instead of starting a new one.
8. Column 28. The comma pushes `Computer` into the next print zone after column 20.
9. Column 31. You must leave one space before each number for the imaginary plus sign of positive values.
10.
```
PRINT ,, "Hello"

PRINT TAB(28); "Hello"

PRINT "                           Hello"
```
11. 86 and 99 are secret agents.

Chapter 7 Answers

1. A. 5
   B. 6
   C. 5
2. A. 5
   B. 7

3. ```
   a, b
   a; b
   ```

   (Don't be fooled. The letters are inside quotation marks, so the variable values cannot be printed.)

4. A. `LET a = (3 + 3) / (4 + 4)`
   B. `x = (a - b) * (a - c) ^ 2`
   C. `f = a^(1/2) / b^(1/3)`
   D. `d = ((8 - x^2) / (x - 9)) - ((4 * 2 - 1) / x^3)`

5. ```
   LET radius = 4
   LET PI = 3.14159
   LET area = PI * radius ^ 2
   PRINT "The area with radius of"; radius; " is: "; area
   ```

6. `PRINT "The remainder is:"; (100 / 4) - (100 \ 4)`

Chapter 8 Answers

1. It can hold 32,767 characters.
2. The dollar sign ($) at the end of the string variable name.
3. Variable-length string variables and fixed-length string variables. Variable-length string variables are easier to work with and are more flexible.
4. + (the plus sign).
5. A, D. `name$` is a command name and `last.name` is a numeric variable name because it does not end in a dollar sign.
6. Double-precision.
   Single-precision.
   String.
   Integer.
   Single-precision.
7. `NAME$` is a QBasic keyword.
8. FALSE. You cannot do math with string constants.

9. `PRINT city$; ", "; state$`

10. `LET filename$ = "C:\" + filename$ + ".DAT"`

Chapter 9 Answers

1. D. `LINE INPUT` does *not* produce a question mark; you must include a question mark in the prompt message.

2. Without a prompt message, the user would not know what to type at the keyboard.

3. TRUE.

4. FALSE.

5. Three. The first `INPUT` produces a question mark and the prompt messages each contain a question mark. The second `INPUT` does not produce a question mark because it uses a comma rather than a semicolon.

6. Four. `a` is numeric, `b$` is string, `c` is numeric, and `d$` is a string.

7. `LINE INPUT` inputs only one variable at a time. You cannot list more than one variable after `LINE INPUT`, but you can after `INPUT`.

8. By enclosing the address in quotation marks when you type it at the keyboard in response to the `INPUT`.

9. `Redo from start`. You must then type the two values from the beginning.

10. `Redo from start`. QBasic never lets you enter incorrect values for the `INPUT` statement.

Chapter 10 Answers

1. The `LPRINT USING` statement.

2. TRUE.

3. 77, 36, 156, 122.
4. C.
5. It prints exactly as you typed it, without performing any print formatting.
6. The number 9,999.99.
7. By overriding the sequential order of the program, control passes to the statement after the GOTO's label.
8. FALSE. BEEP beeps the computer's speaker and not the printer's speaker.
9. %34543. The percent sign warns you that the format was not large enough to hold the output.
10. Blinking light cyan text on a magenta background. (This may not be the prettiest combination you can come up with!)
11. No output is actually produced. However, the next PRINT occurs in the middle of the screen at row 12, column 40.

Chapter 11 Answers

1. A. False.
   B. True.
   C. True.
   D. True.
2. FALSE. 54 is not less than or equal to 50, so the PRINT never happens.
3. A. False. Uppercase characters have lower ASCII numbers.
   B. True. The null string has an ASCII value of 0. The character 0 (zero) has an ASCII value of 48.
   C. False.
   D. False.
4. C.
5. A. False.
   B. False.

C. True.
D. True.

6. C. You cannot compare a numeric variable to a string constant.

7. A. True.
B. True.
C. True.
D. False.

Chapter 12 Answers

1. FALSE. One or more constants must follow `DATA`.

2. One possible pair of statements is

```
READ cust.name$, cust.balance
DATA "1021", 341.76
```

3. Yes, the `READ-DATA` pair simply puts values in variables, just as the assignment statement does.

4. It signals when you just read the last line of data.

5. `DATA "-99", "-99", -99`

6. 6

7. With the `RESTORE` command.

8. The variable `emp.id` must be a string variable. It is not, because there is no dollar sign after it.

9. An `Out of DATA` error appears because the first time the `READ` happens, the `DATA` values cannot be read again. (This is just one of the problems that can happen with an endless loop produced by the unconditional `GOTO` statement.)

10. The `Out of DATA` error does not occur due to the `RESTORE`, which resets the `DATA`. The program still has an endless loop and will run forever unless the user presses Ctrl+Break to stop it.

Chapter 13 Answers

1. A repetition of statements in a QBasic program.
2. The NEXT statement. FOR and NEXT always appear in pairs; you will not see one without the other somewhere in the program.
3. A nested loop occurs when you put one loop inside another.
4. QBasic assumes you want a STEP value of positive 1.
5. The inside loop acts as though it moves fastest because it must complete all its iterations before the outer loop can finish its next one.
6.
```
10
7
4
1
```
7. TRUE. That is why a FOR-NEXT loop is sometimes called a *determinant loop.* A FOR-NEXT loop executes the exact number of times specified by the control constants or variables in the FOR statement.
8. The loop stops execution and the program resumes at the statement following the NEXT.
9. FALSE. The order of the NEXT statements is reversed. You must finish the inside loop before the outside loop can continue.
10.
```
1
2
3
4
5
```

    Remember, the FOR statement looks at the start.val, end.val, and step.val only once: when the FOR statement first begins. Changing those values inside the FOR loop does not affect the control of the FOR loop. Changing the counter variable, however, affects it because the control variable is changed and compared to the ending value each time through the loop.

Chapter 14 Answers

1. TRUE.
2. A. Bottom.
   B. Top.
   C. Bottom.
   D. Top.
3. A. False.
   B. False.
   C. True.
   D. True.

   The UNTIL loops always test for a false condition, whereas the WHILE loops always test for a true.
4. A DO loop performs a relational test. It is an indeterminate loop. A FOR loop, on the other hand, executes the body of the FOR loop a certain number of times controlled by the FOR's control values.
5. Forever. Because A is not changed, the DO WHILE loops endlessly.
6. Here's the loop:

```
QBasic
QBasic
QBasic
   :
   :
```

   This is an infinite loop.

Chapter 15 Answers

1. The colon (:).
2. TRUE if you are using a block IF-THEN-ELSE. Otherwise, the ELSE must be combined with an IF statement on the same line.

3. The separating colon is good for a few short statements. Too many colons, however, can clutter a program and make it less readable.

4. TRUE. The ELSEIF breaks an IF-THEN into more than two possible outcomes.

5. The ELSEIF statement must be one word with no space.

6. QBasic has to know where the block IF ends.

7.
```
IF (A < 2) THEN
   PRINT "Yes"
   GOTO Here
ELSE
   PRINT "No"
   GOTO There
END IF
```

Chapter 16 Answers

1. The SELECT CASE statement.

2. The CASE ELSE option.

3. FALSE. END optionally goes at the end of QBasic programs to signal the end of the entire program. STOP stops the execution at any point within the program.

4. The TO keyword.

5. The IS keyword.

6. The ON GOTO causes multiple branching that can be difficult to follow, whereas the SELECT CASE statement keeps the sections of each CASE code together and more readable.

7. FALSE. Putting the most often-executed CASE option first speeds up your programs. (You do not always know in advance which this will be, however.)

8.
```
SELECT CASE num
   CASE 1
      PRINT "Alpha"
```

```
   CASE 2
      PRINT "Beta"
   CASE 3
      PRINT "Gamma"
   CASE ELSE
      PRINT "Other"
END SELECT
```

9.
```
SELECT CASE code$
   CASE "A" TO "Z"
      PRINT "Code is within range"
   CASE ELSE
      PRINT "Code is out of range"
END SELECT
```

10.
```
SELECT CASE (sales)
   CASE IS > 5000
      bonus = 50
   CASE IS > 2500
      bonus = 25
   CASE ELSE
      bonus = 0
END SELECT
```

Chapter 17 Answers

1. TRUE.
2. By the subscript.
3. No, every element in an array must be the same type.
4. By using the `ERASE` statement.
5. 79. Remember that QBasic begins with a 0 subscript, although many programmers ignore the 0 subscript and start at 1.
6. The `OPTIONS BASE` and the expanded `DIM (... TO...)` statement.

7. By using the SWAP statement.
8. DIM automatically sets all numeric array elements to zero and all string array elements to empty strings when QBasic dimensions the array.
9. Twenty-three elements are reserved (4 - (-18) + 1 = 23).

Chapter 18 Answers

1. `DIM scores(5, 6)`
2. `DIM names$(10, 20, 3)`
3. The first subscript, 5, is the row subscript; the second subscript, 10, is the column subscript.
4. Thirty elements are reserved (5 times 6).
5. A. 2
   B. 1
   C. 91
   D. 8
6. A. 68
   B. 100
   C. 80
7. The nested FOR-NEXT loop is best because its control variables simulate the row and column (and depths, and so on for more than two dimensions) numbers of a matrix.
8. They reserve 552 elements (23 times 6 times 4).

Chapter 19 Answers

1. They are already written for you.
2. It is a constant, a variable, or an expression inside the function's parentheses that the function works on.

3. `ABS()` returns the absolute value, `SGN()` returns the sign of an argument, and `SQR()` computes the square root.
4. There is no way of telling because it is random and based on the `TIMER` return value at the time.
5. `CINT()`, `CLNG()`, `CSNG()`, and `CDBL()`.
6. `-6 -5 -6`
7. Also `.054456`. Passing a positive argument to the `RND` function generates the previous random number.
8. TRUE.

Chapter 20 Answers

1. TRUE.
2. `RIGHT$()` or `MID$()`.
3. The `LEN()` function.
4. `ASC()` returns the ASCII character of whatever number is passed to it. `CHR$()` returns the ASCII number of whatever character is passed to it.
5. TRUE. `MID$()` is one of the few statements that can also be used as a function.
6. When you want to get one character from the keyboard without the user having to press Enter.
7. TRUE. The first `PRINT` prints 10 spaces between the letters, the second `PRINT` prints a string of 10 spaces between the two letters, the third `PRINT` prints 10 ASCII character 32s (spaces) between the two characters, and the last `PRINT` duplicates the first character (the space) in the string 10 times between the two letters.
8. It prints `fun`.
9. It prints `72`.

10. You would use the following statement:

```
PRINT SPACE$(80-LEN("QBasic By Example")/2); "QBasic By Example"
```

Chapter 21 Answers

1. QBasic does not have a built-in function to do everything.
2. FALSE.
3. A. String.
   B. 1
   C. Integer.
4. FALSE. A function can never return more than one value. If it is a multiple-line function with more than one `FN`*num* `=` statement, the data conditionally controls which of the return statements is executed.
5. The square root function (`SQR()`).

Chapter 22 Answers

1. QBasic opens a separate editing window for the subroutine procedure.
2. FALSE. `RETURN` goes at the end of subroutines called by `GOSUB`, not the separate (and better) subroutine procedures fenced from the rest of the program by the `SUB-END SUB` statements.
3. The F2 key (or **V**iew **S**UBs... from the menu).
4. From the data type suffix on the function procedure name. (Putting no data type suffix makes it default to single-precision, just as if you typed the *!* suffix data type character.)
5. If you call subroutine procedures without using the `CALL` keyword, or if your program includes a function procedure.

6. FALSE. Only those variables that exist in both routines need to be shared. If the subroutine procedure uses work variables (for temporary results, or loop counters), no `SHARED` statement is needed.

7. From the parameter list after the function procedure's name. These are the values being passed to the function.

Chapter 23 Answers

1. You can easily change it if the value for `sales.minimum` changes. Instead of changing the value everywhere it appears, you have to change only the `CONST` statement.

2. FALSE. A local variable is local only to the module in which it is defined.

3. You cannot supply the data type suffix character (the $) if you dimension the variable as a specific type.

4. `John L. Ke` is the output because the string is fixed to hold only 10 characters.

5. Never! A global variable does not have to be passed because it is known throughout every procedure in the program anyway.

6. `STATIC`, so it retains its value.

7. Pass by address. Passing by value ensures that arguments will be changed only in the procedure they are sent (copied) to.

8. `-5` and `20`. It does not matter how many elements contain data. `LBOUND()` and `UBOUND()` return the lower- and upper-dimensioned subscripts.

Chapter 24 Answers

1. Sequential access and random access.

2. A. 5
   B. 4
   C. Part No., Description, Quantity, Price.
3. Sequential access and random access.
4. A. There is not enough RAM to hold large amounts of data.

   B. Nonprogrammers cannot always be expected to change the program when the data changes. You want anybody to be able to use your programs without having to know QBasic.
5. Fixed-length records typically require less programming.
6. The file names are technically valid file names. They are not meaningful, however, and do not help describe the data contained in them.
7. The file `sales.89.may` has one too many periods in the name (a file name cannot have more than one file extension). The file called `employees.dec` contains too many letters in the first part of the file name. The rest of the file names are valid.

Chapter 25 Answers

1. The `OPEN` statement.
2. `APPEND`, `INPUT`, and `OUTPUT`.
3. The `INPUT #` statement.
4. TRUE.
5. The `FREEFILE` function.
6. QBasic will create the file.
7. The `PRINT #` writes data to a file, just as `PRINT` writes it to the screen. The more useful `WRITE #` statement inserts commas between fields and puts quotation marks around all string data to make it easier to read later.

8. It tells whether the record just read was the last one.
9. The `FILES=` statement in the CONFIG.SYS file.
10. `LINE INPUT #`

Chapter 26 Answers

1. You can read and write random-access files in any record order without having to read every record up to the one you want.
2. The `TYPE` is much easier and does not require that you convert all fields to string before storing them.
3. `MKI$()`, `MKL$()`, `MKS$()`, and `MKD$()`.
4. `CVI()`, `CVL()`, `CVS()`, and `CVD()`.
5. TRUE.
6. The next record in the file.
7. So that a search on that field will always find the record you are looking for. If more than one record key were the same, you would not know whether you found the record wanted by the user when you found a match of a key value.
8. `LOC(`*`filenumber`*`) / `*`recordlength`*
9. They save space on the disk.
10. By using the `AS ANY` type declaration after the parameter name.

Chapter 27 Answers

1. An adapter card that displays graphics, such as CGA, EGA, VGA, MCGA, or HGA. You must also have a matching monitor.
2. Picture element.

3. The PSET and PRESET commands.
4. FALSE. LOCATE does not work at the pixel level.
5. TRUE. In any graphics mode, you can locate the cursor with the LOCATE command for printing with subsequent PRINT statements.
6. The LINE command with its box-drawing option. You can draw boxes with PSET and with DRAW, but it takes more effort on your part. There is no BOX statement in QBasic.
7. FALSE. The DRAW's B command moves the pixel location *without* drawing. This lets you "pick up" the drawing pen and move it to another location. Subsequent drawing commands will resume the drawing.
8. It stretches the drawn circle, either horizontally (if the aspect is less than 1), or vertically (if the aspect is 1 or more).

Chapter 28 Answers

1. SCREEN mode 0.
2. FALSE. These commands each have color options.
3. Use the COLOR statement.
4. Each color (except black) resides on one of two palettes. Only one palette can be active at a time.
5. FALSE. There is no specified border color on the PAINT statement. Because PAINT assumes a border color of 4 (the same color as the painting color if you do not specify a border), it does not know where to quit filling the circle.

Chapter 29 Answers

1. BEEP produces only one tone. SOUND lets you specify any tone of any duration.

2. `SOUND 440, 36.4`
3. PLAY contains its own miniature musical language that lets you specify much more than SOUND's single note and duration.
4. TRUE. To play while processing the rest of the program, you have to play in background mode. The background mode (MB) buffers the rest of the song so that the program can continue while the song plays simultaneously.
5. There are seven octaves numbered 0 through 6.
6. The pound sign (#) and the plus sign (+).
7. Plays six octaves of the note C.

Keyword Reference

ABS
ASC
ATN
BASE
CALL
CASE
CDBL
CHDIR
CHR$
CINT
CIRCLE
CLEAR
CLNG
CLOSE
CLS
COLOR
COM
CONST
COS
CSNG
CSRLIN
CVDMBF
CVSMBF
DATA
DECLARE
DIM
DO
ELSE
END
EOF
ERASE
ERDEV
ERDEV$
ERL
ERR
ERROR
EXIT
EXP
FILEATTR
FOR
FRE
FREEFILE
FUNCTION
GET
GOSUB
GOTO
HEX$
IF
INKEY$
INP
INPUT
INPUT$
INSTR
INT
KEY
KILL
LCASE$
LEFT$
LEN
LINE
LOC
LOCATE
LOCK
LOF
LOG
LOOP

LPOS
LPRINT
LSET
LTRIM$
MID$
MKDIR
NAME
NEXT
OCT$
ON
OPEN
OPTION
OUT
PAINT
PALETTE
PCOPY
PEEK
PEN
PLAY
PMAP
POINT
POKE
POS
PRESET
PRINT
PSET
PUT
RANDOMIZE
READ
REDIM
REM
RESTORE
RESUME
RETURN
RIGHT$
RMDIR
RND
RSET
RTRIM$
RUN
SCREEN
SEEK
SELECT
SGN
SHARED
SHELL
SIN
SPACE$
SPC
SQR
STATIC
STOP
STR$
STRIG
STRING$
SUB
SWAP
SYSTEM
TAB
TAN
THEN
TIME$
TIMER
TYPE
UCASE$
UNLOCK
USING
VAL
VIEW
WAIT
WIDTH
WINDOW
WRITE

Comparing QBasic and GW-BASIC

You might want to read this appendix if you have programmed in other dialects of BASIC, including GW-BASIC and BASICA. These BASIC programming languages were supplied with previous versions of MS-DOS and PC-DOS. QBasic is a dramatic change from the other BASICs. This appendix explains some of the differences and how to convert programs from a previous version of BASIC to QBasic.

The QBasic Environment

When you first use QBasic, you cannot help but notice the vastly improved interface. Rather than the black GW-BASIC screen editor, you see the colorful opening screen of the QBasic editor. If you have used menus in other programs, you will appreciate QBasic's menus. Instead of having to remember obscure program editing commands such as `LIST`, `RUN`, `SAVE`, `LOAD`, and `LLIST` you simply select program control statements from the menus. You can do so with the keyboard or with a mouse, as described in Part I.

A QBasic program does not require line numbers on every line, as previous versions of BASIC did. Although QBasic allows line numbers, statements should not have line numbers if you never GOTO, GOSUB, or RETURN to that line. Because line labels (descriptive labels on each line) are allowed, line numbers seem to cloud programs instead of making them clearer.

The program shown next is an old GW-BASIC version of a test-averaging program:

```
10 ' Test averaging program
20 CLS
30 INPUT "Please enter three test scores"; test1, test2, test3
40 average = (test1 + test2 + test3) / 3
50 PRINT "The average is"; average
60 PRINT
70 INPUT "Would you like to see three more (Y/N)"; ans$
80 IF (LEFT$(ans$, 1) = "Y") THEN GOTO 30
```

Because you are not limited to line numbers, you can rewrite this program in QBasic as shown:

```
' Test averaging program
CLS

Another:
   INPUT "Please enter three test scores"; test1, test2, test3
   average = (test1 + test2 + test3) / 3
   PRINT "The average is"; average
   PRINT
   INPUT "Would you like to see three more (Y/N)"; ans$
   IF (LEFT$(ans$, 1) = "Y") THEN GOTO Another
```

Notice how much the program's readability is improved, despite the fact that the program is exactly the same in both examples. The QBasic version seems cleaner and "more modern" because the line numbers do not clutter the program. Of course, you can take full advantage of QBasic's control statements and get rid of the GOTO, as shown in this example:

```
' Test averaging program
CLS

DO
   INPUT "Please enter three test scores"; test1, test2, test3
   average = (test1 + test2 + test3) / 3
   PRINT "The average is"; average
   PRINT
   INPUT "Would you like to see three more (Y/N)"; ans$
LOOP UNTIL (LEFT$(ans$, 1) = "Y")
```

The block-structured nature of QBasic (as with most of the newer compiler versions of BASIC that exist today) lets the DO-LOOP span more than one line. You can control an entire block of statements with IF-THEN and DO-LOOP statements.

QBasic offers on-line help (accessed by pressing F1), long integers (32 bits of internal storage), separate subroutine and function procedures, user-defined data types, VGA support, recursion (a subroutine can call itself), and fixed-length strings.

This book is dedicated to each of these new aspects of QBasic as well as the old ones. If you are a veteran GW-BASIC programmer, you can skim some sections and study others.

Whatever you do, remember the on-line help (F1). From the on-line help, you can look at examples of almost every command and function in QBasic.

Don't look for the TRON and TROFF statements. QBasic goes far beyond that simple tracing ability with its **D**ebug pull-down menu. QBasic lets you walk through a program one line at a time, looking at variables and expressions along the way.

The full-screen editor is a must. It offers full mouse support, separate windows for editing and results, a WordStar-compatible speed key command set, a search, and cut-and-paste operations. You can also turn on instant error-checking; *as you type the program,* QBasic can alert you if the line contains an error.

Table D.1 shows a list of all keywords from GW-BASIC that are not supported in QBasic. Although most programs work well without these keywords, if you want to run older BASIC programs that contain any of these statements, you must remove them. Most of the keywords in Table D.1 contain cassette storage commands (cassette storage of programs and data is not supported by QBasic) and editor commands that were replaced by the QBasic pull-down menus.

Table D.1. Keywords not supported in QBasic.

AUTO	LIST	NEW
EDIT	MOTOR	USR
MERGE	SAVE	DELETE
RENUM	DEF USR	LOAD
CONT	LLIST	

There are a few other (minor) differences in some of the statements. The major differences (those having commands better described in this book) are listed in Table D.2.

Table D.2. Statement differences between GW-BASIC and QBasic.

Keyword	*Description*
CHAIN	You cannot specify a line number after CHAIN (only a program name). Do not use the GW-BASIC CHAIN options ALL, MERGE, or DELETE.
COMMON	Must go before any executable statement in your programs (remarks are the only statements that can go before COMMON statements).
DECLARE	Must go before any executable statement in your programs (remarks are the only statements that can go before DECLARE statements).
EOF()	The QBasic EOF() function returns a TRUE result if you just read the last record. GW-BASIC returns a TRUE result if the next record to read is the end of file.
FIELD	You cannot use the values from a FIELD statement if you first close the file. In GW-BASIC, the fielded values would still be in the FIELD variables.

Converting GW-BASIC Programs to QBasic Programs

It is fairly easy to convert a GW-BASIC program to QBasic. You must first remove any of the keywords in Table D.1. You must also convert all CALL statements in the GW-BASIC program to CALL ABSOLUTE statements. (These allow the CALLs to behave the same in both environments. It is usually much better to separate the CALLed subroutines into QBasic subroutine procedures instead.) After removing any of these keywords, you then must save the program as an ASCII file before loading it into QBasic. If you want to save the program under the filename of QFILE.BAS, type

```
SAVE "QFILE.BAS", A
```

The A ensures that GW-BASIC saves the program as an ASCII text file and not as the compacted version that it normally would. If the program reads data files created with GW-BASIC, you must start QBasic with the /MBF option, as in

```
QBASIC/MBF
```

Finally, you might want to run the program through the REMLINE.BAS program supplied with QBasic. REMLINE.BAS removes all unnecessary line numbers to make the program more readable when you load it into the QBasic editor.

Conclusion

Despite the differences, you will find that QBasic offers improvements over the way you programmed in GW-BASIC. The language is similar enough to maintain the familiarity with BASIC that you already have. The differences, such as the on-line help, full-screen editor, debugger, and pull-down menus, are much easier to learn than the cryptic program-editing commands you had to remember for GW-BASIC. The best way to learn QBasic is to start the program and begin running the examples throughout this book.

The Complete Application

```
' Filename: BOOK.BAS
'
' Book Management Database Program
' ---- ---------- -------- -------
'
' This program illustrates using QBasic to create a book-tracking
' database program. You can keep track of your book inventory,
' the authors in your library, the price you paid for each book,
' the condition of the book, and more.

' The program's easy-to-use data-entry screens and reports
' make keeping track of your personal collection of books easy.
'
DECLARE SUB EditData ()
DECLARE SUB ScrnPrintA (init%,author$,title$,edition$,cover$)
DECLARE SUB PrinterPrintA (init%,author$,title$,edition$,cover$)
DECLARE SUB DispScrnTitlesA ()
DECLARE SUB DispScrnTitlesT ()
DECLARE SUB ScrnPrintT (init%,author$,title$,edition$,cover$)
DECLARE SUB PrinterPrintT (init%,author$,title$,edition$,cover$)
DECLARE SUB DispMessage (mess$)
DECLARE SUB PrintBookTitl ()
```

```
DECLARE SUB PressEnter ()
DECLARE SUB PrinterPrint (init%,author$,title$,edition$,cover$)
DECLARE SUB PrintTitles ()
DECLARE SUB ScrnOrPrint (dev$)
DECLARE SUB ScrnPrint (init%,author$,title$,edition$,cover$)
DECLARE SUB DispScrnTitles ()
DECLARE SUB DispFieldData ()
DECLARE SUB ErrorMsg1 (Message$)
DECLARE SUB GetFileName ()
DECLARE SUB PrintBookAuth ()
DECLARE SUB FixTitle ()
DECLARE SUB FileSearch (s.title$)
DECLARE SUB GetLookTitle (s.title$)
DECLARE SUB BadThe ()
DECLARE SUB LookBook ()
DECLARE SUB DispFieldNames ()
DECLARE SUB GetCover (cover$)
DECLARE SUB GetField (row%, col%, data$)
DECLARE SUB DispPrompts ()
DECLARE SUB EnterBook (MaxNumBooks%)
DECLARE SUB DispMenu ()

TYPE bookrec
   title    AS STRING * 30   ' Title of book
   author   AS STRING * 25   ' Author name
   cond     AS STRING * 10   ' Condition
   pubdate  AS STRING * 20   ' Publication Date
   edition  AS STRING * 10   ' Edition (1st, 2nd, etc.)
   cover    AS STRING * 1    ' H/S for Hardcover or Softcover
   notes    AS STRING * 160  ' Misc. notes on the book
END TYPE

' The following are global since almost EVERY procedure needs
' them
COMMON SHARED book AS bookrec          ' A user-defined type
COMMON SHARED bookfile$                ' Book datafile to use

COLOR 7, 1         ' White letters on blue background
CLS
GetFileName        ' Get the filename of the book file
READ MaxNumBooks%  ' Maximum number of books to enter
DATA 500
```

```
DO
   DispMenu       ' Display menu and get menu option
   SELECT CASE menu.option%
       CASE (1): EnterBook (MaxNumBooks%) ' Get a book
       CASE (2): LookBook          ' Look at an individual book
       CASE (3): PrintBookAuth     ' Print book listing by author
       CASE (4): PrintBookTitl     ' Print book listing by title
   END SELECT

LOOP UNTIL (menu.option% = 5)

SUB BadThe
'
' Prints error at bottom of screen if
' they typed The as the first three letters
' of title.
'
   CALL ErrorMsg1("The title cannot begin with 'The'")
   LOCATE 24, 16
   PRINT "Press ENTER to try another one...";
   LINE INPUT ; ans$
   LOCATE 24, 12
   PRINT SPACE$(80)     ' Erase the error messages
   COLOR 7, 1

END SUB

SUB DispFieldData
'
' Displays found book's data in highlighted fields.
'
   COLOR 15, 1        ' Highlight data in fields
   LOCATE 6, 12       ' Print a match from file
   PRINT book.title
   LOCATE 8, 13
   PRINT book.author
   LOCATE 11, 16
   PRINT book.cond
   LOCATE 11, 53
   PRINT book.pubdate
   LOCATE 15, 14
   PRINT book.edition
```

```
    LOCATE 15, 58
    PRINT book.cover
    LOCATE 18, 12
    PRINT RTRIM$(book.notes)

END SUB

SUB DispFieldNames
'
' Simply prints the names of each field
' in their place on the screen, and a
' lot of spaces after them to clear
' whatever may still be on the line.
'
    COLOR 7, 1
    LOCATE 6, 5
    PRINT "Title:" + SPACE$(50);
    LOCATE 8, 5
    PRINT "Author:" + SPACE$(50);
    LOCATE 11, 5
    PRINT "Condition:" + SPACE$(20);
    LOCATE 11, 35
    PRINT "Publication Date:" + SPACE$(20);
    LOCATE 15, 5
    PRINT "Edition:" + SPACE$(20);
    LOCATE 15, 35
    PRINT "Hard/Soft Cover (H/S):" + SPACE$(20);
    LOCATE 18, 5
    PRINT "Notes:" + SPACE$(50);  ' Old notes on the screen may
    LOCATE 19, 1                  ' take more than one line
    PRINT SPACE$(79);
    LOCATE 20, 1
    PRINT SPACE$(79);

END SUB

SUB DispMenu
'
' This subroutine simply displays the book database main menu.
' The user enters the option he or she desires.
' The menu keeps displaying until a valid option is entered.
'
```

```
   SHARED menu.option%    ' Be able to use the main procedure's
                          ' variable

   COLOR 7, 1 ' White letters on blue background
   CLS
   PRINT
   PRINT TAB(20); "*** Book Database Program ***"
   PRINT
   PRINT
   PRINT TAB(10); "Here are your choices:"
   PRINT
   PRINT TAB(20); "1. Enter a new book"
   PRINT
   PRINT TAB(20); "2. Look at a book's information"
   PRINT
   PRINT TAB(20); "3. Print a listing of all books by author"
   PRINT
   PRINT TAB(20); "4. Print a listing of all books by title"
   PRINT
   PRINT TAB(20); "5. Exit this program"
   PRINT
   PRINT TAB(10); "What is your choice? _"
   DO
      ans$ = INKEY$
   LOOP WHILE (ans$ = "")
   LOCATE 17, 31              ' Echo the user's input
   PRINT ans$
   menu.option% = VAL(ans$)

END SUB

SUB DispMessage (mess$)
'
' Displays a red message at bottom of screen
'
   DIM messline AS STRING * 79     ' Message line that will be
                                   ' printed

   COLOR 12, 1   ' Bright red characters on blue
   mess$ = "*** " + mess$ + " ***"         ' Enclose in asterisks
```

```
   mlen = LEN(mess$)      ' Length of error message to print
   MID$(messline, (79 - mlen) / 2) = mess$  ' Center error
                                            ' message

   LOCATE 23, 1
   PRINT messline;

   COLOR 7, 1       ' Restore white on blue

END SUB

SUB DispPrompts
'
' This subroutine is called from the data-entry routine.
' It simply prints the data-entry screen title and prompts
' for each field.
'
   COLOR 7, 1
   PRINT
   PRINT TAB(20); "*** Enter a Book's Information ***"
   PRINT TAB(20); "    -------------------------"

   CALL DispFieldNames     ' Display field names

END SUB

SUB DispScrnTitlesA
'
' Prints new titles on the screen, by Author field.
'
   PRINT "Author"; TAB(27); "Title"; TAB(58); "Edition";
   PRINT TAB(69); "Cover"
   PRINT STRING$(79, "-");

END SUB

SUB DispScrnTitlesT
'
' Prints new titles on the screen, Title field first.
'
```

```
   PRINT "Title"; TAB(32); "Author"; TAB(58); "Edition";
   PRINT TAB(69); "Cover"
   PRINT STRING$(79, "-");

END SUB

SUB EditData
'
' This routine lets the user press ENTER through the data,
' changing whatever needs to be changed on the screen.
'
   COLOR 15, 1        ' Highlight all input

   LOCATE 6, 12
   LINE INPUT title$
   IF (title$ <> "") THEN
      book.title = title$
      CALL FixTitle
      LOCATE 6, 12
      PRINT book.title
   END IF

   LOCATE 8, 13
   LINE INPUT author$
   IF (author$ <> "") THEN book.author = author$
   LOCATE 8, 13
   PRINT book.author

   LOCATE 11, 16
   LINE INPUT cond$
   IF (cond$ <> "") THEN book.cond = cond$
   LOCATE 11, 16
   PRINT book.cond

   LOCATE 11, 53
   LINE INPUT pubdate$
   IF (pubdate$ <> "") THEN book.pubdate = pubdate$
   LOCATE 11, 53
   PRINT book.pubdate
```

```
   LOCATE 15, 14
   LINE INPUT edition$
   IF (edition$ <> "") THEN book.edition = edition$
   LOCATE 15, 14
   PRINT book.edition

   GetCover (cover$)
   IF (cover$ <> "") THEN book.cover = cover$
   COLOR 15, 1
   LOCATE 15, 58
   PRINT book.cover

   LOCATE 18, 12
   LINE INPUT notes$
   IF (notes$ <> "") THEN book.notes = notes$
   LOCATE 18, 12
   PRINT RTRIM$(book.notes)

END SUB

SUB EnterBook (MaxNumBooks%)
'
' This subroutine gets the user's input for a book.
' That information is then written to the file.
'
   OPEN bookfile$ FOR APPEND AS #1       ' Add to end of file
   IF LOC(1) / (LEN(book) + 19) > MaxNumBooks% THEN
      CLS
      ErrorMsg1 ("This file has the maximum number of books")
      CLOSE #1
      EXIT SUB
   END IF

   DO                                ' Repeat until they want to quit
      CLS
      CALL DispPrompts                ' Display the screen prompts
      CALL GetField(6, 12, book.title)   ' Get the title, etc.
      IF (book.title = SPACE$(30)) THEN   ' If they only pressed
                                          ' ENTER,
         CLOSE #1            ' close the data file without writing
         EXIT SUB            ' to it, and return to the Main Menu.
```

```
      END IF
      CALL FixTitle     ' Move 'The' to end of title, if needed
      COLOR 7, 1
      CALL GetField(8, 13, book.author)
      CALL GetField(11, 16, book.cond)
      CALL GetField(11, 53, book.pubdate)
      CALL GetField(15, 14, book.edition)
      book.edition = UCASE$(book.edition)   ' Convert it to
                                            ' uppercase
      CALL GetCover(book.cover)             ' Ensure that an H or
                                            ' S is entered
      CALL GetField(18, 12, book.notes)

      DO
         LOCATE 23, 15
         COLOR 12, 1
         INPUT "Do you want to change anything (Y/N)"; ans$
         IF (UCASE$(LEFT$(ans$, 1)) = "Y") THEN
            LOCATE 23, 15
            PRINT STRING$(60, " ")
            CALL EditData
         END IF
      LOOP UNTIL (UCASE$(LEFT$(ans$, 1)) = "N")

      WRITE #1, book.title,book.author,book.cond
      WRITE #1, book.pubdate,book.edition,book.cover,book.notes

      LOCATE 23, 15     ' See if they want another
      COLOR 12, 1       ' Red on blue
      PRINT STRING$(60, " ")
      LOCATE 23, 15
      INPUT "Do you want to enter another (Y/N)"; ans$
      ans$ = UCASE$(ans$)
   LOOP UNTIL (LEFT$(ans$, 1) = "N")
   CLOSE #1
END SUB

SUB ErrorMsg1 (Message$)
'
' Briefly displays a red error message at bottom of screen.
'
```

```
    DIM errorline AS STRING * 79      ' Error line that will be
                                      ' printed

    BEEP
    COLOR 12, 1    ' Red characters on blue
    Message$ = "*** " + Message$ + " ***"   ' Enclose in asterisks
    lerr = LEN(Message$)      ' Length of error message to print
    MID$(errorline, (79 - lerr) / 2) = Message$   ' Center error
                                                  ' message

    LOCATE 23, 1
    PRINT errorline;

    FOR i = 1 TO 12000    ' Timing loop while user reads error
    NEXT i

    errorline = STRING$(79, " ")    ' Blank the message and return
                                    ' the colors
    LOCATE 23, 1
    PRINT errorline;
    COLOR 7, 1

END SUB

SUB FileSearch (s.title$)
'
' Searches for the title (or partial title) the user entered.
'
    OPEN bookfile$ FOR INPUT AS #1

    DO      ' Search through file for book
       CALL DispFieldNames
       INPUT #1, book.title, book.author
       INPUT #1, book.cond, book.pubdate
       INPUT #1, book.edition, book.cover, book.notes

       IF (LEFT$(UCASE$(book.title), LEN(s.title$)) =
           UCASE$(s.title$)) THEN
          CALL DispFieldData ' Display each field's data
          LOCATE 23, 10      ' Clear bottom message area
          PRINT SPACE$(70)
```

```
        DO                          ' See if this is the correct book
           LOCATE 23, 15
           COLOR 12, 1          ' Bold red on blue
           PRINT "Is this the correct book you were looking for ";
           INPUT "(Y/N)"; ans$
           ans$ = UCASE$(ans$)
        LOOP UNTIL ((ans$ = "Y") OR (ans$ = "N"))
        IF (ans$ = "Y") THEN    ' Wait until they are through
           CALL PressEnter
           CLOSE #1
           EXIT SUB                 ' Return to Main Menu
        END IF
     END IF
  LOOP UNTIL (EOF(1))
  CLOSE #1
  ErrorMsg1 ("There are no more books to search for")

END SUB

SUB FixTitle
'
' If the title starts with "The..." this routine
' will move ", The" to the end of the title.
'
   IF UCASE$(LEFT$(book.title, 4)) = "THE " THEN
      ' Trim any trailing spaces, temporarily, off the title.
      ' Then append ', The' to the end of the book title
      ' and take off the prefix 'The' before actually saving the
      ' "real" title.
      book.title = RIGHT$(RTRIM$(book.title),
LEN(RTRIM$(book.title)) - 4)
      book.title = RTRIM$(book.title) + ", The"
      COLOR 15, 1
      LOCATE 6, 12
      PRINT book.title       ' Display the new title
   END IF

END SUB
```

```
SUB GetCover (cover$)
'
' This routine ensures that the user types either
' an H or an S for Hardcover or Softcover, respectively.
'
   DO
      CALL GetField(15, 58, cover$)
      cover$ = UCASE$(cover$)
      IF ((cover$<>"H") AND (cover$<>"S") AND (cover$<>"")) THEN
         CALL ErrorMsg1("You must type an H or S")
      END IF
   LOOP UNTIL ((cover$="H") OR (cover$="S") OR (cover$=""))
   LOCATE 23, 10  ' Remove error message
   PRINT SPACE$(26)
   LOCATE 15, 58    ' Display uppercase equivalent of the S or H
   COLOR 15, 1      ' Highlight it
   PRINT cover$
   COLOR 7, 1       ' Back to normal characters
END SUB

SUB GetField (row%, col%, data$)
'
' A small function used to place cursor and
' highlight input data for each field.
'
   LOCATE row%, col%
   LINE INPUT data$
   LOCATE row%, col%
   COLOR 15, 1
   PRINT data$; "  "
   COLOR 7, 1

END SUB

SUB GetFileName
'
' Asks the user for the name of the disk file to use.
' This allows for more than one data file. They might have
' a file of technical books, one for fiction, etc.
'
   LOCATE 10, 10
```

```
   INPUT "What is the name of the book file to use"; bookfile$

   IF (RIGHT$(bookfile$, 4) <> ".DAT") THEN      ' Append the
                                                 ' extension
      bookfile$ = bookfile$ + ".DAT"
   END IF

END SUB

SUB GetLookTitle (s.title$)
'
' Get a valid title to look for.
' The user cannot begin a title with 'The' when searching.
'


   DO
      LOCATE 23, 12     ' Bottom of screen message telling user
                        ' what to do
      COLOR 12, 1       ' Red on Blue Colors
      PRINT"* * Type a title, or first few letters of title * *"
      COLOR 7, 1        ' White on blue again
      LOCATE 6, 12
      PRINT SPACE$(60) ' Clear anything that might be onscreen
      CALL GetField(6, 12, s.title$)    ' Get title to search for
      IF (s.title$ = "") THEN EXIT SUB ' If they only pressed
                                       ' ENTER, return
      IF (LEFT$(UCASE$(s.title$), 3) = "THE ") THEN
         CALL BadThe    ' Do not let them start title with The...
      END IF
   LOOP WHILE (LEFT$(UCASE$(s.title$), 3) = "THE ")

END SUB

SUB LookBook
'
' Requests a title, or partial title, and displays that book's
' information.
'
   CLS
   PRINT
   PRINT TAB(20); "*** Look at a Book's Information ***"
   PRINT TAB(20); "    ---------------------------"
```

```
   CALL DispFieldNames              ' Display the field names on
                                    ' the screen
   CALL GetLookTitle(s.title$)      ' Get the title to look for
   CALL FileSearch(s.title$)        ' Search for the title

END SUB

SUB PressEnter
'
' Prompt, in red at bottom of screen, for user to press ENTER.
'
   COLOR 12, 1
   LOCATE 23, 15
   PRINT SPACE$(60)
   LOCATE 23, 20
   LINE INPUT ; "Press ENTER to continue..."; ans$
   COLOR 7, 1

END SUB

SUB PrintBookAuth
'
' Prints a report alphabetically by the author's name. (This
' implies that the user entered them in last name order!)
' The file is read into parallel arrays and sorted.
'
   REDIM author$(500), title$(500)   ' Parallel arrays to hold
   REDIM edition$(500), cover$(500)  ' the data printed

   CALL DispMessage("Please wait while sorting...")    ' Tell
                                                    ' user to wait
   OPEN bookfile$ FOR INPUT AS #1
   num.recs = 1

   DO
      INPUT #1, title$(num.recs), author$(num.recs)
      INPUT #1, cond$, pubdate$, edition$(num.recs)
      INPUT #1, cover$(num.recs), notes$
      num.recs = num.recs + 1
   LOOP UNTIL (EOF(1))
   CLOSE #1
```

```
   FOR i = 1 TO num.recs
      FOR j = i TO num.recs - 1
         IF (author$(i) > author$(j)) THEN
            SWAP author$(i), author$(j)
            SWAP title$(i), title$(j)
            SWAP edition$(i), edition$(j)
            SWAP cover$(i), cover$(j)
         END IF
      NEXT j
   NEXT i

   CALL ScrnOrPrint(dev$)    ' Asks if user wants data on screen
                             ' or printer
   IF (dev$ = "S") THEN
      CALL ScrnPrintA(1, "", "", "", "")  ' Initialize Screen
   ELSE
      CALL PrinterPrintA(1, "", "", "", "")  ' Initialize Screen
   END IF

   FOR ctr = 1 TO num.recs
      IF (dev$ = "S") THEN
         CALL ScrnPrintA(0, author$(ctr), title$(ctr),
                         edition$(ctr), cover$(ctr))
      ELSE
         CALL PrinterPrintA(0, author$(ctr), title$(ctr),
                            edition$(ctr), cover$(ctr))
      END IF
   NEXT ctr
   CALL PressEnter

END SUB

SUB PrintBookTitl
'
' Prints a report alphabetically by the title. The file is
' read into parallel arrays and sorted.
'
   REDIM author$(500), title$(500)  ' Parallel arrays to hold
   REDIM edition$(500), cover$(500) ' the data printed
```

```
CALL DispMessage("Please wait while sorting...")     ' Tell
                                                    ' user to wait
OPEN bookfile$ FOR INPUT AS #1
num.recs = 1

DO
   INPUT #1, title$(num.recs), author$(num.recs)
   INPUT #1, cond$, pubdate$, edition$(num.recs)
   INPUT #1, cover$(num.recs), notes$
   num.recs = num.recs + 1
LOOP UNTIL (EOF(1))
CLOSE #1

FOR i = 1 TO num.recs
   FOR j = i TO num.recs - 1
      IF (title$(i) > title$(j)) THEN
         SWAP author$(i), author$(j)
         SWAP title$(i), title$(j)
         SWAP edition$(i), edition$(j)
         SWAP cover$(i), cover$(j)
      END IF
   NEXT j
NEXT i

CALL ScrnOrPrint(dev$)    ' Asks if user wants data on screen
                          ' or printer
IF (dev$ = "S") THEN
   CALL ScrnPrintT(1, "", "", "", "")    ' Initialize Screen
ELSE
   CALL PrinterPrintT(1, "", "", "", "")   ' Initialize Screen
END IF

FOR ctr = 1 TO num.recs
   IF (dev$ = "S") THEN
      CALL ScrnPrintT(0, author$(ctr), title$(ctr),
                          edition$(ctr), cover$(ctr))
   ELSE
      CALL PrinterPrintT(0, author$(ctr), title$(ctr),
                             edition$(ctr), cover$(ctr))
   END IF
NEXT ctr
```

```
   CALL PressEnter

END SUB

SUB PrinterPrintA (init%, author$, title$, edition$, cover$)
'
' Prints a record on the printer. This subroutine keeps track
' of the printed lines and prints a title at each new page
' (after 66 lines) and form feeds at the end of each page. If
' the init% argument is equal to 1, this routine zeros out the
' printing variables and assumes this call is the start of a new
' listing. Otherwise, the static variables keep their values.
'

STATIC linect AS INTEGER

   IF (init% = 1) THEN     ' If this were called for 1st time...
      LPRINT CHR$(11)      ' Form Feed
      linect = 3
      CALL PrintTitles
      EXIT SUB
   END IF                  ' Else, all future times after 1st...

   IF (linect = 2) THEN
      CALL PrintTitles
      linect = 3
   END IF

   LPRINT title$;TAB(32);author$;TAB(58);edition$;TAB(69);cover$

   linect = linect + 1
   IF linect = 64 THEN
      linect = 2
      LPRINT CHR$(11)
   END IF

END SUB

SUB PrinterPrintT (init%, author$, title$, edition$, cover$)
```

```
'
' Prints a record on the printer. This subroutine keeps track
' of the printed lines and prints a title at each new page
' (after 66 lines) and form feeds at the end of each page. If
' the init% argument is equal to 1, this routine zeros out the
' printing variables and assumes this call is the start of a new
' listing. Otherwise, the static variables keep their values.
'

STATIC linect AS INTEGER

   IF (init% = 1) THEN      ' If this were called for 1st time...
      LPRINT CHR$(11)       ' Form Feed
      linect = 3
      CALL PrintTitles
      EXIT SUB
   END IF                   ' Else, all future times after 1st...

   IF (linect = 2) THEN
      CALL PrintTitles
      linect = 3
   END IF

   LPRINT title$;TAB(32);author$;TAB(58);edition$;TAB(69);cover$

   linect = linect + 1
   IF linect = 64 THEN
      linect = 2
      LPRINT CHR$(11)
   END IF

END SUB

SUB PrintTitles
'
' Prints new titles on the printer
'
   LPRINT "Title"; TAB(32); "Author"; TAB(58); "Edition";
   LPRINT TAB(69); "Cover"
   LPRINT STRING$(79, "-");

END SUB
```

```
SUB ScrnOrPrint (dev$)
'
' Asks the user if he or she wants to print the list
' on the screen or printer.
'
   CLS

   DO
      LOCATE 12, 8
      PRINT "Do you want to see listing on the Screen or Printer ";
      INPUT "(S/P)"; dev$
      dev$ = UCASE$(LEFT$(dev$, 1))   ' Convert single-letter
                                      ' answer to upper
   LOOP UNTIL ((dev$ = "S") OR (dev$ = "P"))
   CLS

END SUB

SUB ScrnPrintA (init%, author$, title$, edition$, cover$)
'
' Prints a record on the screen. This subroutine keeps track
' of the screen lines printed and prints a title at each
' new screen and pauses at the end of each. If the init%
' argument is equal to 1, this routine zeros out the display
' variables and assumes this call is the start of a new
' listing. Otherwise, the static variables keep their values.
'

STATIC linect AS INTEGER

   IF (init% = 1) THEN    ' If this were called for 1st time...
      CLS
      linect = 3
      CALL DispScrnTitlesA
      EXIT SUB
   END IF                 ' Else, all future times after 1st...
```

```
   IF (linect = 2) THEN
      CALL DispScrnTitlesA
      linect = 3
   END IF

   LOCATE linect, 1
   PRINT author$

   LOCATE linect, 27
   PRINT title$

   LOCATE linect, 58
   PRINT edition$

   LOCATE linect, 69
   PRINT cover$

   linect = linect + 1
   IF linect = 22 THEN
      CALL PressEnter
      linect = 2
      CLS
   END IF

END SUB

SUB ScrnPrintT (init%, author$, title$, edition$, cover$)
'
' Prints a record on the screen. This subroutine keeps track
' of the screen lines printed and prints a title at each
' new screen and pauses at the end of each. If the init%
' argument is equal to 1, this routine zeros out the display
' variables and assumes this call is the start of a new
' listing. Otherwise, the static variables keep their values.
'

STATIC linect AS INTEGER

   IF (init% = 1) THEN    ' If this were called for 1st time...
      CLS
      linect = 3
      CALL DispScrnTitlesT
      EXIT SUB
```

```
   END IF                 ' Else, all future times after 1st...

   IF (linect = 2) THEN
      CALL DispScrnTitlesT
      linect = 3
   END IF

   LOCATE linect, 1
   PRINT title$

   LOCATE linect, 32
   PRINT author$

   LOCATE linect, 58
   PRINT edition$

   LOCATE linect, 69
   PRINT cover$

   linect = linect + 1
   IF linect = 22 THEN
      CALL PressEnter
      linect = 2
      CLS
   END IF

END SUB
```

Glossary

active directory The directory the computer first looks to when it is given commands.

active drive The *disk drive* the computer first looks to when given commands.

address Each *memory* location (each byte) has a unique address. The first address in memory is 0, the second *RAM* location's address is 1, and so on until the last RAM location (which comes thousands of bytes later).

analog signals How *data* is transferred over telephone lines. These are different from the binary digital signals used by your PC.

argument The value sent to a *function* or *procedure*. An argument is *constant* or a *variable* enclosed in parentheses.

array A list of *variables*, sometimes called a table of variables.

ASCII An acronym for American Standard Code for Information Interchange.

ASCII file A file containing characters that can be used by any *program* on most computers. Sometimes it is called a text file or an ASCII text file.

AUTOEXEC.BAT An optional *batch file* that *executes* a series of commands whenever you start or reset the computer.

back-up file A duplicate copy of a file that preserves your work in case you damage the original file. Files on a *hard disk* are commonly backed up onto *floppy disks.*

.BAK Common *file extension* for a *back-up file.*

.BAS Common *file extension* for a BASIC *program.*

batch file An *ASCII* text file containing *DOS* commands.

binary A numbering system based on two digits. The only valid digits in a binary system are 0 and 1. See also *bit.*

bit Short for *bi*nary digi*t*, which is the smallest unit of storage on a computer. Each bit can have a value of 0 or 1, indicating the absence or presence of an electrical signal. See also *binary.*

block One or more statements treated as though they are a single statement.

boot To start a computer with the operating system *software* in place. You must boot your computer before using it.

bubble sort A type of *sorting* routine in which values in an *array* are compared to each other, a pair at a time, and swapped if they are not in correct order.

buffer A place in your computer's *memory* for temporary *data* storage.

bug An error in a *program* that prevents the program from running correctly. This term originated when a moth short-circuited a connection in one of the first computers and prevented the computer from working.

byte A basic unit of *data* storage and manipulation. A byte is equivalent to eight *bits* and can contain a value ranging from 0 to 255.

cathode ray tube (CRT) The television-like screen of the computer, also called the *monitor.* It is one place to which the output of the computer can be sent.

CGA Color Graphics Adapter. Defines the *resolution* of the *display* (how many *pixels* show on the screen). CGA graphics have a resolution of 640 x 200 pixels.

click To move the *mouse* pointer over an object or icon and press and release the *mouse button* once.

code A set of instructions written in a *programming language.* See also *source code.*

compile The process of translating a *program* written in a *programming language,* such as QBasic or Pascal, into machine *code* your computer understands.

central processing unit (CPU) The *microprocessor* (central processing unit) responsible for operations within the computer. These operations generally include system timing, logical processing, and logical operations. The CPU controls every operation of the computer system.

clipboard A section of *memory* reserved for *blocks* of *text.* The clipboard holds only one block of text at a time.

clock tick A length of time based on the CPU's built-in timing clock. There are 18.2 ticks in one second.

concatenation The process of attaching one string to the end of another or combining two or more strings into a longer string. You can concatenate *string variables, string constants,* or a combination of both and assign the concatenated strings to a string variable.

conditional loop A series of QBasic instructions that occurs a fixed number of times.

constant *Data* that remain the same during a *program* run.

CPU *Central processing unit.*

crash When the computer stops working unexpectedly.

CRT *Cathode ray tube.*

cursor Located on a *monitor;* the cursor is usually a blinking underline. The cursor denotes the spot where the next character typed will appear on the screen.

cut To remove *text* from your *program.* See also *paste.*

data Information stored in the computer as numbers, letters, and special symbols (such as punctuation marks). *Data* also refers to the characters you input into your *program* so that the program can produce meaningful *information.*

data processing When a computer takes data and manipulates it into meaningful output, which is called *information.*

data record A line of DATA.

data validation The process of testing the values input into a *program*—for instance, ensuring that a number is within a certain range.

debug The process of locating an error (*bug*) in a *program* and removing it.

debugger A special *program* designed to help locate errors in a program.

default A predefined action or command that the computer chooses unless you specify otherwise.

demodulate The process of converting *analog signals* back to digital signals that the computer can understand. See also *modulate.*

dialog box A box-like structure that appears on the screen after the user chooses a *menu* command with an ellipsis (...). You must type more information before QBasic can carry out the command.

digital computer A term that comes from the fact that your computer operates on *binary* (**on** and **off**) digital impulses of electricity.

directory A list of *files* stored on a *disk.* See also *subdirectory.*

disk A round, flat magnetic storage medium. *Floppy disks* are made of flexible material and enclosed in 5 1/4-inch or 3 1/2-inch protective cases. *Hard disks* consist of a stack of rigid disks housed in a single unit. A disk is sometimes called *external memory.* Disk storage is non*volatile.* When you turn off your computer, the disk's contents do not go away.

disk drive A device that reads and writes *data* to a *floppy disk* or a *hard disk.*

diskette Another name for a *floppy disk.*

display A screen or *monitor.*

display adapter Located in the *system unit,* the display adapter determines the amount of *resolution* and the possible number of colors on the screen.

double-click Clicking the *mouse button* twice in rapid succession.

DOS Disk operating system.

dot-matrix printer One of the two most common PC printers. The laser printer is the other. A dot-matrix printer is inexpensive and fast; it uses a series of small dots to represent printed *text* and *graphics*. See also *laser printer.*

drag Pressing and holding the left *mouse button* without letting up while moving the mouse pointer across the screen.

duration The *duration* of a tone in QBasic must be a number from 0 through 65,536. It must be a *constant,* an expression, or a *variable* (any numeric *data* type except an integer, because 65,536 is too large to fit in an *integer variable*). The *duration* measures the length of the note (how long it sounds) in *clock ticks.*

EGA Enhanced Graphics Adapter. Defines the *resolution* of the *display* (how many *pixels* show on the screen). The EGA has a resolution of 640 x 350 *pixels.*

element An individual *variable* in an *array.*

execute To run a *program.*

expanded memory See *extended memory.*

extended memory The amount of *RAM* that is above and beyond the basic 640K in most PCs. You cannot access this extra RAM without special *programs*.

external modem A modem that sits in a box outside your computer. See also *internal modem.*

file A collection of *data* stored as a single unit on a *floppy disk* or *hard disk.* A file always has a *file name* that identifies it.

file extension A suffix to a *file name* consisting of a period followed by up to three characters. The extension denotes what kind of file it is.

file name A unique name that identifies a file. File names can be up to eight characters long and can have a period followed by an extension (which is normally three characters long).

fixed disk See *hard disk.*

fixed-length string variables Variables that can hold only strings that are shorter than or equal to the length you define. These strings are not as flexible as *variable-length strings.*

fixed-length records A record in which each field takes the same amount of *disk* space, even if that field's *data* value does not fill the field. Fixed strings are typically used for fixed-length records.

floppy disk See *disk.*

format The process of creating a "map" on the *disk* that tells the operating system how the disk is structured. This is how the operating system keeps track of where *files* are stored.

frequency The number of cycles per second, in *hertz*. It must be a number from *37* to *32,767* (therefore, it can be an integer *constant*, integer expression, or *integer variable*).

function A self-contained coding segment designed to do a specific task. A function is sometimes referred to as a *procedure* or *subroutine.* Some functions are built-in routines that manipulate numbers, strings, and output.

function keys Keys labeled F1 through F12 (some keyboards go only to F10) that provide special *functions.*

global variable A variable that can be seen from (and used by) every statement in the *program.*

graphics A video presentation consisting mostly of pictures and figures rather than letters and numbers. See also *text.*

graphics monitor A monitor that can display pictures.

hard copy The printout of a *program* (or its output). *Hard copy* also refers to a safe back-up copy for a program in case the *disk* is erased.

hard disk Sometimes called a *fixed disk.* A hard disk holds much more *data* and is many times faster than a *floppy disk.* See *disk.*

hardware The physical parts of the machine. Hardware, which has been defined as "anything you can kick," consists of the things you can see.

hertz A unit of measurement equal to one cycle per second.

hexadecimal A numbering system based on 16 *elements*. Digits are numbered 0 through F, as follows: 0, 1, 2, 3, 4, 5, 6, 7, 8, 9, A, B, C, D, E, F.

HGA Hercules Graphics Adapter. Defines the *resolution* of the *display* (how many *pixels* show on the screen).

hierarchy of operators See *order of operators.*

indeterminate loop A loop in which you do not know in advance how many cycles of the loop will be made (unlike with the FOR-NEXT loop).

infinite loop The never-ending repetition of a *block* of QBasic statements.

information The meaningful product of a *program. Data* goes into a program to produce *meaningful* output (*information*).

input The *data* entered into a computer through a device such as the keyboard.

input-process-output This model is the foundation of everything that happens in your computer. *Data* is input, then processed by your *program* in the computer. Finally, *information* is output.

I/O An acronym for input/output.

integer variable A variable that can hold integers.

internal modem A modem that resides inside the *system unit*. See also *external modem.*

key field A field that contains unique *data* used to identify a *record.*

kilobyte (K) A unit of measurement that refers to 1,024 *bytes.*

laser printer A type of printer that in general is faster than a dot-matrix printer. Laser printer output is much sharper than that of a dot-matrix printer, because a laser beam actually burns toner ink into the paper. Laser printers are more expensive than dot-matrix printers. See also *dot-matrix printer.*

least significant bit The extreme-right bit of a *byte*. For example, a *binary* 00000111 has a 1 as the least significant bit.

line printer Another name for your printer.

local variable A variable that can be seen from (and used by) only the *code* in which it is defined (within a *function* or *procedure*).

loop The repeated circular execution of one or more statements.

machine language The series of *binary* digits that a *microprocessor executes* to perform individual tasks. People seldom (if ever) program in machine language. Instead, they program in assembly language, and an assembler translates their instructions into machine language.

main module The first routine of a *modular program*. It is not really a *subroutine*, but is the main *program*.

maintainability The computer industry's word for the ability to change and update *programs* that were written in a simple style.

math operator A symbol used for addition, subtraction, multiplication, division, or other calculations.

MCGA Multi-Color Graphics Array.

MDA Monochrome Display Adapter.

megabyte (M) In computer terminology, about a million bytes.

memory Storage area inside the computer, used to temporarily store *data*. The computer's memory is erased when the power is turned off.

menu A list of commands or instructions displayed on the screen. These lists organize commands and make a *program* easier to use.

menu-driven Describes a *program* that provides menus for choosing commands.

microchip A small wafer of silicon that holds computer components and occupies less space than a postage stamp.

microcomputer A small version of a computer that can fit on a desktop. The *microchip* is the heart of the microcomputer. Microcomputers are much less expensive than their larger counterparts.

microprocessor The chip that does the calculations for the computer. Sometimes it is called the *central processing unit* (*CPU*).

modem A piece of *hardware* that *modulates* and *demodulates* signals so that your PC can communicate with other computers over telephone lines. See also *external modem, internal modem.*

modular programming The process of writing your programs in several modules rather than as one long program. By breaking a program into several smaller program-line routines, you can isolate problems better, correct programs faster, and produce programs that are much easier to maintain.

modulate Before your computer can transmit *data* over a telephone line, the *information* to be sent must be converted (modulated) into *analog signals*. See also *demodulate, modem.*

modulus This is the integer remainder of division.

monitor A television-like screen that lets the computer display *information*. It is known as an *output device*. See also *cathode ray tube*.

monochrome A single color.

monochrome monitor A monitor that can display only one color, such as green or amber, on a black or white background.

mouse A hand-held device that you move across the desktop to move an indicator, called a mouse pointer, across the screen. The mouse is used rather than the keyboard to select and move items (such as *text* or *graphics*), *execute* commands, and perform other tasks.

mouse button A button on top of a mouse that performs a specific action, such as executing a command, depending on the location of the mouse pointer on the screen.

MS-DOS An operating system for IBM and IBM-compatible computers.

multidimensional arrays Arrays with more than one subscript. Two-dimensional arrays, which have rows and columns, are sometimes called tables or matrices.

nested loop A loop within a loop.

null string An empty string created by typing two quotation marks with no space between them.

numeric functions Built-in routines that work with numbers.

object code A "halfway step" between *source code* and executable *machine language.* Object code consists mostly of machine language but is not directly executable by the computer. It must first be linked to resolve external references and *address* references.

open To load a *file* into an application.

order of operators Sometimes called the *hierarchy of operators* or the *precedence of operators,* it determines exactly how QBasic computes formulas.

output device Where the results of a *program* are output, such as the screen, the *printer*, or a *disk file.*

palette A collection of possible colors, just like an artist's palette of colors.

parallel arrays Two arrays working side by side. Each *element* in each array corresponds to one in the other array.

parallel port A connector used to plug a device such as a *printer* into the computer. Transferring *data* through a parallel port is much faster than transferring data through a *serial port.*

parameter A list of *variables* enclosed in parentheses that follow the name of a *function* or *procedure*. Parameters indicate the number and type of *arguments* that will be sent to the function or procedure.

passing by address By *default*, all QBasic variable *arguments* are passed by address (also called *passing by reference).* When an argument (a *local variable*) is passed by address, the variable's address in *memory* is sent to, and is assigned to, the receiving routine's *parameter* list. (If more than one *variable* is passed by address, each of their addresses is sent to and assigned to the receiving *function*'s parameters.) A change made to the parameter within the routine also changes the value of the argument variable.

passing by copy Another name for *passing by value.*

passing by reference Another name for *passing by address.*

passing by value When the value contained in a *variable* is passed to the *parameter* list of a receiving routine. Changes made to the parameter within the routine do not change the value of the *argument* variable. Also called *passing by copy.*

path The route the computer travels from the root *directory* to any subdirectories when locating a *file.* The path also refers to the subdirectories *MS-DOS* examines when you type a command that requires it to find and access a file.

peripheral A device attached to the computer, such as a *modem, disk drive, mouse,* or *printer.*

personal computer A *microcomputer*, sometimes called a PC.

pixel A dot on the computer screen. The number of dots in a line and in a column determine the *resolution* of the *monitor.* See also *CGA, EGA,* and *VGA.*

precedence of operators See *order of operators.*

printer A device that prints *data* from the computer to paper.

procedure A self-contained coding segment designed to do a specific task, sometimes referred to as a *subroutine.*

program A group of instructions that tells the computer what to do.

programming language A set of rules for writing instructions for the computer. Popular programming languages include BASIC, QBasic, Visual Basic, C, C++, and Pascal.

quick sort A type of *sorting* routine.

RAM *Random-access memory.*

random-access file A file in which *records* can be accessed in any order you choose.

random-access memory (RAM) What your computer uses to temporarily store *data* and *programs*. RAM is measured in *kilobytes* and *megabytes*. Generally, the more RAM a computer has, the more powerful programs it can run.

read-only memory (ROM) A permanent type of computer memory. ROM contains the BIOS (basic input/output system), a special chip used to provide instructions to the computer when you turn on the computer.

real number A number that has a decimal point and a fractional part to the right of the decimal.

record A unit of related *information* containing one or more fields, such as an employee number, employee name, employee address, employee pay rate, and so on. It is an individual occurrence in the *file*.

relational operators Operators that compare *data*; they tell how two *variables* or *constants* relate to each other. They tell you whether two variables are equal or not equal, or which one is less than or more than the other.

resolution The sharpness of an image in print or on the screen. Resolution is usually measured in dots per inch (dpi) for *printers*, and *pixels* for screens. The higher the resolution, the sharper the image.

ROM *Read-only memory.*

scientific notation A shortcut method of representing numbers of extreme values.

sectors A pattern of pie-shaped wedges on a *disk*. Formatting creates a pattern of *tracks* and sectors where your *data* and *programs* will be stored.

sequential file A file that has to be accessed one *record* at a time beginning with the first record.

serial port A connector used to plug in serial devices, such as a *modem* or a *mouse.*

shell sort A type of *sorting* routine in which each *array element* is compared to another array element and swapped if needed to put them in order.

single-dimensional arrays Arrays that have only one *subscript.* Single-dimensional arrays represent a list of values.

software The *data* and *programs* that interact with your hardware. The QBasic language is an example of software. See also *hardware.*

sorting A method of putting *arrays* in a specific order (such as alphabetical or numerical order), even if that order is not the same order in which the *elements* were entered.

source code The QBasic language instructions, written by humans, that the QBasic interpreter translates into *object code.*

spaghetti code A term used when there are too many GOTOs in a *program.* If a program branches all over the place, it is difficult to follow; the logic resembles a "bowl of spaghetti."

string constant One or more groups of characters inside quotation marks.

string literal Another name for a *string constant.*

string variable A variable that can hold string *data.*

subdirectory A directory within an existing directory.

subroutine A self-contained coding segment designed to do a specific task, sometimes referred to as a *procedure.* Subroutines are sections of *programs* you can *execute* repeatedly.

subscript A number inside brackets that differentiates one *element* of an *array* from another.

SVGA Super Video Graphics Array, a nonstandardized type of *display adapter* based on extensions to the *VGA* standard. Defines the *resolution* of the *display* (how many *pixels* show on the screen).

syntax error The most common error a programmer makes. Usually a misspelled word.

system unit The large box component of the computer. The system unit houses the PC's *microchip* (the *CPU*).

text A video presentation scheme consisting mostly of letters and numbers. See also *graphics.*

tracks A pattern of *paths* on a *disk*. Formatting creates a pattern of *tracks* and *sectors* where your *data* and *programs* will go.

trailer data record A special DATA statement that contains specified data values for which to check. Commonly, a trailer data record contains a -99.

truncation When the fractional part of a number (the part of the number to the right of the decimal point) is taken off the number. No rounding is done.

two's complement A method your computer uses to take the negative of a number. This method plus addition enables the computer to simulate subtraction.

unary operator The addition or subtraction operator used by itself.

user-defined functions Functions that the user writes. See also *functions.*

user-friendliness A *program* is user-friendly if it makes the user comfortable and simulates what the user is already familiar with.

variable *Data* that can change as the *program* runs.

variable-length string variables The string *data* stored in the variable can be any length. If you put a short word in a variable-length string variable and then replace it with a longer word or phrase, the string variable grows to hold the new, longer data.

variable-length records A record that wastes no space on the *disk*. As soon as a field's *data* value is saved to the *file*, the next field's data value is stored immediately after it. There is usually a special separating character between the fields so that your *programs* know where the fields begin and end.

variable scope Sometimes called the *visibility of variables,* this describes how variables are "seen" by your *program*. See also *global variables* and *local variables.*

VGA Video Graphics Array, a type of *display adapter*. Defines the *resolution* of the *display* (how many *pixels* show on the screen). This refers to 640 x 480 pixel resolution.

volatile Temporary. For example, when you turn off the computer, all the *RAM* is erased.

word In general usage, two consecutive *bytes* (16 *bits*) of *data.*

Index

Symbols

.BAK, 730
.BAS, 730

A

ABS() function (absolute value function), 420-422
active drive, 729
addition (+) operator, 142
addresses, 28, 729, 738
Alt+key combination (display menus), 40
Alt+MINUS (decrease size of current window) command, 74
Alt+PLUS (increase size of current window) command, 74
analog signals, 25, 729
AND logical operators, 250
angles, 426
APPEND mode, 556, 561, 573-574
application-specific keys, 24
arguments, 525, 729
arrays, 522, 729
  corresponding, 375
  data
    changing, 379
    storing, 369
  dimensioning, 371, 374-377, 380, 389, 395-396
  elements, 368-374, 381-384, 395-400
  erasing, 388
  inputting, FOR-NEXT loop, 374
  known, 378
  matrices, 393
  multidimensional, 393-399, 738
  order, 382
  parallel, 375, 738
  printing, 374, 400-407
  searching, 382
  single-dimensional, 393, 395, 741
  single-precision, 371
  sorting
    bubble, 384-385
    descending, 382
    quick, 384-385
    shell, 384-385

storage, 374, 381
storing
bubble, 386
quick, 386
reverse order, 386
shell, 386
subscripts, 372, 375, 380, 388, 398, 520-522
default values, 396
defining, 530-531
dimensioning, 396, 741
multidimensional, 393-395, 741
numeric, 368-370
OPTION BASE statement, 396
single-dimensional, 393
variables, 367
zero-based, 381
ASC() function, 442
ASCII characters, 221-223
ASCII code character set, 671-675
ASCII file, 729
ASCII table, 220, 353-355, 386, 414, 442-445
aspect ratios, 627-628
Assembler, 13
assignment statements, 93, 171-173, 264, 399-400
ATN() function, 425
AUTOEXEC.BAT, 730

B

back-up file, 730
BASIC (Beginner's All-Purpose Symbolic Instruction Code), 12-14
batch file, 730
BEEP command, 219
BEEP statement, 347
binary, 18, 730
bits, 220, 249, 730
blocks, 68, 332-334, 730
Book Management Database program (BOOK.BAS), 707-727
bookmarks, 68
boot, 730
boxes, 625-626
branching, 84
bubble sort, 384-385, 730
buffers, 730
bugs, 67, 730
bullet proof, 351
bytes, 17, 730

C

C7PAY.BAS program, 146-147
C7PAY2.BAS program, 153
calculations, 152-153
CALL statement, 495
CALL statement format, 495
carriage return–line feed sequence, 128
CASE control value, 351
CASE ELSE statement, 347, 354-356
CASE SELECT statement, 344
cathode ray tube (CRT), 20, 730
CDBL() function, 423
central processing unit (CPU), 16, 731
CINT() function (convert integer), 415-419
CIRCLE statement, 626
CIRCLE statement format, 626
CIRCLE() color function format, 638
circles, 626-627
clicking, 38, 731
clipboard, 69, 731
CLNG() function (convert long integer), 415-419
clock ticks, 656, 731
CLOSE statement format, 560
CLS statement, 85, 93, 110-111
COBOL, 13, 67
code, 731
color
adapters
color, 637-638
Color Graphics Adapter (CGA), 222, 611, 614, 636, 644-645, 731
Enhanced Graphics Adapter (EGA), 611, 614-615, 636, 645-647, 733
Memory Controller Gate Array (MCGA), 611, 614-615, 647, 736

monochrome, 637-638
Monochrome Display Adapter (MDA), 736
Super Video Graphics Array (SVGA), 741
Video Graphics Array (VGA), 611, 614-615, 636, 645-647, 743
adding, 635, 638-641
attributes, 637-638, 637
changing, 643, 647-648
background, 643-647
foreground, 643-645
circles, 639-640, 642, 645
constants, 642
default setting, 648
images, 649
lines, 641
painting, 649-651
rectangles, 639
values, 639, 641-642, 647-648
Color Graphics Adapter (CGA), 222, 611, 614, 636, 644-645, 731
COLOR statement, 223-226, 331, 645
COLOR statement format, 643
command-line options, starting QBasic, 34-36
commands
BEEP, 219
CLS (Clear Screen), 110
FILE NEW, 82-83
FILE OPEN, 80
FILE PRINT, 83
FILE SAVE, 82
FILE SAVE AS, 81
LPRINT, 164
OPEN..., 58
PRINT, 164
SEARCH FIND..., 88-89
SPC, 216-217
START, 59, 68
SWAP, 384
SYNTAX CHECKING, 66
commas, 193-195
COMMON SHARED statement, 522
compile, 731
compound relational operators, 246-250
concatenation, 168-171, 731
conditional loops, 252, 731
conditional statements, 239
CONST statement, 518
CONST statement format, 518
constants, 94, 731
converting, 447
defining, 518-519
double-precision, 93
global, 523
integers, 93
mixing with variables, 171-173
multiples per line, 518
numeric
hexadecimal, 103
octal, 103-105
printing, 131, 152
ranges, 102
single-precision, 93
types, 102
context-sensitive help, 50
copy, passing, 532, 739
COS() function, 425-426
counter variables, 284
counters, 251-254
CPU, *see* central processing unit
crash, 731
CRT, *see* cathode ray tube
CSNG() function, 423
Ctrl+Break (Quit) command, 61
Ctrl+F10 (zoom in or out of active window) command, 74
Ctrl+Ins (Copy) command, 70
Ctrl+K (Set Bookmarks) command, 72
cursors, 20, 199-203, 731
cut, 732
CV*type*() function (convert type), 591

D

data, 732
data processing, 26, 732
data records, 263, 732
DATA statement, 262-278, 398
data validation, 241, 309, 357, 732
DATA value, 290-291
data-driven program, 235

DATE$ function, 460-461
DATE$ function format, 460
dates, 459-463
debug, 732
Debug menu, 39
debugger, 67, 732
decision statements, 238-242
DECLARE statement, 504, 510, 527
DECLARE statement format, 504
DEF FN statement, 470
DEF FN() multiple-line statement format, 479
DEF FN() statement, 474
DEF FN() statement format, 471
default, 732
Del (Clear) command, 71
demodulate, 25, 732
dialog boxes, 42-46, 732
  File Open..., 59
  File Print, 83
  Options Display..., 44
digital computers, 25, 732
DIM (dimension) statement, 371, 375, 380, 387, 395-397
DIM SHARED statement, 521
DIM statement format, 371
directory, 732
disk drive, 732
diskette, 733
disks, 732
  capacity, 545
  fixed, 734
  floppy, 19, 734
  hard, 19, 544
  memory, nonvolatile, 18, 80, 544
  saving, 82
  storing, 18, 543-550
display, 733
display adapters, 21, 733
division (/) operator, 142
DO loops, 311, 374
DO UNTIL-LOOP format, 314
DO UNTIL-LOOP, 314-317
DO WHILE-LOOP, 311-312
DO-LOOP statement, 703
DO-LOOP UNTIL format, 318
DO-LOOP UNTIL loop, 318-320
DO-LOOP WHILE loop, 312-314
DOS, 733
dot-matrix printers, 21, 733
double-clicking, 38, 733
dragging, 38, 733
DRAW statement, 629-631
DRAW statement format, 628
duration, 733

E

Edit menu, 39
editing, 69-70, 73-76
element, 733
ELSE statement, 329
ELSEIF statement, 336-339
empty strings, *see* null strings
END DEF statement, 480
END IF statement, 334
END statement, 93, 110
END SUB statement, 494
end values, 287, 301
endless loops, 276, 310
Enhanced Graphics Adapter (EGA), 611, 614-615, 636, 645-647, 733
EOF() function format, 570
equal to (=) relational operator, 236
ERASE statement, 388-389
ERASE statement format, 388-389
error messages, 196
errors in programs, 65-67
Escape key, 22
exclusive operators, 248
execute, 733
EXIT DEF statement, 482
EXIT DO format, 320
EXIT DO statement, 321-322
EXIT FOR statement, 301-303
EXP() function, 427
expanded memory, 17, 733
exponentiation (^) operator, 142-145
expressions, 98, 105
  converting, 447
  numeric, 344
  printing, 152-153
  text, 344
extended memory, 17, 545, 733
external memory, 18
external modems, 25, 733

F

F5 (Start) command, 68
F6 (move to next window) command, 74
FIELD statement, 589, 596
FIELD statement format, 589
fields, 203
File menu, 39, 58
file name, 734
File New command, 82-83
File Open... dialog box, 59-80
File Print, 83
File Save As command, 81
File Save command, 82
FILEATTR() function, 559
FILEATTR() function format, 559
files, 733
  accessing, 552
  batch, 730
  DOS CONFIG.SYS, 558
  extensions, 551, 734
  fields, 549-550
  loading, 80
  naming, 551
  printing, 562, 600-601
  random-access, 579-592
    advantages, 580
    byte specification, 597
    changing, 602-606
    creating, 581, 593-597
    fixed-length, 580-581, 587
    length, 598
    locating, 601-603
    OPEN statement, 581
    opening, 581-582, 586
    reading, 581, 587-588, 597-601
  records, 549-550
    counting, 572
    defining, 582-589
    fields, 586-589
    fixed-length, 549
    variable-length, 549-550
    variables, 584-586
  saving, 81-83, 552
  sequential
    appending, 556-557, 561, 570-575, 740
    back-up, 557
    closing, 560
    creating, 556-568
    reading, 556, 569-572
    variable-length, 562
  storing, 546
  values, 586
FILES= statement, 558
FIND option, 86
FIX() function, 415-419
fixed disk, 734
fixed-length records, 734
fixed-length string variables, 734
floppy disks, 19, 734
flowcharts, 8
FNnroot() function, 478
FOR loop, 285
FOR statement, 284-287, 300
FOR-NEXT loop, 283, 286, 292-300, 374, 401-402
FOR-NEXT statement, 287-291
form feeding (printers), 222
formats, 734
  CALL statement, 495
  CIRCLE statement, 626
  CIRCLE() color function, 638
  CLOSE statement, 560
  COLOR statement, 643
  CONST statement, 518
  DATE$ function, 460
  DECLARE statement, 504
  DEF FN statement, 471
  DEF FN() multiple-line statement, 479
  DIM statement, 371
  DO UNTIL-LOOP, 314
  DO WHILE-LOOP, 311-312
  DO-LOOP UNTIL, 318-320
  DO-LOOP WHILE, 312-314
  DRAW statement, 628
  EOF() function, 570
  ERASE, 388-389
  EXIT DO, 320
  FIELD statement, 589
  FILEATTR(), 559
  function call, 414
  FUNCTION statement, 508
  GET # statement, 597
  IF-THEN-ELSE block, 332
  IF-THEN-ELSE statement, 329

INPUT # statement, 569
INSTR() function, 454
LINE statement, 622
LINE() color function, 638
MID$() statement, 458
OPEN statement, 556
random-access, 581
random-access, shortcut, 582
shorter, 559
OPTION BASE, 380
PAINT, 649
PALETTE format, 647
PALETTE statement format, 647
PLAY statement, 659
PRESET statement, 616
PRESET() color function, 638
PRINT # statement, 561-562
PSET color function, 638
PSET statement, 616
SCREEN statement, 613
SELECT CASE statement, 343
SELECT CASE statement range format, 355
SOUND statement, 656
STATIC statement, 535
SUB-END SUB, 494
SWAP command, 384
TIME$ function, 460
WHILE-WEND, 308
WRITE # statement, 563
formulas, 145-146
FORTRAN, 13
FREEFILE function, 558
frequency, 734
function call format, 414
function keys, 24, 734
FUNCTION statement format, 508
FUNCTION statement, 508
functions, 221, 734
ABS() (absolute value), 420-422
arguments, 414-415, 421-422, 433, 442
changing values, 416
converting, 424-425
truncation, 416
ASC(), 442
ATN(), 425
CDBL(), 423
CINT() (convert integer), 415-419
CIRCLE() color, 638
CLNG() (convert long integer), 415-419
COS(), 425-426
CSNG(), 423
CV*type*() (convert type), 591
DATE$, 460-461
EOF(), 570
EXP(), 427
FILEATTR(), 559
FIX(), 415-419
FNnroot(), 478
FREEFILE, 558
INKEY$, 464-466
INSTR(), 450-454
INT(), 415-419
integers, 415-419
LBOUND() (lower bound), 530-531
LCASE$(), 447
LEFT$(), 450-453
LEN() (length), 428, 450-453
LOF(), 597
LOG(), 427
LTRIM$(), 450-453
maximum, 477
MID$(), 450-453
minimum, 477
MK*type*$() (make type), 590
noninteger precision, 423
numeric, 413-418
double-precision, 423-424, 428
negative, 417
positive, 417
rounding, 417
single-precision, 423-424, 428
square root, 420
output, 414
return value, 472
RIGHT$(), 450-453
RND, 434, 438
RND() (random-number), 431-432, 437, 620
RTRIM$(), 450-453
SGN(), 420-422
SIN(), 425-426
SPACE$(), 444
SQR(), 420
SQR() (square root), 420
STR$(), 447-448

STRINGS$(), 442-446
strings, 414, 441-443
TAB, 131-134, 217
TAN(), 425-426
TIME$, 460-461
TIMER, 429-430, 435, 460
UBOUND() (upper bound), 530-531
UCASE$() (uppercase), 447-448
user-defined, 469
VAL(), 447-448

G

GET # statement, 597
GET # statement format, 597
GetNums subroutine procedure, 497
global variable, 734
GORILLA.BAS program, 60
GOTO statement, 226-230, 269
Grace Hopper, 67
graphics, 614, 734
  adapters
    Color Graphics Adapter (CGA), 222, 611, 614, 636, 644-645, 731
    Enhanced Graphics Adapter (EGA), 611, 614-615, 733
    Hercules Graphics Adapter (HGA), 611, 614, 735
    Memory Controller Gate Array (MCGA), 611, 614-615, 736
    Video Graphics Array (VGA), 611, 614-615, 743
  aspect ratios
    x-radius, 627-628
    y-radius, 627-628
  boxes
    drawing, 625-626
  circles, 626
    drawing, 627
  drawing, 628-632
  ellipses, 626
  lines
    dashed, 623
    diagonal, 618-620
    dotted, 622
    drawing, 618-619, 622-624
    solid, 618
  margin, 8
  modes, 614-616
  monitor, 611
  pixels, 612, 616-622, 626, 630, 739
    activating, 616
    coordinates, 613
    drawing, 620-621
    home location, 613
  resolution, 612-617, 622, 630
  text, adding, 618
  x-coordinates, 613, 616-618, 620, 625-626
  y-coordinates, 613, 616-618, 620, 626
graphics monitors, 21, 734
greater than (>) relational operator, 236
greater than or equal to (>=) relational operator, 236
GW-BASIC, 701-705

H

hard copy, 734
hard disks, 19, 735
hardware, 15, 735
Help menu, 46-48, 50-52
Help Survival Guide, 46
Hercules Graphics Adapter (HGA), 611, 614, 735
hertz, 656, 735
hexadecimal, 735
hierarchy of operators, 147, 735
home location, 613

I

I/O (input/output), 735
IF statement, 238-245, 327
IF-THEN statement, 326, 329, 703
IF-THEN-ELSE statement, 330-336, 345-347
IF-THEN-ELSE statement format, 329
IF-THEN-GOTO statement, 239
increment values, 292

indeterminate loop, 735
Index to the Icons, 8
infinite loop, 735
information, 735
INKEY$ function, 464-466
input, 5, 735
INPUT mode, 556, 570
INPUT statement, 87, 181-182
  eliminating question marks, 196
  filling variables with values, 182-186
  improving use of, 186-190
  manipulating cursor, 199-203
  prompting with, 186, 191-192
  versus LINE INPUT statement, 197-199
INPUT # statement format, 569
input-process-output model, 26, 735
insert mode, 63
INSTR() function, 450-454
INSTR() function format, 454
INT() function, 415-419
integer division (\) operator, 142-145
integer functions, 415-419
integer variables, 93, 528, 735
integer constants, 93
internal modems, 25, 735

K

key field, 602, 735
keyboard, 22
keyboard shortcuts, 41-43
  Alt+MINUS (decrease size of current window) command, 74
  Alt+PLUS (increase size of current window) command, 74
  Ctrl+Break (Quit) command, 61
  Ctrl+F10 (zoom in or out of active window) command, 74
  Ctrl+Ins (Copy) command, 70
  Ctrl+K (Set Bookmarks) command, 72
  Del (Clear) command, 71
  F5 (Start) command, 68
  F6 (move to next window) command, 74
  Shift+Del (Cut) command, 70
  Shift+Ins (Paste) command, 70
keys
  editing, 74-76
  Escape, 22
  function, 24
keywords, 699-700, 704
kilobytes (K), 17, 735

L

laser printers, 21, 736
LBOUND() function (lower bound), 530-531
LCASE$() function (lowercase), 447-448
leading blanks, 449
least-significant bits, 249, 736
LEFT$() function, 450-453
LEN() function, 428, 450-453
less than (<) relational operator, 236
less than or equal to (<=) relational operator, 236
LET statement, 93, 98-101, 152, 162
LINE INPUT statement, 197-203
line printer, 135, 736
lines
  dashed, 623
  diagonal, 618-620
  dotted, 622
  drawing, 618-619, 622-624
  solid, 618
LINE statement, 622-625
LINE statement format, 622
LINE() color function format, 638
local variable, 736
LOCATE statement, 231, 331
LOF() function, 597
LOG() function, 427
logical operators, 246-250
long integer numbers, 93
loops, 736
  conditional, 252
  DO, 311, 374
  DO UNTIL-LOOP, 314-317
  DO WHILE-LOOP, 311-312
  DO-LOOP UNTIL, 318-320
  DO-LOOP WHILE, 312-314

endless, 276, 310
FOR, 285
FOR-NEXT, 283, 286, 292-300, 374, 401-402
indeterminate, 735
infinite, 735
WHILE-WEND, 308
LPRINT command, 164
LPRINT statement, 135-136, 152-153
LSET statement, 457-458, 591
LTRIM$() function, 450-453

M

machine language, 736
main module, 492, 736
maintainability, 154-156, 736
margin graphics, 8
math operators, 142, 736
addition, 142-143
division, 142-143
exponentiation, 142-145
integer division, 142-145
modulus, 142-145
multiplication, 142-143
subtraction, 142-143
matrices, 393
megabyte (M), 20, 736
memory, 16, 736
arrays, 374, 377
expanded, 17, 545, 733
extended, 17, 545, 733
external, 18
nonvolatile, 18, 80, 544
random-access (RAM), 16, 545
volatile, 18, 743
Memory Controller Gate Array (MCGA), 611, 614-615, 647, 736
menu bar, 37
menu-driven, 736
menus, 736
Debug, 39
dialog boxes, 42-46
displaying, 40
Edit, 39
File, 39, 58
Help, 48-52
Options, 39, 66
pull-down, 39-41
QBasic, 39
Run, 39, 59, 68
Search, 39, 86-87
SELECT CASE, 349-351
View, 39
microchip, 13, 737
microcomputers, 13, 737
microprocessor, 737
Microsoft Disk Operating System (MS-DOS), 11, 27-29
MID$() function statement, 326, 450-453, 458-459
MID$() statement format, 458
MK*type*$() function (make type), 590
modems, 25, 737
modes
APPEND, 556, 561, 573-574
INPUT, 556, 570
insert, 63
music legato, 661
music normal, 661
music staccato, 661
overtype, 63
OUTPUT, 556, 561
SCREEN, 639-640
modular programming, 490, 493, 737
modulate, 25, 737
modulus, 737
modulus (MOD) operator, 142-145
MONEY.BAS program, 58
monitors, 20, 737
graphics, 21
monochrome, 21, 737
Monochrome Display Adapter (MDA), 736
monochrome monitors, 21, 737
mouse, 25, 38, 737
mouse button, 737
MS-DOS, 738
MS-DOS 5.0, 11
MS-DOS Reference Manual, 19
multidimensional arrays, 393-399, 738
multiple-line separators, 326
multiplication (*) operator, 142
music legato mode, 661

music normal mode, 661
music staccato mode, 661
mutually exclusive operators, 248

N

nested loops, 295-300, 738
NEXT statement, 284-287, 292-295
NIBBLES.BAS program, 58
noninteger precision functions, 423
nonprinting characters, 222
nonvolatile memory, 18, 80
not equal to (<>) relational operator, 236
NOT logical operator, 250
*n*th root, 421
null strings, 163, 243, 388-389, 397, 458, 738
numbers, printing, 211
numeric functions, 413-415, 418, 738
numeric keypad, 22
numeric variables, 266

O

object code, 738
ON GOTO statement, 345
on-line help, 47, 703
one-liners, 328
open, 738
OPEN statement, 556
  format, 556
  random-access format, 581-582
  shorter format, 559
OPEN... command, 58
operators
  compound relational, 246-250
  division (/), 142
  equal to (=), 236
  exclusive, 248
  exponentiation (^), 142-145
  greater than (>), 236
  greater than or equal to (>=), 236
  integer division (/), 142-145
  less than (<), 236
  less than or equal to (<=), 236
  logical
    AND, 250
    NOT, 250
    OR, 250
    XOR, 250
  modulus, 142-145
  multiplication (*), 142
  not equal to (<>), 236
  order, 147-149, 250, 738
  overriding, 150-152
  precedence, 149, 739
  relational, 236-238
  subtraction (-), 142
  unary, 143
OPTION BASE format, 380
OPTION BASE statement, 380-381, 387
options
  CASE ELSE, 347
  FIND, 86
Options Display... dialog box, 44
Options menu, 39, 66
OR logical operators, 250
order of operators, 738
output, 5
  devices, 60, 738
  labeling, 121
  programs, 129
OUTPUT mode, 556, 561
overtype mode, 63

P

PAINT statement, 649-651
PAINT statement format, 649
palette, 738
PALETTE statement format, 647
parallel arrays, 375, 738
parallel port, 738
parameters, 472-474, 738
parentheses, 150-152
passing
  arguments, 525, 729
  by address, 738
  by copy, 532, 739
  by reference, 527, 739
  by value, 532-533, 739
passing routine, 525

passwords, 245
path, 739
peripheral, 739
personal computers (PCs), 14, 739
pixels (picture elements), 612, 613, 616-622, 626, 630, 739
PLAY statement, 659, 662
PLAY statement format, 659
precedence of operators, 149, 739
PRESET statement format, 616
PRESET() color function format, 638
primary operators
  addition, 142-143
  division, 142-143
  multiplication, 142-143
  subtraction, 142-143
PRINT command, 164
PRINT statement, 93, 105-121, 126-135, 152-153, 287
  multiple values, 124
  using commas, 125
  using semicolons, 124
  using TAB key, 131, 134
PRINT USING statement, 206, 209-211, 213-216
print zones, 125, 130-133
PRINT # statement format, 561-562
printer, 739
printers, 21
  dot-matrix, 21
  form feeding, 222
  laser, 21
printing, 126
  arrays, 402-407
  calculations, 152-153
  constants, 152
  expressions, 152-153
  numbers, 211
    negative, 127
    positive, 127-128
  special characters, 220-223
  string constants, 121-123
  string variables, 165-166
  strings, 209-211
  to screen
    PRINT statements, 105, 108, 120, 123-126, 132
  variables, 152
  with color, 223-226
  with SPC command, 216-217
PrintNums subroutine procedure, 500
procedure, 739
program editing window, 37, 80, 85
  erasing, 82
  searching for text, 86
program editor, 62
  typing programs, 63-65, 69-76
    errors, 65-67
    practice program, 67-68
programming language, 739
programs, 56-57, 739
  adding REM statements, 120
  Book Management Database (BOOK.BAS), 707-727
  breaking down, 490
  C7PAY.BAS, 146-147
  C7PAY2.BAS, 153
  commands, 94
  comparing TAB and SPC, 217
  control, 345
  counters, 251-254
  creating, 325, 329, 333
  data, 94
  data-driven, 235
  designing, 61-62
  ending, 358
  errors, 65-67
  file names, 117
  GORILLA.BAS, 60
  loading, 81
  locating on disks, 119
  maintainability, 154-156
  modular, 490, 493
  MONEY.BAS, 58
  multiple-choice, 343, 347
  NIBBLES.BAS, 58
  output, 129
  printers, 86
  printing, 83, 165-168
  readability, 337, 345
  REM statements, 116-120
  remarks, 116
  REMLINE.BAS, 58

running, 57-59
saving to disk, 82
sections, 337
spacing, 85
stopping, 60, 358
totals, 251, 255-256
tracing variables, 299-300
typeface, 84
typing, 63-67
user-friendly, 203
with FOR-NEXT statements, 287-291
writing, 84, 490-492
prompts for INPUT statements, 186, 191-192
PSET statement format, 616
PSET() color function format, 638
pull-down menus, 39
choosing options, 40-41
PUT # statement, 594

Q

QBasic, 4-11
converting GW-BASIC to QBasic programs, 705
editing keys, 74-76
environment, 701-702
opening screen, 32
quitting, 51
starting, 32-33
examples, 36
from Windows, 34
with command-line options, 34-36
statements versus GW-BASIC statements, 704
question marks, eliminating, 196
quick sort, 739

R

RAM, *see* random-access memory
random-access file, 740
random-access memory (RAM), 16, 544-545, 739-740
RANDOMIZE statement, 434
READ statement, 262-269, 276, 398
READ-DATA statements combining with FOR-NEXT loops, 290
read-only memory (ROM), 740
real number, 740
receiving routine, 525
record, 740
Redo from start error message, 196
references, passing, 527, 739
relational operators, 236-238, 740
relational tests, 308-309, 313
conditions
false, 329, 333
true, 329, 332-333, 352
REM command, 116
REM command shortcut, 118
REM statement, 116-120
remarks, 119
REMLINE.BAS program, 58
reseeding, 433-434
resolution, 21, 612, 740
RESTORE statement, 276-278
RIGHT$() functions, 450-453
RND (random-number) function, 431-432, 434-438, 620
arguments, 432
numeric
negative, 432
positive, 432
ROM, *see* read-only memory
RSET statement, 457-458, 591
RTRIM$() function, 450-453
Run menu, 39, 59, 68
running programs, 57-59

S

scientific notation numbers, 102, 740
SCREEN mode, 639-640
SCREEN statement, 613-615
SCREEN statement format, 613
screens, 612
scrolling, 20, 24, 44
SEARCH FIND... command, 88-89
Search menu, 39, 86-87
sectors, 740
SELECT CASE statement, 343-359
SELECT CASE statement format, 343, 355

selecting text, 69
sequential file, 740
serial port, 741
SGN() function, 420-422
SHARED statement, 499
shell sort, 741
Shift+Del (Cut) command, 70
Shift+Ins (Paste) command, 70
SIN() function, 425-426
single-dimensional arrays, 741
software, 15, 26, 741
sorting, 741
SortNums subroutine procedure, 500
sound, 655, 661
  background music, 664
  computer-like, 658
  eliminating static, 657
  frequency value, 656
  length, 656-660
  notes, 661-664
  octaves, 659-664
  pauses, 661
  producing, 656-665
  siren, 658
  tempo, 661
  tones, 660
SOUND statement, 655-656
SOUND statement format, 656
source code, 741
SPACE$() function, 444
spaces, 444
spaghetti codes, 227, 741
SPC command, 216-217
special characters, 220-223
SQR() function (square root), 420
square roots, 319-320
START command, 59, 68
start values, 284-289
statements
  assignment, 93, 171-173, 264, 399-400
  BEEP, 347
  CALL, 495
  CASE ELSE, 347, 354-356
  CASE SELECT, 344
  CIRCLE, 626
  CLOSE, 560
  CLS, 85, 93, 110-111
  COLOR, 223-226, 331, 645
  COMMON SHARED, 522
  conditional, 239
  CONST, 518
  DO-LOOP, 703
  DATA, 262-278, 398
  decision, 238-242
  DECLARE, 504, 510, 527
  DEF FN(), 470, 479
  DIM (dimension), 371, 375, 380, 387, 395-397
  DIM SHARED, 521
  DRAW, 629-631
  ELSE, 329
  ELSEIF, 336-339
  END, 93, 110
  END DEF, 480
  END IF, 334
  END SUB, 494
  ERASE, 388-389
  executing, 326
  EXIT DEF, 482
  EXIT DO, 321-322
  EXIT FOR, 301-303
  FIELD, 589, 596
  FILES=, 558
  FOR, 284-287, 300
  FOR-NEXT, 287-291
  FUNCTION, 508
  GET #, 597
  GOTO, 226-230, 269
  GW-BASIC versus QBasic, 704
  IF, 238-245, 327
  IF-THEN, 326, 329, 703
  IF-THEN-ELSE, 330-336, 345-347
  IF-THEN-GOTO, 239
  INPUT, 87, 181-192, 197-203
  LET, 93, 98-101, 152, 162
  LINE, 622-625
  LINE INPUT, 197-203
  LOCATE, 230, 331
  LPRINT, 135-136, 152-153
  LSET, 457-458, 591
  MID$(), 326, 332, 458
  NEXT, 284-287, 292-295

ON GOTO, 345
OPEN, 556
OPTION BASE, 380-381, 387
PAINT, 649-651
PALETTE, 647
PLAY, 659, 662
PRINT, 93, 105-121, 124-135, 152-153, 287
PRINT USING, 208-216
PUT #, 594
RANDOMIZE, 434
READ, 262-269, 276-278, 398
READ-DATA, 290
REM (Remark), 116-120
RESTORE, 276-278
RSET, 457-458, 591
SCREEN, 613-615
SELECT CASE, 343-359
SHARED, 499
SOUND, 655-656
STATIC, 535
STOP, 358-359
SUB, 494
TYPE, 582-583, 594
WEND, 308
WHILE, 308
STATIC statement, 535
STATIC statement format, 535
STOP statement, 358-359
STR$() function, 447-448
string constants, 120, 741
concatenation, 168
labeling output, 121
printing, 121-123, 127-128, 164
storing, 162-163
string functions, 441-443, 448
constants, 447-449
expressions, 447-449
manipulating, 441, 450
multiple characters, 443
string data, 447
variables, 447-449
string literal, 741
string variables, 159, 741
concatenation, 168-171, 731
fixed-length, 160
naming, 160-161
printing, 164-166
storing, 162-164
variable-length, 160
STRING$() function, 442-446
strings, 173-174
characters
returning, 452-453
stripping, 451-453
combining, 449
comparing data, 242-245
enclosing, 193-195
INPUT statement, 193-195
justifying, 457
length, 450
null, 163, 243, 388-389, 397, 458, 738
printing, 209-211
MID$() statement, 459
searching, 454-456
SUB statement, 494
SUB-END SUB format, 494
subdirectory, 741
subroutines, 525, 741
calling routine, 493
keyboard data-entry, 492
length, 493
main procedure, 494
moving, 502
naming, 495-496
opening, 500
primary subroutine-calling, 492
printing, 492
procedures, 494-498, 505-509, 533
deleting, 503
designating, 494
displaying, 503
GetNums, 497
indenting, 495
isolating, 508
PrinNums, 500
searching, 514
SortNums, 500
saving, 494, 497, 503
sorting, 492, 529, 530
variables, 500, 521
writing, 490-491

subscripts, *see* arrays
subtraction (-) operator, 142
Super Video Graphics Array (SVGA), 741
SWAP command, 384
SWAP command format, 384
SYNTAX CHECKING command, 66
syntax error, 741
syntax errors, 65
system unit, 16, 742

T

TAB function, 131-134, 217
TAN() function, 425-426
text, 742
  boxing, 444
  replacing, 89-90
  searching, 86-88
  underlining, 444
time, 459-463
TIME$ function, 460-461
TIME$ function format, 460
TIMER function, 429-430, 435, 460
totals, 251, 255-256
tracks, 19, 742
trailer data records, 269-275, 290, 742
transistors, 18
truncation, 742
truth tables, 246
two's complement, 144, 742
TYPE statement, 582-583, 594

U

UBOUND() function (upper bound), 530-531
UCASE$() function (uppercase letters), 447-448
unary operators, 143, 742
user-defined functions, 475-476, 742
  creating, 469-471
  isolated, 508
  library, 470
  multiple-line, 479, 480, 483-484
  numeric, 469
  parameters, 472-474
  printing, 473
  string, 469
user-friendliness, 203, 742

V

VAL() function, 447-448
values
  assigning, 98-101
  CASE control, 351
  data validation, 241
  increment, 292
  filling variables with, 182-186
  matching variables, 196
  passing, 532-533, 739
  printing, 124-126, 131
variable scope, 517, 524, 743
variable-length records, 742
variables, 742
  adding remarks, 118
  address in memory, 527
  after NEXT statement, 292-295
  automatic default setting, 534-536
  characteristics, 94
  comparing with logical operators, 246-250
  converting, 447
  counter, 284
  defining, 527
  double-precision, 93, 528
  formulas, 145-146
  global, 521-524
  integers, 93, 528, 735
  local, 521-524, 534, 736
  matching values, 196
  mixing with constants, 171-173
  naming, 95-96
  numeric, 94, 266
    converting, 589-591
    ranges, 97, 590
    scientific notation, 102-103
    storing, 162

passing, 525-526
by address, 527-528, 534, 538
by argument, 525
by copy, 532, 739
by reference, 527, 739
by value, 532-533, 739
PRINT statement, 105-107
printing, 152
protecting, 517
records, 584-586
single-precision, 93, 522, 528
STATIC, 534-535
storing, 367
strings, 742
subroutines, 521
testing, 308
tracing through programs, 299-300
types, 96
values, 119, 182-186, 384
visibility, 521, 524
Video Graphics Array (VGA), 611, 614-615, 636, 645-647, 743
View menu, 39
volatile memory, 18, 743

W

WEND statement, 308
WHILE statement, 308
WHILE-WEND loop, 308
Windows, 34
word, 743
WordStar, 703
WRITE # statement format, 563

XOR logical operators, 250

Order Your Program Disk Today!

You can save yourself hours of tedious, error-prone typing by ordering the companion disk to *QBasic by Example*. The disk contains the source code for all the complete programs and many of the shorter samples in the book. Appendix E's complete book-tracking database application is also included on the disk.

You will get code that shows you how to use most of the features of QBasic. Samples include code for graphics and screen control, file I/O, control statements, sound, and more, giving you hundreds of programs that help you learn QBasic.

Disks are available in both 5 1/4-inch and 3 1/2-inch format. The cost is $10 per disk. (On foreign orders, please add $5 for shipping and handling.)

Just make a copy of this page, fill in the blanks, and mail with your check or money order to:

QBasic Diskette
Perry Systems Development
5706 S. Indianapolis
Tulsa, OK 74135

Please **print** the following information:

Payment method: *Check:* ________ *Money order:* ________

Name:____

Street address: ____

City: ___________________________State:__________________

ZIP: __________________ Circle disk size: 3 1/2" 5 1/4" HD DD

(On foreign orders, please use a separate page to give your exact mailing address in the format required by your post office.)

Checks and money orders should be made payable to:

Perry Systems Development

(This offer is made by Perry Systems Development, not by Que Corporation.)

Free Catalog!

Mail us this registration form today, and we'll send you a free catalog featuring Que's complete line of best-selling books.

Name of Book __________

Name __________

Title __________

Phone ( ) __________

Company __________

Address __________

City __________

State __________ ZIP __________

Please check the appropriate answers:

1. Where did you buy your Que book?
   - ☐ Bookstore (name: ________)
   - ☐ Computer store (name: ________)
   - ☐ Catalog (name: ________)
   - ☐ Direct from Que
   - ☐ Other: ________

2. How many computer books do you buy a year?
   - ☐ 1 or less
   - ☐ 2-5
   - ☐ 6-10
   - ☐ More than 10

3. How many Que books do you own?
   - ☐ 1
   - ☐ 2-5
   - ☐ 6-10
   - ☐ More than 10

4. How long have you been using this software?
   - ☐ Less than 6 months
   - ☐ 6 months to 1 year
   - ☐ 1-3 years
   - ☐ More than 3 years

5. What influenced your purchase of this Que book?
   - ☐ Personal recommendation
   - ☐ Advertisement
   - ☐ In-store display
   - ☐ Price
   - ☐ Que catalog
   - ☐ Que mailing
   - ☐ Que's reputation
   - ☐ Other: ________

6. How would you rate the overall content of the book?
   - ☐ Very good
   - ☐ Good
   - ☐ Satisfactory
   - ☐ Poor

7. What do you like *best* about this Que book?

   ____

   ____

8. What do you like *least* about this Que book?

   ____

   ____

9. Did you buy this book with your personal funds?
   - ☐ Yes ☐ No

10. Please feel free to list any other comments you may have about this Que book.

    ____

    ____

    ____

QUE

Order Your Que Books Today!

Name __________

Title __________

Company __________

City __________

State __________ ZIP __________

Phone No. ( ) __________

Method of Payment:

Check ☐ (Please enclose in envelope.)

Charge My: VISA ☐ MasterCard ☐

American Express ☐

Charge # __________

Expiration Date __________

Order No.	Title	Qty.	Price	Total

You can **FAX** your order to **1-317-573-2583**. Or call **1-800-428-5331, ext. ORDR** to order direct.

Please add $2.50 per title for shipping and handling.

Subtotal	
Shipping & Handling	
Total	

QUE

NO POSTAGE
NECESSARY
IF MAILED
IN THE
UNITED STATES

BUSINESS REPLY MAIL
First Class Permit No. 9918 Indianapolis, IN

Postage will be paid by addressee

11711 N. College
Carmel, IN 46032

NO POSTAGE
NECESSARY
IF MAILED
IN THE
UNITED STATES

BUSINESS REPLY MAIL
First Class Permit No. 9918 Indianapolis, IN

Postage will be paid by addressee

11711 N. College
Carmel, IN 46032